ORTHOPRAXIS OR HERESY

American Academy of Religion Academy Series

edited by
Susan Thistlethwaite

Number 63
ORTHOPRAXIS OR HERESY
The North American Theological Response to Latin American
Liberation Theology
by
Craig L. Nessan

Craig L. Nessan

ORTHOPRAXIS OR HERESY
The North American Theological Response to Latin American Liberation Theology

Scholars Press
Atlanta, Georgia

ORTHOPRAXIS OR HERESY
The North American Theological Response to Latin American Liberation Theology
by
Craig L. Nessan

© 1989
The American Academy of Religion

BT
83.57
.N47
1989

Library of Congress Cataloging in Publication Data

Nessan, Craig L.
  Orthopraxis or heresy : the North American theological response to
Latin American liberation theology / Craig L. Nessan
    p. cm. -- (American Academy of Religion academy series ; no.
63)
  Bibliography: p.
  ISBN 1-55540-298-4 (alk. paper). ISBN 1-55540-299-2 (alk. paper:
pbk.)
  1. Liberation theology--Study and teaching--North America.
2. Theology, Doctrinal--Latin America--History--20th century.
I. Title. II. Series.
BT83.57.N47 1989
261.8'098--dc   88-31160
                                                       CIP

Printed in the United States of America
on acid-free paper

τὸν ἄρτον ἡμῶν τὸν ἐπιούσιον

δὸς ἡμῖν σήμερον.

καὶ ἄφες ἡμῖν τὰ ὀφειλήματα ἡμῶν . . .

Give us today our daily bread.

And forgive us our sins . . .

Table of Contents

ix

Abbreviations of Periodicals

Angl Th R	*Anglican Theological Review*
Bib Sac	*Bibliotheca Sacra*
Chr Cent	*The Christian Century*
Chr Cris	*Christianity and Crisis: A Christian Journal of Opinion*
Chr T	*Christianity Today*
Com Via	*Communio Viatorum: A Theological Quarterly*
Conc (USA)	*Concilium—Theology in the Age of Renewal*
Cross Curr	*Cross Currents*
Curr T M	*Currents in Theology and Mission*
Dial	*Dialog*
Duke Div R	*The Duke Divinity School Review*
Ec R	*The Ecumenical Review*
Encount	*Encounter*
Explor	*Explor: A Journal of Theology*
Expos T	*The Expository Times*
Foun	*Foundations: a Baptist Journal of History and Theology*
Horizons	*Horizons: The Journal of the College Theology Society*
IDOC Bul	*IDOC Bulletin: International Documentation Service*
Iliff R	*The Iliff Review*
Int R Miss	*International Review of Mission*
Interp	*Interpretation: a Journal of Bible and Theology*
J A A R	*Journal of the American Academy of Religion*
J B L	*Journal of Biblical Literature*
J Ec St	*Journal of Ecumenical Studies*
J Int Th C	*The Journal of the Interdenominational Theological Center*
J Rel	*The Journal of Religion*
J Rel Thot	*The Journal of Religious Thought*
J Th So Africa	*Journal of Theology for Southern Africa*
Luth Q	*Lutheran Quarterly*
Luth W	*Lutheran World.* Publication of the Lutheran World Federation
Mid-Stream	*Mid-Stream: An Ecumenical Journal*
Missio	*Missiology*
Other Side	*The Other Side*
Past Psych	*Pastoral Psychology*
Perkins J	*Perkins School of Theology Journal*

Princ S B	*The Princeton Seminary Bulletin*
Ref Pres W	*Reformed and Presbyterian World*
Rel Life	*Religion in Life*
Scot J Rel St	*The Scottish Journal of Religious Studies*
Scot J Th	*Scottish Journal of Theology*
Sojourners	*Sojourners*
St Luke J	*Saint Luke's Journal of Theology*
Th	*Theology*
Th Ed	*Theological Education*
Th St	*Theological Studies*
Th Today	*Theology Today*
Thought	*Thought. A Review of Culture and Idea*
Union S Q R	*Union Seminary Quarterly Review*
Wesley Th J	*Wesleyan Theological Journal*
Word World	*Word & World: Theology for Christian Ministry*
Worldview	*Worldview*

Foreword

The following work, under the title *The North American Theological Response to Latin American Liberation Theology. Validity and Limitations of a Praxis-Oriented Theology*, was originally presented to and accepted by the Protestant Theological Faculty of the Ludwig Maximilian University in Munich, West Germany in partial fulfillment of the requirements for the degree Doctor of Theology. In the present edition, two chapters from Part One of the dissertation entitled "Liberation Theology's Understanding of History: Past and Present" and "Theological Reflection and Reformulation: Central Themes" have been omitted.

With the publication of this dissertation in book form, I am acutely aware of the many persons to whom I wish to offer my sincere and heartfelt thanks: Professor Dr. Hans Schwarz, my *Doktorvater*, for the invitation to work as his Assistant at the University of Regensburg from 1982 until 1986 and for his support and guidance of my studies; Frau Bärbel Berger, Chellaian Lawrence, Malar Lawrence, and Professor Dr. Georg Kraus for their encouragement; James W. Erdman for proofreading and constructive comments; Professor Dr. Trutz Rendtorff of the University of Munich for guidance and for serving as a reader of the dissertation; Professor Dr. Horst Bürkle, also of the University of Munich, for likewise serving as a reader; Dr. Susan Thistlethwaite for her helpful service as Editor of the American Academy of Religion Dissertation Series; and Dennis Ford of Scholars Press for ably facilitating the publication process. To these individuals and to others who here remain nameless, I am deeply grateful.

I wish to dedicate this book to my German *Basisgemeinde*—Cathy, Benjamin, Nathaniel, and Sarah—without whose love and support none of this would have come to pass.

Cape Girardeau, Missouri   Easter 1988

Introduction

A. *The Western Theological Tradition and the Claims of Latin American Liberation Theology*

In a gradual but continual process of historical development, Christian theology came to be centered in Europe. When one speaks of "the church" with reference to the entire millennium between Constantine and Luther without further clarification, one tends to speak of the church with its center in Rome.[1] It is the Western tradition which has been authoritative for the history of Christianity,[2] producing such theological classics as Augustine's *The City of God* and the *Summa Theologiae* of Thomas Aquinas. When one examines the sixteenth century and the impact of the Protestant Reformation on Christian theology, one remains within this Western tradition with Europe at the center. The theological writings of Protestantism which are considered classic—whether authored by Luther, Calvin, Schleiermacher, or Barth—all have their origin on the European continent. One cannot begin to understand the history and the content of Christian theology without encountering and grappling with this Western tradition centered, whether Roman Catholic or Protestant, in Europe.

The movement of theological thought has thus been a flow of ideas outward from this center. The migration of peoples to the "New World" of the Americas was accompanied by the transplant of European theology into this new setting. The churches founded there were the

---

[1] This is in no way to denigrate the rich theological tradition of Eastern Christianity. It is only to say that the dominant and normative tradition has been that of Western Christianity. For a discussion of the contribution of Eastern Christianity and its relation to the West, see Jaroslav Pelikan, *The Christian Tradition. Vol. 2: The Spirit of Eastern Christendom* (Chicago/London: University of Chicago Press, 1974), esp. pp. 1-7.

[2] Cf. Adolf Harnack, *History of Dogma*, trans. Neil Buchanon (New York: Dover, 1961), 5:14-22.

1

churches of European immigrants. The missionaries who proclaimed Christianity to the indigenous peoples of America inevitably established the Western tradition as the standard. Both in North and in Latin America, theology stands within this Western tradition. One can understand neither the church nor the theology of the Americas without recognizing their dependence on European origins.[3]

It is only in view of the overwhelming significance of this Western tradition that one can begin to grasp the immensity of the claims which have been made for a new theology which has arisen in the context of Latin America, the theology which has come to be called "liberation theology."[4] The claims made for liberation theology by Latin American theologians have been many and various both in nature and in intensity. They include claims regarding the place of liberation theology in the history of modern theology; the innovativeness of liberation theology's method; the potential contribution of liberation theology to the worldwide church; and the prophetic nature of liberation theology's message.

Juan Carlos Scannone, for example, gives expression to liberation theology's claim to be "at the very least . . . the first major contribution to world theology that is truly original to Latin American theology" if not "the first major current in modern theology to develop outside of Europe."[5] The basis for such a claim is, according to Scannone, grounded in *the innovativeness of liberation theology's very method.*

> It would not be merely a new chapter in theology based on the same old theological methodology. It would not be like a "theology of politics," a "theology of revolution," or a "theology of temporal realities." Instead it would be a completely new reworking and formulation of theological activity as a whole from a completely new standpoint: i.e., the *kairos* of salvation history now being lived on our continent. Its reflection in the

[3] Cf. Enrique Dussel, *A History of the Church in Latin America: Colonialism to Liberation (1492-1979)*, trans. and ed. Alan Neely (Grand Rapids: Eerdmans, 1981), p. 17.

[4] There are in fact many theologies of liberation of recent origin, theologies done from a variety of perspectives—black, feminist, Latin American, African, Asian, etc.—each of which focus on liberation as their central theme. In this study, however, in order to avoid continual repetition of the entire label, "Latin American liberation theology," references to "liberation theology" or "the theology of liberation" refer to the Latin American expression unless otherwise noted.

[5] For this and the following quote see Juan Carlos Scannone, "Theology, Popular Culture, and Discernment," in Rosino Gibellini, ed., *Frontiers of Theology in Latin America*, trans. John Drury (Maryknoll: Orbis, 1979), p. 215.

light of God's word would not just be *about* liberation praxis; it would actually *start from that praxis* to reinterpret the riches of the faith, which itself is praxis.

The self-understanding of liberation theology has been developed in conscious differentiation from that of European theology. These differences can be seen most clearly in liberation theology's claim to an entirely new theological methodology: beginning with the situation of Latin America's poor and oriented towards a praxis designed to change the structural injustice which maintains them in a state of perpetual poverty. Such a starting point and orientation requires a radical break from the Western academic tradition. Insofar as Western theology has confined itself to the apologetical task of rendering the Christian faith intelligible to the questions of modernity, it is a theological approach sharply criticized by liberation theologians.

Another claim for liberation theology has been raised by Enrique Dussel regarding *the significance of liberation theology for the church worldwide.*

> Latin America right now has a fantastic responsibility. If I am correct in saying that the Latin American church is, by a design of Providence, situated within the poverty of the world, not by choice but by birth, then we have a great deal to do in the world of the near future. If the Latin American church does not commit itself to liberation, worldwide Christianity will have nothing to say to Asia or Africa.[6]

Dussel goes beyond Scannone in claiming for liberation theology not only a distinctively new approach to theology but even more a way of revitalizing the Christian message in the Third World context worldwide. Whereas the affluent churches of the First World have increasing difficulty speaking the Christian message with integrity to those living under conditions of poverty and oppression, liberation theology as it is being developed in the Latin American context claims to lead the way toward a renewed and vital proclamation of the Christian gospel.

Beyond the claims to theological innovation and the potential for the renewal of Christian proclamation in the face of Third World reality, Paulo Freire outlines *a prophetic role for liberation theology.*

> Finally, another kind of church has been taking shape in Latin America, though it is not often visible as a coherent totality. It is a church as old as Christianity itself, without being traditional, as new as Christianity, without being modernizing. It is the prophetic church. Opposed and attacked by both traditionalist and modernizing churches, as well as by the elite of the power structures, this utopian, prophetic and hope-filled

---

[6]Enrique Dussel, *Ethics and the Theology of Liberation* (Maryknoll: Orbis, 1978), p. 167.

movement rejects do-goodism and palliative reforms in order to commit itself to the dominated social classes and to radical social change.[7] Freire speaks here of a theology and a church that are not confined to intra-theological and intra-ecclesial concerns. Rather it is a church that is to speak prophetically to the world's power structures and demand social change. This is a way of speaking that is to lead theology out of the academic environment and the church out of the sanctuary. It leads also into the realm of political action and therefore controversy, often to the point of a breakdown in communication with those not sharing the perspective and analysis of liberation theology.

It is not only within Latin America that such claims have been made for liberation theology, however. Theologians outside the Latin American context have also raised numerous claims for liberation theology equal to if not exceeding those made by the Latin Americans themselves. Already this theology, unknown before the mid-1960s, has been described as "the most serious, sustained and theologically informed challenge the Western, dominant Christian paradigm has so far received."[8] While it cannot be denied that Latin American liberation theology continues to be indebted in many ways to this Western tradition (e.g., the influences of Marx, Metz, and Moltmann), at the same time, it is the conviction of many that there is something radically different about the way the theologians of liberation approach and carry out the theological task. Whether characterized as "a watershed for the continuing theological task of the Universal Church,"[9] as "a new way of doing theology,"[10] or as being "at the 'cutting edge' of theological endeavor,"[11] something theologically significant has emerged in liberation theology which calls for reflection, study, and response.

---

[7]Paulo Freire, "Education, Liberation and the Church," *Risk* 9, No. 2 (1973):45.

[8]Beverly Wildung Harrison, "The 'Theology in the Americas' Conference: Challenging the Western Paradigm," *Chr Cris* 35 (Oct. 27, 1975): 254.

[9]J. Andrew Kirk, *Liberation Theology. An Evangelical View from the Third World* (Atlanta: John Knox, 1979), p. 204.

[10]Robert McAfee Brown, "Reflections on Detroit," *Chr Cris* 35 (Oct. 27, 1975):255.

[11]Monika Hellwig, "Liberation Theology: An Emerging School," *Scot J Th* 30 (1977):151.

B. The Purpose and Structure of This Study

With the emergence of what has come to be called "Third World theology" in general and Latin American liberation theology in particular as its most sophisticated current representative, a new situation has also been created for theology in North America. Whereas North American theology has long turned first to the latest issues of European theology for its theological agenda, so much so at times as to be characterized as "mere footnotes to European theology," it is an event of major significance that North American theologians have been extending their view toward new horizons in the Third World and especially in Latin America. No longer is North American theology marked by an almost exclusive interest in dialogue with and commentary upon the European theological tradition and its current representatives. Instead increasing attention has been directed to themes original to North America, e.g., American civil religion, black theology, or feminist theology, and to dialogue with the various Third World theologies originating in Africa, Asia, and Latin America. While the European theological tradition remains the indispensable foundation for North American theology, it is nevertheless of major significance that what was formerly a two-way conversation between North American and European theology (with the former doing most of the listening) has suddenly become a conversation with numerous participants, each making their own original contribution.

It is to one particular coordinate within this new theological constellation that the present work directs itself, the North American response to Latin American liberation theology. How has Latin American liberation theology during its first years of existence impacted and influenced the discussion of theologians in North America? How has liberation theology been received and how has it been criticized? Questions such as these first motivated the present study. Yet, on closer examination, the North American responses to liberation theology have been so diverse, even polarized, that in the course of research a new question pressed itself ever more to the forefront: which, if any, of the North American criticisms of liberation theology are valid on the basis of what has been written by the Latin American liberation theologians and warrant from liberation theology further clarification? In order to address these basic questions, this work consists of three parts.

1. Descriptive Analysis of Latin American Liberation Theology

To undertake an evaluation of the North American response to Latin American liberation theology first requires a fundamental knowledge of the basic tenets of liberation theology itself. Where this fundamental knowledge is absent, the presupposition for serious evaluation and critique is also absent. For this reason, the first part of this work consists of two chapters which analytically describe the starting point and basic presuppositions (Chapter 1) and the method (Chapter 2) of liberation theology. In this first part the attempt is made to represent the viewpoint of liberation theology by paying attention to its own arguments, especially in the literature which has been most readily accessible to North American theologians.

Particularly important for an adequate understanding of liberation theology is its affirmation of praxis as the *sine qua non* of theology. What liberation theology means by praxis, however, is most elusive due to the lack of consensus regarding its definition even among liberation theologians themselves. The reason for this unclarity, as argued in the second chapter, is that praxis refers to nothing less than the very method of liberation theology. To understand the meaning of praxis for liberation theology thus requires an analysis of its entire methodology according to its constitutive elements. Anything less underestimates the significance of praxis for the entirety of the liberation theology viewpoint.

It might be mentioned from the outset that the years between 1968 and 1983, that is, the first fifteen years since the emergence of liberation theology provide the temporal frame of reference for this study. 1968 marks the year of the ground-breaking Medellin Bishop's Conference and also the crucial year for the emergence of liberation theology according to those participating in its formulation. By the year 1983, the literature had grown to immense proportions and the major emphases of liberation theology had become clear. In order to limit the scope of this work, primary attention will be devoted to these years.

2. Responses of North American Theologians to Latin American Liberation Theology

The second part of this study details the most significant North American responses to Latin American liberation theology. These responses are organized into two chapters which represent, first, the response of those theologians generally resonant to the concerns of liberation theology (Chapter 3) and, secondly, those responses raising more critical questions of liberation theology (Chapter 4). Selected to represent the resonant North American responses to liberation theology are the positions of Richard Shaull, James H. Cone, Frederick Herzog, Robert McAfee Brown, Rosemary Radford Ruether, and three evangelical theologians—Ronald J. Sider, Jim Wallis, and Alfred C. Krass—as well as the work of the Theology in the Americas project. Among those theologians raising critical issues of liberation theology from a variety of perspectives are James V. Schall, Michael Novak, Robert Benne, Dennis P. McCann, Richard John Neuhaus, Carl E. Braaten, Daniel L. Migliore, Peter C. Hodgson, John B. Cobb, Jr., Delwin Brown, Schubert M. Ogden, and the evangelical theologians C. Peter Wagner, Carl F. H. Henry, and Donald G. Bloesch. The latter theologians have been organized according to the particular questions which they raise of liberation theology. In examining the positions of these several North American theologians on the question of liberation theology, an interesting spectrum of views and arguments present themselves for critical evaluation.

3. Critical Analysis

The division of North American responses into two distinct chapters indicates the tendency toward polarization among North American responses to liberation theology. Like earlier debates which have polarized North American theology, for example, the question of the appropriateness of the historical-critical method for the interpretation of the Bible (in the nineteenth and early twentieth centuries) or the debate over the theological proposal of the death of God (in the decade of the 1960s), liberation theology is the issue which, perhaps more than any other, polarizes the current North American theological scene. Though it is a massive oversimplification to divide theologians into those who are "for" liberation theology and those who are "against" it, the dynamics of the North American discussion tend to insist upon such neat categories.

Chapter 5 begins with an examination of the dynamics which have led to this polarization of the entire North American discussion of liberation theology. These reflections are then followed by an evaluation of the North American responses to liberation theology in which the critical questions raised of liberation theology by North American theologians are discussed and evaluated. Four issues emerge from this discussion of the North American criticism which warrant further clarification on the part of liberation theology—the questions of its philosophical basis, theological method, theological anthropology, and concept of liberation. These four issues represent the limitations of the praxis-oriented theology of liberation as it has thus far been formulated by Latin American liberation theologians.

At the same time, however, it is further argued that these questions raised of liberation theology in no way negate liberation theology as a significant and valid theological option. Particularly within the context of Latin America, a praxis-oriented theology of liberation is an option validated both by biblical and theological criteria and by the plausibility structure in which this theology is located. By affirming the validity of liberation theology in the Latin American context while also recognizing the relevance of a number of North American criticisms of liberation theology, a position is attained for a more reasonable discussion of the merits and limitations of liberation theology beyond the dynamics of polarization which have characterized the recent discussion.

C. *Responding to the Challenge of Liberation Theology*

Jose Miguez Bonino has argued that theology is always written from a particular point of view.[12] While "we are *situated* by birth, place, education . . . we can *position* ourselves by option." He argues that by positioning oneself "from a conscious and lucid option for the poor," the theologian

(1) views the task of theology from a unique perspective,

(2) establishes definite priorities for reflection, and

(3) clearly defines the goal and purpose of the theological enterprise.

In terms of *perspective*, "the world simply looks differently when seen from an executive's office and from a shanty town. Perspectives hide certain things and make others visible." To proceed theologically from the position of the poor inevitably gives theology a unique vision and content.

In terms of *priorities for reflection*, Miguez Bonino asserts that no theology "can embrace the totality of God's revelation and human need." Therefore it is with care one should decide "what questions

---

[12]For the following quotes, Jose Miguez Bonino, "Doing Theology in the Context of the Struggles of the Poor," *Mid Stream* 20 (1981):369-373.

have priority, what subjects are worth thinking about ("denkwürdig" was Heidegger's expression) and which ones are superfluous, secondary, or alienating."

In terms of the *goal and purpose of the theological enterprise*, Miguez Bonino reminds those who engage in theological discussion of the impact theology inevitably makes in either supporting or challenging the social order of its time. "We cannot anymore ignore the fact that our theological reflection plays such a role and thus, we cannot avoid the question: for whom? for whose sake—in terms of human reality—do we work?"

Latin American liberation theology has raised for theologians in the First World deep and penetrating questions like these about the perspective, priorities, goal, and purpose of the theological task. The challenge is one that deserves response as it positions the poor of Latin America as a mirror in which to examine First World theology and Christian practice.[13] Having encountered in Latin American liberation theology something profoundly *denkwürdig*, it is the hope of the author that this study may contribute in some small way to the ongoing theological, ecumenical, and, simply, Christian task—that we might love because God first loved us (I John 4:19).

---

[13]Thomas E. Quigley, "Latin America's Church: No Turning Back," *Cross Curr* 28, No. 1 (1978):80, makes this statement regarding the importance of the church in the United States listening to the Latin American church: "The Latin American church has more to say to the U.S. church than any other. Christians have more to learn here than any place else about being the church, about community, about what Eucharist means, and about what commitment to the poor has to do with fidelity to Christ."

PART ONE:

DESCRIPTIVE ANALYSIS

OF LATIN AMERICAN LIBERATION THEOLOGY

Chapter One

Starting Point and Basic Presuppositions

A. *A Nontraditional Theological Starting Point*
  1. Poverty as the Motivation for Doing Theology
    a. *A New Correlation: The Question of Poverty*

Paul Tillich, in the introduction to his *Systematic Theology*, describes the method of systematic theology as the "method of correlation."[1]

> In using the method of correlation, systematic theology proceeds in the following way: it makes an analysis of the human situation out of which the existential questions arise, and it demonstrates that the symbols used in the Christian message are the answers to these questions.[2]

According to Tillich, the theologian, analyzing the human situation by means of the materials of human culture (e.g., philosophy, poetry, drama, literature, psychology, sociology), can hear the significant questions being raised by humanity. It then becomes the theological task to answer these questions from the resources of the Christian faith. The theological task is, in short, to apply the answers of Christian revelation to the human existential questions of the day.

A fundamental correlation, mediating between human reality and the Christian faith, also is basic to Latin American liberation theology.[3] The starting point of liberation theology is most definitely the human situation. It begins with questions raised out of human experience. But at the same time it is necessary to make an essential

---

[1] Paul Tillich, *Systematic Theology. Vol. 1: Reason and Revelation and Being and God* (Chicago: University of Chicago, 1951), pp. 59-66.

[2] Ibid., p. 62.

[3] For example, Juan Luis Segundo, *A Theology for Artisans of a New Humanity. Vol. 2: Grace and the Human Condition*, trans. John Drury (Maryknoll: Orbis, 1974), p. 13, makes reference to the correlative nature of the theological task. For more on the role of correlation in the thought of Segundo, especially in contrast to Tillich, cf. David R. Peel, "Juan Luis Segundo's, 'A Theology for Artisans of a New Humanity': A Latin American Contribution to Contemporary Theological Understanding," *Perkins J* 30 (Spring 1977):5.

14 Orthopraxis or Heresy

distinction between the nature of the questions raised by the Latin American context and the questions Tillich, like other theologians, has addressed in the European and North American context. Tillich attempted to answer the question of existential meaning. His theology is an attempt to make the symbols of Christianity intelligible in response to modern humanity's loss of a sense of purpose and direction. His theology is an apologetic theology in which the questioner is the religious skeptic, the "non-believer." It is to the intellectual questions of this modern religious skeptic and the situation of spiritual emptiness in which they are asked that the theology of Tillich most directly addresses itself.

Tillich has been by no means alone in this theological effort. Langdon Gilkey summarizes the aim of twentieth-century theology this way:

> ... the efforts of religious thinkers in our century have by and large been directed at these two inter-related problems: (1) a justification of the meaning and the validity of the concept of God in relation to other, apparently less questionable forms of experience—scientific, philosophical, social, political, artistic, psychological, or existential; and (2) a reformulation of that concept so that it can be meaningful and relevant to the modern world.[4]

The central question that twentieth century theology has tried to answer has been a question about the relevance and the meaning of "God" in the skeptical modern world. It is exactly here, in the nature of the question being asked, where a sharp distinction must be made between these theologies and the Latin American theology of liberation.

The most well-known formulation of the distinctive question which liberation theology attempts to answer is that of Gustavo Gutierrez.

> A good part of contemporary theology seems to have sprung from the challenge of the non-believer. The non-believer questions our religious world and demands from it a very deep purification and renewal. Bonhoeffer took this challenge and sharply formulated the question that is at the heart of many theological efforts of our time: how to announce God in a world that has come of age or become adult ("Mundig")?
>
> In a continent like Latin America, the challenge does not come to us primarily from the non-believer, but from the non-person, that is to say, from him who is not recognized as such by the existing social order: the poor, the exploited, one who is systematically deprived of being a person, one who scarcely knows that he or she is a person. The non-person questions before anything else, not our religious world, but our economic,

---

[4]Langdon Gilkey, "God," Chapter 3 in Peter C. Hodgson and Robert H. King, eds., *Christian Theology. An Introduction to Its Traditions and Tasks* (Philadelphia: Fortress Press, 1982), p. 63.

social, political and cultural world; and thus, a call is made for the revolutionary transformation of the very bases of a dehumanizing society. Our question, therefore, is not how to announce God in an adult world; but rather how to announce him as *Father* in a non-human world.[5] The starting point of Latin American liberation theology is not the question of meaning or unbelief as such. It is, rather, the question of poverty as it is lived and experienced among the majority of the Latin American people. It would be difficult to overstate the significance of poverty as the theological starting point for Latin American liberation theology.[6] Intellectual questions about the meaning and purpose of

---

[5]Gustavo Gutierrez, "Faith As Freedom: Solidarity With the Alienated and Confidence in the Future," *Horizons* 2 (Spring 1975):43.

[6]Throughout the world it has been recognized that it is finally the reality of poverty which has given rise to liberation theology. For example, the North American Richard P. Albertine, "Worship and the Theology of Liberation," *St Luke J* 20 (Mar. 1977):139, writes: "The theology of liberation was born out of the 'deep groanings,' 'los gemidos,' of the people of God of Latin America."
More specific in depicting the starting point of liberation theology is the South African theologian Harold Wells, "Segundo's Hermeneutic Circle," *J Th So Africa* 34 (Mar. 1981):28: "It begins with the situation, one of terrible human need: starvation, stark injustice, political power maintained by tactics of brutal torture and arbitrary imprisonment."
Especially significant for the relatedness of the Latin American to other Third World contexts are the comments of the Indian theologian Sam Amirtham, "Training the Ministers the Church Ought to Have," *Int R Miss* 66 (Jan. 1977):49: "*Experience with the poor is a condition for authentic theological reflection* in the Third World context. I would like to underscore what has been said: that the experience of the *marginals* belongs to the very stuff of theological reflection. Only a direct experience of the poor, from the inside as it were, qualifies one for meaningful theological reflection as to the meaning of the Gospel to the poor. There is a qualitative difference in experience, according to whether it is from inside or outside, and this qualitative difference will be reflected in the theology produced. Being within the struggle, identifying oneself totally with the poor, 'being knit together in friendships, festivities, and funerals,' is essential for this task."
So, too, Latin American liberation theologians witness directly to poverty as the motivating force of their theological concern. Gustavo Gutierrez, "Talking About God," *Sojourners* 12, No. 2 (Feb. 1983):27 thus writes: "The starting point for Third World theologies is the struggle of the poor and oppressed against all forms of injustice and domination."
Lastly, Jose Miguez-Bonino, "Doing Theology in the Context of the Struggles of the Poor," *Mid-Stream* 20 (1981):369, states clearly the context of poverty in which liberation theology has arisen, especially in contrast to other theological viewpoints: "Is there any other context? Poverty is the dominant and growing reality of our world. The 'rich world' is wise in tracing for us itineraries through life which (like those prepared by tourist agents) never cross the paths of the poor. A theologian or a church may choose to keep to those carefully chosen ways, to 'theologize' as if the poor did not exist. It becomes,

modern life lose their priority for those whose daily question is that of
finding something to eat and whose constant struggle is merely to
survive.

b. *The Pastoral Context*

Poverty as a question did not first come to the forefront in Latin
American theology as a result of objective, rational, scientific,
academic inquiry. Unlike the theology often arising in the First
World context, liberation theology does not consider itself to be a
theology which has its roots in the university. It is not a theology which
has had as its ultimate goal the production of statements which "meet
the two criteria of appropriateness or understandability" as the basic
requirements of an "adequate theology."[7] Rather liberation theology
has arisen primarily out of a pastoral situation in which priests and
ministers have been challenged to respond to the life context of their
parishioners.

> The theology of liberation was not invented by theologians. The
> theologians have been able to articulate it in terms of theological doctrine
> or biblical interpretation. But the basic thrust has come from ministers
> and priests actually working with the poor people and among them.[8]

Pastoral ministry in the context of the poor sets new priorities for
theological reflection. "Many intramural questions of the clergy show
up as superfluous and secondary in the face of hunger, sickness, the
mortality rate, ignorance, alienation, persecution, and torture."[9]
These are clearly not the typical materials out of which one constructs a
modern theology. Yet it is this pastoral reality which has been the
catalyst for liberation theology.

Similarly for many bishops of Latin America, a new episcopal
orientation has been called forth by the reality of poverty in their
dioceses and parishes. This new orientation is characterized by the

though, increasingly difficult: the reality of poverty invades the cities, the
parks, the suburbia, even the churches of the rich!"

[7]These are the basic criteria of theology according to Schubert Ogden,
"What Is Theology?" *J Rel* 52 (1972):25.

[8]Jose Miguez Bonino, "Discussion—Selected Extracts," printed text of
discussion extracts from the July 1976 meeting of the Theological Education
Fund Committee, *Int R Miss* 66 (1977):34.

[9]Mendez Arceo, "Address of Bishop Mendez Arceo," in John Eagleson, ed.,
*Christians and Socialism. Documentation of the Christians for Socialism
Movement in Latin America*, trans. John Drury (Maryknoll: Orbis, 1975), p.
155.

demand for pastoral responsibility in defending basic human rights of the members of the church.

[The bishops] did not invent this function, they did not deduce it from some theological principle. It was forced upon them by the piles of letters coming every day, by the people queuing up at the door of the episcopal residence to present their case or to plead for a relative, by the anguished priests from shanty towns and student homes, on the verge of nervous breakdown under the weight of what they saw day after day—and even more, night after night—among their people.[10]

Both bishops and theologians have been summoned to respond to this pastoral reality. It is in the world of the poor and especially in the parishes of the poor where the theology of liberation has its roots. To begin with the poor is a radically different starting point calling for a radically different theological agenda.

c. The Call for Commitment

Liberation theologians, beginning from the reality of poverty, place a high priority on the *commitment* of the theologian toward altering the shape of this reality. They argue that one cannot encounter the devastating effects of poverty in Latin America without being changed by them. Segundo in particular has talked about the compassion of the human heart and the commitment to liberation as prerequisites to the theological task.[11] Raul Vidales similarly speaks of "choice" and "commitment" as basic requisites when faced with Latin American reality.

For our part, we are convinced that this is the inescapable historical "movement" in which we Christians have to make a clear and effective choice: to live the Gospel of Jesus Christ, as a struggle for the liberation of all the poor, as a concrete expression of our faith, and as a permanent commitment to the message.[12]

Much has been written regarding this claim that the reality of poverty demands commitment on the part of the theologian. Suffice it here to say two things. First, this is not a theology that attempts to be neutral and objective in its approach. Rather it is a theology committed to changing the situation of poverty. No attempt is made to claim neutrality. In fact, the very opposite, that is, deliberate commitment

---

[10]Jose Miguez Bonino, "New Trends in Theology," *Duke Div R* 42 (Fall 1977):135.

[11]Cf. Juan Luis Segundo, *The Liberation of Theology*, trans. John Drury (Maryknoll: Orbis, 1976), pp. 81-90.

[12]Raul Vidales, "Peoples' Church and Christian Ministry," *Int R Miss* 66 (1977):39.

and the choice of "solidarity with the poor" are understood to be required in the face of such urgent human needs.[13]

Secondly, the commitment of the liberation theologians to altering the situation of poverty means that this theology does not limit its concern to scriptural interpretation and traditional theological and philosophical topics. Rather, commitment to the poor means for them employing other disciplines and points of view, e.g., political, economic, sociological, and even Marxist analysis, in an attempt to understand and change the harsh living conditions under which so many are forced to exist. The arguments and conclusions of these other disciplines are employed extensively by the theologians of liberation as vehicles necessary for carrying out their criticism of Latin American socioeconomic reality.

d. *Praxis-Orientation*

The Latin American liberation theologians take with utmost seriousness the situation in which they live. "If Latin American theologians have anything original, it is their effort to relate their concept of Christianity to the Latin culture."[14] The one viewing this theology from a distance must never lose sight of the intimate relationship between this theology and the context in which it has emerged. John William Hart, for example, has carefully demonstrated the close connection between "topia" (social-context) and "utopia" (social-vision) in liberation theology by examining the thought of Camilo Torres in his Colombian social milieu and Gustavo Gutierrez in his Peruvian social context.[15] To actually understand liberation theology apart from its historical context is simply not possible.

The word that is most frequently used to describe this persistent orientation of liberation theology to its socioeconomic and historical context is the word *praxis*. Praxis is chosen by the theologians of liberation to express that which is distinctive about their thought. The word praxis incorporates the entire scope of liberation theology as it

---

[13]Gustavo Gutierrez, *A Theology of Liberation*, trans. and ed. Caridad Inda and John Eagleson (Maryknoll: Orbis, 1973), p. 301.

[14]Emilio A. Nunez, "The Theology of Liberation in Latin America," *Bib Sac* 134 (1977):343.

[15]John William Hart, "Topia and Utopia in Colombia and Peru—The Theory and Practice of Camilo Torres and Gustavo Gutierrez in their Historical Contexts," Ph.D. Dissertation (New York: Union Theological Seminary, 1978).

moves from an encounter with the Latin American context of poverty and oppression into socioeconomic analysis and theological reflection and then returns to the task of constructing a more just future for Latin America. Praxis-orientation thus refers to a way of theologizing that never loses sight of its own participation in the liberation process. The word praxis is used repeatedly by the liberation theologians and will be more closely examined in Chapter Two. It is sufficient to note at this point that praxis-orientation encompasses both the starting point (i.e., poverty) and goal (i.e., engagement) of this theology. Theological reflection takes place between these two poles. Liberation theology is thus, in the words of Gutierrez, "critical reflection on praxis."[16]

2. Poverty in Latin America
a. A Situation of Radical Disparity

Phillip Berryman has clearly stated the centrality of the context of poverty for liberation theology.

> . . . its value comes not so much from new "discoveries" in doctrine or ethics as from a new relationship to the social context of oppression-liberation in Latin America. Indeed, it thus makes theological issues out of apparently "profane" realities.[17]

These "profane realities" are not the realities which typically occupy modern theologians. They are, however, the realities which motivate the theology of liberation. They are not pleasant realities. They are realities which the "affluent," that is, those who need not worry about having bread to eat, prefer to avoid. Yet that is all the more reason why the reality of poverty needs to be considered in some detail, since this is the daily experience faced by the majority of human beings who live in Latin America.

Paulo Freire has written:

> It should not be necessary here to cite statistics to show how many Brazilians (and Latin Americans in general) are "living corpses," "shadows" of human beings, hopeless men, women, and children victimized by an endless "invisible war" in which their remnants of life are devoured by tuberculosis, schistosomiasis, infant diarrhea . . . by the myriad diseases of poverty.[18]

Perhaps for those who stand nearer to the Latin American reality such citing of statistics is indeed unnecessary. But for those who stand

---

[16]Cf. Gutierrez, A Theology of Liberation, pp. 6-15.

[17]Phillip E. Berryman, "Latin American Liberation Theology," Th St 34 (1973):383.

[18]Paulo Freire, Pedagogy of the Oppressed, trans. Myra Bergman Ramos (New York: Seabury, 1974), p. 172.

distant it is indeed necessary in order to grasp the dimensions of
poverty and oppression which exist in Latin America.
Some startling statistics provide an initial point of reference.

> In Latin American countries a minority of 5-10% generally controls half
> the wealth, whereas the lower third of the population may receive only 5%
> of the wealth. Similarly the United States, with 6% of the world's
> population, uses 40% of its raw materials.[19]

Here not only the extreme disparity between rich and poor nations but
also the disparity between rich and poor within individual nations is
indicated.

This disparity becomes even clearer when reference is made to
particular countries. El Salvador can be employed as a first example.

> El Salvador has a small group of wealthy families—known apocryphally
> as "The Fourteen"—and a largely impoverished population of 5.2 million.
> Government statistics tell one story: 2 percent of farms occupy 56 percent of
> cultivable land, while 91.4 percent occupy only 21.9 percent of the land; 50
> percent of adults are illiterate; 40 percent suffer seasonal unemployment,
> and chronic malnutrition affects 70 percent of children under the age of
> 6.[20]

Even more startling, however, are statistics stemming from Brazil, a
country which is often noted for its recent economic progress and cited
as an example of the possibility of gradual economic development.

> Take the case of Brazil, the largest nation in Latin America and much
> celebrated in recent years for its "economic miracle." According to the
> military government's figures (which, to say the least, are bound to be on
> the conservative side), one quarter of its population of over 100 million
> belong to the category of "indigent and destitute." Not less than 70% of the
> national income flows generously to the highly privileged 20% of the upper
> echelons of society; whereas 40% of the population survive on a family
> income of less than US $850 a year in a market of international prices.
> And one can extrapolate this appalling imbalance with relative safety to
> most other Latin American countries.[21]

Such statistics speak for themselves. An extreme disparity exists in
Latin America between those who have and those who do not. These
are, moreover, not only statistics. They represent human lives.

b. *A Complexity of Factors*

There exist a multitude of factors which combine to constitute the
reality of poverty in Latin America.

---

[19]Berryman, "Latin American Liberation Theology," p. 386.

[20]Alan Riding, "Latin Church in Siege," *New York Times Magazine*
(May 6, 1979):40.

[21]Aharon Sapezian, "Ministry With the Poor," *Int R Miss* 66 (Jan. 1977):4.

Lack of industries, unemployment, illiteracy, disease, lack of skilled labor and low salaries, lack of roads, obsolete techniques of agriculture, the transformation of vast areas for cattle-raising, and other questions show a pretty complex reality.[22]

In fact, the reality of poverty in Latin America is more than "pretty" complex. When one begins to examine these many factors and the interrelationships between them, it is impossible to establish simple cause and effect equations. What follows is a descriptive sketch of several of the factors contributing to Latin American poverty. They are here artificially isolated from one another in order to give clearer definition to the word "poverty." By identifying the following factors, the attempt is made to make that reality more concrete. No claim is made to be exhaustive. Moreover, one must remain mindful of the interrelationship and dependence of these factors upon one another. These are some of the basic themes which appear often in the literature of liberation theology.

Malnutrition. Poverty is often equated with hunger or malnutrition. It is perhaps the most visible and shocking manifestation of poverty. Numerous studies are available depicting in detail the extent to which hunger and malnutrition stalk the planet and the human toll which is paid.[23] Statistics tell one story, for example, these from the Central American region:

> In El Salvador, according to the most recent data (1973), 72 percent of the population received less than the recommended number of calories for a nutritionally adequate diet as defined by the Food and Agriculture Organization of the United Nations and the World Health Organization. In Guatemala the percentage of the population who were undernourished was 69 percent, in Honduras 60 percent, in the Dominican Republic 58 percent and in Panama 51 percent.[24]

Comparable statistics could be cited for other Latin American countries.

Even more graphic and disturbing is the following description of the process of starvation in which statistics begin to take on human form.

> The victim of starvation burns up his own body fats, muscles and tissues for fuel. His body quite literally consumes itself and deteriorates rapidly. The kidneys, liver and endocrine system soon cease to function properly.

---

[22]Dom Moacyr as quoted by Alvaro Barreiro, "Grass-Roots Ecclesial Communities and the Evangelization of the Poor," *Foun* 23 (Oct.-Dec. 1980):298.

[23]For example, see Ronald J. Sider, *Rich Christians in an Age of Hunger* (Downers Grove: Inter-Varsity Press, 1977).

[24]John P. Olinger, "The Caribbean Basin Initiative: Land & Hunger," *Bread for the World Background Paper* No. 61 (July 1982):2.

A shortage of carbohydrates, which play a vital role in brain chemistry, affects the mind. Lassitude and confusion set in, so that starvation victims often seem unaware of their plight. The body's defenses drop; disease kills most famine victims before they have time to starve to death.[25]

Such is the process of starvation by which millions of human beings in Latin America suffer to various degrees.

Disease. Immunity to disease is significantly diminished as a result of malnutrition.[26] Diarrhea, parasitic infestations, and measles are among those diseases to which the malnourished poor are most vulnerable. The unavailability of adequate health care, immunization, and medication complicates and magnifies the effects of disease on a malnourished population. Especially vulnerable to disease are infants and young children. When analyzing statistics, it is difficult to separate and distinguish between those who die of hunger and those who die from a disease whose onset was given occasion by malnutrition.

Infant Mortality. Infant mortality in Latin America occurs at a rate several times higher than in the First World. In 1973 statistics revealed that in El Salvador the rate is four times higher than that of the United States; in Honduras it is eight times as high; in Nicaragua over nine times greater.[27] The malnutrition of the mother during pregnancy is a major factor in infant mortality. In addition, the trend away from breast feeding to the use of infant formula and the problems that entails in terms of cost, hygiene, nutrition, and loss of immunological protection has played a significant role in the incidence of infant mortality.[28] Undernourished infants are also especially susceptible to fatal disease, a problem compounded by a shortage of medical facilities and medications.

In spite of these problems, significant progress in overcoming infant mortality could be attained at relatively low cost and with immediate results given the introduction of a four-fold program to combat it. The four techniques advocated by the United Nations Children's Fund include oral rehydration therapy, growth monitoring, expanded immunization, and education regarding the

---

[25]*Time*, Nov. 11, 1975, p. 68 as quoted by Jose Miguez Bonino, "Poverty as Curse, Blessing and Challenge," *Iliff R* 34 (Fall 1977):6.

[26]For this and the following cf. Sally Urvina, "Malnutrition in Third World Countries," *Chr Cent* 101 (May 23, 1984):550-552.

[27]Olinger, "The Caribbean Basin Initiative," p. 2.

[28]Urvina, "Malnutrition in Third World Countries," pp. 550-552.

advantages of breast feeding and supplementary nutrition.[29] While the technology for significantly reducing infant mortality is already available, what appears to be lacking is the political will to implement the available methods.

Land Distribution. A factor of major significance is the unequal distribution of land in Latin America. Leopoldo Zea has called this "the central problem of the Americas."[30] According to Zea, redistribution of land ownership is the key to economic and social transformation. The uneven distribution of land in Latin America has its origins in the colonial period following the Iberian conquest. The baronial style of life in which a minority have controlled an inordinate share of the land has survived through the centuries and evolved into ever new forms. Today it is often corporations which possess an inordinate share of the land.

Jacques Kozub cites the example of Haiti where "85 percent of the population of 5 million lives in the most unimaginably squalid conditions in rural areas, while a few foreign firms obtain large land concessions from the state at $3 annually per acre."[31] El Salvador provides an especially acute example of the problem of land distribution "with the wealthiest 2 percent controlling over half the land" and where "fifty percent of the landholders have controlled only 5 percent of the land."[32] El Salvador, though an extreme example of inequity, nevertheless illustrates the nature of the problem of land distribution and ownership. Even in countries such as Mexico, where the inequities are less dramatic and where land reform has been dictated by law, wealthy landowners have been able to employ political influence to thwart enforcement of these laws in order to maintain their advantages.[33]

Export Cropping. Related to the problem of land distribution is the problem of the purpose for which the land is often used. "Export

---

[29]See James P. Grant, "The State of the World's Children 1984," published by the United Nations Children's Fund, esp. pp. 1-26.

[30]See Leopoldo Zea, *Latin America and the World*, trans. Frances K. Hendricks and Beatrice Berler (Norman: University of Oklahoma Press, 1969), pp. 33-51.

[31]Jacques Kozub, "Continuing the Discussion: Liberation Theology and Christian Realism," *Chr Cris* 33 (1973):204.

[32]Lane Vanderslice, "El Salvador: Land & Hunger," *Bread for the World Background Paper* No. 54 (June 1981):2.

[33]Brennon Jones, "Export Cropping and Development. We Need to Know More," *Bread for the World Background Paper* No. 25 (Apr. 1978):2.

cropping" refers to the phenomenon in which the land, instead of being used to grow food staples for an impoverished population, is used to grow export crops such as coffee, cotton, bananas, sugar, or beef that are exported to foreign markets. In Central America roughly half of the cultivated land, and generally the most fertile, is used for such export crops.[34]

Such a system might be justifiable were the income from such export crops in turn used to care for the needs of the people who live in these countries. Unfortunately, however, that is seldom the case and relatively few actually profit from the export crop system. Often the Latin American people are forced to pay higher prices for food which is subsequently imported from other countries rather than using the land of their own country for their own food supply. Ronald J. Sider gives a reminder of the human impact of this problem when he writes that "half of the cultivated land in Central America is used to grow export crops to sell to rich nations, while 60% of their children die of malnutrition before they are five."[35]

A problem somewhat related to that of export cropping involves not only the export of crops but foreign export of natural resources. Precious natural resources such as minerals and oil have been exported to aid in the industrial development of other lands, a process in which relatively few have derived the financial gain and the vast majority have gained nothing. The depletion of these natural resources further retards the economy and minimizes the possibility of future industrialization. The land, depleted of natural resources, is yet poorer.

Inadequate Structures. "The undernutrition of millions of people in developing countries is in most cases not the result of inadequate food supplies in the world or within the countries where they live. Rather it is a product of poverty resulting from the ways in which governments and businesses manage national and international economies. The poor are poor and hunger exists in large part because the continued existence of these poor either serves, or does not threaten,

---

[34]Beverly Keene, "Export Cropping in Central America," *Bread for the World Background Paper* No. 43 (Jan. 1980):1-4.

[35]Ronald J. Sider, *Christ and Violence* (Scottdale, PA: Herald Press, 1979), p. 69.

certain vested economic and political interests."[36] The combined effect of governments, Latin American and foreign, together with business in preserving their vested economic and political interests results for the poor in social structures inadequate in addressing their most basic human needs. The reality of poverty in Latin America is maintained and supported by political and economic systems which function to preserve the status quo and its benefits for the few at the expense of those at the bottom of the socioeconomic ladder.

The most widespread form of government in Latin America and the most effective at maintaining the status quo for the privileged few has been that of the military regime. Through this authoritarian structure, given financial, technical, and military support by foreign governments (in recent times notably by the United States), strict and often repressive control has been enforced. Corporate interests, especially those of foreign concerns, have been defended by the military governments and by the judiciary in most Latin American countries. Thus the existing disparate division of wealth has been maintained. Dissent has been stifled, often violently.[37]

The ways in which governments exercise their power in the repression of political dissent has been capably monitored by the work of Amnesty International.[38] The 1982 report of Amnesty International, for example, thoroughly documents the use of political power in Latin America to quell dissent. Expulsion, imprisonment, torture, disappearances, and execution are means by which systems are maintained and opposition is eliminated. Specific examples of the use of these means can be cited for each Latin American country.

---

[36]"Cultivating Malnutrition," excerpts from the United States Government Accounting Office Study, "World Hunger: Implications for U.S. Policies," *Bread for the World Background Paper* No. 38 (Aug. 1979):1.

[37]For a graphic description of the social, economic, political, military, and religious factors active in recent Latin American history, see Penny Lernoux, *Cry of the People* (New York: Penguin, 1982). Lernoux cites numerous specific cases and data documenting persecution against those who have sought reform, especially those within the church. The involvement of the U.S. government in supporting military rule in Latin America and the preferential treatment given multi-national corporations is amply documented.

[38]*Amnesty International Report 1982. A Survey of Amnesty International's Work on Political Imprisonment, Torture, and Executions* (London: Amnesty International, 1982). See esp. pp. 105-175 on "The Americas." Another more personal account of the effects of political repression is the witness of Argentina's "Mothers of the Plaza de Mayo." See Elizabeth Hanly, "A Seventh Year of Unknowing," *Sojourners* 12, No. 4 (Apr. 1983):21-25.

It is this structural dimension of the problem of poverty in Latin America that the theology of liberation attempts to address most directly. Structural injustice is understood by liberation theology as the fundamental cause of poverty in Latin America. The theology of liberation rejects those models which explain the problems of Latin America as results of "underdevelopment," a situation which can be gradually overcome through a process of development. Rather, the theology of liberation accepts a different theoretical model, that of "dependency" in explaining the structural nature of Latin American poverty. The theory of dependency is, together with the appropriation of the biblical theme of liberation, a basic presupposition of the theology of liberation.

Summary. Some of the basic factors contributing to the existence of poverty in Latin America have here been outlined. They are by no means comprehensive. To these factors many others could be added and documented in greater detail. The following quote suggests still other factors not examined above.

> The socio-economic, political, and cultural situation of the peoples of Latin America poses a challenge to our Christian conscience. Unemployment, malnutrition, alcoholism, infant mortality, illiteracy, prostitution, ever growing inequality between rich and poor, racial and educational discrimination, exploitation, and so forth: these are the factors that go to make up a situation of institutionalized violence in Latin America.[39]

In addition to providing a concise statement of relevant factors, this quotation also directs attention once again to the manifestations of poverty as they might be viewed from a pastoral perspective.

Before turning to a closer examination of the theory of dependency as it is employed by liberation theology in analyzing what it perceives to be a situation of "institutionalized violence," it is important to emphasize once again the human dimension behind the statistics and factors which have been described. The bishops who gathered at Puebla in 1979 provide a first statement which assists in preserving the "human face" of poverty in Latin America.

> This situation of pervasive extreme poverty takes on very concrete faces in real life. In these faces we ought to recognize the suffering features of Christ the Lord, who questions and challenges us. They include:

---

[39]"Final Document of the Convention," from the First Convention of Christians for Socialism, held in Santiago, Chile, Apr. 1972, in Eagleson, ed., *Christians and Socialism,* p. 163. For a more detailed analysis of the various factors see Rodolfo Stavenhagen, "The Future of Latin America: Between Underdevelopment and Revolution," *Latin American Perspectives* 1, No. 1 (Spring 1974):124-148.

—the faces of young children, struck down by poverty before they are born, their chance for self-development blocked by irreparable mental and physical deficiencies; and of the vagrant children in our cities who are so often exploited, products of poverty and the moral disorganization of the family;

—the faces of young people, who are disoriented because they cannot find their place in society, and who are frustrated, particularly in marginal rural and urban areas, by the lack of opportunity to obtain training and work;

—the faces of the indigenous peoples, and frequently of the Afro-Americans as well; living marginalized lives in inhuman situations, they can be considered the poorest of the poor;

—the faces of the peasants; as a social group, they live in exile almost everywhere on our continent, deprived of land, caught in a situation of internal and external dependence, and subjected to systems of commercialization that exploit them;

—the faces of laborers, who frequently are ill-paid and who have difficulty in organizing themselves and defending their rights;

—the faces of the underemployed and the unemployed, who are dismissed because of the harsh exigencies of economic crises, and often because of development-models that subject workers and their families to cold economic calculations;

—the faces of marginalized and overcrowded urban dwellers, whose lack of material goods is matched by the ostentatious display of wealth by other segments of society;

—the faces of old people, who are growing more numerous every day, and who are frequently marginalized in a progress-oriented society that totally disregards people not engaged in production.[40]

Finally, there is this statement describing life in the small city of Tacaimbo, Brazil.

In Tacaimbo, a city of 3,000 inhabitants 165 kilometers from Recife, everything is in short supply: work, housing, food, health, schooling. The people live for the most part in great sacrifice, oppressed, squeezed by the vicious cycle of poverty which spreads, in a cumulative way, like a cancer. . . . The poor majority has no fixed *work*, works by day in the fields for 12.00 cruzeiros a day (early 1976). That work of hoeing does not provide enough to live, only to continue vegetating. That is why many live in hunger. That kind of nourishment does not provide enough to live. One lives by necessity, one lives because somehow one manages to survive. One has meat one day, then eight without. *Health* is poor. A family may have five or six children and four of them will die, die out of needs, die rebuffed, because they cannot get health care. Thus, there are many diseases among the young. Likewise, many adults also live in sickness and cannot buy medicine. In almost any house one finds sick people. The majority of the people here in Tacaimbo live in tight quarters, in houses of cardboard, where hygiene is almost non-existent, for there is no latrine.

---

[40]"The Final Document," in John Eagleson and Philip Scharper, eds., *Puebla and Beyond. Documentation and Commentary*, trans. John Drury (Maryknoll: Orbis, 1979), pp. 128-129 (Nos. 31-40).

The children have bloated bellies, and spells of vomiting and dysentery
without end. Conditions of schooling are precarious. . . . . What is learned
with those resources is almost nothing. . . . "I have a daughter who has
been in school for three years and she is just learning her name."[41]

Here is the human starting point of the theology of liberation.

B. *Two Basic Presuppositions*
1. Dependency Theory

Just as poverty is the starting point for understanding the Latin
American theology of liberation, its two basic presuppositions are: (1)
the socioeconomic theory of dependency and (2) the biblical witness
regarding liberation. These two basic presuppositions are presented in
this section and the next.

Thus far poverty has been described as one encounters it in the
Latin American context. Yet throughout this discussion, one question
has remained unanswered, though in listing the existence of
"inadequate structures" among the factors contributing to poverty, a
preliminary answer has been indicated: how does one interpret the
statistics and human reality of poverty in Latin America?

At what point do we understand the world? Through our senses we acquire
an enormous variety of isolated facts which are apparently independent.
But we still lack an overall comprehension of their *logos*, their structure,
the way in which they are organized—all this is beyond our
understanding. The world is not a collection of atomized facts which
collide and combine somehow, as Democritus thought. Each isolated event
occurs within a certain structure which determines its function and
course, and with it, its meaning. Therefore, in order to understand facts,
one must discover the *model* which governs their functioning.[42]

There are two such models or theories that have most frequently been
employed to interpret the reality of poverty in Latin America, the theory
of development and the theory of dependency. The theology of
liberation has judged the developmental model to be incapable of
adequately interpreting the dynamics of poverty and oppression
operative in Latin America. Instead the theory of dependency has
become a basic presupposition of its theological approach.

Before proceeding to distinguish between these two models, it is
important to notice the significance given to a *socioeconomic*
interpretation of the Latin American reality. The theology of

---

[41]Barreiro, "Grass-Roots Ecclesial Communities and the Evangelization
of the Poor," pp. 297-298.

[42]Rubem Alves, "God's People and Man's Liberation," *Com Via* 14, No. 2-3
(1971):107.

liberation does not immediately set forth a theological interpretation of
poverty but insists on the need for the mediation of socioeconomic
theory. Such an application of insights borrowed from the social
sciences (e.g., economics, sociology, political science) is
characteristic for the theology of liberation. Moreover, in Latin
America a particular importance is given to economic interpretations
as indicated by Miguez Bonino when he writes that "in a capitalist
social formation the economic factor acquires a dominant role,"[43] or
by Osmundo Miranda when he writes that "economic forces do rule
modern life and society."[44] When socioeconomic theory plays such a
large role in the development of liberation theology, it is inevitable that
this theology will also have to reckon with the theoretical and
ideological battle which exists in the modern world between Marxism
and capitalism.

a. Rejection of the Theory of Development

"During the decade of the 50s, many specialists were quite
optimistic about the possibilities rising at that time for Latin America
to break decisively with its situation of dependence and could 'take
off' for development."[45] Indeed during the 1950s the model of
development was predominant for interpreting and offering a solution
to the problems of poverty in Latin America. Gutierrez recognizes the
work of Joseph A. Schumpeter and Colin Clark as significant
contributions to the origin of the developmental model.[46] Schumpeter
had studied the impact of significant innovations, both technico-
economic and politico-social, upon static economic systems which
could disturb the equilibrium of a system and lead to development.
Clark asserted that the goal of economic activity is not wealth but rather
well-being and judged that it is industrialized countries which offer
the highest levels of well-being. Thus Clark went on to propose
industrialization as the way toward progress.

Building upon such economic theories, the theory of development
argues that a solution to the problem of poverty in Latin America lies in

---

[43]Jose Miguez Bonino, "The Human and the System," *Th Today* 35 (Apr.
1978):18.

[44]Osmundo Afonso Miranda, "Aspects of Latin American Revolutionary
Theologies," *J Int Th C* 5 (Fall 1977):8.

[45]Adolfo Ham, "Introduction to the Theology of Liberation," *Com Via* 16,
No. 3 (1973):113.

[46]Gutierrez, *A Theology of Liberation*, p. 23.

the pursuit of a process of development which parallels that of the industrialized nations. In its most comprehensive form, the theory of development encompasses not only exclusively economic factors such as increases in gross national product and per capita income, but it also considers the course of social, political, and cultural development. A strategy for development which incorporates these many different factors is proposed as the solution to the dilemma of poverty in the Third World.[47] The "underdeveloped" nations, through the assistance of the "developed" world, are encouraged along a process of development, particularly through increased industrialization, until they achieve a comparable state of progress.

The Bandung Conference of 1955 has been noted as a significant moment in marking the general acceptance of the model of development.

> A large number of countries met there, especially Asian and African countries. They recognized their common membership in a Third World—underdeveloped and facing two developed worlds, the capitalist and the socialist. This conference marked the beginning of a policy which was supposed to lead out of this state of affairs.[48]

About this time a number of serious economic studies within Latin America proposed that the historical conditions were ripe for a new stage of economic progress, particularly in those countries where the necessary preconditions prevailed.[49]

The developed countries were understood to have a significant role in assisting the "traditional" or "transitional" societies to become "modern" or "industrial."[50] In Latin America a number of programs designed to promote development were established under the auspices of the United Nations, the World Bank, International Aid for Development, and the Alliance for Progress among others.[51] During the same period the concept of development also came to occupy an increasingly important place in the social teachings of the Roman Catholic magisterium, culminating in the central position given to

---

[47]Ibid., pp. 24-25.

[48]Ibid., p. 23.

[49]Ibid., p. 82.

[50]Ibid., p. 82.

[51]Jose Miguez Bonino, "Theology and Theologians of the New World: II. Latin America. Five Theses Toward an Understanding of the 'Theology of Liberation'," *Expos T* 87 (Apr. 1976):197. See also the description of Alan Neely "Liberation Theology in Latin America: Antecedents and Autochthony," *Missio* 6 (July 1978):348.

development in *Populorum Progressio* (1967).[52] It was during this period extending from the 1950s to the mid-60s that the developmental theory prevailed as the standard model for interpreting the fact of Latin American poverty.

Disillusionment with the developmental model began to arise in Latin America when it came to be asked who was primarily benefiting from the economic development under this model. The description by Robert McNamara, former president of the World Bank, expresses the growing skepticism.

> In the last decade (the 1960s) Brazil's gross national product per capita in real terms grew by 2.5% per year. Yet the share of the national income received by the poorest 40% of the population declined from 10% in 1960 to 8% in 1970, whereas the share of the richest 5% grew from 29% to 38% during the same period. . . . In Mexico . . . between 1950 and 1969 the average income per capita grew in real terms, by 3% per year. The richest 10% of the population received half (49%) of the total national income at the beginning of the period and an even larger share (51%) at the end. But the share of the poorest 40% of the people, only 14% in 1950, declined to 11% in 1969.[53]

The economic progress accrued under the developmental model appeared not to improve the lot of the Latin American poor so much as to further improve the lot of those already privileged. It was observed that the gap between rich and poor continued to increase within the individual countries and furthermore that the gap between the developed and underdeveloped countries continued to increase in spite of any progress made by the underdeveloped nations.[54]

It was not only analysis and statistics, however, which altered the Christian consciousness, but also the gradual realization that well-intentioned, philanthropic measures under the developmental model were failing to achieve the desired result of improving the life situation of the vast majority of the population.

> Poverty, hunger, child-mortality, endemic disease, illiteracy began to yield their secret: they grew out of a certain class structure, a "world division of labor" which condemned "third world countries" to permanent dependence, a political system which perpetuates and strengthens these relations, an ideology which justifies it and into which the Christian religion has been co-opted. A serious attempt to practise charity has landed

---

[52]Gutierrez, *A Theology of Liberation*, p. 33.

[53]Robert McNamara, as quoted by Waldron Scott, *Bring Forth Justice* (Grand Rapids: Eerdmans, 1980), p. 133.

[54]Gutierrez, *A Theology of Liberation*, p. 86.

many of these Christians into political and economic analysis and action.[55]

It was not so much the analysis of statistics which prompted Christians to reject the developmental theory but rather frustration over their own firsthand observation of the ineffective results of the process of development, although the data appeared to corroborate their experience.

The essential criticism of the model of development is concisely stated by Ignatio Ellacuria.

> The theory of development has been quick to forget that development often starts out from a basic structure that is marked by sin and injustice. Directing its gaze towards the goal which it seeks—well-being for all and an abundance of the world's goods—the developmentalist outlook is often deluded; it forgets the institutionalized sin at the root of the problem. How can we fashion a better future if we operate with the same egotistical concerns and outlooks, if the craving to possess more goods is stronger than any other motive?[56]

To employ a metaphor, it was asserted that the cancer of poverty in Latin America could not be healed by gradually pouring medications into the system, but instead what was needed was radical surgery. Development could not heal a structure which itself was unsound. Instead what was needed was a new structure to replace the old. The model of development came to be seen increasingly in pejorative terms—as a model promoted by those with a vested interest in maintaining the status quo and as a symbol of timid and ineffective measures.[57] It was perceived that a new language was needed, a new "logos" for interpreting the Latin American economic reality.[58] This is what emerged in the theory of dependency.

b. *The Theory of Dependency*

Even before 1960 there were those who came to be critical of the results of the programs designed to bring development to Latin

---

[55]Jose Miguez-Bonino, "Theology and Theologians of the New World. . . ," p. 196.

[56]Ignatio Ellacuria, *Freedom Made Flesh. The Mission of Christ and His Church*, trans. John Drury (Maryknoll: Orbis, 1976), p. 207-208.

[57]Gutierrez, *A Theology of Liberation*, p. 26.

[58]Rubem A. Alves, "Theology and the Liberation of Man," in Martin E. Marty and Dean G. Peerman, eds., *New Theology No. 9* (New York: Macmillan, 1972), pp. 230-250. See esp. pp. 240-246.

America.[59] It was however in the early 1960s that the developmental model in many circles came to be regarded as "the developmental myth." The growing gap between rich and poor evoked critical language which spoke of developmentalism as a new kind of colonial domination, particularly as a colonialism under the hands of the capitalist system centered in the United States. A study by Paul Baran and Paul Sweezy, entitled *Monopoly Capital* (1966), presented some of the earliest documentation for the charge of economic colonialism against the U.S. in the form of monopolization of the Latin American economy. Since that time a large volume of literature on dependency theory has accumulated with much debate and subtlety among the various theoretical proposals.[60]

The theory of dependency presents an understanding of the causes of Latin American poverty which contrasts dramatically with that of the developmental model.

The dependency model distinguishes underdeveloped Latin America from pre-capitalist Europe. It does not view underdevelopment as an original condition, but instead assumes that nations may once have been undeveloped but never underdeveloped and that the contemporary underdevelopment of many parts of Latin America was created by the same process of capitalism that brought development to the industrialized nations. Latin America is underdeveloped because it has supported the development of Western Europe and the United States. When the center of the expanding world economic system needed raw materials, it was supplied by Latin America. This relationship has not basically changed, even though the United States has replaced Great Britain as the metropolis which dominates over the area, resulting in a strengthening of dependency through foreign corporate and governmental penetration of banking, manufacturing, retailing, communications, advertising, and education. Within each country the pattern of metropolis-periphery relations is replicated as the economic surplus of the countryside drains into urban areas.[61]

Proceeding from this basic understanding of the dependency relationship, the theoreticians of dependency argue that the perpetuation of poverty in Latin America, both rural and urban, can best be explained on the basis of this model. In arriving at their conclusions, these theoreticians have proposed numerous variations of

---

[59]For this and the following comments regarding the growing criticism of the developmental model, see Alan Neely, "Liberation Theology in Latin America," pp. 348-350.

[60]For a comprehensive article reviewing the literature of dependency theory see Ronald H. Chilcote, "A Critical Synthesis of the Dependency Literature," *Latin American Perspectives* 1, No. 1 (Spring 1974):4-29.

[61]Ibid., p. 12.

the dependency theme. Illustrative of this diversity are the four
proposals of Frank, Dos Santos, Cardoso, and Galtung.

An early attempt to offer a new model to replace the model of
development is found in the work of Andre Gunder Frank.[62] Instead of
seeing economic reality as a continuum upon which all nations
equally pursue a steady course of development, Frank divides the
world into strong, metropolitan centers of power and the satellites
whose economies are dependent upon these strong, metropolitan
centers. Such a relationship between centers and satellites is,
furthermore, understood to exist within the individual countries of
Latin America.

> [T]hese metropolis-satellite relations are not limited to the imperial or
> international level but penetrate and structure the very economic,
> political, and social life of the Latin American colonies and countries.
> Just as the colonial and national capital and its export sector become the
> satellite of the Iberian (and later of other) metropoles of the world economic
> system, this satellite immediately becomes a colonial and then a national
> metropolis with respect to the productive sectors and population of the
> interior. Furthermore, the provincial capitals, which thus are themselves
> satellites of the national metropolis—and through the latter of the world
> metropolis—are in turn provincial centers around which their own local
> satellites orbit. Thus, a whole chain of constellations of metropoles and
> satellites relates all parts of the whole system from its metropolitan center
> in Europe or the United States to the farthest outpost in the Latin American
> countryside.[63]

In Frank's system the strong, metropolitan centers drain off the
economic surpluses of the satellites in order to increase their own
wealth and extend their own power. The metropolitan centers of Latin
America drain the wealth from the outlying areas. In turn the wealth
of these Latin American centers is funneled into centers of power
existing in the United States and Europe.

On the basis of this set of dependency relationships Frank draws
this conclusion:

> . . . underdevelopment is not to be attributed primarily to the survival of
> archaic institutions and a lack of capital in territories which have
> remained isolated from the current of world history but is essentially the
> product of and continues to be produced by the same historical process

---

[62]Among the contributions of Frank to the dependency literature are Andre
Gunder Frank, *Latin America: Underdevelopment or Revolution. Essays on
the Development of Underdevelopment and the Immediate Enemy* (New York:
Monthly Review Press, 1969) and *Lumpenbourgeoisie: Lumpendevelopment.
Dependence, Class, and Politics in Latin America*, trans. Marion Davis
Berdecio (New York: Monthly Review Press, 1972).

[63]Frank, *Latin America: Underdevelopment or Revolution*, p. 6.

which also produced economic development, namely, by the development of capitalism itself.[64] The problem is thus not a problem of underdevelopment but rather a problem of dependency, the dependency of the satellites upon external centers of power. Throughout his writings Frank attempts to provide arguments and concrete data in defense of this dependency model.

Theotonio Dos Santos expresses another viewpoint which sees a "new character of dependency" arising in modern times.[65] Earlier in Latin American history there had existed successively a "colonial dependency" under Iberian rule which was followed in the nineteenth century by a "financial-industrial dependency" especially under the domination of Great Britain. Finally since the end of the Second World War a "technological-industrial dependency" has arisen to limit Latin American economic progress. The "new character of dependency" characterized by Dos Santos refers to the functioning of multinational corporations which penetrate into the internal economic systems of the dependent countries. The major contributions of Dos Santos lie in his historical interpretations of the dependency relationship through its successive stages.

A third interpreter of dependency theory, Fernando Henrique Cardoso, holds that the structures of dependency which exist within individual lands are of particular significance for understanding the nature of dependency.[66] This leads him to criticize those who exaggerate the role of external imperialism in dependency theory. Dependency has been internalized within individual lands so fully that it becomes difficult to focus on a single external imperial aggressor which might function to unite the dominated nations into a common front. Cardoso further argues for the complexity of dependency theory and argues against reducing the complexities of empirical economic reality into oversimplified terms.

---

[64]Andre Gunder Frank as quoted by Ulrich Duchrow, "The Church Facing Dependency Structures," *Dial* 20 (Fall 1981):270.

[65]For the theoretical position of Dos Santos, see Chilcote, "A Critical Synthesis of the Dependency Literature," pp. 15-16 and Vitor Westhelle, "Dependency Theory: Some Implications for Liberation Theology," *Dial* 20 (Fall 1981):295.

[66]For this summary of the position of Cardoso see Chilcote, "A Critical Synthesis of the Dependency Literature," p. 17-18 and Westhelle, "Dependency Theory," p. 295. Cf. also Fernando Henrique Cardoso and Enzo Faletto, *Abhängigkeit und Entwicklung in Lateinamerika* (Frankfurt am Main: Suhrkamp, 1976).

An important contribution to the dependency model by one outside
the Latin American context is that of the Norwegian Johan Galtung.[67]
In place of the terms "metropolis" and "satellite" as employed by
Frank, Galtung employs the terms "center" and "periphery." The
world thus exists of center and periphery nations just as individual
nations have within their internal structure both a center and a
periphery.

> In the main, Galtung works with four topographical concepts: (a) the center
> in the center (high income sectors in the rich nations); (b) the periphery in
> the center (low income sectors in rich nations); (c) the center in the
> periphery (high income sectors in poor nations); and (d) the periphery in
> the periphery (low income sectors in poor nations).[68]

After elaborating his basic terms, Galtung proceeds to a description of
the operational dynamics of the system of centers and peripheries.
Such dynamics include: (1) a greater disparity between rich and poor
within poor nations than within the nations of the center; (2) a greater
harmony within the nations of the center because rich and poor alike
benefit from the dependence of the peripheral nations; and (3)
alienation between the poor of the periphery and the poor of the center.
Such alienation occurs because these two peripheries exist in
immediate relationship with their respective centers and fail to
recognize their commonality in that both are dependent realities
within the same system. Galtung further argues (4) against the value
of "free trade" within this system since the trade partners are
themselves not equal in power and the trade benefit tends to accrue to
the most powerful partner.

Domination in Galtung's system should be analyzed on five
levels: communication, cultural, economic, military, and political.
The exchanges between the center and periphery on each of these five
levels reveals the nature of dominance and dependency. Galtung
offers illustrations from recent history to demonstrate the nature of
dependency in these exchanges. Other interpreters share Galtung's
view that dependency theory should incorporate not only economic
aspects but also social and cultural dependencies. In this way
Francois Houtart adds to the economic foundations of dependency
(e.g., imbalance of trade, the problems of developmental aid,
technological dependency, industrial dependency, financial
dependency, and agricultural dependency) the social consequences of

---

[67]Cf. Johan Galtung, "A Structural Theory of Imperialism," *Journal of
Peace Research* 8, No. 2 (1971):81-117.

[68]Duchrow, "The Church Facing Dependency Structures," p. 270.

economic dependency (e.g., breakdown in traditional social structures, rise in unemployment, and reduction in real wages) and the cultural consequences of dependency (e.g., inadequate educational systems and the impact of modern mass media).[69]

Despite the differences which distinguish the various interpreters of dependency theory, there is a consensus regarding the theoretical basics which has found wide acceptance. It is this common ground and not the variety of emphases which has made the theory of dependency a presupposition of liberation theology. Vitor Westhelle summarizes the consensus in four points:

> *First*, dependency has an external dimension manifested in the inter-national division of labor, fixed for Latin America since colonial times. ... *Second*, dependency has an internal dimension, manifested in class struggle and in state intervention in the economy. This dimension is related to the first through the internal intervention of foreign interests, through authoritarian regimes that invite and protect such intervention, and through the external alliances of the national bourgeoise. What is decisive in this context is that the internal dimension of dependency is not mechanically conditioned by the external relation of dependency. The internal structure has a "relative autonomy." *Third*, the dependency situation has to be interpreted on a world-wide scale in both historical and structural terms. Dependency-theorists reject linear views of historical development. ... A *fourth* point of consensus is the necessity of considering also political, ideological, and cultural variables along with the economic factors.[70]

This serves as a concise summary statement regarding the essence of dependency theory as it is employed by the theology of liberation.

The contrast between dependency theory and the previously prevailing developmental theory is great. Since the time of its introduction as an alternate theory for interpreting Latin American poverty, the theory of dependency has drawn extensive criticism not only from defenders of the developmental model but also by leftist defenders of orthodox Marxism.[71] While bearing definite similarity

---

[69]See Francois Houtart, "The Global Aspects of Dependence and Oppression, trans. Francis McDonagh, in Virgil Elizondo and Norbert Greinacher, eds., *Concilium 144: Tensions Between the Churches of the First World and the Third World* (New York: Seabury, 1981), pp. 3-9.

[70]Westhelle, "Dependency Theory," p. 294.

[71]For criticism of dependency theory from a conservative developmental perspective see the article by Joseph Ramos in Michael Novak, ed., *Liberation South, Liberation North* (Washington/London: American Enterprise, 1981). For criticism from an orthodox Marxist perspective see Raul A. Fernandez and Jose F. Ocampo, "The Latin American Revolution: A Theory of Imperialism, Not Dependency," *Latin American Perspectives* 1, No. 1 (Spring 1974):30-61.

to certain aspects of Marxist thought, particularly Lenin's theory of
imperialism, the theory of dependency derives from a variety of
theoretical sources, in particular an analysis of Latin American
economic reality, and is best typified as socialist rather than Marxist
or communist. Nevertheless, the attribution of dependency theory to
Marxist ideology has been a major argument employed by the critics of
liberation theology.

The preference of liberation theology for the theory of dependency
as a "logos" or interpretive key for understanding Latin American
poverty has had decisive implications for the solutions which have been
proposed.[72] By criticizing and rejecting the developmental model, the
theology of liberation denies that the problem of Latin America is one of
retardation that can be solved through a gradual process of
development. In fact such attempts at development have been criticized
as failing to address the root issue. By accepting the model of
dependency as a more accurate diagnosis of the Latin American
problem, a more radical treatment has also been prescribed, a change
in the fundamental political and economic structures of Latin
American society. Thus this theology becomes a theology of *liberation*,
liberation not only from sin as traditionally interpreted by theology but
liberation from the sin of socioeconomic dominance and dependency
which manifests itself in the poverty of the majority of the Latin
American people.

> To characterize Latin America as a dominated and oppressed continent
> naturally leads one to speak of liberation and above all to participate in the
> process. Indeed, *liberation* is a term which expresses a new posture of
> Latin Americans. . . . It is becoming more evident that the Latin
> American peoples will not emerge from their present status except by
> means of a profound transformation, *a social revolution*, which will
> radically and qualitatively change the conditions in which they now
> live.[73]

From the starting point of Latin American poverty, the theology of
liberation has chosen the theory of dependency as the most adequate
available model for interpreting its causes. From the presupposition of
a dependency relationship arises the call for liberation. This first
presupposition finds its complement in a second one which

---

[72]An interesting example of the differing implications of these two models
when applied to a particular Latin American country is found in the report of a
group of European Catholic missionaries entitled, "Guatemala: Development or
Liberation?" *IDOC Bul* No. 13 (Nov. 1973):5-10.

[73]Gutierrez, *A Theology of Liberation*, p. 88.

theologically grounds the goal of liberation in the biblical witness to God's liberating work in history.

2. The Biblical Witness to Liberation
a. *The Bible Through the Eyes of the Poor*

The theology of liberation is specifically theological as it draws on the resources of the Christian tradition to address the issues raised by contemporary Latin American reality. While there are a variety of theological resources upon which the liberation theologians draw—the witness of Bartolome de Las Casas, missionary and defender of the Indians during the Spanish colonial period, the thought of contemporary theologians such as Metz and Moltmann, papal encyclicals and ecclesiastical social teachings—the central theological resource upon which they draw is the Bible.

Rudolf Bultmann made famous the insight that exegesis without presuppositions is not possible.[74] The interpreter of a text always brings along personal or, at least methodological presuppositions which influence how the text is interpreted. The theologians of liberation have made this insight their own and reflected on it at length. Segundo, for example, has used the phrase "hermeneutic of suspicion" to describe his criticism of those interpretations done from the perspective of the economically advantaged. This suspicion is especially directed toward interpretations which purport to be neutral and objective but which in fact tend to support the present social, economic, and political order. The theologians of liberation make no secret of the fact that commitment to the poor is for them the *sine qua non* of biblical interpretation. Jon Sobrino has stated this affirmation quite simply: "You just read the Bible with the eyes of the poor. You read the same Bible, but suddenly you see different things."[75] The liberation theologians claim that interpretation from the context of the poor has a power to reveal aspects of reality which are hidden to those who read the Bible out of another context. Perhaps the most well-known example of this approach is found in the interpretations of the Bible as was practiced at Sunday mass in place of the homily by the peasants of

---

[74]Rudolf Bultmann, "Is Exegesis Without Presuppositions Possible?" in *Existence and Faith*, trans. Schubert M. Ogden (New York: Meridian, 1960), pp. 289-296.

[75]As quoted by Riding, "Latin Church in Siege," p. 38.

Solentiname under the guidance of Ernesto Cardenal.[76] These interpretive discussions of biblical texts as practiced among people and pastor in Solentiname speak with relevance lacking in biblical interpretations which are preoccupied with technical historical-critical questions. There appears to be a revelatory power in this interpretation through the eyes and mouths of the poor that should not be summarily dismissed. The gospel is understood in these conversations in a vital way that has immediate relevance for the lives of the people. There is no apologizing for either the authority or message of the Bible. The texts speak with original force.

This reading of the Bible through the eyes of the poor has been both appreciated and criticized. It has been appreciated for its restoring to the Bible an authority to speak as a Word of God in a way which has been lost in much contemporary theology. It has been criticized for its failure to take seriously the original historical context in which the writings of the Bible are rooted, thereby succumbing to its own unexamined presuppositions.

b. *The Bible as Authoritative Word*

Unlike many contemporary theologians for whom the authority of the Bible has become problematic, liberation theologians to a large degree presuppose the authority of the biblical texts for their theological work. Robert T. Osborn has commented on the "rise and the fall of the Bible in recent American theology."[77] The rise of the Bible which accompanied the rise of neo-orthodox theology as epitomized in Barth has been followed by a period in which the authority of the Bible for theology has been lost or at least set aside. Leaving unaddressed the larger question which Osborn raises regarding the degree to which American theology was ever substantially altered by Barthian neo-orthodoxy and the priority it gave to the Word, the conclusions he draws regarding the authority of the Bible in contemporary American theology merit reflection. According to Osborn, the theologies which culminated in "the death of God" were accompanied by the death of the Bible as the authoritative Word of God. Instead of being perceived as a Word of God which has revelatory power, the Bible has been increasingly perceived as an historical book for which the most

---

[76]Cf. Ernesto Cardenal, *The Gospel in Solentiname*, trans. Donald D. Walsh (Maryknoll: Orbis, 1976).

[77]Robert T. Osborn, "The Rise and Fall of the Bible in Recent American Theology," *Duke Div R* 4 (Sept. 1977):57-72.

appropriate approach is an objective, historical one devoid of explicitly theological questions.

The most appropriate setting for executing such a theology is neither the parish where the preacher must regularly proclaim the Word of God nor the seminary where proclaimers of the Word are trained but the university where objective inquiry is the established method. Thus biblical study has been increasingly relegated in recent times to the university context. Osborn cites the ontological theology of Tillich, the historical-ethical theology of H. Richard Niebuhr, and process theology as examples of how the Bible has been employed primarily in a symbolic and illustrative way in the academic context. When the Bible has been employed in these theologies at all, it is primarily to symbolize or illustrate some aspect of universally true human experience. Authority derives not from revelation but is grounded in human experience. These three theological approaches which have had enormous influence upon recent American theology agree "that human experience itself speaks of God and provides both the necessary sufficient ground of theology without necessary or essential recourse to Scripture."[78]   Contemporary theologians whom Osborn places in this tradition include John Cobb, Langdon Gilkey, Gordon Kaufmann, and Schubert Ogden.

Liberation theology stands in contrast to these theologies in which biblical authority is at best a secondary concern. "For a powerless, marginal, oppressed people caught up in the struggle for their liberation and justice, the Biblical word can become not only viable but necessary."[79]   Latin American liberation theology understands the Bible as a Word addressed from God to God's people, spoken not just long ago into an ancient historical context which can best be interpreted by an objective, historical method, but as a Word which God addresses to people yet today. The Bible speaks. The Bible continues to reveal a Word of God into the contemporary historical context. The primary task of biblical interpretation is neither to derive objective historical information from biblical texts nor to deduce aspects of universal human experience. It is rather to enable the biblical message to address the situation of the poor in Latin America.

Three biblical paradigms are of special importance to the theology of liberation and occur repeatedly in the literature. These paradigms

---

[78]Ibid., p. 65.
[79]Ibid., p. 69.

are understood to be exemplary of God's liberating work in history.
They are: (1) the Exodus of the Hebrew people from slavery in Egypt, (2)
the prophetic tradition of Israel with its criticism of political, social,
and religious injustice, and (3) the liberating work of Jesus with
special attention given to the social and political dimensions of Jesus'
life and passion. Repeated in the writings of liberation theology are
allusions, direct references, quotations, and interpretations of these
three biblical paradigms.

While there is a great variety among the liberation theologians in
their specific use of the Bible, together they share in common this
agreement regarding the authority of the Bible as the Word of God. In
affirming this approach they have made use of one stream of modern
scholarship, the hermeneutical approach to meaning in texts especially
as developed by Paul Ricoeur.[80] The Bible is for liberation theology a
central witness to the liberating activity of God in history, a history
which is not closed but remains open as God continues to participate in
liberation yet today. Liberation theology trusts that God continues to be
active today in liberating deeds which are consistent with those
recorded in the biblical witness. Thus, the theology of liberation
mediates between the reality of poverty in Latin America and the
praxis of participating in changing that reality not only through the use
of social analysis, such as the theory of dependency, but also through an
interpretation of the biblical witness to the liberating activity of God.

---

[80]Cf. J. Severino Croatto, "Befreiung und Freiheit. Biblische Hermeneutik
für die 'Theologie der Befreiung'," in Hans-Jürgen Prien, ed., *Lateinamerika
Gesellschaft—Kirche—Theologie. Band 2: Der Streit um die Theologie der
Befreiung*, trans. Renate Strecker (Göttingen: Vandenhoeck & Ruprecht, 1981),
pp. 39-59. The biblical interpretation of J. Severino Croatto is indicative of a
highly developed hermeneutical method.   Croatto in his approach to
interpretation seeks to emphasize both the original setting of biblical texts and
their contemporary significance for the context of liberation in Latin America.
More than any other Latin American biblical scholar, Croatto has developed the
insights of Ricoeur concerning the "surplus-of-meaning" of biblical texts in
advocating the hermeneutical legitimacy of interpreting the Bible in light of
contemporary Latin America. To this end Croatto has traced the liberating
tradition of the Bible in a trajectory which originates in the Exodus and runs
through the creation narratives, the prophetic witness, the liberating activity of
Jesus, and the "paschal" theology of liberation of Paul.   Throughout his
exposition Croatto returns to the original events and the development of the
biblical tradition itself as the basis for his conclusions. But at the same time he
insists on the ongoing significance of the biblical texts to speak a liberating
word into the Latin American context as a legitimate function of the word itself.
The biblical text grounded in one historical context must also continue to speak
to present reality.

Reflection upon the Latin American reality in light of the biblical witness is essential to the method of liberation theology in proceeding from analysis to action.

C. *A New Point of Departure*
1. Critique of Western Philosophy

Enrique Dussel has drawn attention to the fact that for generations Latin American theology has been imitative of European philosophical and theological thought forms and has not developed those inherently its own.[81] The situation which exists in the economic realm, the dependency of the Latin American economy upon other centers of power, has existed in the philosophical and theological realms as well. By imitating the lead of Europe, and to a lesser extent North America, Latin Americans have paid insufficient attention to their own context and experience. The philosophy and theology of "the center," meaning Europe, has been accepted as the only way of philosophizing and theologizing. This has led to a denial of the particularities of Latin America. In effect it has led to ways of thinking distanced from life as it is lived in Latin America and, due to the particular nature of the European thought forms, has led to a preoccupation with intellectual constructs as opposed to a way of thinking which takes into serious consideration the concrete Latin American context.

Whereas the Medieval world was characterized by an all-pervasive awareness of divine transcendence and by a sense of the presence of God as "other," Western thought no longer shares this world-view. Dussel characterizes the Western philosophical tradition as one which has placed the "I" at its center.[82] This "I" has manifested itself not only as the "I think" of Western philosophy in which the thinking subject came to be the standard for measuring all truth but also in the "I conquer" of Western colonialism, a fact which has had overwhelming significance for Latin America as European "superiority" was imposed upon native American peoples.

---

[81] Cf. Enrique Dussel, *Ethics and the Theology of Liberation*, trans. Bernard F. McWilliams (Maryknoll: Orbis, 1978), Chapter 6, pp. 149-177 and Dussel, *A History of the Church in Latin America: Colonialism to Liberation (1492-1979)*, trans. Alan Neely (Grand Rapids: Eerdmans, 1981), pp. 17, 20, 112, 244, 313, 324, and 330-331.

[82] For this and the following discussion see Dussel, *Ethics and the Theology of Liberation*, pp. 151-153 and Dussel, *A History of the Church in Latin America*, pp. 5 and 11-12.

Martin Heidegger has criticized Western philosophy for the cleavage which he sees existing between subject and object in the mainstream of modern Western thought in a way strikingly similar to Dussel. Throughout his work Heidegger strove to rediscover the horizon of Being as the proper ground which reunites subject and object in a primordial way.[83] Heidegger suggested that the origins of this cleavage between subject and object may be traced back as far as the early Greek philosophers.[84] In the modern period the centrality of thinking subject isolated from the "deceptions" of sense experience is epitomized in the *cogito ergo sum* of Descartes.[85] In Descartes even the existence of God can be demonstrated by the thinking activity of the subject. While Kant took a far more serious view of history, a primary emphasis in his epistemology lies not with objective data but with the categories by which the mind interprets any such data.[86] Thus also in Kant a strong emphasis rests upon the contribution of the rational thinking subject to the process of understanding. In Leibnitz one finds the human subject so active in construing the material basis of human reality that he could affirm this world as the best of all possible worlds, venturing to claim intellectual insight into the mind and purposes of God.[87]

In German Idealism, for example in Hegel, this same tendency is at work. Although the philosophical constructs speak of the activity of an Absolute which is the driving force of history, finally this Absolute comes to be recognized only through the subjective intellect.[88] The very relationship which Hegel methodologically establishes between the thinking subject and human history can also too easily collapse into

[83]A further elaboration of this thrust in Heidegger's philosophy is found in Craig Nessan, "Heidegger, Language and Biblical Interpretation," STM Thesis (Dubuque: Wartburg Theological Seminary, 1978), Chapter 1, esp. pp. 5-7.

[84]Cf. Martin Heidegger, *Early Greek Thinking*, trans. David Farrell Krell and Frank A. Capuzzi (New York: Harper & Row, 1975).

[85]Cf. Rene Descartes, "Meditations Concerning First Philosophy," in *The Essential Writings*, trans. and intro. John J. Blom (New York: Harper & Row, 1977), pp. 180-244.

[86]See Frederick Copleston, *A History of Philosophy. Vol. 6, Part II: Kant* (New York: Image, 1960), pp. 44-47.

[87]See Julian N. Hartt, "Creation and Providence," in Hodgson and King, eds., *Christian Theology*, pp. 127-128.

[88]See Rosemary Radford Ruether, *The Radical Kingdom. The Western Experience of Messianic Hope* (New York: Paulist Press, 1970), p. 95.

mere subjectivism.[89] This is indeed what occurs in the period
subsequent to Idealism. In Feuerbach it is the subject who projects out of
its own subjectivity the existence of God.[90] Nietzsche advocates a
radical subjectivism which finds expression in "the Will to Power."[91]
In phenomenology and existentialism the attempt is made to
philosophize from the very givenness of subjective experience, one such
attempt being Heidegger's own *Being and Time*.[92] Such a
philosophical approach, however, tends to reduce the reality of all
things external to the self to mere perceptions of the self, thus emptying
them of their own independent reality.

These brief references indicate the way in which the *subjective
intellect* has dominated Western philosophy in the modern period.
This emphasis, according to both Dussel and Heidegger, has had
disastrous consequences. According to Heidegger, the cleavage
between subject and object has given rise to a technological approach to
reality by which nature has been used insofar as it has been useful to
the human subject without regard for its own intrinsic value. Nature
has been rendered a thing to be manipulated by the self. According to
Heidegger, nature can regain its own intrinsic value only when
subject and object are reunited in a more comprehensive scheme, i.e.,
Being.

The theology of liberation, however, goes one crucial step beyond
Heidegger and ventures a criticism which turns upon his approach as
well. Jose Porfiro Miranda critiques Heidegger and the Western
philosophical tradition for failing to take seriously the giveness of the
other as an other external to the subjective intellect.

> . . . the outcry of the neighbor in need—the only true content of the voice of
> conscience—absolutely cannot be manipulated. In it there is indeed
> otherness. It is not a branch office of the self and its world and projections.
> It cannot be encompassed. It is not neutral; it demands decision. Its
> otherness cannot be absorbed by the thinker; it remains uncompro-

[89]See James S. Churchill in his Introduction to Martin Heidegger, *Kant
and the Problem of Metaphysics*, trans. James S. Churchill
(Bloomington/London: Indiana U. Press, 1962), p. xi and Dussel, *A History of
the Church in Latin America*, pp. 11-12.

[90]See Ludwig Feuerbach, *The Essence of Christianity*, trans. George Eliot
(New York: Harper & Row, 1957), pp. 33-44.

[91]See Frederick Copleston, *A History of Philosophy. Vol. 7, Part II:
Schopenhauer to Nietzsche*, pp. 181-194 and Dussel, *A History of the Church in
Latin America*, p. 12.

[92]Cf. Martin Heidegger, *Being and Time*, trans. John Macquarrie and
Edward Robinson (New York: Harper & Row, 1962).

misingly exterior to and independent of the thinker. It is truly real and is
not at my disposition; nor does it succumb to my powers of affirmation or
negation or representation. This outcry alone is imperative. Its demand,
insofar as I heed it, increases my responsibility. I am no longer alone. In
a word, it is otherness, and manipulation of otherness is impossible.[93]
It is this reality of "the other" which the theology of liberation finds
crucially absent in the subjective thinking of Western philosophy.

According to Dussel, the rise of the "I" as the dominant mode of
understanding has led to the treatment of persons not as persons but as
mere *cogitatum* to be pondered by the thinking subject.[94] Persons have
been objectified, turned into things. Thus persons have been
transformed into the means by which the "I" can be served. This
turning toward the subject in modern thought is, moreover, preoccupied
with abstract philosophical and intellectual questions at the expense of
the concrete world in which people live. For Dussel, the real world is
not the intellectual world constructed by the philosopher but the world of
the poor of Latin America. In this way Dussel, like Miranda, is also
critical of those like Heidegger who ontologize human existence as
"being-in-the-world."[95] Dussel is critical because "being-in-the-
world" means something vastly different depending on whether one
lives in a privileged academic environment or in an urban slum in
Latin America. The tendency of the Western philosophical tradition
has been to treat reality which fails to correspond to its own categories
of thought as if that reality does not exist. Thus the theology of
liberation is skeptical as to whether this philosophical tradition can
address the concrete reality of Latin America.

2. Critique of Western Theology

The interrelationship and interpenetration of philosophical and
theological approaches to reality make criticisms addressed by
liberation theology to the mainstream of Western philosophy valid also
to a large degree for Western theology.[96] This section redirects this

---

[93]Jose Porfirio Miranda, *Being and the Messiah. The Message of St. John*,
trans. John Eagleson (Maryknoll: Orbis, 1977), p. 55.

[94]Dussel, *Ethics and the Theology of Liberation*, p. 156. See also Dussel's
discussion of "flesh" as the symbol of dominating structures in *A History of the
Church in Latin America*, pp. 8-11.

[95]Dussel, *Ethics and the Theology of Liberation*, pp. 157-159 and Dussel, *A
History of the Church in Latin America*, pp. 15-16.

[96]For example, see the criticisms of the theologies of Bultmann, Barth, and
Moltmann in Rubem A. Alves, "Towards a Theology of Liberation," Th.D.

criticism to address more specifically the questions which liberation theologians raise of the mainstream of Western theology.

In one of his first books, Reinhold Niebuhr described the two-fold problem facing Christianity in the modern world.[97] First, there are the *intellectual* questions raised of Christianity as it encounters the modern scientific world-view. Second, there are the *moral* questions raised of Christianity in the face of the pressing personal and social problems which exist in our modern world. For Niebuhr it seemed the intellectual questions were the easier to address and that they were indeed in the process of being answered. He considered the more urgent modern questions to be those of the moral relevance of Christianity and it is to these questions that he devoted his life's work.

Niebuhr's dual approach can be helpful in understanding the criticism which Latin American liberation theology brings to its encounter with Western theology. Whereas liberation theology directs its primary concern to the moral—one might add economic and political—relevance of Christianity, the mainstream of Western theology has concerned itself primarily with the intellectual challenge to Christianity in the face of a scientific world-view and a modern secularism in which God is no longer a working hypothesis. There are to be sure exceptions to the characterization such as the social gospel movement epitomized by Walter Rauschenbusch.[98] But these remain exceptions to the dominant concern of modern Western theology to render a reasonable, intellectually acceptable account of the Christian faith.

Some examples from the mainstream of Western theology illustrate this dominant concern. The theology of Schleiermacher, often called the father of modern theology, is an attempt to organize Christian doctrine on the basis of the "feeling of absolute dependence." By so doing Schleiermacher hoped to discover a ground upon which theology could be constructed in the modern world and which could answer the questions raised by the cultured despisers of religion.[99]

Dissertation (Princeton: Princeton Theological Seminary, 1969), pp. 57-118 and esp. 112.

[97]For this description and interpretation of Reinhold Niebuhr, see David Ray Griffin, "North Atlantic and Latin American Liberation Theologians," *Encount* 40 (Winter 1979):10-22.

[98]Cf. for example, Walter Rauschenbusch, *A Theology for the Social Gospel* (New York/Nashville: Abingdon, 1945).

[99]Friedrich Schleiermacher, *On Religion: Speeches to its Cultured Despisers*, trans. John Oman (New York: Harper & Row, 1958). Cf. also the

Schleiermacher's theological system is thus constructed around the "feeling of absolute dependence" which not only primarily serves an apologetic function in the face of religious doubt but also constructs theology around a center which emphasizes a strong individualism. The moral power of Christianity is for Schleiermacher subordinate to this apologetic concern with its individualistic tendencies.

Similar concerns motivated Rudolf Bultmann in his program of demythologizing the New Testament in favor of the modern scientific world-view.[100] Bultmann, like Schleiermacher, combined an apologetic concern with a strong individualistic tendency as he reinterpreted Christianity through the individualistic categories of existentialist philosophy. Thus existentialist theology attempted to translate biblical concerns into a language intelligible to the modern individual. Other contemporary theologies are also characterized by their primary concern to render the concept of God meaningful in the face of the modern scientific world-view. The theologies of Tillich and Pannenberg, for example, are masterful attempts to render intelligible the Christian faith in an intellectually responsible way. The central focus, however, in each of these theologies is that of the intellectual challenge to Christianity in the modern period.

Gustavo Gutierrez has strongly objected to such theologies which have "the modern world" as their primary interlocutor. Gutierrez labels such theologies as "progressive" which recognize their primary purpose as an effort "to come to grips with the challenge of the bourgeois, middle-class unbeliever."[101] He argues that such theologies fail to recognize the implicit approval which they offer to the present order in a world which is radically divided between those who are rich and those who are poor. By directing their energy toward reconciling faith in God and the modern spirit, progressivist theology partakes of and supports the existing structure of the world, a world divided into rich and poor, oppressors and oppressed.[102] Gutierrez asserts that for liberation theology the interlocutor is not the modern

---

comments of Frederick Herzog, "Birth Pangs: Liberation Theology in North America," *Chr Cent* 93 (Dec. 15, 1976):1122-1123.

[100]Cf. Rudolf Bultmann, "New Testament and Mythology," in *Kerygma and Myth*, ed. Hans Werner Bartsch and trans. Reginald H. Fuller (New York: Harper & Row, 1961), p. 1-44.

[101]Gutierrez, "The Historical Power of the Poor," in *The Power of the Poor in History*, trans. Robert R. Barr (Maryknoll: Orbis, 1983), p. 93.

[102]Gutierrez, "Theology from the Underside of History," in *The Power of the Poor in History*, p. 193.

"non-believer" but rather "the '*nonperson*,' the human being who is not considered human by the present social order—the exploited classes, marginalized ethnic groups, and despised cultures." The vital question "is how to tell the nonperson, the nonhuman, that God is love, and that this love makes us all brothers and sisters."[103] Thus for Gutierrez there is an urgent need to differentiate liberation theology from progressivist theology which seeks to address the modern world, and which, in the very act of addressing the modern world as its interlocutor, *de facto* supports the status quo. Gutierrez stresses the connection between the choice of the modern non-believer as the central theological concern of progressivist theology and providing theological support, although often unrecognized, for the present socioeconomic structure. Instead liberation theology takes up the cause of the poor. Such a starting point beginning with the poor, the "nonperson," "is a matter of a different theology."[104]

The criticisms which liberation theologians level at the dominant Western theological tradition relate to its failure to address the most urgent questions of Latin America which are neither primarily intellectual nor individualistic. Such intellectual questions are accused of being privileged, bourgeois questions raised by those who need not worry about finding bread to eat. Latin American theologians had attempted for many years to imitate the prevailing theological approach and in so doing avoided the particularity of the Latin American reality. "Being Christian" became equated with "being a European Christian" and little reflection was made concerning the difference between the European and Latin American contexts. For many Latin Americans the Christian faith had been nearly reduced to the memorization of alien catechetical doctrines which had little to do with their own world of experience.[105] Right thinking (orthodoxy) became the measure of Christian faith separated from life lived in the context of oppression (orthopraxis). The moral force of Christianity and its relevance for Latin America were surrendered.

Dussel not only questions the relevance of a theology solely concerned with developing an intellectual apologetic to the modern world. He also questions the validity of European political theology for Latin America. Jürgen Moltmann is criticized by Dussel for failing to make concrete historical and political proposals which can mediate

---

[103]Ibid., p. 193.

[104]Ibid., p. 213.

[105]Dussel, *Ethics and the Theology of Liberation*, p. 154.

between the political order of the present and the hoped-for order of the kingdom of God.[106] Johannes Metz, in spite of correctly appraising the privatization of the Christian faith and the need for a political theology, is criticized for his failure to envision political theory in a context which goes beyond Europe to include a prophetic critique of a world order which consists of center and periphery, rich and poor.[107] Likewise others among the liberation theologians, Gutierrez in particular, have criticized these theologies for their alliance with the modern spirit and failure to radically question the structure of a world which is divided between rich and poor.[108]

Complementing the criticisms of Gutierrez and Dussel and the theology of liberation, Carl Braaten has argued that an important cause of contemporary atheism and the need for a Christian apologetic in response to the modern world-view which goes with it, lies in forgetting the liberating heart of the biblical message,[109] the very message which the theology of liberation attempts to recall. The history of the Christian church has been in many ways a witness less to freedom than to unfreedom. Modern atheism may be itself a reaction against a God who has been perceived as the authoritarian guardian of the status quo. What has been obscured over the centuries is faith in the God of freedom, a God who liberates from every kind of bondage. Braaten suggests that a return to faith in this liberating God as revealed in the Exodus, the prophets, and Jesus, may not only lead the church into new initiatives to achieve liberation but may itself offer a credible answer to the atheistic and intellectual challenges raised against Christianity in the modern world. If this is true, then the theology of liberation becomes not only a theology which is morally relevant but one which also makes an authentic apologetic contribution to authenticating the Christian message in a world characterized by science, secularism, and atheism.

---

[106]Ibid., pp. 159-162 and Dussel, *A History of the Church in Latin America*, pp. 18-19.

[107]Dussel, *Ethics and the Theology of Liberation*, pp. 162-163 and Dussel, *A History of the Church in Latin America*, p. 18.

[108]Gutierrez, "Theology from the Underside of History," in *The Power of the Poor in History*, pp. 182-185.

[109]Carl E. Braaten, "The Future as a Source of Freedom," *Th Today* 27 (Jan. 1971):382-393.

3. Latin America, the Poor, and Praxis: The Distinctive Configuration of Liberation Theology

The criticism which liberation theology makes of the mainstream of Western philosophy and theology can be summarized in a threefold way. *First*, it is critical of the fact that the European context has been established as normative and that the validity of other contexts has been subjected to this norm. *Second*, it is critical because this tradition has been dominated by the inquiry of the thinking subject, a subject who is distanced from objective reality and who turns all of reality, even persons, into things which are thought. *Third*, the theology of liberation is skeptical of a tradition preoccupied with apologetics on an intellectual level which has not taken actual historical life sufficiently into consideration. The theology of liberation understands itself to have a distinctive contribution to make in correcting the limitations of the dominant philosophical and theological tradition of the West on exactly these points.

The theology of liberation no longer accepts uncritically the *European context* as the normative context for theology. The theologians of liberation have criticized their past fascination for European ways of thinking and newly affirmed the theological legitimacy of starting with their own context. The *Latin American context* in all of its particularity has become for them a fertile ground for theological work. Moreover, the theology of liberation understands itself to have a unique contribution to make exactly because it is a theology of the periphery rather than of the center. Theology from the point of view of the periphery reveals aspects of reality which are concealed to those who do theology from the centers of power and who may not even be aware that such a relation between center and periphery exist.[110] Not only is the reality of the Latin American context no longer denied, but it is positively affirmed as a perspective from which the theology of the First World itself needs to learn. Latin American theology in this respect claims to offer a necessary ideological critique of European theology.

Whereas the dominant Western tradition has emphasized the *thinking subject* and has often treated even persons as things to be reflected upon by this thinking subject, the theology of liberation begins from a radically different starting point. Theology for them is neither

---

[110]Dussel, *Ethics and the Theology of Liberation*, p. 166 and Dussel, *A History of the Church in Latin America*, p. 19 and 330-331.

primarily a subjective matter nor exclusively a matter of thought. The liberation theologians seek to move beyond both privatistic and overly intellectual approaches. Instead of beginning with the thinking subject, the theology of liberation begins with *the other* subject to "the one great fact of poverty."[111] In this theology it is the question raised by *a world of human beings living in poverty* which has priority over all other questions. There exists a world of poverty which serves as the focus for theological reflection. Perhaps Gutierrez has done more than any other to emphasize this "new locus for theological reflection."[112] According to Gutierrez it is necessary to "avoid an academic theology dissociated from grassroots work."[113] Theology done in the context of the poor is more than a matter of methodology, more than a way of thinking. To use Gutierrez' own words: "We are talking about a specific way of understanding what it means to be a Christian."[114] In the theology of liberation the theologian is no longer essentially a thinking subject but above all one who is committed to responding to the plight of the poor.

Lastly, the theology of liberation asserts that theology is not so much a matter of *intellectual apologetics* as it is of *praxis*.[115] While the dominant theology of the West has sought primarily to respond to the intellectual challenge arising from the modern, scientific world-view, the theology of liberation continues to a large degree to "presuppose the truth of Christianity."[116] The biblical witness continues to command authority in the Latin American context and thus there has been little interest in demonstrating its intellectual truth to a skeptical modern audience. Accordingly the focus has not been an intellectual defense of biblical and theological truth but rather the application of the moral claims of the biblical message in view of Latin American poverty.

The question of God is raised out of a concrete situation of suffering and that knowledge of God moves consistently from the particular to the

---

[111]Dussel, *Ethics and the Theology of Liberation*, p. 165.

[112]Gustavo Gutierrez, "Talking About God," *Sojourners* 12, No. 2 (Feb. 1983):27.

[113]Ibid., p. 27.

[114]Ibid., p. 28.

[115]Dussel, *A History of the Church in Latin America*, pp. 14, and 18-19.

[116]Griffin, "North Atlantic and Latin American Liberation Theologians," p. 22.

universal, from the concrete situation of suffering to the general context of meaning.[117]

Less urgent philosophical and theological questions pale in the face of the Latin American reality whereas the biblical message regarding liberation and justice is heard to speak forcefully to the concrete historical experience of those who are poor.

Theology in the Latin American context thus lives in intimate relationship to "Christian day-to-dayness."[118] Theology does not derive its subject matter from the history of academic theology. It is not a private conversation among theologians. It is not a matter of offering apologetic answers to intellectual questions unrelated to the Latin American reality. Theology does not employ a method through which it draws its conclusions on the basis of theological axioms. In the words of Dussel, "Theology does not demonstrate from axioms but from the poor. . . ."[119] Repeatedly the theology of liberation returns to this its fundamental starting point.

The theologians of liberation understand their primary task to be not one of offering an apologetic for the truth of the Christian faith against those who doubt it but of reflecting on, promoting, and engaging in *praxis* aimed at altering the context of poverty. Liberation theology has affirmed the eleventh thesis of Marx against Feuerbach and has applied it within the Latin American context: "The Philosophers have only *interpreted* the world, in various ways; the point is to *change* it."[120] Theology is more than interpreting or understanding the world in an intellectual way.

> The theology of liberation does not intend to provide Christian justification of positions already taken and does not aim to be a revolutionary Christian ideology. It is a reflection which makes a start with the historical praxis of people. It seeks to rethink the faith from the perspective of that historical praxis, and it is based on the experience of the faith derived from the liberating commitment. For this reason, this theology comes only after that involvement, the theology is always a second act. Its themes are, therefore, the great themes of all true theology, but the

[117]M. Douglas Meeks, "God's Suffering Power and Liberation," *J Rel Thot* 33 (Fall-Winter 1976):45-46.

[118]Dussel, *Ethics and the Theology of Liberation*, p. 173 and Dussel, *A History of the Church in Latin America*, p. 16.

[119]Dussel, *Ethics and the Theology of Liberation*, p. 175.

[120]Karl Marx, *Karl Marx: The Essential Writings*, ed. and intro. Frederic L. Bender (New York: Harper & Row, 1972), p. 152.

perspective and the way of giving them life is different. Its relation to historical praxis is of a different kind.[121]

The theology of liberation does not exist as a theology executed in a university context.[122] It is rather a theology growing out of pastoral involvement with people, responding to the lives of the poor, and seeking a praxis which will alter their plight. There remains a variety in the ways in which one might choose to become engaged in the cause of changing the Latin American reality. In every case, however, theology is to relate itself to the concrete context. A situation "of mutual interaction" exists "wherein the Christian tradition interprets and is interpreted by the contemporary signs of the times."[123] Theology is to live in direct relationship with praxis.

The distinctive nature of the theology of liberation as here described has not arisen out of a pathological need to be recognized as unique. Rather the distinctive nature of liberation theology has arisen due to the *urgency* of a situation which demands redress. Criticism of the dominant Western philosophical and theological tradition is carried out insofar as this tradition is perceived as having failed to address the context of Latin American poverty and the need for liberating praxis. There is an urgency in this situation which refuses to wait for solutions—philosophical, theological, political, or otherwise—to be introduced from the outside. Therefore the theology of liberation has begun the task of reconstructing theology upon its own turf, beginning with its own starting point and presuppositions. The words of Martin Luther King spoken in another context well articulate the sense of the urgency which has also motivated the emergence of the theology of liberation:

> We are now faced with the fact that tomorrow is today. We are confronted with the fierce urgency of now. In this unfolding conundrum of life and history there is such a thing as being too late.[124]

Under the pressures of time, hunger, repression, injustice, and suffering the theology of liberation has been born and continues to live.

---

[121]Gustavo Gutierrez, "Freedom and Salvation: A Political Problem," trans. Alvin Gutterriez, in *Liberation and Change*, ed. and intro. Ronald H. Stone (Atlanta: John Knox Press, 1977), p. 83.

[122]Cf. the critique of academic theology developed by Jose Comblin, *The Church and the National Security State* (Maryknoll: Orbis, 1979), p. 1-13.

[123]Mary Minella, "Praxis and the Question of Revelation," *Iliff R* 36 (Fall 1979):23.

[124]Martin Luther King, Jr., "A Prophecy for the '80s: Martin Luther King Jr.'s 'Beyond Vietnam' Speech," *Sojourners* 12, No. 1 (1983):16.

Chapter Two

A Theological Method Grounded in Praxis

The first chapter has presented the background necessary for understanding the basic thrust of liberation theology. Having considered poverty as theological starting point and the two basic presuppositions of dependency theory and the biblical witness to liberation in Chapter One, the purpose of this chapter is to examine more closely the specifically theological contribution of liberation theology: its method and theological formulations.

Liberation theology is a theology which orients itself fully towards praxis. This chapter discusses how this is so through an examination of the method of liberation theology. It is only through an examination of the method of liberation theology as it moves from the given reality into social analysis and theological reflection and then returns again to engagement in the project of liberation that the full significance of what liberation theologians mean when they speak of praxis can be realized. In analyzing the methodological elements of liberation theology it becomes clear that liberation theology is indeed "a *new way* to do theology"[1] in its self-understanding as "critical reflection on Christian praxis in light of the Word."[2] These deliberations on liberation theology's method conclude with the formulation of several questions which liberation theology seems to pose to North American theology at the close of the chapter.

A. *A Theology in Search of a Method*

Before setting forth the constitutive elements of the method of liberation theology, it is first necessary to discuss two preliminary matters: (1) the very possibility of identifying a method within the

---

[1] Gustavo Gutierrez, *A Theology of Liberation. History, Politics and Salvation*, trans. and eds. Caridad Inda and John Eagleson (Maryknoll: Orbis, 1973), p. 15.

[2] Ibid., p. 13.

diversity of liberation theology and (2) the primary resources to be used
in this discussion.

1. The Possibility of Discerning the Method of Liberation Theology

Confronted with the immense volume of material bearing the
name of "liberation theology" and the extreme diversity in the
literature sharing that name, it would be easy to despair of the very
possibility of discerning a single method which can adequately
systematize it. Granted, the task is formidable. Methodological
questions have not been central in the first years of liberation theology.
After fifteen years of existence the theology of liberation remains "a
theology in process of discovering its own identity."[3] The ground
swell of theological activity under the name of liberation theology
which erupted in the decade of the 70s ranged from mimeographed
pages exchanged among friends, to occasional writings prepared for
theological conferences, to papers issued by priests concerned about
specific political questions, to documents issued by the official church,
to more formally developed theological essays and full-length
manuscripts and books with an academic theological approach.[4]

Beyond the variety in literary genres, the points of view revealed in
these writings are even more diverse. Hans Schöpfer has assembled
five representative attempts to categorize the theology of liberation
since 1975.[5] Included among the host of distinguishing categories used
to label the various streams of liberation theology are socialist-populist,
Marxist, evangelical, positivist, and structuralist. Distinctions can be
made between those which emphasize method and praxis, culture and
history, or economy and ideology. Viewpoints can be dominated by the
official social teachings of the Roman Catholic bishops, concrete
political praxis, popular pastoral work, or a concern for human rights.
Schöpfer's own conclusion drawn from these various attempts at
classification is that none of them can claim to be definitive and that in
fact future attempts at classification are likely to lead to even more
diversity.

---

[3] J. Andrew Kirk, *Liberation Theology. An Evangelical View from the
Third World* (Atlanta: John Knox, 1979), p. 23.

[4] Cf. Hugo Assmann, *Theology for a Nomad Church*, trans. Paul Burns
(Maryknoll: Orbis, 1976), pp. 43-45 and 51-53.

[5] Hans Schöpfer, *Lateinamerikanische Befreiungstheologie* (Stuttgart: W.
Kohlhammer, 1979), pp. 102-107.

What then becomes of an attempt to identify the method of liberation theology? First, it must be recognized that in spite of all these various genres and identifying categories, there is something basic to all of these diverse viewpoints, that is, their attempt to employ the resources of the Christian tradition to come to grips with the present historical reality of Latin America. Clearly this is done from a variety of perspectives and points of view. But what is even more striking is the consensus of opinion by those who choose to identify themselves under the common banner of liberation theology. On the basis of the same starting point, shared presuppositions, and a common history, these many theologians understand themselves not so much competing with one another in an attempt to gain recognition for their own particular point of view but rather as complementing one another as they each make their own small contribution to the common project of constructing a more just future for Latin America.[6]

> Many thinkers in the West still have difficulties comprehending this watershed of the Spirit. The biggest stumbling block they run into is the fact that they often consider theology to be the work of one individual mind. They fail to appreciate the salient fact of the Third World reality that theology is not the activity of one person's intellect but the product of a given community in which theological reflection is imbedded or "incarnated." Liberation Theology is the expression of an entire community, not the brilliant exercise of some technical expertise.[7]

It is this communal nature of liberation theology in all its diversity which increases the difficulty of speaking of the method of liberation theology. Yet at the same time it is the perception that these many diverse theologians are participating in a common project that offers the possibility of making this affirmation.

The word which recurs throughout the writings of the liberation theologians and serves as the cement which binds them together is the word *praxis*. It occurs repeatedly in the literature as descriptive of the difference of this way of doing theology. At the same time, however, it may appear that there are as many definitions of the word praxis as there are authors who use it. For example, Robert Kress in his

---

[6]See the comments of Leonardo Boff, "Integral Liberation and Partial Liberations," in Leonardo and Clodovis Boff, *Salvation and Liberation. In Search of a Balance Between Faith and Politics*, trans. Robert R. Barr (Maryknoll: Orbis, 1984), pp. 24-30. Cf. also Dennis McCann, *Christian Realism and Liberation Theology. Practical Theologies in Creative Conflict* (Maryknoll: Orbis, 1981), p. 133.

[7]Manfred K. Bahmann, "Liberation Theology—Latin American Style," *Luth Q* 27 (May 1975):145.

evaluation of the use of the word praxis among liberation theologians complains "that this term is so pliable that it can mean almost anything."[8] More elaborate are these criticisms of the use of the term "praxis" by Hector Borrat.

> The bridge between theology and the Latin American process is basically the notion of "*praxis*." What strikes one here is the ambiguity in the use of this word. Even Gutierrez, who observes that the role of praxis in Marx is a controversial question, alternates "praxis," "revolutionary praxis," "historical praxis," "Christian praxis," without giving either the meaning of each expression or the definition of the word. Among less sophisticated supporters of liberation theology, "praxis" seems to be at times an alternative to the faith or to the church (as if faith and church were not history). At other times, it is confused with "*engagement*," a word that by itself has only an existential meaning and therefore could cover any political direction, from the right to the left. If "praxis" gives major patterns for theological thinking, what is it really? Where are these patterns to be found? How can we recognize a "praxis of liberation" when, as in current times, liberation still remains at the level of human expectation and when liberation movements and projects are not only pluralistic but often in mutual opposition?[9]

While it would be possible to argue that such criticisms simply have not looked deeply enough into the historical context of those, like Gutierrez, who use the word praxis, instead it is more to the point to offer an explanation of the word praxis based on its usage by liberation theologians.

Indicative of the use of the word praxis by liberation theology are the following examples drawn from a single collection of essays by prominent liberation theologians. Enrique Dussel comments, "Liberation theology arose in Latin America out of the revolutionary praxis of numerous Christians committedly involved with the people of our continent."[10] Hugo Assmann employs the word praxis in the following way.

> Praxis, then, becomes the basic reference point for any truly contextual theology. Never forgetting the historical implications of our faith and the need for concrete involvement, we are forced to engage in an ongoing process of self-criticism. Praxis cannot come down to some sort of spontaneous generosity. It means that our instruments of analysis must be used both to interpret historical processes below the mere surface level

---

[8]Robert Kress, "Theological Method: Praxis and Liberation," *Communio* (US) 6 (Spring 1979):116.

[9]Hector Borrat, "Liberation Theology in Latin America," *Dial* 13 (Summer 1974):175.

[10]Enrique D. Dussel, "Historical and Philosophical Presuppositions for Latin American Theology," in Rosino Gibellini, ed., *Frontiers of Theology in Latin America*, trans. John Drury (Maryknoll: Orbis, 1979), p. 184.

and to examine the political definition we formulate within the framework of clearly proposed strategic goals.[11]

Juan Luis Segundo also employs the word praxis, but here in a more explicit relationship to theology.

> By "theology," then, I mean here *fides quaerens intellectum* in a much more direct sense. I mean "faith seeking understanding" in order to give guidance and direction to historical praxis. I maintain that not one single dogma can be studied with any other final criterion than its impact on praxis.[12]

Lastly, the following quote is offered which is characteristic of the usage of the term by Gustavo Gutierrez.

> Liberation theology . . . is a process of reflection which starts out from historical praxis. It attempts to ponder the faith from the standpoint of this historical praxis and the way that faith is actually lived in a commitment to liberation. Thus its themes are the great themes of all authentic theology but its focus, its way of approaching them, is different. Its relationship to historical praxis is distinct.[13]

What emerges from a careful examination of these uses of the word praxis and the many others which recur throughout the writings of the liberation theologians is nothing less than the realization that the word praxis is in fact descriptive of a way or process of doing theology that cannot be reduced to a single referent.

> Praxis is not the application of already known truth or the carrying out of a transhistorical ideal; it is that process in and through which one comes to know present reality and future possibilities.[14]

Even though the word praxis refers to a general way or process of theological reflection, it is possible nonetheless to identify specific elements which constitute this way of theologizing in order to provide a more precise definition of what is meant by praxis-orientation. Such elements, as indicated by the previous quotes, include a constant orientation to the life and experience of the Latin American people (cf. Gutierrez), the use of the social sciences as instruments of analysis (cf. Assmann), the reflection upon the Latin American reality using the resources of the Christian tradition (cf. Segundo), and the proposal of courses of action for changing the given reality (cf. Dussel). Such are

---

[11] Hugo Assmann, "The Power of Christ in History. Conflicting Christologies and Discernment," in Gibellini, ed., *Frontiers of Theology in Latin America*, p. 135.

[12] Juan Luis Segundo, "Capitalism Versus Socialism: Crux Theologica," in Gibellini, ed., *Frontiers of Theology in Latin America*, p. 250.

[13] Gustavo Gutierrez, "Liberation Praxis and Christian Faith," in Gibellini, ed., *Frontiers of Theology in Latin America*, p. 22.

[14] Charles Davis, "Theology and Praxis," *Cross Curr* 23 (1973):166.

the elements which begin to precipitate as one clarifies what is meant
by the many uses of the word praxis. Such elements, however, when
analyzed, begin to take shape as something more definite than simply
a "way" of doing theology. Instead these various elements emerge as
the very method of liberation theology. It is a method which is only
gradually taking shape in an explicit way. To this end Juan Luis
Segundo and Clodovis Boff have thus far offered the most important
contributions to a conscious articulation of the method of liberation
theology. Yet already in the use of the word praxis among liberation
theologians can be recognized not only their common participation as
theologians in the project of liberation but also an implicit methodology
which guides their work.

The hypothesis here set forth is that in spite of the great diversity of
liberation theology, it is possible to speak of the method of liberation
theology. It is a method implicit in liberation theology's use of the word
praxis and which is becoming explicit as liberation theologians turn in
a more self-conscious way to this question. That does not mean that
any single liberation theologian adheres exactly to the method here
described. Admittedly this is an attempt to synthesize many diverse
aspects of liberation thought for the sake of a systematic presentation.
Yet it is an attempt which is both grounded in the study of the primary
sources and which corresponds to the conclusions of those who have
most carefully examined the methodological foundations of liberation
theology.

One North American student of liberation theology, Glenn R.
Bucher, offers corroboration for the hypothesis here presented
regarding those elements which combine to constitute the methodology
of liberation theology. Although such elements remain for the most
part implicit due to the fact that "methodological considerations do not
constitute the central concern in a theology that derives its character
from 'the critical reflection on human nature, its basic principles, and
the world in light of the Gospel's transforming liberty' (Gutierrez),"[15]
Bucher goes on to argue that nonetheless the rudiments of a theological
method can be discerned through a closer examination of liberation
theologies.

> Yet implicit in these theologies lies a general method which impinges upon
> both the definition and task of theology, and one which gives to liberation

---

[15]Glenn R. Bucher, "Theological Method in Liberation Theologies: Cone,
Russell, and Gutierrez," *American Academy of Religion. Philosophy of
Religion and Theol. Proceedings* (1976):119.

theologies their distinctive character. As one uncovers in these theologies the relationship between the existential situation of blacks, women, and Latin Americans; the social/political/economic analysis of these social situations; the interpretation and use of the historical theological tradition; biblical material and hermeneutics; an assessment of the Church in history and present; and the meanings in liberation, freedom, and justice for praxis and the transformation of persons and societies, one begins to find a methodology of unique proportions. But that methodology is not located only in the ordering of these essential theological elements, but also in the manner liberation theologians use, interpret, and apply them.[16]

It is exactly those elements identified by Bucher which also play a central role in the elaboration of the method of liberation theology which follows. Bucher, too, recognizes that this is no method in the academic sense of the word. Instead it is much more a "manner," way, style, or art of theologizing, a fact which needs to be taken seriously lest liberation theology be misrepresented. Nevertheless, the theology of liberation can be organized around some constitutive elements which serve as the basis of its method. These elements as indicated by Bucher provide an affirmation of the possibility of speaking of liberation theology's method and point out the direction here to be followed.

2. Primary Resources for a Discussion of Liberation Theology's Method

Having affirmed the possibility of speaking of the method of liberation theology, it is appropriate to note those authors who have led the search for the method of liberation theology. Such a concern for method has only gradually emerged as a question among liberation theologians.

> Everyone is aware of the fact that Latin American theology must confront the whole problem of its methodology and that this problem is acquiring a more pointed urgency every day. Real-life priorities and problems are predominant in its discussions, to be sure. But when these themes are to be turned into organized reflection, there reappears the whole problem of the "reflective approach" and the analytical set of instruments that can give systematic justification to this brand of theologizing.[17]

---

[16]Ibid. Bucher includes in his observations not only Latin American but also feminist and black liberation theologies. Of primary interest in this context is, of course, the application of his insights to the *Latin American* liberation theology.

[17]Raul Vidales, "Methodological Issues in Liberation Theology," in Gibellini, ed., *Frontiers of Theology in Latin America*, p. 34.

Two authors in particular are cited in this discussion for their contributions in articulating the method of liberation theology: Juan Luis Segundo and Clodovis Boff. While C. Boff offers a rigorously academic proposal for what the method of liberation theology ought to become based on an argument which seeks to remain on the epistemological level,[18] Segundo writes out of the conviction that it is necessary to "challenge theological methodology as it is practised in the great centers of learning."[19] Although the approaches of the two authors are strikingly different—C. Boff's reasoned argument which at times appears to be an apology for liberation theology in the face of its "cultured despisers" in the academic world standing in sharp relief to Segundo's more radical and partisan call for a reconstruction of the entire theological enterprise—both contribute insights which cannot be neglected in an attempt to identify the constitutive elements of liberation theology's method. While the work of C. Boff was first published in 1978 (in Spanish) and is only gradually becoming known,[20] Segundo's book first appeared in 1975 (in 1976 in English translation) and has been widely quoted in the literature.

In particular it is the hermeneutic circle proposed by Segundo which has been discussed for its contribution to an understanding of the method of liberation theology.[21] Segundo describes the two preconditions and four movements of his hermeneutic circle in the following way.

> . . . first I think it would be wise for me to reiterate the two preconditions for such a circle. They are (1) profound and enriching questions and suspicions about our real situation; (2) a new interpretation of the Bible that is equally profound and enriching. These two preconditions mean that there must in turn be four decisive factors in our circle. *Firstly*, there is our way of experiencing reality, which leads to ideological suspicion.

---

[18] Clodovis Boff, *Theologie und Praxis. Die erkenntnistheoretischen Grundlagen der Theologie der Befreiung* (Munich/Mainz: Kaiser/Matthias-Grünewald, 1983).

[19] Juan Luis Segundo, *The Liberation of Theology*, trans. John Drury (Maryknoll: Orbis, 1976), p. 5.

[20] At the time of this writing C. Boff's work has not yet appeared in English translation. Some of his basic ideas, however, are available to English speaking readers in Jose Miguez Bonino, *Toward a Christian Political Ethics* (Philadelphia: Fortress, 1983), esp. Chapter 3, pp. 37-53.

[21] For example, Anthony J. Tambasco, *The Bible for Ethics. Juan Luis Segundo and First-World Ethics* (Washington: University Press of America, 1981), pp. 51-55; Harold Wells, "Segundo's Hermeneutic Circle," *Th So Africa* 34 (Mar. 1981):25-31; and Kenneth Leech, "Liberating Theology: The Thought of Juan Luis Segundo," *Th* 84 (July 1981):259-260.

Secondly there is the application of our ideological suspicion to the whole ideological superstructure in general and to theology in particular. *Thirdly* there comes a new way of experiencing theological reality that leads us to exegetical suspicion, that is, to the suspicion that the prevailing interpretation of the Bible has not taken important pieces of data into account. *Fourthly* we have our new hermeneutic, that is, our new way of interpreting the fountainhead of our faith (i.e. Scripture) with the new elements at our disposal.[22]

What should be noted first of all is that the hermeneutic circle of Segundo is proposed specifically as a method of interpreting Scripture and not as a description of the method of liberation theology as a whole. Nevertheless, the hermeneutic circle of Segundo does establish a key element for the method of liberation theology as a whole, that is, ideological suspicion both of the given interpretations of Latin American reality and also of those theological and exegetical approaches which fail to examine their own roles in supporting or criticizing the given ideological superstructure. Only following a thorough-going skepticism and suspicion of the given interpretations of Latin American reality—social, economic, political, and theological—does Segundo believe that liberation theology can succeed in a new interpretation not only of Scripture but also of traditional theological themes. In addition to his articulation of ideological suspicion as a key element for the method of theology of liberation, Segundo also discusses the roles of sociology, commitment, and ideology within liberation theology, each of which makes an additional contribution to understanding the method of liberation theology.[23]

Clodovis Boff's *Theology and Praxis* has made an especially significant contribution to a deeper understanding of method among liberation theologians. It should be kept in mind that C. Boff's proposal is to be understood more as a prescription for what the method of liberation theology should become rather than a description of what liberation theology already is. His proposal is highly theoretical and attempts to prescribe on an epistemological level the further development of liberation theology. Many aspects of C. Boff's work deserve careful attention. In systematic fashion, he sets forth the nature of modern political reality which calls for a new understanding of theological method in conjunction with the use of social-analytical

---

[22]Segundo, *The Liberation of Theology*, p. 9.

[23]Cf. Juan Luis Segundo, *Jesus of Nazareth Yesterday and Today. Vol. 1: Faith and Ideologies*, trans. John Drury (Maryknoll: Orbis, 1984) for a further elaboration of the points first set forth in *The Liberation of Theology*.

mediation. C. Boff develops a proposal for the manner in which such
social-analytical mediation should be linked to hermeneutical
(theological) mediation to clarify the task of liberation theology which
exists in the dialectic between theory and praxis.[24]

Employing the above resources together with a general reading of
the literature, the following five elements are proposed by the present
author to be constitutive for the method of liberation theology.

    1. A Living Encounter with Latin American Reality
    2. Commitment to the Liberation of Latin America
    3. Social Analysis
    4. Theological Reflection and Reformulation
    5. Engagement in the Project of Liberation

The articulation of these elements as integral to the method of
liberation theology corresponds to the explicit assertions increasingly
being forwarded by liberation theologians. L. Boff, for example, has
structured the theology of liberation according to a social-analytic
mediation, an hermeneutic mediation, and a practical-pastoral
mediation (action) which sets forth from a spiritual experience of the
poor.[25] His analysis of the constitutive aspects of liberation theology
corresponds directly to the five elements to be discussed next at greater
length and further legitimizes the presentation of these five elements
as constitutive of the method of liberation theology.[26]

---

[24]Among the other aspects of C. Boff's work which contribute to the
following discussion are his clear distinction between praxis and
interpretation, his discussion of ideology, his criteria for the selection of an
appropriate social theory, his affirmation of methodological objectivity as a
necessary moment in the theological task, his discussion of the political
consequences of theology, and praxis as the ultimate criterion of theological
authenticity. Apart from these individual elements it is, moreover, the very
structure and movement of C. Boff's methodological proposals which are most
helpful: liberation theology sets out from praxis and passes through social-
analytical mediation and hermeneutical (theological) mediation before
returning to praxis. The method which C. Boff proposes as theory correlates at
numerous points to the underlying method which has been implicitly employed
by liberation theologians. Certainly it has nowhere been applied in the thorough
and systematic fashion which C. Boff describes. That is the strength of his work
in challenging liberation theologians to a more conscientious examination of
their methodological presuppositions. Yet in many ways C. Boff's work is itself
a grasping of the method already implicit in liberation theology and thinking it
through in a rigorous way.

[25]Leonardo Boff, "Die Anliegen der Befreiungstheologie," *Theologische
Berichte* 8 (1979):71-103.

[26]Having established the possibility of speaking of the constitutive
elements of the method of liberation theology, a word of caution is in order before

B. *Constitutive Elements for the Method of Liberation Theology*

1. A Living Encounter with Latin American Reality

Latin American liberation theology grows out of its native environment. Therefore the "stuff" of this theology begins with living aspects of Latin American reality as they are encountered there. Several characteristics of the Latin American reality appear thematically in the writings of liberation theologians. They include a wide range of social, economic, political, cultural, and religious factors which together comprise the fabric of Latin American reality.

---

discussing these five individual elements at greater length. That word of caution concerns the resistance of the theology of liberation to being reduced to a method. In no way should the following deliberations be understood as an attempt to pigeonhole liberation theology in order to categorize it and dismiss it. It is not to be seen as just another alternative method which can be set alongside others and evaluated in terms of its relative usefulness. Much more the theology of liberation remains a style or art of theologizing. Just as it is possible to analyze the method of a composer, painter, or poet, at the same time there can be no confusing such analysis with the hearing of a symphony or the experiencing of a painting or poem. This is also the case with liberation theology. While it is possible and helpful to analyze it in terms of its method, the theology of liberation cannot be equated with its method. It is in fact a new *way* of doing theology.

Enrique Dussel helps to express this very point as he characterizes the method of liberation theology as analectic as opposed to epistemological or dialectic.

> Gradually this theology discovers its own methods which I have defined as ana-lectic and not only dialectic, in that it is listening to the trans-ontological voice of the other (*ana-*) and is interpreting its message by means of analogies. . . . For its own part the theology of liberation favours the interpretation of the voice of the oppressed as the basis for its praxis. . . . Starting from a unique position of difference, each theologian, and indeed the whole of Latin American theology, takes a fresh look at traditional themes passed down through history, but enters the interpretive process from the distinct emptiness of his new found liberty (that is, with a blank sheet). ("Domination Liberation: A New Approach," trans. J. D. Mitchell, in Claude Geffre and Gustavo Gutierrez, eds., *Concilium 96: The Mystical and Political Dimension of the Christian Faith* [New York: Herder, 1974], pp. 55-56).

Indeed liberation theology is gradually discovering its own method. It is a method which leads to some distinctive reformulations of the traditional themes of theology. But what is even more decisive is the very way in which this theology carries out its task: through a listening to the voice of the other, searching for analogies with which to interpret this voice, and only then reworking traditional theological themes. It is imperative to keep this awareness of the way or style of liberation theology clearly in view as the attempt is now made to order the constitutive elements of its method.

These factors serve as the basis for theology as the theology of liberation reflects upon its own Latin American context. The following sketch of eight characteristics of Latin American reality is in no way exhaustive. It serves only to indicate some striking aspects of Latin American life which provide the texture of liberation theology as it exists in a living encounter with its environment.

a. *Poverty.* Since the fact of poverty in Latin America serves as the very starting point of this theology as articulated in Chapter One, no lengthy elaboration of this characteristic of Latin American life is necessary. It suffices simply to call to memory the origins of liberation theology as a response to Latin American poverty.

> The roots of the theology of liberation are grounded in the painful perception of the misery to which the great majority of the people are subjected. Its point of departure is therefore its observation of the brutal fact crying out to heaven that in the Christian part of the world which is Latin America the large majority of the population live and die under inhuman living conditions: malnutrition, infant mortality, endemic illness, low incomes, unemployment, and the absence of social security, hygiene, hospitals, schools, housing, in short the phenomenon that the goods which are necessary for a bare minimum of human dignity are not sufficiently available.[27]

One further reference points to the key cause of this enormous poverty as analyzed by liberation theology, that is, a world in which the wealth is unevenly divided between rich and poor, center and periphery.

> The population living under the capitalist system is now about 2.5 billion people. About 800 million live at the center of the system, while 1.7 billion live on its periphery. The gross product of the center is about $1.6 trillion, while that of the periphery is about $340 billion. That comes down to a per-capita income of about $2,000 for those living in the center and an income of about $200 for those in the dependent countries.
>
> Behind these facts and figures lies a tragic human situation of hunger, poverty, marginalization, and exploitation.[28]

The poverty of Latin America calls the theologians of liberation to commitment, analysis, and action.

b. *A History of Domination.* The history of a people shapes both their self-understanding and the structures of the present society. The various periods of Latin American history moving from the domination of colonialism by Iberian conquerors to the domination of the economy beginning in the last century reveal historical forces which continue to shape the present. The history of Latin America

---

[27]L. Boff, "Die Anliegen der Befreiungstheologie," p. 80 (own translation).

[28]Leonardo Boff, *Liberating Grace,* trans. John Drury (Maryknoll: Orbis, 1979), p. 69.

interpreted as a history of domination summons the theology of liberation to participation in the creation of a future which will be liberated from past and present forms of external and internal domination.

c. *Military Rule.* The 1960s marked the beginning of a new political trend throughout Latin America. "Military regimes based on force took control of the government in almost every nation of Latin America."[29] Enrique Dussel has provided a summary of this trend which added the nations of Brazil, Bolivia, Uruguay, Chile, Peru, Ecuador, and Argentina to the already existing dictatorships in Paraguay, Haiti, and Santo Domingo and the "military dictatorships masked as democracies" in Guatemala, Honduras, El Salvador, and Nicaragua.[30] While the political face of Latin America is constantly changing (cf. the Nicaraguan revolution in 1979 and the restoration of democratic rule in Argentina in 1983), the predominance of military rule throughout Latin America remains a distinguishing political characteristic. The linkage of the interests of industry to these governments, together with the role played by the university in providing the expertise needed to keep these regimes functioning, has led to what has been called "a third type of colonial pact rooted in the military-industrial-university complex."[31] The ideology which undergirds these regimes, that of "National Security," has been analyzed and heftily criticized by the theology of liberation.

d. *Cultural Dependence.* The theologians of liberation respond in their writings to a number of cultural phenomena which are here categorized as forms of cultural dependence. Cultural dependence in Latin America has its origins in the imposition of Hispanic civilization upon the indigenous people during the colonial period.[32] In more recent times cultural dependence has been understood as a consequence of the economic dependency of Latin America upon the other centers of power.

First of all, we see the adoption of development models that are out of line with, or even alien to, the socio-cultural reality of our people and nations.

---

[29]Ibid., p. 71.

[30]Enrique Dussel, "Current Events in Latin America (1972-1980)," in Sergio Torres and John Eagleson, eds., *The Challenge of Basic Christian Communities*, trans. John Drury (Maryknoll: Orbis, 1981), pp. 79-80.

[31]L. Boff, *Liberating Grace*, p. 71.

[32]Cf. Enrique Dussel, *A History of the Church in Latin America. Colonialism to Liberation (1492-1979)*, trans. and rev. Alan Neely (Grand Rapids: Eerdmans, 1981), esp. pp. 41-46.

Thanks to the mass media in particular, these models are imposed on us by the "developed" countries. This proves beneficial to their own economic imperialism, generates false values that are alien to our indigenous culture, and provokes frustrating alienating desires. A false model of development intensifies our dependence and does not allow us to grow along our own cultural lines.[33]

A direct correlation is recognized between dependence in the economic realm and the cultural dependence which is nurtured by a capitalist economy.

This economic dependence, in turn, leads to *socio-cultural dependence*. It helps to configure social classes in a particular way. The privileged classes who benefit from economic dependence mimic the values and habits of the economic centers. Their culture is antipopulist, elitist, and imitative. Generations of Brazilians were ashamed to admit their nationality or to speak the language of the country, and we find remnants of the type even today. Industrialization marginalized the majority of the population, luring them from the countryside to the big cities where they formed cordons of poverty. They were not given a role in the dynamic thrust of industrialization, and the ideologists of consumption ignored them because they lacked buying power.[34]

Thus cultural dependency lives as the social complement of economic dependency.

The forces creating cultural dependency have increased in recent decades as the pursuit of economic development has intensified. Juan Luis Segundo has described several interrelated aspects of Latin American cultural dependence as he witnesses "a society undergoing great changes."[35] The recent thrust toward economic development in Latin America has been accompanied by rapid cultural change and an enormous sense of cultural dislocation. Such change is most noticeable in the rapid shift in Latin America from a predominantly rural to a predominantly urban population. The implications of this change in terms of a sense of uprootedness among individuals are numerous. While the new dwellers of the metropolis now live in a highly technological, competitive, mobile, impersonal, and secular society, the values which they retain are those of traditional society: a sense of stability, trust, kinship, and religious piety. This radical conflict of values results in a deep sense of uprootedness and psychic

---

[33]Segundo Galilea, "Liberation Theology and New Tasks Facing Christians," in Gibellini, ed., *Frontiers of Theology in Latin America*, pp. 171-172.

[34]L. Boff, *Liberating Grace*, pp. 69-70.

[35]Cf. for the following Juan Luis Segundo, *The Hidden Motives of Pastoral Action. Latin American Reflections*, trans. John Drury (Maryknoll: Orbis, 1978), esp. pp. 3-23.

insecurity. What modern urban society offers as a substitute for the lost values of traditional society is the deceptive promise of becoming participants in "consumer society." The mass media—television, radio, movies, and the press—communicate this primary value which binds the whole of modern, urban society together, i.e., consumerism, and works to relativize all other values which might contradict consumerism as the highest good. This promise is, however, for most of the population an empty one since their real chances for significant progress in consumer society are negligible. In this whole process through which traditional values are destroyed, the primary benefactors remain hidden behind the ideology of consumer society.

These are some of the factors which comprise the cultural dependence of Latin America as described by the theologians of liberation. On the basis of these factors they recognize the need for striving not only for economic but also for cultural liberation from the cultural dependence which characterizes contemporary Latin America.[36]

e. *Racism*. An awareness of racism as a characteristic of Latin American society has only gradually emerged. Enrique Dussel has chronicled the history of a large number of Africans brought originally to Latin America as slaves and who today live primarily in Brazil, Haiti, and the Caribbean.[37] In addition to the racism experienced by black Latin Americans, racism as a problem for native Indian and mestizo peoples has also been growing in awareness. Especially influential for a growing awareness of racism as a component of Latin American society has been the encounter of Latin American liberation theologians with black liberation theologians from the United States.[38] Special attention has also been given to the problem of racism in the Ecumenical Association of Third World Theologians.[39] The destructive consequences of racial discrimina—

[36]Cf. Gutierrez, *A Theology of Liberation*, esp. pp. 91-92.

[37]Dussel, *A History of the Church in Latin America*, pp. 176-178.

[38]Cf. the documentation from the first "Theology in the Americas" Conference held in Detroit in 1975, esp. the essay by Herbert O. Edwards, "Black Theology and Liberation Theology" and the excerpts entitled "The Black Theology Panel," in Sergio Torres and John Eagleson, eds., *Theology in the Americas* (Maryknoll: Orbis, 1976), pp. 177-191 and 351-356.

[39]Cf. Lloyd Stennette, Mauro Batista, and Barry Chavannes, "The Situation of the Black Race in Latin America and the Caribbean," in Torres and Eagleson, eds., *The Challenge of Basic Christian Communities*, pp. 46-56.

tion and segregation remain an area for continued analysis by liberation theologians which has only begun to be explored.

f. *Oppression of Women.* As was the case with racism, the question of the oppression of women has become an issue for the Latin American liberation theology primarily through its encounter with theologians from other parts of the world. The "Theology in the Americas" conference held in Detroit in 1975[40] and the interchange of theologians through the Ecumenical Association of Third World Theologians have offered the opening of a new awareness to this problem. The first seminar ever held by Christian women of Latin America to reflect in a structured way on the situation of Latin American women was held in October 1979.[41] The final document of this seminar entitled "The Latin American Woman: The Praxis and Theology of Liberation" provided a new challenge to liberation theologians to take up into its considerations the specific forms of oppression suffered by women in the Latin American context. In this document economic, political, ideological-cultural, and ecclesial factors describing the oppression of Latin American women were presented in a series of theses. Also included were a number of theses asserting the importance of the participation of women in the liberation struggle. Most important for the theology of liberation are those statements which are directed to the oppressions suffered by women in the church and the challenge made to liberation theology to incorporate the problems of women in its reflections. To this end some positive suggestions were made for the development both of a biblical theology from a woman's standpoint and of the implications of Christology for women. The final thesis in this report presented a direct challenge: "Every theologian of liberation should be urged to reformulate his or her theological categories from a women's standpoint, and to explore revelation more deeply from that same standpoint."[42] The challenge in regard to the oppression of women in Latin America, like the problem of racism, has only begun to be faced by theologians of

---

[40]Cf. the statements of "The Feminist Theology Panel," in Torres and Eagleson, eds., *Theology in the Americas*, pp. 361-376, esp. the "Statement by Beatriz Melano Couch," pp. 374-376.

[41]For this and the following see Cora Ferro, "The Latin American Woman: The Praxis and Theology of Liberation," in Torres and Eagleson, eds., *The Challenge of Basic Christian Communities*, pp. 24-37.

[42]Ibid., p. 36.

liberation and promises to become a more prominent focus in coming years.

g. *Popular Religion.* A highly significant characteristic of Latin American life which has been discussed frequently by liberation theologians is the popular religion among the common people of Latin America. What is meant by popular religion is a complex mixture of religious elements originating in pagan religiosity, Latin American folk religiosity, and folk Catholicism.[43] Thus the phenomenon of popular religion is not one "diffuse popular religiosity but rather a plurality of popular religions which must be identified and explained."[44] One comprehensive description of popular religiosity was offered as part of the Final Document of the Puebla conference.[45] Among the positive elements mentioned are devotions (such as to the Sacred Heart); iconography; love for Mary; veneration of the saints; remembrance of the dead; an awareness of personal dignity and solidarity; chant; dance; faith situated in time (feasts) and places (sanctuaries and shrines); a feel for pilgrimage; respect for pastors; integration of the sacraments and sacramentals in personal and social life; a capacity for suffering and heroism in withstanding trials; a sense of the value of prayer; and acceptance of other people. Counted among negative aspects are magic, fatalism, fetishism, ritualism, misinformation and ignorance, syncretistic reinterpretation, and a reduction of the faith to a mere contract with God. More recent negative manifestations include secularism, consumptionism, sects, oriental and agnostic religions, various secularized forms of political messianism, and the uprooting and urban proletarianization as the result of cultural change.

As becomes clear from a mere listing of the phenomena included under the category of popular religion, the need has been felt for the development of a systematic approach by which to interpret the many and diverse elements.[46] As was the case with the Puebla document, the

---

[43]Cf. the chart and explanation in Enrique Dussel, *A History of the Church in Latin America*, pp. 82-86.

[44]Jean-Pierre Bastian, "Popular Religion. A Strategic Element for the Formation of a New Hegemonic Block in Latin America," *Foun* 23 (Oct.-Dec. 1980):358.

[45]Cf. "The Final Document" (Nos. 454-456), in John Eagleson and Philip Scharper, eds., *Puebla and Beyond. Documentation and Commentary*, trans. John Drury (Maryknoll: Orbis, 1979), p. 186.

[46]Cf. the categories cited by Bastian, "Popular Religion," pp. 357-363 and by Jose Miguez Bonino, "Popular Piety in Latin America," in Geffre and

final conclusions of such studies generally recognize the ambiguity of popular religion especially in terms of its possible contribution to the process of liberation. "Popular religion remains ambiguous. . . . It is at one and the same time the bearer of dynamic and progressive factors and of reins on the revolutionary process."[47]
One positive aspect of popular religion which has been recognized for its potential contribution to the liberation process is its functioning as "the protest of the natives and the *mestizos*, who have been subjected to a foreign culture, religion and morality, but who use the names and forms of the latter to reconstitute the elements of their own religious and cultural identity."[48] However, it is at the same time recognized that even such a protest "is absorbed by religiosity and toned down into a kind of substitute satisfaction. In the process, alas, it loses all its power to transform the individual and society."[49] Most skeptical about the usefulness of popular religion for liberation has been Juan Luis Segundo who sees a virtual contradiction between popular religion as an expression of mass behavior and the level of commitment required for the liberation struggle which can only be provided through a minority line of conduct.[50] While the final evaluations of the possible role of popular religion range from Segundo's negative judgment to more positive evaluations which stress the need for a deeper encounter by theologians with popular religion in order to make a proper assessment,[51] the theologians of liberation would at least agree that "what is needed is a prophetic critique in order that popular piety or religiosity will begin to move toward a new type of humanity."[52] Popular religion is a characteristic of Latin American life not to be underestimated.

h. *Roman Catholicism*. The final characteristic is the tremendous influence which the institution of the Roman Catholic Church has exercised upon Latin American life throughout the centuries up to and including the present. The influence of Roman

---

Gutierrez, eds., *The Mystical and Political Dimension of the Christian Faith*, pp. 149-150.

[47]Bastian, "Popular Religion," pp. 356-357.

[48]Miguez Bonino, "Popular Piety in Latin America," p. 151.

[49]Ibid.

[50]Cf. Segundo, *The Liberation of Theology*, esp. pp. 183-205. See also the similar conclusions of Miguez Bonino which are grounded on Segundo's line of argumentation in "Popular Piety in Latin America," pp. 154-157.

[51]Cf. the conclusions of Bastian, "Popular Religion," pp. 364-367.

[52]Dussel, *A History of the Church in Latin America*, p. 86.

Catholicism in colonial and neo-colonial periods of Latin American history has been largely of a conservative nature, protective of its own interests in society. This traditionally conservative stance was given a turn with the occurrence of Vatican II and, more immediately in Latin America, the stance taken by the Latin American bishops at the Medellin conference in 1968. In the years following Medellin the way was opened toward a new commitment on the part of the church—bishops, priests, and laity—to the poor. The theology of liberation has itself been supported by this new opening to the poor on the part of a traditionally conservative hierarchy. At the same time reactionary forces have also gathered in opposition to this new direction. Thus liberation theologians have found themselves engaged in the constant process of defending their positions in a church which is thoroughly divided between conservative and progressive forces. The Puebla conference has been noted as a watershed in the encounter between these forces. Since the majority of the liberation theologians are members of the Roman Catholic Church, if not themselves clergy, it is not only the tradition of the Roman Catholic Church which influences them, but also each current development. This interaction between liberation theology and the institutional church promises to continue to mark the future of this theology as it has already marked its past.

These eight characteristics of Latin American society offer an overview of the encounter between the theology of liberation and its environment. This living encounter needs to be recognized as the first element in any explication of the method of liberation. The encounter of liberation theologians with their immediate environment is, moreover, not a neutral one. The aspects of Latin American life listed above are not experienced as objectively given and unchangeable but rather as various aspects of an overall situation of oppression which calls for liberation. The living encounter of liberation theology with Latin American reality thus leads to a second methodological element, that is, commitment to the liberation of Latin America.

2. Commitment to the Liberation of Latin America

Surprising, if not contemptible, to many Western theologians is the claim of liberation theology to include partisan commitment as a fundamental element in its method. Whereas in the West, a neutral, objective, impartial approach has been deemed requisite, liberation theology deems commitment to be of the essence in the Latin American context. The classic expression of the element of commitment as an

integral part of the method of liberation theology is contained in the
assertion of Gutierrez that theology is not the first but the second step for
liberation theology. The first step is instead contained in what
Gutierrez calls *critical* reflection on historical praxis, or what is here
called commitment to the liberation of Latin America. Commenting
on the prophetic function of theology, Gutierrez asserts that "if theology
is based on this observation of historical events and contributes to the
discovery of their meaning, it is with the purpose of making the
Christian's commitment within them more radical and clear."[53]

A concise statement of the centrality of commitment for the
theology of liberation is further articulated by Gutierrez in the
following quote.

> From the beginning, the theology of liberation had two fundamental
> insights. Not only did they come first chronologically, but they have
> continued to form the very backbone of this theology. I am referring to its
> theological method and its perspective of the poor.
>
> From the beginning, the theology of liberation posited that the first act is
> involvement in the process, and that theology comes afterward, as a second
> act. . . .
>
> The second insight of the theology of liberation is its decision to work
> from the viewpoint of the poor—the exploited classes, marginalized ethnic
> groups, and scorned cultures. . . .
>
> This second point, of course, is inseparable from the first. If theology is
> to be a reflection from within, and upon, praxis, it will be important to bear
> in mind that what is being reflected upon is the praxis of liberation of the
> oppressed of this world.[54]

Theology, for Gutierrez, takes place following what he here calls
"involvement in the liberation process" or the "decision to work from
the viewpoint of the poor," that is, a deep commitment, even a
conversion experience, based on an encounter with the world of the
oppressed.

Other theologians use different terms to describe this same
element.   Segundo has asserted that for liberation theology
"commitment is the first step" and he scorns any purported
methodological neutrality.[55] Leonardo Boff has used such phrases as
"intuitive" knowledge or "ethical indignation."

> Many Christians have realized in faith that such a situation contradicts
> God's historical design: poverty represents a social sin which God does not

---

[53]Gutierrez, *A Theology of Liberation*, p. 13.

[54]Gustavo Gutierrez, *The Power of the Poor in History*, trans. Robert R.
Barr (Maryknoll: Orbis, 1983), pp. 200-201.

[55]Cf. Segundo, *The Liberation of Theology*, esp. pp. 39 and 69-81.

want. For this reason a change is urgently required in order to help fellow human beings and to obey the will of God.[56]

Osvaldo Luis Mottesi takes up the same concern using the image of the prophet when he states that the church "must assume the prophetic denunciation of every dehumanizing situation that is contrary to brotherhood, justice and liberty."[57]

Regardless of the words that are chosen to describe this element of the method of liberation theology, the point is the same. There exists an ethical moment of prophetic indignation and protest against the forms of oppression encountered in Latin America which cry out for commitment. Neutrality is seen as an inadequate response to the human suffering which is encountered. A helpful distinction in this respect is the reference of Jose Miguez Bonino to the "double location" of the theologian.

> On the one hand there is the theologian's location with a theological discipline with its particular epistemological conditions and demands; on the other hand the theologian is also a social agent within a particular social formation.[58]

The theology of liberation has been very clear about its social location as a theology carried out from the point of view of the poor. For many this commitment on the part of liberation theologians makes it impossible to distinguish it as theology from ideology. The liberation theologians, however, are not dismayed by such accusations, pointing out the ways in which every theology carries its own ideological weight. Instead of hiding behind a veil of objectivity, the theology of liberation wants to be crystal clear about its bias: "Theological and social location for the Christian are one, unified in the specific commitment to the poor."[59]

While commitment to the liberation process is an essential element of liberation theology, it is at the same time necessary that it move beyond mere denunciation. Important as the initial intuition of liberation theology might be as it leads to commitment, such a first step must necessarily also lead to the next one as well.

> Only when it [Christian faith] is in-formed through love (praxis) is it true faith which works salvation. Otherwise it would be an empty faith which does not lead to the kingdom of God. Where, however, this praxis dispenses of an analysis of the mechanisms, the effectiveness of its

---

[56]L. Boff, "Die Anliegen der Befreiungstheologie," p. 80 (own translation).

[57]Osvaldo Luis Mottesi, "Doing Theology in the Latin American Context," *J Int Th C* (Spring 1978):84.

[58]Miguez Bonino, *Toward a Christian Political Ethics*, p. 42.

[59]Ibid., p. 44.

engagement is paltry and unpredictable in spite of its unequivocal basic option. In this direction it can go no further![60] The encounter of liberation theology with Latin American society does lead to a commitment to liberation. But the act of commitment is not the final step. Appropriate tools of social analysis must be employed to interpret this reality and give direction to its fundamental commitment. Thus the theology of liberation incorporates the mediation of the social sciences as a third element of its method which complements its specifically theological reflections.

3. Social Analysis

a. *The Need for Social Analysis.* The theologians of liberation are unanimous in their affirmation of the need for "social analysis" as an integral element of their theological method.[61] This need is urgent due to the specific nature of the reality which confronts those who set out to do theology in Latin America. Previously a specific example of the use of social analysis by liberation theology has been discussed, i.e., the application of the theory of dependency in analyzing the causation of Latin American poverty. In this section the methodological place and significance of such concrete applications of social analysis are examined more closely.

A representative expression of the need for social analysis by liberation theology are these remarks by Raul Vidales:

> Insofar as the study of Latin American realities is concerned, the analysis of the social sciences leads us toward a very specific perspective. It forces us to view Latin America in terms of overall structures, historical processes, all-embracing factors, and conflict-ridden relationships. The reality which is Latin America cannot be explained as a totality resulting naturally from its own inner evolution in history; nor can internal problems be viewed in isolation from the overall reality as a whole.[62]

Vidales continues regarding the specific contribution which social analysis can make toward the interpretation of this reality.

> The basic contribution of the human sciences is to provide theology with a more clear-eyed view of history, a more critical approach, and a set of analytical instruments. This is particularly true at the present juncture in Latin American history. By providing basic pronouncements about reality, these sciences offer theology diagnostic tools, reveal underlying

---

[60]L. Boff, "Die Anliegen der Befreiungstheologie," p. 82 (own translation).

[61]Followed here is the lead of Jose Miguez Bonino who uses this general term in his *Toward a Christian Political Ethics* to describe the use of the social sciences by liberation theology.

[62]Vidales, "Methodological Issues in Liberation Theology," in Gibellini, ed., *Frontiers of Theology in Latin America*, p. 39.

causes, highlight structural processes and dynamisms, and indicate how systems tend to function. This corpus of data clarifies the situation of people here and now, particularly in the situation of those who have been deprived and impoverished for centuries.[63]

This explanation of the need for and usefulness of social analysis by liberation theology is indicative of a host of references which recur throughout the literature.[64]

In part the liberation theologians have emphasized their use of social analysis in order to make clear the distinctiveness of their theologizing from the traditional approach.

Differing from European schools of theological thought in this respect, it is the first specifically Latin American theology because the distinctive situation of Latin America is part of its intrinsic content and because its

---

[63]Ibid., pp. 41-42.

[64]C. Boff, *Theologie und Praxis*, has offered the most thorough elaboration of the need for social analysis by liberation theology. In particular he stressed the need for what he calls "social-analytical mediation" over against the traditional theological reliance primarily upon "philosophical mediation" in evaluating human reality. Whereas philosophical mediation has in the past rendered a service to an understanding of the political in describing the "essence" of such things as power, the state, conflict, society, the law, etc., such a philosophical description of essences simply does not suffice for a theology which, moving out of a sense of historical urgency, seeks to involve itself concretely in historical praxis (p. 39). Moreover, a philosophical mediation has the dangerous tendency of distancing itself from the concrete historical reality by becoming excessively speculative (p. 40). Such speculation can easily lead to a mystification of the situation of the oppressed which is alienated from practical action to improve their situation. Without a connection to concrete praxis, philosophical theoreticizing may even result in what C. Boff calls "academic cynicism."

C. Boff argues for a use of social analysis that goes beyond former attempts, based on philosophical suppositions, to relate theology and the political by means of ethical principles (pp. 41-47). History is to be understood not just as an open field which awaits the application of ethical ideals but rather is the very ground where revelation is disclosed and which is for that reason in need of hermeneutical interpretation. It is social science which helps provide theology with the appropriate tools for this hermeneutical task. C. Boff also criticizes those attempts to relate theology and the political which fail to consider the impact of social structures and go no further than applying an individual ethic to political issues. Instead theology must go beyond these former approaches to an integration of social analysis as an integral part of its method. The nature of the reality which is to be theologized makes social analysis necessary and the tools of the social sciences make such analysis possible. Without the use of social analysis, he warns that theology falls into the danger of becoming unwittingly ideeological, i.e., an ideological support for the present order.

methodological approach begins with an analysis of this concrete situation with the help of the social sciences.[65]

It is not, however, the sheer need to be different which is decisive but rather the nature of the subject matter to be investigated. The human reality of Latin America calls for the appropriate tools of social analysis in order to intelligently guide theological work.

Having affirmed the need for social analysis, the next issue becomes that of choosing an appropriate form of social analysis, i.e., those conceptual tools which "will pay close attention to all the various aspects of Latin American life, be they historical, anthropological, political, cultural, economic, or social."[66] The social analysis employed by liberation theology tends not to fall neatly into the categories of any one of these disciplines, but rather borrows pertinent elements from the various social sciences in constructing an analysis which seeks to interpret not only individual aspects of Latin American life but the structural dimensions of Latin American reality as a whole.

A fundamental distinction to be made in considering liberation theology's choice of an appropriate form of social analysis is that between "reality" and "interpretation."[67] This seemingly evident but nevertheless essential distinction serves as a reminder of the dialectical relationship which always exists between pure "facts" and the conceptual "theories" used to interpret those facts. The explicit recognition of this distinction allows the theologians of liberation to become conscientious in their evaluation and choice of the theories which are to be used to interpret Latin American reality. Likewise this distinction allows them to become critical of those interpretations of reality which fail to recognize their ideological presuppositions and which thus tend to absolutize their particular interpretation as itself factual truth.

---

[65]Galilea, "Liberation Theology and the New Tasks Facing Christians," in Gibellini, ed., *Frontiers of Theology in Latin America*, p. 166.

[66]Vidales, "Methodological Issues in Liberation Theology," in Gibellini, ed., *Frontiers of Theology in Latin America*, pp. 49-50.

[67]Cf. Miguez Bonino's discussion of "facts and consciousness," *Toward a Christian Political Ethics*, pp. 38-42, in which he makes special use of the work of C. Boff. C. Boff himself differentiates between four levels in the interpre-tation of reality: (1) the real *in se* (the divine viewpoint), (2) the ordinary apprehension of reality (the prevailing ideology), (3) the critical recognition of the distinctions between what is real and its interpretation (the scientific approach) and (4) theological knowledge (the theology of the political). See *Theologie und Praxis*, pp. 64-65.

Clodovis Boff has made a useful presentation of the criteria to be employed in evaluating the relevance of a particular form of social analysis for a theology which attempts to deal with political realities.[68] He distinguishes between two basic theoretical orientations: a functionalist tendency and a dialectical tendency. A functionalist social analysis tends to interpret society as an organic whole divided into sub-units which mutually complement one another. In this form of social analysis it is the order, harmony, and equilibrium of a system which receives primary attention. A dialectical social analysis, on the other hand, emphasizes the conflict, tension, and struggle of a system which is itself understood to be much more complex and marked by inconsistencies. C. Boff goes on to add that these two theoretical orientations are exemplified in the liberal tradition and Marxism, respectively. Taking up C. Boff's argument, Miguez Bonino explains one further distinction:

> It is our contention that these two divergent perspectives have their roots in two specific locations in social reality. The functionalist perspective is a vision "from the top," from the situation of those sectors of society (whether groups, classes, or nations) which exercise power and control and which therefore perceive society as basically a satisfactory organic system that must be preserved and perfected. Dialectical sociologies, on the other hand, express a vision "from below," from those sectors to which society appears as inadequate, badly structured, full of conflict, and in need of transformation.[69]

Given these two basic types of social analysis, C. Boff contends that a decision must be made between them on the basis of both scientific and ethical criteria. A scientific criterion evaluates these theories on the basis of which offers the better interpretation of the data. An ethical criterion bases its evaluation on the values which the interpreter holds for valid.   While advocating the need for a methodological circle which maintains these two sets of criteria in constant tension, C. Boff ultimately argues for the insufficiency of the scientific criterion for rendering a final judgment on the merits of a given form of social analysis.   Thus it is the ethical criterion which is given final preference in the choice of an appropriate form of social analysis. One is finally forced to take a calculated risk and opt for the form of social analysis which is both available in the present historical moment and which best coincides with one's ethical viewpoint. Given the ethical standpoint of the theology of liberation and its commitment to the poor,

---

[68]For this and the following see C. Boff, *Theologie und Praxis*, pp. 114-118.

[69]Miguez Bonino, *Toward a Christian Political Ethics*, pp. 46-47.

its choice is for a dialectical form of social analysis. Thus it is a form of social analysis which makes use of the most highly developed historical expression of this dialectical tendency, i.e., Marxism.[70]

---

[70]When the attempt is made to inquire more specifically what shape this dialectical, Marxist-oriented form of social analysis takes, the answer becomes more difficult. Segundo, *The Liberation of Theology*, Chapter Two, pp. 39-68, has described the theology of liberation as being "in search of sociology." Segundo judges the present positivist or behaviorist sociology (i.e., functionalist) which currently prevails in Latin America to be inadequate. Among the criticisms directed at the prevailing form of social analysis are the following which Segundo borrows from the work of Eliseo Veron.

1. It has shifted from a consideration of a broad field of facts to fragmented specialties.
2. It has shifted from theoretical abstraction to everyday happenings.
3. It has shifted from a consideration of global issues to specific opinions.
4. It has shifted from cognitive categories to evaluative dimensions.
5. It has shifted from "systems of ideas" to isolated opinions.
6. It has shifted from the unconscious level to the conscious level.
7. It has shifted from sociology to psychology.

On each of these seven counts Segundo deems the positivist (i.e., functionalist) forms of sociology to be inadequate for Latin American reality because it is exactly a broad, theoretical, globally-oriented, cognitive, systematic, unconscious-probing sociology which is required for a proper interpretation of Latin American reality.

At the same time Segundo also recognizes a basic inadequacy in Marxist sociology for interpreting Latin America for two basic reasons.

1. Marxist sociology is not consistent in its application of the concept of ideology to religious phenomenon.
2. Marxist sociology has not accepted the relative autonomy of the superstructural levels in its methodology.

The first objection refers to the failure of Marx to proceed to a reinterpretation of religion following his unmasking of its ideological function. Unlike his reinterpretations of philosophy, art, and politics following an unmasking of their ideological uses, Marx asserts that religion is simply to be eliminated. The second objection refers to the inconsistency in Marx's thought between a historical determinism which simply sees history as a machine which is already programmed to run its course and a view of historical change in which the masses serve as key actors. For liberation theology neither of these aspects of the prevailing Marxist analysis can be accepted for obvious reasons. First, the theology of liberation as theology understands religion not only as a potential "opiate of the people" but as a source of liberation grounded in a God who is ultimately a liberator. Second, the theology of liberation seeks to emphasize the role of the people in the liberation process and finds the mechanistic understanding of historical change to minimize the need for human engagement.

These criticisms by Segundo of the inappropriateness of the prevailing positivist (i.e., functionalist) social analysis and the oversimplification of the prevailing Marxist (i.e., dialectical) social analysis leaves the theology of

b. *Marxism as an Instrument of Social Analysis.* "[Liberation] theologians did not set out to become Marxists."[71] It was rather the nature of Latin American reality which led liberation theologians first to commitment and, second, to the recognition of the need for social analysis. It is this need for an appropriate form of social analysis that has, third, prompted "not a few Latin American theologians and ministers to be so uninhibitedly open to Marxist categories, analyses, and interpretations of historical processes."[72] While it is true that liberation theologians are essentially "open to Marxist categories" that does not, however, mean that they have been uncritical or doctrinaire in their use of Marxist thought. The purpose of this section is to draw from the diverse references to Marxism made by liberation theologians, references which reflect the diversity of Marxism itself, in order to typify the way in which liberation theology has employed Marxism as an instrument of social analysis.[73]

---

liberation to develop its own form of dialectical social analysis which, to be sure, builds on these foundations but yet goes beyond them in adapting them from a theological perspective to the concrete reality which is Latin America. Segundo himself sees the forms of analysis employed by Teilhard de Chardin and Max Weber as indicative of the direction in which liberation theology must go in developing its own appropriate sociology.. Yet finally the burden for the development of an appropriate form of social analysis rests upon the liberation theologians themselves: "Right now theologians, except in exceptional cases, must perform the task of introducing the most fruitful elements of the social sciences into their own everyday work of theologizing" (p. 66). Thus the prescriptive model of C. Boff for the type of social analysis needed by the theology of liberation is balanced by Segundo's recognition of the limitations of the present models.

What emerges in fact in the theology of liberation is a social analysis which is indeed dialectical and which draws heavily on Marxist thought. At the same time it is not a doctrinaire Marxist outlook but rather molded to the shape of the Latin American reality. While the theology of liberation remains in the process of searching for appropriate forms of social analysis, some clear guidelines for that search have been established through the work of C. Boff and Segundo.

[71] Phillip E. Berryman, "Latin American Liberation Theology," *Th St* 34 (1973):374.

[72] Aharon Sapezian, "Ministry with the Poor. An Introduction," *Int R Miss* (Jan. 1977):9.

[73] Robert McAfee Brown, "A Preface and a Conclusion," in Sergio Torres and John Eagleson, eds., *Theology in the Americas* (Maryknoll: Orbis, 1976), pp. xviif., warns of the way in which the "Marxist" label is often employed in the U.S. as an appeal to the emotions in order to discredit a threatening position. Brown's comments attempt to defuse this frequent tactic and to encourage an

A helpful starting point for a consideration of the use of Marxism in the theology of liberation is the central thesis offered by Jose Miguez Bonino in his book *Christians and Marxists. The Mutual Challenge to Revolution*, a highly extensive and thorough study of the relationship between Christianity and Marxism.

> It is my thesis that, as Christians, confronted by the inhuman conditions of existence prevailing in the continent, they have tried to make their Christian faith historically relevant, they have been increasingly compelled to seek an analysis and historical programme for their Christian obedience. At this point, the dynamics of the historical process, both in its objective conditions and its theoretical development, have led them, through the failure of several remedial and reformist alternatives, to discover the unsubstitutable relevance of Marxism.[74]

Before describing the selective ways in which liberation theologians employ Marxism as a form of social analysis, one must clarify what is meant by the word "Marxism." Arthur F. McGovern provides the helpful distinction between the terms "Communism," "Socialism," and "Marxism."[75] "Communism" refers to those "actual political-economic systems in countries which claim to have embodied Marxist ideas" (e.g., the Communist Party of the Soviet Union, China, or any other official Communist Party). "Socialism" refers to "any actual or proposed economic system which advocates 'public ownership of property.'" "Marxism" in turn, refers "to the theory or body of ideas originated by Marx and developed by others." While it is impossible to fully separate between these three terms, this distinction of McGovern offers a first level of clarification for what is here meant by the term "Marxist," i.e., the thought tradition founded by Karl Marx.

A second level of clarification is offered by Gregory Baum who further distinguishes between three uses of the word Marxism:

> Marxism can be understood (1) as a philosophy, (2) as a plan of political action, and (3) as an instrument of social analysis.[76]

The theologians of liberation, as shall be further explained, reject the first understanding of Marxism as a philosophy while taking up the

---

evaluation of liberation theology on the basis of its "truth" and not simply to dismiss it on the basis of prejudice.

[74]Jose Miguez Bonino, *Christians and Marxists. The Mutual Challenge to Revolution* (London: Hodder and Stoughton, 1976), p. 19.

[75]For this and the following quotes see Arthur F. McGovern, *Marxism: An American Christian Perspective* (Maryknoll: Orbis, 1980), p. 3.

[76]Gregory Baum, "The Christian Left at Detroit," in Torres and Eagleson, eds., *Theology in the Americas*, p. 423.

second and third understandings and incorporating them into their thought. Marxism as "an instrument of social analysis" is the focus of discussion in this section. The role of Marxism "as a plan of political action" in the project of changing the Latin American social structures will be taken up again in the discussion of the fifth element of the method of liberation theology later in this chapter.

When Christians are faced with Marxism, C. Boff argues that they can react in one of two ways.[77] Confronted by those aspects of Marxism which are irreconcilable with Christian faith they can either totally reject Marxism including its use as a theoretical and practical tool, or they can approach Marxism critically, employing those aspects of Marxist thought which are helpful for social analysis while rejecting those aspects which are contradictory to Christian faith. Clearly it is the second option which has been taken in liberation theology. Before describing those aspects of Marxism which have been positively appropriated by liberation theologians for the purpose of social analysis, it is important to recognize those aspects of Marxism which are criticized or rejected. Here follows a brief typology of the use of Marxism by liberation theology. Six negative criticisms of Marxism by liberation theologians are in turn followed by six positive affirmations of Marxism as an instrument for social analysis.

The *first* and most serious negative criticism of Marxism is that *it cannot be accepted as a comprehensive world-view.* C. Boff distinguishes between Marxism as "historical materialism" and Marxism as "dialectical materialism."[78] By historical materialism is meant Marxism in its capacity as a method for the analysis of society and history. This can be affirmed. What cannot be accepted, however, is Marxism as "dialectical materialism." As dialectical materialism Marxism elevates itself to an all-inclusive world-view claiming ultimacy as an explanation for the totality of human existence. Miguez Bonino explains how this tendency of Marxism transcends its legitimate function as a form of social analysis and in so doing contradicts the Christian faith which itself provides the only legitimate Christian world-view.

> . . . it presents itself as a total, all-embracing, self-sufficient and exclusive understanding of reality; as exhaustive and absolute and therefore ruling out all reality and relationships outside its purview. In so

---

[77]Cf. C. Boff, *Theologie und Praxis*, p. 113.
[78]Ibid., p. 110.

doing it flatly contradicts the Christian faith and raises for itself problems which seem to me unsolvable, as the very history of Marxism indicates.[79] Insofar as Marxism exalts itself into such an all-inclusive world-view, it has been rejected by the theology of liberation.

The *second* negative criticism, related to the first, is that *the atheism of Marxism must be rejected*. This does not mean that the liberation theologians do not make use of Marx's critique of religion. Indeed Marx's critique of the ideological manipulation of religion has been employed extensively to dethrone the many idols which are understood to vie for divinity in the Latin American context.[80] Nevertheless, the liberation theologians go beyond Marxism's rejection of religion which issues in atheism and affirm the God who is truly God.

> Marx is not heterodox because he is an atheist (in regard to the idol, to money). He is heterodox because he is not enough of an atheist, because in his failure to affirm the "God-other" he is left with a system that has no outside support and no radical critique. Christianity is atheistic in regard to every idol—this it shares with Marx; but it is more critical than Marx because, in affirming the "God-other", it is critical of every *possible* system and will be until the eschatological times, until the end.[81]

A major task of liberation theologians is that in "going against the views of dogmatic Marxists, those involved must spell out a *theory of religion* advocating *liberation*."[82] The atheism of Marx must be rejected in favor of a religion which affirms the God who is liberator, the God whom the theology of liberation finds revealed in the Bible.

The *third* negative criticism of Marxism is *a critique of its mechanistic understanding of historical change*.[83] This criticism grows out of an apparent contradiction in Marx's thought between an understanding of historical change which takes place mechanistically and inevitably as a result of the given contradictions of the capitalist system and an understanding which affirms the role of human involvement in accomplishing historical change. Liberation theology is committed to the need for human participation in the liberation

---

[79]Miguez Bonino, *Christians and Marxists*, p. 97.

[80]Cf. Franz Hinkelammert, "The Economic Roots of Idolatry: Entrepreneurial Metaphysics," in Pablo Richard, et al., *The Idols of Death and the God of Life. A Theology*, trans. Barbara E. Campbell and Bonnie Shepard (Maryknoll: Orbis, 1983), pp. 165-193.

[81]Enrique Dussel, *Ethics and the Theology of Liberation*, trans. Bernard F. McWilliams (Maryknoll: Orbis, 1978), p. 17.

[82]Dussel, "Current Events in Latin America," in Torres and Eagleson, eds., *The Challenge of Basic Christian Communities*, p. 100.

[83]Cf. Miguez Bonino, *Toward a Christian Political Ethics*, pp. 40-42 and *Christians and Marxists*, p. 99.

process. "History will not in any fatal or mechanistic way decide for
men; the decision will always be a human decision."[84] Thus any
mechanistic understanding of historical change is understood to be
counterproductive to the liberation struggle.

The *fourth* negative criticism is *a critique of the present historical
systems which claim to embody Marxist thought,* such as China and,
above all, the Soviet Union.[85] Judged as particularly reprehensible is
the form of Communism which prevailed in the Soviet Union under
Joseph Stalin. The price paid for economic "progress" under
Communist regimes has been enormously high.

> We must also record the human cost of these achievements: the liquidation
> of certain social groups, the restrictions to liberty (while we must
> remember that 'liberal freedoms' have little reality for economically,
> intellectually and even biologically submerged masses), the arbitrary
> exercise of power, the disruption of religious and family traditions which
> often give meaning and hope to the life of 'the little in the land.'[86]

In addition to these criticisms, the loss of an ongoing critique of the
revolution and the dominance of self-interest are recognized as signs
of "the deterioration of the historical Marxist movement in terms of its
revolutionary potential."[87] While unwilling to surrender the need for
socialism as an historical project, the present historical forms are
deemed lacking and in need of serious renewal.

> [A]s a whole, Western Marxist countries and parties are rapidly losing
> their credibility in the Third World and their flags are taken up by
> movements which are ready to revise theory and practice in terms of an
> effective revolutionary change and the construction of a genuine
> socialism.[88]

When the theologians of liberation thus speak of socialism it is in
terms adapted to the Latin American context, to be sharply
distinguished from its established Western forms.

The *fifth* negative criticism is *a rejection of the tendency of
Marxism to a materialistic reductionism.* While a primary
contribution of Marxist thought is its analysis of the economic forces
which dominate modern life and while an analysis of the economic
forces which keep Latin America in a state of dependency is vital, the
theology of liberation entertains a broader definition of what is meant

---

[84]Miguez Bonino, *Toward a Christian Political Ethics,* p. 41.

[85]Cf. for the following Miguez Bonino, *Christians and Marxists,* pp. 80-81
and 87-91.

[86]Ibid., p. 88.

[87]Ibid., p. 89.

[88]Ibid., p. 91.

by liberation. Certainly economic liberation is indispensable for the future of Latin America. But the vision of liberation theology goes beyond economic and even beyond social and political liberation. Liberation also means the cultural and spiritual development of human beings: liberation for full human personhood and liberation for deeper human community.[89]

The *sixth* negative criticism is *a rejection of the tendency of Marxism toward authoritarian rule*. The tendency of Marxism to lead to dictatorial or narrowly oligarchical rule stands in contradiction to liberation theology's affirmation of the rights of the Latin American people. In the historical appropriation of Marxism, particularly as interpreted by Lenin, the need was recognized for a vanguard or elite to carry out leadership in the period of transition from capitalism to the final "dictatorship of the proletariat." In the systems, however, which claim to embody Marxism, the role of the elite has tended to degenerate into an inflexible, authoritarian, dictatorial rule. Segundo has been foremost among the liberation theologians who have grappled with this problem.[90]   While there remain a variety of unresolved issues regarding its solution, liberation theologians affirm the right of the people of Latin America to liberation in such a way which precludes the possibility of authoritarian rule.

These six negative criticisms of Marxism help make clearer the critical appropriation of Marxist thought by liberation theologians. Having sketched these six negative criticisms, the following six positive affirmations have been made for Marxism as an instrument of social analysis.

The *first* positive affirmation is a general one, *a recognition of the ethical humanism of Marx*. Especially the writings of the early Marx are understood to be filled with a passionate concern for social and economic justice.[91] "The burning fire of moral indignation at man's inhumanity to man smoulders below the surface of even the most abstruse theoretical analyses of the early Marxists."[92] This sense of

---

[89]Cf. Gutierrez, *A Theology of Liberation*, pp. 36-37. It might be noted that such a vision may not so much stand in opposition to Marx himself as it does to the present historical systems which claim for themselves the name of Marxist.

[90]Cf. Segundo, "Mass Man-Minority Elite-Gospel Message," Chapter 8 in *The Liberation of Theology*, pp. 208-240.

[91]Cf. Jose Porfiro Miranda, *Marx Against the Marxists. The Christian Humanism of Karl Marx*, trans. John Drury (Maryknoll: Orbis, 1980), esp. Chapter 5 entitled "Marx the Humanist," pp. 106-135.

[92]Miguez Bonino, *Christians and Marxists*, p. 76.

moral indignation in Marx corresponds to the experience of liberation theologians as they encounter Latin American reality. Moreover, they realize a deep affinity between the prophetic humanism of Marx and the biblical demand for justice.[93]

The *second* positive affirmation is *the necessity of ideological suspicion for social analysis*. Marx together with Freud have been described as "masters of suspicion." A suspicion of the prevailing ideology on the part of liberation theologians as indicated by Segundo's hermeneutic circle, is directed at the entire ideological superstructure of Latin America including its economic, political, social, cultural, and religious components. Even more, the theologians of liberation exercise decided suspicion over against prevalent theological and exegetical formulations. Due to the significance of ideological suspicion as an element of social analysis, a further discussion will be deferred to the next section. The basis of ideological suspicion for liberation theology, nonetheless, derives from the thought of Marx.

The *third* positive affirmation, related to the previous one, is *the need for a Marxist critique of religion*. Marx heftily criticized the use of religion as an ideological justification of political power.[94] Through the use of religion to lend credence to political power, a mystification was understood to take place in which the really decisive factor, i.e., political support of the economic status quo, became masked. Thus religion could be called the "opiate of the people" in which "religion invests the present misery with a sacred character."[95]

Liberation theology has affirmed the positive service Marx's critique of religion can offer.

> The criticism of religion is valuable in so far as it is a criticism of bourgeois society which unveils its dynamics and provides the revolutionary proletariat with adequate theoretical instruments for carrying out its historical mission of destroying and overcoming this society.[96]

Special application of Marx's critique of religion in Latin America has been made upon the traditional support offered by the Roman Catholic Church to the colonial, neo-colonial, and military forms of domination which characterize Latin American history. Likewise the

---

[93]Cf. Jose Porfiro Miranda, *Marx and the Bible. A Critique of the Philosophy of Oppression*, trans. John Eagleson (Maryknoll: Orbis, 1974), esp. the summation drawn in the Epilogue, pp. 293-296.

[94]Cf. for the following Miguez Bonino, *Christians and Marxists*, pp. 42-51.

[95]Ibid., p. 49.

[96]Ibid., p. 50.

"other-worldly" aspects of Protestantism and popular religion which
tend to ignore or obfuscate historical causes have been subjected to the
Marxist critique. As has been already discussed, however, the Marxist
critique of religion exceeds its legitimate function when it goes so far
as to reject religion altogether and insists upon atheism.[97]

The *fourth* positive affirmation is that *the idea of class struggle is
an accurate description of Latin American reality.*

> The class struggle is a part of our economic, social, political, cultural, and
> religious reality. Its evolution, its exact extent, its nuances, and its
> variations are the object of analysis of the social sciences and pertain to the
> field of scientific rationality.
> It is undeniable that the class struggle poses problems to the universality
> of Christian love and the unity of the Church. But any consideration of this
> subject must start from two elemental points: the class struggle is a fact,
> and neutrality in this matter is impossible.[98]

Following Marx, class struggle is recognized as a given fact.[99] Capitalist society, characterized by the concentration of economic power in
the hands of those who possess the means of production, leads to an
increasing division between rich and poor. This description of the
roots of class struggle is not accepted by liberation theologians because
it is Marxist but because it coincides with their perception of Latin
American reality. When the world is viewed "from below," it appears
as though something like class struggle is at work. Moreover,
neutrality on the part of Christians in the face of the giveness of class
struggle is disallowed. Liberation theologians ascertain in the Bible
no neutral God but a God who shows partiality to the poor. Thus, in spite
of the tension and conflict which this affirmation causes for the church,
the reality of class struggle cannot be ignored. The final unity sought
by the church is achieved only through the conflict-laden process of
overcoming the present historical divisions between those who have
and those who do not.[100]

The *fifth* positive affirmation is *the basic validity of Marx's
analysis of capitalism's structure of oppression.* Most elaborate in his

---

[97]James F. Conway, *Marx and Jesus: Liberation Theology in Latin
America* (New York: Carlton Press, 1973), has argued that liberation theology
itself is evidence for the possibility of religion acting not only as an "opiate" but
also as a force for social change. See esp. pp. 189-194.

[98]Gutierrez, *A Theology of Liberation*, p. 273. Cf. also Gustavo Gutierrez,
"Faith as Freedom: Solidarity with the Alienated and Confidence in the
Future," *Horizons* 2 (Spring 1975):33.

[99]Cf. for the following Miguez Bonino, *Christians and Marxists*, pp. 92-93.

[100]Gutierrez, *A Theology of Liberation*, pp. 277-279.

discussion of capitalism's structure of oppression has been the economist and theologian Jose Porfiro Miranda.[101] The basic features of the Marxist analysis begin with the fact of the private ownership of the means of production. In such a system, made possible by the invention of money as a means of exchange, non-owners are expected to sell their labor to the owners in return for money payments. This is, simply put, the essence of the wage system. The workers in turn exchange their wages for those items which they need to satisfy their material needs. The wage system, however, is only legitimate when it is the result of an agreement between free and equal parties. With capitalism, though, this presupposition is not given. Coercion is exercised both by the ideological superstructure of the capitalist system and, ultimately, by the "hidden persuader" of hunger which compels participation in the system. Moreover, a rule of law is constructed which legalizes the given set of relationships.

The exploitative nature of capitalism becomes more fully exposed with an analysis of the mechanism of "surplus value." Because the logic of capitalism is based upon ever increasing expansion and also because of the recognition of the legitimacy of the owners of the means of production to earn a profit on thier investment, surplus value becomes the means by which capital is "multiplied" for the accomplishment of both expansion and profit. It can be defined as the difference between the actual worth of a worker's labor in terms of what is produced and the amount which a worker is in reality paid for that labor. The goal of ownership becomes the maximization of surplus value and profit which leads to an increasing alienation between owners and workers, seen most clearly in an unequal distribution of wealth. In addition the workers in industrial capitalism are distanced from the creative product of their labor leading to a further sense of alienation. An analysis of the structure of capitalism thus is supposed to reveal its final logic in the pursuit of personal profit and the advancement of self-interest. Given the fundamental inequalities of the actors in this system, capitalism results in the oppression of the "weaker" participants.

Though Miranda is, among the liberation theologians, the most outspoken in articulating this Marxist analysis of the structure of

---

[101]Cf. for the following Jose Porfiro Miranda, "Private Ownership Under Challenge," Chapter 1 in *Marx and the Bible*, pp. 1-33 and "Revolution and Existentialism," Chapter 1 in *Being and the Messiah. The Message of St. John*, trans. John Eagleson (Maryknoll: Orbis, 1977), esp. pp. 1-14.

capitalism, these dynamics are implicitly given in liberation theology's critique of the oppressive nature of capitalism. They are, however, always adapted to the specific face of Latin America (e.g., the modern role of multinational corporations) which calls for certain modifications of Marx's analysis.

The *sixth* and last positive affirmation is *Marx's insistence on praxis as the final criterion of theory*. Theory or social analysis does not contain in itself the final measure of truth. Instead, "theory has meaning only as it leads to a course of action which proves significant and that action itself becomes the test of theory."[102] In this way the theologians of liberation advocate a constant exchange between theory and action, culminating in active participation in the liberation process. The fifth and final element of the method of liberation theology can, following this criterion, be nothing else but engagement in the project of creating a new Latin America.

This brief exposition of six negative criticisms and six positive affirmations illustrates in outline form the nature of liberation theology's critical use of Marxism as an instrument of social analysis. Emphasized have been those aspects of Marxism which are perceived by liberation theologians to render service to a deeper understanding of Latin American reality. These aspects of Marxism have been, for the sake of systematic presentation, separated from the use of Marxism in formulating concrete political options. Such a distinction is a formal one since "the choice of analytical instrument itself implies an ethical and political stance."[103] This distinction is a useful one, however, in clarifying the complex interaction between liberation theology and Marxist thought.

c. *Suspicion and Critical Examination of Ideologies.* Ideological suspicion of the prevailing explanations of the dynamics by which society is ordered is perhaps the most pervasive characteristic which distinguishes liberation theology's method. Already Segundo's hermeneutic circle has indicated the way in which ideological suspicion is applied to society at large, theological formulations, and exegetical interpretations of the Bible. The suspicion which liberation theologians entertain against the given ideologies allows them to depart from many commonplace interpretations of events and often become very original in their theological and exegetical formulations.

---

[102]Miguez Bonino, *Christians and Marxists*, p. 93.

[103]Assmann, *Theology for a Nomad Church*, pp. 38-39.

Clodovis Boff distinguishes between two subtle nuances contained in a definition of the word ideology.[104] First, he affirms ideology as an explanation which gives the appearance of being true, when it is, in fact, erroneous. Ideology is thus, first of all, characterized by illusion. The second nuance, however, goes one step further. Ideology may not only lead to an erroneous understanding, it may also be an illusion which serves as a justifying explanation *for someone.* In this case ideology is not only illusion but also deception. As deception, ideology passes into the moral realm. It becomes subject not only to correction but also to ethical criticism, a criticism which theology must legitimately render.

As is the case with the word praxis, the word ideology is used in a number of related but yet different ways by liberation theologians.[105] The distinction of C. Boff between ideology as illusion and deception provides the basis for a more precise use of the term. An understanding of ideology based on this twofold distinction offers liberation theologians a principle by which to analyze not only the content but also the function of words in society.

> We can now know with a higher degree of precision *what happens* with the words we use, the alliances into which we enter, the ways in which we use our influence and resources. Specifically, in the area of language, we know that the words and expressions we use are not only—and not mainly—received in the context of our own discourse but in the framework of a code prevalent in society, in which they evoke certain connotations. Words, to say it more precisely, have a *performative* function which does not necessarily coincide with their conceptual contents or with our intention.[106]

Such an awareness of the ideological function of words in society allows liberation theologians to penetrate beyond conventional discourse to a highly critical assessment of the way in which words are used to justify social inequity.

Segundo has been foremost among liberation theologians in providing a thorough examination of the functioning of ideology.[107] While recognizing the need for suspicion, criticism, and analysis of the ideologies which prevail in society and theology, Segundo also is aware of the inevitability of human language being clothed in some

---

[104]Cf. for the following C. Boff, *Theologie und Praxis,* pp. 91-95.

[105]Cf. comments of C. Boff, ibid., p. 83.

[106]Jose Miguez Bonino, "New Trends in Theology," *Duke Div R* 42 (Fall 1977):137.

[107]Cf. for the following Segundo, *The Liberation of Theology,* Chapters 4, 5, and 6, pp. 97-182 and *Faith and Ideologies,* esp. pp. 15-20.

form of ideology. This has led one interpreter of Segundo to speak of a
two-fold use of ideology in his theology, i.e., negative and positive
ideology.[108]   Negative ideologies require the unmasking of
illusionary and deceptive explanations of reality as already
described. Segundo exercises suspicion and analysis over against
negative ideologies painstakingly in his work, applying it to such
diverse ideologies as those of the traditional position of the Roman
Catholic hierarchy, Protestant evangelical critiques of liberation
theology, the Lutheran doctrine of the two kingdoms, a facile condemnation of violence, and popular religion.

At the same time, however, Segundo goes beyond a criticism of
negative ideology to the insight that ideology in one form or another is
unavoidable. Even biblical faith is cloaked in ideologies which need to
be recognized for what they are. While it is possible to define faith as
being devoid of ideology, i.e., a purely objective absolute value, such a
faith when translated into human life and history inevitably takes on
an ideological cast. This leads Segundo to the assertion that faith
without ideologies is "dead faith."

> Faith, then, is not a universal, a temporal, pithy body of content summing
> up divine revelation once the latter has been divested of ideologies. On the
> contrary, it is maturity by way of ideologies, the possibility of fully and
> conscientiously carrying out the ideological task on which the real-life
> liberation of human beings depends.[109]

In this light the suspicion, criticism, and analysis of negative
ideologies is only half the task. Given the inevitability of ideology as a
dimension of human discourse, the completion of the task requires a
second step. Once a given ideology has been recognized for what it is, it
must be evaluated solely on the basis of "the reasons or arguments that
support it."[110] Next the process of criticism is followed by a re-clothing
into what can then be called positive ideology, an ideology which has
been reflected upon in a conscious way and intentionally and
deliberately chosen. This does not absolve this "positive" ideology
from future suspicion, critique, and analysis. It is merely what is
necessary given the inevitably ideological character of human
discourse, a risk which must be taken. What is different about positive
ideology, however, is the fact that it is aware of itself as such, has been

---

[108]Cf. Tambasco, "Theology and Ideology in Segundo," Chapter 3 in *The
Bible for Ethics*, esp. pp. 91-106.

[109]Segundo, *The Liberation of Theology*, p. 122.

[110]Ibid., p. 106.

formulated in a critical way, and should remain open to further revision.

Ideological suspicion and analysis are evident throughout the writings of liberation theologians. As a principle of social analysis, they have offered an instrument for criticizing conventional explanations of reality which lend support to injustice and oppression in Latin America. The application of ideological suspicion and analysis also finds a place in the specifically theological reflection and reformulation of liberation theologians.

4. Theological Reflection and Reformulation

a. *The Relationship of Social Analysis to Theological Reflection.* While liberation theologians generally employ social analysis in their theological method, it is not always used in a conscientious and systematic way. C. Boff has been especially critical of the inadequate ways social analysis has often been appropriated for theological use.[111] These include: (1) an empiricism which assumes an immediate apprehension of historical reality by theology without employing social analysis; (2) a methodological purism which consciously excludes social analysis based on the decision that revelation is the only subject matter of theology; (3) a "theologism" which freely associates theological ideas and historical reality in a way which lacks a critical examination of the historical; (4) a semantic mixture which poorly articulates its means of social analysis and fails to conscientiously integrate it into the theological task; and (5) a bilingual approach (i.e., the "language" of sociology and theology) which carries out both a thorough social analysis and clear theological reflection but which fails to bring the two into a fully articulated relationship with each other.

Of the five categories developed by C. Boff, the last two especially characterize the tendencies of those liberation theologians who fail to adequately articulate the relationship of social analysis to their theological work. C. Boff himself mentions the fourth category (semantic mixture) as characteristic of the Roman Catholic Church's recent social documents which have had a considerable influence on liberation theologians.[112] Likewise the fifth category appears to be more applicable to liberation theology than the first three.

---

[111]Cf. for the following C. Boff, *Theologie und Praxis*, pp. 60-74.
[112]Ibid., p. 72.

Methodological consideration of the proper relationship between social
analysis and theological reflection simply has not been a high priority
for liberation theologians given the way in which their theology has
originated.

Clodovis Boff offers not only a critique of the inadequate ways in
which social analysis has been related to theology but also proposes a
positive model for this relationship which has been taken up and
further elaborated by Miguez Bonino.[113] He directs a challenge to
liberation theologians to more explicitly articulate a social analysis
which makes credible its attempt to mediate between theology and
political engagement.[114] The following chart and explanation
summarize C. Boff's proposal for a legitimate relation between social
analysis and theology.[115]

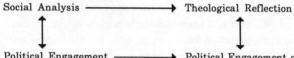

Social Analysis ⟶ Theological Reflection

Political Engagement ⟶ Political Engagement of Christians

In this chart "social analysis" and "theological reflection" are to be
regarded as the theoretical components whereas "political
engagement" and "political engagement of Christians" refer to
concrete involvement in political action.

In studying the dynamics made visual through this diagram, one
must not exaggerate the difference between political engagement and
political engagement of Christians. The Latin American liberation
theology stresses its participation in a common project of liberation
shared by many who do not profess the Christian faith. Nevertheless,
theological reflection is an additional and necessary stage of
reflection for Christians engaged in politics due to their faith in the
God who is also an actor in history—both as revealed in the past and as
discerned in the present. Whereas those who do not profess the
Christian faith simply move in an immediate interaction between
social analysis and political engagement, Christians bring theological and ethical resources to their reflection, introducing what is
sometimes judged by others to be an "alien" element. This alien
element has been the source of much debate and has often led to the

---

[113]Cf. for the following ibid., pp. 339-343 and Miguez Bonino, *Toward a
Christian Political Ethics*, pp. 47-49.

[114]Cf. C. Boff, *Theologie und Praxis*, pp. 307-311.

[115]The following chart appears originally in ibid., p. 340 and is here
modified to reflect the terminology used in this chapter.

charge that Christians are to be held suspect due to the "impurity" of their political (i.e., revolutionary) motives. The faith in God which summons Christians to theological reflection is then seen as a potential obstacle to political (i.e., revolutionary) activity. It might be noted, however, that (non-theological) ethical reflection might be substituted into this chart in the place of theological reflection, which substitution leads to a similar dilemma.

This chart is particularly helpful in articulating the process by which Christians are to incorporate both social analysis and theological reflection as indispensable guides for political engage– ment. Inadequate is any attempt to move directly from theological reflection to political engagement. First of all, such a relation ignores the fact that theological reflection only has demonstrable significance for Christian political engagement. Secondly, theological reflection is in this relation incapable of rendering an adequate appraisal of political reality. It results in a mystification of historical causes and for that reason can be dismissed as irrelevant. Likewise inadequate is an attempt to move directly from social analysis to Christian political engagement. In such a relation the specific contribution of Christian theological and ethical reflection does not enter the process and results in the loss of Christian identity.

Two sets of relations then remain which help clarify the complex relationship of social analysis and theological reflection. The first relation moves along the perimeter from political engagement to political engagement of Christians to theological reflection. This relation reveals the fundamental insight that it is precisely historical reality with its inevitable political character that is the realm in which Christians are to be engaged and which serves as the raw material for theological reflection if the Christian faith is to be relevant to contemporary problems such as poverty or political repression. Otherwise Christian political engagement and theological reflection provide at best a ministry to the victims of political and economic injustice and at worst ideological support for the status quo. Without a full recognition of the significance of the political realm for a solution of these problems, Christian political engagement and theological reflection remain tangential to decisive political and economic factors.

The second relation moves along the perimeter from political engagement to social analysis to theological reflection. This relation illustrates C. Boff's proposal for a clear articulation of the relationship between social analysis and theological reflection. Only as the realm of the political is interpreted through social analysis does it attain a level of theoretical clarity which enables a legitimate and fruitful exchange with theology. This exchange between social analysis and theological reflection can lead in turn to specific implications for Christian political engagement.

The proposal of C. Boff operates by intention on the epistemological level. It might for this very reason be criticized for remaining on the level of abstraction while the actual business of relating social analysis and theological reflection requires a closer connection to political action. While C. Boff may be accused of being overly critical of the lack of methodological sophistication by liberation theologians and of not sufficiently appreciating their achievements, nonetheless his proposal offers a challenge to further reflection upon the relation-ship of social analysis to theological reflection.

b. *The Process of Theological Reformulation.* Liberation theology has as the object of its theological reflection not only traditional theological loci (e.g., God, sin, Christ, church, etc.) but, as has been demonstrated, also what can be considered non-traditional themes (e.g., poverty, politics, social analysis, etc.). In this section liberation theology's reformulation of the more traditional theological themes is to be more closely examined.

Through its analysis of the Latin American context, liberation theology offers a perspective which allows creative reformulation of the Christian faith.

> We will get a new and distinctive theological perspective only when our starting point is the social praxis of the real population of Latin America, of those whose roots are buried deep in the geographical, historical, and cultural soil of our region but who now stand mute. It is from that source that we will get a new reading and interpretation of the gospel message as well as a fresh expression of the experiences it has occasioned throughout history and their meaning.[116]

The recasting of the Christian tradition by liberation theologians always takes place from this starting point. They make no apology for the fact that their interpretation of the traditional Christian faith begins in an encounter with Latin American reality and ends in an insistence upon the creation of a more just Latin America. In this way the Christian tradition is allowed to speak in a living way to the needs

---

[116]Gutierrez, "Liberation Praxis and Christian Faith," in Gibellini, ed., *Frontiers of Theology in Latin America*, p. 25.

of the historical present. By proceeding in this fashion they recover certain aspects of that tradition often obscured by theological reflection beginning with other presuppositions, recognizing "the epistemological privilege of the poor" in opening up new theological horizons.[117]

As liberation theologians undertake the specifically theological task of bringing the resources of the Christian tradition to the Latin American reality, it is necessary to keep in mind the way in which their commitment to and social analysis of that reality form the basis from which they theologize. Any attempt to isolate their theological conclusions apart from an awareness of this foundational concern is destined to end in misunderstanding. Liberation theology consciously distances itself from theological attempts which try to achieve abstract and timeless formulations of Christian truth. Such attempts are judged futile due to the inevitablity of theology serving a socio-political function of one kind or another. The theology of liberation is clear about the socio-political function it attempts to exercise. It places itself at the service of the poor in their struggle for liberation. What is more, it asserts that Christian revelation itself shares this bias in favor of the poor.

Three characteristics mark the distinctiveness of liberation theology's reformulation of traditional doctrine. These three characteristics are next to be outlined.

The *first characteristic* of the process of theological reformulation by liberation theology is once again *ideological suspicion*, this time specifically over against the ideological tendencies of the more traditional theological positions.[118]

> Theology does not live in the clouds but is a social actor which is established in a definite place in society. The accents which it places and the theological subject matter which it selects are determined by viewpoints which appear to be relevant for it on the basis of its social position. In this sense the assertion is valid that there neither is nor can be a neutral theology. Theology is always "partisan" and "engaged." That is even true for the case when it presents itself as purely "theological"—historical, traditional, ecclesial, and apostolic. For then it usually assumes the position of the holders of the ruling power. As soon as another kind of theology, with a corresponding consciousness of its commitment opposes it, however, its social position also becomes immediately evident. Its

[117]Miguez Bonino, *Toward a Christian Political Ethics*, p. 43.

[118]Cf. the discussion of "Theology and Ideology" by Alfredo Fierro, *The Militant Gospel. A Critical Introduction to Political Theologies*, trans. John Drury (Maryknoll: Orbis, 1977), pp. 242-247.

apolitical exterior disappears and it reveals itself as a religious
reinforcement of the current status quo.[119]

Liberation theology undertakes a constant criticism of the
theological tradition on the basis of the ideological bias which often
remains concealed in the customary stating of positions.   Such
ideological suspicion is applied consistently to interpretations of the
Bible, the history of Christian doctrine, ecclesial documents, and
contemporary theology.[120] On its way to a reformulation of Christian
teaching for the Latin American context, the need for ideological
suspicion over against the theological tradition is understood to be
requisite.   Too often theologians have (unwittingly) assumed
theological positions which have had alienating consequences in
serving to bolster the situation of injustice in Latin America.

The use made of ideological suspicion by liberation theology might
be seen by some only in its "destructive" function of calling into
question every theological position. It is true that there exists the
danger that ideological suspicion becomes an end in itself which
leaves no room for constructive theological affirmation. When this
takes place theology can no longer be recognized as such and tends to
lose itself in political activism.   The liberation theologians do,
however, go beyond ideological suspicion. Their own reformulations
testify to a theology which is not only destructive but also constructive.
Liberation theology undertakes ideological suspicion not only in order
to uncover the ideological functioning of other theological positions but
"in order to ensure that every future project of liberation is open-ended,
pointing towards man's total humanization and liberty."[121]

By recognizing the ideological implications of theological
positions, liberation theology makes a genuine contribution to
theological hermeneutics. Not only are the personal presuppositions of
the individual interpreter an influential factor in theological
interpretation but there also exist real social and political
presuppositions which need to be examined. This is as true for
liberation theology itself as for the theologies which it criticizes. C.
Boff thus speaks of the need for "a permanent ideo-political vigilance"

---

[119]L. Boff, "Die Anliegen der Befreiungstheologie," pp. 77-78 (own
translation).

[120]Cf. the way in which Segundo carries out ideological suspicion on the
work of Cox, Marx, Weber, and Cone in *The Liberation of Theology*, pp. 10-34.

[121]Kirk, *Liberation Theology*, p. 40.

on the part of theology.[122] There is a need for theologians to be
cognizant of the institutional and political implications of their
formulations in order to be clear about the role which they play in a
given social structure. Such a permanent ideo-political vigilance has
come to be a distinguishing mark of liberation theology.

The *second characteristic* of the process by which liberation
theology reaches its distinctive theological reformulations is *its
application of the resources of the Christian tradition*. Although
liberation theology makes special use of social analysis in its
theological reflection, that is by no means its only resource. As
theology *per se*, liberation theology brings to its reformulations all the
resources which are distinctive of the Christian tradition.

Foremost among these resources is the interpretation of the Bible as
a living and authoritative voice speaking into the Latin American
context. Liberation theology has been abundant in its use of Scripture
for its theological work as was indicated in Chapter One. New and
creative biblical interpretation is perhaps itself the single most
important contribution of liberation theology as theology.[123] It is the
biblical message of liberation which is the resource that more than any
other shapes the theological reformulations of liberation theologians.

Another resource which occurs noticeably in the theological work of
liberation theologians is the use of the more recent official documents
of the Roman Catholic Church. Already the significance of Vatican II
and the conferences at Medellin and Puebla have been mentioned.
The documents of these ecclesial events continue to be a living resource
for the theological work of liberation theologians as these documents
continue to be appreciated, criticized, interpreted, and reinterpreted.

The history of Christian doctrine also plays an important role as a
resource for liberation theology. An impressive dialogue with church
fathers, ecumenical councils, scholastic theology, and Reformation
thought takes place within the writings of theologians such as
Gutierrez, Segundo, L. Boff, Sobrino, and Miguez Bonino. They
understand themselves as part of a larger tradition which calls for
ongoing criticism and affirmation. Together with their insistence on
contemporary theological relevance, they maintain their identity as
part of this tradition.

---

[122]Cf. C. Boff, *Theologie und Praxis*, pp. 57-59 (own translation).

[123]Cf. the pertinent essays contained in Norman K. Gottwald, *The Bible
and Liberation. Political and Social Hermeneutics* (Maryknoll: Orbis, 1983).

A last resource which shapes liberation theology is its conversation with a host of contemporary authors and theologians. Among the theologians who are most frequently cited by liberation theologians are Dietrich Bonhoeffer, Pierre Teilhard de Chardin, Jürgen Moltmann, Johannes Metz, Paul Ricoeur, and Richard Shaull. Not to be overlooked in this regard is also the considerable influence which the liberation theologians have had upon one another in their common goal of participating as theologians in the project of liberation for Latin America.

The *third characteristic* which marks the theological reformulations of liberation theology is its *praxis-orientation*. This means that the theological reformulations of liberation theology reveal a decided interest in the practice of the Christian faith in contrast to those theologies which have primary interest in an intellectual understanding of the Christian faith.

> Theology, as here conceived, is not an effort to give a correct understanding of God's attributes or actions but an effort to articulate the action of faith, the shape of praxis conceived and realized in obedience. As philosophy in Marx's famous *dictum*, theology has to stop explaining the world and start transforming it. *Orthopraxis* rather than orthodoxy, becomes the criterion for theology.[124]

This distinction between orthopraxis and orthodoxy is one which is frequently cited to qualify the difference of liberation theology. The liberation theologians reformulate Christian doctrine in a way which indicates that it is to be lived rather than merely thought. Although liberation theology does reformulate Christian doctrine, it does so in such a way that its formulations *lean toward active engagement*. Segundo goes so far as to maintain "that not one single dogma can be studied with any other final criterion than its impact on praxis."[125]

Miguez Bonino offers this summary statement of the process of theological reformulation undertaken in the theology of liberation.

> *Starting from this basic outlook, we must critically reread and repossess biblical and theological tradition and also the Christian community to which we belong.* Without going too deeply into this point, I might well mention the following tasks involved: (a) engaging in a critical examination of tradition on the basis of the diagnostic criteria and the suspicions mentioned above; (b) rediscovering the liberative thrust present in that tradition in order to make it available to our Christian praxis in the present; (c) looking to our own religious history in Latin America

---

124Jose Miguez Bonino, *Revolutionary Theology Comes of Age* (London: SPCK, 1975), p. 81.

125Segundo, "Capitalism Versus Socialism: Crux Theologica," in Gibellini, ed., *Frontiers of Theology in Latin America*, p. 250.

specifically in order to find the root causes of the factors which both impede and encourage the dynamics of liberation that are operative in the present-day Christianity.[126]

The way in which liberation theologians reformulate the Christian faith through the use of ideological suspicion, the resources of the tradition, and an orientation toward praxis can be illustrated through an examination of the characteristic way in which the recurring themes in liberation theology are developed, e.g., salvation as historical, Christology, ecclesiology, spirituality, and the kingdom of God.

c. *Is Liberation Theology Still Theology?* Its sharp criticism of the unexamined ideological weight often carried by theology, its partiality and commitment to the poor, its use of Marxism for social analysis, and, not least of all, its singular insistence upon theology's orientation toward praxis, have made liberation theology the object of a host of criticisms which call into question its very identity as theology. Liberation theologians have felt themselves compelled to respond to the question: Is liberation theology still theology?[127]

There are several possible ways to approach such a question. One is to acknowledge the legitimacy of the question due to the fact that liberation theology is still in the process of gaining its maturity. Another is to point to the positive contribution liberation theology has made in questioning inadequate statements of traditional theological problems. Even more basic, however, is to ask *a fundamental question as to the very definition of theology.* In effect, the question as to whether liberation theology is still theology can only be answered after the word "theology" itself has been defined.

Once again it is C. Boff who has offered a number of insights which are helpful in thinking through this question. A first insight is the recognition that "all is theologizable."[128] "If God is really the meaning of the world and history (and he is), then there is in principle really no object or event that cannot be theologized." This means that political reality such as that of Latin America cannot be *a priori*

---

[126]Miguez Bonino, "Historical Praxis and Christian Identity," in Gibellini, ed., *Frontiers of Theology in Latin America*, pp. 262-263.

[127]Cf. for this and the following Assmann, *Theology for a Nomad Church*, pp. 56-59 and Miguez Bonino, *Revolutionary Theology Comes of Age*, pp. 72-73.

[128]For this and the following quote see C. Boff, *Theologie und Praxis*, p. 77 (own translation).

excluded as an object of theological inquiry simply because it has not been the standard subject matter of theology.

Clodovis Boff continues from this assertion to make a distinction between two types of theology which he calls Theology 1 and Theology 2.[129] Theology 1 corresponds to theology as it has developed in its classical form. It has as its subject matter specifically "religious" themes such as God, creation, Christ, grace, sin, eschatology, etc. It is an approach to theology which attempts to achieve a certain autonomy and objectivity in its presentation of these aspects of divine revelation through a use of a theological method which concentrates on that which has been revealed. Theology 1 thus attempts to remain objective and neutral in its formulations over against political matters. Theology 2, on the other hand, has as its themes "worldly" realities such as culture, sexuality, history, and politics. It is a theological approach in which theologians make conscientious use of social analysis in their examination of themes. Moreover, theologians operating under the norms of Theology 2 are challenged to engaged and committed involvement in seeking to alter conditions of social injustice.

Clodovis Boff himself presents a case for a dialectic between Theology 1 and Theology 2 as two necessary components of theological method.[130] According to C. Boff, Theology 1 represents a necessary complement to Theology 2 in that it maintains within theological method the idea of objectivity on the theoretical level which counteracts the danger that theology be reduced to ideology. Insofar as theology is defined exclusively or primarily in terms of a Theology 1, liberation theology does not deserve the name theology, or does so only to a very limited extent. Insofar, however, as theology is defined in terms of a Theology 2, the theology of liberation must be recognized for the contribution it has made in employing the resources of the Christian tradition in addressing nontraditional themes. Moreover, through its examination of these nontraditional themes, it offers a perspective which also allows for a fresh reformulation of the so-called traditional themes of theology.

Clearly it is possible to ask for more precision from liberation theology in terms of its method and its elaboration of the theological task. Not only those outside liberation theology but also a theologian like C. Boff who stands within the liberation theology movement have

---

[129]Cf. ibid., pp. 27-29.

[130]Cf. ibid., pp. 51-59 and 145-152.

raised such criticisms. Not only has C. Boff called for a deliberate inclusion of Theology 1 as a necessary component of Theology 2, but he has also extended his criticism to the failure of liberation theology to make a clear distinction between faith, theological discourse, and theology proper.[131]   Theology proper, according to C. Boff, is systematic, disciplined, and follows its own distinct method and must be distinguished from other kinds of religious and theological discourse.

The work of C. Boff offers one possible direction to be followed in moving beyond the polemic which has often characterized the discussion between academic and liberation theologians.[132] The danger, however, is that the achievements of liberation theology be sacrificed in an attempt to retain academic theology as its final criterion. It is important to remain mindful of the fact that liberation theology arose in many respects precisely as a reaction against a theology which was perceived as being overly abstract, non-committal, disengaged, "methodological," and, thus, remote from the Latin American context. Liberation theology has challenged the purely academic exercise of theology by insisting on a theology which both takes up nontraditional themes and which reformulates traditional themes on the basis of its central concern for justice. Insofar as this definition of theology is a valid one, liberation theology can indeed claim the name of theology—a theology from the perspective of the poor of Latin America.

5. Engagement in the Project of Liberation

Having begun in an encounter with Latin American reality and moved through social analysis and theological reflection, the methodological circle of liberation theology returns to the Latin American reality with a call for participation in changing the existing injustices. Together with the use of Marxism as an instrument of social analysis, this insistence upon active engagement in the liberation of Latin America may be the most controversial aspect of liberation theology. It is controversial because it sees the necessity for a radical change in the political and socioeconomic structures which presently rule in Latin America. Those who profit from or are protected by the present structures are thus threatened by this call for

---

[131] Cf. ibid., pp. 186-193.

[132] For a survey of this discussion see Assmann, *Theology for a Nomad Church*, pp. 56-59.

radical change. Likewise those who hold theology to be an apolitical discipline are offended by liberation theology's highly partisan outlook. Liberation theology, however, does not shun controversy. It persists in its claim that theology, in the face of Latin American reality, must lead to active engagement just as Christian faith itself must become active in love.

What do the liberation theologians mean, however, when they speak of engagement? Jürgen Moltmann has raised, among other points, the question of a lack of specificity in liberation theology's call for engagement.[133] Moltmann asserts that for all their criticism of European theology's approach, it is difficult to discern what is specifically Latin American in their proposals. Furthermore, their use of Marxism is far more European than seems to be realized and there exists the genuine danger of liberation theology becoming elitist in its positions at the expense of the Latin American people.

In regard to these criticisms, it is surprising that Moltmann does not recognize the development of thousands of basic Christian communities as a specifically Latin American achievement. These communities are fully supported by the liberation theologians and their existence answers to a large extent each of Moltmann's criticisms. The vital role which these communities play in the thought and life of liberation theology is a concrete example of the way in which liberation theology expresses itself in engagement.

Moltmann's exchange with liberation theology, nevertheless, indicates the ongoing need for liberation theology to further specify what it means by engagement. Beyond the role of the basic Christian communities, it is only possible to outline in broad strokes what liberation theology means by engagement. To call for increased specificity is certainly desirable. But the difficulty lies in that the specifics border on a realm which only individuals standing within a very specific and concrete context can offer for themselves. The particularity of the different contexts calls for particular kinds of engagement based on an analysis of the concrete situation. These are the decisions which liberation theologians must make for themselves in the course of their participation in a specific situation. What can be described, however, are the general parameters of what is here called "the project of liberation."

---

[133]Cf. Jürgen Moltmann, "An Open Letter to Jose Miguez Bonino," *Chr Cris* 36 (Mar. 29, 1976):57-63.

Leonardo Boff has described the mutual interaction between the given project of an individual and the overall project of a given society.[134] Each culture has its own ethos, its own "way of being with and relating to others, nature, and the transcendent. Hence it implies a particular way of living out political, economic, and religious relationships. The resultant values both express these relationships and serve as their ideological justification. And the relationships are perpetuated and legitimated by social institutions (which are both functional and symbolic), juridical bodies, ethical codes, and a given hierarchy of values."[135] Individuals with their own understanding of their own personal project interact with the cultural project of a society, accepting and rejecting it to varying degrees.

The theology of liberation, on the basis of both social analysis and theological criteria, rejects the cultural project as it is presently formulated in Latin America. The prevailing political and socioeconomic structure together with its supportive ideology are judged bankrupt when measured by the standards of human decency and divine justice. Moreover, the liberation theologians hold little hope for the possibility of reforming the given structure. Therefore they understand that they must themselves participate in a project which has a different vision of Latin America's future. It is a vision they share with others who do not call themselves Christian. Nevertheless, it is a project that they trust is in greater accordance with God's intention than the project which presently rules over Latin America.[136]

The project of liberation to which liberation theology commits itself has several discernible features. It is, first of all, a project which is decidedly ideological, political, and conflict-laden. It is, moreover, a project which describes itself as a form of socialism. Lastly, it is a project which raises the question of violence as a means of attaining political change.

a. *A Project Which Is Ideological, Political, and Conflict-Laden.* In considering ideological suspicion as a part of liberation theology's social analysis, the distinction was made between positive and negative *ideology*. By a positive understanding of ideology is meant

---

[134]Cf. L. Boff, *Liberating Grace*, pp. 142-144. Cf. also Miguez Bonino, *Toward a Christian Political Ethics*, p. 52, who describes a historical project as falling between the extremes of an "utopia" and the elaboration of specific strategies and tactics.

[135]Ibid., pp. 142-143.

[136]Cf. ibid., pp. 146-147.

"the theoretical and analytical structure of thought which undergirds successful action to realize revolutionary change in society."[137] Liberation theology sees its task not only in criticizing the negative ideologies which support an unjust status quo but also in developing a positive ideology which insists upon structural change. Segundo has been the most thorough in his explanation of the inevitability and necessity of theology playing an ideological role.[138] A conscious awareness of the ideological weight carried by one's chosen position must be developed in order for a particular stance to escape absolutization and remain open for revision and correction.

Not only does liberation theology affirm that its project must be ideological but it goes on to affirm that its project must be *political*.[139]

> For a long time, the area of the political seemed an area apart, a sector of human existence subsisting alongside of, but distinct from one's family, professional, and recreational life. Political activity was something to be engaged in during the time left over from other occupations. Furthermore, it was thought, politics belonged to a particular sector of society specially called to this responsibility. But today, those who have made the option for commitment to liberation look upon the political as a dimension that embraces, and demandingly conditions, the entirety of human endeavors. Politics is the global condition, and the collective field, of human accomplishment. Only from a standpoint of this perception of the global character of politics, in a revolutionary perspective, can one adequately understand the legitimate narrower meaning of the term—orientation to political power.[140]

Liberation theology recognizes the necessity of entering into political action if it is to address the root causes of Latin America's poverty and oppression. It is not so much a matter of drawing conclusions for politics on the basis of theological work but rather the realization that, as was the case with ideology, that theology also bears an inevitable

---

[137]*Christians in the Technical and Social Revolutions of Our Time*, World Conference on Church and Society, The Official Report, with a description of the Conference by M. M. Thomas and Paul Abrecht (Geneva: World Council of Churches, 1967), p. 202, as quoted by Hans-Werner Gensichen, "Revolution and Mission in the Third World," *Luth W* 16, No. 1 (1969):17.

[138]In addition to his argument in *Faith and Ideologies* and *The Liberation of Theology*, cf. Juan Luis Segundo, *A Theology for Artisans of a New Humanity. Vol. 3: Our Idea of God*, trans. John Drury (Maryknoll: Orbis, 1974), pp. 127-133.

[139]For a broad explanation of the mediating role of politics for theology which complements that of liberation theology cf. Fierro, *The Militant Gospel*, pp. 28-33.

[140]Gutierrez, "Liberation Praxis and Christian Faith," in *The Power of the Poor in History*, pp. 46-47.

political weight.[141] Theology must, in lieu of Latin American poverty, surrender its futile attempts to remain politically neutral and make a conscious decision for a politics which takes the side of justice for the poor.

Liberation theology's conscious option for politics has been, together with its use of Marxism, the cause for sharp criticism. Bishop Alfonso Lopez Trujillo and Roger Vekemans have been among the most influential critics of liberation theology on these counts.[142] While focusing their arguments against the involvement of priests in politics, their arguments also have negatively critical implications for liberation theology with its insistence on political activism. As if in direct reply to such critics, Gustavo Gutierrez makes the following defense of the political dimension of the gospel.

> Are we in a time of political "reductionism" of the gospel? The answer is yes for those who use the gospel in the service of the powerful; the answer is no for those who are moved by the gospel, experienced as a gratuitous and liberating message, to denounce that type of use. Yes, for those who put it and put themselves in the hands of the great powers of this world; no, for those who identify themselves with the poor Christ seeking solidarity with the dispossessed of the continent. Yes, for the ones who maintain the gospel as a prisoner of an ideology serving the capitalist system; no, for those who are freed by the gospel and in turn try to free it from any slavery. Yes, for those who want to neutralize the liberation of Christ reducing it to a religious state tangential to the concrete world of men; no, for those who believe that the salvation of Christ is so total that nothing escapes it.[143]

Taking the side of the poor means, for the theologians of liberation, risking difficult but necessary political decisions—even if those decisions make them vulnerable to a host of negative criticism.

The previous quote by Gutierrez also establishes that liberation theology sees its historical project for liberation not only as necessarily ideological and political but also as *conflict-laden*. The project of liberation inevitably creates conflict because it collides with those in the established order who desire above all else to preserve their present advantages. The world is perceived by liberation theology not as a harmonious whole but rather as the scene of conflict between those who

---

[141] Cf. Assmann, *Theology for a Nomad Church*, pp. 34-36.

[142] Cf. Alfonso Lopez Trujillo, *Liberation or Revolution? An Examination of the Priest's Role in the Socioeconomic Class Struggle in Latin America* (Huntington, IN: Our Sunday Visitor, Inc., 1977) and Roger Vekemans, *Caesar and God. The Priesthood and Politics*, trans. Aloysius Owen and Charles Underhill Quinn (Maryknoll: Orbis, 1972).

[143] Gutierrez, "Faith as Freedom: Solidarity with the Alienated and Confidence in the Future," *Horizons* 2 (Spring 1975):55-56.

hold power and those who suffer in poverty.[144] Class struggle is, for liberation theology, an expression of conflict that was not created by Marx but which is an appropriate description of the conflict between those who have and those who do not.[145] Moreover, class struggle is not only descriptive of Latin American society but also of a basic conflict which expresses itself within the church.[146] A church which attempts to impose an artificial sense of conciliation may be out of touch with the conflict history depicted in the Bible.[147] Unity and conciliation are not so much already present in a divided world as they are both a gift of God and a goal to be achieved through the conflict-laden movement of human history.[148]

Gutierrez gives eloquent expression to the painful necessity of liberation theology entering into the conflicts which characterize Latin American life.

> But what is perhaps most difficult for the Christian who openly and devotedly takes the side of the poor and exploited and commits himself to the struggle of the proletariat is the conflictive character which his social praxis acquires in that context. Politics today involve confrontations—in which there are varying degrees of violence—between groups of people and between social classes with opposing interests. To be an "artisan of peace" does not excuse one from being present in those conflicts, but demands that one take part in them in order to overcome their root causes; it requires understanding that there is no peace without justice.[149]

Insofar as conflict is an unavoidable part of attaining justice for the poor, liberation theology chooses to enter into the fray.

Liberation theology supports the project of liberation for Latin America. It is a project which is ideological, political, and conflict-laden as it collides with the project which presently rules over Latin America embodied in political, social, economic, and religious structures. In rejecting the structures of the capitalist project, liberation theology advocates another project which is seen as the only other available historical option. Liberation theology thus opts for socialism to describe the project which best matches its aspirations for liberation.

---

[144]Cf. Assmann, *Theology for a Nomad Church*, pp. 65-66.

[145]Cf. Gutierrez, *A Theology of Liberation*, pp. 273-274.

[146]Cf. ibid., pp. 137-138 and Assmann, *Theology for a Nomad Church*, pp. 138-139.

[147]Cf. Assmann, *Theology for a Nomad Church*, pp. 98-99.

[148]Cf. Gutierrez, *A Theology of Liberation*, pp. 277-279.

[149]Gutierrez, "Faith As Freedom . . .," p. 35.

b. *Advocacy of Socialism*. Liberation theology names its project socialism. In so doing it affirms socialism as, at least in theory, better matched to its humanitarian and religious ideas than the present system under the influence of capitalism.[150] As already elaborated, that does not mean liberation theology advocates socialism in an uncritical fashion. When it names socialism as its project, that does not mean the Communism of the Soviet Union or the countries in its orbit. Liberation theology entertains a much broader vision of the meaning of liberation than is manifested in the atheistic and materialistic reductionism of socialism in Soviet Communism. It affirms much more the development of a socialism which is appropriate to Latin America.

In naming its historical project socialism, liberation theology makes use of Marxist thought in a way which goes beyond social analysis. Marxism is employed here in a second sense which assists in giving content to its vision for a more just future.

> The theology of liberation acknowledges its debt to Marxism. If it makes revolution its first subject matter, then it has to accept Marxism as the ideology and tool that has interpreted in the best way this revolutionary fact. It takes from Marxism its political and economical analyses, its praxis and its revolutionary tradition. It is a creative dialogue with Marxism not only on a theoretical basis but on the practical level of the actual revolutionary engagement.[151]

The theology of liberation makes use of Marxism in this way not only theoretically (i.e., as an instrument of social analysis) but also on the practical level of engagement.

What is the content of liberation theology's use of Marxism in envisioning a socialist project for Latin America?

> The decision for Marxism is therefore an option for structural over against purely individual change, for revolution over against reformism, for socialism over against capitalist development or "third" solutions, for "scientific" over against idealistic or utopian socialism.[152]

Choosing socialism as a project means, first of all, the necessity of radical, structural change from the present capitalist economic order and the forms of government which support it and the erection of a socialist form of government and economic system in which the means of production will no longer be privately but rather publicly

---

[150]Cf. L. Boff, "Die Anliegen der Befreiungstheologie," p. 90 and McGovern, *Marxism: An American Christian Perspective*, pp. 199-200.

[151]Adolfo Ham, "Introduction to the Theology of Liberation," *Com Via* 16, No. 3 (1973):115.

[152]Miguez Bonino, *Christians and Marxists*, p. 19.

owned. It is to be a system in which the basic human needs for food, health care, clothing, and shelter are to be established as the highest priority and are not merely the supposed consequences of a system which establishes profit as its highest good. Furthermore socialism means for liberation theology a system in which fundamental human rights are guaranteed and in which there is cultural freedom for the development of the individual.

In putting such ideals into words it may appear that they are more utopian than scientific. Utopia is a word often used to denigrate the aspirations of liberation theology. Liberation theology, however, has taken up the word utopia in a positive sense to express that which lends vision and hope to political action.[153] Utopia opens up an alternative view of what historical reality might become which counters the cynicism which defines the present as that which must be. The biblical notion of the kingdom of God is often described by liberation theology as an utopian vision which lies at the very heart of the Christian faith.

While liberation theologians are not dismayed at the use of the word utopia to describe their vision, that does not mean, however, that they have nothing more to say about socialism as a project for Latin America. There are in fact a variety of ways in which liberation theologians express their understanding of the meaning of socialism. Gutierrez speaks of the need for a socialism which is fully adapted to the particularity of the Latin American context[154] and sees "social ownership of the means of production" as a key element which is finding increasing attention among Christians in Latin America.[155] Dussel defends socialism as the only viable option for Latin America over against critics who either charge the ineffectualness of any noncapitalist option or who seek to find some third way.[156] Segundo describes how, at least for Latin American liberation theology, the

---

[153]Cf. Gutierrez, *A Theology of Liberation*, pp. 232-239.

[154]Cf. ibid., pp. 90-91.

[155]Ibid., p. 112. Cf. also pp. 111-113. For Gutierrez's use of Marxism and socialism see also John William Hart, "Topia and Utopia in Colombia and Peru—The Theory and Practice of Camilo Torres and Gustavo Gutierrez in their Historical Contexts," Ph.D. Dissertation (New York: Union Theological Seminary, 1978), pp, 234-244.

[156]Cf. Dussel, "The Kingdom of God and the Poor," *Int R Miss* 68 (Apr. 1979): 125-127 and "An International Division of Theological Labor," *Foun* 23 (Oct.-Dec. 1980):350-351.

decision between capitalism and socialism is "a theological crux."[157]
On the basis of biblical and theological arguments Segundo makes a
case for socialism as a project which, at least in an anticipatory way, is
in greater accord with what the Bible means by the kingdom of God.
Most extreme in taking this line of argumentation has been Miranda
whose works consistently seek to document the parallels between
biblical faith and Marxism and who goes so far as to title one of his
books *Communism in the Bible*.[158] Miranda argues that justice, in the
fully historical sense of the word, is the central concern both of
Marxism and the Bible. Thus, according to Miranda, socialism
emerges as the project commended by rigorous biblical study. A last
representative, Miguez Bonino, having offered a critical affirmation
of Marxism in his book *Christians and Marxists*, also recognizes the
tremendous ambiguity involved for Christians who opt for the socialist
project.[159] His voice sounds a warning to those who might overlook
those aspects of socialism which stand in tension or conflict to
Christian faith. Foremost among those aspects is the use of violence as
a means of attaining social change.

The most concrete and controversial example of the option by
liberation theologians for socialism is that of the Christians for
Socialism movement. In this movement a significant number of
Latin American Christians, occasioned by the rise of Salvador
Allende to power in Chile during the early seventies, declared
themselves as Christians to be supportive of the Marxist program he set
forth. The "Final Document" of the convention held in April 1972
included the following affirmations:

> Socialism presents itself as the only acceptable option for getting beyond a
> class-based society. . . . Only by replacing private ownership with the
> social ownership of the means of production do we create objective
> conditions that will allow for the elimination of class antagonism.
>   The construction of socialism is a creative process that has nothing to do
> with dogmatic schemas or an uncritical stance. Socialism is not a
> complex of historical dogmas but a constantly developing critical theory of
> the conditions of exploitation and a revolutionary praxis. Operating

---

[157]Cf. Segundo, "Capitalism-Socialism: A Theological Crux," trans. J. P.
Donnelly, in Claude Geffre and Gustavo Gutierrez, eds., *Concilium 96: The
Mystical and Political Dimensions of the Christian Faith* (New York: Herder,
1974), pp. 105-123.

[158]Jose Porfiro Miranda, *Communism in the Bible*, trans. Robert R. Barr
(Maryknoll: Orbis, 1982). Cf. also the two works already cited, *Marx and the
Bible* and *Being and the Messiah*.

[159]Cf. Miguez Bonino, *Marxists and Christians*, pp. 122-125.

through the takeover of power by the exploited masses, this praxis leads to social appropriation of the means of production and financing and to comprehensive, rational economic planning.[160]

Such statements are representative of the socialism advocated by the Christians for Socialism.

The flood of criticism which has been directed against this movement need not be repeated in this context. What is most significant, however, is to recognize the way in which the option for socialism as advocated by liberation theology took concretion in this movement. Nothing could be more specific than the support given by the Christians for Socialism movement for the program of Allende's Popular Unity coalition in Chile during its brief existence. Similarly the program of the Sandinista government in Nicaragua in the early eighties provides a concrete example of the way in which socialism, according to liberation theology, is to be implemented in Latin America. There is, however, an important distinction to be made between Allende's government in Chile in the early seventies and the Sandinista government in Nicaragua in the early eighties. The first came to power through the democratic process and was toppled by military coup.[161] The second has come to power by violent revolution against the Somoza dictatorship and it remains to be seen if democracy can in turn be established.

The ambiguities in liberation theology's advocacy of socialism as a project for the future of Latin America are numerous. A host of unanswered questions remain.[162] Is it in fact possible to distinguish in Marxism between those aspects which can be critically employed and those which must be rejected? Does the implementation of socialism not necessitate the establishment of a repressive authoritarian regime which by its very nature violates human rights? Is it realistic to believe, in light of the present global context which is so sharply divided between capitalist and communist spheres of influence, that it is possible to break from dependency upon capitalism without inevitably falling into a new form of dependency upon the

---

[160]"Final Document of the Convention," in John Eagleson, ed., *Christians and Socialism. Documentation of the Christians for Socialism Movement in Latin America*, trans, John Drury (Maryknoll: Orbis, 1975), pp. 169-170.

[161]Cf. Penny Lernoux, *Cry of the People* (New York: Penguin, 1982), p. 410, who asserts, "The record in Chile shows that the poor, if given the opportunity for self-development and expression, will choose socialism."

[162]Cf. the questions raised by Jose Comblin, *The Church and the National Security State*, pp. 47-48.

Soviet Union? Can violent means ever be employed by Christians in achieving social change? To these and other questions which can be raised against liberation theology's option for socialism as a project for the future of Latin America, the answer which is given in return is that for the sake of the poor, socialism is the historical choice which must be made in spite of the risks involved.

c. *The Use of Violence as a Means of Social Change?*[163] The question of the use of violence by Christians to achieve socio-political change emerged into international theological discussion in the mid-sixties. A significant impetus to this discussion was given at the World Conference on Church and Society held in Geneva in 1966, particularly by the address "The Revolutionary Challenge to Church and Theology," of Richard Shaull.[164] Because Shaull, although North American, based his address on his personal experiences in Latin America, the views he represented have come to be associated with Latin American liberation theology. Liberation theologians such as Gutierrez, however, have found it necessary to distance their own position from this "theology of revolution."

> In 1966 another line of theological reflection emerged, again with strong biblical overtones. It was known as the theology of revolution. It included, as a segment, a theology of violence, and this was the tree that often hid the forest. The theology of revolution had been developed initially by theologians who were very familiar with certain countries then engaged in a process of revolution. But it was eventually removed from its context and found a sounding board in certain currents of thought in Germany. In this latter form it was reintroduced into Latin America.[165]

Gutierrez is critical of the theology of revolution for several reasons. Although it served as a challenge to theology to recognize its connection to unjust social orders, it went too far when it claimed that "the gospel is not only not at odds with revolution but actually calls for revolution."[166] Such a "baptizing" of revolution, however, could easily be reduced to an uncritical ideology based on a misuse of biblical texts. Even more objectionable was the way in which the theology of

[163]For general discussions of this problematic, cf. McGovern, *Marxism: An American Christian Perspective*, pp. 285-292, and Fierro, *The Militant Gospel*, pp. 201-207.

[164]Cf. the accounts of this conference by J. M. Lochman, "Ecumenical Theology of Revolution," *Scot J Th* 21 (June 1968):170-186 and "Peace and Revolution," *Ref Pres W* 30 (Summer 1968):108-114.

[165]Gutierrez, *The Power of the Poor in History*, p. 43.

[166]Ibid.

revolution came to be carried out in distant academic centers and was theoretically applied to revolutionary contexts whereas, according to Gutierrez, the only legitimate context for such reflection must come "*from within* the liberation process" itself.[167]

Others, like Monika Hellwig, observing this process as outsiders have come to conclusions similar to those of Gutierrez.

> My own incomplete survey of positions suggests that those more distant from the Latin American scene are willing to condone more violence than those actually engaged in it, perhaps because they feel it ill becomes them to prescribe for others in a far more difficult situation than they face themselves. . . . Almeri Bezerra de Melo, points out that there is almost no published Latin American discussion on the question of violence from a theological perspective, and very little from either Africa or Asia, while there is a flood of literature from Europeans and North Americans interested in Latin America.[168]

Regardless, however, of who first initiated and gave impetus to the discussion of violence, the Latin Americans found themselves in the midst of a debate which stimulated their own reflection on the use of violence as a means of social change.[169]

Within Latin America what might be called a "classical" statement of the issues has come to prevail among liberation theologians.[170] A central figure in elaborating this position has been Dom Helder Camara.[171] Describing the Latin American situation of injustice as one of "institutional violence," the viewpoint articulated by Helder Camara attained authoritative status at the Medellin Conference and came to exercise a major role in shaping an understanding of the violence problematic among liberation theologians.[172] This "classical" position begins with the crucial

---

[167]Ibid., p. 44.

[168]Monika Hellwig, "Response of Monika Hellwig to Avery Dulles," in Torres and Eagleson, eds., *Theology in the Americas*, pp. 103-104.

[169]Cf. the variety of viewpoints assembled in *Chr Cris* 32 (July 10, 1972): 163-172, especially the final contribution by Jose Miguez Bonino, "Violence and Liberation," pp. 169-172.

[170]For a concise statement of the basic features in this position, see Berryman, "Latin American Liberation Theology," p. 367.

[171]Cf. Dom Helder Camara, "Violence in the Modern World," in *Between Honesty and Hope. Documents from and about the Church in Latin America*, issued at Lima by the Peruvian Bishops Commission for Social Action, trans. John Drury (Maryknoll: Maryknoll Publications, 1970), pp. 47-54.

[172]Medellin Documents: "Peace" (esp. Nos. 15-19), in Joseph Gremillion, ed., *The Gospel of Peace and Justice. Catholic Social Teaching Since Pope John* (Maryknoll: Orbis, 1976), pp, 459-461.

recognition that revolutionary violence is not itself the only form of violence which needs to be examined in the Latin American context. Instead it must be recognized that there are three kinds of violence.

The *first violence* which must be recognized as such is *the institutionalized violence* which prevails in Latin America. This first violence, "practiced routinely by the power structure, is usually perfectly legal; it takes place in the haciendas and factories, banks and government ministries, the White House or Pentagon. . . . It is what gives the upper 5% control over half the wealth, and the lower 35% of the people 5% of the wealth."[173]

> The first and most inhuman violence that exists is that which destroys millions of people, whole generations: the violence of the oppressors, of the dominators, of the empires which is objectified in the unjust and oppressive structures that do not allow a human being to be human. And, what is worse, it makes the oppressed, because of their desperation, into oppressors themselves—as is seen in the foreman over the worker, the police over the people, and the middle class over the lower classes.[174]

The reality of violence institutionalized into Latin American structures has become the fundamental starting point for the reflections of liberation theologians on violence.[175]

In response to institutionalized violence arises what can then be called a *second violence*, that is *counterviolence* or *revolutionary violence*. This is the violence "practiced in order to take power and establish a just order."[176] It is the violence which motivates a Camilo Torres or Nestor Paz to come to the conclusion that only violence can achieve the measure of change required in Latin America.

> Reacting to this oppressive violence is the violence of a small number who courageously challenge egoistic conformity, risk their own well-being and even their lives in order to transform the oppressor-oppressed dialectic into a relationship of brother-with-brother.[177]

The liberation theologians have taken up this understanding of counter-violence as a second form of violence in their theological viewpoint. It finds a variety of applications ranging from those which

---

[173]Berryman, "Latin American Liberation Theology," p. 367.

[174]Dussel, *A History of the Church in Latin America*, p. 174.

[175]Cf. Galilea, "Liberation Theology and New Tasks," pp. 174-177 and Miguez Bonino, "Violence and Liberation," pp. 169-170 in Gibellini, ed., *Frontiers of Theology in Latin America*; and Rubem Alves, "Towards a Theology of Liberation," Ph.D. Dissertation (Princeton: Princeton Theological Seminary, 1969), pp. 193-198.

[176]Berryman, "Latin American Liberation Theology," p. 367.

[177]Dussel, *A History of the Church in Latin America*, pp. 174-175.

tend to use it as a righteous justification of revolutionary violence[178] to those who are far more aware of the ambiguity of all violence.[179]

Responding to the threat of counterviolence, there emerges what can be called yet a *third violence*, that is, *repressive violence*. It is that violence employed by a system to suppress those who have taken up revolutionary violence. Included are those repressive measures which might be enacted by a Latin American government in order to preserve national security. In the process basic human rights are violated and dissent becomes criminal. The experience of this form of violence became intense in Latin America during the mid-seventies and has had a significant impact on liberation theology.

Beginning with this shared understanding of the diverse forms which violence takes, the individual liberation theologians arrive at a number of diverse conclusions regarding the use of violence as a means of social change.[180] Segundo, for example, seeks to broaden the definition of violence in such a way that human existence itself cannot be lived without a certain measure of violence.[181] The very limitedness of human energy means that some persons are always treated more as things than with the full respect due to human beings and this he describes as an inevitable form of violence. Moreover, to be honest in one's reading of the gospels, Jesus must be seen as exercising violence not only in this way but also in the sharp words he directs at those like the Pharisees and scribes. Segundo comes to the conclusion that life must be honestly appraised according to its inherent violence. The gospel itself serves not as an absolute value but to show the way in which it is possible in an historical process to learn to overcome the violence which is given. In this way the gospel:

> . . . is meant to orient us in the right direction through the course of history, so that we will look for ways to replace violence with love insofar as new possibilities open up to us.[182]

In this way Segundo brings his own theological understanding of history as process to his treatment of the question of violence.

---

[178]Cf. Alves,"Towards a Theology of Liberation," pp. 218-222.

[179]Cf. Miguez Bonino, "Violence and Liberation," in Gibellini, ed., *Frontiers of Theology in Latin America*, pp. 170-172.

[180]McGovern, *Marxism: An American Christian Perspective*, p. 193.

[181]Cf. Segundo, *Our Idea of God*, pp. 163-169 and *The Liberation of Theology*, pp. 156-165.

[182]Segundo, *Our Idea of God*, p. 169.

Ignacio Ellacuria is another liberation theologian who gives considerable attention to the question of violence.[183] Similar to Segundo, Ellacuria seeks to broaden the definition of what is meant by violence to include biological and psychoanalytical viewpoints which witness to the basic aggressiveness of human behavior. In its most extreme form, however, the existence of violence reveals a context of injustice. A Christian response to the violence caused by injustice must have its aim in what Ellacuria calls "the redemption of violence." He offers three examples of those who have come to strikingly different conclusions about how that redemption must take place: Charles de Foucauld, Martin Luther King, Jr. and Camilo Torres. In a carefully worded summary, Ellacuria comes to the following conclusion:

> The eradication of violence in all its forms is an urgent task that cannot be postponed. But stress must be placed on that form of violence which is protected by legal forms, which entails the permanent establishment of an unjust disorder, which precludes the conditions required for the human growth of the person, and which therefore gives rise to strong reactions. Our rejection of violence must be absolute. The paradox is that the absolute character of this rejection calls for attitudes and lines of action that cannot help but be extreme.[184]

The ambiguous yet possible use of violence as a means of social change is, among liberation theologians, perhaps nowhere better expressed than by Ellacuria.

Miguez Bonino shares Ellacuria's sense of the ambiguity of violence but goes on to recognize the ambiguity of nonviolence as well.

> Seen in this perspective, the often-debated question of nonviolence takes on a different aspect. It ceases to be a question of "personal purity." Strictly speaking, we do not deal with nonviolence but with qualities, forms, and limitations of violence present in a conflict of oppression and liberation.[185]

Miguez Bonino thus seeks to move beyond the absolutizing of any single position into an abstract principle which neglects a consideration of the concrete situation.

When one surveys the conclusions drawn by the various liberation theologians regarding the use of violence as a means of social change, they range from Galilea's call for a "theology of reconciliation" as the

[183]Ignacio Ellacuria, *Freedom Made Flesh. The Mission of Christ and His Church*, trans. John Drury (Maryknoll: Orbis, 1976), pp. 167-231.

[184]Ibid., p. 230.

[185]Miguez Bonino, "Violence and Liberation," in Gibellini, ed., *Frontiers of Theology in Latin America*, p. 172. Cf. also *Marxists and Christians*, p. 124.

only Christian solution[186] to Dussel's hard opinion that he does "not
believe that nonviolence is a viable option for Latin Americans who
want to effect change."[187] It is somewhat surprising that, given the
foundational significance of Helder Camara's statement of the
problematic of violence in Latin America, that his own conclusions
regarding nonviolence have not received more serious consideration.
Likewise the possibility of strategic nonviolence as a means of
attaining social change as it has been practiced by the 1980 winner of
the Nobel Peace Prize, Adolfo Perez Esquivel, is noticeably absent from
their reflections.[188] In Argentina, Peru, Ecuador, Paraguay, and
throughout Latin America, Perez Esquivel has provided a nonviolent
model for social change which deserves further reflection among
liberation theologians for its potential application to the broader
liberation struggle. Likewise the models of Mahatma Gandhi and
Martin Luther King, Jr., although perhaps not immediately applicable
to the Latin American context, would seem to merit more thorough
examination than they have thus far received.

It is in the question of the use of violence as a means of social
change that the heritage of Marx collides most forcefully with the
Christian tradition. Liberation theology has provided a statement of
the problematic of institutionalized, counter, and repressive violence
which is most insightful. In addition liberation theologians have
struggled and will continue to struggle with the question of violence in
the Latin American context.[189] This survey illustrates the hard
question which violence has put to the liberation theologians and shows
that any attempt to make a simple equation of liberation theology with
the advocacy of violence is a gross oversimplification. The use of
violence as a means of social change remains an open and troubling
question.

---

[186]Galilea, "Liberation Theology and New Tasks," in Gibellini, ed.,
Frontiers of Theology in Latin America, pp. 176-177.

[187]Dussel, *A History of the Church in Latin America*, p. 173.

[188]Cf. Adolfo Perez Esquivel, *Christ in a Poncho. Testamonials of the
Nonviolent Struggles in Latin America*, ed. Charles Antoine, trans. Robert R.
Barr (Maryknoll: Orbis, 1983).

[189]Cf. the exchange between Dan R. Ebener, "Is there a Future for
Nonviolence in Central America?", and Mano Barreno, "A Latin American
Response," *Fellowship* 49, No. 10-11 (Oct./Nov. 1983):6-7, 28.

C. *Theological Method and Praxis-Orientation*

In the preceding elaboration of the five elements which constitute the method of liberation theology, the word praxis has been employed sparingly and that by intention. Only through an examination of these five elements can what the liberation theologians mean by praxis come to be understood. In the writings of the various liberation theologians praxis can refer to any one of these five elements individually. Much more, however, praxis refers to that method which emerges when these elements are considered in mutual interaction.

It would be mistaken to assume that any single liberation theologian precisely follows the five methodological elements here described. It is rather the case that their separate contributions combine to compose a whole which is greater than the sum of the individual parts. Also mistaken would be any attempt to view the five elements here presented in a strict sequential order. In the writings of the liberation theologians, method has not been, with the exceptions already noted, a matter of explicit interest. Nevertheless the word praxis itself as used by liberation theologians points toward these five elements described above.

Praxis in liberation theology refers to a method which is exercised in a fluid interchange between thought and action, theory and practice. It is not the application of a preconceived theory upon practice[190] but instead an *encounter with historical reality which itself gives rise to thought within the context of engagement.* Gregory Baum offers the following description of praxis as it is used by liberation theologians:

> What does this strange word mean anyway? The English word "practice" refers to any action that applies a particular theory. Praxis, on the other hand, is practice associated with a total dynamics of historical vision and social transformation. Through praxis people enter their historical destiny. Since praxis changes the world as well as the actors, it becomes the starting point for a clearer vision and a more correct understanding of history. Praxis is the precondition of knowledge, even though in turn this knowledge issues forth into a new praxis. The dialectics of truth begin with praxis. [191]

Letty Russell describes praxis-orientation as "action that is concurrent with reflection or analysis and leads to new questions, actions, and

---

[190] Cf. the distinction between "theory *for* practice" and a "theory *of* practice" presented by McGovern, *Marxism: An American Christian Perspective*, pp. 180-181.

[191] Gregory Baum, "The Christian Left at Detroit," in Torres and Eagleson, eds., *Theology in the Americas*, p. 407.

reflections."[192]   Similarly Philip Hefner has grasped the dynamic
nature of what liberation theology means by praxis when he writes:
"Practice-becoming-aware-of-itself and thereby contributing both to
our store of knowledge and also to the humanization of the world is
praxis."[193]

Liberation theology as theology brings something unique to Latin
American praxis. It brings a tradition which can perhaps itself best be
understood not as doctrine or theory but as the praxis of faith in the
living God. The Christian tradition, grounded both in the history of
Israel and in Jesus and his church, itself witnesses to the dynamic
synthesis of action and reflection which liberation theology calls
praxis.

> The word of God is no longer a fixed absolute, an external proposition we
> receive before analyzing social conflicts and before committing ourselves
> to the transformation of historical reality. God's summons to us, God's
> word today, grows from the collective process of historical awareness,
> analysis, and involvement, that is, from praxis. The Bible and the whole
> Christian tradition do not speak directly to us in our situation. But they
> remain as a basic reference about how God spoke in quite a different
> context, which must illuminate his speaking in our context.[194]

In their participation in Latin American praxis, liberation theologians
bring the resources of the Christian tradition to this task. They attempt
to listen not only to God's word in Scripture and tradition but also to
God's word in contemporary history in order to discern God's living
word for Latin American praxis today.

In concluding this discussion of the method of liberation theology
and the five elements which constitute it, it is well to become mindful
once again of who the prime actors in this praxis really are. They are
not so much the liberation theologians themselves, although they have
played a significant role in articulating and encouraging a praxis
which they hope will lead to a more just future. In the last analysis,
however, it is the poor themselves who are the only ones who have the
power to "subvert" history and turn it upside down.

> We shall not have our great leap forward, into a whole new theological
> perspective, until the marginalized and exploited have begun to become the
> artisans of their own liberation—until their voice makes itself heard

[192]Letty M. Russell, *Human Liberation in a Feminist Perspective—A
Theology* (Philadelphia: Westminster, 1974), p. 55.

[193]Philip Hefner, "Theology Engaged: Liberational, Political, Critical,"
Dial 13 (Summer 1974):191.

[194]Hugo Assmann, "Statement by Hugo Assmann," in Torres and
Eagleson, eds., *Theology in the Americas*, p. 299.

directly, without mediations, without interpreters—until they themselves take account, in the light of their own values, of their own experience of the Lord in their efforts to liberate themselves. We shall not have our quantum theological leap until the oppressed themselves theologize, until "the others" themselves personally reflect on their hope in a total liberation in Christ. For they are the bearers of this hope for all humanity.[195]

It is in this context that Gutierrez's statement about the final value of all theologies, including liberation theology, becomes clear.

They are not worth one act of faith, love, and hope, committed—in one way or another—in active participation to liberate man from everything that dehumanizes him and prevents him from living according to the will of the Father.[196]

Neither theological method nor theology itself has intrinsic value for liberation theology in Latin America. The final measure of their worth is praxis itself as it contributes to justice for the poor.

D. *Questions Raised by Latin American Liberation Theology for North American Theologians*

Ignacio Ellacuria makes the following remark in his discussion of the meaning of the term "liberation" for the present mission of the church:

The work of Christian liberation opens up a privileged field of action for the Church in its work of proclaiming the gospel. At the present stage of history this liberation must be liberation from injustice and for love. The struggle against injustice and the effort to facilitate love are two signs of credibility that dovetail perfectly with the sign of credibility embodied in Christian liberation.[197]

As the theology of liberation reads "the signs of the times" as they appear in the Latin American context, it has concluded that the term liberation most fully expresses the meaning of the gospel message for its time and place. Salvation for this theology means liberation. It means a liberation which does not negate the traditional notion of salvation from sin, but rather expands it to include and accent the sinfulness of social and political structures which create and perpetuate the poverty and exploitation of millions.

In the previous pages the basic features of this theology have been outlined in an attempt to carefully analyze that which the theologians

---

[195]Gutierrez, "Liberation Praxis and Christian Faith," in *The Power of the Poor in History*, p. 65. Cf. also pp. 105-107 and 201-202.

[196]Gutierrez, *A Theology of Liberation*, p. 308.

[197]Ignacio Ellacuria, *Freedom Made Flesh. The Mission of Christ and His Church*, trans. John Drury (Maryknoll: Orbis, 1976), p. 109.

of liberation have been saying. The assumption is that what they are saying about the contemporary state of the world and of theology is of vital importance not only to those in Latin America but also to those in the North American context. It has been asserted that it is most necessary first to understand what these theologians are themselves saying before proceeding to any premature conclusions and criticisms.

In examining the theology of liberation one discovers that a variety of different viewpoints and outlooks merge together to form a unified voice. It is a voice which speaks for the poor of Latin America. It speaks of their struggle for life and for justice. The differences which exist between the various individual liberation theologians are not nearly so great as that which unites them, i.e., their concern for a praxis which they believe can help to create a more just future for the poor and oppressed people in their lands.

Poverty is truly the starting point for understanding this theology. One who does not or cannot see this poverty and conclude that it represents an intolerable situation cannot begin to understand the difference of liberation theology and the impact it is making in Latin America and throughout the Third World. Moving out from the reality of the poor, the question is being raised in a new way as to the causes of this poverty. The theory of dependency has been developed as an initial answer to this question. What is more, the biblical message has spoken with existential relevance to those who suffer as the poor of the earth. These basic presuppositions of liberation theology indicate a new point of departure for theology, one which stands in stark contrast to the predominant Western paradigm.

The single word which best symbolizes the difference of this theology is the word "praxis." For liberation theology, praxis means a new method and a reformulation of basic theological themes. Chapter Two has detailed what the theology of liberation means by praxis in an attempt to examine this central concern. The insistence on praxis, however, can never be separated from the concrete situation of the poor who are the reason for this theology's very existence. Thus one comes full circle: from an encounter with the poor, through social analysis and theological reflection, to social-political engagement for the poor. The circle does not end but goes on and on.

Before turning in the next chapters to an examination of the responses which North American theologians have made to Latin American liberation theology, it may be helpful to summarize in a concise way some of the central questions which liberation theology raises of North American theologians. The following is a series of twelve questions which liberation theology poses to theologians in North America and throughout the First World. They are questions to which North American theologians have responded in a variety of ways. They serve as a final point of reference for the subsequent discussion of North American responses to Latin American liberation theology.

1. Is liberation theology taken seriously as a theological approach or treated superficially as a passing fad? How well do North American theologians understand the fundamental issues of liberation theology?

2. How is the task of theology itself defined? Is all of history, including the contemporary reality of poverty, to be interpreted theologically?

3. Are the issues addressed considered in a global context or confined to a more immediate (i.e., North American) one?

4. What stance is taken to the Western theological tradition?

5. Is theology to remain neutral and objective in its methodology or does theology entail the subjective commitment of the theologian to theology's subject matter?

6. What theological significance is given to the fact of poverty in the world?

7. What is the theological starting point? How are social, eco-nomic, and political questions addressed by theology?

8. What use is made of social analysis for theology? Does philosophy, perhaps, provide the primary analytical paradigm?

9. How does theology function in political terms? Is it supportive, critical, revolutionary in relation to the status quo?

10. Is the Bible a source for theology which continues to speak in a living way, or primarily interpreted as an historical document?

11. What is the nature of the theological reformulations made by theology? Which questions motivate them? Which conclusions are drawn for the present?

12. Does theology insist upon engagement and praxis, or is its primary aim understanding, insight, or knowledge?

These are the kinds of pointed questions which liberation theology raises for North American theologians. Only by taking seriously the questions raised by liberation theology can a genuine dialogue take place which bases itself upon the explicit arguments of the dialogue partner.

PART TWO:

RESPONSES OF NORTH AMERICAN THEOLOGIANS

TO LATIN AMERICAN LIBERATION THEOLOGY

Chapter Three

Finding a Resonance

Latin American theologians have at times been skeptical about the capability of North American and European theologians to adequately understand and respond to liberation theology. Jose Miguez Bonino, for one, raises the fundamental question of whether it is possible for those living in the affluent world to begin to envision the world from the "location of the poor."[1] Enrique Dussel further sharpens this question when he asserts that most theologies in the United States, Germany, and other European countries in fact play an ideological role in confirming "the legality of the system," a system in which the situation of the poor is simply ignored.[2]

Gustavo Gutierrez has raised a somewhat different yet related point when he cautions against the cooptation of the central issues of liberation theology by those who adopt a "liberation" vocabulary while leaving the content of their thought virtually unchanged.

> Facile attitudes, coupled with a certain "trendiness," or penchant for the newest vogue, have encouraged some persons simply to tack on the word "liberation" to whatever they have always been saying anyway and go on saying it, hoping to update a sluggish old inventory by slapping a new label on obsolete goods.[3]

In this way liberation theology becomes emptied of "its human and historical content, so that now it can be accepted by the political and ecclesiastical system."[4]

The skepticism of Latin American liberation theologians about the ability of North Americans to grasp and respond to what they are

---

[1] Jose Miguez Bonino, "Doing Theology in the Context of the Struggles of the Poor," *Mid-Stream* 20 (1981):373.

[2] Enrique Dussel, "An International Division of Theological Labor," *Foun* 23 (1980):346.

[3] Gustavo Gutierrez, "Liberation Praxis and Christian Faith," in *The Power of the Poor in History*, trans. Robert R. Barr (Maryknoll: Orbis, 1983), p. 64.

[4] Ibid.

saying finds a certain counterpart among those in North America who insist that Latin American liberation theology cannot simply be translated from its original context into the North American one. The process which led to the first Theology in the Americas Conference in Detroit in 1975 serves to amply document the significant differences which exist between the North and South American continents and the reluctance of North American theologians to attempt any facile application of Latin American theology to their own context.[5]

Such words of caution or even skepticism need to be taken seriously in examining the ways North American theologians have in fact responded to Latin American liberation theology. Taken by themselves these warnings could well lead to a total impasse, the breakdown of communication altogether. Indeed one way of responding to liberation theology has been to remain silent and to continue to carry out theology now as before. Yet in spite of the difficulties entailed in understanding a theology which has arisen in such a radically different context, the challenge which liberation theology raises for the North American understanding of the method, content, and even definition of theology is so great that some sort of a response seems to be called for. The next two chapters of this work will document the many and various responses that have been made.

The responses of North American theologians can be divided into two general categories corresponding to the distinction made here between Chapters Three and Four. As one examines the literature written by North Americans in response to Latin American liberation theology, a most striking phenomenon becomes apparent, that is, a decided polarity between those responses which for the most part resonate with liberation theology, accepting its claims on the basis of its own presuppositions and arguments, and those responses which have raised major critical questions about these same presuppositions and arguments, often sharply so. This is not to say that those making resonant responses raise no critical issues. It is rather that the critical questions which they do raise do not prevent them from affirming the fundamental validity of the position of liberation theology. At the other pole are those whose criticisms of liberation theology are so severe that they either reject it altogether as a legitimate theological option or could only affirm its adequacy given a clarification or modification of its deficiencies. A fuller analysis of this phenomenon of polarization

---

[5]See Sergio Torres and John Eagleson, eds., *Theology in the Americas* (Maryknoll: Orbis, 1976), esp. 242-252 and 431-436.

will be offered in Chapter Five.

The present chapter proceeds with a description of the resonant responses several North American theologians have made to Latin American liberation theology. Those who are examined in more detail—Richard Shaull, James Cone, Frederick Herzog, Robert McAfee Brown, and Rosemary Radford Ruether—have been singled out due to both the breadth and depth of their response. They are those whose contributions occur early and consistently in the pertinent theological literature and serve to provide an interesting variety among the resonant responses.

A. *Richard Shaull: The Latin American Challenge to North American Church and Society*

To speak of Richard Shaull's "response" to Latin American liberation theology is in itself a complicated matter. This is due to the fact that Richard Shaull's personal history and the development of his theology are fully interwoven with the course of events taking place in Latin America in the decades prior to the emergence of liberation theology. It is therefore virtually impossible to differentiate between Shaull as one who was an active participant in the origin of liberation theology and Shaull as one who has made a significant North American response to liberation theology. Due to his unique involvement in the Latin American context itself, it becomes particularly important in the case of Shaull to pay due attention to his biography as the essential background for understanding his theology.

Born in 1919 to "a staunchly Calvinist family in an isolated rural community in Pennsylvania,"[6] Shaull went on to graduate from Princeton Theological Seminary and was ordained as a minister of the United Presbyterian Church. While at Princeton, Shaull was especially influenced by the thought of Karl Barth, Emil Brunner, Josef Hromadka, and John Dewey among others, and by the specter of the imminent Second World War. Already the seeds began to be planted for what would later constitute the leitmotif of Shaull's theology—that "God's ongoing transformation of the world would flow out of the new

---

[6]Richard Shaull, "Reflections on My Years in Brazil" (unpublished manuscript), p. 2. Cf. also Carl-Henric Grenholm, *Christian Social Ethics in a Revolutionary Age. An Analysis of the Social Ethics of John C. Bennett, Heinz-Dietrich Wendland and Richard Shaull* (Uppsala: Verbum, 1973), p. 210, for a brief biographical sketch of Shaull.

life lived in the church."[7] With this theological background and an
evangelical concern for mission, Shaull and his wife went to Colombia
as missionaries in 1942. This turn to Latin America would prove to be
decisive for Shaull for the next five decades. While in Colombia the
Shaulls were "engaged in many diverse activities in evangelism and
the renewal of the church."[8] In 1950 Shaull returned to the U.S.A.
studying briefly at Union Theological Seminary with Reinhold
Niebuhr before going to Princeton to begin doctoral studies with Paul
Lehmann whose thought would come to profoundly influence his own.[9]

Shaull returned to Latin America in 1952, this time to Brazil where
he began to teach at the Campinas Theological Seminary. Through an
intense involvement with his students and the Brazilian environment,
Shaull became increasingly aware that the rapid social changes
sweeping through Latin American society demanded new and creative
responses from both the church in Brazil and in the U.S.A.[10] Shaull's
understanding of the missionary task underwent a significant
transition during these years from a more evangelistic model toward a
model which had as its primary aim the equipping of mission churches
for dealing with the social and political challenges of a world
becoming rapidly secularized.[11]

Shaull's first book, *Encounter with Revolution* (1955), appeared
during these years and documents the increasing application of
Shaull's authentic evangelical concern to the urgent social issues
emerging in Latin America at this time.[12] In this book Shaull was
particularly interested in communicating to a North American
audience the appeal made by communism among those daily facing
"the grim reality" of "imminent hunger, poverty, sickness, and

---

[7]Shaull, "Reflections on My Years in Brazil," p. 4.

[8]Richard Shaull, "Introduction," in Hyla Stuntz Converse, ed., *Raise a
Signal. God's Action and the Church's Task in Latin America Today* (New
York: Friendship Press, 1961), p. 108. On his years in Colombia see also Shaull,
"Reflections on My Years in Brazil," p. 5.

[9]Shaull, "Reflections on My Years in Brazil," p. 6.

[10]See ibid., pp. 7-12.

[11]Cf. Shaull's early evangelistic concern in Richard Shaull, "Evangelism
and Proselytism in Latin America" and "Letter to the Editor," *Student World*
46 (1953):14-20 and 49-51, with the concern for social questions which come to
dominate his later thought.

[12]Richard Shaull, *Encounter With Revolution* (New York: Association
Press, 1955).

death."[13]   While arguing that communism ultimately betrays the revolution it sets out to achieve by degenerating into the totalitarianism of a closed society, Shaull sought to challenge North American Christians to their own creative response to this revolutionary situation. Shaull called Christians to perceive God's activity in the political movements of the present and, moving away from a privatistic approach to religion, to commit themselves to political action in league with God's purposes. Shaull sought to raise for North American Christians both a political and spiritual challenge in light of his encounter with the revolutionary situation in Latin America. It was, however, the spiritual challenge which Shaull still emphasized as the fundamental one in 1955.

> Those nations in which the consequent crisis is most acute urgently need economic help, and must develop new structures of social and political life. Yet in the last analysis, their fundamental need is a spiritual one and their hope of finding permanent solutions to their most urgent problems lies in the discovery of those moral and spiritual resources adequate for the task.[14]

In the years to follow, however, it was the need for change in the political and social structures to which Shaull would devote the major share of his attention.

In the middle of 1957 Shaull left Campinas for a year's study leave at Princeton to work on his dissertation.[15]   Upon returning to Campinas in 1958, he encountered growing opposition to the social and political orientation of his theology and its influence upon students. Eventually Shaull was prompted to accept a new position. Thus in 1960 he became Vice-President of the Mackenzie Institute in Sao Paulo. This new position allowed Shaull to devote more of his attention to the political issues facing the church and to participate more directly in the Brazilian Student Christian Movement. The more Shaull confronted the political and social challenges facing the church, however, the more critical he became of traditional theological and ecclesial forms and the more convinced of the need for fundamental structural change if a solution to Latin American social problems was to be found.[16] Politically this led him to a reevaluation of the relationship between Christianity and Marxism which had once appeared to be a settled

---

[13]Ibid., p. 4.

[14]Ibid., p. 132.

[15]For the following cf. Shaull, "Reflections on My Years in Brazil," pp. 12-17.

[16]For the following cf. ibid., pp. 19-27.

matter for him in *Encounter with Revolution*. Ecclesiologically it led him to search for a new form for the church via small groups which could give sustenance to the needed political engagement. On the basis of his increasing political and social concern, Shaull began to arrive at a new appreciation for the ministry of Roman Catholics on these issues, an appreciation which has grown ever stronger with the emergence of liberation theology and the basic Christian communities within the Roman Catholic church in Latin America.[17]

Alan Neely has forcefully argued that Shaull's years in Brazil should be understood as an important antecedent of Latin American liberation theology especially along the Protestant line of development.[18] Through his teaching, publications, and his involvement in both the Student Christian Movement and I.S.A.L. ("Church and Society in Latin America"), Shaull made a lasting impact on Latin American church and theology. Rubem Alves, Jose Miguez Bonino, and Julio de Santa Ana are among those to have been influenced by Shaull during these years. Though Shaull's thought has also been criticized by several Latin American theologians,[19] this has been done with an accompanying recognition of Shaull's contribution in turning the Protestant vision away from its traditional isolationism to an encounter with the social and political problems facing Latin America in a period of rapid change.

As Shaull became "Professor of Ecumenics" at Princeton Theological Seminary in 1962, he continued to devote the majority of his attention to the interface between the Latin American social and political context and its significance for North American church and society. Even a cursory examination of his writings during this period reveals Shaull's ongoing interest in challenging North Americans to their own response in light of the implications drawn from the Latin American context. Two books were written during Shaull's years at Princeton which extended to 1980: *Containment and Change* (1967) together with Carl Oglesby and *Liberation and Change* (1977) together with Gustavo Gutierrez. Perhaps most significant of all, however, was the lecture which Shaull gave to a gathering of the World Council of

---

[17]Ibid., p. 27-29.

[18]See Alan Neely, "Protestant Antecedents of the Latin American Theology of Liberation," Ph.D. Dissertation (Washington, D.C.: The American University, 1977), pp. 253-268, for a lengthy analysis of Shaull as an antecedent of Latin American liberation theology.

[19]Ibid., pp. 266-268.

Churches at Geneva in 1966 which was subsequently published with the title "The Revolutionary Challenge to Church and Theology."[20] Given impetus by this presentation of Shaull and the themes it raised for theological discussion, "political theology" and the "theology of revolution" emerged into heated debate, especially within the European context.[21] Subsequently a volume of Shaull's essays were translated into German under the title *Befreiung durch Veränderung* (1970).

Before turning to a synopsis of Shaull's theology as it developed during his years at Princeton and a comparison between his position and that of Latin American liberation theology, some final biographical information is in order. In 1980 Shaull resigned from his professorship at Princeton after a period of growing disenchantment with the ability of the mainline Protestant churches and academic theology to adequately respond to the challenges raised by the marginal and the poor both in the U.S. and abroad.[22] Since that time Shaull has begun to travel extensively throughout Latin America under the sponsorship of the International Subsistence Service Program of the Presbyterian Church, U.S.A. and also works with the Program of Theological Education of the Instituto Pastoral Hispano in New York. The book *Heralds of a New Reformation. The Poor of South and North America* (1984) was written as part of this renewed effort "to become much more involved in Latin America and take on the task of communicating to North Americans something of the richness of theological thought and Christian life so evident there." It is in this book that Shaull deals most explicitly with liberation theology *per se* as it has come to be articulated by the major Latin American theologians.

In examining the central theological themes which dominate Shaull's writings during his years at Princeton, two clarifying remarks are necessary regarding the interpretation of Shaull's

---

[20]Richard Shaull, "The Revolutionary Challenge to Church and Theology," *Th Today* 23 (Jan. 1967):470-480.

[21]Cf. the volumes by Trutz Rendtorff and Heinz Eduard Tödt, *Theologie der Revolution. Analysen und Materialen* (Frankfurt am Main: Suhrkamp, 1969) and Ernst Fiel and Rudolf Weth, eds., *Diskussion zur "Theologie der Revolution"* (Munich/Mainz: Christian Kaiser, 1969).

[22]For this and the following quote, Richard Shaull, *Heralds of a New Reformation. The Poor of South and North America* (Maryknoll: Orbis, 1984), back cover. On Shaull's disenchantment with the institutional church and academic theology respectively, see the comments in "Does Religion Demand Social Change?" *Th Today* 26 (Apr. 1969):13 and "The Challenge to the Seminary," *Chr Cris* 29 (Apr. 14, 1969):81-86.

writings. First, it is important to remember that Shaull has written no
systematic theology. His theology is dispersed in a variety of
publications written on an *ad hoc* basis. Secondly, from his earliest
book *Encounter with Revolution* in 1955 to his 1984 volume *Heralds of a
New Reformation*, it has been Shaull's consistent passion to make
North American church and society aware of the challenge raised by
the social, political, and ecclesial situation in Latin America. If there
is a constant theme in Shaull's writings it is his conviction of the
urgency of the issues raised in the Latin American context also for
North America.[23] While interpreters of Shaull have recognized the
first of these concerns, they have tended to proceed to criticize Shaull as
if his theology were of a more systematic nature.[24] Regarding the
second concern, Shaull's consistent interest to reach a North
American audience has been largely overlooked.

Upon becoming professor at Princeton in 1962, Shaull brought with
himself experiences from Latin America and a theological outlook
which he continued to develop and articulate. The basic elements of
this theological viewpoint recur throughout his writings during this
period and can be summarized under a few major themes.

Undergirding Shaull's entire theology is the affirmation that *God
is at work in history*. In this affirmation Shaull takes up the
theological program of his teacher Paul Lehmann especially as it was
developed in the book *Ethics in a Christian Context* (1963).[25] Shaull,

[23]Numerous articles by Shaull during this period center explicitly on the
Latin American context and its implications for North American church and
society. See, for example, "The New Revolutionary Mood in Latin America,"
Chr Cris 23 (Apr. 1, 1963):44-48; "Christian Participation in the Latin-
American Revolution," in Creighton Lacy, ed., *Christianity Amid Rising Men
and Nations* (New York: Association Press, 1965), pp. 91-118; "Christian
Initiative in Latin American Revolution," *Chr Cris* 25 (Jan. 10, 1966):295-298;
"Next Stage in Latin America," *Chr Cris* 27 (Nov. 13, 1967):264-266; "The New
Latin Revolutionaries and the U.S.," *Chr Cent* 85 (Jan. 17, 1968):69-70; and
"Repression Brazilian Style," *Chr Cris* 29 (July 21, 1969):198-199.

[24]Cf. the study and critique of the ethics of Shaull by Grenholm, *Christian
Social Ethics in a Revolutionary Age*, and the examination of the "theology of
revolution" by Gerd-Dieter Fischer, *Richard Shaulls "Theologie der
Revolution." Ihre theologische und ethische Argumentation auf dem
Hintergrund der Situation in Lateinamerika* (Frankfurt am Main: Peter
Lang, 1984).

[25]Cf. Grenholm's description of the influence of Lehmann on Shaull,
Christian Social Ethics in a Revolutionary Age, pp. 218-222. See also Shaull's
review, "Discussion of Paul Lehmann: *Ethics in a Christian Context*," *Princ S
B* 58 (1964):46-49.

like Lehmann, finds in the Bible the basis for a theology of God's ongoing action in history. This divine action is not privatistic but rather "political," taking place through historical events and carried out to the goal of human maturity or, to use a familiar phrase of Lehmann, "to make and to keep human life human."[26] This theology of history can also be described as messianic as it is oriented toward the arrival of God's messianic kingdom of justice and peace. In a passage which summarizes the biblical basis for this theology of history, Shaull writes:

> Israel meets and knows God in the midst of her history, in her involvements in political crises and complex social and cultural problems. In the Incarnation, this God relates himself once and for all to man within a dynamic process. As God's action in the world aims at its transformation, the coming of Christ and the work of the Holy Spirit release new and disturbing forces in history that affect the process itself. As the influence of Christ grows, old stabilities are swept away, and the struggle for humanization moves to new frontiers; at the same time, new threats appear, and the forces that resist Christ become stronger and more manifest. Along this road, there can be no turning back; those who would participate in God's work cannot seek refuge in old ways nor draw back from the front lines because the situation is becoming increasingly dangerous. For it is in this struggle that the battle for the future of man is being waged.[27]

In this theology a continuity is seen between God's activity recorded in the events of the Bible and God's ongoing activity throughout history even up to the present.

The importance given here to God's ongoing activity in history leads directly to a second theme which is crucial for Shaull, that is, *the task of discerning what God is doing in contemporary history*. Once again Shaull leans heavily on the work of other thinkers as he analyzes contemporary events for their theological meaning, in this case Arend Th. van Leeuwen and Herbert Marcuse.[28] From van Leeuwen Shaull takes over the distinction between an "ontocratic" view of reality and society in which all of reality is understood to be part of a single, unchangeable, cosmic system and a "theocratic" view of history and society based upon the history of Israel in which

---

[26]Paul Lehmann, *Ethics in a Christian Context* (New York: Harper & Row, 1963), p. 101.

[27]Richard Shaull, "Revolutionary Change in Theological Perspective," Chapter 1 in John C. Bennett, ed., *Christian Social Ethics in a Changing World. An Ecumenical Inquiry* (New York: Association Press, 1966), pp. 26-27.

[28]For more on the influence of van Leeuwen and Marcuse on Shaull see Grenholm, *Christian Social Ethics in a Revolutionary Age*, pp. 213-218.

criticism and change of the existing social structure is possible.[29] It is
affirmed that Western civilization has been dramatically shaped by
this theocratic understanding of reality and that the resulting
desacralization of the world and its history has become a
presupposition of Western thinking. History has become subject, in the
West, to human innovation and manipulation free from divine
sanctions which hold static a particular social order.

Shaull has found these formulations particularly insightful in
understanding both Latin American and North American society.
The secularization of the world and the application of human
technology in shaping that world are in this way for Shaull the marks
which most characterize modern society.

> Recent developments in our technological society have brought man to a
> new stage in his struggle to create more tolerable conditions for life
> through the ordering of his social existence. Social evils, once accepted as
> inevitable, can now be overcome by organized human endeavor; we have
> the resources and the power to create the type of society we want. . . .
> Technology tends to shatter old forms of social organization and cause
> constant changes in our way of life. But it does not automatically create a
> society that offers increasing opportunities either for material well-being
> or for human liberation.[30]

It is in this world, marked by the ambiguity of the secularization
process and its technological mentality, that God too, according to
Shaull, continues to be active to accomplish his purposes.

Shaull's evaluation of the achievements of technology become
increasingly negative as he makes use of the social analysis of
Herbert Marcuse. Marcuse's book *One-Dimensional Man* (1964) was
employed by Shaull to argue that technological society has fateful
consequences for the deepest needs of human persons. In a one-
dimensional society, the total orientation of the system toward
material progress is accompanied by conformity to the status quo, the
development of an unmanageable bureaucracy, and an overall
reduction in human freedom.

> . . . advanced technology, together with the ideological *ethos* accompany-
> ing it, is producing a system which tends to be totalitarian. The
> development of ever larger economic and political units, together with the
> integration of the economic and political orders, create a society in which

---

[29]See, for example, Shaull's extensive use of van Leeuwen's book
Christianity in World History (1964) in "The Christian World Mission in a
Technological Era," *Ec R* 17 (July 1965):205-218.

[30]Richard Shaull, "Revolution: Heritage and Contemporary Option" in
Carl Oglesby and Richard Shaull, *Containment and Change* (New York:
Macmillan, 1967), p. 179.

certain material needs of a large percentage of the people are met, but they have no significant opportunity to participate in the decisions regarding their own future. The system not only has tremendous power but it also reduces to ineffectiveness those forces which might otherwise bring constant pressure for social transformation.[31]

The emergence of a one-dimensional technological society has had, according to Shaull, disastrous implications both for the continued exploitation of the poor in the underdeveloped world and for the loss of meaning sensed within the developed world, especially among the younger generation.[32] For this reason, contemporary discernment of what God is doing in the world to make and to keep life human, turns Shaull's attention to the need for resistance to these totalitarian trends. Revolutionary strategies become essential.

Within the historical process there exist two competing tendencies: the first toward autocracy and the attainment of total systems, the second the revolutionary tendency toward social change.[33] It is the authentic contribution of the revolutionary impulse to counter, temper, and humanize the tendency toward autocracy which in recent times manifests itself in the form of a one-dimensional technocracy. By *revolution* Shaull thus means the impulse and pressure toward radical social change. Therefore he speaks of the need for "permanent revolution."

> Instead of *total* revolution in the sense of a head-on assault on the total structure of the established order, we can work for *permanent* revolution by which the entire structure is confronted by an increasing number of challenges at those points where changes are most imperative. Our goal is not primarily that of overthrowing the present structures but rather of forcing them to be more open and flexible, and to respond to new problems in more creative ways.[34]

The strategy for such a permanent revolution Shaull describes as the "*political equivalent to guerilla warfare.*"[35] By this he means political pressure on the part of numerous small groups of individuals both to provoke social transformation and to awaken the masses to the need for social change.[36]

---

[31]Shaull, "The Revolutionary Challenge to Church and Theology," pp. 474-475.

[32]Shaull, "Revolutionary Change in Theological Perspective," pp. 24-25.

[33]See Shaull, "Revolution: Heritage and Contemporary Option," pp. 203-208.

[34]Ibid., p. 238.

[35]Ibid., p. 239.

[36]See ibid., pp. 239-243.

The ambiguity of Shaull's understanding of revolution becomes most acute when he addresses the question of *violence* as a means of social change. Shaull does not himself so much advocate the choice of violence as a means of social change as argue that violence will inevitably be employed when change by other means has been stifled. In his reading of history Shaull observes, with reference to the view of Rosenstock-Huessey, "that the history of the West can only be understood as the history of revolutions."[37] The ultimate responsibility for the choice of violence rests with those who hold power and can therefore choose to allow change to take place by other means. Shaull is, however, most sober about the willingness of governments to permit change by peaceful means.

> . . . we will recognize that at certain times and places the introduction of incoherence and violence is essential. Admittedly, this is a risky business, something to be undertaken with fear and trembling. But . . . we can perceive that upheavals which all but wreck the societies in which they occur are often the occasion for major advances of civilization.[38]

The extreme ambiguity of Shaull's position becomes most clear in this quote. On the one hand, history is understood to progress through revolution—and by violent revolution if necessary. On the other hand, violence is abhorrent to the Christian consciousness. It is no wonder that Shaull, on the basis of his understanding of history, leaves the question of violence clouded in ambiguity, preferring to search for a "political equivalent to guerrilla warfare" while at the same time leaving open the possibility of the use of violence when "absolutely necessary."[39]

The connecting link between the Christian faith and the need for permanent revolution in society Shaull locates in a new form for the church. Just as the pressure for change in society is to be exerted by "small nuclei with revolutionary objectives"[40] so also the *form of the church* which corresponds most adequately to the demands of the present historical moment takes the shape of *small groups oriented toward achieving social change.* Throughout his writings Shaull

---

[37]Richard Shaull, "A Theological Perspective on Human Liberation," Chapter 3 in H. Wendland, ed., *When All Else Fails: Christian Arguments on Violent Revolution* (Philadelphia: Pilgrim Press, 1970), p. 56.

[38]Richard Shaull, "The Christian in the Vortex of Revolution," in Thomas F. O'Meara and Donald M. Weisser, eds., *Projections* (New York: Doubleday, 1970), pp. 64-65.

[39]See the discussion in Shaull, "The Revolutionary Challenge to Church and Theology," pp. 474-475.

[40]Ibid., p. 475.

repeatedly challenges the institutional church to develop such new forms in order to be responsive to the revolutionary demands of the present.

> Any hope for a significant Christian contribution to the revolutionary struggles going on around the world will depend, I believe, on the emergence of new forms of Christian community on the front lines of revolution. Such groups can have no pretension of being political movements. . . . But they can offer the context for a continual running conversation between our theological and ethical heritage and the major human issues that arise in the attempt to transform society. [41]

The precedents upon which Shaull draws in proposing this new form of church can be found both within the worker-priest model originally developed in France and his own experiences with small groups of students in Brazil as part of the Student Christian Movement.[42] In such groups Christ's presence in the world can be experienced in a new way: first, as Christ makes himself known "in the midst of those who are hungry and exploited" and, second within the community itself.[43] Shaull also saw the counterculture movement of the late sixties in its search for life in communes as a sign of the need for new forms of social existence.[44] One of the most explicit descriptions of this new form of church given by Shaull is the following:

> Such groups may take shape around some aspect of the present revolution, of the struggle for national development, or of political action. They may be composed of those in the same profession or in a variety of fields of work who are concerned about the concrete form of Christian presence in their work. They may be temporary groups that come into existence in order to study a specific problem and discover ways of meeting it.
>
> What is important here is that each group be composed of those who accept a specific ministry in a specific place. It must be concerned about relating the Christian faith to its problem and about developing the type of pastoral community that will sustain them in their efforts. The exact shape of such a koinonia will be discovered as experimentation takes place along the road.[45]

---

[41] Shaull, "Revolution: Heritage and Contemporary Option," p. 247.

[42] See Richard Shaull, "The New Challenge Before the Younger Churches," Chapter 14 in Edwin H. Rian, ed., *Christianity and World Revolution* (New York: Harper & Row, 1963), p. 203.

[43] Ibid., p. 204.

[44] Cf. Richard Shaull, "The End of the Road and a New Beginning," in John C. Raines and Thomas Dean, eds., *Marxism and Radical Religion. Essays Toward a Revolutionary Humanism* (Philadelphia: Temple University Press, 1970), pp. 44-46.

[45] Richard Shaull, "Crisis in the Young Churches," *World Encounter* 6 (Oct. 1968):11.

In his effort to communicate a vision for this new form of community, Shaull also turns to the sectarian tradition for precedents.[46]

The last major theme to be mentioned in discussing Shaull's thought during this period is his *reevaluation of the definition and task of theology.* In light of Shaull's understanding of contemporary history and the need for the church to partake in the revolutionary movements of the present, it follows that his understanding of theology also undergoes significant revision.

> For this to happen would require something of a revolution in the life and work of the theologian himself. By this I mean several things: the willingness to do theology in the midst of revolutionary praxis; the experience on the part of the theologian of a real *exodus* and *exile* in relation to the prevailing culture and dominant social system; a rich knowledge of our theological heritage combined with a full awareness of the bankruptcy of its traditional terms and systems and of the need for the creation of new paradigms; most important of all, perhaps, a willingness to dare to allow dead theological systems to be buried, to stand before the world empty-handed, and to expect a theological resurrection.[47]

The model of an academic or professional theologian is cast aside. Instead the theologian is envisioned as an active participant in the revolutionary ferment.

In a parallel way, the task of theological education becomes that of preparing ministers for engagement in the struggle for social change and not "to prepare ministers as middle-class professionals with the expectations of status, economic rewards and professional role that go with this way of life."[48] Theologians and theological institutions are both called to a radical turn from old to new models if they are to keep pace with the revolutionary challenge of the present.

Shaull's reevaluation of the theological task also entails a *rethinking of the relationship between theology and ideology.* In order to contribute to the process of social transformation, theology must begin to take on the characteristics of an ideology. By ideology Shaull does not mean a total view of reality which has been assumed uncritically. Rather Shaull means by ideology a critically appropriated point of view in the service of social change.

> This is precisely what ideology is all about. It is essentially historical reason, a way of analyzing and interpreting from a situation of

---

[46]Cf. Richard Shaull, "A New Look at the Sectarian Option," *Student World* 61 (1968):294-299.

[47]Shaull, "The Christian in the Vortex of Revolution," pp. 55-56.

[48]Richard Shaull, "The Challenge to the Seminary," *Chr Cris* 29 (Apr. 14, 1969):86.

involvement, the concrete cultural, social, and economic phenomena around us. . . . . [I]deological thought focuses attention on the concreteness of the present in the light of its future transformation. It therefore aims at the definition of goals and the determination of strategy for the achievement of social change.[49]

For theology itself this means taking the risk of making theological judgments about "the more immediate history of which we are a part" under the provision that they "must always remain tentative and open to constant revision."[50] The immediate participation of the theologian in the process of social change as proposed by Shaull means that:

Theological reflection on history will be most relevant to the ideological struggle when it is willing to become something of an ideology itself.[51]

The contrast with an academic model of theology whose ideals include historical objectivity and methodological neutrality is dramatic.

During the decade of the seventies Shaull underwent a period of increasing disillusionment over the ability of the present ecclesial and theological institutions to respond to contemporary challenges. Two images which appear in his writings at this time are especially indicative of Shaull's disenchantment. The first image is that of a "prisoner" trapped within immovable, unresponsive institutions.[52] The second image is that of "death and resurrection," that only after the death of old perspectives and structures can new values and social relationships arise which are more responsive to human needs.[53] A new inwardness appears in Shaull's thinking at this time which speaks of the need for grace in the face of frustration and the need for sharing personal faith stories with those who can offer sustaining community. Shaull also sounds an apocalyptic note as he speaks of the collapse of the American dream and points to the signs within American society which already witness to that collapse.[54] In the face of collapse Shaull would begin to establish a new vision for America's

---

[49]Richard Shaull, "The Rehabilitation of Ideology," in J. Rose and M. Ignatieff, eds., *Religion and International Affairs* (Toronto International Teach-In, 1968), p. 101.

[50]Shaull, "Revolution: Heritage and Contemporary Option," p. 227.

[51]Ibid., pp. 226-227.

[52]See Richard Shaull, "Grace: Power for Transformation," in Thomas M. McFadden, ed., *Liberation, Revolution and Freedom: Theological Perspectives* (New York: Seabury, 1975), pp. 76-82.

[53]See ibid., pp. 84-87 and Richard Shaull, "The Death and Resurrection of the American Dream" in Gustavo Gutierrez and Richard Shaull, *Liberation and Change* (Atlanta: John Knox, 1977), pp. 95-184.

[54]Cf. Shaull, "The Death and Resurrection of the American Dream," pp. 105-119 and 146-147.

future and a new proposal for an "evocative" theology to arise from the ashes of the old. People's faith stories, supportive communities, and a new Christian consciousness are among the characteristics which are to contribute to this new theological outlook. It was consistent with the pursuit of this new theology that Shaull resigned as professor at Princeton in 1980.

The similarities and differences which exist between the theological viewpoint of Shaull, which came to be known as the "theology of revolution," and the theology of liberation emerging in Latin America during the same period need to be carefully noted. This is especially true since the interpreters and critics of liberation theology have often confused the two, attributing to liberation theology the content of the theology of revolution without differentiation. This, however, has served to distort both the theology of liberation and the uniqueness of Shaull's own perspective. While it is vital to a correct understanding of Shaull to recognize the impulses which the Latin American context have given to his thought, the Latin American liberation theologians have developed their own viewpoint with arguments, emphases, and interpretations often quite different from Shaull's. The confusion of the two has led to a sometimes serious misunderstanding of liberation theology.

The similarities between the theology of Shaull and liberation theology become most clear in the essay, "Toward a Reformation of Objectives."[55] In Shaull's theology of God's ongoing work in history are echoes of the thought of Gustavo Gutierrez on themes such as the difference between a quantitative and a qualitative understanding of salvation or Gutierrez's affirmation that history is one.[56] Likewise there is a resemblance between Shaull's understanding of the function of the new form of the church in small groups and the reflections of Juan Luis Segundo on the church as a creative minority in his book *The Liberation of Theology*.[57] Shaull's ecclesiological emphasis on the importance of small groups might also suggest comparison with the emergence of the basic Christian communities within the Roman Catholic Church of Latin America.[58]   Other more occasional

---

[55]Richard Shaull, "Toward a Reformation of Objectives," in Norman A. Horner, ed., *Protestant Crosscurrents in Mission. The Ecumenical-Conservative Encounter* (Nashville: Abingdon, 1968), pp. 81-107.

[56]Cf. ibid., pp. 83-84 and 96-98, respectively.

[57]Cf. ibid., pp. 90-91.

[58]Cf. ibid., pp. 105-107.

references in Shaull's writings—to the motifs of liberation[59] and praxis,[60] to the need for a critique of the theory of development[61] and the need for structural change,[62] and to the usefulness of social analysis for theology[63]—each demonstrate that the direction of his thought runs parallel to that of liberation theology. This is also true of Shaull's criticisms of academic theology and his call for the development of a new theological paradigm.

Nevertheless, while the similarities in concern between the theology of Shaull and the theology of liberation are at times striking, the differences which exist between them should likewise be made clear.

1. Shaull's thought finds its point of departure in a comprehensive theology of God's ongoing work in history characterized by the attempt to obtain an overview of how historical change takes place. In examining the process of historical change "from above," as it were, historical tendencies, impulses, and categories are discerned by which contemporary history should, in its turn, also be interpreted.

Liberation theology begins, by contrast, not with a comprehensive theology of history and historical change but instead has as its primary point of departure the concrete historical context of the poor in Latin America. It then proceeds on the basis of its encounter with the actual poor to make proposals for social change. Liberation theology thus begins "from below" and not with a preconceived theology of history as does Shaull. To express this contrast another way, Shaull's theology approaches the need for historical change deductively from his theology of history whereas liberation theology advocates the need for social and political change inductively beginning with its experience of the poor. While the need for change is a conviction of both, the consequences of this fundamental difference in orientation are significant.

2. One of these consequences is contained in the contrast between the names borne by these two theologies—"theology of revolution" as compared to "theology of liberation." Shaull's understanding of history, deduced from an examination of the movement of history in

---

[59]Cf. Shaull, "Does Religion Demand Social Change?", pp. 9-10.

[60]Cf. Shaull, "The Challenge to the Seminary," p. 82.

[61]Cf. Shaull, "The End of the Road and a New Beginning," p. 28.

[62]Cf. Shaull, "A Theological Perspective on Human Liberation," p. 61.

[63]Cf. Richard Shaull, "Liberal and Radical in an Age of Discontinuity," *Chr Cris* 29 (Jan. 5, 1970):344.

the past, asserts that historical change inevitably takes place through the revolving process of ontocratic systems giving way to revolutionary upheaval followed by new attempts at ontocratic control. Thus revolution becomes a necessary part of the flow of history—a part of the flow of history with which Christians need to remain in tune. For this reason Shaull's thought rightly came to be characterized as a "theology of revolution."

For a theology of liberation, however, the option for or against revolution as a means of social change cannot be made apart from a careful analysis of the social, economic, and political situation in a particular place and time. The option for revolution is not necessitated by a fixed theology of history but rather a specific historical conclusion based on a critical reading of the historical moment. The importance which liberation theology gives to the social analysis of a particular context finds no comparable significance for Shaull. On the basis of its analysis of the particularities of Latin American society, politics, and history from the perspective of the poor, the Latin American theologians call first for liberation and not for revolution. That revolution may also prove necessary in attaining political and economic liberation is a subsequent decision and not a matter of theological necessity as it appears to be with Shaull.

3. The ambiguity of Shaull in relation to the question of the use of violence as a means of social change also needs to be compared to the elaborate analysis of violence on the part of the liberation theologians. The distinctions between institutional, counter, and repressive violence by liberation theologians move the entire discussion of this question to a new level of clarity. The diversity of opinion among liberation theologians on this question also indicates that they, in contrast to Shaull, tend to avoid categorical statements about the inherency of violent revolution to the movement of history.

4. In spite of the similarities between the small group ecclesiology advocated by Shaull and the basic Christian community movement in Latin America, here too, several contrasts need to be made. For Shaull, the small communities of Christians which he proposed must be seen in relation to his theology of history and historical change as a whole. Their very identity depends to a large degree on their self-understanding as contributors to the ongoing activity of God in the world. The small groups envisioned by Shaull need not bear any formal relationship to specific institutional churches. In fact, Shaull came to draw more and more on the sectarian tradition in describing

this ecclesiological form. Alienation from the institutional church comes almost to characterize the small groups described by Shaull, at least as a result of the failure of the institutional churches to develop this form.

In Latin America, however, the basic Christian communities did not originate as the result of a theology of history which calls them forth in order to exert pressure for historical change. Rather the communities arose to fulfil a specific need within the Roman Catholic Church there under the reality of immensely large parishes and a shortage of priests. They arose to provide a more intimate and socially relevant form of Christian community where the institutional structure has not been able to do so. The basic Christian communities have not arisen in alienation from the institutional church but rather have been nurtured by it.

5. A final point of comparison lies in the intentionally spiritual character of the base communities which is funded by a new interpretation of the biblical message. That the basic Christian communities, like the small groups of Shaull, seek to be active for social change is undeniable. But the spirituality of the basic Christian communities, the fact that the interpretation of the Bible is at the center of their existence, is an emphasis which remains for the most part implicit in Shaull's deliberations on the new form of the church in small groups.

Such distinctions between the theology of Shaull and liberation theology should prevent any simple equations between the two. Gutierrez and Segundo have, among others, been very concerned to make such differences clear lest their own position be misunderstood.[64] While Shaull has made his own real and lasting contribution to the development of liberation theology, especially among Protestants, and while his own theology was dramatically changed by his experiences in Latin America, his theological

---

[64]See the comments of Gustavo Gutierrez, "Liberation Praxis and Christian Faith," pp. 43-44. It is essential for Gutierrez that liberation theology arises *within* its own historical context and not be an *application* of theological reflection from the outside. Cf. also the criticism of Shaull's idea of revolution by Juan Luis Segundo, *The Liberation of Theology*, trans. John Drury (Maryknoll: Orbis, 1976), pp. 147-149, as well as the comments of Hugo Assmann, *Theology for a Nomad Church*, trans. Paul Burns (Maryknoll: Orbis, 1976), pp. 87-92, which further document the need for a clear distinction between the theology of revolution and liberation theology.

viewpoint must be seen as parallel to and not coinciding with the theology of liberation.

Shaull himself has indicated that he is aware of the differences between his own theological perspective, which continued to develop after he left Latin America to return to North America, and the theology of liberation.[65] In recent years he has attempted to more directly learn from and appropriate liberation theology and to articulate its implications for those in the North American context. His book *Heralds of a New Reformation* (1984) documents Shaull's most recent encounter with liberation theology as it has been formulated by its major proponents.

In this book Shaull once again returns to the interest which is discernible in his writings from beginning to end, i.e., to raise for North American church and society a challenge based upon Latin American reality. Three chapters are devoted to an exploration of the biblical themes—the exodus of Israel and its unique egalitarian social structure, the witness of the prophets to God's demand for justice, and Jesus understood as the Messiah of the poor—which undergird liberation theology. Likewise the base communities of Latin America are examined anew by Shaull on the basis of his own experiences and encounters with them. While traces of his own theology of history remain,[66] Shaull, more than ever before, explicitly takes up the themes and language of liberation theology itself in order to address an audience of North American Christians. Thus Shaull speaks of "looking at the world from below" as a challenge to "change values" or even "change sides." The events taking place in Nicaragua following its revolution serve as a frequent example of the direction which Shaull believes might lead to a better future for Latin America. Citations from the major liberation theologians punctuate the book.

In many ways it appears that with this book Shaull has come full circle. Having begun his career in Latin America and received impulses which shaped his later career as a professor in the United States, he has put his ear once again to the Latin American context to discern and interpret the latest developments in Latin American liberation theology as a challenge for North American church and society.

---

[65]See Shaull, "The Death and Resurrection of the American Dream," p. 180.

[66]Cf. especially Richard Shaull, *Heralds of a New Reformation*, Chapter 4, "When Empires Decline," pp. 58-75.

B. *James Cone's Black Theology of Liberation: From Confrontation Toward Convergence*

At first examination it would appear that the black theology of liberation, whose key proponent has been James H. Cone, has much in common with the Latin American theology of liberation. Yet in the interchange between these two theologies, that has not always been self-evident. It has required a lengthy and difficult process for these two theologies of liberation to move from mutual distrust and confrontation toward increasing commonality and even convergence.

James H. Cone has since 1969 taught theology at Union Theological Seminary in New York City, holding the position as Charles A. Briggs Professor of Systematic Theology. In the background of Cone's theological program stands the figure of Karl Barth whose theology of the Word of God in its threefold form—preached, written in Scripture, and revealed in Jesus Christ—has provided Cone with his basic theological orientation.[67]

The influence of Barth and other European theologians—Tillich, Bonhoeffer, Bultmann—on Cone's thought is most pronounced in his first two books, *Black Theology and Black Power* and *A Black Theology of Liberation*. However, from the very titles of those books it becomes clear that Cone has made a very precise use of these theologians in addressing theologically the situation of blacks in the United States. That situation is, according to Cone, the situation of black people in a racist society struggling to survive.

> Black theology must take seriously the reality of black people—their life of suffering and humiliation. This must be the point of departure of all God-talk which seeks to be black-talk. . . .
> The task of Black Theology, then, is to *analyze the black man's condition in the light of God's revelation in Jesus Christ with the purpose of creating a new understanding of black dignity among black people, and providing the necessary soul in that people, to destroy white racism.*[68]

The Black Power Movement as it developed in the U.S. in the late sixties provided a mighty impulse to this predominant emphasis in Cone's thought and even led Cone to the affirmation that "for twentieth-century America the message of Black Power is the message of Christ

---

[67]See James H. Cone, *My Soul Looks Back* (Nashville: Abingdon, 1982), pp. 80-83. This book provides an autobiographical overview of the entirety of Cone's life and theological career.

[68]James H. Cone, *Black Theology and Black Power* (New York: Seabury, 1969), p. 117.

himself."[69]   Black Power became for Cone the form of the gospel in the context of black oppression in the U.S.

In his early writings Cone juxtaposed these two concerns: a theology of the Word of God and the experience, history, and culture of black people in a racist society.[70] Responding to criticism that his first two books were more influenced by the former than the latter, Cone consciously sought in his next two books to further appropriate black experience as a source for his theology, especially as black experience can be discerned in the spirituals and blues sung by black people.[71]

In Cone's choice of themes for theological reflection and also in the content of those reflections, there appear some striking parallels with the central theological emphases of Latin American liberation theology. This can be briefly demonstrated by a few examples. First of all, the three central biblical paradigms undergirding Cone's theology are identical to those most prominent in Latin American liberation theology: the exodus of Israel from Egypt, the prophetic advocacy of social justice, and the good news to the poor in Jesus Christ.[72] Cone's thoroughgoing critique of traditional, academic, "white" theology in its ideals of neutrality and objectivity in favor of a theology which is passionate and committed to liberation is likewise reminiscent of similar critiques of Western theology made by Latin American theologians.[73]   Moreover, the reaction against such an understanding of the task of theology has led both black and Latin American liberation theology to be accused of being captive to an ideology alien to the Christian faith.[74]

---

[69]Ibid., p. 37. For an elaborate documentation of the relationship between the black power movement and black theology see Gayraud S. Wilmore and James H. Cone, eds., *Black Theology: A Documentary History, 1966-1979* (Maryknoll: Orbis, 1979), pp. 1-359. See also Gayraud S. Wilmore, *Black Religion and Black Radicalism. An Interpretation of the Religious History of Afro-American People*, 2nd ed. (Maryknoll: Orbis, 1983), pp. 192-219.

[70]Cf. James H. Cone, *A Black Theology of Liberation* (Philadelphia/New York: J. B. Lippincott, 1970), pp. 53-74.

[71]Cf. James H. Cone, *The Spirituals and the Blues: An Interpretation* (New York: Seabury, 1972) and *God of the Oppressed* (New York: Seabury, 1975), pp. 1-38.

[72]Cf. Cone, *Black Theology and Black Power*, pp. 44-45, *A Black Theology of Liberation*, pp. 18-20, and *God of the Oppressed*, pp. 63-81.

[73]Cf. Cone, *A Black Theology of Liberation*, pp. 34-53, and *God of the Oppressed*, pp. 39-61 and 82-83.

[74]For Cone's reply to this charge see *God of the Oppressed*, pp. 84-107.

Christology has also been a central theological topic for both of these liberation theologies with Jesus Christ interpreted in terms of liberator.[75] For both it is the historical Jesus and his proclamation of the kingdom of God to the poor which receives special, though not exclusive, attention. Other common themes include an emphasis on the corporate and structural dimensions of human sin[76] and comparable deliberations on the possible use of revolution and violence as means of accomplishing social change.[77] Even Cone's emphasis on a church which is involved in the struggle for liberation in the world[78] and on an eschatological orientation which is not an escape but an impetus to this struggle[79] find their parallels in the concern of Latin American liberation theology. While there are also differences in emphasis, for example, Cone's response to critics on the questions of the role of theodicy and reconciliation in his theology,[80] nevertheless the overwhelming impression in comparing these two liberation theologies is that of their affinity for one another. Nowhere does that become more apparent than in the very choice of the theme "liberation" as the organizing principle of each of these theologies.

Cone has written that both "black and Latin theologians began to use the term 'liberation' almost simultaneously but independently of each other."[81] Given their similar reading of the Bible as a message of God's liberation and a common commitment to the liberation of an oppressed community (i.e., blacks in the U.S. and the Latin American poor, respectively), the theme of liberation became the label chosen to characterize both of these movements.[82]

> Christian theology is a theology of liberation. It is *a rational study of the being of God in the world in light of the existential situation of an oppressed community, relating the forces of liberation to the essence of the gospel, which is Jesus Christ.*[83]

---

[75]Cf. Cone, *A Black Theology of Liberation*, pp. 197-227 and *God of the Oppressed*, pp. 108-137.

[76]See Cone, *A Black Theology of Liberation*, pp. 186-190.

[77]See Cone, *Black Theology and Black Power*, pp. 136-143 and *God of the Oppressed*, pp. 217-225.

[78]See Cone, *A Black Theology of Liberation*, pp. 228-238.

[79]See ibid., pp. 238-249 and *The Spirituals and the Blues*, pp. 86-107.

[80]Cf. Cone, *God of the Oppressed*, pp. 163-194 and 226-246, respectively, for these two issues.

[81]Cone, *My Soul Looks Back*, p. 103.

[82]Cf. Cone, *A Black Theology of Liberation*, pp. 11-12 and 17-30; and *God of the Oppressed*, esp. pp. 138-162.

[83]Cone, *A Black Theology of Liberation*, p. 17.

The theology of liberation attempts to reflect on the experience and meaning of the faith based on the commitment to abolish injustice and to build a new society; this theology must be verified by the practice of that commitment, by active, effective participation in the struggle which the exploited social classes have undertaken against their oppressors.[84]

The first of these quotes is taken from the black theologian of liberation, Cone, from a book published in 1970 and the second is a formulation of Gustavo Gutierrez of Peru published in Spanish in 1971. Both began virtually simultaneously, though independently, to rethink the Christian faith under the rubric liberation and in so doing crossed the threshold into a theology of advocacy on behalf of an oppressed people. Herein lies the ground for a tremendous sense of common cause which at the same time has paradoxically served as the basis for initial distrust and even confrontation between these two theologies.

The earliest direct encounter which has been documented between black theology and Latin American liberation theology took place in Geneva in May 1973 at a symposium on black theology and Latin American liberation theology under the auspices of the World Council of Churches.[85] Prior to this time the development of these theologies had taken place in virtual isolation from one another, apart from the possible awareness of some of the early writings by theologians in the other context.[86] At Geneva the symposium was designed to introduce black and Latin American liberation theologies to a predominantly European and North American audience. In the course of the discussion, however, it was the differences between these two theologies which came to be stressed rather than their common concerns. The mutual unfamiliarity with the situation of the other led to the discovery of the need for ongoing dialogue between black and Latin American theologians. During the symposium itself, however, a sense of "incommunication" between these two theologies emerged leaving many European and North American participants with the impression that irreconcilable differences existed between them. Among black

---

[84]Gustavo Gutierrez, *A Theology of Liberation. History, Politics, and Salvation*, trans. and eds. Caridad Inda and John Eagleson (Maryknoll: Orbis, 1973), p. 307.

[85]See James H. Cone, "From Geneva to Sao Paulo: A Dialogue between Black Theology and Latin American Liberation Theology," in Sergio Torres and John Eagleson, eds., *The Challenge of Basic Christian Communities*, trans. John Drury (Maryknoll: Orbis, 1981), pp. 266-267, for this and the following description of the Geneva symposium.

[86]See ibid., pp. 265-266.

and Latin American participants, by contrast, a primary insight was of the need for more dialogue between them.

The first "Theology in the Americas" conference held in Detroit in August 1975 would demonstrate how difficult this dialogue could become.[87] In part the difficulty lay in the emphasis given to the dialogue between Latin American theologians and white North American theologians in the preparation for the conference. Black theologians, especially in view of their experience in Geneva, strongly objected to this thrust, arguing for a more central role for black theology at the conference as exemplary of a North American theology done from the point of view of the oppressed. The conference itself took place, nevertheless, with a primary emphasis on the exchange between the Latin American theologians present and a predominantly white audience of theologians and church people.[88] The failure to sufficiently incorporate the viewpoint of black and other racial minorities into the structure of the conference led to deepening distrust and further "incommunication." The confrontational nature of the encounter between black and Latin American theologians became apparent not only at the formal conference sessions but also at a private caucus at which once again the differences in the two perspectives became highlighted at the expense of a recognition of their common concerns. In the words of Cone:

> Blacks came close to saying that the Latin Americans were white racists, and the Latin Americans accused blacks of being North American capitalists. . . . This late night discussion did more to alienate blacks and Latin Americans then any other encounter during our eight years of dialogue.[89]

In the eyes of many this Detroit conference marked the low point of misunderstanding and confrontation between black and Latin American liberation theologians.

---

[87]For the following description of the first Detroit conference see ibid., pp. 267-270.

[88]Materials from this conference are available in Sergio Torres and John Eagleson, eds., *Theology in the Americas* (Maryknoll: Orbis, 1976). Especially relevant regarding the interchange between black and Latin American liberation theology at the conference are the contributions of Herbert 0. Edwards, pp. 177-191; Manuel Febres, pp. 329-340; The Black Theology Panel, pp. 351-356; and Gregory Baum, pp. 408-410.

[89]Cone, "From Geneva to Sao Paulo," p. 269. Cone also refers in his footnote 12 to the more positive interpretation of this caucus given by Enrique Dussel. See ibid., p. 281.

What were the reasons for this distrust and confrontation in light of the many common theological concerns already indicated between these two liberation theologies? Besides the relative unfamiliarity of these theologians with each other, two central issues can be cited in order to explain their initial antipathy. The first and most important factor was the conflicting interpretations of the final cause of oppression. For the Latin Americans class analysis and an economic interpretation of oppression were central whereas for black theologians it was race analysis and a racial interpretation of oppression which were predominant. Especially at Detroit these two forms of analysis became established in opposition to one another setting aside all other reasons for mutual understanding. Gregory Baum describes the confrontation this way:

> The blacks felt that a class analysis is not enough. The name of the oppression under which they suffer is racism, and while racism is related to economic exploitation and class identification, it cannot be reduced to economic oppression. . . . The blacks feared, moreover, that arguments over the economic system might divide the black community and weaken them in the face of the white majority. For the blacks the primary enemy is racism; and since the Latin Americans defined as principal enemy the economic imperialism of the Northern nations, especially the U.S., the blacks could not declare themselves in solidarity with them.[90]

From the side of the Latin Americans black theology's use of the symbol "black" to describe God and Christ was symptomatic of that which divided them.[91] At Detroit the crucial importance of the differences between race and class analysis came to the fore and became the focal point for subsequent discussion.

The second reason for the initial confrontation between these two theologies, not unrelated to the first, was the different weight which they gave to social analysis. For Latin American liberation theology social analysis in the form of a critique of developmentalism and an affirmation of dependency theory occupied an integral part in its methodology. For black theology, however, social analysis through the use of comparable social scientific and economic theories played a much more limited role.[92] Instead black theology sought to draw upon

---

[90]Gregory Baum, "The Christian Left at Detroit," in Torres and Eagleson, eds., *Theology in the Americas*, pp. 409-410.

[91]Cf. The Black Theology Panel, "Excerpts from the Discussion," in Torres and Eagleson, eds., *Theology in the Americas*, pp. 353-354.

[92]For the following see James H. Cone, *For My People. Black Theology and the Black Church* (Maryknoll: Orbis, 1984), pp. 88-96 and James H. Cone,

"black experience" in a less analytical way. Cone writes in retrospect on this issue:

> We were naive, because our analysis of the problem was too superficial and did not take into consideration the links between racism, capitalism, and imperialism, on the one hand, and theology and the church on the other. . . . If we had used the tools of the social sciences and had given due recognition to the Christian doctrine of sin, then it is unlikely that we would have placed such inordinate dependence on the methodology of moral suasion.[93]

Though Cone also mentions that black theology is primarily Protestant in origin while Latin American liberation theology is predominantly Roman Catholic, as well as the fact that there exists a significant difference in revolutionary consciousness in the two contexts of North and Latin America, it is the two previously mentioned reasons which appear as primary causes for the initial confrontation between black and Latin American liberation theologies.

Since the Detroit conference, through many opportunities for ongoing contact and dialogue, a process of mutual convergence has begun between the position of Cone and that of Latin American liberation theology. On the primary point of contention between race and class analysis, that has meant a broadening on both sides toward an incorporation of the other's concern. Cone notes that for him the mediation of both Sergio Torres and Gustavo Gutierrez was crucial in keeping the lines of communication open subsequent to the first Detroit conference.[94] Contact with Gutierrez was enhanced when he served as visiting professor at Union Theological Seminary in 1976, whereas Torres, as director of Theology in the Americas (TIA), helped reorganize the various projects of TIA to expand the roles of the various racial minorities. Cone became an active participant in the programs of the reorganized TIA. He cites conferences in Atlanta in August 1977 and Mexico City in October 1977 as key moments for a new appreciation of Latin American liberation theology by black theology and vice versa.

> We must seek ways of expressing our solidarity with the poor throughout the world. Indeed we can no longer speak of racism as if it is the only problem in the United States and the world. For if the black poor in the

---

"Introduction," in Wilmore and Cone, eds., *Black Theology. A Documentary History, 1966-1979*, p. 455.

[93]Cone, *For My People*, p. 88.

[94]Cone, "From Geneva to Sao Paulo," in Torres and Eagleson, eds., *The Challenge of Basic Christian Communities*, pp. 270-271.

154   Orthopraxis or Heresy

United States are to achieve freedom, the achievement will take place only in solidarity with other poor people in the U.S. and the world context.[95] While Cone began at this time to raise the issue of socialism versus capitalism and to suggest the usefulness of Marxism as a tool of social analysis, among Latin Americans the factor of racial injustice began to receive more serious consideration.

In addition to Cone's continued participation in the Black Theology Project of TIA, his involvement in the Ecumenical Association of Third World Theologians (EATWOT) has also been vital to the growing convergence between the concerns of his black liberation theology and the Latin American theology of liberation. This organization, founded in 1976, has brought together for numerous conferences theologians from throughout Asia, Africa, and Latin America, and has come to also include North American blacks within its membership (in spite of certain initial resistance from some Latin Americans).[96] Conferences of EATWOT have been held thus far in Dar es Salaam, Tanzania (1976); Accra, Ghana (1977); Wennappuwa, Sri Lanka (1979); Sao Paulo, Brazil (1980); New Delhi, India (1981); and Geneva, Switzerland (1983). Through these conferences and other related meetings,[97] a basis has been established for increased understanding not only between black theologians from North America and Latin American theologians but the dialogue has also been broadened to include Asian and African points of view. This process has served to temper the tendency to absolutize any single viewpoint and to encourage the search for factors of shared social and theological interest. That these encounters have significantly altered the position of black liberation theology in general and Cone's theology in particular can be seen both from the place given to "Black Theology and Third World Theologies" in Wilmore and Cone's *Black Theology. A Documentary History, 1966-1979*[98] and to the new emphases emerging in Cone's most recent writings.

---

[95] Ibid., p. 271.

[96] For the following cf. ibid., pp. 272-279.

[97] Cone also mentions specifically a meeting held at Mantanzas, Cuba in February-March 1979 as a key moment in this entire process. Cf. ibid., pp. 274-275 and Cone, "Introduction," in Wilmore and Cone, eds., *Black Theology. A Documentary History, 1966-1979*, pp. 452-453.

[98] Cf. the section "Black Theology and Third World Theologies," in Wilmore and Cone, eds., *Black Theology. A Documentary History, 1966-1979*, pp. 445-608, which comprises one quarter of the entire volume.

In his book *For My People. Black Theology and the Black Church* (1984), Cone develops at length the new themes which began to appear in his thought as early as 1977 in response to the challenges of Third World Theology in general and Latin American liberation theology in particular. Cone has come to the firm conviction of the need for unity between black North Americans and the people of the Third World.[99] To this end he sees the need for the establishment of an ecumenical organization among U.S. blacks that can serve as a liaison with corresponding organizations in the Third World. Cone would have black churches become aware of the history, publications, and central theological concerns of the EATWOT both because of the importance of being linked with others who are involved in the common struggle for liberation and also in order to be challenged by the analysis which others have made of the causes of poverty on a global scale, especially the critique of international capitalism.

As Cone describes the theological method which undergirds both black and Third World theology, the influence of his encounter with Latin American liberation theology becomes most clear.[100] Cone has been prompted by this encounter to articulate his theological method in terms that are particularly reminiscent of the formulations of Gustavo Gutierrez. Thus Cone speaks of "both a religio-cultural affirmation and a political commitment" as the "first act" of "doing theology." "Praxis" in this way "comes before theology in any formal sense." Theology begins with this prior commitment and enters into "critical reflection" beginning with "concrete historical events." "*Orthopraxis* in contrast to orthodoxy" has become the final "criterion of theology."

Cone has, in addition, begun to explicitly articulate several of the themes shared in common between his black theology and Latin American and other Third World theologies. The common critique of Western academic theology, a shared rereading of the Bible from the point of view of the poor, and a mutual commitment to praxis as the final norm of theology are no longer just an implicit basis for unity but are rather recognized and stated explicitly.

Even more, Cone has been prompted by Latin American liberation theology to take up Marxism as a tool for social analysis and to apply it

---

[99]For the following see Cone, *For My People*, pp. 140-147 and 153-156.

[100]For the following see ibid., pp. 147-153. The cited references are from pages 147-148.

to the situation of North American blacks.[101]   Realizing the
unfamiliarity of North American black churches with Marxism as
well as the North American "taboo" on socialism (R. Bellah) and
Marxist analysis, Cone nevertheless asserts that a reappraisal of
Marx's thought can provide new impulses to black theology. Cone
finds Marx's critique of religion and his insistence upon praxis as
valid insights which can serve to critique any possible ideological role
played by white American churches.

> When North American blacks and Third World peoples evaluate
> Marxism in the light of the behavior of white American churches, they
> usually side with Marx and against white Christianity. Marxism is
> viewed as an internal critique of Euro-American churches, whose "gos-
> pel" has served as an opium of the people in its support of the status quo.[102]

According to Cone, religion which does not manifest itself in
liberating praxis for the poor rightly falls under Marx's critique of
religion.

Not only is the importance of Marx's critique of religion for black
churches emphasized by Cone, but also Marxism's critique of
capitalism.[103] Once again Cone is cognizant of what he describes as
"the pervasive and irrational anticommunism of the churches" in the
U.S. which inhibits discourse about "any form of socialism."[104] Still
Cone has come to see in Marxism a critique of capitalistic values and a
method of social analysis which can help to disclose the dynamic of
oppression hidden in capitalism. Like Latin American liberation
theologians, Cone seeks to employ Marxism critically. For example,
he rejects Marx's atheism, Marxism as a total philosophy which is
opposed to Christian faith, and the abuses of European systems which
claim to be Marxist. Instead Cone looks to the Third World for a model
where "they are now remaking Marxism in the light of their own
history and culture."[105]

The impact and influence of Cone's encounter with Latin
American and other Third World theologies has been most
significant. The concentrated focus on the specific dilemmas of black
people in the U.S. in his early writings has not been abandoned so
much as broadened to encompass the situation of the poor throughout the

---

[101]For the following cf. Chapter IX, "Black Christians and Marxism," in
ibid., pp. 175-188.

[102]Ibid., p. 183.

[103]For the following cf. ibid., pp. 184-188.

[104]Ibid., p. 185.

[105]Ibid., p. 187.

world. The symbol of a black God and a black Christ have in this way become transformed into the God of the poor and Jesus the Messiah of the poor. The original intention of these symbols has not been so much abandoned as broadened to be inclusive of the poor throughout the world. Cone continues to challenge other Third World theologians to take more seriously a racial analysis of their own contexts. But he himself now has come to affirm that the solidarity of black Christians in the U.S. with Christians throughout the Third World is essential. Race analysis versus class analysis are in this way not exclusive alternatives but two equally necessary aspects of any adequate social analysis.[106]

The shift in Cone's thought from confrontation with Latin American liberation theology toward a convergence with its main concerns is well summarized as he looks toward the future of black theology and asks the question, "Where do we go from here?" While continuing to ground his theology on the experience, history, and culture of black people, a new analysis of the relationship between black people in the U.S. and the poor throughout the world has led Cone to an increasing convergence with the concerns of Third World people, especially as these concerns have been articulated by the Latin American theology of liberation. In listing six elements which he considers necessary for shaping the vision of black theology's future, the final three bear directly upon the convergence of Cone's thought with Latin American liberation theology.

> 4. The new social order should be democratic and socialist, including a Marxist critique of monopoly capitalism. . . .
>
> 5. The new black perspective must be a global vision that includes the struggles of the poor in the Third World. African-Americans are linked in countless ways with their brothers and sisters in Africa, the Caribbean, Latin America, Asia, and the Pacific. . . . There will be no freedom for anybody until all are set free.
>
> 6. Any new vision of a just social order must affirm the best in black religion and embrace the creative elements in the religions of the poor who are struggling for freedom throughout the globe. Any social order that excludes religion or ignores it is doomed to failure from the start.[107]

Through these affirmations of Cone, black and Latin American liberation theologies attain a common vision which leaves behind the suspicion and misunderstanding which marked their earliest encounters.

---

[106]Cf. Cone, "From Geneva to Sao Paulo," p. 279.

[107]Cone, *For My People*, p. 204.

C. Frederick Herzog: God's Liberating Word for a Justice Church

One of the first North Americans to begin formulating a response to the theology of liberation was Frederick Herzog. As member of the theological faculty at the Duke University Divinity School since 1960 and as one active on a variety of theological commissions for both the World Council of Churches and his own United Church of Christ, Herzog has provided a unique response initially to black but also subsequently to Latin American liberation theology. Herzog has understood the issues raised by these liberation theologies as an occasion for developing a liberation theology appropriate to the particularities of his own North American context.

Theological influences upon Herzog include a host of twentieth-century thinkers among whom Karl Barth, Rudolf Bultmann (as well as Bultmann's students who further developed his thought in the direction of a "new hermeneutic"), and, above all, Paul Lehmann deserve special mention.[108] These influences become important for understanding the unique thrust of Herzog's response to liberation theology which has insisted upon the priority of God as the agent of liberation especially as God has spoken the Word of liberation in Jesus Christ. This emphasis has perhaps characterized Herzog's response to liberation theology more than any other. At the same time Herzog has proceeded from this central theological point to examine what God's Word of liberation also means for the church within a particular context. Increasingly in his recent writings and in more immediate interaction with Latin American liberation thought, Herzog has begun to reflect at greater length on the political and ecclesial mediations of liberation theology. The church thus becomes for him a "justice church," living in obedience to God's Word in the midst of the contingencies of history in a particular time and place.

Already in his book *Understanding God. The Key Issue in Present-Day Protestant Thought* (1966), Herzog pursued a new method for systematic theology, a concern which ties his earliest writings to his most recent ones.[109] In search of a valid option for contemporary

---

[108]Herzog himself studied theology at Bonn and Basel, and received his doctoral degree from Princeton Theological Seminary under Paul Lehmann.

[109]See Frederick Herzog, *Understanding God. The Key Issue in Present-Day Protestant Theology* (New York: Charles Scribner's Sons, 1966), pp. 11-15. Cf. also Frederick Herzog, *Justice Church. The New Function of the Church in*

theological method, the "new quest for God" undertaken in recent theology was understood by Herzog to have arrived at an "ontological aporia" just as the research undertaken to discover the historical Jesus proved to be an "historical aporia" from the perspective of systematic theology.[110] One constructive result emerging from these approaches was, however, the development of new insights into the meaning of theological hermeneutic.[111] Herzog found in the ontology of language—fundamental to reflections of such theologians as Ebeling and Fuchs on the new hermeneutic—a key to overcoming both the ontological and historical aporias confronting systematic theology in the present. These aporias have been, in effect, overcome from the side of God in the Word which has been spoken by God in Christ.

> In the primordial Word God himself is present as he was present in Jesus. His presence with man is Wordpresence. The embodiment of God's Wordpresence in the incarnation is the fulfillment of man's quest for the presence of meaning in his life. Understanding in this respect is tied to certain texts, the texts of the Bible. After the incarnation God's Wordpresence became concrete once more in the biblical word.[112]

In the Word God has made himself present in a way which answers both the ontological and the historical questions of contemporary systematic theology.

In *Understanding God* Herzog developed three additional and related themes which are significant in light of his subsequent interest in liberation theology. First, Herzog discovered in the Fourth Gospel a biblical source well-suited to both his formal concern for theological method as well as his material concern for the political implications of the gospel.[113] The coupling of a Logos Christology with an emphasis upon the diakonic deeds of Jesus in the Gospel of John provided Herzog with a theologically charged resource for addressing these two concerns. The importance of the Fourth Gospel for the response of Herzog to liberation theology becomes plain in his next major work, *Liberation Theology: Liberation in the Light of the Fourth Gospel* (1972).

North American Christianity (Maryknoll: Orbis, 1980), p. xiii, where he writes: "The principal thrust of the book is the attempt to develop a new theological method that can overcome the systems of a controlling reason still prevalent in the church."

[110]See Frederick Herzog, *Understanding God*, esp. pp. 40-43 and 60-64.

[111]For the following cf. ibid., pp. 14-15 and 89-109.

[112]Ibid., p. 104.

[113]For the following cf. ibid., pp. 65-88.

A second theme which received prominence in the last chapters of *Understanding God* is Herzog's emphasis on the ethical and political dimensions of the Word in the face of contemporary reality.

> The communal nature of man is threatened most severely today in the realm of politics, local, national and international. Since God in his Wordpresence shares himself with all men, proclamation cannot but seek to draw out the creative possibilities this presence affords for man's social relationships.[114]

Most immediately for Herzog, the Word of God (which is in itself a "word-deed") has a political application within the context of race relations in the South of the U.S., although other ethical applications also remain within view.[115] Herzog notes that taking seriously the political implications of the Word would mean significantly revising the current approach to the teaching of theology.[116]

The third theme which in effect sums up the entire book is Herzog's proposal of a bi-polar method for systematic theology.

> Systematic theology is the critical restatement of the Gospel for today with reference to the interpretation of the Gospel in the history of dogma. It is bi-polar. As a restatement of the Gospel it is concerned with the New Testament texts reflecting the Gospel, just as much as is exegesis. But it has to consider in equal measure the contemporary factor. Here the problem of translation is introduced.[117]

Herzog concludes that systematic theology is essentially hermeneutic, i.e., the translation of God's Word into the contemporary context with all the political consequences implied therein. On the basis of this understanding of the method of systematic theology, Herzog's response to liberation theology becomes clarified. He is attracted to liberation theology as a theology which expresses the most urgent issues within contemporary life. These issues are, however, to be addressed on the basis of the Word of God already spoken in Jesus Christ and the Bible which are only in need of translation into contemporary idiom and action.

Keeping in mind this bi-polar approach to systematic theology, Herzog's earliest responses to liberation theology decidedly place their emphasis on the fact that it is *God* who is the one who through his Word works liberation. In one of the first North American articles explicitly exploring a "theology of liberation," Herzog wrote:

---

[114]Ibid., p. 109.

[115]See ibid., pp. 119-122.

[116]See ibid., pp. 128-129.

[117]Ibid., p. 130.

And yet the emphasis on the Word—as much as it may stand in need of some American corrective—challenges the one-dimensional understanding of attaining God's kingdom on earth through human effort. The Word does not deny that God's kingdom comes to this world. But it does deny that it comes through human effort alone. It liberates man from the illusion that everything depends on him. It calls attention to two dimensions. God's initiative as well as man's response.[118]

This emphasis on God as the primary agent of liberation is reechoed throughout Herzog's writings from this period.[119] This emphasis does not, however, prevent Herzog from drawing implications from God's liberating Word for a "liberated theology, a theology in which the initiative and power of God's liberation unite the theologian more fully with the lot of the disadvantaged."[120]

In his early writings dealing with liberation theology, Herzog's primary orientation was not toward Latin American theology of liberation but rather toward European political theology and the black theology of liberation.[121]   Nowhere in his writings is the connection with black liberation theology so apparent as in his 1972 theological commentary on the gospel of John entitled *Liberation Theology*. In this volume Herzog experimented with the medium of theological commentary after the genre of Karl Barth's *The Epistle to the Romans* as a form for systematic theology. For Herzog, however, the primary interlocutor was understood to be "White Christian America" which in the context of the contemporary racial struggle needed "to be confronted point-blank with the biblical Word."[122] Only an argument based on the biblical Word could, according to Herzog, rise above "the morass of complete subjectivity and privacy" which currently was seen to cloud the vision of white Christianity.[123] To this end the gospel of John was

---

[118]Frederick Herzog, "Theology of Liberation," *Continuum* 7 (Winter 1970): 521.

[119]See Frederick Herzog, "God, Evil, and Revolution," *J Rel Thot* 25, No. 2 (1968-69):5-28, especially his reference's to Shaull and Lehmann and the emphasis on "God's revolution," pp. 20-24. Cf. also Frederick Herzog, ed., *Theology of the Liberating Word* (Nashville: Abingdon, 1971), especially Herzog's "Introduction: A New Church Conflict?" pp. 11-24, where he raises up the importance of "the liberating Word" as the foundation for any participation by the church in contemporary liberation movements.

[120]Herzog, "Theology of Liberation," p. 524.

[121]Cf. Frederick Herzog, "Political Theology," *Chr Cent* 86 (July 23, 1969): 975-978 and also the footnote references in "Theology of Liberation."

[122]Frederick Herzog, *Liberation Theology: Liberation in the Light of the Fourth Gospel* (New York: Seabury, 1972), p. viii.

[123]Ibid., p. ix.

perfectly matched both to Herzog's concern for theological method and his concern for contemporary relevance. "The Fourth Gospel" thus comes to function "as interpretive key to liberation history."[124]

Herzog begins the introduction to his book with an argument for the need of contemporary theology to "begin with an identification with the wretched of the earth"[125] which issues in a liberation theology over against the academic God-talk of liberal theology whose theological starting point is "the Cartesian self," i.e., the private, bourgeois, white self.[126] By "thinking black" (i.e., from the point of view of the oppressed) in proceeding to interpret the Bible, Herzog is convinced that a breakthrough is possible from liberal theology which can lend impetus to the creation of a "liberation church." To this end Herzog proceeds to translate, reread, and interpret the Fourth Gospel in order to allow God's living Word of liberation to address the racial struggle.

Herzog divides his commentary into six parts and provides an original translation and theological commentary on the successive texts of John's gospel. In this commentary the work of Jesus is interpreted in terms of liberation. Jesus' cleansing of the temple indicates his challenge to the status quo of his time. Nicodemus' query about becoming born again is rendered by Herzog as "becoming black" in accordance with Jesus' own blackness (or redness). The opponents of Jesus in the gospel of John are transformed into organization churchmen. Jesus comes into the world bringing freedom, freedom from privatism (cf. Jesus' discourse on freedom with the Jews), from the blindness of racism and militarism (cf. healing of blind man), from bondage to the forces of death (cf. raising of Lazarus). Those who recognize God's unconcealment in Christ become participants in the way of love, servanthood, and discipleship within the liberation church. They are promised the Spirit who will continue to counsel them in the way of resistance to the world and positive involvement in the cause of liberation in the world. The final demonstration of the way of liberation is witnessed in the passion of Jesus. Jesus, after resisting every temptation to turn to a form of self-liberation, fulfilled in his crucifixion all that is necessary for human liberation. As the resurrected Christ, Jesus lives again to commission

[124]Ibid.

[125]Ibid., p. 2.

[126]For the following cf. ibid., pp. 10-17. Herzog also states in this context that the theological starting point of Schleiermacher is that of the Cartesian self.

and empower his disciples to carry on his liberating work, a work which continues throughout history.

Throughout Herzog's commentary there occur allusions to the formulations of thinkers as varied as Soren Kierkegaard, Karl Barth, Martin Heidegger, Rudolf Bultmann, and James Cone. Together their thoughts contribute to "an experiment in a new form of Christian theology"[127] which emphasizes the political implications of John's gospel with special reference to the need for black liberation. At the close of the volume, Herzog raises once more his central theological point. While not denying the need for change in the structures which inhibit the attainment of justice in society, the primary theological task is a different one: to point to the one who is the final source of liberation.

> Initially...liberation theology is interested in radically witnessing to the power of liberation, the grounds on which the goals of liberation can be tackled sanely, with a measure of effectiveness. This calls for stressing the core point of the Fourth Gospel once more: *we* cannot generate the power of liberation—God liberates.[128]

All Christian involvement in liberation movements follows from the prior fact of God's liberation.

The publication of *Liberation Theology* occasioned numerous responses including "The Kearns Seminar on *Liberation Theology*" held at Duke University in March 1973.[129] In his response to the papers delivered at this seminar, Herzog emphasized the importance of context for liberation theology and explained how it is the particularly Southern (U.S.) context which was the backdrop for his book.[130] Interestingly, Herzog also made passing reference to his preference for socialism in this response.

In his next publications, Herzog continued to develop his critique of white, liberal theology and further stressed the necessity of taking one's own context seriously as the proper arena for theology.[131] In the

---

[127]Ibid., p. 254.

[128]Ibid., p. 265.

[129]See "The Kearns Seminar on *Liberation Theology*," *Duke Div R* 38 (Fall 1973):125-150, with contributions by Frederick Herzog, Susan H. Lindley, George Lea Harper, Robert T. Osborn, and James L. Price.

[130]Frederick Herzog, "The Burden of Southern Theology: A Response," *Duke Div R* 38 (Fall 1973):151-170. The reference to socialism appears on p. 161.

[131]Cf. Frederick Herzog, "The Liberation of White Theology," *Chr Cent* 91 (Mar. 20, 1974):316-319; "Liberation Theology or Culture Religion," *Union S Q R* 29 (1974):233-244; "Liberation Theology Begins at Home," *Chr Cris* 34 (May 13, 1974):94-98; "Responsible Theology," in James Wm. McClendon, Jr., ed.,

United States this means taking seriously the issue of black-white relations before all other issues, a goal toward which Herzog himself continued to strive.[132] At times this led Herzog to take a critical stance toward Latin American liberation theology as a political diversion from the centrality of one's own North American context. Herzog thus referred to the danger of taking "flights into the Third World" and insisted on the priority of a liberation theology which "begins at home."[133]

> The primary context for theological reflection in the U.S. is not the Third World but the black-white confrontation in our own world.[134]

In the same vein Herzog, in dependence on Richard John Neuhaus, at one point even came to criticize the theology of Gustavo Gutierrez as a theology of revolution (!) which is distanced from the North American context and which stresses human liberation at the expense of the liberation which only God can bring.[135]

Up to 1975 the references to Latin American liberation theology in the writings of Herzog are rather sparse and critical insofar as the Latin American context is seen as a way of avoiding more immediate issues in the North American context. While his interpretation of the Bible as a living Word of God and his promoting of liberation as the central theological paradigm would appear to offer much in common with the thought of the Latin American liberation theologians, it was only with his participation in the first Theology in the Americas conference at Detroit in 1975 that Herzog began to more explicitly address the relevant issues raised by Latin American liberation theology for North American theology.

In a paper presented at the conference, Herzog summarized much of his previous thought and brought it into more direct dialogue with Latin American liberation thought. Herzog reiterated that liberation

---

Philosophy of Religion and Theology: 1974 Proceedings. American Academy of Religion Annual Meeting 1974 (Tallahassee: American Academy of Religion, 1974), pp. 159-173; and "Liberation Hermeneutic as Ideology Critique?" *Interp* 28 (Oct. 1974):387-403.

[132]See Frederick Herzog, "Theology at the Crossroads," *Union S Q R* 31 (1975):59-68, for his contribution to a symposium held on the thought of James H. Cone.

[133]Regarding this question see Herzog, "The Liberation of White Theology," p. 317, and "Liberation Theology Begins at Home," p. 94. Both passages make reference to the warning of Hugo Assmann against turning Latin American liberation theology into U.S. "consumer goods."

[134]Herzog, "Liberation Theology Begins at Home," p. 94.

[135]Cf. Herzog, "Responsible Theology?" pp. 166-168.

theology is "no consumer good" and firmly insisted that North American theology concentrate on its own particular context. Only in this way could a constructive interchange with Latin American liberation theology take place with *"experience challenging experience."*[136] Herzog argued that the global issues of liberation theology find a counterpart in local issues at home in the U.S. In contrast to liberal theology, liberation theology strives to participate in what *God* is doing for liberation in history.

> *Thus liberation theology is Christian theology* responding *to God's commission under the pressure of the global process of inter-dependence.*[137]

From these few sentences the continuity of this paper with Herzog's previous writings can be seen: the emphasis on God as the primary agent of liberation, the insistence on the priority of the North American context for North American theology, and the critique of liberal theology.

Herzog went on to delineate four points which should clarify the relationship between North American and Latin American theology.[138] The very occurrence of such a dialogue was noted as significant due to the traditional orientation of U.S. theology toward Europe. Moreover, the encounter was described as promising because of the common interest in an action-reflection model. The four points which Herzog made can be briefly summarized: (1) the priority of the divine mandate and divine activity in the liberation process; (2) the North American "blind spot" to the importance of black theology which can only undermine a genuine recognition of the issues raised by Latin American liberation theology; (3) the functioning of North American Protestantism as a cultural religion and ideology for the status quo; and (4) the need to recover a "liberation tradition" which is inherently North American. Expanding on this fourth point, Herzog criticized American civil religion and particularly its notion of a divine covenant between God and America as an abuse of the Christian faith.[139] The limitations of American civil religion become, for Herzog, most pronounced when the United States is placed within a

---

[136]Frederick Herzog, "Pre-Bicentennial U.S.A. in the Liberation Process," in Torres and Eagleson, eds., *Theology in the Americas*, p. 142.

[137]Ibid., p. 143.

[138]For the following cf. ibid., p. 144-149.

[139]For the following cf. ibid., pp. 149-156.

global context which today calls for the interdependence of nations in stark contrast to all imperialistic attitudes.

Herzog's elaboration of the need for criticism of the ideological use of theology and also of the importance of an "American socialism" demonstrate further affinity between his thought and Latin American liberation theology. Although Herzog does not develop these themes at length, his treatment of these issues reveals a recognition of new connections between the meaning of liberation for North America and Latin America. This is especially true when Herzog writes:

> At least four issues need tackling: (1) the definite class structure in the United States; (2) social analysis issuing in political action; (3) public ownership and public planning as foci in this move; (4) a coherent strategy of the churches to meet the challenge of American socialism.[140]

Like Cone, Herzog's ongoing encounter with Latin American liberation theology prompted new reflections on the meaning of socialism for the North American context. So too Herzog began to speak in an initial way of the usefulness of the social sciences to a theology which is involved in the liberation process.[141]

The emphases of Herzog's paper prepared for the first Theology in the Americas conference remain predominantly those he brought with him to the conference. This is exemplified in his description of the essence of liberation theology:

> The new vision of God (*visio Dei*) and the new image of the human person (*imago Dei*) issuing in the liberating mission (*missio Dei*) are dependent on the sovereign God (*regnum Dei*).[142]

The central theological point Herzog wants to make about God's liberation remains firm. Nonetheless, Herzog was encouraged by this conference to enter into dialogue with Latin American liberation theology on a deeper level than he had previously done.[143] That Herzog was altered by this encounter becomes obvious in contrasting his writings before this conference to those after it.

In an introduction written for the North American edition of Hugo Assmann's *Theology of a Nomad Church* (1976), the impact of the Detroit conference on Herzog's thinking becomes most clear. What is new is not his ongoing critique of liberation theology nor his continued stress on the uniqueness of the North American context for North

---

[140]Ibid., p. 160.

[141]See ibid., p. 164.

[142]Ibid., p. 162.

[143]Cf. the numerous references to Latin American theologians in ibid., pp. 162-163.

American theology.[144] What is most original is Herzog's drawing new connections between the North and Latin American contexts.

> Due to the increasing interdependence of peoples the question we face in theology is this: In what sense can we in the U.S. learn from sisters and brothers struggling in dire circumstances. Can we take over their theology? Or are they challenging us to develop a theology our very own, yet true to their plight for which we, too, are accountable?[145]

Whereas previously Herzog had tended to see Latin American liberation theology as a diversion from the North American context, he now recognizes that it is exactly Latin American liberation theology's insistence on the priority of its own context of poverty and political repression that encourages North American theology to take seriously its own context. It is on this basis that Herzog once again critiqued the covenant concept within American civil religion, emphasizing the God who judges all injustice and laying new stress on the need to free the Bible from subservience to capitalistic ideology.[146]

In reflecting upon the Detroit conference, Herzog made new connections between what he describes as the race, sex, and class conflicts within North American reality.

> The recovery of the Bible as the empowerment of the just church compels us to go through history also as race, sex, and class conflict and thus to discover the unity of liberations. Here theology does not appear as adjunct of liberation struggles in general, but as the praxis of God's liberation in global history.[147]

For Herzog as for Cone, the recognition of the interrelationship of the various forms of oppression was a major insight resulting from the "conflict" which took place at the Detroit conference. In order to allow this conflict to become creative, there arose an awareness of the need to combine racial analysis with a critique of capitalism (as well as an analysis of sexual oppression). Herzog writes:

> Blacks struggle with whites, women with men, native Americans with foreign Americans, and Latin Americans with North Americans in order that one people may arise: *God's* people.[148]

The global dimensions of liberation theology here came to be expressed in Herzog's theology in a new way.

---

[144]Cf. Frederick Herzog, "Introduction: On Liberating Liberation Theology," in Hugo Assmann, *Theology for a Nomad Church*, trans. Paul Burns (Maryknoll: Orbis, 1976), pp. 4-11.

[145]Ibid., p. 2.

[146]See ibid., pp. 5-7 and 10-11.

[147]Ibid., p. 15 (italics deleted).

[148]Ibid., p. 18.

These new awarenesses on the part of Herzog continued to ferment and mature. Hereafter he began to articulate liberation theology in terms increasingly inclusive of Latin American liberation theology. Thus he could now write of such themes as (1) "the objective claims of the poor," (2) the praxis method as "the interaction of deed and thought, the holistic embodiment of meaning," or (3) the crucial role of Marxist thought for systematic theology in understanding North American society, in terms clearly resonant with Latin American liberation theology.[149] This trend was continued in greater detail in his book, *Justice Church. The New Function of the Church in North American Christianity* (1980).

If in his earlier work Herzog had strongly emphasized that liberation takes place by God's initiative and activity, it is in *Justice Church* that Herzog takes up more directly the political and ecclesial mediations of God's liberating activity. Already in the "Introduction" Herzog lays new stress on praxis orientation in the church and in theology. The Gospel story is termed a "praxis-test" even as the church is described as the "praxis context" for theology.[150] The six chapters of the book are to serve to examine different aspects of the church as the praxis concept of theology.

In the first three chapters Herzog grapples with the issue of power in the church and in theology. Whereas the church has been thoroughly analyzed for its role in either comforting or challenging the status quo, Herzog asks whether a more pertinent dilemma in the present might not be the distinction between an ideal (Tillich) and an actual (Gilkey) church. By the actual church Herzog understands a church fully involved in contemporary history, i.e., a church taking up the cause of the marginals in history. In affirming the choice of an "actual" church, Herzog offers three principles for a liberation doctrine of the church.[151]

1. The need to overcome the denominational divisions of the churches in favor of an interdenominational praxis which can unite them.

2. The need to recognize that ministry in the U.S. today can only be seen as subversive due to its insistence upon interethnic praxis in the face of the prevalence of ethnic nationalism.

---

[149]Cf. Frederick Herzog, "Birth Pangs: Liberation Theology in North America," *Chr Cent* 93 (Dec. 15, 1976):1120-1125.

[150]Herzog, *Justice Church*, pp. 3-5.

[151]For the following cf. ibid., pp. 9-27.

3. The need to recover theology's proper theme which is not the question of cultural pluralism (vs. Cobb) but the praxis of God within history for justice.

Herzog argues, moreover, that the crucible for such an understanding of the church is the reorientation of theological education.

The Christological basis for this new understanding of the justice church is located in a reevaluation of the significance of the historical fact that Jesus was a Jew.[152] By rooting Jesus the Jew in the history of Israel, theological mystification of such matters as Jesus' ministry to the poor and his crucifixion as a religious and political subversive can, according to Herzog, be avoided. Herzog employs examples from contemporary theology (Bultmann, Barth) to illustrate the tendency of Western theology to cloud Jesus' rootedness in the particularities of the historical context in which he lived. Recovering the Jewishness of Jesus is thus crucial not only as a correction to contemporary theology but also for reestablishing the church in a "Christopraxis" on behalf of the poor and outcast. A Jewish Jesus can likewise serve to draw together diverse ethnic groups, e.g., Jews and Christians in the time "after Auschwitz," uniting them in a Jesus-like praxis for the sake of justice.

Herzog also continued in this book his critique of liberal theology, making special reference to Schleiermacher whose theological program is understood to be decisive for a host of contemporary theologians.[153] A central criticism of Schleiermacher must be, according to Herzog, his unexamined assumption of the normative status of the culture in which he lived, the consequence of which is his assumption of the harmonious nature of human society. This leads Schleiermacher to bifurcate history into the separate realms of spiritual and secular power. External history, i.e., Old Testament history or the history of the crucified Jesus, thus becomes subordinated to the inward realm of religious experience and feeling. On the basis of this interpretation, Herzog calls contemporary theologians to recognize that the late twentieth-century situation is not directly equatable with that of Schleiermacher's. Instead Herzog affirms:

> Communicating to the despisers of religion today involves listening to the uncultured and regarding their lot as the crucial orientation point of culture.[154]

---

[152]For the following cf. ibid., pp. 30-51.

[153]For the following cf. ibid., pp. 55-68.

[154]Ibid., p. 67 (italics deleted).

In the contemporary context, it is the recovery of external history and the struggle of the historical poor which are indispensable to theology.

In the last chapters of *Justice Church* Herzog deals with the meaning of the American revolution in light of both the Marxist revolution and the biblical mandate against poverty; the correct interpretation and appropriation of Latin American liberation theology in the North American context; and a case study on creating a justice church (based on a study document of the United Church of Christ). At one point Herzog argues that both the Marxist revolution and the biblical "antipoverty program" should serve to remind Americans of their own revolutionary tradition and the absolute priority of eliminating poverty in today's world.[155] This reference indicates the degree to which Herzog has been prompted by Latin American liberation theology to rethink theology in global terms. The polemic against the Latin American context as a diversion from the North American one has fully disappeared. Instead Herzog calls for the use of imagination in differentiating the different theological challenges of the Latin and North American contexts while affirming their common struggle for liberation.[156]

While within Latin America Herzog recognizes the importance of social analysis alongside the task of biblical interpretation, in North America he sees a danger that too much dependence upon social analysis could become coopted by capitalist culture.

> In the North American situation we cannot take over Jose Miranda's claim that a person must regard human history "as his only church." We cannot make Gustavo Gutierrez's "self-liberation" or Juan Segundo's notion of this world becoming the new heaven of God our own. We need to focus on God's struggle in history creating a church in history that stands against our sinful history.[157]

The complexity and particularity of the North American context requires a careful articulation of its own theological tasks. These tasks include: (1) "the praxis task" of moving beyond intellectualism to actual involvement by the theologian in the cause of the "nonperson"; (2) "the dogmatic task," not of providing coherent worldviews but of participation in "God's battle for justice"; and (3) "the social analysis task" of making rational, though risky, choices about a particular political course. For Herzog that finally means the risky option of becoming a "Christian for socialism" based on the conviction

---

155Cf. ibid., pp. 72-84.
156For the following cf. ibid., pp. 86-101.
157Ibid., pp. 95-96.

that "it is impossible to remain silent about religious blasphemy in U.S. capitalism."[158]

The response of Frederick Herzog to Latin American liberation theology is one marked from beginning to end by the insistence that liberation is first of all *God's* liberation. The activity of God for liberation has been revealed in his liberating Word who is Jesus. This word, moreover, continues to speak today in the Bible. Primary attention has been given by Herzog to what this liberating Word means in the North American context. That has meant taking seriously the situation of blacks in the U.S. and, since his participation in the first Theology in the Americas conference in 1975, a new and expanding appreciation for the global connectedness of the liberation struggle, especially the issues which have been raised by Latin American liberation theologians. The "justice church" which Herzog has come to envision for the North American context and the theology which is to be in service to this justice church are thus to be fully cognizant of their time and place in the international context. Where Herzog differs most noticeably from Latin American liberation theology has been in the lesser role given to social analysis in his thought. While his book *Justice Church* has begun to move in the direction of greater political and ecclesial concretion, the greatest contrast between Herzog and the Latin American liberation theology occurs on this issue, a fact which Herzog would attribute to the differences which exist between the two contexts. Both fully agree, however, that it is praxis on behalf of the world's poor which is the final measure of church and theology.

D. *Robert McAfee Brown: Herald and Apologist for Liberation Theology*

The entire career of Robert McAfee Brown provides antecedents for his fervent interest in Latin American liberation theology.[159] Presbyterian churchman and past professor at Macalester College, Union Theological Seminary, and Stanford University, Brown has most recently served as Professor of Theology and Ethics at the Pacific School of Religion in Berkeley, California. A prolific writer, his numerous publications document the theological interests which have

---

[158]Ibid., p. 99.

[159]For an autobiographical account of his career see Robert McAfee Brown, *Creative Dislocation—The Movement of Grace* (Nashville: Abingdon, 1980).

led Brown, since the seventies, to become a herald and apologist for
Latin American liberation theology in the North American context.

Brown's special interest in liberation theology can be understood
on the basis of several of his earlier books and personal involvements.
For example, in 1955 Brown published *The Bible Speaks to You*, an
introduction to the Bible in which Brown's interest in communicating
the biblical word as a living and contemporary message finds a recent
parallel in liberation theology's biblical hermeneutic and especially
in the biblical interpretation carried out among the basic Christian
communities of Latin America.[160]

Brown's active participation in the worldwide ecumenical
movement also indicates his interest in a church and theology which
thinks in global terms.[161] As a Protestant observer at Vatican II in
1963, Brown was able to broaden and deepen his understanding of
Roman Catholicism in direct contact with the liberalizing forces which
would also come to strongly influence the origin and development of
Latin American liberation thought.[162] Another vital impulse to
Brown's ecumenical awareness has come from his participation in
conferences and programs of the World Council of Churches which has
brought him into frequent contact with representatives of Third World
thought.[163] An additional "ecumenical" dimension was provided by

---

[160]Robert McAfee Brown, *The Bible Speaks to You* (Philadelphia:
Westminster, 1955). It is especially interesting to consider the similarities in
style and thrust between this early work of Brown and his more recent volume,
Unexpected News. Reading the Bible with Third World Eyes (Philadelphia:
Westminster, 1984), in which Brown, through a series of ten Bible studies,
attempts to communicate the living voice of Scripture in light of Third World
liberation theology.

[161]For a summary of Brown's ecumenical involvement up to the early
seventies cf. John T. Carmody, "The Development of Robert McAfee Brown's
Ecumenical Thought," *Rel Life* 43 (Aug. 1974):283-293.

[162]For the development of Brown's ecumenical thought in this period cf.
Robert McAfee Brown and Gustave Wiegel, *An American Dialogue* (Garden
City: Doubleday, 1960), Robert McAfee Brown, *Observer in Rome* (Garden City:
Doubleday, 1964), and Robert McAfee Brown, *The Ecumenical Revolution*
(Garden City: Doubleday, 1967), which document his growth in understanding
of Roman Catholicism and his positive assessment of the reforms of Vatican II.

[163]Cf. Brown, *The Ecumenical Revolution*, for his brief description of the
history of Protestant ecumenism and the contemporary challenge to ecumenism
provided by the more secular issues of poverty and war. One especially
noteworthy presentation by Brown in the context of the World Council of
Churches was his address, "Who is this Jesus Christ who Frees and Unites?" *Ec
R* 28 (Jan. 1976):6-21, given at a plenary session of the World Council of
Churches Fifth Assembly at Nairobi in November 1975. This address has been

Brown's decision to teach at the non-church-related Stanford University during the decade of the sixties at which time the civil rights struggle and the war in Vietnam further widened Brown's understanding of the meaning of ecumenism.[164]

The commitments Brown made as a theologian to both the civil rights movement and opposition to the war in Vietnam provide special insight into his later interest in liberation theology.[165] From these involvements Brown began to recognize in an existential way the need for a theology which listens not only to the Bible and the church but also to the world.[166] The relevance of political events for theology which Brown first learned from Reinhold Niebuhr began to take on new immediacy and complexity. From both of these movements Brown learned to look at history from a new point of view, i.e., "from below," from the point of view of black Americans, Vietnamese peasants, and North American youth conscripted to fight in the war in Vietnam. Brown was also prompted to begin to examine the effects of American power in global terms which led to an increasingly critical conclusion.

> If the "system" remains as resistant to change in other areas as it has proved to be in Vietnam, if genteel protest fails to produce change, and if one believes (as I think one must) that Vietnam is a symptom of a much deeper malaise in our American way of life, is one not called upon to escalate the number and intensity of his political acts, including civil disobedience—to move, in other words, from the liberal toward the radical camp, recognizing that what is at fault is not just little inadequacies in the system that can be eliminated by tinkering, but the system itself?[167]

Brown's critical analysis of the exercise of American power in Vietnam found renewed relevance as he examined the ongoing use of American power in Latin America, particularly in Chile, El Salvador, and Nicaragua.

As a result of Brown's commitment to the interface between theology and contemporary events, his writings often assume a form

---

especially remembered due to Brown's delivery of the largest portion of the address in Spanish as "a symbol of my desire to enter into closer solidarity with my sisters and brothers in the Third World, and especially in Latin America . . . " (p. 12).

[164]On the significance of his move from Union Theological Seminary to Stanford University see Brown, *Creative Dislocation* pp. 30-37.

[165]For his involvement in these movements see Robert McAfee Brown, *The Pseudonyms of God* (Philadelphia: Westminster, 1972), esp. pp. 33-45.

[166]See ibid., pp. 21-22.

[167]Ibid., p. 42.

which he himself once described as "theological journalism."[168] This popular style of writing has continued to mark Brown's work and has made his thought particularly accessible to those with no claim to professional theological training. This has in no way, however, prevented Brown from taking the increasingly critical stance which he believed necessary in the face of the abuses of American power.

Two other characteristics also mark Brown's thought and writings and act as a counterbalance to the weightiness of the issues with which he deals and which in themselves could lead to cynicism and despair. The first characteristic which has consistently marked his writings has been his ongoing concern for the institutional church and his unspoken confidence that through this church, minds and hearts can be reached to become a force for countering the negative effects of American power both domestically and abroad. Brown's writings have, thus, been addressed primarily to the American churches and church people. He has shown special interest in addressing the issues, questions, and possible objections raised by "average" American church members to his challenging some of their fundamental presuppositions about the Christian faith.[169] A second characteristic of Brown's writings in this regard has been his use of humor and wit to temper the harsher tones of his message.[170] This has been combined with an admission of his own vulnerability to the very same

---

[168]Ibid., p. 44.

[169]On his concern to address the possible questions and objections of American church people see, for example, Robert McAfee Brown, *Frontiers for the Church Today* (New York: Oxford University Press, 1973), pp. 19-24, on the meaning of Christian mission; *Religion and Violence. A Primer for White Americans* (Philadelphia: Westminster, 1973), pp. 98-101, on the response of white American churches to the issue of revolutionary violence; *Is Faith Obsolete?* (Philadelphia: Westminster, 1974) which as an entirety grapples with the difficulty of faith in the modern world; *Theology in a New Key. Responding to Liberation Themes* (Philadelphia: Westminster, 1978), esp. pp. 155-188, which searches for an authentic response by the North American church to Latin American liberation theology; *Making Peace in the Global Village* (Philadelphia: Westminster, 1981), esp. pp. 105-112, which emphasizes the role the church can play in global peace-making; and *Unexpected News*, esp. pp. 157-161, which addresses possible negative reactions of church people to the challenges raised by a Third World reading of the Bible. The last two of these books can also be seen in their entirety as suitable for use in adult education in American churches.

[170]See, for example, the Saint Hereticus writings of Brown including "Theological Gamesmanship: Disposing of Liberation Theology in Eight Easy Lessons," *Chr Cris* 38 (Aug. 21, 1978):200-202.

challenges he raises of others in the church.[171] In humor Brown has
discovered a "saving grace," a sign of the presence of God which
assists in keeping the seriousness of human life in its proper
proportion.[172]

Of the several "frontiers for the church today" which Brown
surveyed in his 1973 book by the same title, the frontier which he then
described as "the frontier of revolution" came to obtain a central place
in his subsequent writings. It is along this frontier that Brown arrived
at an ever deeper recognition of the significance of Latin American
thought for the North American context. Already in 1973 Brown
demonstrated his theological openness to some of the central issues
which have occupied liberation theology: the material disparity
between First and Third Worlds, the fundamental limitations of a
developmental approach to Third World poverty which instead calls
for structural change, and the problem posed by revolutionary violence
to Christian theology.[173] Brown characteristically took special care in
this book to emphasize the humanizing, prophetic, political, economic,
and pastoral functions which the church could offer in light of this
Third World reality.[174]

> The American church, as an institution of one of the most powerful nations
> on earth, clearly has a role to play, a role that it will embrace to the degree
> that it remembers that it is part of a worldwide fellowship with loyalties
> much more encompassing than mere national loyalties.[175]

If the future of the church lay not "in Europe or North America, but in
Asia, Africa, and Latin America" (Paul Albrecht), then Brown saw the
necessity of solidarity between the American church and those in the
context of revolution. Especially interesting in light of his subsequent
writings on liberation theology are the early references by Brown to the
literature of the theology of liberation in this book and particularly his
inclusion of Gustavo Gutierrez's *A Theology of Liberation* in the
annotated bibliography.[176]

---

[171]That Brown himself also feels implicated by the challenges of Latin
American liberation theology is apparent from both the "Foreword" to *Theology
in a New Key*, pp. 11-15 and the "Introduction" to *Unexpected News*, pp. 11-17.

[172]Cf. Brown, *Creative Dislocation—The Movement of Grace*, pp. 133-139.

[173]Cf. Brown, *Frontiers for the Church Today*, Chapter 4, "The Frontier of
Revolution," pp. 48-64.

[174]See ibid., pp. 53-54 and 61-64.

[175]Ibid., p. 64.

[176]Ibid., p. 140.

The problem raised by both the Third World context and by the North American racial struggle which initially drew a large portion of Brown's attention was that of a Christian response to the question of violence.[177] In his book *Religion and Violence* (1973) Brown attempted to communicate to an anticipated audience of white Americans what he had learned about the meaning of violence, especially from his encounter with the meaning of violence in the context of the Third World.[178] From the outset Brown noted that it was especially the reality of violence in the Third World context that prevented him from proposing an absolute pacifist position as the exclusive alternative for religious people. What this meant for Brown was that he had discovered the critical importance of the insight that in the Third World context of poverty and oppression there already exists a situation of "institutionalized violence," either overt or covert, which necessitates a broadening of the very definition of the term "violence."[179] In dependence upon the thought of Dom Helder Camara, Brown articulated the spiral of violence which was initiated when institutional violence leads successively to revolt and repression. It is on this basis that he understood the dynamics of violence in the Third World context.

After examining traditional criteria employed to evaluate "just war," Brown took a closer look at the meaning of structural violence in contemporary society both for those who benefit from and for those who are victims of the present structures. Probing to the roots of the problem, the issue of violence was seen to revolve around the question of power, i.e., who has the power and on whose behalf is it exercised. Brown then proposed that by paying attention to the exercise of U.S. power in the Third World context, new awareness could be attained not only about how structural violence actually functions but also about how Americans themselves are implicated by the use of American power in that context.[180] In order to raise this awareness, he cited a number of examples from Latin America—deliberations from the Medellin Conference and the contrasting case studies of Camilo Torres and Dom Helder Camara—to demonstrate how others have come to understand the dynamics of violence in their own context.

---

[177]Cf. ibid., pp. 56-61, and Brown, *Religion and Violence.*

[178]For the following see Brown, *Religion and Violence*, p. xv.

[179]Cf. ibid., pp. 7-13.

[180]For the following cf. ibid., pp. 41-53.

As Brown surveyed the arguments presented on the issue of violence, especially from a Third World perspective, he found himself compelled to return once again to the traditional criteria of a just war but this time with a significantly different question: "can there be a 'just revolution'?"[181] Brown found the traditional criteria to be a constructive tool for analyzing the conditions under which a revolution might be justified: is it (1) declared by a legitimate authority, (2) waged with a right intention, (3) undertaken only as a last resort, (4) weighed on the basis of the principle of proportionality, (5) likely to have a reasonable chance of success, and (6) waged with all possible moderation? Brown was, however, ready to make no apodictic conclusions on the basis of such deliberations. Different contexts call for different responses, and Brown especially stressed the substantial difference between the contexts of North and South America.

Nevertheless, according to Brown, there could be no compromising the fact that structural change is absolutely necessary both in the structures which govern life within the U.S. and in those which order the exercise of American power abroad.[182] To support this conclusion he again called upon the critique of developmentalism undertaken by Latin American theologians who have concluded that significant change can only be achieved through a change in the structures which presently order Latin American society. Seeing a direct relationship between the structures which order life in the U.S. and the effects of these structures in the Third World, Brown concluded this book with a discussion of present alternatives available to Americans in order to achieve social change: from working to reform existing structures from within, to employing nonviolent means to challenge the present system, to engaging in violent struggle to overthrow the system. Brown wrote:

> So to our initial question, "Are there alternatives to violence?" the answer is "Yes." To the subsequent question, "Can we avail ourselves of those alternatives to violence?" the answer is, "If we do not, we will thereby contribute to the necessity of the violent alternative."[183]

In a world where so many hunger and suffer as a consequence of unjust social structures, there was for Brown no question about the necessity of structural change. The only question was the sobering one of motivating those who benefit from the present equilibrium to choose

---

[181]For the following cf. ibid., pp. 55-61.

[182]For the following cf. ibid., pp. 73-88.

[183]Ibid., p. 85.

another alternative in order to avoid the eventual option for violence by
the oppressed when all other means toward change have failed.

Having entered deeply into the thought world of liberation theology
via the question of violence, Brown turned in his next writings to a
more comprehensive depiction and defense of liberation thought. In a
book *Is Faith Obsolete?* (1974), written to reappraise the meaning of
faith in a world where faith was seen to be in decline, Brown
introduced liberation theology as an example of a vital and living
form of faith among many in the Third World context today.[184] After
explaining some of the basic concepts of liberation theology—its
critique of the theory of development, its biblical orientation on behalf
of the poor, its insistence on breaking with the status quo and changing
sides, and its engagement for revolution and conscientization—Brown
asked what such a faith option could mean for those in the North
American context. Anticipating the common objections which might
be raised against liberation theology, Brown next engaged in what
might be called apologetics for liberation theology for those in the North
American context. As will also be seen in his future writings, this
became an approach which Brown has used frequently to communicate
the importance of liberation theology for those who as North Americans
might have a natural resistance to its confrontative message. Brown
advised instead a more positive approach in appropriating liberation
theology which he summarized under five basic guidelines.

1. The first thing we can do is indicate our willingness to listen and be
ready to *listen* for a long time. . . .

2. As we listen, we must pay liberation theology the respect of *taking it
seriously*. . . .

3. As we listen seriously, we must acknowledge that liberation theology is
a *genuine Christian theology* and not a contrived importation. . . .

4. As we listen seriously to this genuine Christian theology, we need to
recognize that not only does it describe a situation somewhere else, but that
it describes our own situation as well. . . .

5. To the degree that we do some or all of the above, we will be better
equipped to face the basic question, already asked: *can a theology for the
oppressed also become a theology for the oppressors?*[185]

These are the ground rules which Brown has consistently sought to
enact for the dialogue between North Americans and liberation
theology. Only so can the urgent message of liberation theology
penetrate beyond established defense mechanisms to alter the
consciousness and practice of North American Christians.

---

[184]For the following cf. Brown, *Is Faith Obsolete?* pp. 120-137.

[185]Excerpted from ibid., pp. 131-133.

Like Cone, Herzog, Ruether, and many other North American theologians, Brown's understanding of Latin American liberation theology was furthered by his participation in the first Theology in the Americas conference at Detroit in 1975. Some of his reflections on this conference and the entire Theology in the Americas process were collected in his introduction to the published edition of the papers and materials from the conference.[186] Brown described the Detroit conference as an initiation into "a new way of 'doing theology'." In contrast to the academic rigors of a theology written by experts, the Detroit conference was itself an experiment in theology as a process— an open-ended, corporate, self-correcting, and engaged process. Brown acknowledged the contribution made by Latin American liberation theology to this process and laid particular stress on the praxis-orientation of this new theological form.

Just as he had earlier tried to establish ground rules for the encounter between liberation theology and North American Christians, Brown, reinforced by his experience of the tensions between various participants at the Detroit conference, saw the need to propose even more stringent ground rules if the more threatening aspects of liberation theology were not simply to be evaded.

1. A threatening position can sometimes be disposed of simply *by calling it a "fad" and those who espouse it "naive"*. . . .

2. A threatening position can sometimes be disposed of by *co-opting it*. Third World theologians are legitimately nervous as they look at what North Americans are doing with their terms. . . .

3. A threatening position can sometimes be disposed of by *keeping it at a safe distance*. We can examine oppression far away . . . and never have to confront the denial of civil rights to Spanish-speaking poor in the central valley of California. . . .

4. A threatening position can sometimes be disposed of *by describing it in emotionally discrediting terms*. In the United States, this means disposing of liberation theology by applying Marxist or communist tags to it.[187]

Here Brown's apologetical arguments appear to have been sharpened by his encounter with the ongoing criticism of liberation theology.

In the remainder of his introduction to this volume Brown addressed the question of what would be necessary for an authentic appropriation of the insights of liberation theology for the very different

---

[186]For the following see Brown, "A Preface and a Conclusion," in Torres and Eagleson, eds., *Theology in the Americas*, pp. ix-xxviii.

[187]Excerpted from ibid., pp. xv-xviii.

context of North America.[188] Among Brown's proposals were: (1) the
need to combine an adherence to one's particular context with a global
vision, (2) the need to recognize the relationship between one's
communal (i.e., ideological) identification and one's theological
viewpoint, (3) the necessity of recognizing the direct correlation
between Third World oppression and the exercise of U.S. power, and
(4) the indispensability of theology's employing appropriate forms of
social analysis. Especially interesting in this regard was Brown's
suggestion that within recent European theology there also exist
materials relevant to a North American construction of liberation
theology, e.g., the experience of Bonhoeffer in resisting National
Socialism, the religious socialism of Tillich and Barth, and
Moltmann's theology of hope. In conclusion, Brown encouraged those
who, from a global perspective, live as "oppressors" to learn from the
oppressed what it means to do theology. Required more than anything
else in order to reach that goal would be "our willingness to risk our
security on behalf of the insecurities of others."[189]

Brown's most extensive treatment of liberation theology and its
implications for North Americans appeared in 1978 under the title
Theology in a New Key. The subtitle of the book, "Responding to
Liberation Themes," expresses the essence of what Brown has
attempted to evoke from others with regard to liberation theology even
as he himself has attempted to make an authentic response.
Throughout this book Brown utilizes musical images to communicate
the qualitative difference of liberation theology from all other
alternatives. A major portion of the book is devoted to communicating
to a North American audience just what the theology of liberation
really says. Brown, on the basis of his deep conviction that the message
of Latin American liberation theology is vital to Christian faith also in
the North American context, proceeded to elaborate the historical
background and basic concepts of which the theology of liberation
consists.[190]

In his heralding of liberation theology, Brown emphasized the
context in which this theology has arisen, the context of poverty for
which North Americans are also implicated. Brown also reviewed
several pertinent factors in the historical development of liberation

---

[188]For the following cf. ibid., pp. xix-xxiii.

[189]Ibid., p. xxvii.

[190]For the following cf. the first three chapters in Brown, *Theology in a New Key*, pp. 19-100.

theology—its relationship to Roman Catholic social teaching, its relatedness to recent developments in the World Council of Churches, and the significance of both the Medellin bishops conference and the Christians for Socialism movement in Chile.   Certain basic characteristics of Latin American liberation theology are elaborated in some detail including its starting point with the poor, its primary interlocutor as the nonperson, its use of the social sciences and Marxist thought for social analysis, its insistence on praxis, and the place of theology as a "second act" which follows the "first act" of commitment to the poor. Brown laid special emphasis on the Scriptural hermeneutic of liberation theology which challenges more conventional North American interpretations. The hermeneutic employed by liberation theology was presented by Brown as an occasion for discovering the "ideological captivity" of much traditional biblical interpretation and as an opportunity for hearing Scripture speak from the perspective of the poor.   Several biblical passages were examined by Brown to illustrate how the Bible has been heard to speak among the poor in a new and vibrant way.

Following this exposition of some of the major aspects of liberation thought, Brown turned next to the apologetic task.[191] Already in 1978 a variety of critiques of liberation theology had been offered.   Brown categorized the critiques of liberation theology into eight groups and proceeded to respond to each of them. "Defensive critiques" were described by Brown as those based primarily on a defensive emotional reaction to liberation theology's accusation of North American responsibility for Third World poverty. "Total rejection critiques" derive from a fundamentally different understanding of the essence of Christian faith, especially from those who see the primary mission of the church in evangelistic activity toward the end of obtaining eternal salvation. "Oversimplified critiques" are characterized, according to Brown, by their oversimplification and thus misrepresentation of liberation theology. "Pseudo-issue critiques" single out one issue, most often the issue of violence, making premature assumptions about what liberation theologians have actually said about that issue and abstracting the discussion from the concrete context in which it originated.

"Reductionist critiques" argue that liberation theology has reduced the full meaning of Christian faith into an inappropriate substitute,

---

[191] For the following cf. ibid., pp. 101-131.

e.g., politics, sociology, or Marxism, and no longer represents the gospel in its wholeness. "Methodological critiques" charge the inadequacy of the method of liberation theology, e.g., that it is overly bound to a particular social context, that it makes a superficial use of social analysis, or that its method is finally utopian. "Co-optation critiques" are those which continue to use liberation language while substituting a spiritualized content for what is meant by liberation. Lastly, "dialogical critiques" are those undertaken in a mutual exchange of views in which both critic and liberation theology are partners in a serious dialogue. For each of the eight categories Brown offered specific examples of those who have exercised the various types of criticism. Apart from the final "dialogical critique" it is clear that Brown found them to be inadequate responses to the complex and urgent message of liberation theology for those in the North American context.

In the remainder of *Theology in a New Key* Brown indicated what could be learned from honestly listening to Latin American theology.[192] An encounter with liberation theology could lead to a new appreciation of the stories of those often neglected by North American Christians—the stories of blacks, Native Americans, women, and the poor in the Third World. Likewise new attention could be aroused for neglected portions of Christian history such as the pre-Constantinian church, the radical Reformation, the U.S. social gospel movement, and the religious socialism of a Tillich or Barth. Brown even described how American civil religion might be reevaluated in the light of liberation theology. The common concerns which exist between North Americans and the Third World people in the realms of work, power, and human rights were each explored as potential bridges for spanning the gap between First and Third World concerns. Finally, Brown searched for new images of the church which could assist it in the transition to a new self-understanding in closer alliance with liberation thought (e.g., the church as "remnant within the remnant" or as an "Abrahamic minority"). The challenge of liberation theology to the North American church was finally understood as the challenge to enter into solidarity with the oppressed in concrete ways. Brown encouraged the church to take this challenge earnestly.

Of all Brown's writings on liberation theology, *Theology in a New Key* is the most comprehensive and demonstrates most fully his role as a North American herald and apologist for Latin American liberation

---

[192]For the following cf. ibid., pp. 132-188.

theology. Since that time Brown has continued to maintain a steady interest in new developments both in liberation theology and in the Latin American church. In his interpretation of the 1979 Puebla bishops conference, for example, Brown continued to articulate new emphases in Latin American thought for the North American churches, highlighting the Puebla document's emphasis on basic Christian communities, its criticism of the doctrine of "national security," and its "preferential option for the poor."[193] Frequent articles in religious periodicals have also continued to call attention to such issues as the interrelatedness between the U.S. economic system and Third World poverty, or the destructive consequences of U.S. foreign policy in Nicaragua.[194]

A new book devoted exclusively to liberation theology's interpretation of Scripture appeared in 1984 bearing the title *Unexpected News. Reading the Bible with Third World Eyes*. This volume is a collection of ten Bible studies which Brown undertook in an attempt to "see the world the way others do."[195] In it Brown sought to present for North American readers the rereading of often familiar Bible passages which have begun to speak with new accents and implications in the Third World context. References to recent events in places like Chile and Nicaragua are frequent in this book and Brown's effort to awaken North American Christians to the urgency of liberation thought is relentless.

> The great hope, surely, is that we *can* begin to be liberated from some of the false gods—the Bible calls them "idols"—that have held us in captivity. We know their names: fear of change, the need to conform, the burden of success expectations programmed into us from childhood, the stigma of being thought of as "unpatriotic," the terror of becoming vulnerable. . . .
>
> If we could face the question of the effects our allegiances have, we could begin the painful but necessary process the Bible talks about, that of "changing sides." We could begin to reread and reappropriate the long heritage that is ours, preserved in the book we have been studying, enshrined also in our history and our tradition, but always more powerful

---

[193]Cf. Robert McAfee Brown, "The Significance of Puebla for the Protestant Churches in North America," in John Eagleson and Philip Scharper, eds., *Puebla and Beyond. Documentation and Commentary*, trans. John Drury (Maryknoll: Orbis, 1979), pp. 330-346.

[194]See, for example, Robert McAfee Brown, "Appreciating the Bishops' Letter," *Chr Cent* 102 (Feb. 6-13, 1985):129-130 and "Nicaragua: On Saving Us from Ourselves," *Chr Cent* 102 (Jan. 2-9, 1985):6-7.

[195]Brown, *Unexpected News*, p. 12.

than any of the vessels in which it is contained, more powerful even than our own attempts to reduce it to nonthreatening platitudes.[196]

Worthy of note is Brown's inclusion of himself among those to be challenged by a reading of the Bible through Third World eyes.

One personal relationship has been especially significant for Brown's interest in Latin American liberation theology, that is, his personal friendship with Gustavo Gutierrez. This personal relationship was nurtured when Gutierrez taught for two semesters as a colleague of Brown at Union Theological Seminary in the late seventies.[197] That he has been profoundly affected not only by the thought but also the person of Gutierrez, becomes evident from Brown's short introduction to the theology of Gutierrez, *Gustavo Gutierrez* (1980), in which the subject of the book is affectionately addressed on a first name basis as "Gustavo."[198] In this short volume Brown presented both a sketch of the thought of Gutierrez and a short biographical account, placing Gutierrez's thought in its Peruvian context where he is intimately involved in the world of the poor. Special attention is given to the method of Gutierrez's theology which insists upon the "first act" of "commitment to the poor" (praxis) as the presupposition for the "second act" as "critical reflection on praxis in the light of the Word of God." As in his other writings on liberation theology, Brown also devotes attention to refuting the critics of liberation theology and to raising for North American readers the significance of this theology for their own context.

> We too need the three kinds of liberation of which Gustavo speaks: liberation from oppressive systems, liberation from the notion that we are powerless to bring about change, and liberation from the sin that dominates our lives. Every time this begins to happen, new doors open.[199]

Brown has continually searched for the connecting links between North American and Latin American experience.

In his preface to a North American edition of Gutierrez's essays, Brown has taken the opportunity of introducing the "subversive" thought of Gutierrez to North American readers.[200] At the appearance

---

[196]Ibid., pp. 160-161.

[197]Brief reference is made to this time in Brown, *Creative Dislocation*, p. 44.

[198]Robert McAfee Brown, *Gustavo Gutierrez* (Atlanta: John Knox, 1980).

[199]Ibid., p. 75.

[200]Robert McAfee Brown, "Preface: After Ten Years," in Gustavo Gutierrez, *The Power of the Poor in History. Selected Writings*, trans. Robert R. Barr (Maryknoll: Orbis, 1983), pp. vi-xvi.

of the North American edition of Gutierrez's work on Latin American spirituality, *We Drink From Our Own Wells*, Brown has pointed out the deeply spiritual and biblical quality of Gutierrez's thought over against the charge that Gutierrez represents an errant form of theology, corrupted by Marxism and advocating violent revolution.[201] This charge, buttressed by an official inquiry by the Roman Catholic church into Gutierrez's theology, Brown found preposterous in any fair reading of Gutierrez's own writings.

> Realizing the gifts he brings us, I find it both dismaying and disheartening to see Gutierrez once again under attack by heavy theological artillery from within his own church. Not only Catholics but all of us need his words, his witness and the example of his life. . . . We are all deprived when he has to turn his energies from struggling for the poor in order to defend himself against attack. We must work, hope and pray for his release from such constraints, so that he—and we—can turn with renewed commitment to the holy tasks of justice and love.[202]

Brown's personal commitment to liberation theology, nurtured by his relationship with Gutierrez and other Latin Americans, adds human depth and a sense of urgency to Brown's writings on the entire subject.

Brown's publications in the eighties have not dealt exclusively with Latin American liberation theology. Yet even when turning to other contemporary issues such as peacemaking in the nuclear age or post-holocaust Judaism and the writings of Elie Wiesel, these topics have been approached with an eye toward their connectedness with the poor and oppressed throughout the world for whom the theology of liberation has arisen.[203] In this way Brown has continued to serve as herald and apologist for Latin American liberation theology in ever new contexts and connections. On the basis of his passionate articulation of the content and significance of liberation theology for those in North America and his defense of this theology against its critics, it is with some justification that Jorge Lara-Braud has named Brown "the ablest U.S. interpreter of third world Christianity."[204]

---

[201] Robert McAfee Brown, "Drinking from Our Own Wells," *Chr Cent* 101 (May 9, 1984):483-486.

[202] Ibid., p. 486.

[203] See, for example, Robert McAfee Brown, *Making Peace in the Global Village* (Philadelphia: Westminster, 1981) and *Elie Wiesel: Messenger to All Humanity* (Notre Dame: University of Notre Dame Press, 1983).

[204] Jorge Lara-Brand in Brown, *Unexpected News*, back cover.

E. *Rosemary Radford Ruether: Toward a Holistic Theology of Liberation*

The theology of Rosemary Radford Ruether has consistently pressed forward on numerous fronts toward a holistic theology of liberation. While the focal point of her theology must be seen to lie with feminist liberation, one among the several fronts which she has integrally incorporated into her thought has been Latin American liberation theology. In many ways her appropriation of the Latin American theology of liberation into a more holistic liberation theology has been the most original response among all North American theologians.

Ruether comes from a Roman Catholic religious background which she has critically reappropriated as her own. Having a strong academic background in both classical studies and patristics, Ruether has taught at Howard University (1965-76), as visiting lecturer at Harvard Divinity School (1971-72), and Yale Divinity School (1973-74), and since 1976 at Garrett Evangelical Theological Seminary in Evanston, Illinois where she is both Georgia Harkness Professor of Applied Theology and simultaneously a faculty member in the joint doctoral program at Northwestern University.[205] Important influences on Ruether serving to heighten her interest in a theology which addresses the political questions of the day were the civil rights movement of the sixties; the peace movement (beginning with opposition to the war in Vietnam and followed by an ongoing critique of the use of U.S. power in the world); and an ever increasing recognition of the oppression of women throughout history, especially in the Christian tradition, the effects of which persist into the present.[206]

Consistently throughout her career, it has been concrete existential questions such as these which have motivated Ruether's intellectual interests and academic research in an attempt to attain clarity over against prevalent societal and ideological presuppositions.

> In this sense all my varied intellectual interests have cohered in one way or another as an interaction of reflection and practice. This may actually be true of all intellectual life, although our concepts of "pure research" tend to deny it. But I suspect that it tends to be more consciously and concretely

---

[205]For an autobiographical account of her personal and academic career cf. Rosemary Radford Ruether, *Disputed Questions: On Being a Christian* (Nashville: Abingdon, 1982).

[206]Cf. ibid., pp. 76-85 and 109-141.

the case with those whose identities do not cohere readily with the dominant systems of thought and society.[207]

The affinity with Latin American liberation theology, both in its concern for a theology grounded in practical questions and in its critique of an academic theology unaware of any possible ideological functioning on behalf of the status quo, is readily apparent.

In order to appreciate Ruether's creative response to Latin American liberation theology, certain basic concepts undergirding her thought deserve special recognition. For Ruether perhaps the most fundamental problem facing theology has been historically and continues to be the bifurcation of thought into various dualistic categories.[208] Through a long and complex historical process which Ruether has detailed through numerous studies, human relationships have come to be structured in terms of hierarchy and domination.[209] Philosophically speaking, the most significant of these dualisms include the apocalyptic dualism between good and evil, the gnostic dualism between soul and body, and the modern conceptual dualism between subject and object.[210] In each of these respective dualisms it is important to note that the contrasted pairs do not exist as equal partners but rather that a value judgment is made. Just as in the apocalyptic dualism good is clearly superior to evil, so also in the gnostic dualism soul is superior to body and in the modern conceptual dualism the subject is valued more highly than the object. Simultaneously Ruether has noted the existence of other comparable philosophical dualisms such as spirit-matter, reason-emotion, sacred-secular, individual-community, or transcendent world-this world.[211] Each of these philosophical dualisms has in turn contributed in its own peculiar way

---

[207]Rosemary Radford Ruether, "Asking the Existential Questions," *Chr Cent* 97 (Apr. 2, 1980):375.

[208]For an excellent discussion of the criticism of dualistic thinking in Ruether's thought see Judith Vaughan, *Sociality, Ethics, and Social Change. A Critical Appraisal of Reinhold Niebuhr's Ethics in the Light of Rosemary Radford Ruether's Works* (Lanham, MD: University Press of America, 1983), pp. 103-145.

[209]For example, cf. Rosemary Radford Ruether, "Paradoxes of Human Hope: The Messianic Horizon of Church and Society," *Th St* 33 (June 1972): 235-252 and "Outlines for a Theology of Liberation," *Dial* 11 (Autumn 1972):252-257.

[210]Rosemary Radford Ruether, "Foundations for a Theology of Liberation," in *Liberation Theology. Human Hope Confronts Christian History and American Power* (New York: Paulist, 1972), pp. 10-22, and "Outlines for a Theology of Liberation," pp. 255-256.

[211]Ruether, *Liberation Theology*, p. 6.

to the structuring of human relationships under the pattern "oppressor-oppressed."[212]

These various philosophical dualisms have found expression in manifold ways throughout history both in Christianity and other world-views. In Christianity, the incorporation of such dualistic thinking contradicted what was for Israel and the Hebrew mind an essentially holistic world-view. While tensions between such concepts also clearly exist in Hebrew thought, they did not acquire radically dualistic proportions until a relatively late date under the influence of Persian apocalyptic thinking and Platonic philosophy.[213]

The consequences of dualistic thinking become most ominous in its various historical concretions. For Ruether the primary and in many ways paradigmatic form of hierarchical domination between human beings is the relationship between man and woman.

> Sexual or male-female dualism was the original model for this social projection of psychic dualism. Classical Christian spirituality viewed man as a "rational spirit." The male alone was said to fully possess this "human nature" in its essence. The male alone was made in the "image of God," modeled in his inward being after the intellectual *Logos* or "mind" of God (which was also the theological identity of Christ). The female was said to lack this full "image of God" in herself, and to possess it only when taken together with the male "who is the head." Likewise, women were seen as possessing no rights over their own bodies, but as standing under the tutelage and being possessed as the private property of a particular male, first their fathers, and then their husbands. Male-female dualism was seen as a social extension of subject-object dualism, so the male alone was the perceiver and the articulator of the relationship, while the woman was translated into an "object" in relation to this male perception and "use." Thus women were seen, literally, as "sexual objects," either to be used instrumentally, as a "baby-making body," or else to be shunned as the incarnation of tempting, debasing "sensuality."[214]

The superiority of good over evil, soul over body, spirit over matter, reason over emotion, etc., from a philosophical viewpoint became, through a complex historical process, intertwined with Christian thinking and constitutive for the relationship between man and woman, i.e., man over woman. This hierarchical domination of man over woman became, in multiple ways throughout the course of history, a structured component of human relationships. In numerous studies Ruether has detailed various oppressive attitudes held toward women throughout history—from tribal times, the history of Israel, the origins

---

[212]Ibid., p. 1.

[213]Ibid., pp. 10-16.

[214]Ibid., p. 19.

of Christianity, the patristic period, monasticism, medieval thought and society, the industrial revolution, up to the present century.[215] This particular male-female dualism serves for Ruether as the model for understanding the other historical concretions of dualism which have come to characterize human relationships.

A second historical form in which dualistic thinking has come to be structured in human relationships is that of racism. In this manifestation it is especially the dualistic assertion of white over black which has had fateful consequences for American history. The relationship oppressor-oppressed which emerges from dualistic thinking finds a direct historical concretion in the history of black people in the United States and comparably wherever racism prevails. Ruether has included in her thought a concern for overcoming this form of domination as another component of her attempt to develop a holistic theology of liberation.[216]

A third component of Ruether's holistic understanding of liberation theology arises in response to anti-Semitism, especially as it has theological roots in the Christian tradition. Dualistic thinking has had tragic consequences for the relationship between Christians and Jews in that here too human relationships have been structured in a hierarchy of domination, i.e., Christians over Jews. In a number of essays and especially in a seminal work, *Faith and Fratricide. The Theological Roots of Anti-Semitism* (1974), Ruether has documented and analyzed the history of Christian anti-Semitism—its Greek and Jewish antecedents, its New Testament basis, the vilification of the Jews in the Church Fathers, and the incorporation of a negative myth of

---

[215]For example, cf. Rosemary Radford Ruether, "Is Christianity Misogynist? The Failure of Women's Liberation in the Church" in *Liberation Theology*, pp. 95-114; "Misogynism and Virginal Feminism in the Fathers of the Church," in Rosemary Radford Ruether, ed., *Religion and Sexism. Images of Woman in the Jewish and Christian Traditions* (New York: Simon and Schuster, 1974), pp. 150-183; and *New Woman New Earth. Sexist Ideologies and Human Liberation* (New York: Seabury, 1975), pp. 1-85.

[216]Cf. Rosemary Radford Ruether, "Is There a Black Theology? The Validity and Limits of a Racial Perspective," in *Liberation Theology*, pp. 127-145, in which she also warns against the danger of black theology's simply reversing the dualism into a new form of domination without overcoming it; and "Crisis in Sex and Race: Black Theology vs. Feminist Theology," *Chr Cris* 34 (Apr. 15, 1974):67-73, in which she attempts to address the issues which tend to drive black and feminist theologies into competition rather than cooperation with one another. In addition to critiquing both black and feminist theologies for possible blind spots, Ruether also points toward the contribution which could be made by black feminism in overcoming such weaknesses.

the Jews into Christendom.[217] For Ruether a holistic theology of
liberation must consciously take steps toward first recognizing, then
admitting and overcoming the despicable anti-Semitic attitude held by
Christians against Jews throughout history which has led to so many
unspeakable crimes.

In a holistic theology of liberation Ruether would also include an
overcoming of the dualism which pits one class against another.
Classism is yet another historical concretion of dualistic thinking
which has become embedded in social structures establishing rich
versus poor, i.e., the domination of the rich over the poor. It is under
this category which Latin American liberation theology is included by
Ruether. Once again she has addressed herself to this essential
component of a holistic liberation theology in a number of writings
which will be examined in greater detail following this brief overview
of Ruether's thought as a whole.[218]

As a final component of a comprehensive theology of liberation
Ruether finds indispensable a concern for overcoming the domination
and exploitation of nature itself by human beings in the modern
world.[219] In this regard it is the dualism between subject and object in
both post-Cartesian thought and technologism which is of primary
relevance. Even as the preponderance of dualistic thought has led to the
structuring of human relationships into hierarchies of oppression in
sexism, racism, anti-Semitism, and classism, so too nature has been
subordinated to human whim without taking sufficient consideration
of the negative consequences to the delicate ecological balances upon
which life itself depends.

The nineteenth-century concept of "progress" materialized with the Judeo-
Christian God concept. Males, identifying their egos with transcendent

---

[217]Cf. Rosemary Radford Ruether, "Judaism and Christianity: A
Dialogue Refused" and "Christian Anti-Semitism and the Dilemma of
Zionism," in *Liberation Theology*, pp. 65-93; and *Faith and Fratricide. The
Theological Roots of Anti-Semitism* (New York: Seabury, 1974).

[218]For example, cf. Rosemary Radford Ruether, "Latin American
Theology of Liberation and the Birth of a Planetary Humanity," in *Liberation
Theology*, pp. 175-194.

[219]Cf. Rosemary Radford Ruether, "Mother Earth and the Megamachine:
A Theology of Liberation in a Feminine, Somatic and Ecological Perspective,"
in *Liberation Theology*, pp. 115-126; "New Woman and New Earth: Women,
Ecology, and Social Revolution," in *New Woman New Earth*, pp. 186-211; and
"Ecology and Human Liberation: A Conflict between the Theology of History
and the Theology of Nature?" in *To Change the World. Christology and
Cultural Criticism* (New York: Crossroad, 1981), pp. 57-70.

"spirit," made technology the project of progressive incarnation of transcendent "spirit" into "nature." The eschatological god became a historical project. Now one attempted to realize infinite demand through infinite material "progress," impelling nature forward to infinite expansion of productive power. Infinite demand incarnate in finite nature, in the form of infinite exploitation of the earth's resources for production, results in ecological disaster: the rapid eating up of the organic foundations of life under our feet in an effort to satisfy ever-growing appetites for goods. The matrix of being, which is no less the foundation of human being, is rapidly depleted. Within two centuries this pattern of thought and activity has brought humanity close to the brink of the destruction of the earth and its environment.[220]

Ruether here pays special attention to the historical development of dualistic thinking which has resulted in devastating consequences for the earth's ecosystem.

Together these five components—sexism, racism, anti-Semitism, classism, and the exploitation of nature—provide the parameters of Ruether's proposal for a holistic liberation theology. Each of these has been examined by Ruether in their historical development (especially in their relatedness to philosophical dualistic thinking) and in their contemporary manifestations. Taken together they witness to a modern world fundamentally characterized by social structures in which domination and hierarchy are the norm.[221] In effect this means the modern world, standing at the end of a long history of dualistic thinking, is permeated by false consciousness and alienation. This reality contradicts an ideal of salvation in which domination and oppression give way to reconciliation and mutuality. In the modern world the polarization of thought into the various philosophical and historical dualisms has resulted in the alienation of human beings from themselves, from each other, and from the world. It is to the overcoming of these basic alienations, rooted as they are in dualistic thought patterns, that Ruether addresses her theology seeking a holistic approach to liberation at each of these various levels.

In addition to the major place Ruether has given to countering the effects of dualistic thinking in her theology, another basic concept which undergirds her writings is the affirmation that the prophetic tradition must be recognized as the normative tradition for the interpretation of the Bible and thus for Christianity itself. In this way it is the prophetic tradition which functions as Ruether's "canon within

---

[220]Ruether, *New Woman New Earth*, p. 194.

[221]For the following cf. Vaughan, *Sociality, Ethics, and Social Change*, pp. 105-112.

the canon." This affirmation is particularly important for Ruether due
to the fact that it is precisely in the prophetic tradition that the distortions of dualistic thinking have been for the most part overcome.[222]

> At its best, prophetic faith represents a decisive break with the pattern of
> religion that makes the divine a confirming theophany of the existing
> social order. Instead, the existing social order as a hierarchy of rich over
> poor, the powerful over the weak, is seen as contrary to God's will, an
> apostasy to God's intent for creational community.[223]

It is this prophetic tradition that is also a resource for overcoming the
effects of dualistic thinking today.

Ruether goes on to affirm that while the prophetic tradition is for the
biblical faith the normative tradition, the prophets themselves have not
always drawn all the necessary consequences of their fundamental
understanding of God as advocate of the oppressed.

> But even when biblical texts are most clearly in this prophetic mode, not all
> dimensions of unjust relations may be discerned. The prophet may see
> clearly the injustice of rich urbanites against impoverished countryfolk,
> or of imperial nations against the small and scattered nations, but may
> miss entirely the injustice of master-slave relations, of male-female
> relations in patriarchal, slave-holding society, or else ameliorate these
> relations in more conventional ways that still take the basic system for
> granted.[224]

It remains the task of a critical theology to proceed on the basis of the
God of the prophetic tradition who is the advocate of the oppressed to
draw all consequent conclusions for contemporary life even when the
prophets themselves did not do so.

> Prophetic critique as the norm of biblical faith, therefore, is not limited to
> the insights of the societies that produced the biblical texts. Rather, this
> principle goes out ahead of us, allowing us to apply it in new ways in new
> contexts. Only in this way is biblical faith a living faith and not a dead
> letter.[225]

Time and again Ruether has sought to explore how this prophetic
tradition has remained alive, expressing itself ever anew in history.
It is within history itself and not in some trans-historical realm that
the prophets looked for the arrival of God's salvation. On this
particular point Ruether and the Latin American liberation
theologians fully agree, i.e., that "history is one" and itself the raw

---

[222]For the following see Ruether, *Disputed Questions*, pp. 30-35. Cf. also
Ruether, *Liberation Theology*, pp. 7-9; "Individual Repentance Is Not Enough,"
Explor 2 (1976):50-52; and "Asking the Existential Questions," p. 376.

[223]Ibid., pp. 32-33.

[224]Ibid., p. 33.

[225]Ibid., pp. 34-35.

material for God's salvation.[226] Thus current history also becomes the
realm in which social change for the sake of justice is to be achieved.
Especially in her book, *The Radical Kingdom. The Western Experience of Messianic Hope* (1970), Ruether has examined a variety of
movements in which the prophetic hope for the historical arrival of the
messianic age revived itself, appearing in ever new forms—e.g., the
radical reformers, the nineteenth century utopian socialists, the Social
Gospel movement, Marxism and Christian Socialism, the theology of
hope, etc. In reflecting on this radical, prophetic, messianic hope,
Ruether writes of the task of the present:

> Yet within the bounds of present life, the struggle itself is its own reward.
> It is in the process of struggle against debased existence, with the attendant
> demands for moral sensitizing, self-discipline, and constant resetting of
> one's sights upon the vision of salvation, that one is closest to the secret of
> human life.[227]

It is in commitment to the struggle for justice that life itself finds its
meaning.

This thought leads to the consideration of a final basic concept
which undergirds Ruether's theological work, her conviction that "all
liberation scholarship is advocacy scholarship."[228] For Ruether this
does not mean a loss of objectivity, rather clarity about one's
commitment to the struggle for justice insofar as "neutrality hides a
commitment to the status quo."[229]

> The theological questions have to do with the fundamental tension between
> the "is" and the "ought" of human life. They rise from the fundamental
> contradiction between man's existence and his aspirational horizon of
> meaning and value. Out of this tension and contradiction arise the
> fundamental theological questions about a man's "nature," his "origin"
> and his "goal;" how man can transform himself in his personal and
> social history and what "power" and from whence mediates between this
> "transcendent nature," "ground" and "goal," and his "fallen"
> reality.[230]

Ruether calls theologians to take up this critical and prophetic task and
to understand their work in terms of contributing to the goal of social

---

[226]Cf. Rosemary Radford Ruether, *The Radical Kingdom. The Western
Experience of Messianic Hope* (New York: Paulist, 1970), pp. 1-18, and Vaughn,
Sociality, Ethics, and Social Change, p. 194.

[227]Ruether, *The Radical Kingdom*, p. 288.

[228]Ruether, *New Woman New Earth*, p. xii.

[229]Ibid.

[230]Ruether, *Liberation Theology*, p. 3.

transformation.[231] In this way theologians are to combine their skills
with other disciplines in promoting human liberation on all its various
levels.[232]

Clearly it is to this very task that Ruether has committed her own
scholarship.

> I would regard my own mode of thinking as dialectical. I see negation not
> as an attack on someone else's person or community, but as a self-
> criticism of the distortions of one's own being and community. Criticism
> of these distortions opens up the way for a positive reconstruction of the
> healing and liberating word of the tradition and capacities of human life.
> This is the healing and liberating word that I have heard emerge from the
> Christian tradition, once freed of its distorted consciousness. This is the
> healing and liberating word I would hope to communicate to others. But
> this healing and hope is available only through the cross of negation.[233]

Holistic liberation is to be advocated by the theologian in opposing all
philosophical dualism in thought and all historical dualisms
structured into hierarchical relationships of domination. Thus
theology is both an intellectual (ideological) task in challenging false
consciousness and a practical task in serving social transformation
on behalf of justice.

Several of Ruether's writings elaborate in greater detail how she
understands Latin American liberation theology to belong to the
historical struggle toward holistic liberation. Already in 1972 Latin
American liberation theology was established as an integral part of
her concern for a holistic liberation theology in her book *Liberation
Theology*. In her essay "Latin American Theology of Liberation and
the Birth of a Planetary Humanity," Ruether articulates how liberation
theology must be seen "in a global context" pressing forward to "a new
awareness of the universal *humanum*."[234] Latin American liberation
theology is seen to play a major role in the development of this
planetary consciousness.

Ruether pays special attention to the praxis-orientation of Latin
American liberation theology as it has arisen in its own historical
context under the influence of its own particular history, the history of
colonialism. Particular attention is devoted to the contrast between the
traditional Constantinian identification of the church in Latin

---

[231] Cf. Rosemary Radford Ruether, "What Is the Task of Theology?" *Chr
Cris* 36 (May 24, 1976):121-125.

[232] Cf. Ruether, *Liberation Theology*, pp. 1-4.

[233] Ruether, *Disputed Questions*, pp. 141-142.

[234] Ruether, "Latin American Theology of Liberation and the Birth of a
Planetary Humanity," in *Liberation Theology*, p. 175.

America with the existing hierarchical social structure and the rising revolutionary consciousness among many Latin Americans. Among the various aspects of Latin American liberation thought, Ruether especially emphasizes the process of conscientization and liberation theology's critical use of Marxist analysis. In this early essay Ruether showed familiarity with a number of specific movements within the Latin American scene including the Golconda movement in Colombia, the impact of Camilo Torres' decision to engage in violent revolutionary activity, and the Medellin bishops' conference. In the Latin American context which is marked by extreme polarization, Ruether examines most carefully the debate about Christian participation in violent revolution. Citing both Torres and Dom Helder Camara, Ruether saw a direct parallel between guerrilla violence in Latin America in opposition to oppressive regimes and the war in Vietnam which was still being waged at the time this essay was written. In both contexts U.S. power was seen to be discredited insofar as it was exercised in an attempt to defeat "a genuinely popular struggle for national liberation."[235]

Latin American liberation theology was seen by Ruether in this essay as a harbinger of the awakening of a revolutionary consciousness throughout the globe. In the Third World, the sophistication of Latin American thought was evaluated as particularly significant for its potential role in stimulating the development of this consciousness also in Asia and Africa. In the "development toward a planetary humanity" it is, moreover, necessary there be cooperation with "every oppressed group, in demands for national, class, racial, and sexual integrity, and identity."[236] The holistic thrust of Ruether's thinking is thus very much present. In fact, Ruether's concern for a holistic liberation even leads her to warn against the danger of a narrow "Christocentrism" which would fail to work in alliance with secular liberation movements for the attainment of the liberation which God intends for all people.[237]

In other writings Ruether has also incorporated the Latin American theology of liberation into her proposal for a holistic

---

[235]Ibid., p. 188.
[236]Ibid., p. 189.
[237]Cf. ibid., pp. 190-191.

liberation theology.[238] Like Cone, Herzog, and Brown, Ruether
encountered Latin American liberation theologians at the first
Theology in the Americas conference at Detroit in 1975 where she
emphasized the importance of intrastructuring race, class, and sex as
mutual components in a comprehensive liberation outlook.[239] At the
time of the Puebla bishop's conference in 1979, Ruether was involved on
location together with the Latin American based Project on Women
(Mujeres para el Dialogo) in offering educative seminars on
feminism and liberation theology.[240] Her linkage of feminist
liberation theology with Latin American liberation theology thus
united with those having similar concerns in the Latin American
context in an attempt to broaden the horizons of Latin American
bishops, priests, theologians, and laity to include a greater awareness
of women. In this context it is worthy of note that her book, *The Radical
Kingdom*, has also appeared in Spanish translation facilitating an
exposure to her thought in the Latin American setting.[241]

In her volume on Christology, *To Change the World. Christology
and Cultural Criticism* (1981), Latin American liberation theology
once again takes its place alongside chapters on political theology,
Christology and Jewish-Christian relations, Christology and
feminism, and the ecological implications of Christology. The Jesus
of this Christology is one who stands firmly in the prophetic tradition of
the Bible and who continues to inspire a prophetic response to the
challenges of the contemporary world.

> The teachings and liberating praxis of Jesus prove to be a focal point for
> this critical and transforming vision. Jesus discloses the transformatory
> and liberating patterns of relation to each other and, through them, to God,

---

[238]For example, cf. Rosemary Radford Ruether, "Monks and Marxists: A
Look at the Catholic Left," *Chr Cris* 33 (Apr. 30, 1973):75-79 and "The
Foundations of Liberation Languages: Christianity and Revolutionary
Movements," *J Rel Thot* 32 (1975):74-85.

[239]Cf. "Letter of Rosemary Ruether to Sergio Torres and the Planners of the
Conference" and "Response by Rosemary Ruether," in Torres and Eagleson,
eds., *Theology in the Americas*, pp. 84-86 and 372-373, which both in their own
way plead for an inclusive and holistic understanding of the total liberation
task which incorporates a "very complex intrastructuring of race, class, and
sex" without reducing the importance of the various components (p. 373).

[240]Cf. Rosemary Radford Ruether, "Consciousness-Raising at Puebla:
Women Speak to the Latin Church," *Chr Cris* 39 (Apr. 2, 1979):77-80.

[241]Published as *El Reino de los Extremistas* (Buenos Aires: La Aurora,
1971).

not only for his situation, but also in ways that continue to speak to our situation.[242]

One of the several movements which exists in continuity with the liberating praxis of Jesus in the contemporary world is Latin American liberation theology.

In her discussion of Latin American liberation Christologies, Ruether characteristically stresses the goal of liberation theology to overcome dualistic thought in a more holistic vision. With regard to the Latin American context, that means a theology which entails not only the personal but also the political dimension.[243] Ruether proceeds to offer a concise summary of the most salient points of Latin American liberation Christologies—their starting point with the liberating praxis of Jesus, their preferential option for the poor, the centrality of Jesus' gospel of God's kingdom, the call to discipleship, the criticism of the ideological tendencies of most dominant Christologies, the meaning of Jesus' cross. Just as Jesus engaged in liberating action with preference for the poor, so too "the liberation of the poor becomes the critical locus of God's action in history."[244] With Jesus' proclamation and deeds of the kingdom there was no bifurcation between spiritual and material salvation. *This* world is the world into which God brings salvation wherever justice and mutuality among human beings reigns. Ruether affirms that it is Latin American liberation theology which has been instrumental in returning the idea of the kingdom to the central position it deserves in interpreting the Christian gospel.

In her discussion of Latin American thought Ruether does not abstract from the particular history of Latin America and the challenges raised within the present social, political, and economic context. The debit of traditional Catholicism in Latin America which exploited the colonial situation to its own advantage has begun to be paid as the church has begun to turn to the poor. The martyrdom of Christians for their participation in the liberation struggle is a sign of this new commitment among many in the Latin American church.

At the end of this elaboration of Latin American liberation theology Ruether sounds a warning against two dangers in the Latin American context: first, that of absolutizing one's own revolutionary cause and

---

[242]Rosemary Radford Ruether, *To Change the World*, p. 5.

[243]For this and the following cf. ibid., pp. 19-30, which apart from a different introduction also appears in Ruether's *Disputed Questions*, pp. 90-107.

[244]Ruether, *To Change the World*, p. 20.

failing to remain open to ongoing criticism, and, secondly, to fear risking involvement at all. What Ruether has learned from her historical study of movements for social transformation is the need for them to remain self-critical lest the last fate be worse than the first.

It is important to underline this warning because it is one which occurs not only in this context but time and time again in her writings.[245] A holistic liberation theology must beware of the trap of submitting to new forms of dualistic thinking which only lead to new forms of interhuman domination and oppression.

> Quite simply, what this means is that one cannot dehumanize the oppressors without ultimately dehumanizing oneself, and aborting the possibilities of the liberation movement into an exchange of roles of oppressor and oppressed. By projecting all evil upon the oppressors and regarding their own oppressed condition as a stance of "instant righteousness," they forfeit finally their own capacity for self-criticism. Their revolt, then, if successful, tends to rush forward to murder and self-aggrandizement, and the institution of a new regime where all internal self-criticism is squelched.[246]

That liberation movements remain self-critical and avoid setting themselves up as the final and ultimate expression of human salvation is of paramount importance to Ruether.[247] Liberation theology too must avoid new forms of dualistic thinking.

Ruether's ideal in terms of the goal of the liberation struggle in her own North American context would be a form of socialism which is at once democratic, intrinsically American, nonsectarian, and politi-cally engaged.[248] Her vision for an ideal society would thus be that of a communitarian socialism which should be sharply differentiated from both Soviet totalitarianism and Western capitalism. [249]

> This means the economic and political sectors of local communities are run on the principles of subsidiarity, self-ownership, and self-management. Planning, distribution, and enforcement of standards need to be ceded to larger units: metropolitan regions, states, nations, and international bodies. But these levels of government must be rooted in strong self-governing local communities, with representatives elected from the base. Only in this way can socialism be kept from becoming total alienation of the atomized individual in huge impersonal corporatisms. An urgent task for those concerned about the society of the future is the

---

[245]For example, cf. Ruether, *Liberation Theology*, pp. 12-16, 129-138, and 190-191; *New Woman New Earth*, p. 132; *Faith and Fratricide*, pp. 228-232 and 248-249; and *To Change the World*, pp. 53-56.

[246]Ruether, *Liberation Theology*, p. 13.

[247]See Ruether, *New Woman New Earth*, p. 132.

[248]Cf. Ruether, *Disputed Questions*, pp. 85-90.

[249]Cf. Ruether, *New Woman New Earth*, pp. 206-211.

development of viable forms of local communalization on the level of residential groups, work places, and townships that can increase our control over the quality of our own lives.[250]

In the idea of communitarian socialism relationships of domination— man over woman, white over black, Christian over Jew, rich over poor, human beings over nature—are overcome and replaced by relationships of mutuality and justice. The Hebraic concept to describe this ultimate goal is *shalom*, an ideal toward which the struggle for social transformation in history ever presses forward.[251]

The response of Rosemary Radford Ruether to Latin American liberation theology is one which aims at a more comprehensive and holistic liberation theology which is simultaneously active on several levels. It should be reiterated in conclusion that for Ruether it is feminist liberation which is the paradigmatic form of liberation theology. That the primary interest of Ruether is focused on the liberation of women is documented once again in a major work, *Sexism and God-talk. Toward a Feminist Theology*, published in 1983. In this volume Ruether reflects on a number of systematic loci— methodology, sources, and norm; the doctrines of God and creation; anthropology; Christology; mariology; theodicy; ministry; social ethics; and eschatology—in the pursuit of a systematic and feminist theological viewpoint. The feminist focal point of Ruether's work needs to be highlighted lest it appear that Latin American liberation theology occupies a position in her work out of proportion to that which is actually the case. Nevertheless, even as Ruether keeps a focus on feminist liberation, it is always for the sake of a liberation viewpoint which is inclusive of others as well.

> Women are sociologically a sexual caste within every class and race. All women share certain common oppressions as women: dependency, secondary existence, domestic labor, sexual exploitation, and the structuring of their role in procreation into a total definition of their existence. There is, in this sense, a common condition of women in general. But women are also divided against each other by their integration into oppressor and oppressed classes and races. This makes the protest of the middle-class American white woman, in rebellion against the stifling horizons of bedroom suburbia, very different from the poor Indian woman of the Latin American favela on the bottom of the hierarchies of class, race, and sex. Women of oppressed classes and races cannot separate their struggle as women from their struggle as poor people

---

[250]Ibid., p. 207.
[251]Cf. Ruether, *To Change the World*, pp. 69-70.

of oppressed races. Rather, they must seek to lead their class and racial struggle out beyond the limits of patriarchal concepts of liberation.[252]
The creative thrust of Ruether's response to Latin American liberation theology occurs in her integration of the Latin American viewpoint into a holistic theology of liberation which she is convinced is apropos to the North American context. While this context requires a strong emphasis upon feminist liberation, the challenges of racism, anti-Semitism, classism, and the exploitation of nature each must also be addressed in a comprehensive liberation theology if the contemporary ramifications of dualistic thinking are to be overcome. In turn Ruether would encourage other liberation theologies toward a more holistic understanding of the total task of human liberation with a special challenge to awaken to the need for the liberation of women.[253]

F. *An Evangelical Affirmation: The Biblical Basis for Liberation*

A serious examination of Latin American liberation theology has also taken place among evangelical theologians in North America. Two characteristics mark the chief concern of evangelicals in this discussion: (1) that the Bible be understood as norm and standard of liberation theology and (2) that liberation theology be examined in relationship to the history and current theology of evangelical missions in the Third World context. Beyond these two characteristics, however, what could be said of the papers delivered at the Annual Conference of the Evangelical Theological Society held in April 1976 on the theme "The Theology of Liberation" also applies to the overall response of evangelical theologians to liberation theology, i.e., that there exists no "uniform or doctrinaire approach to the subject".[254]

In spite of general agreement that the Bible as the Word of God must serve as the final norm for measuring the validity of liberation theology, there nevertheless exists no consensus on what that means concretely for the evaluation of liberation thought. In this way the condemnation of liberation theology as "heresy" by the evangelical

---

[252]Ruether, *New Woman New Earth*, p. 30. See also Rosemary Radford Ruether, *Sexism and God-talk. Toward a Feminist Theology* (Boston: Beacon Press, 1983), p. 222.

[253]Ruether, *Sexism and God-Talk*, p. 32.

[254]Carl E. Armerding, "Introduction," in Carl E. Armerding, ed., *Evangelicals & Liberation* (Phillipsburg, NJ: Presbyterian and Reformed Publishing Co., 1979), p. vii.

theologian Kenneth Hamilton[255] can exist side by side with the judgment of another evangelical theologian, Clark H. Pinnock, who calls North American Christians to more radical discipleship on the basis of liberation theology since it "is in reality God's instrument for the refinement of our own commitment to the gospel."[256] It would appear that although evangelicals uniformly call upon the Bible as the final authority for faith and life, the hermeneutical problem regarding which tradition(s) within the plurality of biblical traditions is (are) to be recognized as normative remains unsolved. Thus there emerge distinctions such as "new evangelical" or "radical evangelicalism" to describe an evangelical position which gives special authority to the biblical traditions which speak of God's demand of justice for the poor and of radical discipleship over against a more conservative evangelical theology oriented toward those biblical passages supporting the concern for the conversion of individuals to a personal relationship with Jesus Christ for the sake of eternal salvation. While all evangelicals acknowledge the central importance of conversion for Christian existence, the "radical" evangelicals most strongly emphasize a conversion which leads to discipleship on behalf of the poor and oppressed in this world, even as a more conservative evangelicalism emphasizes to a greater extent the transcendent and other-worldly nature of salvation.

Nowhere is the evangelical community more divided than on the question of liberation theology. As is the case with North American churches and theologians in general, a polarization of views on the issue of liberation theology cuts through all positions which otherwise claim allegiance to the selfsame tradition. This is not to say that no attempt has been made by evangelicals to provide a balanced presentation and evaluation of liberation theology. On the contrary, many evangelical theologians have been extremely serious in striving to understand and fairly critique liberation theology.[257] Even so, it seems to be the nature of liberation theology itself to evoke either a

---

[255]Kenneth Hamilton, "Liberation Theology: Lessons Positive and Negative," in ibid., p. 124.

[256]Clark H. Pinnock, "A Call for the Liberation of North American Christians," in ibid., p. 128.

[257]For example, cf. the thoughtful paper by Stephen C. Knapp, "A Preliminary Dialogue with Gutierrez's *A Theology of Liberation*," in ibid., pp. 10-42.

radical resonance on the basis of its presuppositions and proposals or
an equally stringent critique.

In this section and again in the next chapter, the positions of
representatives from the North American evangelical tradition
standing on both sides of the liberation theology debate are presented.
The positions of Ronald J. Sider, Jim Wallis and the Sojourners
community, and Alfred C. Krass serve to represent the reception of
Latin American liberation theology in North America while the
positions of C. Peter Wagner, Carl Henry and *Christianity Today*, and
Donald C. Bloesch have been selected to represent evangelical
critiques of liberation theology.

In considering the evangelical reception of liberation theology, the
contribution of Orlando E. Costas can be mentioned by way of
introduction to the evangelical discussion. Costas, a native of Puerto
Rico and recently Thornley B. Wood Professor of Missiology at
Eastern Baptist Theological Seminary, has been a widely quoted
spokesman for the concerns of liberation theology to North American
evangelicals, especially insofar as Latin American liberation
theology requires a rethinking of the meaning and task of North
American missions.[258] Costas has been an advocate of a holistic
approach to Christian missions which seeks to hold together both
commitment to evangelization and a prophetic social concern.

> If we can enable Christian women and men around the world to see the
> billions who have yet to hear the good news of salvation, to commit their
> lives to their integral evangelization, and to acquire the necessary
> analytical tools and communication skills to facilitate such a task; if we
> can enable them to have prophetic courage and confront social institutions
> with the demands of the gospel; and if we can foster in them a "spirituality
> for combat" (M.M. Thomas), we shall have been indeed faithful to the
> whole gospel and sensitive to the fullness of the world to which God has
> sent us.[259]

On the basis of this holistic approach to missions Costas has also raised
the question if, on the basis of the experience of the gospel among the
poor in the Third World, the U.S. itself might not be in need of

---

[258]Cf. Orlando E. Costas, *Christ Outside the Gate. Mission Beyond
Christendom* (Maryknoll: Orbis, 1982).

[259]Ibid., p. 172. In this book Costas also draws special attention to the
parallels between the modern missionary movement and the "business
enterprise" model of emerging capitalism (pp. 58-70) and also to the need for an
authentic North American response to the cry of Latin America (pp. 103-116). In
addition Costas interprets for North American readers what he calls the
"prophetic significance of Third World liberation theologies" (pp. 117-134).

missionizing by Third World Christians.[260] In these ways Costas, former colleague of Ronald J. Sider at Eastern Baptist Theological Seminary, has raised a number of pointed questions regarding the meaning of missions in the North American context on the basis of a theology which has been significantly shaped by the viewpoint of Latin American liberation theology. These are important concerns which recur throughout the evangelical discussion of liberation theology.

1. Ronald J. Sider

Ronald J. Sider, a professor of theology at Eastern Baptist Theological Seminary in Philadelphia who has also served as president of Evangelicals for Social Action, is a highly respected evangelical scholar and author. A mere survey of his writings indicates his interest in the social concerns which also motivate Latin American liberation theology, particularly the problem of Third World poverty, though Sider approaches these issues in a distinctively evangelical fashion. Indicative of Sider's approach is the following passage excerpted from "The Chicago Declaration of Evangelical Social Concern" of which Sider was both co-author and signer:

> We must attack the materialism of our culture and the maldistribution of the nation's wealth and services. We recognize that as a nation we play a crucial role in the imbalance and injustice of international trade and development. Before God and a billion hungry neighbors, we must rethink our values regarding our present standard of living and promote more just acquisition and distribution of the world's resources.[261]

This document points to a strong concern among evangelicals for the problems of world poverty and structural injustice which are also the starting points of Latin American liberation theology.

Sider's genuine concern for and knowledgeableness on the problems of hunger and poverty in the world is best documented by his book, *Rich Christians in an Age of Hunger: A Biblical Study* (1977).[262] Central issues behind this book are the immense disparity between rich and poor, and Christian responsibility in the face of a hungry world. Employing a variety of concrete examples to press into consciousness the dimensions of the problem of world hunger, Sider undertakes a

---

[260]Cf. ibid., pp. 71-85 and 183-186.

[261]"The Chicago Declaration of Evangelical Social Concern," in Alfred C. Krass, *Evangelizing Neopagan North America. The Word That Frees* (Scottsdale, PA: Herald Press, 1982), pp. 187-188.

[262]For the following cf. Ronald J. Sider, *Rich Christians in an Age of Hunger: A Biblical Study* (Downers Grove, IL: Inter-Varsity, 1977).

careful examination of numerous biblical passages pertinent to the issue of poverty and wealth. Among the images which occur in his study of biblical texts are several which are directly paralleled in the writings of Latin American liberation theologians, e.g., the "God of the poor." It is striking how such biblical passages, long dormant, have received new prominence not only from Latin American liberation theologians but also from a North American evangelical theologian like Sider. It is therefore not surprising that Sider, like the Latin American liberation theologians, is led to investigate the causes of the poverty which exists on such a massive global scale. At this point Sider, like Latin American liberation theologians, begins to speak about the meaning of "structural evil," i.e., "evil social systems and societal structures that unfairly benefit some and harm others."[263]

Sider examines both the biblical evidence and the contemporary phenomenon of "structural evil." Contemporary examples include the high rate of return gained on U.S. investments in Latin America and the participation of the U.S. secret service in the overthrow of the Allende government in Chile in 1973.[264] Sider draws the following conclusion from such evidence:

> The proper conclusion is that injustice has become embedded in some of our fundamental economic institutions. Biblical Christians—precisely to the extent that they are faithful to Scripture—will dare to call such structures sinful.[265]

The question of structural evil and especially its relationship to the theory of development is one which has occupied Sider and other evangelicals in depth.[266] An analysis of structural evil has led Sider to call for "a new praxis" on three levels: personal lifestyle, ecclesial commitments, and political involvement. In the final chapters of *Rich Christians in an Age of Hunger*, Sider offers encouragement and concrete suggestions to those who would take seriously the biblical call to repentance on each of these levels. Especially relevant in light of

---

[263]Ibid., p. 133.

[264]See ibid., pp. 160-163.

[265]Ibid., p. 162.

[266]Cf. Ronald J. Sider, ed., *Evangelicals and Development. Toward a Theology of Social Change* (Philadelphia: Westminster, 1981). This volume is a compilation of papers from a "Consultation on the Theology of Development" sponsored by the Unit on Ethics and Society of the Theological Commission of the World Evangelical Fellowship of which Sider has been the convener. Especially interesting in this context is Sider's reference in his "Introduction" to "the strong insistence of Third World leadership that the question of social structures which create poverty must receive new attention" (p. 10).

Latin American liberation theology's political commitments is
Sider's proposal that North American Christians need to begin to think
politically. What that entails for Sider includes support for such
measures as a foreign policy which takes up the cause of the poor, the
reform of international trade conditions, policies which give priority to
the world hunger problem, and efforts to curb the arms race which
diverts precious resources away from food programs to armaments
production.[267]

At this point, however, the views of the North American evangelical
Sider part company from many Latin American theologians of
liberation. Sider in his North American context with one eye on world
hunger and another on the nuclear arms race, has offered biblical
arguments for the normative status of nonviolence for Christians and
has sought to provoke new thought on how nonviolent strategies might
be creatively employed.[268]   Many Latin American liberation
theologians have in contrast, come to entertain violent resistance to
structural evil as a tragic but possibly necessary option if positive
social change in the situation of the poor is to be realized. In a similar
way many Latin American liberation theologians have come to agree
that an option for socialism is necessitated in the Latin American
context as a concrete political position. This contrasts to Sider's
reluctance to identify his thought with any one concrete political or
economic option. For him commitment to specific issues takes
precedence over participation in the struggle of political movements to
obtain political power. Sider's focus remains on a praxis for North
America and for him that means efforts to reform inadequate social
structures especially by nonviolent means.[269] In Latin America
however, mere reform measures have come to be deemed insufficient
and the call has been raised for more radical structural change.

A concise summary of Sider's thought with regard to liberation
theology has been written in essay form under the title "An
Evangelical Theology of Liberation."[270]   The central question

---

[267]Cf. Sider, *Rich Christians in an Age of Hunger*, pp. 206-223.

[268]Cf. Ronald J. Sider, *Christ and Violence* (Scottsdale, PA: Herald Press,
1979) and Ronald J. Sider and Richard Taylor, *Nuclear Holocaust and
Christian Hope: A Book for Christian Peacemakers* (Ramsey, NJ: Paulist,
1982).

[269]See Sider, *Rich Christians in an Age of Hunger*, pp. 207-208.

[270]For the following see Ronald J. Sider, "An Evangelical Theology for
Liberation," *Chr Cent* 97 (Mar. 19, 1980):314-318.

addressed is that of the biblical legitimacy of liberation theology's claim that God takes the side of the poor. While Sider takes exception to liberation theology's tendency "to blur the distinction between the church and the world," nevertheless Sider, on the basis of Scriptural argument, agrees with liberation theology's fundamental affirmation that "God *is* on the side of the poor and the oppressed."[271] Sider is careful to distinguish what he means by this affirmation, however. It does not mean, for example, the idealization of the poor or any exclusion of the rich from the purview of God's concern as a matter of principle. Neither does it mean a reduction of all biblical truth to this single affirmation nor submitting to any nonscriptural, ideological interpretation of oppression (e.g., Marxism). Rather it is on the basis of Scripture itself—Sider considers specifically the Exodus, the prophetic interpretation of the destruction of Israel and Judah, the incarnation of God in Jesus, the biblical witness on riches, and the biblical teaching that the people of God are to imitate God in taking the side of the poor—that an evangelical theology of liberation has its foundation.

In referring to numerous biblical texts, Sider writes:

> . . . [T]he words are plain. What do they mean for Western Christians who demand increasing affluence each year while people in the Third World suffer malnutrition, deformed bodies and brains, even starvation? The text clearly says that if we fail to aid the needy, we do not have God's love— no matter what we may say. The text demands deeds, not pious phrases and saintly speeches. Regardless of what we do or say at 11 A.M. Sunday morning, those who neglect the poor and oppressed are not the people of God.[272]

On the basis of Scripture Sider raises a challenge to the evangelical community in North America to reexamine the faithfulness of its words and deeds in relationship to the God who takes the side of the poor. He asks whether evangelical Christians who place such great stress on biblical orthodoxy have not themselves succumbed to a non-biblical "theological liberalism" which plays an ideological role in supporting a materialistic society.

> [W]e must teach and live, in a world full of injustice and starvation, the important biblical doctrine that God and his faithful people are on the side of the poor and oppressed. Unless we drastically reshape both our theology and our entire institutional church life so that this fact becomes as central to evangelical theology and evangelical institutional programs as it is in Scripture, we will demonstrate to the world that our verbal commitment to

---

[271] Ibid., p. 314.
[272] Ibid., p. 317.

sola scriptura is a dishonest ideological support for an unjust, materialistic status quo.[273]

To such an assertion Latin American liberation theology could only add its agreement.

The resonant response of Ronald J. Sider to liberation theology finds its foundation in the biblical passages which witness to the commitment of God and God's people to justice for the poor. In applying such biblical insights to his own North American context of evangelical Christianity, the concrete proposals Sider makes move in the direction of Christian support for political and economic reform measures rather than more radical means of social change. Still Sider has acknowledged the structural dimensions of human sinfulness and thus recognizes the importance of Christian support for the nonviolent change of social structures. The response of Sider to the central concerns of Latin American liberation theology has been most significant in his attempt to raise the awareness of North American evangelicals of the devastating effects of world hunger, their own responsibility for this problem as U.S. citizens, and especially the biblical witness to a God who takes the side of the poor. It is on the basis of their understanding of the biblical witness to justice that the concern of Sider and Latin American liberation theology merge, whereas they diverge in terms of the strategies which may be necessary for achieving change in social structures. This divergence is in part attributable to the very different social contexts in which they operate as well as to Sider's pacifist interpretation of the Christian imperative.

2. Jim Wallis and the Sojourners Community

Jim Wallis, pastor of the Washington, D.C. based Sojourners Community, preacher, activist, author, and editor of *Sojourners* magazine, has, since the early seventies, exercised considerable influence on the thinking of North American evangelicals. Wallis, raised in Detroit within the Plymouth Brethren church, became sensitized early in his life to racism against black people and during his college years was active in opposing the U.S. war in Vietnam.[274] Upon entering Trinity Evangelical Divinity School he joined with others in combining an activist social concern with an evangelical

---

[273]Ibid., p. 318.

[274]For an autobiographical account cf. Jim Wallis, *Revive Us Again. A Sojourner's Story* (Nashville: Abingdon, 1983).

theology in what was to later become the distinguishing mark of the
Sojourners community.

The position of Wallis and the Sojourners community might be
characterized as consistently pro-life. What this means is that on
every social issue, the attempt is made to discern how the life which God
has created can best be preserved and enhanced. In this way pro-life
does not exclusively refer to opposition to abortion. Rather a host of
issues are included under the pro-life umbrella including opposition to
the nuclear arms race, supporting the rights of blacks and women,
criticizing both right-wing military dictatorships and left-wing
totalitarian governments, and defending the earth's environment.[275]
It also means advocacy on behalf of the poor and oppressed.

> Christian conscience is especially sensitive to those who are the victims of
> the prevailing social order. The poor, the marginalized, the political
> prisoners, the oppressed race or class, women, the ethnic minority—these
> are the ones Christians should be particularly attentive to in any society.
> Christians must see the view from the outside, learn from the perspective of
> the bottom, hear the voices of the forgotten ones.[276]

It is with this concern for the "victims of the prevailing social order"
and the poor, that Wallis and the Sojourners community have devoted
considerable attention to the Latin American context and to the views of
Latin American liberation theology.

The earliest roots of the Sojourners community date back to the
early seventies where a number of evangelical Christians in the
Chicago area began to experiment in new forms of community
living.[277] In 1975 the move was made to the present location of the
community in a poor section of Washington, D.C. In addition to the
many social ministries of the Sojourners (e.g., peace ministry,
organizing renters, day care, book service), it is common participation
in prayer and worship which is the center of the community's life.

> We seek...to live in such a way that our personal and corporate spiritual
> disciplines help us see and understand the movement of the Spirit in our
> inner lives, our community, the churches, and history. To sustain us over
> the years, our disciplines must not be used to protect us from the world or
> from one another, but to deepen our faith so that we can give more of our
> lives for the sake of Christ.
> These disciplines include prayer, solitude, and spiritual direction. The
> relationship that each of us has with Jesus Christ is the building block of

[275]Cf. Jim Wallis, "The Rise of Christian Conscience," *Sojourners* 14, No.
1 (Jan. 1985):16.
[276]Ibid.
[277]For the following cf. Wallis, *Revive Us Again*, pp. 92-108.

community, and that relationship needs to be affirmed and renewed in prayer.[278]

The social involvements of the community are in these ways directly related to an evangelical piety and community worship. Especially in light of the combination of worship and social concern it might be possible to draw a certain parallel between this form of Christian community and that of the basic Christian communities of Latin America.

Jim Wallis has been the author of two books in addition to an autobiography.[279] As was the case with Sider, Wallis seeks to ground his theology in an evangelical understanding of the Bible. Also like Sider this has meant recovering certain biblical themes which have not been typical of evangelical thought in recent times. Criticizing what he calls "evangelical nationalism," Wallis writes:

> The problem is not that they mix faith and politics; biblical faith has political meaning. The problem is that this patriotic religion does not stand for the same things as the original evangel, the original good news. If we evaluate every claim of Christian politics by the standard of the gospel, this evangelical nationalism is neither Christian nor genuinely evangelical. The longtime accommodation of evangelicalism to the values of American power, and especially its recent hardening into a religious vision of zealous nationalism, has all but destroyed the integrity of the term evangelical.[280]

Wallis' critique of an extreme American nationalism by evangelicals is carried out on the basis of an attempt to look at the world "from below." Such a perspective is one Wallis can affirm as genuinely biblical insofar as God has been revealed as one who takes the side of the poor.

In *The Call to Conversion*, Wallis includes—alongside other chapters on the biblical foundations of radical evangelical faith, the nuclear threat, Christian community, worship, and resurrection hope—a chapter which is simply titled "The Injustice."[281] It is in this chapter that one sees the affinity of Wallis' thinking for the issues which also motivate liberation theology. It also clearly illustrates how Wallis' concern for the poor is established within a comprehensive evangelical world-view. Wallis emphasizes the disparity between rich America and the poor, whether they are within the U.S. itself or in

[278]Ibid., pp. 104-105.

[279]Jim Wallis, *Agenda for Biblical People* (New York: Harper & Row, 1976) and *The Call to Conversion* (San Francisco: Harper & Row, 1981).

[280]Wallis, *The Call to Conversion*, p. 26.

[281]For the following cf. ibid., pp. 38-72.

a foreign land. On the basis of biblical teaching Wallis calls, first, for
the solidarity of Christians with the poor and, second, for American
Christians to convert from life-styles of over-consumption and waste to
the relinquishment of wealth on behalf of the majority of the world's
people who are poor. The choice, as Wallis sees it, is between the God of
the poor or mammon. According to Wallis the biblical evidence is
clear as to which choice conforms to the will of God.

Wallis employs a vivid image to express his view of the current
state of the world:

> The relationship of the poor to the rich today can be illustrated by two
> hands. An outstretched hand is rising up from the South, seeking
> liberation. As the hand moves outward, it encounters another hand, made
> into the palm-forward sign to halt; it is a wall blocking the movement of
> the outstretched hand. The open hand moves against the wall, again and
> again, gradually becoming a fist pounding on the hand that refuses to
> yield. Soon the second hand also clenches and hardens into a fist. This is
> how we must characterize the world today, as the two fists pounding
> against one another.[282]

Wallis recognizes that the "word *liberation* expresses the deepest
aspiration in the hearts of the poor and powerless around the world."[283]
He is also convinced that the movements for liberation which are al—
ready in motion will not rest until they have achieved their goal.

Wallis also serves as the editor of *Sojourners* magazine (formerly
the *Post-American*) and it is through this medium that the Sojourners
community has played a significant role in bringing an awareness of
current Latin American issues and Latin American liberation
theology before its readership (the circulation of *Sojourners* magazine
is approximately 55,000 per issue). Through feature articles on such
topics as a response to the National Bipartisan Commission on Central
America, the situation of political refugees from El Salvador,
Honduras, and Guatemala, the witness of Argentina's mothers of the
Plaza de Mayo, or an outline for an evangelical liberation theology;[284]

---

[282]Ibid., p. 156.

[283]Ibid.

[284]Cf. "Changing Course. A Response to the National Bipartisan
Commission on Central America," *Sojourners* 13, No. 3 (Mar. 1984):10-12;
"Breaking the Veil of Darkness," *Sojourners* 12, No. 11 (Dec. 1983):16-21;
Yvonne Dilling, "Baby Jesus in a Hammock," *Sojourners* 12, No. 11 (Dec.
1983):20-21; John Hammond, "A Word Out of Silence," *Sojourners* 12, No. 11
(Dec. 1983):22-24; Elizabeth Hanley, "A Seventh Year of Unknowing,"
Sojourners 12, No. 4 (Apr. 1983):21-25; and Clark H. Pinnock, "An Evangelical
Theology of Human Liberation," *Sojourners* 5, No. 2 (Feb. 1976):30-33 and
Sojourners 5, No. 3 (Mar. 1976):26-29.

through articles by Latin American theologians such as Elsa Tamez and Gustavo Gutierrez;[285] through interviews with key Latin American figures as Ernesto Cardenal and Samuel Escobar;[286] and through book reviews of titles relevant to Latin American theology,[287] *Sojourners* has addressed the issues which it believes are vital to an adequate North American response to the movement for liberation within Latin America. *Sojourners* has given much critical coverage to U.S. policy in Nicaragua with two cover stories devoted to this concern as well as many other articles.[288] With regard to Nicaragua, *Sojourners* has both co-sponsored the "Witness for Peace" program whose aim was to give North American Christians first-hand involvement in the Nicaraguan context and co-organized "A Pledge of Resistance," a contingency plan for civil disobedience in the event of a U.S. invasion of Nicaragua.[289] In these ways *Sojourners* has offered a response to the concerns of Latin American liberation theology, especially as that theology has called for a praxis involvement in liberation which goes beyond theological reflection.

Jim Wallis and the Sojourners community exemplify a second resonant response by evangelical Christians in North America to Latin American liberation theology. Like the response of Sider (who himself serves as a contributing editor of *Sojourners* magazine), it is grounded in the biblical teaching regarding God's concern for social justice and the poor. Similar to Sider, the response of Wallis and the Sojourners community is one which avoids partisan political

---

[285]Cf. Elsa Tamez, "Dear Brother Job. . .," *Sojourners* 12, No. 8 (Sept. 1983):23 and Gustavo Gutierrez, "Talking About God," *Sojourners* 12, No. 2 (Feb. 1983):26-29.

[286]Cf. "A Priest in the Ministry," *Sojourners* 12, No. 3 (Mar. 1983):22-23 and "Interview with Samuel Escobar," *Sojourners* 5, No. 8 (Sept. 1976): 15-18.

[287]For example, cf. Joyce Hollyday, "The Bleak Landscape of El Salvador. A Review of Joan Didion's *Salvador* and James R. Brockman's *The Word Remains: A Life of Oscar Romero*," *Sojourners* 13, No. 3 (Mar. 1984): 35-36; Danny Collum, "Two Theologies in Contrast. Review of Dennis C. McCann's *Christian Realism and Liberation Theology*," *Sojourners* 12, No. 2 (Feb. 1983):35-36; and Frederick Herzog, "The Imperative of Praxis. Review of Torres and Eagleson, eds., *Theology in the Americas*," *Sojourners* 11, No. 9 (Oct. 1982):37-38.

[288]Cf. *Sojourners* 12, No. 3 (Mar. 1983) and 13, No. 7 (Aug. 1984) as well as Richard J. Barnet and Peter Kornbluh, "Contradictions in Nicaragua," *Sojourners* 13, No. 5 (May 1984):8-10 and Jim Wallis, "In Defense of CEPAD," *Sojourners* 13, No. 10 (Nov. 1984):4-5.

[289]Cf. "Witness for Peace," *Sojourners* 12, No. 10 (Nov. 1983):3-4 and Jim Wallis, "A Pledge of Resistance," *Sojourners* 13, No. 7 (Aug. 1984):10-11.

commitments and which advocates pacifism as the normative
Christian position, especially in the light of U.S. commitments to
nuclear defense. Wallis and the Sojourners community go beyond
Sider, however, in embedding their concern for the poor in what they
describe as a consistent pro-life theology, and in their high level of
radical social activism.

3.   Alfred C. Krass

A consistent theme of the writings of Alfred C. Krass, a minister of
the United Church of Christ and former missionary in Ghana, has
been an evangelical concern for the meaning and practice of
evangelism with special attention directed to the particular
contributions and liabilities of U.S. church and society.[290] In recent
years Krass has also served as an editor for *The Other Side* magazine
and been deeply involved in the Jubilee Fellowship, a house church
with numerous ministries in the Philadelphia area. Like others
mentioned in this chapter, Krass has also been a participant in the
Theology in the Americas process.[291]

In a book published in 1982, *Evangelizing Neopagan North
America. The Word that Frees*, Krass has explicitly incorporated
liberation theology into his understanding of the full meaning of
evangelism which includes working for social justice. In this book
Krass focuses on the U.S. as a context for evangelizing in light of what
he perceives to be the prevalence of a new North American
neopaganism. Indications of this neopaganism are, for Krass, the
priority given to military buildup while programs to benefit the poor
languish, the thriving of American corporations while thousands go
unemployed, and the captivity of religion in America to consumerism
as a way of life. In such a context the meaning of evangelism must be
totally rethought. Evangelism must be undergirded by a holistic
theology which unites the proclamation of the gospel with the struggle
for social justice. Krass sees this very issue to be occupying an ever
more central position on the evangelism agenda in recent years.[292]

---

[290]Cf. Alfred C. Krass, *Beyond the Either-Or Church* (Nashville: Tidings,
1973) and *Five Lanterns at Sundown: Evangelism in a Chastened Mood* (Grand
Rapids: Eerdmans, 1978).

[291]Cf. Alfred C. Krass, "Living in Resurrection Reality," *Other Side*, No.
110 (Nov. 1980):44-47.

[292]Cf. Krass, *Evangelizing Neopagan North America*, pp. 46-68.

One key resource for a new holistic understanding of evangelism is Latin American liberation theology.[293]

A prime contribution of liberation theology to a new concept of evangelism has been, according to Krass, its relating an eschatological understanding of the kingdom of God to the present historical context which is marked by injustice. Without identifying earthly progress with the coming of the kingdom of God, liberation theologians have insisted that working for human liberation in the present is inseparable from faithfulness to the biblical notion of God's kingdom. By contrast, the North American church has been dominated by otherworldly and individualistic ideas of the kingdom which, in effect, serve the interests of the world's ruling elites by failing to challenge the temporal status quo.

Krass has also laid stress on the contribution of Latin American liberation theology to the recovery of a contextual biblical hermeneutic.[294] Going beyond the illusion of a value-neutral, ahistorical understanding, Krass believes liberation theology can be instructive regarding a hermeneutic which intentionally includes ideological suspicion as part of its methodology. Since there is no escape from the fact that the Bible was written in a number of definite historical contexts by authors influenced by their own ideological viewpoints, these insights need to be consciously incorporated into a contextual hermeneutic which is thoroughly attentive to the particularities—historical, ideological, etc.—which are given with every biblical text. An important example of the functioning of ideological presuppositions in the interpretation of Scripture is the contrast between a traditional evangelical understanding of what the Bible means by "the poor" and the understanding of poverty which has emerged under the influence of liberation theology.

Krass has, moreover, borrowed Segundo's differentiation between faith and ideologies to make the point that the efficacy of faith can only be realized when faith avails itself of time-bound and relative ideologies for its historical embodiment. This insight also has importance for the development of an adequate conception of evangelism today. This means evangelism must be fully incarnate in a particular time and place just as Jesus' own evangelism was fully contextual.

---

[293]For the following see ibid., p. 29 and pp. 60-63.
[294]For the following cf. ibid., pp. 93-117.

With reference to the Latin American bishops' conference at Puebla, Krass sees immediate relevance for the critique of the idolatrous abuse of political power not only for the Latin American but also for the North American context.

> For a long time we in North America have thought of atheism as a "religious matter." We tend to analyze oppression and injustice in a secular way, on a purely human level. We think they concern human relationships alone. The bishops challenge this kind of analysis, and this is where they speak to us as well. If oppression and injustice exist, then it's because of idolatry, the true atheism. Idolatry and atheism have immediate consequences for this-worldly human relationships.[295]

On the issue of idolatry, Krass' concern for the verbal proclamation of the gospel for the sake of conversion merges with his concern for a social commitment to justice in society. Atheism is not simply a matter of false belief but a matter of practical devotion to false gods.

Each of his references to liberation theology supports the overall argument of Krass for evangelism in North America which combines kerygmatic proclamation of the gospel with an active participation in the struggle for justice for the poor. Noteworthy in the response of Krass to liberation theology is his slightly different emphasis among the elements which also distinguish the evangelical responses of Sider and Wallis to liberation theology. Once again the main source of commonality is their fundamental agreement regarding the central importance of those biblical texts which call for interhuman justice on behalf of the poor. Where the response of Krass is most unique is in his reinterpretation of the task of evangelism to explicitly include participation in the struggle for social justice. Like Sider and Wallis, Krass' concern for social justice has not only been a theological emphasis but a commitment in which he has actively participated individually and ecclesially. It is perhaps in their concrete engagement on behalf of social justice that these evangelical theologians demonstrate most fully their response to Latin American liberation theology. Theology and praxis are to remain inseparable.

G.   Theology in the Americas

Many of the theologians whose thought has already been examined, Latin American and North American alike, have participated at various points in the conferences and projects of the Theology in the Americas process. Organized in 1974 under the leadership of the Chilean priest and theologian, Sergio Torres, who served as its first

---

[295]Ibid., p. 136.

executive secretary, the foundational event for Theology in the Americas was a conference held at Detroit in August 1975. Because of the catalytic nature of Theology in the Americas in promoting an encounter between Latin American liberation theology and North American theology, it warrants separate consideration for its role in promoting the reception of Latin American liberation thought by North American theologians.

"The original intention of the planners of the 'Theology in the Americas: 1975' conference was to invite a group of Latin American theologians, representing the theology of liberation, to dialogue with North American theologians concerning the content and methodology of this new theological current."[296] Due to such critical feedback, however, this original goal began to be rethought and the Theology in the Americas process underwent a transformation which eventually led to its current shape.[297] Instead of an encounter in which the Latin Americans were the presenters and the North Americans the receptors, new emphasis was placed on the particularity of the U.S. context—its own history; social, economic, and political dynamics; and theological resources—as the locus for North American theologizing. Instead of exclusively involving professional theologians, participation was extended to include Christian activists who had a strong interest in social change. Moreover, the conference was not to be an entity in itself but rather the culmination of a process of group work and reflection. The critical comments and reactions of these groups then became the basis for further modification in the planning for the conference.

The materials from the first Theology in the Americas conference have been published under the title, *Theology in the Americas*, and document the various currents of thought which flowed together to compose Theology in the Americas at its time of origin. Many of the conference papers and responses have been made available in this volume. A central focus of the conference remained the encounter between several Latin American liberation theologians and various North American theologians both professional and lay. However, this dimension of the conference was counterbalanced by the concern of many for the development of a liberation theology which is indigenously North American and not imported from outside. Thus

---

[296]Sergio Torres and John Eagleson, eds., *Theology in the Americas* (Maryknoll: Orbis, 1976), p. 3.

[297]Cf. ibid., pp. 3-5.

an attempt was made to give the concerns of black and feminist theology greater attention at the conference even as there was a growing recognition of the need for even more emphasis upon other nonwhite racial and national minorities. Another notable aspect of the conference was its initial effort at a sociological interpretation of North American society.

Worthy of mention in this context is the transformation of Theology in the Americas from a program with its major emphasis on the passive reception of participants to one of active involvement in shaping its content. Very important was the insistence of the participants on a greater inclusion of ethnic and racial minorities and a lesser emphasis on dialogue with white professional theologians.[298] Greater emphasis was also to be placed on the contextualization of theology in North America which was seen to require greater attention to: (1) the experience of ordinary Christians, (2) the inclusion of social analysis within theological methodology, and (3) the criterion of praxis as the final measure of theology. At the same time that the particularity of the North American context was to be stressed, however, the North American context was to be continually examined in terms of the global situation. With these objectives in place, approximately sixty "reflection groups" were formed to continue and deepen the experiment in theologizing given impetus by the first Detroit conference.

With its headquarters in New York City, the Theology in the Americas process in the years following the Detroit conference divided into nine distinct yet inter-related projects which continued to "do theology" in the North American context from their own unique viewpoints.[299] They were: (1) The Black Project, (2) The Hispanic Project, (3) The Women's Project, (4) Quest for Liberation in the White Church, (5) Asian Americans in the North American Context, (6) The Task Force of Professional Theologians, (7) Labor and Church Dialogue, (8) Land, Native Americans and Red Theology, and (9) Ecumenical Dialogue with Third World Theologians. Each of these projects organized its work independently, coming together for various meetings, workshops, and conferences as a basis for their common

---

[298] For the following cf. ibid., pp. 433-436.

[299] For the following cf. "Towards a North American Theology of Liberation: Theology in the Americas Process," Theology in the Americas Documentation Series No. 1, pp. 1-13.

work. At the same time each of the individual projects shared in the
objectives of a common process.

As articulated in 1978, these objectives were:

1. To develop a new way of doing theology that

a) grows out of the different social, ethnic, racial, economic, and
sexual realities.

b) incorporates as theological themes our own histories, the
demands and challenges of the Third World and the structural
complexities of this country.

c) exemplifies a communal or collective process.

2. To explore new methodologies in dealing with the relationship
between

a) truth and practice.

b) faith and praxis.

c) ideology and faith.

3. To confront the dominant theological mainstream with this
new way of doing theology, of participating with God in history.[300]

According to these objectives, the meaning of Christian discipleship
was to be considered in light of contemporary social reality. Both
personal and structural conversion were recognized as integral
components in this process which aimed toward the formation both of a
new people and a new order. A key concept for the entire process was
that of "praxis" which pointed toward a new epistemology and a new
emphasis on the action which is to result from theological reflection.
In the development of a new methodology, social analysis,
contextualization, and an international perspective were to contribute
to a new theological outlook. Seen to be in formation was nothing less
then the emergence of a theological paradigm which sought to offer an
alternative to academic theology.

Occurring simultaneously with the development of the various
projects of Theology in the Americas, was the origin of the Ecumenical
Association of Third World Theologians under the organization of
Sergio Torres, which had its first international conference at Dar es
Salaam, Tanzania in August 1976. This organization would act in the
ensuing years as an informal dialogue partner with Theology in the
Americas and through its conferences and official statements
continue to raise to the forefront the global implications of North
American theology.   In 1983 at Geneva, Switzerland, theologians

---

[300]Ibid., p. 1.

active in the Theology in the Americas process—Rosemary Radford
Ruether, Letty Russell, Don Prange, Jim Wallis, Lee Cormie,
Elizabeth Schussler Fiorenza, Shiela Collins, James Cone, and
Jacquelyn Grant—took part in a dialogue between First and Third
World theologians at the sixth Conference of the Ecumenical
Association of Third World Theologians. This ongoing exchange
with the Ecumenical Association of Third World Theologians has
added to the global awareness of the Theology in the Americas process.

Representative of the continuing work of Theology in the Americas
are the papers from a workshop held at New York City in June 1978
which were published under the title, *Is Liberation Theology for North
America? The Response of First World Churches*.[301] As reflected in
these papers, the Theology in the Americas process has sought to
conscientiously incorporate a spectrum of "minority" viewpoints
(black, native American, feminist, Third World, etc.) together with
social analysis of North American reality and "usable" elements
from the Christian tradition to work to create a more just and equitable
society. Subsequently the papers from this workshop were made
available to others for study and reflection in printed form. It is
through numerous workshops such as this one that the bulk of the work
of the various Theology in the Americas projects has been carried out.

A second major conference was again held at Detroit in August
1980.[302] Once again it was a conference which brought together the
diverse liberation perspectives of the various Theology in the Americas
projects on the basis of a common attempt at social analysis and a
shared Christian faith. As at the first Detroit conference, considerable
attention was given to the presentation from representatives of a
variety of Third World situations. Yet at Detroit II the primary focus
remained on the role of the U.S. and especially the role of U.S.
churches. By comparison to the first Detroit conference, the papers
delivered at Detroit II indicate increasing politization within the
Theology of the Americas process and a growing emphasis upon
socialism as a political option.[303] Also by comparison to the first

---

[301]*Is Liberation Theology for North America? The Response of First
World Churches* (New York: Theology in the Americas, n.d.).

[302]Cf. Cornel West, Caridad Guidote, and Margaret Coakley, eds.,
Theology in the Americas. Detroit II Conference Papers (Maryknoll: Orbis,
1982).

[303]Cf. the analysis of the conference by Cornel West, "Prospects for the
North American Christian Left," in ibid., pp. 165-169.

Detroit conference, the prominence earlier given to white male professional theologians yielded to contributions from non-male and non-white theologians both professional and lay. The papers of the second conference reveal a pluralism of views consistent with the division of Theology in the Americas into its nine different projects. Also emerging from the second Detroit conference was an Inter-Ethnic/Indigenous Coalition which sought to further coordinate the work between the Black, Hispanic, Asian, and Native American projects.

As Theology in the Americas entered the decade of the eighties, a new "Vision Statement" was drafted to express the continuing aims of the process.

> Our vision is rooted in the affirmation that TIA is called to discern the social and political signs of the times from the perspective of the poor and the exploited, who constitute the majority of North America and the global population. We therefore, believe that the primary agenda of TIA should be informed by the agendas of the poor and oppressed peoples throughout the world.[304]

By comparison with earlier statements of objectives and purpose, this 1981 Vision Statement also suggests the increasing politicization of the Theology in the Americas process and thus an increasing departure from traditional forms of theological reflection. Among the issues which are listed as potentially important for common reflection are unemployment, militarization, labor, liberation struggles throughout the world, pre-party work or party building as an independent political response, racism, sexism, land abuse, and nuclear proliferation. The once explicit theological dimension of these issues within the methodology of Theology in the Americas, however, receives only implicit mention. While activism in social causes received high priority, the rootedness of such activism in Christian identity, by comparison with earlier statements, seemed to be losing in significance.

In the eighties the work of Theology in the Americas has continued to encourage a North American encounter with liberation theologies throughout the world including the Latin American theology of liberation. This work is now coordinated by a National Committee composed of representatives from the various projects as well as by a "Coordinating Team." Workshops and conferences continue to comprise the bulk of Theology in the Americas activity. In addition a

---

[304]From "Theology in the Americas. Vision Statement. 1981," Theology in the Americas pamphlet.

newsletter, "Doing Theology in the Americas" has been printed
regularly since 1975 offering updates on the work of the various
projects, reports on workshops and conferences, and news about
liberation struggles throughout the world. Theology in the Americas
has also made available a number of study resources which coincide
with its interest in the liberation struggle. In these ways Theology in
the Americas has had a considerable impact upon the reception of Latin
American liberation theology in North America.[305]

---

[305]In no way do the views of the theologians selected for more extensive
treatment in this chapter exhaust the resonant responses made to Latin
American liberation theology by North American theologians. The pertinent
literature is immense. Those chosen to represent the North American reception
of liberation theology have been selected due to both the breadth and depth of their
own particular responses. It is appropriate, however, also to note briefly several
other resonant contributions made by North American theologians.

Harvey Cox is especially noteworthy in this regard beginning with his book
The Secular City. Secularization and Urbanization in Theological Perspective
(London: SCM, 1965) which has also been widely read in Latin America. Cox's
proposals for the roles of the church and theology in a secularized world
described in this book have contributed much to the discussion of the
secularization process, ecclesiology, and a political theology, striving to
discern the presence of God in contemporary history also in the Latin American
context. Because Cox's response to Latin American liberation theology has in
many respects been as much personal through his many contacts and travels in
Latin America as literary—cf. his autobiography *Just As I Am* (Nashville:
Abingdon, 1983), pp. 95-113—a discussion of that response remains in many
ways intangible. Nevertheless, with the publication of *Religion in the Secular
City. Toward a Postmodern Theology* (New York: Simon and Schuster, 1984),
Cox makes clear his appreciation for Latin American liberation theology and
the basic Christian community movement as models for theology and the
church in a "postmodern" world.

Glenn R. Bucher has in a number of essays provided another interesting
North American response to liberation theology by beginning to formulate the
outlines of a North American, white, male answer to the challenge of liberation
theologies, whether black, feminist, or Latin American. See Glenn R. Bucher,
"Liberation, Male and White: Initial Reflections," *Chr Cent* 91 (Mar. 20,
1974):312-316 and "Toward a Liberation Theology for the 'Oppressors'," *J A A R*
44 (Summer 1976):517-534.

Phillip E. Berryman has in *The Religious Roots of Rebellion: Christians
in Central American Revolutions* (Maryknoll: Orbis, 1984) brought years of
experience in Latin America and reflection on the history and theology of the
Latin American church into a comprehensive description of recent events in
Central America. This work, together with other articles, e.g., "Latin
American Liberation Theology," *Th St* (1973):357-395, has made Berryman into
one of the foremost interpreters of Latin American liberation theology and the
Latin American church in the North American context.

Among feminist liberation theologians Letty M. Russell's book *Human
Liberation in a Feminist Perspective—A Theology* (Philadelphia:

Westminster, 1974) articulates the common characteristics shared by the various liberation theologies, i.e., the common methodology, perspectives, and themes in feminist, black, and Third World liberation theologies. She does so, however, with her own primary focus on the concerns of women in the church as have been described at greater length in her subsequent books, *The Future of Partnership* (Philadelphia: Westminster, 1979) and *Growth in Partnership* (Philadelphia: Westminster, 1981).

Two works have especially dealt with Latin American liberation theology in appreciation of its insights in overcoming the Marxist critique of religion as ideology. William Hordern in *Experience and Faith. The Significance of Luther for Understanding Today's Experiential Religion* (Minneapolis: Augsburg, 1983), esp. Chapter 6, pp. 106-119, finds in liberation theology a key for recognizing and overcoming tacitly assumed ideologies which condition thought. More extensive regarding this problem and informed by a thorough reading of sociological literature from a theological perspective is Gregory Baum, *Religion and Alienation: A Sociological Reading of Theology* (New York: Paulist, 1975). Liberation theology is interpreted by Baum as an attempt at "critical theology," a theology which is methodologically aware of the ideological implications of its stance.

Also based largely on the field of sociology is Marie Augusta Neal, *A Socio-Theology of Letting Go. The Role of a First World Church Facing Third World Peoples* (New York: Paulist, 1977). In the essays collected in this volume, Neal presents sociological analysis in critique of American civil religion and argues for the development of a global perspective for theology which transcends a privatistic viewpoint uncritical of American policy. Neal calls the church to a prophetic stance in the North American context and to what she describes as "a theology of relinquishment."

In addition to the works of Baum and Neal, other Roman Catholic theologians have also made important contributions to the North American discussion. Two of these deal primarily with the theology of Juan Luis Segundo. Alfred Hennelly, *Theologies in Conflict. The Challenge of Juan Luis Segundo* (Maryknoll: Orbis, 1979), provides an introduction and a basically appreciative analysis of both liberation theology in general and the thought of Segundo in particular. Hennelly finds in liberation theology many significant challenges for North American theology which call for response. Concentrating more directly on the ethics and exegesis of Segundo is Anthony J. Tambasco, *The Bible for Ethics: Juan Luis Segundo and First World Ethics* (London: University Press of America, 1981). Although primarily appreciative of Segundo's efforts, Tambasco also raises some critical questions, especially regarding Segundo's exegetical work as will be further discussed in the next chapter.

Ronald J. Schreiter, *Constructing Local Theologies* (Maryknoll: Orbis, 1985) provides yet an additional Roman Catholic response to the impulses which find their expression in liberation theology. Schreiter deals with the problems involved in a theology which seeks to be faithful not only to the Christian witness but at the same time to the context in which it arises. Schreiter's is a creative contribution to the question of theological method which remains an outstanding issue for, among others, liberation theology.

Latin American liberation theology has also begun to find a resonance in the United States among Spanish-speaking North Americans. Virgil Elizondo, *Galilean Journey. The Mexican-American Promise* (Maryknoll: Orbis, 1983) relates specifically to the experience of Mexican-Americans and a theology which responds to that experience. For Elizondo, the symbol of Galilee in contrast to the symbol of Jerusalem as the center of power is used to describe Jesus' status as an outsider who proclaims the coming of God's kingdom to those rejected by society. One can note especially in Elizondo's Christology the strong influence of liberation theology.

Another author whose work in the North American context should not be overlooked, although she is West German, is Dorothee Soelle. Throughout Soelle's work, which has become widely known in the United States through her teaching and lecturing there, exist references and allusions pertinent to the North American discussion of liberation thought. Particularly worthy of mention are her books *Political Theology* (Philadelphia: Fortress, 1974) and *Choosing Life*, trans. Margaret Kohl (Philadelphia: Fortress, 1981). The major portion of the latter title was first delivered as lectures in 1979 in Buenos Aires, Argentina.

Chapter Four

Critical Issues

There have not only been resonant responses to Latin American liberation theology among North American theologians. There have also been a number of serious critical questions and issues raised over against this theology. They range from virtual rejection of the social analysis, Marxist influence, exegetical basis, and/or methodology of liberation theology to critical proposals for the development of a more adequate conceptuality. This chapter documents the critical issues raised by North American theologians with regard to Latin American liberation theology by examining the main arguments that have been presented. Particularly striking is the tendency toward polarization between the views of liberation theology presented in this chapter and those in the previous one. In the next chapter this polarization will itself be taken up thematically together with an evaluation of the entire North American discussion of the Latin American theology of liberation.

A. *Questioning Liberation Theology's Use of Marxist Thought*

One of the central factors in the polarization of North American responses to liberation theology has been the differing appraisals of its use of Marxist thought. For those most negatively critical of the Marxist influence upon liberation theology, this has meant a virtual rejection of liberation theology as a legitimate option for Christian theology. The contradiction between Marxist thought, as it is seen to influence liberation theology, and the Christian tradition is simply irreconcilable. This criticism is not only significant to varying degrees in the arguments of the three theologians considered in this section—James V. Schall, Marc Kolden, and Rosemary Radford Ruether—but is also an essential component of the arguments of others to be considered in subsequent sections of this chapter. Michael Novak, Robert Benne, Thomas G. Sanders, Dennis P. McCann, Richard John

Neuhaus, and Carl E. Braaten as well as the evangelical theologians
C. Peter Wagner, Carl F. H. Henry, and Donald G. Bloesch, each
incorporate into their own critique of liberation theology objections to
its use of Marxism. This contrasts dramatically to the understanding
of liberation theology—with the exception of Rosemary Radford
Ruether and the evangelical theologians—of the main theologians
resonant to liberation theology considered in the previous chapter. The
criticisms of liberation theology's use of Marxism must thus be seen as
a, if not the, critical issue in the polarization of North American
responses to the theology of liberation.

1. James V. Schall

In his book, *Liberation Theology in Latin America* (1982), James
V. Schall has collected a number of essays by various authors critical
of liberation theology and has himself offered an introductory essay
which is particularly critical of liberation theology's Marxist
tendencies. As he surveys the Latin American scene, Schall sees the
spread of leftist dogma to be pervasive. Under a strong European
influence, Schall understands liberation theologians, due to their
adoption of Marxist concepts, to be offering an ultimately illusory
solution to the real and serious problem of poverty in the Latin
American context.

> The question to which this discussion will principally address itself is
> this: Does the Christian religious analysis currently gaining dominance
> in Latin America explain either why the poor are poor or how to alleviate
> their condition? Further, does it retain the central beliefs and ideas and
> practices Christianity is committed to preserve and hand on? I hold that it
> does not explain the poverty of the poor, nor even less make a positive
> contribution toward its alleviation. It does maintain that it changes no
> central Christian doctrine or practice, though this is questioned. In any
> case, it interprets Christianity radically so that it appears to be a this-
> worldly doctrine whose principal tendency is an economic and political
> one, explained in a fashion that would reunite religion and politics. This
> does not mean that we are not dealing mostly with sincere people, nor that
> problems of corruption and ignorance and political power do not exist. But
> it does mean that concern for the poor in Latin America and elsewhere is
> not best served by the present kinds of analysis we find formally presented
> as the answer to the questions of the human condition there.[1]

Throughout his essay, Schall returns to the influence of Marxism as
the cause for this faulty social analysis and distortion of Christian
doctrine which has taken place in liberation theology.

---

[1]James V. Schall, *Liberation Theology in Latin America* (San Francisco:
Ignatius Press, 1982), p. 9.

In an initial chapter, Schall illustrates the growing "concern over Latin America," its present social, economic, and political problems, on the part of Latin Americans.[2] New interpretations of Latin American history and social problems have been growing in influence, not least of all those of a Marxist persuasion. Because of the interrelatedness of the North and South American continents, these new currents of thought ought to also be of interest to U.S. citizens and Christians. This is especially the case insofar as the U.S., its corporations and government policies, has been implicated by many Latin American theoreticians, including liberation theologians, as an important factor in causing Latin America's plight. The theory, however, which liberation theology has overtaken to analyze the Latin American condition is judged to be a deficient one. Instead of authentically leading to "liberty" as it is understood in the U.S. political traditions, the "liberation" promised by liberation theology is seen to lead to new forms of oppression, i.e., "absolutism or even totalitarianism."[3]

In a chapter entitled "What Liberation Theology Maintains" Schall explains in greater detail how liberation theology has gone about transforming theology into a comprehensive system of thought in accordance with Marxist logic.[4] Once again Schall notes the significant Germanic and European influence upon Latin American liberation theology.[5] Chief among these influences is that of Marx which, in spite of claims that it has been purged of its anti-Christian aspects, is seen to provide the intellectual foundation for liberation thought.

> In this light, therefore, liberation theology proposes to rewrite or reinterpret all the major elements and themes of Christianity. This does not take the classic form of "heresy" or "protestantism" because it does not claim to deny classical Christianity. Rather, it claims to explain what Christianity "really" believes if it only knew its mind. Moreover, liberation thought accepts all or part of the Marxist analysis as being "scientifically" true. The conclusion from this is that Marxism is necessarily conformable with Christianity. To what degree this renovation is at all compatible with traditional Christianity is subject to considerable debate.[6]

---

[2]For the following cf. ibid., pp. 11-26.
[3]Cf. ibid., p. 22.
[4]For the following cf. ibid., pp. 27-44.
[5]Cf. ibid., p. 31. Cf. also pp. 50 and 61.
[6]Ibid., p. 34.

From Schall's subsequent discussion of the praxis and conscientization emphases of liberation theology it is clear he does not think the two, liberation theology and traditional Christianity, are compatible.

Although taking as its initial starting point the condition of the poor, the logic which unfolds from this starting point reveals the actual nature of liberation theology: "Poverty—Dependence—Exploitation—Conscientization—Revolution—Socialism—this is pictured as the natural sequence so that any other view which might propose a different logic to the same end is more or less equivalent to rejecting the dire needs of such peoples."[7] In this way such Christian ideas as the kingdom of God and charity are replaced by efforts to improve the lot of the poor and attain justice respectively, i.e., a political and economic agenda rather than an individual and religious one. In addition the analysis of liberation theology results in an anti-American and anti-capitalist bias which denies capitalism has a role to play in "the solution of the world's and Latin America's poverty problems."[8] Throughout its doctrinal formulations and even in its spirituality liberation theology results in a new politicization of Christian thought which is high on "religious enthusiasm and earnestness" but "dangerous" as a proposal for actually solving the problems of the Latin American poor.[9]

Schall's most aggressive critique of liberation theology is contained in the chapter, "Where Liberation Theologies Lead."[10] In its variance from traditional Christian teaching, this time on the basis of Marxism, liberation theology joins the series of heretical movements which have challenged the Church throughout its history. Related to other modern intellectual currents such as existentialism, the "death of God" theology, and the theology of "secularization," liberation theology is understood, moreover, to incorporate ecological arguments based, for example, on the "'limits of growth,' after a notoriously biased pseudo-study by the Club of Rome."[11] Together these influences are seen to contribute to the rejuvenation of Marxism by liberation theology in seeking to offer an option for Latin America's future. Through its rhetoric against "capitalism" and the resulting

---

[7]Ibid., p. 38.

[8]Ibid., p. 41.

[9]Cf. ibid., pp. 43-44.

[10]For the following cf. ibid., pp. 45-62.

[11]Ibid., p. 52.

"theory of collective guilt" now baptized under the term "sinful structures," liberation theology's chosen option, however, undermines the legitimate option of gradual economic development under a democratic model.[12] In doing so liberation theology goes beyond European political theology in its positive assessment and advocacy of socialism. Furthermore, it ignores the wisdom of classical Christian political theories which are reserved in their expectations of what can be achieved in the political realm. Its hope, however, in the potential of socialism to benefit the poor is contradicted by the non-existence of a system which validates its option in practice.

These various arguments lead Schall to the conclusion that liberation theology, in spite of good intentions, offers Latin America an empty promise.[13] Although endorsed by many American and European intellectuals, Schall contends that the hard evidence about the actual causes of Latin American poverty is against liberation theology's analysis which puts the blame on the First World and particularly on the United States. Schall offers instead a counter-thesis to the Marxist claims of liberation theology.

> The basic view that shall be argued here is that liberation theology is, in its essential outlines, itself a cause of continued underdevelopment, that its eventual growth and success would institutionalize in Latin America a life of low-level socialist poverty enforced by a rigid party-military discipline in control of economic enterprise and the movement of peoples.[14]

Insofar as the Latin American church overtakes the analysis of liberation theology, it is in danger of once more coming to identify itself with an authoritarian and totalitarian movement.

The viable alternative to liberation theology's utopian vision is that of a progressive economic development for which Brazil offers one example. Such development can provide tangible economic gains for the poor which are not to be dismissed by reference to any supposed "gap" which exists between the rich and the poor. Schall introduces economic statistics which suggest this development is already taking place. An economy based on the incentive of the profit motive and competition is both much more realistic in its theory and successful in its outcome than is allowed for by liberation theology's references to capitalist exploitation. The benefits provided by multi-national corporations are further cited by Schall in defense of the developmental

---

[12]Cf. ibid., pp. 53-56.

[13]For the following cf. ibid., pp. 63-82.

[14]Ibid., p. 67.

approach. For these fundamental reasons, for which he claims the support of other contemporary authorities, Schall must reject liberation theology due to its "impractical *praxis*."[15] The kingdom of God simply cannot be ushered in by social or political means as is advocated by liberation theology.

At the close of his essay, Schall turns to an examination of the response of Pope John Paul II to liberation theology.[16] As one coming from the Marxist-controlled country of Poland, Schall understands the pope to be particularly well-suited for recognizing the theological aberrations of liberation theology. The pope's "decision" regarding liberation thought on the occasion of the Puebla bishop's conference was one which, according to Schall, in the face of the Marxist threat insisted upon the "purity of doctrine" especially by reaffirming the divinity of Christ in the face of the current proclivity toward Christ's "over-humanization." In addition the pope stressed doctrinal clarity against a confusion of the kingdom of God with movements for justice, an ecclesiology reduced to the role of social activism, and an anthropology which is not based upon Christian teaching. Special stress is made by Schall on the pope's caution against the threat to religious and human freedom posed by authoritarian states and also against political activism by the clergy.

As exemplified by Puebla, Pope John Paul II is cited by Schall as properly situating the Christian idea of liberation within the whole of traditional Christian doctrine. When he speaks of liberation, the pope thus means *God's* liberation, an emphasis which does not deny the need for love of the neighbor and just institutions but which locates such concerns in an appreciation of divine transcendence. This understanding of a truly Christian redemption is opposed to contemporary currents of thought such as liberation theology which hold "that 1) man wholly liberates himself from any presumed bondage or restriction, 2) that this is a collective effort which subordinates the individual to the group, 3) that this is achieved by hatred, violence, or class struggle, 4) that therefore Christ is either not necessary or merely a model of a revolutionary person, and 5) that the goal of liberation is a perfect worldly order."[17] By maintaining that the first human bondage is to sin and death, John Paul II corrects the obscuring of religious truth

---

[15]Ibid., p. 82.

[16]For the following cf. ibid., pp. 83-121.

[17]Ibid., p. 111.

which occurs when liberation is understood in primarily political and ideological terms.

James V. Schall presents a critique of liberation theology which places its greatest stress on the captivity of liberation thought to Marxist thought and analysis. While admitting liberation theology's genuine concern for the Latin American poor, its analysis of poverty's causes is seen to divert from the real issues and result in a political option which will lead inevitably to yet worse forms of authoritarian oppression.[18] Furthermore its political reduction of Christian doctrine is understood to be a distortion of the authentic Christian teaching. In searching for a more viable alternative to solve Latin American poverty, he proposes development under the model of democratic capitalism.[19] In this way his critique of liberation theology indicates affinity to that of Michael Novak whose defense of democratic capitalism receives further elaboration later in this chapter.

2. Marc Kolden

As Professor of Systematic Theology at Luther Northwestern Theological Seminary in St. Paul, Marc Kolden participated in a five-year study process as a member of the Task Force on Marxism sponsored by Lutheran World Ministries. As his contribution to a book examining many facets of Marxism and the Marxist-Christian dialogue, Kolden has written a concise essay entitled "Marxism and Latin American Liberation Theology." This essay serves as the focus of this section.

Kolden describes liberation theology as arising "from a concern to understand the meaning of the biblical message and to construct a position about the church's mission in a situation of great economic and political oppression."[20] To that end Marxism has been employed by liberation theology as an aid to understanding the interconnections between Latin American "poverty and dependence" and the "economic and political domination by North Atlantic nations."[21] Liberation theology has furthermore criticized the theologies of churches which have aligned themselves to authoritarian regimes and the concomitant

---

[18]Cf. ibid., p. 124.

[19]Cf. ibid., pp. 125-126.

[20]Marc Kolden, "Marxism and Latin American Liberation Theology," in Wayne Stumme, ed., *Christians and the Many Faces of Marxism* (Minneapolis: Augsburg, 1984), p. 123.

[21]Ibid.

status quo. Kolden notes, moreover, that the socialism of Chile under
Allende and the communism of Cuba under Castro have been given a
positive appraisal by liberation theology. Yet liberation theologians
have been involved to differing degrees in actual political movements;
many have confined themselves to specifically ecclesial participation
in the cause of the poor. Such commitments are characteristic of both
the majority of liberation theologians who are Roman Catholic and of
their Protestant counterparts.

In comparison to Schall, Kolden's critique of the use of Marxism by
liberation theologians is much more differentiated. He recognizes the
continuity of many liberation themes with that of the biblical concern
for justice expressed in the exodus narratives, the prophetic corpus, and
the teachings of Jesus, especially as they are expressed by the
evangelists Matthew and Luke. "Yet the uses to which these themes are
put are new, for they challenge the ways in which Christians have so
often domesticated the biblical cries for peace and justice and have
made liberation into something which is possible only in heaven."[22]

Before proceeding to an evaluation of liberation theology on the
basis of its use of Marxism, Kolden first identifies five "main ideas"
of liberation theology which serve to illustrate how liberation
theologians have actually done so. The first of these ideas is its
critical stance toward both society and previous theological
positions."[23] Liberation theologians have applied Marx's critique of
religion to theologies which have served a legitimizing function in
upholding the status quo of unjust social relations. In this way they
have challenged the notion that North American theology, for example,
is "theology" while their own theology must be qualified as "Latin
American." This acts then as a self-critical principle for
understanding how theology can be affected by the social location of its
author.

A second idea is liberation theology's contention "that the purpose
of the Christian faith is to *transform the world*."[24] To "know God" in
this view is "to do justice" (cf. Jer. 22:16) and to do justice requires not
only acts of charity but also just social structures in terms of property
ownership, production relations, and government. In this context
Kolden introduces liberation theology's notion of structural violence
which is necessary for a proper understanding of the context in which

---

[22]Ibid., p. 124.

[23]Ibid.

[24]Ibid., p. 125.

liberation theologians consider violence as a means of social change. He recognizes further that liberation theologians have applied ethical criteria, e.g., "the good of the 'neighbor'" and the risk that one unjust system replace another as the result of the revolutionary activity, in their deliberations.

A third idea is liberation theology's "distinction between 'development' and 'liberation.'"[25] Here Kolden briefly explains the role of dependency theory in liberation theology which draws a causal connection between the wealth of the developed world and the poverty of the poor nations. Yet liberation means more than economic development for liberation theology and in this way it goes beyond both Marx and capitalist economics. Liberation instead aims toward the biblical vision of *shalom* which also includes communal, racial, and sexual justice. Kolden recognizes this third main idea of liberation theology to be a key one insofar as it does not avoid admitting that conflict with oppressor groups will be necessary in arriving at the required change in social structures. Still Kolden also sees a biblical warrant for this idea in "the way in which the God of the Bible is seen to use groups and movements to bring judgment on those who serve themselves rather than God and the people."[26]

That *"the God of the Bible takes sides"* is a fourth main idea of liberation theology. Evidence for this claim is drawn from God's partiality to the Hebrew slaves over against the Pharaoh, the prophetic defense of the poor over against the rich and powerful, and from Jesus' good news to the poor (cf. Luke 4:18). Liberation theology thus rejects any spiritualizing of the biblical idea of poverty in favor of its socioeconomic meaning. Because God sides with the poor, liberation theology claims a hermeneutical privilege for the poor as interpreters of Scripture.

The fifth idea emphasized by Kolden is that the *"meaning of salvation is broadened* in liberation theology. "[27] Salvation is not just reserved for the next world but includes a "greater fullness of life here on earth. Liberation theologians criticize much traditional belief, which has made salvation overly individualistic and otherworldly. At times it sounds almost as if liberation theologians equate salvation with political liberation because they have stated their case for having salvation *include* economic and political liberation with such

---

[25]Ibid.

[26]Ibid., p. 126.

[27]Ibid., p. 127.

sharpness."[28] Human beings are understood by liberation theology to
participate in God's salvific process by their engagement in the world.
While the realization of the kingdom of God in history is not possible,
even partial fulfillments are a real gain. Kolden refers to the thought
of Gustavo Gutierrez in this regard for the tension between God's final
bringing of salvation and the vital importance nevertheless of human
efforts to approximate that final kingdom. Gutierrez's description of
these interrelated levels of liberation illustrates how liberation
theology's "broadened idea of salvation clearly has much in common
with a Marxist understanding of human fulfillment," yet "is also
critical of Marxism's truncating of reality to include only the
historical process. "[29]

In evaluating liberation theology's use of Marxism Kolden insists
that it is imperative to keep in mind the context in which it has arisen.
Thus no simple rejection of its revolutionary implications is
appropriate. The Bible has too much to say about God's concern for
justice and the liberation theologians have been too thorough in
reaching their conclusions to allow for a blanket condemnation. The
key question becomes "whether theology can use a Marxist analysis of
society without also sharing in other Marxist ideas which are clearly at
odds with Christian faith."[30] While to Kolden this appears to be
possible with regard to the atheism of Marxism, nevertheless the
danger exists of a reduction of Christian thought to a consideration of
economic factors, for example, the class struggle, at the expense of a
fuller understanding of God's work in history. In their use of
Marxism, liberation theologians have been sensitive to this issue and
"clearly intend to be Christian theologians and not simply to give a
religious rationale for a Marxist political program."[31] At the same
time they are aware of theology's unavoidable connection to the social
context in which it arises and this is an insight which can be valuable
to any critical theology.

Kolden proceeds next to certain critical points made over against
Marxism which may have validity for liberation theology as well.

> Both are more concerned about the community than about the individual,
> and both would claim that authentic individuality is found only in
> community. Both see evil as primarily systemic rather than rooted in

---

[28]Ibid.
[29]Ibid., p. 128.
[30]Ibid.
[31]Ibid., pp. 128-129.

individuals, and both hold that the overcoming of evil is not primarily found in forgiveness or regeneration but in the transformation of the system. One might wish to give equal time to the sinfulness of the individual, to the extent that no system will ever be sinless nor will it ever be able to offer liberation from death. Liberation theologians know this but they do not stress it. Finally, both Marxism and liberation theology share in the criticism of traditional religion for merely legitimizing injustice and inaction.[32]

From these deliberations a key factor for evaluation becomes liberation theology's very definition of theology, i.e., "critical reflection on liberating activity, aimed not merely at understanding the world but at transforming it in accord with the revelation in Christ."[33] Kolden sees a danger in this definition that liberating action becomes the single norm of truth. Truth tends to become then equated not only with human action but also with a definite kind of political engagement. This, however, threatens to short-change the biblical idea of a theology of the cross in which "power is seen in weakness, in love, and in losing oneself for another."[34] While most liberation theologians are cognizant of such a danger, nevertheless caution against identifying the church with a partisan cause and the kingdom of God with a revolutionary movement remains in order. This danger becomes especially acute when liberation theology, in accordance with Marx, polarizes reality into oppressors and oppressed and identifies the cause of God only with the latter. In lieu of Marx's critique of religion and his reduction of liberation to an exclusively human work, the introduction of the Christian idea of liberation into this framework tends to mean sacrificing the Christian content (i.e., "as service losing one's life, going the second mile, turning the other cheek, living with the ambiguity of being in the image of God but not being one's own God"[35]) to the Marxist content.

The problem for liberation theology may be that its major focus for understanding reality (oppressor/oppressed or dependence/liberation) implies a liberation different from that of the God "in whose service is perfect freedom." Another way of making this criticism is to say that liberation theology's Marxist method threatens to undercut its biblical content, even though it is that method which has allowed its content to speak so powerfully in the present situation.[36]

[32]Ibid., p. 129.
[33]Ibid.
[34]Ibid.
[35]Ibid., p. 130.
[36]Ibid.

Kolden here finds the central grounds for criticism in the tendency of a Marxist concept of liberation to supplant the Christian concept by virtue of liberation theology's very method. This criticism echoes that of Dennis P. McCann to be examined in greater detail later in this chapter.

Kolden's critique of liberation theology's use of Marxism is one which appreciates the positive contributions of liberation theology while calling into question any use of Marxist categories for the purpose of norming the content of Christian theology. He sees both legitimate insights and definite dangers in a reliance upon Marxism, dangers especially when Marxism becomes a hermeneutical key for interpreting Christian thought. He also affirms the integrity of liberation theologians in their awareness of this tension and recognizes the basis of their theology not only in Marxism but in the biblical witness. In doing so Kolden has offered a differentiated critique of liberation theology which avoids a rejection of liberation theology on the basis of its use of Marxism while fully aware of the dangers when it becomes the methodological principle of liberation theology.

3.   Rosemary Radford Ruether

Although, as seen in the previous chapter, Rosemary Radford Ruether is in agreement with the basic concerns of liberation theology for social justice in Latin America, she has in her writings nevertheless raised concern about the dangers of an uncritical use of Marxist ideology. This corresponds both to her concern for the need to overcome dualistic thought and to her vision of a communal socialism. Marxism is understood to reintroduce dualistic categories of thought which both absolutizes one's own revolutionary cause and at the same time demonizes the enemy. This is an especially perfidious result of the transformation of Marx's vision for an ideal communist society into the totalitarianism of real communist states due to an inner contradiction within Marx's own thought. Moreover, Marxist states have followed the road of industrialization with disastrous consequences for the environment in a way which equals or surpasses the damage done to the environment in the capitalist West. These criticisms of Marxism recur in different forms throughout her writings and will here receive further clarification.

In *The Radical Kingdom* Ruether, in a chapter on Marx, argues that there exists within his thought an internal contradiction which leads directly to the totalitarianism of the communist states which are based upon his thought.[37] Although especially in his earlier writings Marx recognized the basis for human alienation to be traceable to an inner contradiction *within* the human being, this insight was left behind in the attempt to overcome human alienation by analysis and change of *social* relations. "This dilemma of man, unsolvable within the critique of political economy, thus forms the point of mystification of Marx's thought into an ideology, as that thought became the basis of the ruling parties of actual socialist states."[38]

By virtue then of a deficient anthropology, instead of ushering in the ideal society of communism which Marx envisioned, his thought

> became an ideology of preindustrial states that were attempting to pass with rapid strides to industrialization by means of collectivized property and centralized control. In practice communism came to mean, not an advance beyond capitalism, but a way of introducing capitalism, bourgeois values, and lifestyles by political force. Not the higher communism, in which all alienated authority disappears, but the most authoritarian type of economic and political life in the form of state capitalism was the social reality of the Marxist states. But since the social reality was in fundamental contradiction to Marxian eschatology, and since the claim to be on the road to the achievement of this eschatology was the basis for the legitimacy of the party's power, the result was an extraordinary and intricate mystification of Marxism as party doctrine.[39]

Instead of leading to the ideal communist society, industrialization led to the reality of dictatorial control and tyranny. The state did not wither away but rather became the means of brutally enforcing an orthodox ideology in contradiction with its own theoretical ideal for communist society. By failing to admit the inner contradiction within the human person, Marxism remains unable to identify the fundamental source of human alienation which it has so desperately sought to overcome. Ironically the road of industrialization and technologization followed by communist states has also led to the same ecological problems encountered in the West.[40]

---

[37]For the following see Rosemary Radford Ruether, *The Radical Kingdom. The Western Experience of Messianic Hope* (New York: Paulist, 1970), pp. 106-109. Cf. also Rosemary Radford Ruether, *Liberation Theology. Human Hope Confronts Christian History and American Power* (New York: Paulist, 1972), pp. 147-148.

[38]Ibid., p. 107.

[39]Ibid., pp. 107-108.

[40]Cf. Ruether, *Liberation Theology*, pp. 152-153 and Rosemary Radford Ruether, *Sexism and God-Talk. Toward a Feminist Theology* (Boston: Beacon Press, 1983), p. 253.

In spite of its own serious difficulties, Ruether nevertheless understands the appeal of Marxism and communism to the nationalist aspirations of the Third World.

> First, because communist states prove to be the states most sympathetic to this national and social struggle in practice, while Western nations are both the present and former colonialists and the counter-revolutionaries. Secondly, Communism, despite its original belief that it was the ideology of post-capitalistic society, has in practice, from the time of the Russian revolution, been primarily the vehicle for pre-industrialized states to make rapid industrial revolution under authoritarian, centralized state control. That this contradiction between original Marxist theory and actual communist practice has produced all the obfuscation that presently dominates Marxist thought is true, but that is of less and less interest to Third World revolutionaries who are primarily interested in Marxism because it has some methods which work.[41]

In their desire to improve their economic status, Third World revolutionaries are thus understood to be willing to overlook the contradictions in Marxist theory and practice in the hope for an overall positive advance in solving the social and economic problems which confront them. It is with this promise of social transformation that Marxism has also appealed to Latin American liberation theology.[42]

In spite of her understanding the nature of this appeal, Ruether has still raised serious questions about the negative consequences of dependence upon Marxist thought. In one context she questions whether Christian Marxism in Latin America has sufficiently considered the full implications of its use of Marxism.

> Marxism comes on the scene as a panacea of relevance, but not enough attention is paid to the dilemma of Marxism itself today. Why did the Communism of the Third International so quickly convert itself into a byzantinism every bit as rigid as that of Christendom? What does it mean that Marxism, so far, has been able to mediate only the traditional revolutions: the anti-feudal, anti-colonial revolutions of rapid industrialization?[43]

While sharing the goal of achieving greater justice in Latin America, Ruether, with reference to the arguments of Phil and Daniel Berrigan, asks about "the ways in which the Marxist adopts the political, economic and, finally, the military means of the enemy."[44]

> Power may change hands, but has its character really changed? It is good that Cuban children no longer starve, but when Cuban poets must pay for

---

[41]Ibid., pp. 161-162.

[42]Cf. ibid., pp. 177-180.

[43]Rosemary Radford Ruether, "Monks and Marxists: A Look at the Catholic Left," *Chr Cris* 33 (Apr. 30, 1973):79.

[44]For the following quotes see ibid.

this by suppression, is such a revolution radical enough to respond to the crisis of our times?

The relationship between such questions about the Marxist alternative and Ruether's own vision of a scaled-down communal socialism should be here kept in mind. Ruether agrees that Latin American social structures should be altered. The issue is that of the means for arriving at social change and the envisioned goal which guides the revolution.

In more recent writings Ruether has raised another related issue which is directed at Marxism's tendency to so absolutize the revolution that it loses the ability to remain self-critical.[45] The proponents of the revolution become absolutized as the epitome of goodness whereas any defects are attributed to either an external or an internal enemy. With regard to Latin American liberation theology Ruether makes these comments:

> [T]he real point of danger comes when victory becomes possible. How can one avoid the temptation of the victorious poor to become the avengers? Is it possible to dethrone the mighty and still exercise forgiveness towards the people? Here is where the Christian character of the struggle is really tested.[46]

While Marxism tends to absolutize between those for and against the revolution in a way that makes reconciliation impossible, Ruether argues for an overcoming of such dualistic thinking through the Christian concept of forgiveness. Any reintroduction of dualistic thinking ultimately undermines a revolution by cutting it off from the self-criticism which is indispensable to all human ventures. A dialectic must be forever maintained between the "already" of the positive achievements of a revolution and the "not yet" of what remains outstanding and thus calls for ongoing criticism.[47]

Throughout Ruether's writings are interspersed both critical evaluations of Marxism like those noted here and also more appreciative ones.[48] Those most related to the use of Marxism by liberation theology, however, are of a critical cast: (1) the danger of

---

[45]Cf. Ruether, *Sexism and God-Talk*, p. 253.

[46]Rosemary Radford Ruether, *To Change the World. Christology and Cultural Criticism* (New York: Crossroad, 1983), pp. 29-30.

[47]Cf. Ruether, *The Radical Kingdom*, pp. 286-288.

[48]For example, cf. Ruether's appreciative comments on the importance of Marx's critique of religion in *Sexism and God-Talk*, pp. 42-43, and her evaluations of the Marxist analysis of the subjection of women as well as women's liberation in communist societies in *New Woman New Earth. Sexist Ideologies and Human Liberation* (New York: Seabury, 1975), pp. 166-183.

reintroducing a dualistic thinking which absolutizes the revolution without provision for ongoing self-criticism and (2) the betrayal of Marx's own vision for a communist society by the erection of totalitarian communist states bent on rapid industrialization without regard for negative environmental consequences. Theoretically, these deficiencies are traceable to an internal contradiction in Marx's thought about the ultimate cause of human alienation. As an alternative vision Ruether would raise up a communal form of socialist society which goes beyond dualistic thought to inclusive categories in accordance with a more holistic theology of liberation.

B. *Defending Democratic Capitalism*

The emergence of Latin American liberation theology into the North American theological discussion has served as one important factor in recent efforts to examine and defend the system which has been called "democratic capitalism." Liberation theology's critique of capitalism and especially its use of dependency theory for its socioeconomic analysis have prompted several responses among North American theologians in defense of the historical, philosophical, economic, social, political, ethical and religious underpinnings of democratic capitalism. The work of two North Americans has been outstanding in this discussion, Michael Novak and Robert Benne, whose arguments in defense of democratic capitalism in response to the critique of liberation theology here represent this critical line of argument.

1. Michael Novak

Michael Novak, lay Catholic theologian and author of numerous books, occupies the George Frederick Jewett Chair at the American Enterprise Institute in Washington, D.C. The American Enterprise Institute for Public Policy Research, founded in 1943, is an institution which describes itself as "a publicly supported, nonpartisan, research and educational organization" whose "purpose is to assist policy makers, scholars, businessmen, the press, and the public by providing objective analysis of national and international issues."[49] To this end the American Enterprise Institute represents a point of view which has been traditionally described as conservative on a variety of social,

---

[49] Michael Novak, ed., *Liberation South, Liberation North* (Washington/London: American Enterprise Institute, 1981), inside cover.

political, and economic issues.

Although coming from a background of university teaching and authorship oriented toward the left of the political spectrum,[50] further examination of the democratic socialist position gradually led Novak to a reevaluation of the virtues of democratic capitalism and finally to its defense.[51] An essential component of this defense has been directed against liberation theology's critique of capitalism insofar as Novak perceives the pervasive influence of this theology and its socialist outlook, especially within influential circles within the Roman Catholic church.[52] In this regard Novak has made special reference to the influence of the Vatican Commission on Peace and Justice.[53]

Already in 1975, Novak began to assert his reservations regarding liberation theology.[54] In 1979 on the occasion of the trip of Pope John Paul II to Mexico, Novak highlighted the Pope's opposition to the Marxist tendencies both of the documents of the Medellin Conference of the Latin American bishops and of liberation theology in general.[55] Against the logic of liberation theology which is supposed to lead to the affirmation of a state organized on Marxist principles, the Pope was understood to defend genuine freedom and human rights.

In this 1979 article Novak cited the Maryknoll missioners and their Orbis publishing house as "the headquarters for liberation theology in the United States, and perhaps in the entire world."[56] In a survey of liberation theologians and sympathetic bishops, Novak pointed out the Marxist leanings of the entire movement as well as some observations on their possible motivation. Novak asserts that the Marxism which is the chief identifying characteristic of liberation theology is of a very particular kind, not the result of academic study

[50]Cf. Michael Novak, *A Theology for Radical Politics* (New York: Herder and Herder, 1969).

[51]For a more extended description of this reevaluation process see Michael Novak, *The Spirit of Democratic Capitalism* (New York: Simon & Schuster, 1982), pp. 22-28.

[52]See ibid., pp. 248-249.

[53]See ibid. and Michael Novak, *Freedom with Justice. Catholic Social Thought and Liberal Institutions* (San Francisco: Harper & Row, 1984), pp. 209-218.

[54]Cf. Michael Novak, "Theology of Liberation," *National Catholic Reporter* 11 (Nov. 21, 1975):12.

[55]For the following cf. Michael Novak, "Liberation Theology and the Pope," in James V. Schall, *Liberation Theology in Latin America* (San Francisco: Ignatius Press, 1982), pp. 278-290.

[56]Ibid., p. 281.

but rather a "populist" Marxism in solidarity with "the people." On this point Novak writes:

> It is difficult to take liberation theologians seriously as theoreticians of Marxism. One can grant that they are "populist Marxists," using Marxist slogans to ventilate some of the frustrations and aggressions of people whose aspirations have long been colored by external propaganda.
>
> There is a second sense in which they are Marxists. Marxism in Latin America is not just a theory. It is a well-financed, well-organized political institution, with parties, officials, printing presses, secret agents, operatives, intellectual sympathizers, international connections, and designated politicians. To be a Marxist, as the liberation theologians say, is not merely to hold a theory but to be committed to praxis. Yet the innocence with which the liberation theologians are committed to the Marxist praxis speaks volumes.[57]

The Marxism of liberation theology is thus understood by Novak to be unwittingly cooperating in a much more comprehensive Marxist conspiracy. It is important to note Novak's critique on this point for a clear understanding of the background of his defense of democratic capitalism.

In his "Introduction" and "Postscript" to a volume of essays which he edited in 1981 under the title *Liberation South, Liberation North*, Novak begins to develop a more positive argument against liberation theology. Here Novak writes of two theories of liberation, a South American one which has emerged as the theology of liberation and a North American one based on "a new conception of political economy," i.e., democratic capitalism.[58] Novak compares the histories of South and North America saying "South America chose to embody the political economy of Latin Europe" while "North America was more experimental and broke more thoroughly from Europe."[59] On this basis Novak contrasts the development of the two American continents over the centuries, citing their relative unfamiliarity with one another and even certain cultural hostilities. It is to the end of advancing "the study of two quite different theories of liberation" on the two continents that Novak cites as the rationale for the entire volume.[60]

The essays presented in this volume, apart from an initial one by Juan Luis Segundo, represent various positions which are highly critical of liberation theology. The arguments advanced by authors such as Ralph Lerner (on the American republic's "new man" of

---

[57]Ibid., p. 287.

[58]Novak, "Introduction," in *Liberation South, Liberation North*, p. 2.

[59]Ibid., pp. 1-2.

[60]Ibid., p. 4.

commerce) or the economist Joseph Ramos provide the foundation for many of the arguments which Novak himself subsequently takes up in his own criticism of liberation theology.[61] At the conclusion of this book, Novak mentions that in the current discussion of capitalism versus socialism, there exists "a general lack of clarity about the moral ideals of democratic capitalism."[62] This is a void Novak has attempted to fill by his next book, *The Spirit of Democratic Capitalism* (1982).

What does Novak mean when he speaks of democratic capitalism?

> I mean three systems in one: a predominantly market economy; a polity respectful of the rights of the individual to life, liberty, and the pursuit of happiness; and a system of cultural institutions moved by ideals of liberty and justice for all. In short, three dynamic and converging systems functioning as one: a democratic polity, an economy based on markets and incentives, and a moral-cultural system which is pluralistic and, in the largest sense, liberal.[63]

The first half of this book is devoted to an explication of the ideals of this democratic capitalist system—its historical achievements, its high idealism, its realistic anthropology, its terminology, its practicability and proven effectiveness. Composed of the three interlocking subsystems—political, economic, and moral-cultural—democratic capitalism has, according to Novak, proven itself superior to all other available alternatives.[64] Thus it is necessary to stress the virtuous spirit of democratic capitalism, in a time when it is attacked on many sides. One area of special concern for Novak is the attack on democratic capitalism by socialism and particularly by liberation theology which is considered an especially virulent exponent of socialism in the present context.

The second section of Novak's book concentrates on what he calls "the twilight of socialism," i.e., its failure to offer a practicable alternative to democratic capitalism in spite of its high aspirations. References to Latin America are interspersed throughout this discussion. In the present context, however, it is most important to concentrate attention on the specific arguments which Novak directs to

---

[61]Cf. Ralph Lerner, "Commerce and Character: The Anglo-American as New-Model Man," in ibid., pp. 24-49 and also the various essays by Joseph Ramos, in ibid., pp. 50-81.

[62]Michael Novak, "Editor's Postscript," in ibid., p. 98.

[63]Novak, *The Spirit of Democratic Capitalism*, p. 14.

[64]Cf. ibid., pp. 172-186.

liberation theology in three chapters of the third and final section of
this book.

It is important to note that although Novak criticizes liberation
theology and its advocacy of a socialist option for Latin America as a
way toward alleviating poverty and the other social, political, and
economic problems of Latin America, he nevertheless claims a
genuine interest in the solution of these problems. His criticism is
directed therefore at the means chosen for their solution and not at the
end itself.

At the center of Novak's criticism of liberation theology is his
challenge to the legitimacy of dependency theory as an interpretation
of the cause of Latin American poverty.[65] Novak is skeptical of
dependency theory which is said to project blame for Latin American
poverty away from Latin America toward the United States and the
economically developed world. Instead, Novak points to other factors
than does the Marxist inspired dependency theory: the recent
population explosion of Latin America, the failure of Latin America to
develop its own industrial and manufacturing potential, and a
different ethos from that which undergirds the Anglo-American
world.

Novak explains that neither the volume of trade between the U.S.
and Latin America nor the amount of total U.S. investments in Latin
America suffice to account for Latin American poverty or dependency.
Instead Novak looks to the history of Spanish colonialism and its
introduction of both feudalism and the Spanish ethos into Latin
America, a combination which the Roman Catholic church
unfailingly supported for centuries. Thus Novak calls into question
any analysis by Roman Catholic bishops which blames Latin
American poverty on dependency to the First World without
recognizing their own historical complicity in supporting the colonial
system to their own advantage. Two documents, one by the Peruvian
bishops and one by North American bishops, are cited by Novak for
their faulty analysis.

In turning to the dependency theory's categories of dividing the
world into center and periphery, Novak finds such a division much
more cogent when applied to socialist states than to the democratic
capitalist world. Novak ridicules such categories and their proponents
for their indefiniteness and inspecificity.

---

[65]For the following cf. ibid., pp. 272-286.

The theory of the "center" and the "periphery" is merely a clever restatement of the proposition that the poverty of the poor is explained by the wealth of the wealthy. For this there is not a shred of evidence. What causes wealth is intelligent economic activity. Societies can become wealthy through the blessings of nature. . . . Societies may lack resources and, nevertheless, become wealthy, like Hong Kong and Japan. Societies may be colonies or former colonies, like the United States. Others, like some in Latin America, blessed with climates that make subsistence relatively easy, can languish without significant development for generations. Theories of wealth which try to ignore cultural factors miss the central point. Theories which overlook the importance of a system of liberty miss a crucial lesson of economic history.[66]

It is factors internal to Latin America, its ethos and lack of liberty, which Novak emphasizes as the causes of Latin American poverty.

The objections of Novak to liberation theology, which revolve around this central critique of dependency theory, are many.[67] It would appear to Novak that the pursuit of liberty in Latin America would have led "away from socialism and toward 'the natural system of liberty' described so often in the Anglo-Saxon Whig tradition."[68] It did not, however, and Novak feels this latter tradition is not well known in Latin America, especially among European educated Catholic theologians. The absence of the commercial virtues of this liberal tradition, moreover, contributes greatly to the lethargy of the Latin American economy.

In surveying the main tenets of liberation theology, Novak comments on its theoretical utopianism, its Marxist illuminism, its elitist character, and its antipathy to things North American. Repeatedly, however, he returns to his central charge regarding the deficiency of liberation theology's critique of the idea of development and its preference for dependency theory and socialism. The socialism which liberation theology advocates is described as "vague and dreamy" and "derivative of European socialist ideas."[69]

> From the Latin American theologians one learns little about the actual political and economic realities of the diverse societies of Latin America. One finds in them minimal concrete description of persons, events, and institutions. Their tone is inspirational and hortatory, marshaling the "awakening" masses in rebellion against "oppressors." Liberation theology is remarkably abstract.[70]

---

[66]Ibid., p. 285.

[67]For the following cf. ibid., pp. 287-297.

[68]Ibid., p. 288.

[69]Ibid., p. 392.

[70]Ibid.

This abstraction is further demonstrated, according to Novak, by the absence of reflection on the nature of the institutions which are to replace the existing ones following the proposed revolution. Cuba is cited as an example of the way of socialism which may provide some "direct assistance to the poor" but "at the cost of economic stagnation and the deprivation of liberties."[71] By contrast democratic capitalism offers a way toward development which is concrete and proven.

Novak concludes his criticism of liberation theology in *The Spirit of Democratic Capitalism* with a final line of argument directed once more at the inadequacy of dependency theory in interpreting Latin America's history and present condition.[72] Novak stresses the importance of differing ethos and cultural values in North and South America as a significant factor in explaining their different developments.

> Latin Americans do not value the same moral qualities North Americans do. The two cultures see the world quite differently. . . . The "Catholic" aristocratic ethic of Latin America places more emphasis on luck, heroism, status, and *figura* than the relatively "Protestant" ethic of North America, which values diligent work, steadfast regularity, and the responsible seizure of opportunity.[73]

Novak feels such factors are greatly underestimated in explaining the differences in North and South American achievements.

Novak especially employs the work of Joseph Ramos, a Chilean economist, to counter the dependency theory defended by Gustavo Gutierrez.[74] Ramos has presented six statistics which serve to call into question the assertion that Latin American underdevelopment is caused by dependency on the United States, e.g., the relatively low level of U.S. trade with Latin America or the low rate of return on those investments which have been made. Ramos has gone on to ask if there are not factors internal to Latin America which are not more fundamental obstacles in achieving development. Perhaps the most crucial oversight of Gutierrez is, according to Ramos and Novak, capitalism's discovery of the logic behind the creation of wealth lying in a dynamic, expanding economy which is insufficiently acknowl-edged in Gutierrez's appeal to class conflict.

Novak proceeds to quote the work of Ramos regarding the actual success of Latin America in attaining sustained economic growth in

---

[71]Ibid., p. 297.

[72]For the following cf. ibid., pp. 298-302.

[73]Ibid., p. 302.

[74]For the following cf. ibid., pp. 304-312.

the period from 1945-1975. According to Ramos, growth in real wages, manufacturing and agricultural income, and output per worker have been accompanied by decreases in the rates of illiteracy and infant mortality. The conclusion drawn by Novak from these indicators is that Latin America is a "late starter" and basically should continue on its present economic course. The "failure" of Latin America is not in terms of economic growth but rather in terms of the actual distribution of the wealth. Novak follows Ramos again in calculating the need for a $5 billion annual redistribution of wealth in order to bring all Latin Americans above the destitution line and another $11 billion to raise all those classified as poor in Latin America above the poverty line. Both Ramos and Novak are convinced that such a redistribution of wealth in the Latin American context might be possible through various reform measures and they suggest a few possibilities. For Novak it is democratic capitalism which offers the means to this end.

Throughout his critique of liberation theology Novak repeatedly expresses his conviction that the socialist option advocated by liberation theology would inevitably lead Latin America to both a surrender of liberty and a stagnant economy under a real state of dependency on the Soviet Union.[75] The examples of Cuba and Nicaragua are several times noted in this regard.[76] Over against this real threat to the liberation of Latin America, Novak sees the choice of the democratic capitalist alternative as the real crux facing Latin America today.

> Latin America does face a crux. Shall the church in Latin America encourage its people along the road of unitary socialism—or along the road of pluralistic democratic capitalism? More than good intentions and high motives are needed. Decisions about the shape of the system *qua* system, about the political economy *qua* economy, will have consequences far beyond those willed by individuals. The people desire bread. They also desire liberty. Not only is it possible to have both, the second is a key to the first.[77]

In effect liberation theology by neglecting the democratic capitalist alternative and opting for socialism has betrayed the deepest aspirations of the Latin American people for liberty.

The argumentation against liberation theology is taken up once again by Novak in his book *Freedom With Justice. Catholic Social Thought and Liberal Institutions* (1984). In this book Novak defends

---

[75]See ibid., pp. 312-314.

[76]For example, see ibid., pp. 272, 282-283, 286, 293-294, and 312-314.

[77]Ibid., p. 314.

the main thesis that Roman Catholic social teaching in the modern
period has been gradually moving toward a position which has
considerable affinity with "liberal institutions" and which in fact
logically requires concrete embodiment in liberal institutions.

> Catholic social thought has yet to discover the practical secrets of the
> human spirit which infuse liberal institutions, but the course we have
> followed shows clearly enough that this discovery lies just around the next
> turn, just over the crest, along the road so arduously followed. For the
> Catholic commitment to the dignity of each individual person now
> demands as its institutional expression a full panoply of liberal
> institutions: in the polity, in the economy, and in the domain of
> conscience, ethos, virtues, ideas, and information.[78]

By "liberal institutions" it is clear Novak means the system which he
has also called "democratic capitalism."

Once again in this volume, references to Latin America and the
danger of the Marxist option for the Latin American context as
advocated by liberation theology are interspersed throughout.[79] Novak
stresses repeatedly the crucial decision which lies before Latin
America: the choice between socialism which leads to a stagnant
economy and tyranny under dependency on the Soviet Union or the
Anglo-American model of freedom under the governance of liberal
institutions.

An increasingly emphasized motif in Novak's explanation of
Latin American poverty is that of "ethos."

> Latin America is a region of immense geographical and cultural
> diversity. Yet virtually all its nations share Latin culture, languages,
> and Catholic faith. The continent is rich in natural resources of many
> kinds. Every nation among them has sufficient arable land and a
> sufficiently favorable climate to be able to feed itself. If Latin Americans
> shared the ethos, virtues, and the institutions of the Japanese, they would
> assuredly be among the economic leaders of the world.[80]

In weighing the factors which have produced Latin American poverty,
Novak emphasizes neither the aftermath of Latin American
colonization nor the disparity between rich and poor embedded in the
present Latin American social structures as does liberation theology,
but rather he faults Latin Americans for their choice of an ethos
inappropriate to the creation of wealth.

In a chapter entitled "Liberation Theology in Praxis" Novak
concentrates a new line of argument against the theology of

---

[78]Novak, *Freedom With Justice*, p. 218.
[79]Cf. ibid., pp. 35-38, 48, 56, 78, 120, 162-164, 174-176, and 195.
[80]Ibid., p. 174.

liberation.[81]   While recognizing the honorable intention of liberation
theology to "lift up the poor," its fatal flaw lies in its proposal of the
wrong praxis. Because liberation theology emphasizes praxis to such a
large degree, it is on the basis of its praxis which he argues it should be
evaluated. For Novak this means particular attention should be paid to
two points.

> The two most insistent *practical* claims of liberation theology are the
> following: first, that its basic insights are validated by the "expressed
> conscience" of "the poor," testifying to one another in their *comunidades
> de base*; second, that liberation theology offers a *praxis* which flows from
> the consciences so expressed.[82]

To the first of these claims Novak responds that no uniform public
opinion exists among the poor of Latin America and that the public
opinion surveys which do exist seldom conform to the views of
liberation theology. Moreover, Novak disputes liberation theology's
claim that the poor have any special insight into their own condition
and that "the 'analysis' of the situation given by the poor is *ipso facto* a
true analysis."[83] While the poor deserve to be heard with sympathy,
this does not "suffice to still critical and practical inquiry. The poor
may have things wrong. Their opinions are not necessarily God's,
nor do they necessarily carry the warrant of truth."[84]

With regard to the second practical claim which Novak sees
liberation theology making, he believes it is necessary to evaluate
liberation theology on the basis of its praxis. Nicaragua is cited as an
example of the results of this praxis which, according to Novak,
indicates the betrayal of liberation by the Sandinistas to a new form of
oppression "held in power and ideologically held in line by Cuban and
Soviet financing, military power, and secret police."[85] The
abstractness of liberation theology is cited over against the diversity of
the thirteen nations of South America. In reference to the dependency
theory employed by liberation theology, Novak believes the resentment
it creates is not conducive to the creation of new wealth in Latin
America regardless of any possible validity this theory might have. In
any case he says that colonialism under Spain and Portugal would be a
more justifiable target for blame than the United States. What is more,

---

[81] For the following cf. ibid., pp. 183-194.

[82] Ibid., p. 184.

[83] Ibid., p. 185.

[84] Ibid.

[85] Ibid., p. 186.

the ethos of Latin America inhibits its development in spite of its rich natural resources.

Novak also comments on the lack of statistical evidence to substantiate the dependency theory's claim of U.S. exploitation. He in turn offers his own statistical argument against dependency theory based on the comparatively low level of U.S. investments in Latin America. Japan is noted as an example of a nation which, in spite of the devastation of World War II, does not view itself as a victim of oppression but instead has put its energy to work in revitalizing its economy.

Novak also seeks to answer the charges that Latin America's economic problems are the consequence of unfair international terms of trade. Insofar as such charges are true, Novak would see them remedied. But even so these charges draw attention away from the more pressing need for Latin America to develop its manufacturing sector. Manufacturing means jobs, a reduction in imports, and the production of goods needed by the domestic markets of Latin America. Latin America need only reach its economic "take-off" point in order to raise the living standard of the poor. And it is raising the poor's standard of living that should be the number one priority rather than the "red herring" of focusing on the gap between rich and poor.

In conclusion, Novak reiterates that liberation theology fails exactly at the point it has itself emphasized, that is, praxis.

> If liberation theology is for what works, it will one day discover that Marxist-Leninism is incompatible not only with the generation of broad, popular prosperity, but also with the practice of democracy. For only democracy guarantees associations of persons the power to defend their own human rights institutionally and with effect. In practice, private ownership, differential incentives, markets, and institutions of sustained economic invention and creativity seem to be necessary (if not sufficient) conditions for a practical, functioning democracy. This is because, without private ownership, citizens and their families have no substantial independence from the state.[86]

Latin America has, according to Novak, yet to try the way of a democratic capitalism which is both genuinely capitalist and genuinely democratic. It needs to finally leave behind the ethos of the past and the illusionary proposals of liberation theology which only lead to new forms of tyranny, and to open itself to the promise of prosperity and liberty which only democratic capitalism offers.

---

[86]Ibid., p. 192.

Michael Novak has written a many-faceted defense of democratic capitalism which has attempted to respond to the challenge of socialism, particularly as that challenge has been articulated by the Latin American theology of liberation. His is a response to liberation theology which has found much support among the ranks of religious and political conservatives in the United States during the decade of the eighties and which in its argumentation has shown great affinity to the viewpoint of the Reagan administration in its foreign policy in Central America.

2. Robert Benne

Robert Benne is professor at Roanoke College at Salem, Virginia and former Professor of Church and Society at the Lutheran School of Theology at Chicago. Benne's major contribution to the defense of democratic capitalism has been his book entitled *The Ethic of Democratic Capitalism. A Moral Reassessment* (1981). As indicated by the title, Benne, in comparison to Novak, lays greater stress on the ethical legitimacy of democratic capitalism.

> Positively stated, my thesis argues that the combination of democracy and market economy peculiar to the United States is a morally defensible arrangement. Further, it has a good deal of promise in dealing with its many challenges if it proceeds in accordance with gifts and possibilities inherent in democratic capitalism. . . .
>
> Negatively stated, my thesis argues that all moral authenticity is not on the side of the sharp critics of democratic capitalism, especially on the second part of the combination. It *is* possible to prize justice and at the same time support market arrangements, particularly if these arrangements, are qualified by democratic polity.[87]

In using Novak's term "democratic capitalism" to describe the American political economy, it is the practical and ethical possibilities of democratic capitalism which are Benne's primary concern.

Benne has been moved to the ethical defense of democratic capitalism by what he considers the facile critique of capitalism by those employing broad generalizations based upon Marxist analysis, especially by those among the church.[88] This includes the position of liberation theology and in particular its use of dependency theory.

> To the left, the field is dominated by the various strands of liberation theology. Bonino, Segundo, Assmann, Gutierrez, and others take as their prime target the capitalism represented by American multinational

---

[87]Robert Benne, *The Ethic of Democratic Capitalism. A Moral Reassessment* (Philadelphia: Fortress, 1981), pp. vii-viii.

[88]For the following cf. ibid., pp. 1-19.

> corporations. They have swallowed the Marxist analysis of dependent
> capitalism and hope for a revisionist socialism in Latin America. . . .
> The social ethics of both the World Council and the National Council of
> Churches are hostile toward Western capitalism and partisan toward the
> socialist movements of the developing world. Marxist thought has become
> the major tool of economic analysis and prescription for Christian
> liberation theology and ethics.[89]

While asserting a personal commitment to an ethical and theological
position which seeks to be critical of all systems and especially
democratic capitalism, Benne at the same time believes that solid
economic and ethical arguments exist in favor of the system of
democratic capitalism. The historical "track record" of socialism
belies its actual ability to compete with democratic capitalism in
categories such as "liberty, democracy, equality, quality of life,
productivity, peaceful intentions and actions, cultural creativity, and
others."[90] While the morality of democratic capitalism is more subtle
and complex than the rhetoric of socialism, it is nevertheless to be
preferred on the basis of its accomplishments. Thus in the present time
there is an urgent need to return to sound and reasonable ethical and
economic arguments in the face of the wide appeal of the "socialist
myth" (P. Berger). Benne writes his book then in order "to establish
an ethical perspective—in this case one derived from Christian
theological ethics—that transcends democratic capitalism and
provides grounds for criticism."[91] On the basis of this perspective he
asserts: "Democratic capitalism can be legitimated as a relatively just
form of society now, with the prospect of significant improvement in the
future."[92]

The theoretical foundations for Benne's ethical perspective derive
primarily from two authors, Reinhold Niebuhr and John Rawls.[93] It is
interesting to observe how Reinhold Niebuhr has served as a central
resource for several of those who have most severely criticized Latin
American liberation theology. In addition to Benne both Michael
Novak and Dennis McCann have turned to the thought of Niebuhr,
emphasizing his theological anthropology which itself stresses the
fallenness of human existence into the condition of sin and the
consequent egoism of human behavior especially in its social forms.

---

[89]Ibid., p. 4.

[90]Ibid., p. 9.

[91]Ibid., p. 16.

[92]Ibid., p. 18.

[93]For the following cf. ibid., pp. 23-87.

Benne differs from Novak and McCann, however, in also turning to Rawls' theory of justice in constructing his own ethical perspective. Rawls' theory of justice is employed by Benne in translating the intention of Christian agape, itself most applicable to the personal realm or very small groups, to the social realm. Rawls' theory of justice is hypothetically based upon what Rawls' calls an "original position." Rawls hypothesizes a set of conditions which would be reasonably included in a social contract among persons seeking to establish a just society. Presupposed is that the participants in this contract are free and equal rational beings endowed as well with self-interest. Two principles emerge from Rawls' deliberations.

> First: each person is to have an equal right to the most extensive basic liberty compatible with a similar liberty for others.[94]

This principle is one Rawls then further qualifies in his book in order to explain its applicability. After revision, the second principle of Rawls affirms:

> Social and economic inequalities are to be arranged so that they are both (a) to the greatest benefit of the least advantaged and (b) attached to offices and positions open to all under conditions of fair equality of opportunity.[95]

After undertaking an extensive discussion of Rawls' work, Benne concludes that Rawls' theory of justice "provides a suitable complement to a basically Niebuhrian approach to justice in society."[96]

Both Rawls and Niebuhr in this way provide the foundation for the principles of a just society which Benne proposes.[97] In critical dialogue with their thought, these principles are to include: (1) economic efficiency and growth (undervalued by Niebuhr and Rawls), (2) subsidiarity (i.e., protecting the equilibrium of power by insisting on its exercise on the lowest possible level of society and resisting its relinquishment to the larger community), and (3) a clearly defined understanding of the role of the state (i.e., resolving conflict, performing functions impossible at the lower levels, and correcting injustice). Benne argues for realistic, not perfectionist, expectations in the application of these principles to actual societies. On the basis of this criterion he then goes on to deem the actual achievements of democratic capitalism superior to those of the socialist alternative.

---

[94]John Rawls, *A Theory of Justice* (Cambridge: Harvard University Press, 1971), p. 60, as quoted in Benne, *The Ethic of Democratic Capitalism*, p. 54.

[95]Rawls, A Theory of Justice, p. 83, as quoted by Benne, *The Ethics of Democratic Capitalism*, p. 55.

[96]Benne, *The Ethics of Democratic Capitalism*, p. 67.

[97]For the following cf. ibid., pp. 69-87.

Benne's primary argument against the dependency theory
employed by liberation theology occurs in the second and third parts of
his book which he entitles "The Case for Democratic Capitalism" and
"The Challenges and Possibilities of Democratic Capitalism,"
respectively. In a chapter on "The Virtues of Capitalism," which
applies the three principles mentioned above to democratic capitalism
as it is practiced in the United States, Benne cites the correlation
between economic growth in the advanced countries and the rate of
growth in the lesser developed countries as an initial argument
against dependency theory. This fact "belies the stock criticism that
development of the richer countries is at the expense of the poorer" and
he quotes the economist Arthur Lewis in support of this view.[98]

This argument is expanded upon in the chapter entitled "The
Challenges Surrounding Efficiency and Growth."[99] Although the
"theory of dependent capitalism" has gained widespread acceptance
even by Americans who are the primary objects of its critique and
although it may be called "*the* dominating frame of reference for the
'progressive' edge of theological social ethics,"[100] Benne remains
unconvinced by its arguments. Benne finds the counter-theory of
Arthur Lewis a more plausible alternative for interpreting the causes
of underdevelopment. The theory of Lewis first contradicts the thesis
that the raw materials of the Third World enabled the industrial
revolution in the First World. Instead the First World is claimed to
have been self-sufficient in raw materials and, moreover, it is
asserted that the trade between First and Third Worlds at this time was
minimal. The divergent developments of First and Third Worlds are
in fact attributable to economic reasons. Political explanations are
insufficient since colonialism cannot explain the underdevelopment
of those Third World nations which already in the nineteenth century
were independent. "Brazil, Argentine, and all the rest of Latin
America were independent political entities which were free to
industrialize but did not."[101]

Lewis explains that this failure to industrialize is the key to Third
World underdevelopment. Industrialization can only take place
subsequent to or simultaneous with an agricultural revolution which
enables and undergirds industrial revolution. This agricultural base

---

[98]Ibid., p. 133.

[99]For the following cf. ibid., pp. 194-208.

[100]Ibid., p. 195.

[101]Ibid., p. 199.

for industrialization was in the Third World impossible, however, due to the existence of "landed classes, who benefitted from cheap imports and saw no reason to support an emerging industrial order."[102] Benne at this point briefly suggests that Catholicism reinforced these patterns and thus served to impede development. He then goes on to quote a summary of the argument of Lewis.

> The principle cause of the poverty of the developing countries, and of their poor factoral terms of trade is that half their labor force (more or less) produces food at very low productivity levels. This limits the domestic market for manufacturers and services, keeps the propensity to import too high, reduces taxable capacity and savings, and provides goods and services for export on unfavorable terms. To alter this is the fundamental way to change Less Developed Countries/More Developed Countries relations. But this takes time.[103]

This argument Benne finds representative of the position of many other economists as well.

While Benne recognizes certain instances of abuse by the industrialized West, these abuses finally are deemed insufficient explanations of Third World problems. The Third World is finally "dependent because it is underdeveloped, not underdeveloped because it is dependent."[104] A further argument which reinforces this explanation is that of the actual benefits accrued by the Third World through their trade with the First World. Only by an accurate appraisal of the causes of underdevelopment can the proper measures be taken toward its elimination. And this is not assisted by placing blame for Third World problems on the economic exploitation of the First.

After briefly reiterating three scenarios which possibly describe the future course which may be taken by the Third World, Benne offers some proposals for development which he sees going beyond the oversimplification of dependency theory. Although the road to development will be a difficult one, the democratic capitalist model offers concrete proposals with a promise of effectiveness absent in the socialist alternative. In encouraging Third World development America should:

---

[102]Ibid.

[103]W. Arthur Lewis, *The Evolution of the International Economic Order* (Princeton: Princeton University Press, 1978), p. 26, as quoted by Benne, ibid., p. 200.

[104]Benne, *The Ethics of Democratic Capitalism*, p. 201.

(1) "Continue its good record of emergency aid to nations and peoples who experience serious crises, regardless of their ideological commitments."[105]

(2) Support in its foreign policy "political leadership in the less-developed countries that genuinely represents the interests of all their people, but especially their poor."[106]

(3) "Work to remove trade barriers to imports from developing countries."[107]

(4) "Gradually raise the proportion of its GNP for foreign aid from the current 0.25 percent to the United Nations target of 0.7 percent."[108] Following the theory of Lewis this increase should aim especially at agricultural development in order to establish a base for industrialization.

In concluding his discussion of Third World economic growth, Benne notes that the continued economic strength of the First World is a necessary presupposition for Third World development. The apparent imbalance between U.S. population size and U.S. consumption (i.e., that 6 percent of the world's population consumes 37 percent of the world's goods and services) should not obscure the economic benefits of U.S. productivity to the rest of the world.

Although at one point in his book Benne concedes that in situations of extreme poverty and oppression the way of revolutionary socialism may seem to be a tragically necessary option, he has strong reservations against such "shortcuts" to progress.[109] The danger of the erection of new forms of oppression which contradict the norms of efficiency and growth, subsidiarity and equality, and liberty are extremely great in such cases. For this reason Benne has argued for the practical and ethical legitimacy of the democratic capitalist system and the possibility of its being reformed where challenges to its ideals remain.

Together Benne and Novak have sought to provide a theoretical defense of democratic capitalism. They have done so as theologians attempting to make primary use of philosophical, historical, economic, and ethical in addition to theological arguments. A central occasion for their defense has been the emergence of liberation theology and its

---

[105]Ibid., p. 204.

[106]Ibid., p. 205.

[107]Ibid., p. 206.

[108]Ibid., p. 207.

[109]Cf. ibid., pp. 86-87.

employment of the theory of dependency as a critique of the capitalist economic system.

C. *The Challenge of Christian Realism*

In the autumn of 1973 an extensive North American discussion of Latin American liberation theology ensued in the journal *Christianity and Crisis* precipitated by the publication of an article by Thomas G. Sanders with the title "The Theology of Liberation: Christian Utopianism."[110] The theological basis for Sander's critique of liberation theology was the "Christian realism" of Reinhold Niebuhr which was understood to call into question both liberation theology's anthropology and its view of history. Since the time of this initial debate, the thought of Niebuhr has been frequently cited by the North American critics of liberation theology. Both Michael Novak and Robert Benne have in their respective defenses of democratic capitalism used Niebuhr as a theological source. Likewise Dennis P. McCann has written an elaborate work employing the thought of Niebuhr to contrast and critique the Latin American theology of liberation. In this section the arguments of Sanders and McCann are examined in order to describe the challenge which Christian realism has set before liberation theology in the North American context.

1. Thomas G. Sanders

Thomas G. Sanders, most recently of the Institute of World Affairs at Salisbury, Connecticut and previously with the American Universities Field Service as well as a former associate professor at Brown University, provided an early critique of liberation theology on the basis of Christian realism which was published in a 1973 issue of *Christianity and Crisis*. After a brief survey of Latin American history and some of the main tenets of liberation theology, Sanders proceeded in his essay to criticize the "'soft' utopianism" represented by liberation theology which "was repeatedly criticized by Reinhold Niebuhr in working out his interpretation of Christian realism."[111] Sanders explains the similarity between liberation theology and the concern of Niebuhr this way:

> That a comparable phenomenon should appear 40 years later in a different geographical context and largely under Catholic auspices does not mean

---

[110]Thomas G. Sanders, "The Theology of Liberation: Christian Utopianism," *Chr Cris* 33 (Sept. 17, 1973):167-173.

[111]Ibid., p. 169.

that history repeats itself. A better explanation seems to be that the
religious outlook on reality lends itself to a "moralistic" ideology in
utopian form as a reaction to a legalistic and conservative ethic, guilt over
the complicity of the church in social evils, discovery of the radicalness of
biblical ethics and dialogue with non-Christian movements of social
criticism like Marxism. Latin American Christianity has passed
through these creative but painful experiences during the past decade, just
as North American Protestantism underwent them earlier in this
century.[112]

Having identified liberation theology as a "moralistic ideology" and a
"utopian moralism," Sanders raises two chief objections of Niebuhr
against such thinking. First, it contradicts, according to Niebuhr, the
biblical view both of human nature and of history. Human nature in
the Pauline-Augustinian-Lutheran tradition, even when forgiven by
Christ, remains captive to sin which continues to significantly
influence human action. History is thus a dialectic between the
strivings of human hope and the actual condition of human sinfulness
which limits such strivings. History continues to exist in this dialectic
and is misunderstood when conceived as the "progressive unfolding of
moral aspirations."[113]

Sanders' second major objection to liberation theology on the basis
of Christian realism is that "utopianism gives insufficient
consideration to the moral ambiguity that characterizes all forms of
social existence."[114] Social systems and governments are always
imperfect due to the delicate balances of power upon which they are
based. That any nation attains even a relative degree of justice is
attributable to the restraints which are made upon the egoism inherent
in all human efforts. Niebuhr's achievement was his realistic
apprehension and analysis of the struggle for power within all social
systems.

Such a realistic Niebuhrian outlook on the potential of human
individuals and nations to attain their highest aspirations finds the
division of people, classes, and nations into good and bad, oppressed
and oppressor, socialist and capitalist, overly simplistic and incapable
of rendering intelligible the complexity of factors contributing to Latin
American dependence.

The ascription of responsibility for regional problems to outside
"domination" obscures the real characteristics of Latin American
dependence, the function of foreign capital and technology in

---

[112]Ibid., p. 170.
[113]Ibid.
[114]Ibid.

development, the responsibility and sovereignty of these nations in their decisions and the limitations on U.S. influence in Latin America.[115]
The incapability of rendering the necessarily complex and ambiguous moral decisions is further enhanced by introducing concepts like liberation and the kingdom of God into the political sphere. The gap between the symbolic value of these legitimate Christian symbols and the risky concrete business of proposing and carrying out an effective policy is simply too great. The tendency of liberation theology toward rationalization and moralizing does not satisfy the need for an actual course of action, a program and a policy. Sanders employs examples from Panama and Argentina to illustrate this point.

Sanders further affirms the inevitability of disillusionment among those who aspire to establish the kingdom of God in the political realm. In this regard he cites liberation theology's growing disillusionment with "revolution" and "socialism."[116] Sanders also explains the favorable reception of liberation theology among North American Protestants as at least partially an aftermath of the optimism about social change of the sixties in a period which has become generally disillusioned about U.S. policies.

A more realistic approach to Latin America and the theology of liberation would, according to Sanders, move beyond moralistic dichotomies to an assessment of the variety and particularity of the different Latin American nations. An examination of the differences between countries like Chile, Cuba, and Brazil means leaving behind stereotypes, e.g., that Latin America as a whole is in "revolutionary ferment." A more realistic view would see that in comparison to the rest of the Third World "most Latin American nations have achieved a relatively advanced level of development, while continuing to have serious injustices, social problems, and what social scientists call 'political underdevelopment.'"[117] A realistic approach takes seriously such complexities in making ethical decisions and attempts on the basis of the given particularities to make the concrete decisions of exercising political power.

In conclusion, Sanders affirms that the church must also learn the complexities of the political process which leads to effective policies. While utopianism can at times positively open the church to new possibilities, the danger lies in its tendency to absolutism which fails to

[115]Ibid.
[116]Ibid., p. 171.
[117]Ibid., p. 172.

carry out the harder work of developing concrete strategies. An example of the latter has been the Christians for Socialism movement in Chile during the period of the Allende government. Sanders encourages the church, especially the Latin American church, to move beyond utopianism to a realistic appraisal of its limited role in shaping Latin America's future. Where the church's tradition and established structure offer opportunities for "defending human rights, strengthening the family or 'awakening consciousness'" beyond its "preeminent theological and pastoral obligations," these should be pursued.[118] Sanders goes on, however, to say:

> In the final analysis the effectiveness of Christianity will depend on its capacity to understand the issues that decision-makers confront and to speak with knowledge on the morally and politically ambiguous, but real, questions faced by each national society. The church does not help by pointing to a religious reality beyond the possibilities of Latin American countries and making it into a political program. Rather, it must discern the moral implications underlying existent societal processes and alternative uses of power.[119]

Liberation theology, according to Sanders, falls short on the basis of these criteria.

A reply to Sanders' essay appeared in the same issue of *Christianity and Crisis* by the Brazilian theologian Rubem A. Alves in which he attacked Christian realism as an "ideology of the establishment."[120] A subsequent issue presented brief statements pertinent to the exchange between Sanders and Alves by John C. Bennett, John Plank, Robert McAfee Brown, Thomas Quigley, Jacques Kozub, and Alexander Wilde.[121] Finally Sanders wrote a brief reply to these critiques which served as a conclusion to the published discussion.[122]

In this reply Sanders was most responsive to the statement of John C. Bennett who had written:

> This article [Sanders'] confirms a conviction, which I have had before, that Christian Realism is not a self-sufficient theology; it is a corrective theology that at its best incorporated something of the spirit and dynamism of the Social Gospel and the Christian Socialism of the Niebuhr of *Moral*

---

[118]Ibid., p. 173.

[119]Ibid.

[120]Rubem A. Alves, "Christian Realism: Ideology of the Establishment," *Chr Cris* 33 (Sept. 17, 1973):173-176.

[121]"Continuing the Discussion: Liberation Theology and Christian Realism," *Chr Cris* 33 (Oct. 15, 1973):196-206.

[122]Thomas Sanders, "Thomas Sanders Replies," *Chr Cris* 33 (Nov. 26, 1973): 249-251.

Man and Immoral Society for which it was a corrective. Without the continuing influences of those sources, latter day Christian Realism often is the North American ideology that Rubem Alves finds it to be.[123]

Bennett further remarks that the social concern for the poor and oppressed expressed by liberation theology is the larger context in which it must be seen. Only with an appreciation for that larger context can the genuine insights of Christian realism avoid functioning as an ideology for the present social order. Bennett concludes his statement:

> Sanders is right in saying that "no Latin American decision maker can base judgments on liberation or on the Kingdom of God." But the real question is: What influence do liberation and the Kingdom of God have on the vision, the presuppositions and the accompanying awareness according to which he makes decisions? Sanders seems to forget that Christian Realism in its early days had a much more dialectical view of the relation between the Kingdom of God and historical decisions or institutions than that which informs his article.[124]

In his reply to the entire discussion Sanders further explained his own involvement in Latin American affairs and his growing conviction as a result of that involvement that the church needs to realistically grasp both the importance of power in political decision making and the dynamics of its use. Whereas the theology of liberation had, according to Sanders, emphasized the moral imperative of the Latin American situation, his attempt was to call for more specificity in the liberationist analysis. He admits, however, his vulnerability to Bennett's charge that he had in his article sacrificed the "dialectic." In conclusion, Sanders reformulates many of the points made in his first article no longer as statements of fact but now as questions aimed at deepening the valid insights of liberation theology. Practical and effective political action by Christians can only be enhanced by grappling with the issues which are faced daily by those responsible for public affairs.

2. Dennis P. McCann

The most elaborate exposition of the contrast between Niebuhr's Christian realism and Latin American liberation theology has been authored by Dennis P. McCann, currently Assistant Professor of Religious Studies at DePaul University in Chicago. His book, *Christian Realism and Liberation Theology. Practical Theologies in Creative Conflict* (1981), takes as its point of orientation the debate

---

[123]John C. Bennett, *Chr Cris* 33 (Oct. 15, 1973):197.
[124]Ibid., p. 198.

emanating from the Sanders article[125] and develops what he sees to be the valid insights of Christian realism in order to critique liberation theology.

> After wrestling with this issue for a number of years, I conclude that Niebuhr's "paradoxical vision" of the Hidden God's relationship to human history is a more adequate basis for practical theology and Christian social actions than the vision of Christ the Liberator proclaimed by Latin Americans like Gustavo Gutierrez. While Niebuhr's vision is more promising, the theology and ethics that he develops from it are not without their deficiencies. I shall try to show what these are and why they give the charge "ideology of the Establishment" some plausibility. But I shall also argue that in light of the even more severe problems facing liberation theology, these deficiencies do not warrant the repudiation of Christian realism. For Gutierrez's vision is of dubious origin, and his theology consequently is vitiated by a critical ambiguity: a failure to clarify the theological relationship between "liberation" and "salvation." As liberation theologians continue their "critical reflection on praxis," Gutierrez's ambiguity becomes a dilemma: either the content must be politicized or the method trivialized. I shall give reasons why this dilemma rules out liberation theology, as it stands, as an alternative to Christian realism. Its structural failure means that this theology possesses no theoretical resources for distinguishing religious transcendence from political enthusiasm, a distinction that practical theologians and Christian social activists must make if they are to remain recognizably Christian.[126]

At the heart of McCann's critique of liberation theology on the basis of Christian realism is his argument against its method.

The first half of McCann's book is a detailed examination of Reinhold Niebuhr's Christian realism: the context in which it arose, its method, its theological emphases, the framework it offers for social ethics, as well as a critique thereof. McCann notes the pragmatism of Niebuhr's position, his combination of faith with experience, which eventually led him to abandon the Marxist position due to its deficient apprehension of human nature, i.e., human sinfulness, and his disillusionment about the actual praxis deriving from Marxism especially in Stalin's Russia.[127] Niebuhr's break with Marxism on the basis of new emphasis upon "God's otherness" and its correlate of a "religious disinterestedness" which refuses to identify with any one political movement is particularly emphasized by McCann.[128]

---

[125]Dennis P. McCann, *Christian Realism and Liberation Theology. Practical Theologies in Creative Conflict* (Maryknoll: Orbis, 1981), pp. 1-3.

[126]Ibid., p. 4.

[127]Cf. ibid., pp. 15-19.

[128]Cf. ibid., pp. 27-37.

Central to Niebuhr's method is his interpretation of the central Christian "myths" of Creation, Fall, and Atonement.[129] Together the truth of these myths is summarized by McCann under two aspects which reveals the core of Christian realism: "an unflinching realism about human nature ultimately inspired by a religious awareness of its limits and possibilities, and an uncompromising loyalty to the absolute moral demands of Jesus qualified by a humble recognition of our inability to fulfill them."[130]

Niebuhr's theological anthropology and theology of history received its most thorough elaboration in his major work, *The Nature and Destiny of Man* (1941/43).[131] In discussing this work it is McCann's judgment that Niebuhr's "theological anthropology dominates the structure of Christian realism at the expense of its theology of history"[132] and this is a point for criticism. Likewise McCann notes a frequent objection of liberation theology to liberal anthropologies which also has validity for Niebuhr's theological anthropology.

> It is possible to dismiss his theological anthropology as ahistorical, as so restricted to the inner world of private religious experience that it provides no adequate perspective for interpreting either society or history. As we shall see, liberation theologians make this kind of claim against both progressive Catholic and liberal Protestant theologies: abstract generalizations about human nature represent an obstacle to critical historical consciousness. Their anthropologies, in other words, inhibit an awareness of the dialectical patterns of social development—the role of political, economic, and social structures, technological advances, as well as geographic, ethnic, and linguistic differences—and their significance for interpreting social change. If this objection is valid, it also holds for Christian realism.[133]

McCann describes this as the "gap" in Niebuhr's thought between "self and society." He explains, furthermore, the way Niebuhr attempted in part to bridge it by speaking of an "equality of sin" among all human beings coupled with an "inequality of guilt," more guilt being attributable to those apportioned greater power and responsibility in a given society.

In discussing Niebuhr's theology of history, McCann pays special attention to his Christology and eschatology. With regard to the latter,

---

[129]For the following cf. ibid., pp. 37-50.
[130]Ibid., p. 44.
[131]For the following cf. ibid., pp. 52-78.
[132]Ibid., p. 53.
[133]Ibid., p. 62.

McCann stresses the tension in Niebuhr's concept of the kingdom of God between its present possibilities for realization and its future arrival through God alone. Niebuhr consequently described history as an "interim" with a "paradoxical interpretation of salvation as realizable 'in principle but not in fact.' Implied by it is Niebuhr's 'religious reservation' about collective human endeavors: no human association, Christian or otherwise, can claim to have established a perfect society—a kingdom of God—on earth. All such assertions are rejected as either 'ideological' pretensions or 'utopian' projections."[134] In criticism of Niebuhr's *The Nature and Destiny of Man*, McCann finds its theological anthropology to be plausible while its theology of history is inadequate.

> [T]he connection between the history of theological concepts and the processes of social development remains for the most part unanalyzed. Thus instead of correlating his religious insights into the paradox of sin and grace with some form of critical social theory, he restricts the reference of his theology of history to the history of ideas.[135]

According to McCann the gap between an essentially valid theological anthropology and the contingencies of human history remains, in Niebuhr, unbridged.

As a theological framework for social ethics, Christian realism is, according to McCann, more suggestive of a "dispositional ethic" for individual moral agents rather than a genuine social ethic.[136] As a political ethic Niebuhr's emphasis on the relation between love and justice leads McCann to a similar conclusion. While useful for critiquing political "illusions," it has limited applicability for the larger task of social ethics. Likewise Niebuhr's analyses of the "middle axioms," i.e., "the test of tolerance" over against the intolerance of ideology and the balance of power, reveal their weakness in their greater usefulness to a dispositional ethic for individuals rather than to a comprehensive social ethic. It is this deficiency which makes Niebuhr's theology vulnerable to the charge of serving "as an ideology of the Establishment."[137]

That this deficiency is actually at work in Niebuhr's thought, McCann seeks to demonstrate in a chapter critical of the praxis of Christian realism.[138] In its practical application to specific historical

---

[134]Ibid., p. 73.

[135]Ibid., p. 75.

[136]For the following cf. ibid., pp. 79-104.

[137]Ibid., p. 103.

[138]For the following cf. ibid., pp. 105-130.

situations, e.g., the "cold war," British colonialism, the prospects for democracy in Latin America, and the war in Vietnam, Niebuhr's thought exhibits an increasing drift toward conservatism which McCann attributes to the prominence of his theological anthropology over theology of history. Of special interest in this context is Christian realism's conviction that centrist parties would offer the most promise to Latin America's future (with special reference to Chile in the late sixties).[139]   Likewise pertinent is Niebuhr's skepticism that Third World poverty has been primarily caused by Western exploitation.[140] Such a view is instead attributed to the influence of Marxist thinking. Third World poverty is, according to Niebuhr, rooted in such factors as an uneven distribution of the world's resources, differences in productivity standards between nations, and the initially negative influence which nations with a higher level of technology have had upon non-technical societies.

McCann concludes this chapter with a summation of his critique of the weaknesses of Christian realism.[141]   Building especially on Ronald H. Stone's work on Niebuhr, McCann focuses his criticism once again on the theoretical weakness of Niebuhr's thought which issues in what he sees as the practical weaknesses of Christian realism in its concrete applications. This means the failure of Niebuhr to establish a theology of history commensurate to his basically valid theological anthropology.   This failure leaves Christian realism abstract in its actual political proposals and more useful as a dispositional ethic for individuals than as a comprehensive social ethic.

The second half of McCann's book turns to an examination of liberation theology and a critique based primarily on the valid insights ascertainable from Christian realism.   Initially McCann devotes his attention to an overview of the context in which liberation theology has arisen.[142]   The Latin American history of colonialization, the Medellin bishops conference, the "basic communities" (for which the thought of Camilo Torres is chosen to represent their theological viewpoint), the "conflicting ideologies" of developmentalism versus dependency, a brief examination of liberation theology's orientation, and a comparison with the context of

---

[139]Cf. ibid., pp. 116-121.

[140]For the following cf. ibid., pp. 112-114.

[141]For the following cf. ibid., pp. 121-129.

[142]For the following cf. ibid., pp. 131-155.

Christian realism are covered by McCann in this overview.
Indicative of his interpretation of liberation theology are his emphases
upon the radicality both of what he calls the "basic communities" and
liberation theology as a whole. What most characterizes both is their
"ideology," their "common social commitment, presumably as
defined by the pastoral guidelines of the church."[143]

> Doing theology in the context of solidarity with the oppressed places great
> importance on the modes of analysis used to interpret the situation of
> oppression. Accordingly, the critical theories that support the paradigm of
> dependence/liberation are transposed into principles of theological
> interpretation. They circumscribe a "hermeneutic circle," which in turn
> is validated by the community's experience of and reflection upon the
> struggle against oppression. There is nothing surprising about this, when
> viewed in relation to the usual circular processes of modern ideological
> thinking. Questions are raised, however, whether or not there is any
> justification for this as a distinctively theological method.[144]

McCann proceeds to describe how "the Bible is invoked as the ultimate
warrant for this shift (i.e., to a focus on the struggles of the oppressed):
through a highly selective reading of certain texts, liberation
theologians understand their commitment as essentially an imitation
of Yahweh's historic concern for the poor."[145] In contrast to Christian
realism the key issue which divides it from liberation theology is the
question: "Is American neocolonialism really the primary cause of
the misery among the oppressed peoples of Latin America, or is it
not?"[146] Moreover, Christian realism's primary emphasis on
theological anthropology contrasts with liberation theology's stress on
a theology of history beginning with the oppressed.

The crucial chapter in McCann's analysis of liberation theology is
entitled "Liberation Theology as a Method."[147] It is McCann's thesis
that ultimately the method of liberation theology, in its appropriation of
the theory of conscientization, makes actual theologizing impossible.

> It is clear that Paulo Freire's theory of conscientization provides the
> distinctive methodological principle. But since the logic of
> conscientization in itself appears to be more subversive than constructive, I
> shall argue that it promises not just to detoxify but to eliminate theological
> reflection entirely. If this point can be made persuasively, it will mean
> that liberation theology from the beginning is marked by an internal
> difficulty, a tension between its subversive method and its constructive

---

143 Ibid., p. 143.
144 Ibid., p. 150.
145 Ibid.
146 Ibid., p. 153.
147 For the following cf. ibid., pp. 156-181.

theological intention, which makes it at once dynamic and yet vulnerable to dissolution.[148]

McCann sets out to demonstrate this thesis by examining Gutierrez's description of theology as "critical reflection on praxis."[149] In doing so, however, McCann sees Gutierrez introducing a Marxist mode of social analysis into theological reflection which itself in effect becomes the norm for scriptural and theological interpretation. That this new norm is at work can be further seen in its shift from the criteria of orthodoxy to that of orthopraxis. In this way not only the task of academic theology has been subverted but even more importantly the ultimate norming of theology by "the Word of the Lord." This tendency is further demonstrated by liberation theology's criticism of Metz's "new political theology" for not proceeding beyond "denunciation" of the status quo to "annunciation" of "the establishment of the kingdom of God on earth in the struggle for liberation. "[150]

The primary source for the method of liberation theology is, according to McCann, Paulo Freire's theory of conscientization.[151] Little did the bishops at Medellin realize all they were endorsing when they incorporated this theory of Freire into their official statements, a theory which liberation theologians have, citing the authority of Medellin, used as the basis for developing their theology.

> The theory of conscientization, as Freire presents it in *Pedagogy of the Oppressed*, is fundamentally three things: (1) a description of the practice of a literary training program designed to trigger a social awakening among oppressed peasants and barrio dwellers; (2) a revolutionary theory of education derived from this practice; and (3) a global perspective on history as a whole—what I shall call the "dialectical vision"—which grounds the substantive values that inspire both the practice and the theory. . . . When I suggest that conscientization threatens to eliminate theological reflection entirely, I am interested primarily in the third meaning, the dialectical vision and its subversive implications for theology as such. The methodological question for liberation theologians—assuming that an analysis of conscientization will show that the dialectical vision is incompatible with the religious visions of Christianity in general and Catholicism in particular—thus is whether a conscienticizing evangelization can appropriate the first and second meanings (as Gutierrez attempts to do) without accepting necessarily the third and the problems of coherence that go with it.[152]

---

[148]Ibid., p. 157.
[149]Cf. ibid., pp. 157-160.
[150]Ibid., p. 164.
[151]For the following cf. ibid., pp. 164-172.
[152]Ibid., pp. 165-166.

In elaborating the significance of these three aspects of
conscientization, McCann concludes that liberation theology does not
and cannot separate between them. The incorporation of Freire's
essentially Marxist dialectical vision necessitates, according to
McCann, the sacrifice of the Christian faith to Marxist praxis.[153]
Marx's critique of religion which is implicit in the method of
liberation theology means human existence is stripped of all "limit-
situations," i.e., situations in which human beings are limited in their
ability to transcend them. If Christianity, however, is understood as
nothing more than mythicization where it affirms that such limits do
exist, then it is deprived of its own essential substance.

> The claim . . . is a general one: if there are no limit-situations, theological
> reflection eventually becomes meaningless. If there are no genuine
> limit-situations, any discourse presupposing the reality of God—the
> biblical God, at least—necessarily is an instance of mythicization,
> however liberating its intent. As Marx said, religion may even be "the
> *protest* against real distress," but the sincerity of the protest makes its
> expression in religious symbols no less alienating and its theological
> reference no less illusory.[154]

McCann finds confirmation of liberation theology's denial of all
limit-situations in its rejection of the "eschatological proviso" of
Christianity when it is consistent to its methodological commit—
ments.[155]

A comparison with the method of Christian realism further
convinces McCann of the correctness of this interpretation.[156] "If
rigorously adhered to, conscientization recognizes no limit to
demythicization, and in principle there is no reason not to demythicize
any theology, including liberation theology."[157] In this way the
method of liberation theology in its appropriation of the theory of
conscientization subverts not only those theologies which it would
choose to criticize as ideologies of the status quo but also its own
intention to offer a theological alternative. This is a defect which, by
way of contrast, is not inherent to Christian realism in its clear
espousal of genuine limit-situations.

In a chapter entitled "The Theology in Liberation Theology"
McCann seeks to illustrate the logical dilemma into which liberation

---

[153]For the following cf. ibid., pp. 172-175.

[154]Ibid., p. 173.

[155]Cf. ibid., pp. 174-175.

[156]Cf. ibid., pp. 175-180.

[157]Ibid., p. 179.

theology succumbs on the basis of its chosen method.[158] A primary
example to demonstrate this thesis is taken from theological
formulations of Gutierrez in *A Theology of Liberation*. In this work
Gutierrez attempts to distinguish between liberation (the human task)
and salvation (the divine gift) while bringing them "into the closest
possible correlation (but not identification)."[159] McCann raises the
question, however, of whether this distinction can be logically
maintained on the basis of the theory of conscientization which is seen
to be integral to liberation theology's method.

> The basic agenda of Gutierrez's theology of liberation, then, is both clear
> and difficult. He seeks to proclaim the reality of Christ the Liberator as the
> ultimate fulfillment of the struggles of the oppressed, by constructing a
> theology based on a correlation of the themes of "liberation" and
> "salvation." The difficulty is that each of these themes emerges from a
> distinctive world-vision which may not be reconcilable with the other.
> The tensions between the epiphanic vision underlying the theme of
> liberation, in other words, make Gutierrez's theology radically
> ambiguous or unstable.[160]

This is the thesis McCann seeks to demonstrate in the remainder of
this chapter.

McCann notes a total lack of a theological anthropology in
Gutierrez's theology. Gutierrez simply speaks of "a new man" without
sufficient theological elaboration. Rather Gutierrez turns to the
development of a theology of history without this anthropological
groundwork. The basis for this theology of history is found instead by
Gutierrez in the biblical narrative. References especially to the
Exodus paradigm, the prophets, and the ministry of the historical Jesus
are used to warrant liberation praxis. No mention is made by
Gutierrez, however, of the biblical story of the fall and its introduction
of the idea of original sin. Once again McCann claims this
corresponds to the absence of a theological anthropology. Sin is rather
emphasized with regard to social structures. Likewise the work of
Christ corresponds not primarily to the condition of fallen human
beings but rather to the condition of a fallen creation. Throughout
Gutierrez's theology McCann thus sees an irreconcilable and
ambiguous tension between human liberation and divine salvation.

If Gutierrez were to be consistent to the theory of conscientization,
however, he would have to resolve this ambiguity in favor of the purely

---

[158]For the following cf. ibid., pp. 182-207.

[159]Ibid., p. 183.

[160]Ibid., p. 186.

human task of liberation. Any remnants of talk about salvation as a divine gift should be logically seen—via the theory of conscientization—as nothing more than "mythicized reality" (Freire). By continuing to appeal to biblical warrants from the Exodus paradigm and other passages, McCann is convinced Gutierrez has not been consistent to "the logic of conscientization" but rather remains trapped in a new form of "supernaturalism" and "mythicization."

> All three...points—first, the existential problem of reconciling "a liberating God" with the project of "man's" becoming the Subject of history; second, the inability to establish the relevance of salvation-history to the praxis of liberation except on "subjectivist" theological grounds and third, the epistemological difficulty of reconciling the biblical narratives in question with the modes of analysis characteristic of critical history—all three suggest that Gutierrez's theology of history itself is not an interpretation of history consistent with the logic of conscientization, but a religious myth about history.[161]

If Gutierrez were to be consistent to the theory of conscientization, he would, according to McCann, have to decode all limit-situations. Gutierrez either has to follow the theory of conscientization to its logical end or his theology remains immersed in religious myth. Other liberation theologians remain caught in this dilemma as well. Stated bluntly: liberation theology cannot employ conscientization as its theological method without sacrificing its rootedness in the Christian tradition. Yet without conscientization liberation theology is nothing more than another progressive theology. Its distinctiveness is then gone. This dilemma is only further confirmed for McCann when he compares liberation theology with Christian realism which is judged to be a more coherent and adequate theological orientation both on theoretical and practical grounds.[162]

In terms of its praxis liberation theology is led, on the basis of this theological dilemma, into a practical dilemma as well: either it must politicize theology or trivialize what it means by liberation.[163] The basic communities have been forced to choose in their praxis between these two irreconcilable alternatives of liberation theology. Insofar as liberation theology has been politicized, opposition has arisen to both the basic communities and liberation theology which has led to their increasing marginalization. This tendency toward marginalization leads to the risk of sectarianism and McCann identifies Segundo in

---

[161]Ibid., pp. 196-197.

[162]Cf. ibid., pp. 204-206.

[163]For the following cf. ibid., pp. 208-233.

this regard as advocating an ecclesiology more consistent with Lenin's "revolutionary vanguard" than with Catholic ecclesiology. Such a development is, however, according to McCann, more consistent to the theory of conscientization than other attempts which simply "theologize liberation."[164] The theology of Jon Sobrino is employed to illustrate the latter approach which does not carry conscientization through to its logical end, therefore resulting in the exposition of new myths. Segundo, on the other hand, represents a more thorough-going conscientization in his emphases on an "elite of mature Christians," ideology, and the role of violence in the liberation process. Gutierrez's thought, by comparison, is caught in ambiguity between these two logical alternatives which on the basis of its method demands resolution in favor of Segundo's "total conscientization."

In concluding his book, McCann returns to the contrast between Christian realism and liberation theology.[165] Both perspectives illustrate "the essential problematic of modern theology," i.e., "the relation of the Absolute and the relativities of history."[166] Yet in responding to this problem Niebuhr has maintained the normativeness of the Christian world-view in a way that liberation theology has not.

> The dilemma is that liberation theologians must choose between either the method or the content as outlined by Gutierrez. If they choose the method, then liberation theology becomes increasingly distant from the mainstream of Catholic life and thought; if they choose the content, then liberation theology becomes increasingly indistinguishable— methodologically, if not thematically—from the progressivism of Vatican II. In either case its distinctive program, the new way of "doing theology in a revolutionary situation," is sacrificed.[167]

Although Christian realism may be faulted for having lost its critical and prophetic edge, especially in Niebuhr's later years, and therefore suffer from an "ideological drift," nevertheless it does not sacrifice the reality of religious transcendence as liberation theology necessarily must if it is consistent to its method. This leads McCann to the following succinct statement in concluding his comparison of these two practical theologies in conflict:

> [O]n the one hand, the weaknesses of Christian realism are not sufficient reason to reject the spirituality that inspired it; on the other hand, even as a

---

[164]Cf. ibid., pp. 216-217.

[165]For the following cf. ibid., pp. 227-240.

[166]Ibid., p. 228.

[167]Ibid., p. 230.

timely protest against those weaknesses, liberation theology is faced with a
dilemma that undercuts its status as a promising alternative.[168]
Liberation theology, on the basis of the theological and practical
consequences which must derive from a logically consistent execution
of its method grounded in the theory of conscientization and on the
basis of the valid insights of Christian realism, particularly its
theological anthropology, is rejected as a valid alternative for contem—
porary Christian theology. In coming to this conclusion McCann has,
on the basis of Christian realism, developed the most extensive and
complex of all current arguments against liberation theology.

D. *Liberation Theology and the Kingdom of God*

Two North American Lutheran theologians, Richard John
Neuhaus and Carl E. Braaten, have subjected Latin American
liberation theology to a rigorous theological critique primarily on the
basis of the New Testament idea of the kingdom of God. With special
reference to the theology of Wolfhart Pannenberg, Neuhaus and
Braaten above all object to what they see as a too narrow identification
of the kingdom of God with one particular political option, in this case a
revolutionary socialist one. Moreover, liberation theology's advocacy
of revolutionary socialism in conjunction with a Marxist social
analysis contains its own inherent difficulties due to the
contradictions between a Christian theological conceptuality and a
Marxist one. In this regard Braaten has especially questioned the
notion of praxis employed by liberation theology.

1.   Richard John Neuhaus

Richard John Neuhaus, Lutheran churchman and theologian,
editor of *Worldview, Lutheran Forum*, and since 1984, *The Religion
and Society Report* of the Institute on Religion and Society, has offered
a critique of liberation theology primarily on the basis of what he
perceives to be an inadequate idea of the kingdom of God. An early
expression of this criticism was published already in the June 1973
issue of *Worldview* in the form of a review of Gutierrez's *A Theology of
Liberation* shortly after its publication in English translation. In this
review Neuhaus draws parallels between earlier cultural "captivities
of Jesus" and liberation theology's tendency to hold Jesus captive to a
new form of ideology, this despite certain acknowledged cautionary
words of Gutierrez to the contrary.

---

[168]Ibid., p. 240.

In describing Gutierrez's theology Neuhaus emphasizes his politicizing of the idea of the kingdom of God, his ambiguous use of Marxist thought, his repudiation of a distinction between secular and salvation history, and his optimism about the possibility of historical progress. The mission of the church is to entail conscious involvement in the political realm. To this end Gutierrez incorrectly claims, according to Neuhaus, the authority of Jesus.

> While Gutierrez appears to have an unseemly confidence in his locating of the Christic action and tends to propose the Church as a recruitment office for the revolution, one should also keep in mind that not everywhere have "the political options become radicalized" as they have in many Latin American countries. Fastidiousness about maintaining the Church's critical distance from the parties that would capture it is perhaps a luxury that can be afforded only in societies where the options are not so restricted as to force to the forefront the revolutionary alternatives. Nonetheless, there is, one hopes, an approach between fastidiousness and recklessness.[169]

It is in Gutierrez's tendency to identify Jesus and the church's very mission with the revolutionary cause that Neuhaus sees the danger of a new and reckless captivity of Jesus to an alien ideology.

Neuhaus raises a number of additional questions of Gutierrez's theology which proceed from this reading of his work.[170] He sees a fundamental unclarity in Gutierrez's idea of freedom, i.e., between freedom's individual and communal aspects. Neuhaus fears this unclarity leaves Gutierrez vulnerable to new forms of repression and authoritarianism. The lack of criteria for distinguishing between legitimate and illegitimate revolutionary causes is an additional serious deficiency in the thought of Gutierrez which "comes close to providing carte blanche legitimization for joining almost any allegedly revolutionary struggle to replace almost any allegedly repressive regime."[171] Although at times Gutierrez would guard himself against the excess of generalized and uncritical approval of all revolutionary struggles, Neuhaus perceives nevertheless a loss of the critical tension necessary for a Christian critique of the liberation process in Latin America. In so doing Gutierrez tends to let his thought serve as a mere "chaplaincy" to a revolution whose prime motivations

---

[169]Richard John Neuhaus, "Liberation Theology and the Captivities of Jesus," reprinted in Gerald H. Anderson and Thomas F. Stransky, eds., *Mission Trends No. 3. Third World Theologies* (New York: Paulist, 1976), p. 52.

[170]For the following cf. ibid., pp. 55-61.

[171]Ibid., p. 56.

come from non-Christian sources. The final confirmation of this
tendency is, according to Neuhaus, Gutierrez's admission of class
struggle as a valid interpretive category. For Neuhaus, however, the
idea of class struggle negates the inclusiveness of the gospel which is
directed toward all persons and not just toward some as the idea of
class struggle suggests.

Many of these ideas, first raised in criticism of the theology of
Gutierrez, received more systematic form in subsequent writings of
Neuhaus. In his 1975 essay "Liberation As Program and Promise: On
Refusing to Settle for Less," for example, Neuhaus examines and
criticizes five key themes of liberation theology: the unity of history,
the insistence upon historical fulfillment, the understanding of man
as the maker of history, the redemptive history of the poor, and the
distinction between the church and the kingdom of God. While each of
these are in themselves to be recognized as valid theological themes,
Neuhaus questions certain aspects of liberation theology's formulation
of these themes, especially what he suspects as a too facile transition
from theological to political categories.

Most elaborate is Neuhaus' evaluation of liberation theology's
thematic emphasis on the unity of history. By differentiating between
the unity of history and the "uniformity" of history, Neuhaus seeks to
point out a too narrow identification in liberation theology between its
political project and the arrival of the kingdom of God. The apocalyptic
elements within the New Testament, for one, argue against an
understanding of the kingdom ushered in purely by human political
effort. Liberation theology is characterized throughout by a lack of
modesty in its claims to be realizing God's kingdom in history.

> The sense of political urgency that liberation theology would generate is
> indeed necessary. But it cannot be based upon lies; theology should not be
> reduced to political propaganda. This is precisely what happens, however,
> when it is suggested that the experience we call alienation can be resolved
> by anything short of the coming of the Kingdom.[172]

Beneath liberation theology's optimism about bringing forth the
kingdom of God lies hidden an even more questionable optimism about
human nature itself.

> Any diagnosis of alienation that traces its roots to anything less than the
> radical evil we call original sin is a superficial diagnosis. The "new
> man in the new society," to use one of the favored phrases of liberation
> theology, still stands under the sign of death. . . . Any liberation theology

---

[172]Richard John Neuhaus, "Liberation As Program and Promise: On
Refusing to Settle for Less," *Curr T M* 2 (Apr. 1975):95.

that skirts this fact or that even implies a resolution of alienation through political action represents a premature synthesis, that is a false religion that distracts us from seeking first and last the Kingdom of God.[173]

Neuhaus thus questions the adequacy of liberation theology's anthropology for its optimism in the potential of human beings to create both a "new man" and a "new society." The provisionality of all human accomplishments in history is in this way underestimated.

Neuhaus insists, in contrast to liberation theology, that the transcendent dimension remain transcendent in order to critique all human historical achievements. A proper understanding of the relationship between the transcendent and human history holds them in a dialectical tension whereas liberation theology collapses them into a virtual identification. An authentic grasp of the transcendent dimension would require a greater tentativeness in liberation theology's political agenda; a recognition that while politics is indeed important, Christianity is not reducible to politics; an affirmation of the propriety of the worship of God apart from any possible political consequences. In this concern for the preservation of the transcendent in theology, there are clear parallels to "The Hartford Declaration" which also appeared early in 1975 and for which Neuhaus was a primary catalyst.[174] Reading the Hartford Declaration in terms of Neuhaus' critique of liberation theology assists one in understanding which specific forms of modern thought were implicitly rejected by that highly publicized declaration.

The four other themes of liberation theology criticized by Neuhaus in this essay are each handled more briefly and each related to his primary concern for greater differentiation between the political ambitions of liberation theology and the coming of God's kingdom.[175] As a second theme, the historical fulfillment sought by liberation theology must remain at best a foretaste, a tentative approximation of God's final kingdom lest the reality of God's transcendence be sacrificed. In order to maintain this emphasis, Neuhaus suggests to liberation theology a greater appreciation of the meaning of the cross and resurrection as it points to divine redemption, rather than an

---

[173]Ibid.

[174]Cf. "The Hartford Declaration," *Th Today* 32 (Apr. 1975):94-97. Themes 4, 6, 7, 8, 9, 10, 11, 12, and 13 of the Hartford Declaration seem to indicate a direct correspondence to the explicit critique of liberation theology by Neuhaus in the essays considered here.

[175]For the following cf. Neuhaus, "Liberation As Program and Promise: On Refusing to Settle for Less," *Curr T M* 2 (June 1975):152-158.

excessive emphasis on the Exodus interpreted in terms of the human role in this redemptive act. In regard to the third theme, that man is the maker of history, Neuhaus reiterates his concern that liberation theology confuses human with divine responsibility for the final outcome of history and questions once again liberation theology's "anthropological optimism."

In response to a fourth theme, the redemptive mystery of the poor, Neuhaus senses a romanticizing of the poor by liberation theology which awakens highly unrealistic expectations for what the poor are likely to accomplish through revolutionary change. Neither the revolution in the Soviet Union, nor in Cuba, nor in Allende's Chile, nor in China validate liberation theology's hopes for revolution in Latin America. Neuhaus finds more plausible a scenario "in which, for the next century or so, the 'haves' continue to have things more or less their way, exploiting the 'have nots' when that is convenient and ignoring them when it is not."[176] In light of this scenario Neuhaus would find more constructive authentic appeals to the justice and compassion of the rich rather than attempts at intimidating them through "revolutionary bravado."[177]

Finally, as a fifth theme Neuhaus finds it necessary to insist once more upon a clear distinction between the church and the kingdom of God, a distinction too easily obscured by the political program which liberation theology has set before the church. As a corrective to the theology of liberation, Neuhaus suggests a "theology of vindication" which would seek to respond to the urgent issues raised by liberation theology but yet do so in terms genuine to Christian theology and not through the incorporation of an alien notion of liberation.

> A theology of vindication speaks to all the sweating, itching, smelling, uncertain stuff that is history's struggle. It comprehends our partial and often perverse ideas of freedom and liberation. Vindication is judgment, a theme richly and variously served by the Christian tradition. It is the promise of the theodicy that must ever elude us until the Kingdom comes in its fullness.[178]

Only by preserving God's prerogative in ushering in the kingdom can liberation theology be delivered from sacrificing Christian theology to errors which seriously distort its most genuine truth about God, humanity, and the nature of their encounter in history.

---

[176]Ibid., p. 156.

[177]Cf. ibid., p. 157.

[178]Ibid., p. 158.

2. Carl E. Braaten

Carl E. Braaten is Professor of Systematic Theology at the Lutheran School of Theology in Chicago and a widely published Lutheran theologian. As was the case with Neuhaus, Braaten has been greatly influenced in his thought by the theology of Wolfhart Pannenberg and it is primarily on the basis of the idea of the kingdom of God that he has formulated his criticism of the theology of liberation. Although there is much in Braaten's theology which would suggest a resonant response to liberation theology, since the time of the publication of his book, *The Future of God* (1969), his criticism of liberation theology has steadily increased both in complexity and intensity. In *The Future of God*, for example, Braaten, in his eschatologically oriented reformulation of Christian doctrine, expressed concern and even affinity for the then-current theology of revolution, critiquing Luther's doctrine of the two kingdoms and proposing a reevaluation of the contributions of "Christian prophets of revolution."[179] Yet even in *The Future of God* Braaten's theological emphasis was upon *God's* activity in revolutionary movements both past and present and not upon the human role in those same revolutions. Thus in the earliest writings of Braaten, even in their advocacy of a theology of revolution, there exists a basis for his later critique of liberation theology due to what he perceives to be its excessive emphasis on the human role in ushering in God's kingdom.

It would appear that their exists between Braaten's thought and liberation theology much basis for agreement on the content of what is meant by and hoped for in the coming of God's kingdom.

> A real historical grounding of eschatology is needed today as a corrective to the church's tendency to relate gospel hopes to purely private concerns, thus ignoring the public issues of human life. The gospel is the good news of the advent of God's kingdom. The purely personal and interpersonal sphere cannot contain the full meaning of the kingdom, minus all social, political, economic, and cultural realities which determine the contexts and possibilities of human existence. . . .
>
> The Christian hope drives us to seek ever more adequate actualization of God's kingdom in the open fields of public life, so that the vision of freedom, peace, and justice may achieve provisional embodiment in institutional structures that determine the conditions under which individuals exist in society. Without this political grounding, the

---

[179]Cf. Carl E. Braaten, *The Future of God. The Revolutionary Dynamics of Hope* (New York: Harper & Row, 1969), pp. 141-166.

Christian hope runs the risk of becoming a palliative, an opiate, an ideological servant of the status quo.[180]

Yet in spite of this fundamental agreement regarding a political grounding of the kingdom in a concern for justice and just social structures in this world, Braaten believes liberation theology has distorted the genuinely Christian hope for God's kingdom in a variety of ways. First, Braaten asserts that liberation theology has stressed the kingdom as arriving through human effort at the expense of God's divine activity. This affirmation of liberation theology threatens the divine prerogative in the salvation event and so too the gospel character of the gospel. Second, it has tended to reduce the full meaning of the kingdom, which also contains such affirmations as hope in eternal life, to a political program. Third, liberation theology in its stress on the human role in liberation has overtaken Marxist categories, particularly the Marxist idea of praxis, in a way which threatens to compromise the content of a genuinely Christian hope for God's kingdom.

These objections to liberation theology began to be expressed by Braaten already in his book *Eschatology and Ethics* (1974). In reflecting upon the ethical relevance of the eschatological kingdom, Braaten is in agreement with those who object to a too narrow identification between the coming of God's kingdom and human ethical activity.[181] Instead Braaten explains the relationship between human love and the kingdom of God this way:

> It would be both too presumptuous and too burdensome for people to build up the future kingdom of God's love through their loving actions. There is a critical distance between God's love and human love that can never be bridged from the side of man. The real aim of liberated love is not to build up the kingdom of God; it is indeed sufficient of itself. Neither God nor his kingdom are in need of man's love. Rather, it is always the other person who needs our love.[182]

Braaten would establish a "critical distance" between what God does, i.e., bring the kingdom, and what human beings do, i.e., love the neighbor. No facile transition dare be made between the two. This leads Braaten to speak of a "proleptic ethics" and of "eschatopraxis" in order to insist both upon the ethical importance of eschatology and the

---

[180]Carl E. Braaten, "The Kingdom of God and Life Everlasting," in Peter C. Hodgson and Robert H. King, eds., *Christian Theology. An Introduction to its Traditions and Tasks* (Philadelphia: Fortress, 1982), pp. 294-295.

[181]Cf. Carl E. Braaten, *Eschatology and Ethics. Essays on the Theology and Ethics of the Kingdom of God* (Minneapolis: Augsburg, 1974), pp. 108-112.

[182]Ibid., p. 112.

necessary differentiation between the priority of the divine activity and the subordinate role of the human response.[183] Human ethical striving is not equatable with the arrival of the kingdom but is at best a prolepsis of the final kingdom which in its fullness is reserved for the future under God's transcendent initiative. The term "eschatopraxis" is introduced to define the proper relationship between human ethical effort and God's final kingdom, that is, that Christian ethics involves "doing the future now ahead of time"[184] in anticipation of God's final eschatological rule.

As a Lutheran theologian Braaten has had special concern that the gospel character of the Christian gospel has been compromised by liberation theology's emphasis on praxis. In contrast to the Lutheran insistence on the pure proclamation of the gospel of justification by faith alone, liberation theology is thought to obscure and even legalize the gospel.

> In liberation theology the "gospel" represents the ideal state of affairs, which hopefully will come about some day, and for which we ought to fight. We hear about the *demands* of the gospel which prescribe for Christians the kind of liberating praxis to which they ought to commit themselves. The future kingdom comes about through a synergism of divine grace and good works, in this case the right kind of political praxis. The notes of *sola gratia* and *sola fide* are simply not to be found in the score played by the liberation theologians.[185]

Liberation theology is in danger of transforming the gospel into a new synergistic scheme of salvation, a new form of revolutionary works righteousness. According to Braaten in liberation theology:

> Eschatology is reduced to ethics. The kingdom of God arrives as a result of the ethical achievements of mankind. The gospel of the kingdom of God is removed to the future as a goal to be attained by the right kind of ethical activity. The gospel is not thought of as a present reality in history, already prior to human action, in the person and ministry of Jesus Christ.[186]

Just as liberation theology threatens to turn the coming of the kingdom into a human work, at the same time Braaten sees the gospel turned into a new form of works righteousness. The two concerns are directly interrelated one with the other. In place of liberation theology's synergism, Braaten would propose a clearer articulation of the *ordo salutis* in which the act of God's justifying the sinner is clearly

---

[183]Cf. ibid., pp. 116-122.

[184]Ibid., pp. 121-122.

[185]Carl E. Braaten, "The Gospel of Justification Sola Fide," *Dial* 15 (Summer 1976):208.

[186]Ibid.

differentiated from the works of love which flow from justification. Only on the basis of a monergistic model (cf. Braaten's proposal in *Eschatology and Ethics*) can the theological deficiencies of liberation theology be overcome.

Braaten's most extensive treatment of the content and theological difficulties of liberation theology are contained in his book, *The Flaming Center. A Theology of Christian Mission* (1977). In this book which strives to rethink the central position of mission for church and theology, Braaten seeks to negotiate between what he perceives to be a false dichotomy currently made between the "vertical" and a "horizontal" dimension of salvation.[187] Braaten would hold together both "personal salvation and human liberation," both "forgiveness and freedom, both faith and food."[188] Such an inclusive approach, however, leaves him critical of any liberation theology where the gospel is endangered by an "ideological captivity where the vision of Marx outweighs the message of Jesus."[189]

Braaten's constructive proposal for a proper understanding of the idea of the kingdom of God in history reiterates his criticism of those theologies which make the arrival of the kingdom contingent on human effort.[190] Among those theologies criticized is the one he calls the "revolutionary model" which, in accordance with the thought of Karl Marx, affirms that "this world is evil but it can be changed."[191] This view of the world contrasts with the Christian model which affirms that "in Jesus Christ we have received the word of God's promise that this world will be changed under the impact of his approaching rule."[192] It is clear that in Braaten's estimation liberation theology falls under the critique of the Christian model by belonging to the Marxist type.[193]

Similar to Neuhaus, Braaten also raises questions relevant to liberation theology on the basis of Christology.[194] He asks whether the

---

[187]See Carl E. Braaten, *The Flaming Center. A Theology of Christian Mission* (Philadelphia: Fortress, 1977), pp. 1-8.

[188]Ibid., p. 4.

[189]Ibid., p. 7.

[190]Cf. ibid., pp. 39-44 and 101-102.

[191]Ibid., p. 48.

[192]Ibid.

[193]Cf., for example, Braaten's reference to Gutierrez as a "neo-Marxist," ibid., p. 84.

[194]Cf. ibid., p. 74-76.

revolutionary position of Jesus does not transcend the revolutionary spirit of modern times especially in his revolutionary teaching about loving even the enemy. Because of Jesus' own spirit which was iconoclastic of both the right and the left, the church too must steer a course guided solely by the freedom of the gospel.[195] This is particularly urgent by virtue of the attacks on the traditional understanding of Christian mission originating in the Third World. In response to the present identity crisis in missions, Braaten again proposes a bifocal approach: both "words and deeds," "evangelization and humanization," "gospel and social concern, faith and political action, religious worship and secular work" belong together.[196] This approach would respond to the critiques of the Third World in favor of the horizontal dimension of Christian mission without sacrificing the vertical dimension upon which the horizontal is grounded.

In the midst of Braaten's multifold critique of liberation theology, it is interesting to note his basic affirmation of the correctness of dependency theory for interpreting the relationship of the U.S. to Third World countries.[197] Braaten is sharply critical of the domination of the underdeveloped world by international capitalism. At the same time, however, unlike liberation theologians, Braaten is equally critical of the socialist option. Neither system merits endorsement by the church. While nations may have to decide between such concrete political choices, the church must remain distanced from such decisions in order to preserve its own authentic vision of God's kingdom. A community like the church "must straddle all the parties so that its members may be drawn from the left and the right and the middle, thus finding a fellowship of reconciliation in the midst of conflicts."[198] Both the idea of the kingdom of God which transcends all present political programs and the inclusiveness of the gospel lead Braaten to this position on the provisional nature of all present political options whether of the left or the right.

Braaten's most concentrated discussion of liberation theology is written in the final chapter of *The Flaming Center*. Liberation theology is recognized by Braaten as no passing theological fad but a lively and original option in the context of the Third World.[199] In this

[195]For the following cf. ibid., pp. 76-92.

[196]Ibid., p. 91-92.

[197]For the following cf. ibid., pp. 132-137.

[198]Ibid., p. 137.

[199]For the following cf. ibid., pp. 139-148.

section Braaten demonstrates his solid knowledge of the dynamics of liberation theology. The theology of liberation in its praxis orientation and critique of dominant theological paradigms is understood to be a genuine challenge to theological business as usual. In his interpretation Braaten emphasizes liberation theology's employment of a Marxist social analysis. In addition he explains a number of key aspects of the theology of liberation: its method insisting on praxis, its interpretation of Scripture from the point of view of the poor, its understanding of the oneness of history, its preference for the idiom of politics over that of metaphysics, its understanding of salvation in terms of liberation entailing a more social and this-worldly reading, and its rejection of all attempts to privatize the gospel for functioning in support of the status quo (e.g., the doctrine of the two kingdoms). In each of these ways liberation theology has raised issues for the church and theology which cannot go unanswered.

While Braaten in this context appreciates liberation theology in many ways for its emphasis on the horizontal dimension of salvation and for providing the occasion for reexamining the present meaning of Christian mission, he nevertheless also finds much that is in need of criticism.[200] Foremost is again a critique from the point of view of a Christian eschatology. In reasserting the horizontal dimension of salvation, Braaten believes liberation theology has succumbed to an over-reaction which now undervalues the validity of the vertical dimension. Instead Braaten would hold the two dimensions together in a more holistic view.

> In an eschatological interpretation both aims are valorized. Holistic salvation is both other-worldly and this-worldly, present and future, somatic and spiritual, personal and social, religious and secular, historical and eschatological.[201]

In this view the social meaning of salvation raised up by liberation theology would be recovered without sacrificing the individual meaning stressed by the Reformation doctrine of justification. Braaten argues for the perennial importance of the pure gospel and its message of the forgiveness of sins to the individual and fears this gospel is endangered by liberation theology's turning the gospel into a new law with its own inherent demands. Braaten once again names this tendency "synergism" and subjects liberation theology to critique accordingly.

---

[200]For the following cf. ibid., pp. 148-158.
[201]Ibid., p. 150.

Braaten, moreover, notices in liberation theology a loss of transcendence in its eagerness to make theology relevant to the present historical struggle. This leads to a leveling out of the biblical understanding of such ideas as history and sin. With regard to history, biblical eschatology tends to be reduced to its utopian function. "This means that the symbols of hope in biblical eschatology are used to picture a promising future *in* history, but not a fulfilling future *of* history."[202] With regard to sin, the deeper roots of human sinfulness are obscured by liberation theology's tendency to reduce sin to its social expressions.

> Sin provokes the wrath of God; it is slavery to Satan; it is a state of spiritual death; it is a disease of the whole person—a sickness unto death. It is a state of corruption so profound that the elimination of poverty, oppression, disease, racism, sexism, classism, capitalism, etc., does not alter the human condition of sinfulness in any fundamental way. . . . There is no liberation from this universal human condition through social and political praxis of whatever magnitude.[203]

Here Braaten joins others like Sanders, McCann, and Neuhaus in questioning the anthropology upon which liberation theology is based. Braaten goes on to assert that liberation theology surrenders too much to Marxism in its understanding of human being. This is illustrated by its failure to adequately maintain the Christian hope in eternal life.

In summing up his argument, Braaten echoes Neuhaus in fearing liberation theology leads to "a new Constantinianism of the socialist left,"[204] a new captivity of the church and its Christ to an alien ideology. He is wary of liberation theology's too narrow identification of the immanent and transcendental aspects of God's dealings with history and would raise up the transcendent dimension of the idea of the kingdom of God over against liberation theology's failure to do so. On the basis of his reflections, Braaten proceeds to offer his own evangelical approach to Christianity's liberating mission in the present context.[205] It is an approach which moves from the proclamation of the gospel to engagement for interhuman justice, yet which seeks to avoid the pitfalls of liberation theology. This engagement is to take place in the church as a whole, however, in accordance with a reformist model rather than a revolutionary one.[206] Only individual

---

[202]Ibid., p. 154.

[203]Ibid., p. 155.

[204]Ibid., p. 157.

[205]Cf. ibid., pp. 160-162.

[206]Cf. ibid., pp. 166-167.

Christians may opt for the revolutionary approach; otherwise there exists the real and present danger of new schism within the church. The church must become increasingly responsive to the liberation struggles of the present time without sacrificing its own identity in the person of Jesus Christ.

Since writing his comprehensive critique of liberation theology in *The Flaming Center*, Braaten has introduced similar arguments in subsequent writings.[207] In addition Braaten has expanded on an earlier criticism of liberation theology by further calling into question liberation theology's idea of praxis as deriving from the Marxist notion. Whereas earlier Braaten warned against a one-sided emphasis on the Marxist idea of praxis by liberation theologians in favor of the proper place of theoretical work as a check on praxis,[208] more recently he has identified the Marxist idea of praxis as "the Trojan horse of liberation theology."[209] By this figure Braaten argues that liberation theology has surrendered too much of its own identity in the Christian tradition to the alien ideology of Marxism. A crucial issue is, according to Braaten, liberation theology's failure to realize that no human praxis can usher in God's kingdom. Salvation arrives only as a gift of God and praxis must remain at best a second step which derives subsequently from what God himself does in the gospel. "Otherwise we are faced with a legalization of Christian faith, whereby the kingdom of God generates no gospel, but only the new law of transformative praxis."[210]

It is as a Lutheran theologian schooled in the doctrine of justification by grace through faith alone in conjunction with a contemporary reappropriation of the New Testament idea of the kingdom of God that Braaten has criticized the theological formulations of liberation theology. Braaten has accordingly raised questions especially about liberation theology's understanding of salvation, history, and anthropology. Moreover, it is the thought of

---

[207]For example, cf. Carl E. Braaten, *Principles of Lutheran Theology* (Philadelphia: Fortress, 1983), pp. 37-38 (liberation theology and synergism), 69-71 (liberation theology and the Christian idea of salvation), 75-78 (liberation theology and justification by faith), and 107-108 (liberation theology and a confusion between law and gospel).

[208]Cf. Carl E. Braaten, "Theory and Praxis: Reflections on an Old Theme," in *Eschatology and Ethics*, esp. pp. 139-146.

[209]Carl E. Braaten, "Praxis: The Trojan Horse of Liberation Theology," *Dial* 23 (Autumn 1984):276-280.

[210]Ibid., p. 279.

Marx which poses a particular threat to Christian theology in the formulations of liberation theology. At the same time as he criticizes liberation theology, however, Braaten would share the conviction that the church cannot remain apart from the political issues of the present.[211] It must enter the political realm, however, on the basis of its own belief in the coming of *God's* kingdom and for no other reason.

E. *The Question of Exegesis*

While on the one hand liberation theologians have been praised by some for restoring to the Bible a measure of authority perceived to be absent from the mainstream of contemporary theology, on the other hand serious questions have also been raised about the exegetical accuracy and depth of their use of Scripture. Perhaps it is even fair to say that insofar as the Bible has authority for them in their commitment to liberation, they are vulnerable to the charge of misusing biblical authority.[212] Because the theologians of liberation insist so strongly that commitment to the cause of liberation must come prior to theological reflection, they are subject to the charge that their theology is "the mere rationalization of positions already taken."[213] This has been said in various ways about the exegesis of liberation theology.

At times this critique has been made in a generalized way both by evangelical and mainline theologians. For example, the evangelical C. Peter Wagner writes of "the theology of the radical left:"

> If their understanding of the Biblical world view seems deficient, it is usually not because they fail to acknowledge the authority of the Bible as the Word of God. . . . It lies rather in the extreme degree to which their understanding of the secular world has influenced their understanding of Biblical truth. In many instances (but not all), truth is not denied so much as it is distorted. Priorities are often shifted out of Biblical focus. At times one gets the feeling that the starting point of this group has been an a priori socio-economic theory, and that theology has been called in only as an afterthought, not to say rationalization. The Bible seems to be used very

---

[211]Cf. Braaten, *Principles of Lutheran Theology*, pp. 137-138.

[212]Cf. the argument of David H. Kelsey, *The Uses of Scripture in Recent Theology* (Philadelphia: Fortress, 1975).

[213]Schubert M. Ogden, "The Concept of a Theology of Liberation: Must a Christian Theology Today Be So Conceived?", in Brian Mahan and L. Dale Richesin, eds., *The Challenge of Liberation Theology: A First World Response* (Maryknoll: Orbis, 1981), p. 134.

often as a source book for proof texts rather than the touchstone of all doctrine.[214]

In a parallel way Dennis P. McCann subjects Gutierrez's use of Scripture to criticism:

> . . . Gutierrez's rendering of the Exodus paradigm and the ministry of Jesus, for example, are open to serious question on historical grounds. Sometimes Gutierrez assumes the historical reliability of the biblical narratives without question; often he seems to know more about these episodes than any reliable historian would care to assert; and consistently he reshapes their details to fit the pre-established requirements of the theme of liberation.   These tactics suggest that whatever the historical authenticity of the biblical narratives may turn out to be, Gutierrez's use of them is not disciplined by the usual canons of historical scholarship. On the contrary, they suggest that Gutierrez's theology of history is an exercise in reconstructing a biblical myth.[215]

While such criticisms are indicative of the question raised about the exegesis of liberation theology, they do not, however, proceed to a concrete demonstration of their case and thus have limited value beyond raising attention to the exegetical question.

More specific are the cases made by Carl E. Armerding and John Howard Yoder with special reference to liberation theology's use of the Exodus paradigm. Armerding, like Wagner an evangelical, and also an Old Testament scholar, raises more specific questions about liberation theology's exegesis drawing examples from Gutierrez and Miranda.[216] On Gutierrez's use of the Exodus paradigm, Armerding emphasizes its thematic use by Gutierrez in accordance with modern conditions of oppression and the contemporary language of liberation. This minimizes the particularity of the Exodus narrative itself and obscures such distinctive factors as covenant theology, the divine initiative (cf. Gutierrez's emphasis on human participation), and Israel's sacralized world-view. While Armerding shows great respect for Miranda's exegetical work, he still raises some specific exegetical points. For example, Armerding questions Miranda's judgment on the absence of covenant theology in the earliest Yahwist material and,

---

[214]C. Peter Wagner, *Latin American Liberation Theology: Radical or Evangelical. The Struggle for the Faith in a Young Church* (Grand Rapids: Eerdmans, 1970), p. 21.

[215]McCann, *Christian Realism and Liberation Theology*, p. 196. One wonders that McCann does not apply a comparable critical standard in his evaluation of the exegesis of Reinhold Niebuhr.

[216]For this and the following see Carl E. Armerding, "Exodus: The Old Testament Foundation of Liberation," in Carl E. Armerding, ed., *Evangelicals and Liberation* (Phillipsburg, NJ: Presbyterian and Reformed Publishing Co., 1979), pp. 51-58.

in general, the attempt by Old Testament scholars (e.g., Noth) to radically separate between the Exodus and Mt. Sinai traditions. In conclusion Armerding writes:

> The problem, of course, is that we all tend to come out of our exegetical house pretty much where we have gone in, whereas the real task of exegesis is to illuminate the text in its own setting. . . . Biblical theology, if it ultimately forces exegetical reconstructions into forms alien to the text and its world, has become just as guilty of proof-texting as was classical dogmatics.
>
> In liberation theology, the starting-point is clearly situational, but what of its method? It seems to me that, as a broad hermeneutical principle, the concept of loose analogy between the Exodus-salvation event and the contemporary oppression-liberation struggles is dominant. No real attempt is made to allegorize the biblical events; there are simply too many points at which the experience of slaves of the Late Bronze Age are not paralleled by any of our twentieth-century phenomena.[217]

In this exegetical dilemma Armerding does not so much single out liberation theology for its failures as to note that it simply has not overcome the exegetical problems shared by all those who attempt to use the Bible in an authoritative way.

John Howard Yoder has likewise joined those raising critical questions about the use of the Exodus paradigm by liberation theologians.[218] Two questions especially guide Yoder's critique. First, he questions the appropriateness of calling upon the Mosaic model in support of revolution. Secondly, he asks (together with Miguez Bonino) about the relevance of other biblical models less cited by liberation theology (e.g., captivity, cross, the giving of the law, the taking of the land, etc.). In discussing the first question, Yoder notes the divine intervention in the Exodus event which will not allow it to be equated with a revolutionary movement. For Israel the Exodus resulted not from an uprising of the oppressed through violent action but from the formation of a creative counter-community which then was set free through divine intervention.

> The old tyranny is destroyed not by beating it at its own game of intrigue and assassination, but by the way the presence of the independent counter-community (and its withdrawal) provokes Pharaoh to overreach himself.
>
> There would never have been a Red Sea experience if there had not previously been the willingness to follow Moses out of Goshen. This was a leap of faith, made in common by the Hebrew people, not on the basis of any

---

[217]Ibid., pp. 57-58.

[218]For the following see John Howard Yoder, "Probing the Meaning of Liberation," *Sojourners* 5 (Sept. 1976):27-29.

calculation of their capacity to destroy the Egyptians, but fully trusting in the transcendent intervention of Yahweh.[219]

Yoder suggests that according to this model the liberation movements of our time should devote far more energy to creating a cohesive and solidary group identity rather than prematurely grasping for arms. Even so, however, Yoder is wary of identifying Israel as God's chosen people in the Exodus narratives with "any and all suffering peoples. 'The people of God' is not everybody. To transpose the motif of liberation out of that distinct historical framework and thereby also away from the distinct historical identity of the God of Abraham, Isaac, and Jacob, into some kind of general theistic affirmation of liberation, is to separate the biblical message from its foundation."[220]

It should be noted that Yoder argues against warranting violent revolution through the use of the Exodus paradigm on the basis of his own Mennonite pacifist convictions. His deliberations lead him to the conclusion that there exist situations in which "no liberation is possible because no peoplehood has been formed."[221] For Yoder liberation can only take place in conjunction with the formation of a community. This corresponds to his reading of the Exodus narratives. In order for the liberation of Exodus to be fulfilled it must be accompanied by a Sinai experience in which a people is formed. Yoder fears revolutionary theologies propose only the former without its necessary complement.

Yoder's second point asserts that there exist yet other biblical models which can have meaning for oppressed people. Most important is the Diaspora model whose biblical representatives include Joseph, Daniel, and Mordecai. In this model the community receives its proper due. It is a model, moreover, in accordance with the Bible's own understanding of what liberation entails.

> The *form* of liberation in the biblical witness is not the guerrilla campaign against an oppressor culminating in assassination and military defeat, but the creation of a confessing community which is viable without or against the force of the state, and does not glorify that power structure even by the effort to topple it.[222]

In the biblical view, says Yoder, liberation occurs when a community makes itself available to be an agent of God's action in history. This contrasts radically with the revolutionary model taken up by many

---

[219]Ibid., p. 28.
[220]Ibid.
[221]Ibid.
[222]Ibid., p. 29.

contemporary liberationists who more mimic the power relations of the world than follow God's way toward liberation.

Another position relevant to the question of liberation theology's exegesis is that of the New Testament scholar Leander E. Keck. Although he makes no special reference to liberation theology, Keck's caution against the use of the New Testament in support of violence seems to be directed at issues raised by some Latin American and black theologies of liberation. Keck protests against all attempts to claim the New Testament for one particular ideology whether of the left or the right.

> The New Testament is misused ideologically when it is interpreted in such a way that it sanctifies the values, power, and worldview of its readers. Times of conflict, like our own, are marked by extreme polarization, with each side constructing an ideology to justify its power or its struggle to seize it.[223]

The characteristic way of misusing the New Testament ideologically is through the use of proof-texting. The most important check on proof-texting is, according to Keck, the careful use of the historical-critical method of interpretation. Properly applied, the historical-critical method does not supply conclusions to warrant any specific type of contemporary action. Instead it can stimulate the reflection process and enable free decisions apart from claims to Scriptural justification.

This places the modern interpreter very much in the realm which was once also occupied by Jesus himself. Keck notes Jesus' own freedom from the various ideological options of his day. Jesus attained to this freedom by virtue of his intense belief in the imminent arrival of God's kingdom. This conviction served to motivate his action apart from any of the then-popular ideological positions. By returning to "Jesus' own center—the Kingdom of God as the alternative to every human tyranny and injustice—one is freed first of all from sanctifying extant systems of power, including revolutionary power."[224] Keck sees in the freedom of Jesus from the ideological alternatives of his time a real possibility for a corresponding freedom among Jesus' modern followers. It is a freedom from bondage to systems and ideologies and a freedom for both loving individual persons and changing the systems which may hold them in bondage. Attaining to this position of freedom apart from all ideologies is for

---

[223]Leander E. Keck, "The Church, the New Testament, and Violence," *Past Psych* 22 (Oct, 1971):7.

[224]Ibid., p. 14.

Keck a prerequisite for the correct interpretation of the New Testament which goes beyond the need to seek biblical warrant in proof-texting.

Finally, two additional authors should be cited for their contributions to the exegetical debate concerning liberation theology. Both Steven Phillips and Anthony J. Tambasco have examined in some detail the use of Scripture by one particular Latin American liberation theologian, Juan Luis Segundo. Phillips has examined and compared the use of Scriptural authority; the Scriptural foci; the dialectic between Scriptural authority and the authority of other socio-political ideologies; and confluence in the selection and use of Scripture not only in the theology of Segundo but also James H. Cone and Jürgen Moltmann. At the end of his work Phillips draws the following conclusion:

> There has been a tendency within the movement to profess alliance with those who share the same political objectives, to the exclusion of basic theological convictions. In view of the real danger that biblical foundations may easily be subsumed under pragmatics, the continuing dialectic between Scripture and context becomes even more necessary and valid.[225]

Phillips sees the danger that liberation theologies use the Bible in such a way that it no longer exerts a critical function.[226] In part this is due to their selectivity in choosing certain passages of Scripture to the exclusion of others. Moreover, the original context in which a text originated often deserves greater attention. This is not to exclude the role of present experience in the process of interpretation but rather to insure that present experience does not manipulate the integrity of Scripture in its own original meaning. While generally appreciative of the vitality of Scripture in liberation theology, Phillips still raises

---

[225]Steven Phillips, "The Use of Scripture in Liberation Theologies: An Examination of Juan Luis Segundo, James H. Cone, and Jürgen Moltmann," Ph.D. Dissertation (Louisville: Southern Baptist Theological Seminary, 1978), p. 241. Cf. also the even more pointed remarks by the British theologian, J. Andrew Kirk, *Liberation Theology. An Evangelical View from the Third World* (Atlanta: John Knox, 1979), esp. pp. 190-194. Kirk calls for a critical analysis of all pre-understandings which color biblical interpretation, and particularly what he sees as the Marxist pre-understanding of the theology of liberation. In criticism of liberation theology Kirk proposes that interpretation must "be conducted with the greatest possible objectivity" (pp. 192-193). He sees the need for the maintenance of two distinct poles in the process of biblical interpretation, the pole of contemporary reality and the pole of the biblical message understood as objectively as possible. His criticism of the theology of liberation is in its failure to maintain the second of these two poles.

[226]For the following cf. Phillips, "The Use of Scripture in Liberation Theologies," pp. 241-244.

these cautions. The tension between exegetical integrity and present meaning cannot be broken on either side of the dialectic.

Anthony J. Tambasco has likewise paid special attention to Segundo's use of the Bible especially in its relationship to Christian ethics. Following an examination of Segundo's social analysis and the relationship between theology and ideology in his thought, Tambasco reflects on Segundo's Scriptural exegesis.[227] He finds in Segundo a highly sophisticated hermeneutic in which social analysis and ideology (understood in its positive function) "are necessary preunderstanding to discover the liberating message of the Bible."[228] This leads Segundo to differentiate between a "proto-learning" from the Bible, i.e., what can be positively learned from the Bible on the basis of its own faith content, and a "deutero-learning," i.e., the contemporary application made of that faith content in the current situation and context.[229] Segundo's methodological proposals are found helpful by Tambasco in preserving "the distance between the biblical times and our own, while at the same time making application of the Bible to the present."[230]

In examining the specific ways Segundo has interpreted Scripture, Tambasco looks at Segundo's deliberations on the words "flesh" in the Pauline epistles, "world" in the Johannine writings, and the word "salvation" especially with regard to eschatology. Regarding the biblical idea of *sarx*, Tambasco finds Segundo's exegesis "misdirected."

> It is an attempt to derive from the text what one wants to find. . . . [W]hile Segundo's insight into massification may be valid, its application to Paul's notion of *the flesh* seems to be more eisegesis than exegesis, at least in this particular aspect.[231]

Tambasco has a similar criticism of Segundo's application of the Johannine concept of the "world."

> Segundo has valuable insights into John and has valid insights into massification. The social analysis may even help in reading John, but this particular aspect seems again to be a reading into the text and not a good application of his hermeneutic circle.[232]

[227]For the following cf. Anthony J. Tambasco, *The Bible for Ethics. Juan Luis Segundo and First-World Ethics* (Washington, D.C.: University Press of America, 1981), pp. 135-176.

[228]Ibid., p. 141.

[229]Cf. ibid., pp. 143-145.

[230]Ibid., p. 145.

[231]Ibid., p. 155 and 157.

[232]Ibid., p. 164.

While Tambasco makes these criticisms of Segundo's exegesis, he does not, however, do so without an overall positive estimation of the new insights gained into the biblical text as the result of Segundo's hermeneutic.[233]

In summing up Tambasco's evaluation of Segundo's exegesis, it is fair to say he reaches a conclusion parallel to that of Phillips. Tambasco is most appreciative of the general integrity of Segundo's exegesis. Nevertheless, there are several points at which Segundo needs to approach the exegetical task with greater rigor. These include the need for a greater emphasis on the Old Testament and, correspondingly, a broader understanding of the biblical idea of *sarx*.[234] Tambasco, like Phillips, points to the need for a dialectical tension between the original meaning of the biblical text and its contemporary relevance, a problem Segundo together with contemporary theology in general has not yet satisfactorily solved.

> A second major area of interest . . . is that of biblical interpretation. We have found it necessary to challenge and modify Segundo here also, but he has offered insights that are at the heart of biblical hermeneutics these days. It seems fairly clear that current exegetes are wrestling with how to make the Bible relevant in today's world, while still respecting the biblical world. They are also wrestling with the problem of maintaining objectivity in biblical interpretation while also acknowledging the subject who does the interpreting. It is a thorny problem without immediate solution. Neither Segundo nor our own modifications of Segundo pretend to give the full answer.
>
> Nevertheless, Segundo has forced us to confront the question directly and has offered some insights into the answer. He frankly acknowledges that we bring presuppositions to the biblical text and wants to work with that. He also tries to maintain distance between the text and our own history while still keeping the Bible as norm. We have modified his circle to get more of a dialectic, but we respect his sensitivity to the delicate balance between objectivity and subjectivity and the need to work toward the balance.[235]

Tambasco, like Phillips, would challenge liberation theologians to a greater appreciation of the independence of the exegetical task. At the same time he appreciates the difficulty of the task in achieving this ideal if the Bible is to function with authoritative status at all. Because this issue remains outstanding not only for liberation theology but also for contemporary theology in general, Tambasco and Phillips are not

---

[233]Cf. the comments in ibid., p. 173.

[234]Cf. ibid., pp. 233-240.

[235]Ibid., pp. 257-258.

overly critical of Segundo in pointing out the need for integrity in carrying out exegetical work.

It appears in surveying the various criticisms made by North American theologians regarding the exegesis of liberation theology that most helpful are those analyses which have moved beyond blanket generalizations to the examination of the exegesis of specific individual liberation theologians. This has been done most extensively with regard to the thought of Juan Luis Segundo, which has been deemed if not better, at least no worse than other contemporary theologians in its theological use of biblical exegesis. Outstanding remain additional critical studies of other individual liberation theologians with regard to the exegetical question.

F. Evangelical Critiques

Several well-known evangelical theologians have joined the ranks of those critical of liberation theology. Although they develop various arguments in making their case, the primary authority upon which they call is that of the Bible as the Word of God. Unlike those evangelical theologians responding more favorably to liberation theology, these theologians see significant contradictions between the proposals of liberation theology and the biblical message. Three viewpoints serve here to represent the evangelical criticisms of liberation theology: C. Peter Wagner, Carl F. H. Henry and *Christianity Today*, and Donald G. Bloesch.

1. C. Peter Wagner

The book by C. Peter Wagner, *Latin American Theology: Radical or Evangelical?* (1970), was an early response to the theological impulses which became identified as Latin American liberation theology. It has not only prompted discussion in the North American context but also responses from Latin American liberation theologians as well.[236] The central thrust of Wagner's critique of liberation theology entails a divergent understanding of the central mission of the church and the nature of the salvation it proclaims. It is important to recognize from the outset that Wagner himself has been a proponent of the philosophy of "Church Growth" whose most prominent North

---

[236]For example, see Juan Luis Segundo, *The Liberation of Theology*, trans. John Drury (Maryknoll: Orbis, 1976), pp. 134-138.

American representative is Donald McGavran.[237] In an era where the
theology and practice of Christian missions has undergone much
circumspection, McGavran has maintained the primary importance of
church growth through individual conversions to Jesus Christ in order
to obtain eternal salvation. Thus the central mission of the church is to
press for numerical increase in the number of individuals converting
to personal faith in Jesus Christ who thereby obtain eternal salvation.

One central purpose of Wagner's book is to defend McGavran's
understanding of mission as "Church Growth" against what he calls
"radical theology" in Latin America with its differing understanding
of the church's mission and message of salvation. Noting both
psychological and theological reasons for opposition to church growth
among Latin American theologians, Wagner affirms finally that it is
a matter of setting the proper priorities which gives the edge to the
philosophy of church growth over its radical critics.

> Here the choice is not between good and evil, but in the familiar terms of the
> Sears Roebuck catalog: good, better, and best. The New Testament
> commands us to love our neighbor. What we are here discussing is a
> matter of priority.[238]

It is interesting that Wagner engages in no excessive polemic against
the viewpoint of radical theologians. He even admits that under
certain circumstances, the use of violence to achieve political goals
may be justified even by Christians.[239] His argument is rather that
any political agenda undertaken by Christians must take a secondary
place to the priority of church growth.

> All of what the church does in the world—building schools and hospitals,
> dialoging with non-Christians, joining civil rights marches, lobbying in
> congress, bandaging the sores of lepers, teaching peasants how to grow
> bigger crops, distributing contraceptives—all these are good, and if
> Christians feel led to do this they should receive all possible
> encouragement. But the error is to describe these activities as "mission" to
> the exclusion of church growth or just to add church growth to the long list of
> other good things the church should do in the world.[240]

Wagner bases his argument for this setting of priorities on the basis of
Christ's commission in Matthew 28:19-20 to "go," "make disciples,"

----

[237]For the following cf. C. Peter Wagner, *Latin American Theology:
Radical or Evangelical? The Struggle for the Faith in a Young Church* (Grand
Rapids: Eerdmans, 1970), pp. 67-74.

[238]Ibid., p. 72.

[239]Cf. ibid., pp. 25, 51, and 108.

[240]Ibid., pp. 72-73.

"baptize them," and "teach them all things." Any other priority distorts even good intentions into "sin."[241]

Wagner's primary criterion for critiquing radical theology is therefore his theological concern that the church's primary mission is that of church growth and the "salvation of souls," a concern repeated throughout his book.[242] It is on the basis of this criterion that Wagner accuses radical theology of "syncretism," i.e., incorporating issues alien to the Christian mission, or even secondary Christian concerns, into the center of theology so as to distort Christianity's genuine mission.[243] In his survey of the "rise of the new radical left in Latin America" and its theology, Wagner points out how he sees this syncretism taking place. Among the Protestant radical left there has been a shift from Protestantism's original mission in Latin America in working for conversions to a new understanding of mission as participating in the social revolution.[244]

This trend toward syncretism is argued by Wagner through a lengthy analysis of the thought of several radical Latin American theologians. Indicative of Wagner's critique are the following quotations. Regarding the thought of Gonzalo Castillo Cardenas, Wagner writes:

> When evangelicals begin to formulate their theology, they have evangelism in mind as the primary responsibility of the church in the world. Their problem is often that they do not get around to articulating the secondary responsibility of social service with a comparable degree of enthusiasm and skill. But the more radical theologians tend to look at social service as the *primary* responsibility of the church. Unhappily, rather than just bypassing a theology of evangelism they at times set forth an anti-evangelistic theology. . . . From that point of view, they judge evangelical theology not in terms of how true it is to the Bible or how it will result in the salvation of souls, but what it will do to promote social justice.[245]

With reference to the thought of Jose Miguez Bonino, Wagner comments:

> The weapons of the radical left seem consistently to be study and analysis, social action and economic reform, revolution and renewal. Seldom are prayer, the Word of God, the preaching of the Gospel, and the work of the

---

[241]Cf. ibid., pp. 73-74.

[242]For example, see ibid., pp. 10, 23, 44, and 46-47.

[243]Ibid., p. 10.

[244]Ibid., pp. 18-20.

[245]Ibid., pp. 25-26.

Holy Spirit in individual hearts and lives mentioned as valid or useful resources for the Christian in the world.[246]

Finally, Wagner's criticism of radical theology's reversal of priorities is reflected in this remark on the Scriptural interpretation of Rubem Alves:

> The Bible naturally recognizes that man is not, as someone has facetiously said, "A soul with ears." It recognizes man's need of food, drink, clothing and shelter. It recognizes that every man has a right to share the physical and material blessings of nature, and that social justice is a worthy goal. But the order again is important. The Bible does not indicate that Christians should fight in the Marxist revolution, or should agitate in labor unions, or should publish self-righteous declarations against the large world powers, and then "all these things shall be added unto you." If the Incarnation means anything, it at least means that Christians should obey the words of the Master who said, "Seek ye first the kingdom of God." Any other point of view risks disobedience to God.[247]

These quotations well illustrate Wagner's argument with radical theology and its theologians.

Wagner believes there are other evangelical theologians in Latin America who at least in an initial way have begun to address the issues raised by radical theology without sacrificing the focus on evangelistic mission.[248] He sees, furthermore, the need for evangelicals to develop "an evangelical view of social service" which takes seriously the radicals' critique of evangelism for lacking a social vision without surrendering to the radicals' excessive social activism.[249] Wagner's own proposal stresses the "primary relationship of the church to the world" in proclaiming the gospel and gaining new members for the Christian church with the "secondary relationship of the church to the world" consisting of social service, first within one's own family, then to other members of the church, and finally in the world. By maintaining this order, Wagner seeks to respond to the radical critique without losing the church's foremost mission of evangelism and church growth.

Wagner sees the rise of radical theology as both a genuine challenge and a threat to the church's mission in the present time. In its syncretistic tendencies, radical theology poses a threat to what he understands to be "Biblically revealed Christian truth."

> Those theologians who feel that proclaiming salvation, persuading men and women to become Christ's disciples, baptizing them, and building the

---

[246]Ibid., p. 30.

[247]Ibid., p. 43.

[248]Cf. the chapter "Evangelical Alternatives," in ibid., pp. 81-99.

[249]For the following cf. ibid., pp. 100-109.

church is either irrelevant, superfluous, peripheral, or even secondary to
the social ministry of the church in the world are guilty of reconciling
Biblically revealed Christian truth with the diverse and opposing tenets of
secularism, which according to our definition is syncretism by
accommodation.[250]

In its general concern, however, radical theology challenges
evangelicals to reevaluate their understanding of social ministry and
social service to the world. In criticizing liberation theology on the
basis of the idea of church growth and a theology of personal conversion
to Jesus Christ, Wagner represents a theological point of view
influential in many evangelical circles in North America.

2. Carl F. H. Henry and *Christianity Today*

Another evangelical viewpoint critical of liberation theology is
represented specifically by the theology of Carl F. H. Henry and
generally by the editorial position of the evangelical publication
Christianity Today. Carl F. H. Henry is a highly published and
respected evangelical scholar who also acted as editor and editor-at-
large of *Christianity Today* for many years. Together Henry and
Christianity Today represent the mainstream of evangelical
scholarship in criticism of liberation theology.

An early indication of Henry's theological objections to a
liberation theology is his critique of the preparatory documents for the
World Council of Churches' World Conference on Church and Society
held at Geneva in 1966. Henry observed a "revolt against fixed
revelational principles in ecumenical social theory" which has "led
on toward an unprincipled, situational ethic."[251] The phrase "fixed
revelational principles" indicates Henry's theological position which
favors an understanding of the Bible as the source of "propositional
revelation."[252] In this theological understanding, the Bible functions
as the literally true, verbally inspired, inerrant Word of God
containing divine truths which are both cognitive and intelligible.
The propositions derived from the Bible serve furthermore as the basis
for the development of both Christian doctrine and Christian ethos.
This understanding of Scripture as the source of propositional truth

---

[250]Ibid., p. 78 (italics deleted).

[251]Carl Henry, "The World Council and Socialism," *Chr T* 10 (July 8,
1966):3.

[252]For an elaboration of "The Bible as Propositional Revelation" see Carl
F. H. Henry, *God, Revelation and Authority* (Waco: Word Books, 1976-1983),
3:455-481.

stands at the heart of the theological position in the United States which
is commonly known as fundamentalism.[253]

Henry's major multi-volume work, *God, Revelation and Authority*
(1976-1983) contains many critical references to liberation theology.
In light of the critical things Henry says about liberation theology, it is
interesting to note his own use of the theme "liberation" to describe the
messianic work of Jesus for the hungry, poor, suffering, and
oppressed.[254] Nevertheless, these remarks must be seen in light of
Henry's subsequent comments about "civil government as a divinely
purposed instrument for justice in fallen society"[255] and the responsibility of Christians "in and through civil authority to work
aggressively for the advancement of justice and human good" through
"critical illumination, personal example, and vocational leadership."[256]

> Christ's disciples are to guard against two serious errors: first, that the
> world by structural changes can be turned into the new society or the
> kingdom of God; and second, that improving sociopolitical structures is
> unimportant in the distinctive call to proclaim the gospel.[257]

Henry holds that Christians are to carry out responsibly their political
duties within the given political structures. This political involvement
does not, however, entail the arrival of God's kingdom and can be
undertaken neither apart from personal regeneration nor divine
revelation in Scripture.[258] While Henry does not rule out the
possibility of Christians participating in revolutionary movements
except where there exists a claim to "messianic fulfillment,"[259] he is
most cautious about this possibility.

It is especially with regard to the influence of Marxism upon
liberation theology that Henry draws his major line of criticism. In
spite of a legitimate and biblical concern for the poor and oppressed,[260]
liberation theology has incorporated ideas from Marxist thought in a
way which undermines its noblest intentions. Marxism offers utopian

---

[253]For a thorough interpretation of the definition and meaning of
fundamentalism see James Barr, *Fundamentalism* (London: SCM, 1977).

[254]Henry, *God, Revelation and Authority*, 3:63-68, with special references to
Isaiah 61:1-3 and Luke 4:16-18.

[255]Ibid., 3:69.

[256]Ibid., 3:70.

[257]Ibid., 3:71.

[258]Cf. ibid., 3:72.

[259]Ibid., 3:71.

[260]Cf. ibid., 4:543.

promises for a more just society which are contradicted by the oppressive reality of actual socialist societies.[261] This should be seen in conjunction with Henry's claim that the concrete shape of the society promised by liberation theology is left vague and indefinite.[262] The contrast between liberation theology's vaguely defined utopian socialism and the oppressive reality of Marxist-inspired societies is a point of emphasis for Henry.[263]

Another way in which Henry sees liberation theology supplanting Christian truth with Marxism is in its very understanding of the liberation process. Gutierrez, for example, is understood by Henry to advocate the emergence of "a new man and a new society" primarily if not exclusively through "the revolutionary process."[264] In this way Gutierrez is seen to substitute a humanly wrought form of social salvation understood in Marxist terms for the Christian salvation which takes place through the person of Jesus Christ. The gap between the teaching and ministry of Jesus and the liberation program of liberation theology is, according to Henry, vast.

Given Henry's particular understanding of the Bible as the source of propositional revelation, it follows that he is especially critical with regard to liberation theology's exegesis. In a chapter entitled "Marxist Exegesis of the Bible" Henry deals at length with what he sees as the fundamental issues involved in an evangelical critique of liberation theology.[265] Henry faults Gutierrez and liberation theology for focusing primarily on "existing social and political conditions" rather than "on Christ and the Bible as the revelational center of human history and destiny."[266] He attributes this reversal in traditional priorities to liberation theology's use of Marxist interpretation. This is seen further in liberation theology's use of the Marxist critique of ideology and its allowing Marxism to supply "the scientific content of Christian social ethics."[267] In terms of its interpretation of Scripture this means:

> By appealing to the present historical milieu as the only legitimate context
> for theological reflection, liberation theology thus readily colors, limits

---

[261] Cf. ibid., 4:547.

[262] Cf. ibid., 4:523.

[263] Cf. ibid., 4:571.

[264] For the following see ibid., 4:584.

[265] For the following cf. ibid., 4:555-577.

[266] Ibid., 4:556.

[267] Ibid.

and even subverts the scripturally given revelation even while it does not necessarily displace it. The appeal to Scripture and to Christ becomes a hermeneutical veneer; the biblical heritage is glossed over to advance the modern ideology of socialism.[268]

Although liberation theology wants to distinguish itself from the theology of revolution on this and other points, Henry finds the similarities in their exegesis and outlook greater than their differences.

In part Henry is willing to attribute liberation theology's divergence from Scriptural authority to the influence of the Roman Catholic understanding of revelation in tradition and history. But the primary reason for this divergence is nevertheless due to the influence of Marx.

> Like Marx, liberation theology presupposes that social classes are by-products of a capitalistic society, and that all ecclesiastical thought and effort must promote the overthrow of that society and replace it with a socialist alternative. . . . [W]e ask, what biblical basis exists for transmuting all this into the Marxist motif of "a classless society in which there is a collective ownership of the means of production?"[269]

By turning to Marxist thought for political solutions, liberation theology ignores "a third way that is open to evangelical Christianity on a genuinely biblical basis, that is, one which refuses to baptize either Marxist socialism or secular capitalism as Christian."[270]

Henry criticizes at length what he understands to be the overwhelming Marxist influence on the thought of Gustavo Gutierrez.[271] In addition Henry objects to Gutierrez's promotion of the idea of universal salvation. Other liberation theologians undergo similar criticism for their dependence on Marx rather than biblical revelation, for example, Hugo Assmann.[272] In effect, liberation theology "results in a redefinition of salvation, Christology, eschatology and the church."[273] According to Henry, in each article of doctrine Marxist ideology comes to replace the genuinely Christian content revealed in biblical teaching.[274] The root cause for this transformation is liberation theology's Marxist exegesis.[275] Marxist

---

[268] Ibid., 4:556-557.

[269] Ibid., 4:558-559.

[270] Ibid., 4:560.

[271] Cf. ibid., 4:560-562.

[272] Cf. ibid., 4:564-565.

[273] Ibid., 4:562.

[274] Cf. ibid., 4:563 and 570-571.

[275] Cf. ibid., 4:562-563.

presuppositions make legitimate exegesis impossible. Even an evangelical scholar basically sympathetic to liberation theology such as Orlando Costas "considers dangerous the liberation theology emphasis that theology is grounded in the concrete historical situation . . . so that Scripture retains only a secondary comparative and descriptive function."[276]

In response to the challenge of liberation theology and Marxism in general, Henry sees the need for the development of a sound evangelical alternative.

> It is imperative that we forge a socially concerned biblical alternative, a comprehensive scriptural vision of society, even if it may appear astonishingly new and perhaps even radical alongside some current evangelical traditions. . . . The alternative must be biblically authentic, and also "possible" (likewise defined biblically) of realization in any given situation. We need a biblical frame of reference that also knows how to use the sociological tools at our disposal. Such a theology will be more durable and genuinely transformational than either the theology of revolution or that of liberation, since its aims include the spiritual transformation of man and society.[277]

The challenge of liberation theology is a real one and, like Wagner, Henry begins to outline what he sees as an authentic evangelical response.[278] Foremost in this evangelical response must be a correct apprehension of the biblical revelation now distorted by the Marxist exegesis of liberation theology. This means beginning with the personal regeneration of the sinner through the evangel and proceeding to social action under the continual test of Scriptural truth.[279]

The evangelical periodical *Christianity Today* has likewise published many articles in criticism of liberation theology which, together with Henry, represent the viewpoint of a large segment of the North American evangelical community. They range from more generalized reactions to the potential distortions of evangelical thought by the movements of recent times[280] to specific critiques of the theology of liberation. It is the latter which warrant primary attention in the present context.

---

[276]Ibid., 4:567.

[277]Ibid., 4:570.

[278]Cf. ibid., 4:570-577.

[279]Cf. ibid., 4:576-577.

[280]For example, see Joel H. Nederhood, "Christians and Revolution," *Chr T* 15 (Jan. 1, 1971):7-9 and Vernon C. Grounds, "Bombs or Bibles? Get Ready for Revolution!", *Chr T* 15 (Jan. 15, 1971):4-6.

C. Rene Padilla, for example, echoes Henry's charge that liberation theology overtakes the Marxist understanding of revolutionary praxis and thereby uses theology and biblical exegesis merely for the purposes of rationalization.[281]

> The result is an "ideologization" of the faith that is entirely consistent with a Marxist philosophical framework but bears little resemblance to the Gospel of Christ.[282]

At the same time Padilla, like Henry, encourages evangelicals to learn from liberation theology the danger of ideologizing theology and to develop a Scripturally sound position in response to the present historical situation.

A somewhat different critique is that offered by Rene De Visme Williamson. Following an exposition of his understanding of the basic aspects of liberation theology, Williamson proceeds with a six-point evaluation of its deficiencies. First, liberation theology has a faulty understanding of liberty. "Liberty is *not* the central theme of the Christian faith,"[283] rather to glorify God must have top priority. Second, liberation theology has a defective concept of equality. Williamson affirms against liberation theology "that inequality of some kind is an inescapable fact of life."[284] Third, Williamson objects to liberation theology's claim that the poor are in any way "privileged recipients of the Gospel" since in the Bible "God is no respecter of persons."[285] Fourth, "the advocacy of subversion and revolution runs counter to Romans 13, which instructs us to obey the powers that be."[286] Fifth, liberation theology does away with the notion of original sin which places a real limit on the human ability to eliminate poverty and injustice. Sixth, liberation theology espouses secularization which can be understood to be neither Christian nor even religious. For all these reasons, liberation theology must be soundly rejected from an evangelical point of view.

---

[281] C. Rene Padilla, "The Theology of Liberation," *Chr T* 18 (Nov. 9, 1973):69.

[282] Ibid., p. 70.

[283] Rene De Visme Williamson, "The Theology of Liberation," *Chr T* 19 (Aug. 8, 1975):12.

[284] Ibid.

[285] Ibid.

[286] Ibid., p. 13.

W. Dayton Roberts has offered another account of where liberation theology has gone wrong within the pages of *Christianity Today*.[287] Among the eleven points elaborated by Roberts, he notes liberation theology's turning to human history (especially as interpreted according to Marxist principles) as its theological locus at the expense of divine revelation. Roberts also claims that liberation theology fails to acknowledge "the active presence of the Holy Spirit" and therefore "personal devotion, mysticism, the disciplines of piety, prayer, and meditation are also incidental" to it.[288] A major point of criticism is liberation theology's redefinition of salvation "in collective terms to the virtual exclusion of individual redemption."[289]

> Evangelicals have good reason to be suspicious of this kind of soteriology— because it is a direct throwback to the "modernists" and "social gospelers" of a past generation. It undercuts the personal encounter with Jesus Christ and the "justification by faith" that have always been the cherished hallmarks of evangelicalism.[290]

All of these distortions are finally traceable to liberation theology's displacement of the authority of the Bible and its insufficient understanding of the person and ministry of Jesus Christ. For an evangelical theology such distortions are simply unacceptable, even heretical.

A final example from *Christianity Today* is the article by Walter W. Benjamin, "Liberation Theology: European Hopelessness Exposes the Latin Hoax."[291] In it Benjamin compares the drabness, oppression, and economic problems of Eastern European countries under communist rule to the vitality, freedom, and material plenty of the capitalist West. The stark contrast which Benjamin describes between life in the East and West ought to be instructive for liberation theology. It should force liberation theologians to recognize there exists another form of oppression than the one which exists in Latin countries, a form of bondage under Soviet tutelage. Such a recognition should then prompt liberation theology to move beyond romanticizing revolution to a serious critique of all revolutions. As a correlate this means for liberation theology surrendering its hypercritical attitude

---

[287]W. Dayton Roberts, "Where Has Liberation Theology Gone Wrong?" *Chr T* 23 (Oct. 19, 1979):26-28.

[288]Ibid., p. 27.

[289]Ibid., p. 28.

[290]Ibid.

[291]For the following see Walter W. Benjamin, "Liberation Theology: European Hopelessness Exposes the Latin Hoax," *Chr T* 26 (Mar. 5, 1982):21-23.

toward the United States. American virtues and not only vices need greater appreciation in liberation circles. This entails for Benjamin assent to Michael Novak's thesis that "capitalism works better than its circumspect ideology; socialism far worse than its romantic hopes."[292] Finally, Benjamin chides liberation theologians to "beware of irrational guilt" which leads them to overcompensate for their perceived responsibility for the world's problems.[293] In these several ways liberation theology might benefit from a comparison between liberation theology's naive hopes for a socialist society and the bleak reality of existing communist societies in Eastern Europe. Implicit is Benjamin's conviction that liberation theology's socialist option is leading Latin America toward a society similar to the one he experienced during his travels through Czechoslovakia and Hungary.

These articles in criticism of liberation theology published in *Christianity Today* together with the more scholarly approach of Carl F. H. Henry represent a second evangelical viewpoint over against liberation theology. Against the primarily Marxist tendencies of liberation theology, these evangelicals raise up their understanding of the Bible's authority over all Christian doctrine and practice. The theology derived from the Bible interpreted as the source of propositional revelation conflicts dramatically with the theological understanding of liberation theology rooted in its own historical context and theological understandings. This confrontation takes on still other contours in the critique of liberation theology by Donald G. Bloesch.

3. Donald G. Bloesch

Professor of theology at the University of Dubuque Theological Seminary, Dubuque, Iowa, and prolific Reformed and evangelical author, Donald G. Bloesch offers a more nuanced and sophisticated critique of liberation theology from an evangelical perspective. In part this is due to Bloesch's understanding of Scriptural authority which in a qualified way affirms the use of the historical critical method[294] and

---

[292]Ibid., p. 23.

[293]Ibid.

[294]Cf. Donald G. Bloesch, *Essentials of Evangelical Theology* (San Francisco: Harper & Row, 1978-79), 1:70-74. Bloesch's understanding of "the hermeneutical task" witnesses to a depth and complexity lacking in many other evangelical theologies.

his general openness to dialogue with other currents of contemporary theology.

A good introduction to the views of Bloesch on liberation theology is contained in his response to a 1979 symposium on "Theological Education and Liberation Theology."[295] In this article Bloesch first admits his own basic agreement with a theology which has a political dimension and takes the concern for social justice seriously. Nevertheless Bloesch disagrees with certain affirmations of those challenging theological education in the name of liberation theology on several important points. First, Bloesch objects to the equation between "knowing God" and "doing justice." On both sides of the equation there are difficulties. On the one hand, there are those who believe in God and are incapacitated in one way or another from working for justice. On the other hand, there are those (e.g., secular humanists) who work for justice without knowing God. In the place of this equation, Bloesch hearkens theology back to a grounding in the doctrine of justification out of which works of love and justice flow. Without this grounding liberation theology is in danger of succumbing to a new form of legalistic works righteousness.

Secondly, Bloesch questions liberation theology's claim to innovation as "a new way of doing theology." Citing historical examples ranging from Augustine and Luther to Wesley and Bonhoeffer, Bloesch argues that classical theology has always entertained the ethical dimension, also in the social realm. As a third point, Bloesch criticizes liberation theology's too narrow identification of a particular social program with the kingdom of God. Over against this tendency Bloesch cites Reinhold Niebuhr regarding the necessity of a transcendent dimension which critiques all social agendas.

Fourthly, Bloesch warns against erecting a "canon within the canon" for the purposes of biblical interpretation which may introduce a contemporary ideology as hermeneutical key. Bloesch encourages an appreciation for the entire canon and prefers speaking of Scripture in terms of "center and periphery" rather than "canon within the canon" in order to make this point.

Fifthly, Bloesch sees not only a danger that theological education become captive to ideologies of the right or the middle, but also to those of the left. Liberation theology, in this regard, impresses Bloesch as

---

[295]For the following see Donald G. Bloesch, "Response," *Th Ed* 16 (Aut. 1979):16-19.

being "under the spell of messianic socialism,"[296] a critique to which Bloesch returns in other writings. Because of this danger Bloesch urges liberation theology to heed not only the social critiques of Marxist scholarship, but also those of Jacques Ellul and Alexander Solzhenitsyn.

In terms of setting theological priorities, Bloesch, sixthly, asks whether there is not first a need for "a new consciousness that will lead people to identify with the poor and oppressed" which is prior to "new programs to insure a just distribution of goods."[297] Here Bloesch raises the issue of the root problem underlying unjust society which he sees as "sin in the human heart" rather than merely "an oppressive social environment."[298] Bloesch connects this issue with liberation theology's tendency toward utopianism which is negated by the insight that in this world at most a proximate level of justice can be achieved. This Reformation insight, renewed in recent times by Emil Brunner and Reinhold Niebuhr, needs to be recaptured by liberation theology along with its clearer distinction between law and gospel and between civil and spiritual righteousness.

> My quarrel with liberation theology is that it tends to confuse the roles of church and state, civil and spiritual righteousness, sacred and universal historicity, law and gospel.[299]

Thus Bloesch seeks greater dogmatic clarity about the proposals of liberation theology lest essential Reformation and evangelical insights be lost. At the same time Bloesch admits his own gratitude to the theology of liberation for reminding theology of the world context in which theology is today carried out.

> But I am grateful to liberation theologians for impressing upon us that the Christian hope concerns progress toward righteousness in this world as well as the perfect righteousness in the world to come. Liberation theology bids us recapture the millennial vision of the kingdom of God on earth, and unless we incorporate this vision in our theological perspectives, we will end up with an otherworldly theology and an otherworldly church whose message will seem irrelevant if not incredible to the impoverished masses of contemporary humanity.[300]

Bloesch balances his dogmatic criticisms with the recognition that the present world situation of poverty calls forth the theological impulse and vision offered by liberation theology.

---

[296]Ibid., p. 18.
[297]Ibid.
[298]Ibid.
[299]Ibid., p. 19.
[300]Ibid.

In Bloesch's major dogmatic work, *Essentials of Evangelical Theology* (1978-79), Bloesch integrates references to liberation theology into various discussions of evangelical doctrine. In his treatment of the doctrine of "total depravity," for example, Bloesch mentions liberation theology in relation to the optimism of the Social Gospel movement. Because of human sinfulness Bloesch is skeptical of the position of theologians such as Shaull, Alves, and Gutierrez who "urge the violent overthrow of existing orders of oppression so that the kingdom of God can be manifested in the realization of man's hopes for liberation."[301] In his pursuit of doctrinal clarity Bloesch would insure that "an optimism based on grace must be sharply distinguished from an optimism based on man's resources."[302]

This reservation about the optimism of liberation theology is repeated in Bloesch's discussion of the Christian meaning of "new birth." Against liberation theology and other related positions Bloesch writes:

> Conversion is seen as involving a decisive break not with man's inherent drive for power but with the conditions that hold people in economic and political bondage. . . . What is disturbing about this point of view is that it locates the misery of man in oppressive conditions in society rather than in the concupiscence within the heart of man and sees revolution by violence as a way to salvation.[303]

With others, Bloesch questions liberation theology's anthropology in general and in particular its idea of human sinfulness. The roots of sin penetrate deeper into human existence than liberation theology will acknowledge.

In his discussion of "the church's spiritual mission" Bloesch discusses and criticizes liberation theology's contribution to the contemporary meaning of mission. Once again Bloesch is critical of liberation theology's preoccupation with the social dimension of mission at the expense of its individual dimension. "In this kind of thinking," writes Bloesch, "the self-development of the oppressed peoples of the Third World, in effect, supplants the call to evangelize the heathen."[304] In response to this challenge Bloesch would follow Hans Küng in clearly differentiating between redemption and emancipation.

---

[301] Bloesch, *Essentials of Evangelical Theology*, 1:112.
[302] Ibid., 1:114.
[303] Ibid., 2:24.
[304] Ibid., 2:165.

Redemption "means liberation of man by God, not any self-redemption on
man's part." Emancipation, on the other hand, means the "liberation of
man by man, it means man's self-liberation." Emancipation should
grow out of redemption, but it must never be confused with the latter, for
otherwise we are again in the morass of Pelagianism.[305]

In this criticism Bloesch also echoes Schubert Ogden who has made this
point at greater length.

In a 1981 article in which Bloesch evaluates the soteriology of
liberation theology, related doctrinal concerns have been raised.[306]
Following a brief survey of salient aspects of liberation theology,
Bloesch proceeds to an evaluation of its soteriology. While
appreciative of liberation theology's "rediscovery of Hebraic holism
where man is conceived of as a unity and salvation is understood as
encompassing both body and soul" as well as its recovery of "the idea of
a servant church," Bloesch at the same time sees certain
weaknesses.[307] They include the danger of losing the significance of
the gospel of what *God* has done to achieve salvation in Christ to ethics.

Liberation theology thereby falls into a new kind of works-righteousness
in which the struggle for justice is seen as a necessary preparation for
faith. The emphasis is on the sanctification of the socially involved, not
the justification of the ungodly.[308]

Among the criticisms of liberation theology which Bloesch has already
made in earlier contexts, this one takes a central position. This can
also be seen insofar as Bloesch includes liberation theology among the
contemporary forms of "heroic" religion which confuse the proper
relationship between the priority of God's gift of salvation by grace and
the secondary place of human works.[309]

In comparison to other evangelical critiques of liberation theology,
Donald G. Bloesch offers a doctrinally precise, and balanced point of
view. While admitting certain positive insights of liberation theology,
Bloesch draws a critical line where it endangers what he sees as the
valid dogmatic foundations of evangelical theology. Most especially
this means clarity with regard to the doctrines of sin and soteriology.

---

[305]Ibid., 2:167. Quoted references are from Hans Küng, *On Being a
Christian*, trans. Edward Quinn (Garden City, NY: Doubleday, 1976), p. 430.

[306]For the following see Donald G. Bloesch, "Soteriology in Contemporary
Christian Thought," *Interp* 35 (Apr. 1981):137-139.

[307]Ibid., p. 138.

[308]Ibid.

[309]Donald G. Bloesch, *Faith and Its Counterfeits* (Downers Grove, IL: Inter-
Varsity Press, 1981), p. 92.

G. *Toward a More Adequate Conceptuality*

With the theology of Bloesch it is possible to detect a certain change not only in the tone but also the nature of the critique of liberation theology. Bloesch not only negatively criticizes liberation theology but also is able to recognize some positive contributions. The attempt is made to include not only negative but also positive criticisms. Unlike several other critiques of liberation theology, here the effort is made to offer constructive proposals toward a more adequate conceptuality for liberation theology. Criticism remains and often it is a serious criticism. But nevertheless the criticism is in service of constructive proposals for responding to the perceived inadequacies of liberation theology. This approach especially characterizes the approach of the North American theologians examined in the following section: Daniel L. Migliore, Peter C. Hodgson, John B. Cobb, Jr., Delwin Brown, and Schubert M. Ogden. These theologians clearly offer their criticism with the intent of contributing to a more adequate theological conceptuality both for North American and for Latin American liberation theology.

1. Daniel L. Migliore

Daniel L. Migliore, Professor of Theology at Princeton Theological Seminary, has in his book *Called to Freedom. Liberation Theology and the Future of Christian Doctrine* (1980), offered a constructive proposal for the interaction of liberation theology with traditional Christian doctrine, toward the achievement of a more adequate theological conceptuality. In Migliore's book this is done by incorporating liberation perspectives into the consideration of five basic Christian doctrines: Scripture, Jesus Christ, God, spirituality, and eschatology. Migliore recognizes "both the importance and the limits of interpreting the gospel today as God's liberating activity in which we are called to take part."[310] On the positive side, Migliore sees liberation theology as "by far the most creative and penetrating"[311] theological development of the last decade which assists in recovering social and this-worldly aspects of Christian teaching too long obscured. On the negative side, liberation theology needs the breadth of perspective offered by traditional doctrinal formulations lest it slip into uncritical or reductionistic thinking.

---

[310]Daniel L. Migliore, *Called to Freedom. Liberation Theology and the Future of Christian Doctrine* (Philadelphia: Westminster, 1980), p. 14.
[311]Ibid.

The central thesis which guides Migliore's doctrinal reformulations is:

> . . . that the freedom of God is not sheer arbitrariness; it is preeminently the freedom to love. In like manner, the perfection of human freedom is to be seen not in the total absence of limitations but in openness to and solidarity with others, and especially with the poor, the despised, and the oppressed.[312]

In his consideration of each of the five doctrines, this central, guiding thesis comes to expression in various ways. The theocentric emphasis of Migliore's thought (cf. K. Barth) is readily apparent.

The first doctrine considered by Migliore is that of "Scripture as Liberating Word."[313] Here Migliore draws explicitly on Barth's theology of the Word of God for his primary model. In this model the Bible functions as Word of God in its witness to Jesus Christ. In Barth's theology of the Word of God, Migliore sees the basis for a truly liberating theology grounded in the primacy of God's liberating acts in human history. Although liberation theologians in their historical context have criticized Barth's connection of a theology of the Word of God with a theology of reconciliation which they feel shortchanges the reality of conflict in arriving at liberation, Migliore believes the two themes of liberation and reconciliation serve to complement one another.

> Liberation and reconciliation presuppose each other. Reconciliation presupposes liberation in execution. Liberation presupposes reconciliation in intention. The biblical understanding of God's liberating activity is characterized by this bond between liberation and reconciliation. For the Bible bears witness to God who is free for others.[314]

In proposing principles for the interpretation of Scripture today, Migliore incorporates both Barth's emphasis on a "theocentric" interpretation which can critique all political movements and liberation theology's emphasis on a "contextual" interpretation which takes the social location of theology with utmost seriousness.[315] This approach is characteristic of Migliore's irenic intention in appropriating liberation insights into contemporary formulations of Christian doctrine.

Similarly, Migliore sees both a gain and a limit in liberation theology's contribution to a contemporary understanding of

---

[312]Ibid., p. 16.

[313]For the following cf. ibid., pp. 23-42.

[314]Ibid., p. 32.

[315]Cf. ibid., pp. 36-40.

Christology.[316] The gain is seen in recovering the New Testament foundations for an understanding of Jesus as liberator alongside other legitimate Christological titles. This is especially important given the reality of the contemporary struggles for liberation in the modern world. The limit of a liberation Christology must be seen, however, in that the content of Jesus Christ as Liberator must derive from the early Christian understanding and not from any other source. After reviewing the traditional understandings of Christ's work and certain characteristics of the freedom discernible in the ministry of Jesus and the community created by his spirit, Migliore argues for an understanding of liberation which is holistic in including many different kinds of liberation in its purview, cautious in seeking to avoid a mere exchange of one kind of bondage for another, and gospel-oriented in acknowledging liberation not only as a human task but especially as a gift of God.[317] Migliore seeks to incorporate and at the same time balance the liberation perspective of liberation theology within a broader scope.

In discussing the doctrine of God, Migliore joins other modern theologians in recognizing the doctrine of the Trinity as the foundation for a theology of human freedom. In reference to the Third Person of the Trinity, Migliore encourages a greater appreciation of "social" analogies of the Trinity as opposed to "psychological" analogies. He cites Segundo regarding the way in which a triune understanding of God "criticizes the image of God that is reflected in the oppressive social and economic structures of the affluent nations of the world."[318] In the Christian idea of the Trinity, liberation theology can doctrinally establish its concern for human freedom.

Migliore sees no fundamental opposition between a liberation theology and an authentic Christian spirituality.[319] In fact, the insights of liberation theology can assist North Americans in overcoming a spirituality too often conceived in privatistic, ahistorical, consumer-oriented terms. Hearing the Bible "from below," from the viewpoint of the marginal of society, can offer not only a new appreciation of the Bible's message but can also prompt a reevaluation of the meaning of conversion, prayer, and holiness. In this way a liberation theology can contribute to the formation of an

---

[316]For the following cf. ibid., pp. 43-62.

[317]Cf. ibid., pp. 60-62.

[318]Ibid., p. 74.

[319]For the following cf. ibid., pp. 81-99.

authentically North American spirituality, one which is political
without being partisan, one which is costly in biblical terms. This
Migliore sees as especially urgent since "the old forms of spiritual life
are dead, and the new ones . . . are often more alienating than life-
transforming."[320]

As a fifth and final doctrinal focus, Migliore examines the
contemporary meaning of Christian hope in the face of death.[321] In
comparing the most common "images of death in American society
today" to the emphases of liberation theology, Migliore sees the
emergence of a more wholesome understanding. With regard to an
image of death as an enemy to be overcome through technology,
Migliore asks about the limits of technology and the costs which are
paid by the poor in the pursuit of this goal. With regard to an image of
death as a natural "fact of life," Migliore warns against masking the
fact that the death of the poor through oppressive political systems is no
natural death. With regard to an image of death as the moment of
release of the immortal soul, Migliore counters with the Christian hope
of the resurrection of the body which affirms God's will for the
liberation of the entire creation. In these ways a liberation perspective
can contribute to the deepening of the North American understanding
of Christian eschatology.

While borrowing from liberation theology in his various doctrinal
formulations, at the same time Migliore sees certain dangers should
the idea of God's liberating activity be misunderstood.

> There is the temptation to identify political programs with the kingdom of
> God and to assume human liberation can be accomplished entirely by
> social or political change; there is the tendency to fall into a simplistic
> dualism of oppressed and oppressors; there is the danger of a spirit of self-
> righteousness and legalism in working for a more just and equitable
> social order; there is the inclination to discount the theological tradition as
> irrelevant to present revolutionary praxis; there is the possibility of subtly
> transforming the Christian message of salvation by grace through faith
> into a religion of works; there is the danger of emphasizing only the bright
> symbols of exodus, resurrection, and hope while forgetting the dark
> symbols of journey through the wilderness, crucifixion, and costly
> discipleship.[322]

In spite of such potential misunderstandings by liberation theology,
however, Migliore affirms it as a legitimate and needed challenge to
theology in the present global context. Through the process of mutual

---

[320]Ibid., p. 99.

[321]For the following cf. ibid., pp. 101-120.

[322]Ibid., pp. 123-124.

learning and dialogue between First and Third worlds, theology can move "toward a more adequate understanding of the freedom of God and of the new human freedom rooted in faith in God."[323] Migliore believes this is especially true for theologians in his own North American context.

2. Peter C. Hodgson

Professor of Theology at Vanderbilt Divinity School, Peter C. Hodgson has long been interested in the theological currents which collectively are called liberation theology. In particular Hodgson has striven to offer one white theologian's response to the challenge of the North American black theology of liberation.[324] The focus on black liberation theology recurs in the major work of Hodgson to be considered here, *New Birth of Freedom. A Theology of Bondage and Liberation* (1976), but not without significant references to Latin American liberation theology as well. It can be assumed that Hodgson's proposals for a more adequate theological conceptuality in *New Birth of Freedom* are applicable to black and Latin American liberation theologies alike.

The immediate context for the publication of this volume by Hodgson was the celebration of the bicentennial of the founding of the United States. Therefore there are numerous references to the definition and meaning of freedom within the history of the U.S. political experience. Hodgson wants to make clear from the outset his own theological location as "a white American male" which establishes certain parameters around his theological efforts.[325] This means he "cannot *do* black theology, or feminist theology, or third world theology."[326] Nevertheless, Hodgson seeks to be in dialogue with these movements as much as possible and does draw "extensively from the literature" of liberation theologians.[327] In so doing Hodgson remains convinced that "good theology . . . must transcend regional

---

[323]Ibid., p. 124.

[324]See especially Peter C. Hodgson, *Children of Freedom. Black Liberation in Christian Perspective* (Philadelphia: Fortress, 1974).

[325]Peter C. Hodgson, *New Birth of Freedom. A Theology of Bondage and Liberation* (Philadelphia: Fortress, 1976), p. xiv.

[326]Ibid., pp. xiii-xiv.

[327]Ibid., p. xiii.

and national identities, although it may well arise out of the determinate situation of a people, a place, or an epoch."[328]

Hodgson's response to the current theological ferment in *New Birth of Freedom* is that of "a foundational theology of freedom."[329] In this way Hodgson seeks to ground the quest for liberty, whether in the U.S. or Europe or Latin America, in a more comprehensive theology of freedom. The choice of the word "freedom" in Hodgson's project points to his primary aim at providing a more comprehensive philosophical foundation. The word "liberation," by contrast, indicates a conflictual approach which does not reflect Hodgson's intention. To this end Hodgson believes it is necessary to be in dialogue not only with the Third World but also with German idealism, French and German existential and social phenomenology, and contemporary Continental theology and biblical scholarship.[330] Among the various Continental sources upon which Hodgson draws most extensively for his philosophical framework are Hegel and Ricoeur.

Hodgson outlines in an initial chapter the vision, failings, and unfinished work in the U.S. experiment in freedom. In Abraham Lincoln's phrase, "a new birth of freedom," taken from his Gettysburg Address, Hodgson discovers a symbol to express, in effect, the scope of his entire book. This phrase:

> suggests that freedom, once granted to humankind in the original act of creation, has been lost and must now be reborn. This birth, like all births, is a painful one, entailing suffering, dedication, sacrifice. The symbolism of Jesus' death on the cross, and of his resurrection from the dead, is just below the surface. The new birth of freedom occurs "under God," meaning liberation from bondage, like resurrection from the dead, is not an autonomous human achievement. The finishing of freedom is the work of God, but "under God" it is also to become a human work.[331]

In coming to understand the full depth of freedom's meaning, several dimensions of freedom must be investigated: freedom as created, fallen, redeemed, and restored. Hodgson names these four dimensions essential freedom, bound freedom, liberated freedom, and final freedom, respectively, and devotes chapters to each dimension. By thoroughly exploring the various dimensions of freedom, Hodgson

---

[328]Ibid.
[329]Ibid.
[330]Cf. ibid.
[331]Ibid., pp. 40-41.

seeks to ground contemporary liberation movements in the broader panorama of universal history.[332]

Hodgson contrasts the concept of freedom he seeks to establish with several "rival" meanings which exist in the contemporary world: political-economic, pragmatic-technocratic, rational-psychoanalytic, tragic-existential, and ecstatic-vitalistic.[333] Among these rival meanings, most pertinent is the political-economic type whose intellectual antecedents include Greek democracy and Marxism and whose current expressions include third world liberation. Hodgson's critique of Marxism is especially interesting at this point since it is a critique frequently applied to liberation theology as well. Marx's crucial, and false, assumption, according to Hodgson, is that Marx assumed that alienation can be eliminated by the "abolition of private property and the establishment of a socialist economic system."[334] The deeper roots of human alienation in human selfishness and will to power, i.e., sinfulness in theological terms, are neglected. For this reason Marxism offers an attractive but ultimately deceptive solution to the dilemma of human alienation. Each of the rival freedoms are discussed by Hodgson at length and he argues that each of them alone is at best a partial manifestation of that freedom to which human beings are finally called. It is the Christian understanding of freedom which transforms, fulfills, and transcends each of these partial manifestations.[335]

In a complex philosophical argument which draws heavily from phenomenology, symbolics, and idealism, Hodgson proceeds to a discussion of the meaning of "essential freedom."[336] The "structures" of freedom which Hodgson incorporates and elaborates as belonging to essential freedom are autonomy (subjective freedom), community (both intersubjective and objective freedom), and openness (transsubjective freedom). Because of the "fragility" of freedom, however, essential freedom falls into the various forms of bondage which mark human existence.[337] "Bound freedom" is characterized both subjectively by a "servile" will and objectively by estrangement, exploitation, and oppression. In his discussion of the objectification of

---

[332]Cf. ibid., pp. 267-271.

[333]Cf. ibid., pp. 42-50.

[334]Ibid., p. 57. Cf. also pp. 58-61 and 175.

[335]Cf. ibid., pp. 111-112.

[336]For the following cf. ibid., pp. 114-165.

[337]For the following cf. ibid., pp. 168-206.

oppression, Hodgson refers to the dependency theory employed by Latin
American liberation theologians to illustrate the institutional forms in
which oppression comes to be structured.[338]

To describe the possibility of "liberated freedom," Hodgson turns
next to the meaning of "Jesus the Liberator" in the Christian
tradition.[339] Here Hodgson draws upon his own studies in the
historical Jesus and Christology to formulate an exegetically
sophisticated definition of the freedom which became realized in Jesus
Christ.[340] Hodgson makes reference to Leander Keck in expressing
his concern for the misuse of the New Testament through "proof-
texting" and for this reason seeks to base his investigations on sound
exegetical arguments.[341] He nevertheless is convinced that sound
exegesis can arrive at a number of conclusions which warrant an
understanding of Jesus in terms of liberation. These include Jesus'
own "radical freedom" in his relationship to God as son, his attitude
and actions towards others, and his claim to a unique identity and
authority. This radical freedom of Jesus is furthermore established in
his proclamation of the kingdom of God, or, as Hodgson terms it, the
"kingdom of freedom." The symbol of the kingdom is, for Hodgson,
both political and postpolitical or eschatological.

> "Postpolitical" is a helpful expression because it reminds us that what we
> are speaking of is post*political*, not apolitical or unworldly. When we
> describe an idea or cultural epoch as *post-*, we usually mean that the
> preceding reality (in this case, "politics") does not cease to exist but
> furnishes the foundation for a further development and thus is included in
> a new framework.[342]

In this way Jesus' proclamation of the kingdom has most definite
political implications without being reduced to politics. What this
means for liberation movements which call upon the authority of Jesus
is that they must advocate a form of "critical partisanship": *partisan*
in accordance with Jesus' ministry to the poor and outcasts (e.g., blind,
lepers, deaf, etc.) of his time and *critical* in standing under the
eschatological proviso which allows for no identification between
God's kingdom and any one political ideology.[343] The legitimacy of

---

[338]Ibid., p. 203.

[339]For the following cf. ibid., pp. 208-264.

[340]Cf. also Peter C. Hodgson, *Jesus—Word and Presence. An Essay in
Christology* (Philadelphia: Fortress, 1971).

[341]Cf. Hodgson, *New Birth of Freedom*, pp. 209-216.

[342]Ibid., p. 231.

[343]Cf. ibid., pp. 238-240 and 316-319.

the position of critical partisanship is further demonstrated by Hodgson in Jesus' own attitude toward the Zealots.[344]

The key chapter in Hodgson's work for his treatment of liberation theology is entitled "The Dialectics of Liberation."[345] In it Hodgson addresses the dialectic process in which the freedom engendered by Jesus comes to be actualized in history. Affirming the validity of Marx's insight regarding the structural nature of social and political oppression, liberation too must take place on the structural and not only the psychic level. The liberation engendered by Jesus must accordingly have both socioeconomic/political and personal/psychic dimensions. Moreover, this liberation in the historical process must be viewed both as a human project and as the advent of divine redemption. These various aspects are developed by Hodgson with special reference to Hegel's philosophy of history. History obtains meaning as it moves forward in a dialectical process toward ever higher realizations of liberation. This dialectical movement takes place through the negation of inadequate historical expressions toward ever higher syntheses of liberation. Liberation theology serves to illustrate the nature of this dialectic which includes both the liberation of consciousness (cf. Freire's method of conscientization) and the liberation of socioeconomic and political structures. Where some liberation theologies may require critique is in their tendency to overemphasize liberation as a human project while minimizing liberation as a divine act.[346] Liberation in its fullest sense must strike a balance between emancipation (human) and redemption (divine). The formulations of Gutierrez are cited approvingly in having achieved this balance with theoretical precision.[347]

The power which energizes the liberation process belongs ultimately to God. Hodgson employs a Hegelian interpretation of the dialectics of the Trinity in history in order to conceptualize the divine role in accomplishing liberation. Liberation theology is introduced to exemplify the working out of this ongoing historical process. The resurrection of Jesus plays a crucial role in activating human praxis on behalf of liberation, especially through his communal body, the church. The agency of Jesus is understood by Hodgson to be fundamental to the actualization of the liberation process. Jesus as

---

[344]Cf. ibid., pp. 240-243.
[345]For the following cf. ibid., pp. 265-321.
[346]Cf. ibid., pp. 280-290.
[347]Ibid., pp. 288-290.

liberator models the dialectics of freedom through his crucifixion and resurrection, the content of his earthly proclamation and ministry, and his openness toward the future eschatological fulfillment. Simultaneously Jesus as liberator already grounds present efforts to approximate the transcendent possibility. Even more, Jesus as liberator addresses both the personal/psychic need for liberation by setting free from sin and death and the socioeconomic/political need for liberation by freeing from the law and the powers. Hodgson goes on to point out how the very freedom from the self obtained through personal/psychic liberation from sin and death opens an individual to participation in working for liberation in the socioeconomic/political sphere. This is to take place always on the basis of an attitude of critical partisanship. What that means personally for Hodgson is the option for democratic socialism under the condition that the means chosen for attaining structural change remain nonviolent.[348] In his insistence on nonviolent means there is again a tacit point of criticism of some liberation theologies. But in making this personal option, Hodgson insists that a critical attitude not be sacrificed.

Hodgson concludes his book with a discussion of "final freedom," the eschatological freedom toward which the historical process presses.[349] The anticipated kingdom of freedom exerts in the present a pressure for political action, yet should not be identified with any preliminary manifestations short of the eschaton. The time between the present and final fulfillment belongs to the work of the Spirit in increasing faith, love, life and hope. Hodgson describes the work of the Spirit in opening human beings to God, each other in community, their own authentic selves, and, finally, in attaining to the perfect freedom of the kingdom of God. This is so because the reality of God "must in some sense *be* freedom. . . . He is *the Free One*, the One who 'has' freedom absolutely; his freedom is the event or power that clears a free realm in which human beings can dwell."[350]

Hodgson, in his proposal for a foundational theology of freedom, embeds liberation theology within a comprehensive philosophical and theological framework. He affirms the basic thrust of liberation theology while at the same time situating it within a more adequate conceptuality. In this way his response contains an implicit critique of

---

[348]Ibid., pp. 317-321.

[349]For the following cf. ibid., pp. 324-355.

[350]Ibid., pp. 335-336.

liberation theology together with a constructive proposal for its correction from a North American perspective.

3. John B. Cobb, Jr. and Delwin Brown

Process theologians have in recent years been increasingly interested in both European political theology and the theology of liberation. Burton Cooper has offered a concise explanation for this interest and suggested the need for more dialogue.

> Process theology needs a concrete social and political gospel to protect it from the danger of fascination with its own brilliant, abstract conceptuality; and the liberation theologies can gain in strength by the insights that an innovative, theological system throws upon the unjust political and social realities of our time.[351]

This invitation to dialogue has been accepted by several North American theologians who have been greatly influenced by process thought. Besides Cooper, theologians such as John B. Cobb, Jr., David Griffin, Delwin Brown, and Schubert M. Ogden share the belief that an exchange between process and liberation theologies can have mutual benefits.

John B. Cobb, Jr., Ingraham Professor of Theology at the School of Theology at Claremont and Director of the Center for Process Studies, has made his initial contribution to this dialogue with his book *Process Theology as Political Theology* (1982). Cobb takes up the thematic of political theology as a process theologian due to his recognition that "process theologians have lagged far behind in the discussion of Christian responsibility for public affairs, especially as these are politically conceived."[352] Most process studies have remained abstract in comparison to the themes handled by the various liberation theologies and political theology and this is a situation Cobb would like to see altered. As a starting point, Cobb in this book chooses European political theology as conversation partner due to the intellectual nature of political theology, its more immediate transfer value "to the situation of whites in the United States, among whom process theology

---

[351]Burton Cooper, "How Does God Act in Our Time?: An Invitation to a Dialogue between Process and Liberation Theologies," *Union S Q R* 32 (Fall 1976):35. This invitation to dialogue between process and liberation theologies has issued in numerous responses, for example, see the articles in *Process Studies* 14 (Summer 1985):73-181.

[352]John B. Cobb, Jr., *Process Theology as Political Theology* (Philadelphia: Westminster, 1982), p. vii.

so far has its primary home,"[353] and because other process theologians
(e.g., Ogden, D. Brown) have already begun the dialogue with
liberation theologians. The thought of three political theologians—
Jürgen Moltmann, Dorothee Soelle, and especially Johann Baptist
Metz—is therefore chosen by Cobb for primary treatment in this
volume.

While Cobb believes process theology needs to be opened to both the
themes and the concreteness of political theology, the overriding thesis
of this book is that process theology can offer a more adequate
conceptual framework for political theology. Following introductory
chapters on political theology and the "Chicago school" of process
thought, Cobb proceeds to a discussion and eventual process critique of
the method, doctrines of God and eschatology, politics, ecological
awareness, and theology of history in political theology. In each
context Cobb argues that a process perspective can contribute
constructively to a deepening and broadening of the insights of
political theology.

There are some especially salient points not only for the encounter
of process theology with political theology but also for that with
liberation theology as well. These include Cobb's recognition of the
danger that liberation theology be reduced to propaganda when
distanced from an adequate conceptuality;[354] discussion of the idea of
the kingdom of God in political and liberation theologies;[355]
reservations against combining theology with partisan politics in
favor of the task of balanced criticism;[356] and preference for
persuasion rather than violence as a Christian means of social
change.[357] It is, however, above all Cobb's conviction of the relative
adequacy of process conceptuality in comparison to liberation and
political theologies which is the decisive argument of this work.
Whereas liberation theologies have a major contribution to make in
concretizing and localizing theology in a particular context and
whereas political theology assists in theoreticizing the praxis
connection of liberation theology, process theology can offer an even
broader and more comprehensive conceptual framework in which both

---

[353]Ibid., p. viii.

[354]Cf. ibid., pp. 72-73.

[355]Cf. ibid., p. 77.

[356]Cf. ibid., pp. 83-92.

[357]Cf. ibid., pp. 106-108.

of these theologies can better locate themselves.[358] If political theology
can serve as the foundational theology for the praxis-orientation of
liberation theology, then process theology can in turn offer to political
theology its comprehensive philosophical world-view. Such is the
thrust of Cobb's argument.

In *Process Theology as Political Theology* Cobb made reference to
other works from a process perspective which have already dealt more
directly with liberation theology.[359] One of these was the book, *To Set at
Liberty* (1981), by Delwin Brown, Professor of Religious Studies at
Arizona State University. Cobb's "Foreword" to Brown's book offers
some additional and interesting observations about Cobb's
understanding of the significance of liberation theology for the North
American context.

> [W]e must recognize that while liberation theology advances in the Third
> World, First World churches are drawing back from their supportive
> interest. This is equally true of Catholics and Protestants, of Germans
> and North Americans. Churches in the First World are attending to
> increasing demands of their more conservative constituencies and seem
> less and less able to adopt positions that transcend economic and national
> interests. It seems all too likely that in the eighties a politicized Third
> World Christianity will confront a First World church concerned for
> otherworldly salvation and peace of mind and whose political dimension
> is exhausted by its nostalgia for an older morality and its sanctification of
> existing structures of power. . . .
> [M]ost of the response in English-language contexts [has been] of two
> types: one, a largely uncritical adulation, and two, a rather
> condescending dismissal of the central thrust of liberation theology while
> approving of limited contributions. Neither of these responses could have
> much effect upon actual church life in this country.[360]

Given this analysis of the current situation (which tends to confirm the
emphasis on polarization in the North American responses to Latin
American liberation theology to be discussed in the next chapter), Cobb
makes three constructive proposals.[361] First, there needs to be a greater
appropriation of the importance of black theology in the North
American context rather than the mere importation of Latin American
liberation theology. Second, liberation theology must be allowed to
challenge North American thought to reflect upon the total global
situation, yet do so in a way which is fitting to the particularities of life

---

[358]Cf. ibid., pp. 14-16.

[359]Ibid., pp. viii-ix.

[360]John B. Cobb, Jr., "Foreword," in Delwin Brown, *To Set at Liberty.
Christian Faith and Human Freedom* (Maryknoll: Orbis, 1981), p. xi.

[361]Ibid., p. xii.

in the United States. "Third, there is need for a critical appraisal of the more strictly theological achievement of liberation theology."[362] It is into this third category that Cobb's own book falls as well as the volume of Delwin Brown, *To Set at Liberty*.

Brown describes his book as "an essay on freedom."[363] In this respect the direction of his work is not unlike that of Hodgson to whom he makes numerous references throughout the text. Brown argues that the question of freedom in the intensity and fashion in which it is posed today is a peculiarly modern question. His investigation is to explore this modern question of freedom from a particularly Christian perspective and to ask "whether a Christian analysis can provide a basis for, and can strengthen, a secular understanding of freedom and the pursuit of that freedom's realization."[364] In answering this question in the affirmative, Brown finds the conceptuality of process thought, and especially of Alfred North Whitehead, to be extremely valuable in clarifying a number of dilemmas remaining unsolved on the contemporary theological agenda.

In two initial chapters Brown presents and defends his thesis that the question of freedom, unlike any other question, characterizes the modern period and affirms that it is the modern intellectual task to respond to this question as it reflects upon the meaning of the will.[365] Brown finds the changes which took place in the development of the philosophy of Jean Paul Sartre particularly instructive in exploring the nature of freedom. It is, however, the conceptuality of Whitehead which is the most satisfying in resolving the intellectual problems connected with thinking a freedom which is both actually free and yet finite. Brown identifies the two primary elements constituting freedom as creativity and context. Both elements are essential for a definition of freedom which is adequate to its reality. The element of creativity points to the spontaneity, innovativeness, and possibility of newness which belongs to freedom. Context refers to the existing conditions which act to limit the exercise of creativity. Both elements participate continuously in the ongoing processes of nature, life, and history through an infinite series of moments in which ever new and varied resolutions between creativity and context come into existence.

---

[362]Ibid.

[363]Delwin Brown, *To Set at Liberty*, p. xv.

[364]Ibid.

[365]For the following cf. ibid., pp. 3-39.

Brown next addresses the problems raised for the idea of human freedom given in the traditional understanding of God, particularly such ideas as God's unchangeable nature or foreknowledge which tend to trivialize the significance of human freedom.[366] At issue are the various claims which have been made in the tradition to the *aseity* and the *agape* of God. Brown argues for a very definite way of relating these two divine attributes.

> The *aseity* of a loving God cannot be allowed to obscure God's genuine relatedness to the world. Although independent, unconditioned, and absolute in existence and character, God, precisely because that character is constituted as *agape*, is also dependent, conditioned, and related in the concreteness of the divine experience. Moreover, because God is *always* self-constituted—is *a se*—as love, and because love requires an object, it follows that God always needs a world in order to love.[367]

In order to express these affirmations about the divine nature and its relationship to the world, Brown turns to the process conceptuality of freedom to also describe the freedom of God which is likewise composed of the elements of creativity and context. While the divine creativity works unceasingly toward actualizing the freedom latent in the world, the exercise of divine creativity is conditioned by the context in which it operates. This context is marked by the existence of other free beings who can not only choose to cooperate with the divine intention but can also choose to contradict it. Brown describes how such an idea of divine freedom responds to the dilemmas entailed in traditional theological conceptuality. God, in a process conceptuality, acts as "the lure toward freedom" which yet leaves room for the functioning of the freedom of others as well.

In analyzing sin as that which denies the actualization of freedom, Brown develops Reinhold Niebuhr's understanding of anxiety and the traditional understandings of sin as pride and sensuality.[368] Especially pertinent to the insights of liberation theology is Brown's assertion that sensuality as a form of sin may be particularly important today insofar as it expresses itself either as resignation to one's fate (e.g., that one is poor) or as a "habit" of indifference to the world's injustice. Moreover, Brown's discussion of "the social objectifications of sin" in unjust social structures parallels to a large degree the emphasis in liberation theology upon social sinfulness.[369]

---

[366]For the following cf. ibid., pp. 43-63.

[367]Ibid., pp. 49-50.

[368]For the following cf. ibid., pp. 64-87.

[369]See esp. ibid., pp. 78-81.

Brown introduces a number of statistics to concretize what he means by the social objectification of sin. Nevertheless, the final irony is that in spite of an awareness that such structures ought to be changed, "we *willingly remain* in the bondage wherein we unwillingly find ourselves. We wish we were not here, but we choose to stay."[370] The theological symbol which designates the final consequence of human sinfulness in its various manifestations is death.

Brown's Christology explicates the meaning of Christ as the one who offers "the confirmation of freedom."[371] In this context Brown draws extensively from modern scholarship in articulating freedom as the most fitting category to describe the significance of Jesus—his proclamation of the kingdom of God in his proverbs, parables, and person. "The freedom Jesus proclaims and personified" was furthermore given as a gift to those who followed him.[372] His community is thus to be a liberated one, open to all. The freedom given by Jesus also entails an obligation for this community to participate in the freeing of all those held in bondage. This includes the obligation to pursue freedom in the political sphere, though it is not reducible to the political dimension. Brown argues, in a way reminiscent of Hodgson, that the ministry of Jesus most definitely had and has political implications. Anything less atrophies the full meaning of the freedom Jesus offers. In this way Brown is open to the emphasis of liberation theology on a human role in the liberation process.

Even more, Brown argues that in order for the freedom which Jesus brings to be effective today, it is necessary to begin with an analysis of the nature of contemporary bondage and not be limited to seeking freedom from forms of bondage which may or may not address contemporary experience.

> A theology of freedom from *our* bondage must begin with an analysis of our bondage, captivity as it is experienced by us. This means, in the first place, that a description of unfreedom is to be validated, not by its conformity to some authoritative notion of the enslaved experience (not even Paul's notion), but rather by its adequacy to our experience of captivity, reflectively considered.[373]

This means further that Brown affirms the primacy of the fact *that* Jesus brings freedom while the questions of *how* Jesus does so depends on the nature of the bondage under which human beings are currently

---

[370]Ibid., p. 81.

[371]For the following cf. ibid., pp. 88-107.

[372]Ibid., p. 92.

[373]Ibid., p. 100.

suffering. Jesus empowers to freedom under the conditions of bondage prevailing now. The significance of this insight for liberation theology is that attempts to achieve liberation from social structures of injustice in the present are therefore theologically legitimate. The confirmation of the fact that Jesus indeed brings freedom, an affirmation called into radical doubt by Jesus' death on the cross, lies in God's raising Jesus from the dead. The resurrection confirms both that God is a God of freedom and that Jesus is God's agent of that freedom.

It is in the final chapter of Brown's essay on freedom where the positive contributions of liberation theology to a contemporary understanding of salvation are most explicitly recognized.[374] In this chapter Brown traces the historical development in which the kingdom of God proclaimed and personified by Jesus came to be emptied of its significant content in terms of human history. Although Jesus' own unique understanding of the kingdom as both already inbreaking and still not yet fulfilled was in part retained in the shift to a primarily apocalyptic understanding of history in the generations which immediately succeeded him, the significance of the kingdom for history was almost totally obscured when Christian theology came to be interpreted in the individualized and spiritualized categories of Greek philosophy.

> The early Christian hope which, following Judaism, had longed for the renewal of persons in the totality of their relationships—physical, social, political—became a Hellenized longing for the eternal future of the soul in separation from its body and its world.[375]

It is especially in recent times, beginning with the rediscovery of the apocalyptic in the thought of Johannes Weiss and Albert Schweitzer and further developed in the theology of hope, that the original significance of the kingdom of God for history in this world has come to be recaptured. Yet even in the thought of a Moltmann, for example, there remain vestiges of the view which robbed human initiative of its ultimate worth. It is liberation theology in its insistence on the oneness of history which has helped to a large degree in recovering the dynamic significance of the kingdom of God for human history.[376] Liberation theology has done so by reestablishing the importance of human action and the exercise of human freedom for the development of history

---

[374]For the following cf. ibid., pp. 108-133.

[375]Ibid., p. 112.

[376]Cf. ibid., pp. 116-120.

without sacrificing the equally important affirmation of the liberation only God can deliver.

In spite of his appreciation for this major achievement by liberation theology, Brown still notes unclarity in liberation theology's formulation of this indispensable insight into the integral relationship between the renewal of this world and the coming of God's kingdom.

> The point is that in addition to the welcomed breadth of their vision of salvation and their courageous application of this vision to their own concrete circumstances, there is also, if only secondarily, a need for more systematic reflection upon the meaning of that to which they give witness. . . . We mean only to suggest that such a witness to the Word will be strengthened if, in its "critical reflection," a socio-economic and cultural analysis is supplemented with a search for greater conceptual clarity.[377]

Brown finds this more adequate conceptuality in the categories of process thought derived from Whitehead. His constructive proposal therefore consists in a process understanding of the interchange between the often stifled but real possibilities of human freedom (cf. Niebuhr's critique of historical optimism) and the activity of God in luring history toward ever greater realizations of freedom. In this conceptuality, history remains open to innovation and progress while taking seriously that the intention of God for the attainment of freedom can either be assisted or hindered by the human will. The possibility that human efforts at liberation may finally undermine the actual attainment of a higher level of freedom does not negate the task itself. The future remains open both to failure and success. God wills, however, that freedom reign as has been confirmed in the reality of Jesus. For Brown, this vision coincides with the Bible's own hope for the future of human history.

Delwin Brown represents an additional North American response to liberation theology in which the achievements of liberation theology are appreciated while continuing to call for the development of a more adequate conceptual framework. He, like Cobb, argues that this conceptuality is available in the constructs of process thought. By setting forth this constructive proposal he invites response from representatives of liberation theology in order that the dialogue between North American theology and the Latin American theology of liberation might continue.

---

[377]Ibid., p. 121.

4. Schubert M. Ogden

Professor of Theology at Perkins School of Theology and Director
of the Graduate Program in Religious Studies at Southern Methodist
University, Schubert M. Ogden has set forth as a primary line of
argumentation in his published writings the need for theology to
undertake a consistent program of demythologizing.[378] This means
theology should carry forward the basic program of Rudolf Bultmann,
going beyond him, however, in continuing to demythologize the
mythological remnants which abide in Bultmann's thought and
translating the entirety of theology's content into non-supernatural,
non-mythological categories.[379] In pursuit of this goal Ogden has
called for the rigorous use of reason, self-consistency, and logic in
theological argument, criteria which he himself has applied in his own
theological writings. Like Cobb, D. Brown and others, Ogden has
found in process philosophy useful conceptual categories to assist him
in carrying out this program, especially in considering the doctrine
most central to his theology, the doctrine of God. Once again with
Ogden, the openness of process theologians for liberation theology is
documented, although again with a plea for greater conceptual clarity
in its theological formulations.

A preliminary understanding of Ogden's critical response to
liberation theology can be gained by examining Ogden's very
definition of the theological task and particularly the dual criteria he
has established to measure the adequacy of theological statements.

> Because theological understanding itself must therefore be correlative in
> structure, it is subject to assessment by dual criteria of adequacy, which
> are likewise variable as well as constant in their specific requirements;
> accordingly, to be assessed as adequate, a theological statement must meet
> the two criteria of appropriateness and understandability as these may
> require in the given situation.[380]

By "appropriate" Ogden means that a theological statement must
accurately represent the same understanding of faith belonging to the
original Christian kerygma. By "understandable" he means it must
be communicated in language which is both existentially and
metaphysically meaningful in addressing the human condition.

---

[378]Cf. the programmatic proposals in Schubert M. Ogden, *The Reality of
God. And Other Essays* (New York: Harper & Row, 1966), p. 20.

[379]Cf. Schubert M. Ogden, *Christ Without Myth: A Study Based on the
Theology of Rudolf Bultmann* (New York: Harper & Row, 1961).

[380]Schubert M. Ogden, "What Is Theology?" *J Rel* 52 (1972):25 (italics
deleted).

These criteria become important for the present discussion as they are applied by Ogden to the formulations of liberation theology.

Ogden's basic openness to the concerns of a liberation theology can already be traced in the writings which predate the formal emergence of the Latin American theology of liberation. Thus in an essay published in 1967, Ogden wrote:

> But no less clear is the response of Christian faith to the presence of genuine freedom, whether of the heart or of the mind, wherever it encounters such freedom. Because faith knows that the God revealed to it is the great emancipator of mankind—not only of Christians but *of every child of man*—it cannot but note the presence and working of that God wherever men are free and engaged in the one task worthy of men: the task of witnessing by word and deed to the great movement of emancipation that is how God functions in human life.[381]

Ogden here affirms God's functioning in human life to work "emancipation." The basic correspondence with liberation theology's insistence upon human liberation is clear. However, within this apparent correspondence are also contained the seeds for an important critique by Ogden of liberation theology: that human participation in God's work of emancipation is theologically subsequent to the redemptive work of God in setting humans free to undertake that task. This distinction is one of several Ogden would seek conceptually clarified by liberation theology.

Ogden has responded directly to Latin American liberation theology and its theologians in a variety of contexts.[382] Most important of these is his book *Faith and Freedom. Toward a Theology of Liberation* (1979) in which Ogden elaborates an understanding of the relationship of liberation theology to the rest of contemporary theology, a fourfold critique of liberation theology, and his own proposals for a liberation theology more adequately conceived. Interestingly Ogden does not stress liberation theology as a "new way of doing theology" as the Latin Americans themselves have frequently done, but rather he places liberation thought among the contemporary currents of liberal

---

[381]Schubert M, Ogden, "How God Functions in Human Life?" *Chr Cris* 27 (May 15, 1967):108.

[382]For example, cf. his contribution to the discussions of the 1973 Faith and Order Conference of the Texas Conference of Churches and especially the critique of Juan Luis Segundo's *The Community Called Church* contained therein, in Schubert M. Ogden, "The Gospel We Hold in Common—Or Do We?" 35 pp. (unpublished manuscript); his review of Jon Sobrino's *Christology at the Crossroads: A Latin American Approach* in *Perkins J* 31 (1978): 47-49; and his contribution to the symposium on "Theological Education and Liberation Theology" in Schubert M. Ogden, "Response," *Th Ed* 16 (Autumn 1979):48-50.

theology.[383]   More specifically, it is expressive of one particular
subphase of the liberal project, namely "social Christianity" or the
"social gospel." Ogden interprets liberation theology in terms of
continuity with the liberal tradition. Yet one vital difference separates
this theological perspective from its antecedents which likewise sought
the meaning of theology for social action and the pursuit of justice.
Liberation theologies are an achievement, not of the advocates of the
poor and oppressed, but rather of these groups themselves.

> [W]hereas the social gospel, after all, was typically a movement from
> within the relatively advantaged human group to take account of the
> differing historical situations and needs of persons belonging to
> disadvantaged groups, the theologies of liberation are typically
> movements within the disadvantaged groups themselves to provide a
> theological self-interpretation of their own situations and needs.[384]

Arising out of the context of the "disadvantaged," these theologies raise
a challenge to any theology which strives to be adequate according to
the dual criteria of appropriateness and understandability.[385]
However, due to certain deficiencies, the current theologies of
liberation challenge theologians to work out "a still more adequate
theology of liberation than any of them has yet achieved."[386]

While Ogden appreciates the "successes" of liberation theologies,
e.g., their liberal theological outlook and their profound concern for
action and justice, nevertheless according to the criteria of adequacy
already cited, some crucial "failures" yet mar them.[387]   Ogden
concisely identifies four of these failures. First, according to the
criteria of appropriateness and understandability, liberation
theologies are typically more a form of witness than they are theology
proper. "The evidence for this is that they tend rather to be the
rationalization of positions already taken than the process or the
product of critical reflection on those positions."[388]   Although Ogden
recognizes this is a charge which may be applicable to many other
theologies as well, he nevertheless believes it applies to liberation
theologies. Ogden argues that liberation theologians have not been
critical enough in testing the veracity of the Christian witness; rather

---

[383]For the following cf. Schubert M. Ogden, *Faith and Freedom. Toward a
Theology of Liberation* (Nashville: Abingdon, 1979), pp.18-25.

[384]Ibid., pp. 23-24.

[385]For the following cf. ibid., pp. 25-32.

[386]Ibid., p. 32.

[387]For the following cf. ibid., pp. 32-39.

[388]Ibid., p. 33.

they have simply assumed its claims are true. This leaves them
vulnerable to the charge of an ideological use of theology.

A second failure of liberation theologies is their insufficient
reflection on the metaphysical being of God in favor of a focus on God's
existential meaning. The emphasis on the ethical and the existential
aspects of the Christian faith does not, however, excuse theology as
theology from articulating the critical concepts by which the Christian
faith's talk of God can be expressed in an intellectually adequate way.
This requires critical metaphysical deliberation on the meaning of
God. Theology proper cannot avoid this task simply by appealing to
existential and practical relevance.

The third and perhaps most significant failure of liberation
theology is, according to Ogden, its confusion of two interrelated yet
distinct forms of liberation, i.e., redemption and emancipation.
Although the same God indeed functions both as Redeemer and
Emancipator, these two works of God must for theological purposes be
distinguished from one another. The redemptive work of God in
overcoming sin and death needs to be differentiated from God's work
in emancipating from political, economic, cultural, racial, or sexual
bondage. In fact the redemptive work of God must, on the basis of the
apostolic witness, be given a certain priority, although it ought not be
separated from works of emancipation which flow from the reality of
redemption. Ogden devotes a major portion of his attention in the
remainder of the book to a clarification of this issue.

Finally, the fourth failure of liberation theologies is their too
limited understanding of the diverse forms bondage can assume. The
idea of bondage is not reducible to any of the concrete forms currently
championed by the various liberation theologies, although they give
expression to certain aspects of what is meant by bondage. Ogden
would argue for a more comprehensive definition of bondage than he
perceives is currently functional among theologies of liberation.

Following these critical remarks, Ogden proceeds to offer his own
proposal for a theology of liberation which answers the failures he has
noted.[389] In a chapter entitled "Faith as the Existence of Freedom: In
Freedom and For Freedom," Ogden first argues that the ultimate norm
of Christian theology be located in what he calls the "Jesus-kerygma,"
that is, the very earliest stratum of kerygma witnessing to Jesus which
can be reconstructed by historical critical investigation. Next Ogden

---

[389]For the following cf. ibid., pp. 43-65.

argues that theological reflection, properly understood, consists primarily in the explication of the existential meaning of religious statements. This task implies furthermore the need for reflection on the metaphysical being of God who is the ultimate legitimation of all such statements. Given these preliminary considerations Ogden then will examine both the existential meaning of God and the metaphysical being of God and relate these examinations to the issues involved in a more adequate theology of liberation. By focusing on the reality of God as the key issue also for liberation theology, Ogden returns the discussion to the theological problem he has repeatedly defended as the most crucial one of all for contemporary theology, that is, the problem of God.[390]

Christian existence is, according to Ogden, existence *in* and *for* freedom. The apparent contradiction in the New Testament between Paul and James over the relationship of faith and works reflects the tension between these two aspects of freedom and, finally, the need to affirm both of them as rightly belonging to Christian freedom. Still, in the apostolic witness, and especially as it was explicated by the Reformers, a priority is given to existence *in* freedom *through* "trust in the promise of God's love declared to us in Jesus Christ."[391] By existence "in" freedom, Ogden means something more than belief "about" God. Christian existence means existence in the freedom God gives in Jesus Christ. This freedom includes both freedom *from* all things other than the love of God when determining the ultimate meaning of life and freedom *for* the love and service of others. Ogden calls upon Luther's treatise *The Freedom of a Christian* in further exemplifying what is meant by a freedom which is both a freedom from and a freedom for. Ogden summarizes the discussion this way:

> [F]aith in God is indeed the existence of freedom in the twofold sense that it is both existence *in* freedom and existence *for* freedom. Because faith is utter trust in God's love as well as utter loyalty to him and his cause, it is both the negative freedom *from* all things and the positive freedom *for* all things—to love and to serve them by so speaking and acting as to respond to all their creaturely needs. In this respect faith is existence *in* freedom, and so a *liberated* existence—an existence liberated by God's redeeming love. But because faith is utter loyalty to God and his cause as well as utter trust in him, it is also existence *for* freedom, and so also a *liberating* existence— an existence devoted to so bearing witness to God's love by all that we say

---

[390]Cf. esp. the programmatic essay, "The Reality of God," in Ogden, *The Reality of God*, pp. 1-70.

[391]Ogden, *Faith and Freedom*, p. 53.

and do as to optimize the limits of other's freedom in whatever ways this can be done.[392]

Ogden believes such conceptual clarity between freedom "in" and freedom "for" would be a real gain for liberation theology.

In the following chapter entitled "God as the Ground of Freedom: The Redeemer and the Emancipator," Ogden directs his attention to an understanding of the nature of God as the ground of freedom.[393] Due to other priorities, liberation theologies have neglected for the most part "the questions of fundamental theology concerning the concept and existence of God, and even more properly systematic questions of the being and action of God."[394] By neglecting these questions they presuppose the constructs of classical metaphysics, however, and thereby also inherit the inherent liabilities of that metaphysics. It is here that Ogden, like Cobb and D. Brown, would introduce process metaphysics in order to supply liberation theology the conceptual categories for fulfilling this remaining task. The idea of freedom as it is expressed in a process understanding of God which simultaneously allows for the existence of other forms of freedom is defended by Ogden as a conceptuality more adequate than that of classical theism.

In applying this process understanding of God to the twofold idea of freedom as "freedom in" and "freedom for" already elaborated, Ogden arrives at a twofold affirmation about God—God is the Redeemer and God is the Emancipator. By virtue of the process conceptuality redemption becomes "the unique process of God's self-actualization, whereby he creatively synthesizes all other things into his own actual being as God."[395] Redemption involves the fact of God's unbounded acceptance of others. Such redemption works salvation when God's acceptance of others is not rejected by them (sin) but rather accepted. Redemption is, moreover, God's work and God's work alone. This work is to be differentiated from the second aspect of God's work, that of emancipation, in which human beings do have a participatory role.

In process terminology Ogden explains this difference as follows:

> It belongs to this concept that God is to be conceived not only as the one to whom all things make a difference—or, in theological terms, as the Redeemer—but also as the one who himself makes a difference to all

---

[392]Ibid., p. 64.

[393]For the following cf. ibid., pp. 69-95.

[394]Ibid., p. 71. The one notable exception mentioned by Ogden is Juan Luis Segundo's *Our Idea of God* which he also critiques.

[395]Ibid., p. 83.

things, the one whose own self-creation in response to his creatures in part determines all of their self-creations by optimizing the limits of their free decisions.[396]

For process theology God functions to maximize the possibility that freedom will take place. In the work of emancipation, unlike the work of redemption, God's creatures are able to make use of their own finite freedom to cooperate with God in, for example, achieving higher levels of justice. It is here that liberation theologies have made their greatest contribution according to Ogden's schema. They have pointed toward the need for structural change in unjust social systems and called those most affected to become active agents in changing these structures instead of merely submitting as passive objects. Even more, a process conceptuality calls all God's creatures to join God in taking "sides with the oppressed against all who oppress them."[397] Interestingly Ogden does not rule out the use of force for achieving this end, although he remains cautious in suggesting the limits of this possibility.

The final chapter of *Faith and Freedom* deals with what Ogden calls "Subtler Forms of Bondage and Liberation."[398] Not only can a process conceptuality assist in distinguishing between the two different processes of redemption and emancipation contained in the term liberation, it can also uncover other forms of bondage obscured in present theologies of liberation. Most especially this means for Ogden moving beyond a homocentric approach which is forgetful of the bondage under which nature also suffers. Ogden rejects a homocentrism which issues in a dualism between nature and history. He offers process metaphysics as a resource for a more holistic understanding of the need not only for human liberation but also for the liberation of nature from human manipulation and the disastrous environmental consequences resulting therefrom.

An "emancipation of theology" can only result when theology undertakes the critical task of seriously reflecting on the truth of the Christian witness and not merely rationalizing on the basis of that witness. Thus far liberation theologies have not sufficiently undertaken this critical task in their advocacy of a liberation praxis. Ogden summons all of theology, including liberation theologies, to the more rigorously critical approach which lies at the heart of the liberal

---

[396]Ibid., p. 88.

[397]Ibid., p. 94.

[398]For the following cf. ibid., pp. 99-124.

theological project. This can be achieved only by submitting theological method to the test of adequacy under the dual criteria of appropriateness and understandability. By avoiding this methodological rigor, theology, including liberation theology, is little more than rationalization. Only a critical theology which also relentlessly asks about the truth of its claims can ultimately be of lasting value to the praxis which liberation theologies strive to engender. Unless this level of critical reflection is attained, theologies of liberation themselves remain in a kind of bondage to their own presuppositions.

Ogden's proposals for a more adequate conceptuality for liberation theology have not gone without critical comment.[399] Nevertheless, Ogden has continued to defend his definition of the critical theological task under the dual criteria of adequacy against what he perceives to be the danger that liberation theologies become "the mere rationalization of positions already taken."[400] Yet at the same time that Ogden argues that the formal definition of theology should not be coopted into an advocacy position which neglects the critical question of truth, Ogden still believes that the exigencies of the present historical context do require the material content of theology to, insofar as it is critically demonstrable, assume the form of a liberation theology.[401] What is more, Ogden believes the fundamental concerns of a liberation theology are indeed critically demonstrable.

In many ways Ogden's own book *The Point of Christology* (1982) itself attempts to supply a critical demonstration that the Jesus-kerygma does allow for the construction of a theology of liberation.

---

[399]For example, cf. Dorothee Soelle, "'Thou Shalt Have No Other Jeans Before Me' (Levi's Advertisement, Early Seventies): The Need for Liberation in a Consumerist Society," in Brian Mahan and L. Dale Richeson, eds., *The Challenge of Liberation Theology. A First World Response* (Maryknoll: Orbis, 1981), esp. pp. 10-14; Elisabeth Schüssler Fiorenza, "Toward a Feminist Biblical Hermeneutics: Biblical Interpretation and Liberation Theology," in Mahan and Richeson, eds., *The Challenge of Liberation Theology*, esp. pp. 94-95, 100, and 107; and James H. Cone, "A Critical Response to Schubert Ogden's *Faith and Freedom: Toward a Theology of Liberation*," *Perkins J* 33 (Fall 1979): 51-55. Ogden has replied directly to Fiorenza's criticisms in a paper delivered at a symposium on "Women and the Canon" held at Perkins School of Theology, February 5-6, 1980, entitled "Women and the Canon: A Response to Elisabeth Schüssler Fiorenza," 3 pp. (unpublished manuscript).

[400]Schubert M. Ogden, "The Concept of a Theology of Liberation: Must a Christian Theology Today Be So Conceived?" in Mahan and Richeson, eds., *The Challenge of Liberation Theology*, p. 134.

[401]Cf. ibid., pp. 135-139.

The evidence for this assertion is only introduced, however, after Ogden first thoroughly analyzes what is really intended in making Christological claims. It is important at this point to recall Ogden's overall theological program to provide a consistently demythologized interpretation of Christian truth. This program of consistent demythologizing also stands behind Ogden's proposals for a revisionist Christology.[402] This means in Ogden's analysis that behind the initial Christological question, "Who is Jesus?," two other questions are indicated: "Who is God?" and, even more basic, the existential question, "Who am I?"[403] The Christological question becomes in this way the religious question, i.e., the question about the ultimate meaning of life and the ultimate reality which both warrants a claim to ultimate meaning and undergirds both morality and metaphysics. Insofar as the Christological question is posed in relationship to Jesus, it is furthermore not only a question about ultimate reality but also an historical question about Jesus. Such are the parameters of the Christological question explored by Ogden.

As he had already briefly asserted in *Faith and Freedom*, Ogden argues here at greater length, following Willi Marxsen, that it is the earliest Jesus-kerygma which serves as "the subject of the Christological assertion."[404] This is the case due to the fact that while knowledge about the historical Jesus himself is theologically desirable for norming Christology, such knowledge is not accessible on the basis of the available historical sources. It is "the existential-historical Jesus" who emerges from the earliest Christian kerygma and who therefore grounds all Christological statements. Ogden contends, furthermore, that this earliest Christian witness to Jesus is sufficient and appropriate for norming Christology.

Having identified the Christological "subject" as the earliest accessible Christian witness to Jesus, Ogden proceeds to identify the Christological "predicate."[405] Once again the nature of the available historical sources make impossible any grounding of this predicate in the being of Jesus himself and his own self-understanding, no matter how desirable such a grounding might be theoretically. What is possible is to recognize that the necessary and sufficient basis for

---

[402]Cf. Schubert M. Ogden, *The Point of Christology* (San Francisco: Harper & Row, 1982), p. 11.

[403]Cf. ibid., pp. 22-30.

[404]For the following cf. ibid., pp. 41-63.

[405]For the following cf. ibid., pp. 64-85.

asserting a Christological predicate today is the same as it was for the various writings of the New Testament: the claim "that he is the decisive re-presentation of God, in the sense of the one through whom the meaning of God for us is made fully explicit."[406] By formulating the problem in this way Ogden places the burden of truth not on the recovery of Jesus' own self-understanding but on the veracity of the claims made for Jesus according to that which is ultimately real. Do the claims made for Jesus and the God he represents provide finally the ultimate answer to the human quest for authentic existence, or do they not? This means that verification of the Christological predicate involves more than historical inquiry into the historical Jesus. It requires, even more essentially, both metaphysical inquiry into the very nature of ultimate reality and also moral inquiry into the manner of life which is consistent with that which is affirmed to be ultimately real.

It is the remaining chapters of *The Point of Christology* which have the most immediate relevance for liberation theology. Ogden begins by asking how the point of Christology, i.e., the question about ultimate reality which makes a claim on us through the Jesus-kerygma, is to be made credible in the modern period.[407] Ogden characterizes the modern period under two aspects: (1) the modern quest for freedom and (2) the modern scientific world-view. Modern theologies have, however, for the most part recognized only the challenge of the modern scientific world-view and the accompanying secular culture in making their formulations. Liberation theologies have, however, poignantly raised the other aspect to prominence. Ogden cites Gutierrez here to make the point that it is not just the "non-believer" who poses a challenge to Christian theology but rather the "non-person," the one existing under conditions of economic, social, political, and cultural degradation who also poses inescapable questions to theology.

For this reason Ogden proposes that an appropriate method must be developed to respond to these issues, a method of "deideologizing" and political interpretation, which parallels the method of demythologizing developed in response to the challenge of the scientific world-view.

By "deideologizing" I mean the method of so interpreting the meaning of the christology of witness as to disengage it from the economic, social,

---

[406]Ibid., p. 77.

[407]For the following cf. ibid., pp. 86-105.

political, and cultural world whose injustices it is used, negatively if not positively, to sanction.[408]

Through deideologizing, Ogden seeks to counteract all ideological tendencies which would rationalize the particular interests of some at the expense of others. Together the two methodological approaches, demythologizing and deideologizing, must not only make understandable the Christological witness but must continue to conform to the criterion of appropriateness to the original witness as well. While the criterion of credibility (earlier called by Ogden the criterion of understandability) today requires a method of deideologizing to complement the method of demythologizing, the criterion of appropriateness requires conformity to the earliest apostolic witness as its norm.

On the basis of the two criteria of adequacy—credibility and appropriateness—Ogden will next make a contribution to the development of what he calls "a christology of liberation."[409] In so doing Ogden wants to incorporate the primary concern of liberation theologies for secular freedom within a more comprehensive understanding of Christian freedom. This is indeed a legitimate possibility, according to Ogden, through the understanding of freedom contained in the New Testament, especially in Paul and John, and finally through the earliest kerygmatic witness to Jesus. Even a "minimalist" position in interpreting the Jesus material of the New Testament provides sufficient warrant for grounding a Christology of liberation. Through the kerygmatic witness to Jesus as an eschatological prophet and teacher, one can unmistakably discern his witness to the God of boundless love. Ogden expresses this point through the summary statement, "Jesus meant love."[410] But that is not all that may be said about Jesus. With Ernst Käsemann and others, Ogden goes on to explain how the Jesus who meant love is also the Jesus who meant freedom.

> [T]he claim is commonly made that Jesus not only meant freedom by proclaiming the liberating love of God and summoning his hearers to live in the freedom of God's children but himself also lived in such freedom, to the extent, indeed, of perfectly actualizing it in his own life. . . . But even if one argues, as I have argued earlier, that any such claim about Jesus' own perfect freedom is as theologically unnecessary as it is historically

[408]Ibid., p. 94.
[409]For the following cf. ibid., pp. 106-126.
[410]Cf. ibid., pp. 118-120.

impossible, one can still join in affirming that the meaning of Jesus for us
is precisely the possibility of the existence of freedom.[411]

Because "Jesus means freedom," a "christology of liberation that is
demanded today by the pervasive concern for freedom is no less
clearly supported by the apostolic witness."[412]   Both criteria of
adequacy are therefore satisfied.

Having defended the thesis that a Christology of liberation is
historically warranted by the apostolic witness, Ogden also seeks to
argue for the metaphysical credibility of such a Christology.[413] Ogden
states his own growing appreciation for the value of analogy, metaphor,
and symbolic language in carrying forth metaphysical affirmations
about God. It is therefore a "symbolic metaphysical" argument in
defense of the assertion, "God is boundless love," that Ogden would
now propose in undergirding his Christology of liberation.

The final problem Ogden addresses involves the practical
application of a Christology of liberation to the demands being made
for liberation in the present historical context.[414] How is it possible to
bridge the gap between the freedom which Jesus offers and the concrete
call for freedom in our time? Ogden responds to those, like Edward R.
Norman and Wolfhart Pannenberg who have criticized liberation
theologies for their politicizing of Christianity, by arguing for an
interpretation of the kingdom of God which neither identifies it with
politics nor totally separates it from political responsibility.[415]

In an argument which in many respects parallels his discussion
in *Faith and Freedom*, Ogden would distinguish between the freedom
given in Christ Jesus ultimately grounded in the love of God for all
creatures, and the freedom which seeks justice for the neighbor in the
world. Nevertheless, these two different forms of freedom should not be
separated from one another even though they remain distinguishable.
Rather, even as God's love for his creatures is a boundless love, so also
the love of God's creatures for one another should reflect the
boundlessness of God's own love. Applying this insight to a world
where injustice yet remains, this means "that the moral implications
of Christian freedom are always to seek justice, in the broad sense of so
acting toward all others as to secure what is due them—to meet any and

---

[411] Ibid., p. 122.

[412] Ibid., pp. 125-126.

[413] For the following cf. ibid., pp. 127-147.

[414] For the following cf. ibid., pp. 148-168.

[415] Cf. ibid., pp. 151-164.

all of their real human needs and thus to realize the whole of their
human good."[416] This does not mean that the modern quest for the
attainment of justice is itself authorized by the historical Jesus (cf.
Sobrino). But it does mean that there exists a moral responsibility in
the modern context in which significant numbers are affected by
unjust political and social structures to advocate and participate in the
transformation of those structures.

> The conclusion to which the argument leads, then, is that the freedom we
> have in Christ Jesus implies our specifically political responsibility for the
> achievement of secular freedom. Actually, the implication here is
> twofold. For if Christian freedom means that there should be justice, and
> hence freedom and equality, throughout society and culture, it also means
> that the majority who are more the victims than the agents of society's
> decisions have the *right* to demand such freedom and equality, even as the
> minority who are more the agents than the victims of the same decisions
> have the *responsibility* to help the majority to achieve this right. Thus,
> although the two kinds of freedom are different and never to be identified,
> they are also conjoined and never to be separated—not at least by modern
> Christians like ourselves, now that we have become conscious of our proper
> human role as agents of history who bear full responsibility for the whole
> social and cultural order.[417]

By distinguishing between these two forms of freedom while
continuing to insist on their necessary interrelatedness, Ogden seeks
to contribute to the clarification of a crucial problem which has led to
increasing polarization between liberation theologies and their critics.
The final measure of the credibility of a Christology of liberation thus
becomes for Ogden the degree to which "we ourselves, as individuals
and as the community called church, also live up to the demand that it
strictly implies—by involving ourselves in the ongoing struggles for
basic justice, in solidarity with all who suffer from the oppressions of
the existing order or are working to overcome them. To do anything
less than this is to leave room for the question whether the freedom we
have in Christ Jesus is not ideological, after all, whatever the
conclusion of our christology of reflection."[418]

---

[416]Ibid., p. 159.
[417]Ibid., pp. 163-164.
[418]Ibid., p. 167.

With the publication of *The Point of Christology* Ogden has further
demonstrated his growing concern not only for a theology which
responds to the modern secular challenge to the meaningfulness of the
Christian witness but also his concern for a theology which
appropriately and credibly serves the cause of liberation.[419] This has
been done by a rigorous application of the results of modern biblical
and theological scholarship to what he sees as the outstanding issues
and problems of contemporary liberation theologies. With Migliore,
Hodgson, Cobb, and D. Brown, Ogden has in this way attempted to raise
the current discussion of liberation theology to a *niveau* beyond the
polarity of either apologetics for or negative rejection of liberation
theology, toward the construction of a more adequate theological
conceptuality.[420]

---

[419]Cf. his personal reflections on the development of his theology in
Schubert M. Ogden, "Faith and Freedom," *Chr Cent* 97 (Dec. 17, 1980): 1241-
1244.

[420]Among other North American theologians who have raised critical
questions of liberation theology, several merit recognition and brief comment
for their contributions to the discussion. Several responses deal with the method
of liberation theology. David Tracy, for example, in *Blessed Rage for Order.
The New Pluralism in Theology* (New York: Seabury, 1975), esp. pp. 244-248,
asks whether liberation theology has not underestimated the problematic nature
of Christian symbols in the modern period. He therefore challenges liberation
theology to a more sophisticated consideration of its own methodological
approach especially with regard to the questions posed by modernity to the very
meaningfulness of Christian symbols which are often presupposed to be true by
liberation theology. These methodological issues are further broadened and
deepened in his *The Analogical Imagination. Christian Theology and the
Culture of Pluralism* (New York: Crossroad, 1981), esp. pp. 69-79 and 390-398.
Here Tracy examines the importance of a praxis-oriented theology in the
present theological situation as a complement to manifestation-oriented and
proclamation-oriented theologies.
    Charles R. Strain has proposed an interpretation of liberation theology
which identifies its characteristics and functions in analogy to secular
ideologies. Following Ogden and Tracy, Strain furthermore argues for the
need for a more extensive set of criteria for evaluating liberation theologies. To
the criteria of "appropriateness" and "adequacy" articulated by Ogden and
Tracy, Strain adds that of "dialectical inclusiveness," meaning the ability of
one particular liberation theology to also incorporate the particular perspectives
of other liberation theologies as well. See Charles R. Strain, "Ideology and
Alienation: Theses on the Interpretation and Evaluation of Theologies of
Liberation," *J A A R* 45 (Dec. 1977):473-490.
    Also raising questions about the method of liberation theology, from its
understanding of the theological task to its critique of academic theology, is
Robert T. Osborn, "Some Problems of Liberation Theology: A Polanyian
Perspective," *J A A R* 51 (Mar. 1983):79-95. The methodological problems

Osborn raises are subsequently addressed by him in a constructive way borrowing from Michael Polanyi's theory of knowledge.

A different line of criticism has been indicated by M. Douglas Meeks, "God's Suffering Power and Liberation," *J Rel Thot* 33 (Fall-Winter 1976): 44-54, who proposes the need for deeper reflection by liberation theology on the trinitarian nature of God in order to ground liberation theology's identification with those who suffer in the very suffering of God. The temptation of liberation theology to adopt a concept of power alien to the Christian understanding can thus be checked through measuring it against the power of the God who suffers on the cross.

Finally, a pacifist critique has been directed at liberation theology by a few North American pacifist thinkers. Gordon C. Zahn, "The Bondage of Liberation: A Pacifist Reflection," *Worldview* 20 (Mar. 1977): 20-24, has in this way questioned liberation theology's tendencies to reduce and minimize the traditional just war criteria, to aggravate rather than improve the condition of the oppressed through an elitist understanding of conscienticization, and to nurture the idea of nationalism which finally inhibits the attainment of peace with justice. The most well-known of North American pacifist theologians, John Howard Yoder, likewise makes numerous critical references to the problematic of violent revolution in his writings which have relevance in light of the openness of some Latin American liberation theologians to the option for revolutionary violence as a means of social change. Among Yoder's most pertinent titles are *The Original Revolution. Essays on Christian Pacifism* (Scottdale, PA: Herald Press, 1971), *The Politics of Jesus. Vicit Agnus Noster* (Grand Rapids: Eerdmans, 1972), and *When War Is Unjust. Being Honest in Just-War Thinking* (Minneapolis: Augsburg, 1984). What is actually quite surprising, however, in the literature on Latin American liberation theology is how infrequently the critique of violence as a means of social change appears from the side of North American theologians.

PART THREE:

CRITICAL ANALYSIS

Chapter Five

Critical Analysis of an Intercontinental Theological Disputation

The Latin verb "*disputare*" means "to debate, discuss, argue; literally to reckon up." The intercontinental discourse concerning liberation theology has involved all of the above. The responses presented in the preceding two chapters amply document the discussion, debate, and arguments which have been set forth in the North American context in recent years. This final chapter deals more directly with the literal meaning of *disputare* indicated above, that is, "to reckon up." What assessment can be made of the diverse—indeed conflicting—opinions and arguments presented with regard to Latin American liberation theology on the North American continent in the last two decades? Which issues emerge warranting further clarification and constructive work?

Through a critical analysis of the North American arguments pro and especially con Latin American liberation theology, this chapter proposes that the North American discussion of liberation theology calls for a twofold conclusion:

1. That certain limitations in method and theological formula-tion require further reflection and clarification on the part of liberation theology. Most important among these, according to the present analysis, are the questions of liberation theology's relation to philosophy, its theological method, its theological anthropology, and its concept of liberation.

2. That a praxis-oriented liberation theology is, given the histori-cal, political, socioeconomic, and cultural dimensions of Latin American reality, a highly significant and valid theological proposal. While the Latin American plausibility structure provides the primary condition for Latin American liberation theology, the biblical witness and Christian tradition provide a legitimate warrant for the fundamental formulations of liberation theology.

The major portion of this chapter is devoted to elaborating and defending this twofold conclusion.

There remains, however, another pressing issue facing the intercontinental discussion of liberation theology. That issue is the tendency toward an extreme polarization of viewpoints which often inhibits and even prevents reasoned discourse of the relevant issues. Several of the dynamics of this tendency toward polarization are to be examined next, together with some basic suggestions for counteracting this negative tendency. Only in moving beyond polarization can the international disputation of liberation theology evolve in the direction of creative dialogue rather than degenerate in the direction of an uncritical espousal of preestablished positions.

A. *The Impasse of Polarization*
1. The Dynamics of Polarization

"Are you for liberation theology or against it?" In discussing most contemporary theological positions, e.g., those of Barth, Tillich, or Rahner, such an oversimplified query would be quickly passed over in favor of an examination of the relevant arguments and an appraisal of the relative gains and liabilities of a particular position.   There occasionally arises a theological issue, however, in which such a "passing over" proves to be virtually impossible. In the recent past in North America such issues have included the virtual impasse between liberals and fundamentalists regarding the use of "higher" historical criticism as a method of biblical interpretation and that between traditional and radical theologians over the "death" of God. In the present such an impasse threatens to engulf the entire North American discussion of liberation theology. Why is this so?

It is not enough to account for the polarization of positions around liberation theology by referring to the inevitable resistance afforded every form of innovation, although to a certain degree this too may play a role. Instead there appear to be a number of factors both conscious and perhaps also unconscious which contribute to the dynamics of polarization. An initial factor would have to be the sometimes brazen claims which have been made for liberation theology both by the liberation theologians themselves and by their interpreters especially in its earliest period of development.   The claims made by this "upstart" theology for the renewal of theology and church and even for a prophetic mission have been met with skepticism by those who have learned that claims in themselves mean very little until they have been thoroughly examined and put to the test.

Another key factor contributing to polarization from the side of liberation theology has been its sharp critique of the Western philosophical and theological tradition, in particular the latter as it has been identified as "academic" theology. Those who have invested their lives in the pursuit of an intellectually responsible academic theology with its respective methods and modes of reflection can make claim to a long and respected tradition for their discipline.[1] For this reason liberation theology's critique of this tradition appears in part presumptuous. However, insofar as this critique has been made by liberation theology, a critique which calls in question not only the discipline of academic theology but also accuses theologians engaged in such an academic theology of themselves performing an ideological function in supporting an unjust international social order, the stage has been set less for dialogue than for the polemics which have been consequently acted out on numerous occasions.

There is yet another level on which the critique of liberation theologians has contributed to the dynamics of polarization, that is, its critique of the role of the United States in perpetuating poverty in Latin America and supporting authoritarian regimes unresponsive to the needs of the majority of the population. Such a critique implicates theologians of the United States on a level which reaches deep into their identity, an identity which goes beyond their identity as theologians. Liberation theology's use of certain Marxist categories, particularly that of class conflict, and their advocacy of socialism stir up an anticommunist sentiment which has deep roots in the American psyche.

The sociologist Robert Bellah has explicated as an integral component of American civil religion what he calls "the American taboo on socialism."[2] The connotations of socialism in American culture summon forth images of the "foreign" and "alien;" of "collectivism" as opposed to the hearty individualism of American belief; and of the atheistic and "antireligious." Such a taboo on socialism has, moreover, been intensified once again in the decade of the eighties. The return to prominence of the main themes of American civil religion under the influence of what has been called

---

[1]Cf. Wolfhart Pannenberg, *Theology and the Philosophy of Science*, trans. Francis McDonagh (Philadelphia: Westminster, 1976), esp. pp. 228-296 and Gerhard Ebeling, *The Study of Theology*, trans. Duane A. Priebe (Philadelphia: Fortress, 1978).

[2]Robert N. Bellah, *The Broken Covenant. American Civil Religion in Time of Trial* (New York: Seabury, 1975), pp. 112-138.

the "New Right" has even been heralded as a "fourth Great Awakening."[3] Liberation theology with its use of Marxist categories and advocacy of socialism as a project for the future of Latin American society has been radically iconoclastic in breaking this American taboo on socialism. By its criticism of the U.S. role in the perpetuation of social injustice it has furthermore challenged other basic tenets of American civil religion: that America is the "New Israel," the "Chosen People," the "Promised Land," the "New Jerusalem."[4] By striking out at the heart of one of the most powerful and pervasive tenets of American civil religion, liberation theology hits upon a raw nerve in American social identity. The central assertion of liberation theology that God takes the side of the poor clashes forcefully with the assertion of American civil religion that America is God's chosen land. What is more, liberation theology not only radically questions America's privileged status in the divine scheme of things but dares to propose that God, by siding with the poor, may be against the United States—and it dares to do so, moreover, with biblical arguments! In this way liberation theology raises a contemporary challenge to the legitimacy of the myth of American civil religion in a period where this myth has once again attained a high level of credibility in American society.[5]

Theologians in the United States are to various degrees inevitably influenced by the tenets of American civil religion. Certainly the similarity of the arguments used by theologians as diverse as Michael Novak, Richard John Neuhaus, and Carl F. H. Henry in their rigorous opposition to liberation theology must be at least in part explained by their general agreement on the positive value of religion in helping to provide a "sacred canopy" over the pluralism of American society, whether that conviction has been carefully examined or not.[6] On the other side of the spectrum, it is

---

[3] See Paul Johnson, "The Almost-Chosen People: Why America Is Different," The First Annual Erasmus Lecture (Rockford, IL: The Rockford Institute, 1985), pp. 11-12.

[4] Cf. Robert N. Bellah, "Civil Religion in America," Chap. 9 in *Beyond Belief. Essays on Religion in a Post-Traditional World* (New York: Harper & Row, 1970), pp. 168-189.

[5] Bellah's comments on "the third time of trial" for American civil religion are particularly interesting in light of its subsequent revival little more than a decade later. See ibid., pp. 183-186.

[6] The term "sacred canopy" is that of Peter L. Berger, *The Sacred Canopy. Elements of a Sociological Theory of Religion* (Garden City, NY: Doubleday,

understandable that in spite of their diverse theological backgrounds several of those theologians most receptive to liberation theology have expressed their preference for a form of socialism, e.g., James H. Cone, Frederick Herzog, and Rosemary Radford Ruether among others. The observation of Gregory Baum is most pertinent:

> It is not surprising, therefore, that in the present the division among Christians no longer follows the inherited, confessional boundaries but passes right through the various churches. The cultural crisis has its theological equivalent. Christians are divided, it seems to me, on whether they should regard it as their religious duty to shore up the inherited social consensus and the cultural values that are being questioned, or whether they should join the critical forces in society and work for the re-creation of social life in greater accord with the future promises.[7]

This is not to say that there is not also a confessional component to the polarization of views on liberation theology. The contrast, for example, between the Protestant understanding of the gospel as a matter of "justification by grace through faith" and the insistence of liberation theology upon the gospel as primarily "good news for the poor" is a confessional difference of the first order which requires careful consideration in its own right. The point here to be made is, however, a different one, i.e., that in the North American discussion of liberation theology the impact of American civil religion plays a significant role in the polarization of positions. In addressing the phenomenon of polarization on this level therefore the insights of the discipline of the sociology of knowledge might prove particularly relevant.[8]

On each of these levels then—on the basis of the extraordinary claims which have been made for liberation theology, on the basis of its critique of Western "academic" philosophy and theology, and on the basis of its criticism of the role of the United States in the causation of Latin American poverty and political repression which attacks the core beliefs of American civil religion—liberation theology tends to provoke a defensive response from North American theologians and

---

Anchor, 1969). Among these three the most elaborate defense of the idea that religion should provide a sacred canopy for American society is Richard John Neuhaus, *The Naked Public Square. Religion and Democracy in America* (Grand Rapids: Eerdmans, 1984).

[7] Gregory Baum, *Religion and Alienation. A Theological Reading of Sociology* (New York: Paulist, 1975), p. 212.

[8] The fundamental insights of the sociology of knowledge have been elaborated by Karl Mannheim, *Ideologie und Utopia*, Sixth Edition (Frankfurt am Main: G. Schulte-Bulmke, 1978) and Werner Stark, *The Sociology of Knowledge* (London: Routledge and Kegan, 1958).

feed the dynamic of polarization. Each of these factors contributes to the tendency toward polarization even before any reasonable discussion of the pertinent arguments can take place. Each to varying degrees tends to prevent the discussion from moving beyond polemic to authentic dialogue.

Before reflecting on the measures which need to be taken in moving beyond the impasse of polarization, there is one final factor contributing to the dynamics of polarization which deserves consideration. Walter Brueggemann has pointed out that two primary trajectories of covenant tradition underlie the Old Testament, the Mosaic and the Davidic.[9] While the biblical tradition presents itself in terms of one unified tradition, "critical scholarship, however, has now made it reasonable to assume that these two articulations of covenant are not only distinct but also came from very different centers of power and very different processes of tradition building."[10] The first of these trajectories, the Mosaic, "tends to be a movement of protest which is situated among the disinherited and which articulates its theological vision in terms of a God who intrudes, even against seemingly impenetrable institutions and orderings. On the other hand, the Davidic tradition tends to be a movement of consolidation which is situated among the established and secure and which articulates its theological vision in terms of a God who faithfully abides and sustains on behalf of the present ordering."[11]

Brueggemann together with other biblical scholars recognizes tension and even conflict between these two trajectories of tradition within the biblical narrative. After an enlightening examination of these two traditions from the origins of the Mosaic tradition in the pre-monarchial period of the "conquest" and the origins of the Davidic tradition at the time of the institutionalization of the monarchy to their contention with each other in the periods of the divided kingdom, the exile and the postexile, Brueggemann identifies the basic characteristics of what he labels the "royal" trajectory and the "liberation" trajectory. In schematic form these characteristics are:[12]

---

[9]Walter Brueggemann, "Trajectories in Old Testament Literature and the Sociology of Ancient Israel," *J B L* 98 (June 1979):161-185.

[10]Ibid., p. 161.

[11]Ibid., p. 162.

[12]The following schema is that of Brueggemann, ibid., p. 180.

A. *The Royal Trajectory*
(1) prefers to speak in myths
of unity
(2) speaks a language of fertility
(creation) and continuity
(royal institutions)
(3) preferred mode of perception
is that of universal compre-
hensiveness
(4) appears to be fostered by
and valued among urban
"haves"
(5) tends to be socially conserving
with a primary valuing of
stability
(6) focuses on the glory and holiness
of God's person and institutions
geared to that holiness

B. *The Liberation Trajectory*
(1) prefers to tell concrete
stories of liberation
(2) speaks a language of war
and discontinuity

(3) preferred mode of perception
is that of historical specificity

(4) appears to be fostered by
and valued among peasant
"have nots"
(5) tends to be socially revolutionary with a primary
valuing of transformation
(6) focuses on the justice and
righteousness of God's will

Given the validity of this "paradigm" for biblical interpretation, Brueggemann draws two general conclusions. First, he notices the relatedness of a Marxist class reading of the Bible to this paradigm. Second, he suggests an affinity between these two distinct trajectories and "various alternatives in current theological discussion."[13] Using the example of the contrast between process hermeneutics and liberation hermeneutics, Brueggemann proposes that process theologies:

> may be generally placed in the trajectory of royal theology which is concerned with large comprehensive issues, which regards the concreteness of historical memory as a matter of little interest and which is concerned with the continuities of the process. Current scholarly investigation within this trajectory: (a) is likely seeking meaningful interface with current cultural forms; (b) is most likely to be lodged in university contexts and their epistemological commitments and not primarily interested in the forming of the synagogue/church as an alternative and distinct community of faith; and (c) is likely to have an inherent bias toward social conservatism. Of course, persons engaged in this scholarship may indeed be found elsewhere, but the reference group is likely to be the same. It is equally clear that persons in this scholarly tradition may themselves be concerned for an ethical radicalness, but it is not likely to be rooted in this epistemological tradition.[14]

[13]Ibid., p. 184.
[14]Ibid., p. 184.

By contrast, liberation theologies refer to the Mosaic trajectory for their legitimation.

> They are inclined to focus on the concreteness of historical memory and regard more sweeping, unitive statements as less important and compelling. Current scholarly work in this trajectory: (a) is likely not so directly concerned with contact with cultural forms and values but is addressed to a particular faith community living in uneasy tension with the dominant cultural forms and values; (b) is most likely to be lodged in a confessing community or a school of it. It is inclined to be concerned primarily with the faithful effectiveness of the confessing community and to believe that the dominant rationality will permit no ready point of contact without coopting. And, if the scholar is lodged in a university context, it is still likely the case that the main referent is a confessing group; (c) is likely to have an intrinsic bias toward social, ethical radicalness. This does not mean, of course, that in every case the person involved is socially radical for he/she may in fact be conservative. But the practice of this scholarship will predictably lead to the surfacing of such issues, even without the person intentionally doing so.[15]

The paradigm presented by Brueggemann has several immediate implications for understanding the tendency toward polarization in the North American discussion of liberation theology. Not only process theologies may be the heirs of the trajectory of royal theology. In fact as the previous chapter has shown, individual process theologians (e.g., D. Brown, Ogden) have been more receptive to the insights of liberation theology than the representatives of several other positions. Instead it appears that those North American theologians who value the tenets and role of American civil religion could be more accurately seen as the modern counterparts of the royalist trajectory (e.g., Novak's appeal to a theology of creation in defending democratic capitalism) whereas the defenders of liberation theology call upon the liberation trajectory for their legitimation.

What is of particular importance in this paradigm is to recognize how social location has impacted the development of the biblical tradition itself. In this way the current polarization between certain academic theologies with their royalist tendencies and liberation theology can be understood to be as old as the Old Testament traditions themselves. Even more, the contemporary theological rivals can each call upon a significant biblical trajectory in buttressing their arguments. It does not suffice therefore to dismiss either the modern defenders of the royalist trajectory or the modern representatives of the liberationist trajectory by accusing them of "the mere rationalization

---

[15]Ibid., p. 185.

of positions already taken."[16] That is due to the fact that the two conflicting biblical trajectories serve not only as a source for arguments in defense of a preconceived position but may themselves be creative of the conflicting positions in the first place. The royalist trajectory fosters the development of a socially conservative theology which values stability and supports the established institutions while the liberationist trajectory fosters a socially radical theology which values transformation and supports movements for greater social justice. The relationship between the origins of a particular contemporary theological option in one particular biblical trajectory and the warrants drawn from that particular biblical trajectory in defense of a particular contemporary theological option is thus a circular one.

Since each trajectory tends to make exclusive claims to divine favor upon its own theological position, the tendency toward polarization which characterizes the current discussion of liberation theology seems to be inherent to the Bible itself. The most relevant arguments therefore become those not based solely on appeals to biblical authority. Rather appeals to biblical texts always need to be considered with reference to historical context—both their original one and the contemporary one—in the course of interpretation. The impasse of polarization can in part be dismantled by recognizing the complexity of the hermeneutical process in which all appeals to Scripture take place.

2. Beyond Polarization

Proceeding under the supposition that the present tendency toward polarization in the North American discussion of liberation theology serves no one but the ideologue of whatever persuasion, the issue becomes that of developing an approach which moves beyond the impasse of polarization to a reasonable discussion of the relevant arguments. Polarization feeds on its own certainty both of the rightness of its own position and the wrongness of that of its opponent. There is no escape from this vicious circle unless critical thought can

---

[16]The phrase is that of Schubert M. Ogden, "The Concept of a Theology of Liberation: Must a Christian Theology Today Be So Conceived?" in Brian Mahan and L. Dale Richesin, eds., *The Challenge of Liberation Theology: A First World Response* (Maryknoll: Orbis, 1981), p. 134. Although Ogden employs the phrase in reference to liberation theology, it would appear to be just as applicable in this context to its royalist counterpart.

emerge which moves beyond the polemics of polarization to both a critical appreciation of the valid insights of the other and a self-critical appraisal of one's own position. While such an approach is ill-suited to the maintenance of the ideological certainty often reigning in contemporary political discourse, it does seem more appropriate to the discussion of the ideas of this earth where the basis for such certainty is absent. In this respect "deideologizing"—not only critique of the other but also of one's own position—as a component of contemporary theological method seems to be called for especially in view of the tendency toward polarization in the recent international discussion of liberation theology.[17]

A more constructive approach to the impasse of polarization would involve two complementary aspects. First, there is a need for a *critical appreciation* of the countervailing position. Such a critical appreciation begins with an authentic encounter with the fundamental logic and arguments of the other position and a genuine attempt to understand it on its own terms. With regard to Latin American liberation theology, that means encountering and understanding its arguments within its own historical context. This requires the interpreter to make the same kind of effort at bridging the hermeneutical gap between her/his own context and that of liberation theology as is made at bridging the hermeneutical gap between her/his own context and that of an ancient text. A similar effort would be expected of liberation theologians in their interpretation of "academic" theology. No valid critique of another position can take place which does not first fairly represent the views of that position. Otherwise the critique is merely directed at a caricature, a "straw man," in order to bolster one's own preconceived notions.

Part One of this work in its descriptive analysis of Latin American liberation theology intends to provide the basis for just such a critical appreciation of liberation theology. Through a descriptive analysis of liberation theology the stereotypes which sometimes appear in the arguments of those opposed to liberation theology lose much of their force. For example, the generalization that the writings of liberation

---

[17]The proposal of Schubert M. Ogden, *The Point of Christology* (San Francisco: Harper & Row, 1982), pp. 93-96 and 164-168, for "deideologizing" in analogy to what Bultmann called demythologizing and "political interpretation" as components of theological method deserves careful consideration not only for the tasks of biblical interpretation and Christological construction but for the overall task of theological formulation.

theology are "formal attempts to translate Christianity into Marxist categories"[18] does not coincide with an examination of the critical negations and affirmations which liberation theologians have made regarding the use of Marxism. Similarly, the accuracy of the generalizations raised against liberation theology contained in the following quote become most questionable.

> Essentially, again, these are the views that 1) man wholly liberates himself from any presumed bondage or restriction, 2) that this is a collective effort which subordinates the individual to the group, 3) that this is achieved by hatred, violence, or class struggle, 4) that therefore Christ is either not necessary or merely a model of a revolutionary person and 5) that the goal of liberation is a perfect worldly order.[19]

None of these five views accurately represents the positions of liberation theology. One need only recall the differentiated understanding of violence in the writings of the various liberation theologians or their expositions of Christology to realize the invalidity of such generalizations.

The occasional suggestion or outright charges of heresy against liberation theology also deserve reflection. If these are to be proven, they need to be based upon arguments directed against positions actually represented by the liberation theologians. In a fascinating historical examination of heresy, Norbert Brox has assembled a number of characteristics of the polemic often employed against heresy in the history of the church.

> The long and intensely argued disputes have led to a constant stock of antiheretical types and motifs. Typical are simplified conceptuality, uncompromising directness, and aggressive sharpness even up to the cursing of the heretics. The linguistic form of the combat against heretics has its own history. The antiheretical terminology in its ongoing usage developed "into a kind of generalized ecclesiastical and emotive . . . specialized language," into the stereotype of an "ars maledicendi." Constants are the accusations of posteriority and inferiority, of deficient originality, and of the falsification of the Bible and the tradition. Polemical in a narrower sense are the invectives which in themselves are not really argumentative. The attack upon person and subject matter with preference for the means of word play, proverb, irony and caricature, antithesis and paradox, the discriminating comparison, and metaphor (e.g., wolf in sheep's clothing, weeds in the wheat, poison, snake, vermin, sickness, plague, adultery, fox, robber, thief, beast) are of service for the

---

[18]Michael Novak, "Liberation Theology and the Pope," in James V. Schall, *Liberation Theology in Latin America* (San Francisco: Ignatius Press, 1982), p. 279.

[19]James V. Schall, *Liberation Theology in Latin America*, p. 111.

purpose of moral and intellectual disqualification.[20]
This description of the nature of the polemic used against ancient
heresies is reminiscent of the polemic which sometimes enters the
North American discussion of liberation theology. While such
polemical language and tactics have a long history of use in the
church, one wonders about their usefulness in contemporary
theological discourse.

Beginning with a genuine attempt at understanding, critical
appreciation entails not only a negative critique of the other position but
simultaneously a positive appreciation of its achievements. This by no
means is to suggest the elimination of criticism. Critical arguments
need to be raised on both sides of the debate over liberation theology. But
it does mean that criticism needs to be based upon an authentic
encounter with the actual position of the dialogue partner.

The second aspect of an approach which can lead beyond the
impasse of polarization involves the application of *self-criticism*.
Critical thought does not begin and end with criticism of the arguments
of others. Critical thought must also, if not primarily, be directed at an
examination of one's own arguments. As Trutz Rendtorff has written
regarding the scientific character of theology:

> . . . the critical meaning of science is not attainable without the ethos of the
> scientific method which consists of being critical not only and not
> primarily over against "others" but in relationship to one's own
> standpoint.[21]

One's own tendency toward absolutistic thinking in this way is in
need of scrutiny as an integral part of theological method.

It is the absence of self-critical thought which has perhaps more
than anything else marred the North American discussion of
liberation theology. And this lack of self-criticism is not only
characteristic of the most ardent North American opponents of
liberation theology. Rosemary Radford Ruether also identifies this
danger in the thinking of liberation theology.

> The Western apocalyptic model of liberation theology polarizes the world
> into "light" and "darkness," elect and damned, good and evil.

---

[20]Norbert Brox, "Häresie," in Theodor Klauser et al., eds., *Reallexikon
für Antike und Christentum. Sachwörterbuch zur Auseinandersetzung des
Christentums mit der Antiken Welt* (Stuttgart: Anton Hiersemann, 1984),
13:283 (own translation).

[21]Trutz Rendtorff, *Ethik. Grundelemente, Methodologie und Konkretionen
einer ethischen Theologie* (Stuttgart: W. Kohlhammer, 1980), 1:29 (own
translation). See also Peter L. Berger, *Pyramids of Sacrifice. Political Ethics
and Social Change* (Garden City, NY: Doubleday Anchor, 1974), pp. 109-110.

Liberation movements draw on the same tendency to absolute polarity, but in a reverse form. To recognize structures of oppression within our own group would break up this model of ultimate righteousness and projection of guilt upon the "others." It would force us to deal with ourselves, not as simply oppressed or oppressors, but as people who are sometimes one and sometimes the other in different contexts. A more mature and chastened analysis of the capacities of human beings for good and evil would flow from this perception. The flood gates of righteous anger must then be tempered by critical self-knowledge. This is a blow to the ego of adolescent revolutionary personalities. But, in the long run, only this more complex self-knowledge gives us hope that liberation movements will not run merely to the reversal of hatreds and oppressions, but rather, to a recovery of a greater humanity for us all.[22]

The impasse of polarization which often inhibits a constructive discussion of liberation theology can only be dismantled given a mutual commitment to both critical appreciation of the arguments of the other and self-criticism of one's own position.

B. *Critical Analysis of the North American Arguments*

The arguments raised by North American theologians in criticism of liberation theology have been diverse, as has been documented in the previous chapter. Having presented the various arguments in some detail, this section proceeds to their critical analysis. Which of the lines of argumentation are the most valid based upon the actual assertions of liberation theology?

The arguments here to be analyzed are primarily those raised in Chapter Four in criticism of liberation theology. Although there also occur among the resonant responses to liberation theology discussed in Chapter Three occasional critical points, e.g., Herzog's insistence upon the priority of God's Word in the process of liberation, the resonant responses as a whole support the contention to be made in the final section of this chapter that liberation theology is, beyond the various critical arguments, a highly significant and valid theological option in light of the Latin American plausibility structure. It is in arguing for the appropriateness and validity of Latin American liberation theology in its historical context that the resonant responses are once again brought to bear on the conclusions drawn in this chapter.

---

[22]Rosemary Radford Ruether, *New Woman New Earth. Sexist Ideologies and Human Liberation* (New York: Seabury, 1975), p. 132.

1. Liberation Theology's Use of Marxist Thought

In evaluating the criticisms of liberation theology based on its use of Marxism, it is first of all important to pose the question whether the North American critics have accurately assessed the place of Marxism in liberation theology. It is important to recall that liberation theology has not only made a positive appropriation of certain aspects of Marxism but has also firmly rejected others.

Among the three North American critics of liberation theology's use of Marxism discussed in the previous chapter only Kolden and Ruether recognize the differentiated approach to Marxism advocated by liberation theologians. James V. Schall's arguments, that liberation theology is virtually identifiable with a Marxist interpretation of Christianity and that the Marxism advocated by liberation theology leads inevitably to the erection of a totalitarian society with an accompanying low level economy, are simply not directed at positions actually defended by liberation theologians. By employing a dogmatic understanding of Marxism and the abuses of totalitarian Communist regimes as hermeneutical keys by which liberation theology and its use of Marxism have been interpreted, Schall has reduced liberation theology to a caricature. By so doing the convincingness of his entire argument has been weakened.

The most persuasive arguments raised are those of Kolden and Ruether who base their criticisms on a prior attempt to fairly represent the position of liberation theology with regard to Marxism. Interestingly, two of Kolden's arguments, (1) that liberation theology may tend to sacrifice the Christian emphasis on the theology of the cross to a human attempt to usher in the kingdom of God and (2) that the method of liberation theology may ultimately surrender too much to that of Marxism, have been elaborated at greater length by other North American theologians (the first by Neuhaus and Braaten and the second by McCann) and will be further discussed in the context of their more extensive treatment of these issues.

A crucial question in approaching the entire issue of liberation theology and Marxism is that raised most poignantly by Kolden: "The question that arises then is whether theology can use a Marxist analysis of society without also sharing in other Marxist ideas which are clearly at odds with Christian faith."[23] Stated in a more general

---

[23]Marc Kolden, "Marxism and Latin American Liberation Theology," in Wayne Stumme, ed., *Christians and the Many Faces of Marxism* (Minneapolis: Augsburg, 1984), p. 128.

way: Is a differentiated approach to Marxism even possible? On the surface an affirmative answer would seem apparent. Theology has always attempted to make a discerning use of philosophy whether it be that of Greek philosophy in the patristic period or existentialist philosophy in the twentieth century. Yet in the polarities of the present world where the ideologies of capitalism and communism virtually insist upon an alignment with one camp or the other, such a differentiated approach to Marxism is rendered exceedingly difficult. Any positive reference to Marx is, at least in the United States, likely to be interpreted as a wholesale endorsement of communism.

Even beyond the prevailing ideological polarities, there is in the thought of Marx himself, particularly in his later writings, a deterministic logic claiming the status of science which presents itself as a comprehensive system and which therefore resists dissection into separate individual elements.[24] This too renders a differentiated approach to Marxist thought most difficult. Although liberation theologians have indicated their non-acceptance of Marx's determinism in their effort to make a critical application of certain of his insights, further attempts to clarify their position in its affirmations and negations can only be welcomed.[25]

Besides the formal question regarding the possibility of a critical use of Marxism by liberation theology, two essential material questions also emerge from the North American discussion. The first of these is the acceptability of Marxist anthropology for Christian theology. Kolden and Ruether, as well as Schall, are joined by Hodgson in questioning Marx's anthropological optimism which held that by overcoming the oppressive social relations of capitalism the root cause of human alienation would be eliminated. The Christian tradition, however, affirms that the root cause of human alienation goes much deeper than the social relations which structure human

---

[24]Karl R. Popper, *The Open Society and Its Enemies. Vol. II: The High Tide of Prophecy: Hegel, Marx, and the Aftermath* (Princeton: Princeton University Press, 1962), pp. 81-211, documents this deterministic logic and describes it as Marx's "historicism." While Popper appreciates much in Marx's social analysis and his moral radicalism, he is convinced of the disastrous consequences of Marxist determinism and its scientific pretensions.

[25]The criticism of the "Marxist analysis" in liberation theology by the Sacred Congregation for the Doctrine of the Faith, *Instruction on Certain Aspects of the "Theology of Liberation"* (Vatican City: Vatican Polyglot Press, 1984), makes a further clarification of liberation theology's use of Marxism not only desirable but an apologetic task of the first order.

affairs. The fundamental cause of human alienation exists, rather, in the contradiction between the human self as created by God and the self which wills to live for itself as its own god. It is this contradiction which has been traditionally expressed in Christian theology by the doctrine of human sinfulness.

It should be noted that this criticism is directed primarily at Marx's anthropology. It would be directed at liberation theology only insofar as liberation theologians may have uncritically assumed this anthropology in their own theological formulations. In addition to further general clarification of the use of Marxism by liberation theology, a crucial specific point in that clarification needs to be liberation theology's position with regard to Marxist anthropology.

A second important and related material question follows. Again both Kolden and Ruether, together with Schall and others, have questioned the viability of a liberation program which does not address the root cause of human bondage in human sinfulness. This criticism is again directed primarily at the Marxist idea of "salvation" and at liberation theology only insofar as it has uncritically overtaken the Marxist notion. Ruether has been particularly critical of the paradox between the liberated society envisioned by Marx and the reality of totalitarian Communist states. By pursuing a program of liberation exclusively on the level of social structures, a new mystification of the root cause of human alienation takes place which manifests itself in both the rhetoric and oppressiveness of the social structures established in Communist countries. This does not mean that liberation is not also needed on the level of social structures. It does mean, however, that the relationship between liberation from the dilemma of human sinfulness and liberation from unjust, "sinful" social structures needs to be carefully elaborated.

These two questions are of paramount importance for the future dialogue between Latin American liberation theologians and North American theologians. Other issues raised with regard to Marxism, for example, Ruether's question about the destructive consequences of choosing violent means for achieving social change, also deserve careful deliberation. Likewise both Kolden and Ruether have pointed out the tendency of Marxist categories to polarize discourse. A critique of this tendency has been discussed in the previous section. The two most pressing issues for liberation theology which arise from its attempt to make a critical use of Marxism remain, however, the questions of its theological anthropology and its concept of liberation.

2. Defense of Democratic Capitalism

In turning first to Novak's defense of democratic capitalism and his concomitant critique of liberation theology, one notices immediately the discrepancy between his own presentation of the nature of liberation theology and that of the liberation theologians themselves. Novak virtually ignores the biblical arguments and theological reformulations of liberation theology in order to concentrate his critique on the social analysis and political proposals (i.e., "praxis") of liberation theology. By so doing it is questionable if Novak has fairly represented the fullness of their position. For Novak liberation theology is, whether unwittingly or not, the pawn of an international Marxist conspiracy which can only lead Latin America into new forms of poverty and totalitarian domination within the orbit of the Soviet Union. In making his case Novak therefore holds liberation theology worthy of ridicule and demeaning.

Overlooking Novak's polarizing discourse, however, attention needs to be paid both to his arguments for democratic capitalism and those against liberation theology. Novak is convinced of both the moral and practical superiority of democratic capitalism. Yet at the same time there are significant problems with the capitalist system itself even in those nations where it is most highly developed, particularly the United States, which raise questions about a facile recommendation of capitalism as the solution to the poverty of the Third World. There continues to exist an "other America" more than twenty years after Michael Harrington first used this phrase to describe the fact of poverty in the U.S.[26] Moreover, as the U.S. Roman Catholic bishops have noted in their pastoral letter on the U.S. economy, in the first half of the decade of the eighties there has been a significant increase (9 million between 1979 and 1983) in the number of those classified below the official poverty level.[27] A central argument Novak employs to explain such anomalies in the progress of democratic capitalism is that of the different ethos of those who are poor. Such an argument, which in effect is a sophisticated form of

---

[26]Cf. Michael Harrington, *The Other America. Poverty in the United States* (New York: Macmillan, 1962) and *The New American Poverty* (New York: Holt, Rinehart & Winston, 1984).

[27]First Draft of the U.S. Bishops' "Pastoral Letter on Catholic Social Teaching and the U.S. Economy," *Origins, NC Documentary Service* 14, No. 22/23 (Nov. 15, 1984):362 (No. 187), which cites statistics provided by the U.S. Bureau of the Census.

"blaming the victim,"[28] apart from its racist implications, cannot account for such systemic problems as the underemployment and unequal pay for working women in the U.S. or the growing unemployment and poverty of those formerly employed as industrial workers, especially among those who share the Anglo-American ethos Novak esteems so highly. Perhaps more than anything else, it is Novak's uncritical certainty about the unmitigated benefits of democratic capitalism which needs to be challenged by recognizing counter-indications like these.

Novak's interpretation of the history of Latin America and his social analysis of its problems also raise a number of difficulties. To write, as Novak does, that "South America *chose* to embody the political economy of Latin Europe . . .," is a serious distortion of the history of Latin American colonialization and exploitation.[29] Likewise the primacy of ethos in Novak's explanation of Latin American poverty, an ethos which was also apparently chosen,[30] inordinately emphasizes a factor at best tangential to the existence of exploitation in Latin America both in the colonial and modern periods.

Novak's critique of the theory of dependency deserves special attention in its challenging an integral component of liberation theology's social analysis. As Novak understands it, the theory of dependency ignores the history of Iberian colonialization as a cause of Latin American poverty in attributing poverty almost exclusively to capitalist exploitation in the modern period. This is, however, a misunderstanding of dependency theory insofar as the theory of dependency asserts that contemporary forms of capitalist exploitation are in continuity with the colonial past, making use of past feudalistic structures where they remain in place as well as manipulating the often feudal-like nature of newer structures. Dependency theory is in this way more complex and sophisticated than Novak's presentation thereof.

Novak also points to other factors which cause Latin American poverty, e.g., overpopulation and the failure to industrialize. While

---

[28]Cf. William Ryan, *Blaming the Victim* (New York: Pantheon Books, 1971).

[29]Michael Novak, "Introduction," in Michael Novak, ed., *Liberation South, Liberation North* (Washington: American Enterprise Institute, 1981), p. 1 (emphasis added).

[30]Cf. Michael Novak, *Freedom With Justice. Catholic Social Thought and Liberal Institutions* (San Francisco: Harper & Row, 1984), pp. 173-176.

both of these factors need to be taken into consideration in a comprehensive understanding of the causes of Latin American poverty, they are not of themselves sufficient to explain either the history or present extent of Latin American poverty. Indeed a strong case can be made that overpopulation is equally explainable as the result of poverty as it can be understood as its cause. For example, statistics demonstrate a close correlation between an improved standard of living, measured in terms of a reduced infant mortality rate, and a reduction in population growth.[31] To identify a simple cause and effect relationship between poverty and overpopulation is therefore difficult.

To point to the failure to industrialize as the cause of Latin American poverty or, as Benne does in dependence upon the thought of Arthur Lewis, to point toward a prior failure to develop an agricultural base upon which industrialization could take place, is ultimately to point to the colonial structures which originally prevented such a development and to the consequences of such colonialism in terms of unequal land distribution and disparity of wealth which persist in the present. Thus to refer to the failure to industrialize may do more to support the theory of dependency than to refute it. Such an argument also overlooks, moreover, the human cost (e.g., the working conditions prevalent in the early stage of capitalist society) which accompanied the industrialization of the West as it is offered as a model for the future of the Third World.[32] It furthermore neglects the question of whether a comparable process of industrialization by the Third World is even an historical possibility given the current power relations between First and Third Worlds.[33]

> A crucial circumstance of original capitalist development in the West was that it was the *first* such case in history. Conversely, it is decisive for the Third World that it is *not* first, but that a fully developed and enormously powerful international capitalist system already exists—and that the Third World is painfully dependent upon this system. This makes for an entirely different situation, rendering the argument from Western

---

[31] United Nations Children's Fund—James P. Grant, Executive Director, "The State of the World's Children 1984" (New York: UNICEF, 1984), pp. 32-35.

[32] For an exposition of some of these human costs see Julio de Santa Ana, ed., *Separation Without Hope? Essays on the Relation between the Church and the Poor During the Industrial Revolution and the Western Colonial Expansion* (Maryknoll: Orbis, 1978).

[33] This question is raised by Peter L. Berger, *Pyramids of Sacrifice*, pp. 57-58.

history almost completely irrelevant.[34]
This is to leave untouched the arguments against industrialization based on its negative ecological consequences.

Novak employs an additional argument against the theory of dependency which requires closer examination. Novak argues that the amount of U.S. investments in Latin America are not sufficiently large to support the contention that the U.S. economy is dependent on Latin America.[35] While that may be true, this in no way discounts the theory that the Latin American economy may itself be dependent upon such investments. Moreover, Novak overlooks the factor of the enormous indebtedness of Latin American countries to Western banks which seems to indicate there is more validity to the notion of dependency than Novak is willing to admit.[36] It would appear that Novak's preference for the system of democratic capitalism leads him to a certain selectiveness in his choice of statistics and their interpretation.

For these several reasons Novak argues that the praxis advocated by liberation theology ultimately proves false. The question arises, however, as to where the praxis of liberation theology has yet to be tested. In discussing the praxis of liberation theology Novak fails to mention the basic Christian communities of Latin America as a central example of the praxis it supports. Otherwise, apart from the present government in Nicaragua and possibly the government of Allende in Chile toppled by the military in 1973, it would appear the praxis advocated by liberation theology has yet to be tried. It is both anachronistic and contrary to its own affirmation to hold liberation theology accountable for the crimes committed by communist regimes throughout the twentieth century. Moreover, the conflicting reports on the achievements and failures of the Sandinista government in Nicaragua seem to indicate that no final verdict can yet be rendered on the attempt to establish socialism there.

Novak understands Latin America to be standing before a choice of momentous proportions: either democratic capitalism or authoritarian socialism (i.e., communism). According to Novak, liberation theology has opted for the latter, a choice which is wrong on both moral

---

[34]Ibid., p. 58.

[35]Michael Novak, *The Spirit of Democratic Capitalism* (New York: Simon & Schuster, 1982), pp. 304-305, and *Freedom With Justice*, p. 188.

[36]Stephen Koepp, "The Gathering Storm" *Time* 124, No. 27 (July 2, 1984): 4-7.

and practical grounds. The history of Latin America, its present political situation, and the position of liberation theology are, however, each far more complex than Novak depicts them. If liberation theology is ever in danger of oversimplifying the political and economic options confronting Latin America, the proposal of Novak is no less oversimplified. For one, it is not clear that either of Novak's options, either the implementation of genuine democratic capitalism or socialism, could be enacted without radical change in the present Latin American political structures, i.e., without revolution. Secondly, it should be recognized that a capitalism patterned after the United States or a communism modelled after the Soviet Union are not the only two options before Latin America and the rest of the Third World. As an important step in overcoming such oversimplifications, one must ask, with Peter L. Berger, "*what kind* of capitalism" and "*what kind* of socialism" are under discussion.[37] A host of options thus appear to be available where once it seemed there were only two.

A similar point needs to be made about the debate surrounding the theory of dependency. Neither the theory of dependency nor the theory of development are descriptions of "reality" as such. They are rather attempts to interpret a complex of factors which in their complexity confound every theory. The above questions raised in criticism of Novak do not purport either to disprove the theory of development or to prove the theory of dependency. They rather point out the "awe-full" complexity of the factors which contribute to the misery of thousands, even millions, of human beings in Latin America. Their misery should not be a matter of debate. Rather the issue remains one of interpreting the maddening complexity of factors which cause that misery in order to alleviate it.

As Peter L. Berger has argued forcefully in *Pyramids of Sacrifice*, there is a desperate need to get beyond myth and ideology in analyzing the causes of Third World poverty. While he firmly defends the basic appropriateness of capitalism for the West, Berger nevertheless admits a certain legitimacy to the theory of dependency in explaining the dilemma of the Third World, providing this theory is stripped of its dogmatism.

> Polarization between rich and poor nations, polarization within the latter between relatively affluent factors and sectors of massive misery, growth in the major indicators of this misery (from downright starvation to pervasive unemployment), growing economic dependency of poor nations

---

[37]Berger, *Pyramids of Sacrifice*, pp. 62-64.

364   Orthopraxis or Heresy

upon the rich (as reflected in mounting debts, deteriorating terms of trade
and balances of payment, vulnerability to decisions made by governments
and nongovernmental bodies in the rich nations)—all these are not
inventions of Marxist ideologists, but empirical facts readily available to
any objective observer. It is, therefore, of the greatest importance that the
no to various theoretical affirmations of Marxist critique be balanced by
an emphatic *yes* to many of its specific empirical assessments.

Both economically and sociologically, a key test for the critique is the
question of the "spread effect" of the benefits of development. There is
little disagreement about the present facts. The disagreement rather
concerns the projections of these facts into the future. How much of a time
span is one to allow for the "spread effect" to become manifest? Advocates
of the capitalist model are vague about this. "In the long run," they
maintain, all these good things will happen. But as Keynes pointed out in
another context, "in the long run" we'll all be dead. The evidence in this
matter to date, in most parts of the Third World, supports the Marxist
critique rather than the capitalist apologetic. It is difficult to see by what
mechanisms this trend is to be reversed, unless one considers *political*
mechanisms that are normally excluded by capitalist ideologists (such as,
needless to say, the politics of revolution).[38]

The question thus becomes in many ways one of measuring urgency.
At what point does the misery caused by poverty in Latin America
become so great that the gradual reformist measures proposed by the
theory of development become ludicrous? At what point do the costs of
revolution and the risks to individual freedom entailed in a centrally
managed economy and political system seem worth taking in
exchange for the promises of a more equitable distribution of wealth,
whether or not those promises will ultimately be fulfilled?[39]

One gain in the position of Robert Benne in his defense of
democratic capitalism, over that of Novak, is his much stronger
emphasis upon the question of justice (e.g., his consideration of Rawls'
theory of justice) in evaluating the competing claims of political and
economic systems. This leads Benne to make some very constructive
proposals for the formulation of U.S. foreign policy in the developing
world.[40] It also leads Benne at one point in his argument to
countenance the possibility that in certain situations of extreme
injustice, revolutionary change may be a tragic necessity.[41] The Latin
American liberation theologians do not dispute that revolutionary
change is in itself a tragic choice. Those liberation theologians who

---

[38]Ibid., pp. 56-57.

[39]On the costs of revolution and socialism see ibid., pp. 80-98.

[40]Robert Benne, *The Ethic of Democratic Capitalism. A Moral
Reassessment* (Philadelphia: Fortress, 1981), pp. 204-207.

[41]Ibid., p. 86.

admit the possible use of violence as a means of social change do not do so frivolously. They do, however, believe that for the poor of Latin America, the promises of capitalism have proved empty and they are willing to enter upon the risks involved in the construction of a Latin American socialism.

The defenses of democratic capitalism by Novak and Benne, perhaps against their own intention, help to reveal the complexity of Latin American "reality" and the insufficiency of any single theory to comprehend it. The plausibility of a particular system, i.e., capitalism/socialism, or of a particular form of social analysis, i.e., theory of development/dependency, depends in many ways upon the "facts" which are selected for interpretation and the "perspective" from which one does the interpreting. To return to a phrase of Miguez Bonino which expresses a basic insight of contemporary sociology: "The world simply looks differently when seen from an executive's office and from a shanty town."[42] If it does nothing more, the defense of democratic capitalism forces those on all sides of the liberation theology debate to a deeper recognition of the complexity of Latin American poverty, its causes and possible solution. The need for rigorous thought, beyond the throes of oversimplification and polarization, is great.

3. Challenge of Christian Realism

An important and valid point made by Thomas G. Sanders in his criticism of liberation theology is the need to develop specific proposals and concrete strategies for responding to the social, political, and economic problems in the various diverse contexts which compose Latin America as a whole. Praxis-orientation must be context specific, and those proposals for engagement which may be applicable to Colombia may not be applicable to Chile just as those relevant to an urban *favela* in Sao Paulo, Brazil may not be relevant to the rural areas of El Salvador. By labeling liberation theology as a Christian utopia in a derogatory sense, however, Sanders fails to appreciate the extent to which such context specificity is already at work in liberation theology, particularly through the grass roots organizing of basic Christian communities. Likewise he may minimize the context specificity of the active engagement of individual liberation theologians which does not necessarily become the subject matter of

---

[42]Jose Miguez Bonino, "Doing Theology in the Context of the Struggles of the Poor," *Mid-Stream* 20 (1981):370.

books and articles about liberation theology.[43]

Liberation theology admits the importance of an utopian element
for its thought. Gutierrez has clearly delineated how the idea of utopia
serves as a mediating concept for his liberation theology between the
kingdom of God and the given historical situation, a mediating
concept to be revised as the situation changes. Utopia as a mediating
concept serves both as a means to critique the inadequacies of the
present social structure and as motivation for participating in social
change. Liberation theologians like Gutierrez and Miguez Bonino are
nevertheless careful to avoid an identification between human utopia
and God's ultimate kingdom which comes as a gift. In the Latin
American context they understand utopian thought to play an
important role in leading to the erection of more just social structures.
That does not mean, however, the erection of the kingdom of God.

If a danger facing liberation theology is the extreme of an
unrealistic utopia, then that confronting Sanders and the position of
Christian realism in general is an unmovable cynicism which has
lost all impetus for social change. This is the point made by Rubem
Alves in his response to the original Sander's article. But in making
this point, a new polarity is established which leads no further than
mutual accusation. Gregory Baum suggests, however, that there exists
a wide diversity in the forms which utopian thought may take and that
all of them should not be categorically denied.

> The bearer of the charism, in touch with the alienation of his community,
> produces a new imagination with varying effects; it may lead his
> followers into blind alleys or actually make them agents of significant
> social change. The spectrum is very wide here. Each social order creates
> its own opposing movements, but these may vary from irrational sectarian
> protest groups to revolutionary movements and reformist parties; the form
> of the countervailing trend depends on the utopian imagination that has
> produced it.[44]

Recognizing that utopian thought expresses itself in diverse forms
opens discussion to a consideration of the particular affirmation of
utopia made by liberation theology in lieu of the specifics of the Latin
American context.

Dennis P. McCann's critique of liberation theology on the basis of

----

[43]For example see the context specific interpretation of the thought of Camilo
Torres and Gustavo Gutierrez by John William Hart, "Topia and Utopia in
Colombia and Peru—The Theory and Practice of Camilo Torres and Gustavo
Gutierrez in their Historical Contexts," Ph.D. Dissertation (New York: Union
Theological Seminary, 1978).

[44]Baum, *Religion and Alienation*, p. 173.

Christian realism goes beyond that of Sander's on a number of levels. McCann has demonstrated in the volume *Christian Realism and Liberation Theology* a depth of knowledge of the position of Reinhold Niebuhr and Christian realism which does raise important questions for liberation theology. It is somewhat surprising, however, that McCann does not hold the flaw which he discovers in Niebuhr's thought, i.e., the failure to develop an adequate theology of history (which leads to an increasing ideological drift in the practical application of his thought) to be deserving of the same kind of radical criticism which he directs at liberation theology. Instead McCann proceeds to use the position of Christian realism, especially its theological anthropology, as norm for critiquing liberation theology without sufficiently pursuing the more radical question of whether Niebuhr's theological anthropology may not itself necessarily lead to this inadequate theology of history. A recent study of Niebuhr's thought, *Sociality, Ethics, and Social Change* by Judith Vaughan, makes a strong case that a more serious reappraisal of Niebuhr's anthropology and ethics is necessary due to its insufficient concept of human sociality.[45] The individualism of Niebuhr's theological anthropology—which McCann himself recognizes as being more appropriate to a dispositional ethic for individuals than to a bona fide social ethic—may thus prove so inherent to Niebuhr's position that it becomes impossible to construct an adequate social ethic from this basis.

More immediate to the present concern, however, is McCann's treatment of liberation theology. Unfortunately McCann does not demonstrate the same depth of understanding in his discussion of liberation theology that he shows in his elaboration of Niebuhr's thought, to say nothing of critical appreciation. This leads McCann to make a number of questionable interpretations of the basics of liberation theology. Four of these deserve mention.

First, McCann shares a common North American misunder—standing of dependency theory which perceives dependency theory to assert that Latin American poverty has as its exclusive cause in what McCann calls "American neocolonialism." Dependency theory, however, does not deny that the history of colonialism was a major factor in creating the current misery in Latin America. Rather, it

---

[45]Judith Vaughan, *Sociality, Ethics, and Social Change. A Critical Appraisal of Reinhold Niebuhr's Ethics in the Light of Rosemary Radford Ruether's Works* (Lanham, MD: University Press of America, 1983).

asserts that the present nature of dependency which includes dependency on the American capitalist system, perpetuates in various ways the situation of dependency which has long existed in Latin America. Liberation theology's explanation of the dependency relationship is more sophisticated than McCann's interpretation thereof.

Second, McCann's interpretation of the basic Christian communities, emphasizing their ideology and radical politicization, stands in need of serious correction. McCann goes so far as to use the thought of Camilo Torres in his option for revolutionary activity to represent the general position of the basic Christian communities. While in certain instances such an appraisal may be accurate, the description of the basic Christian communities offered by liberation theologians reveals a commitment to Bible study and community building as the foremost characteristics of the basic Christian communities. So too the forms of practical engagement chosen by the basic Christian communities are rarely so radical as McCann envisions them. Moreover, the growth of the majority of these communities has been encouraged and nurtured by the Roman Catholic bishops in Latin America.

Third, the key argument of McCann in rejecting liberation theology as a valid option for contemporary Christian theology is his understanding of its method. As demonstrated in the previous chapter, McCann argues that the essence of liberation theology's method is derived from Paulo Freire's theory of conscienticization. By elevating conscienticization to its central methodological principle, McCann believes liberation theology must either eliminate all references to the transcendent realm as remnants of ideological thought or be inconsistent to its primary methodological affirmation. In effect, McCann in this way reduces the content of liberation theology's method to a Marxist critique of the ideological function of religion.

The description of liberation theology's method in the second chapter of this work argues that ideology critique or conscienticization plays a more modest, though still very significant role, for liberation theology. Ideology critique serves liberation theology in examining how a particular theology or doctrine functions in legitimizing or challenging a given social order. Thus ideology critique has assisted liberation theology in assessing not only the ideological commitments of other theologies but also its own ideological tendencies. Liberation theology does not claim to eliminate through ideology critique all vestiges of ideology and certainly does not thereby purport to eliminate all vestiges of the transcendent. References to the activity of God by liberation theologians continue to have a significant meaning which cannot be reduced to synonymity with human activity. Certainly liberation theology seeks to draw a much closer—even sacramental—relationship between the activity of God and human history than has been typical of the scholastic theology often prevalent in Latin America. But this is a concern also shared by other contemporary theologians who have different theological interests than liberation theology.[46]

By exaggerating the importance of conscienticization for the method of liberation theology, McCann skews the position of liberation theology so that he can no longer take seriously its own theological affirmations, considering them instead to be remnants of the theological myth which should have been excised through a more consistent application of the method of conscienticization. This is, in essence, to claim that liberation theologians no longer have a place for God or the biblical witness to God's activity if they are true to their methodological commitments. This argument, however, is so contrary to the actual affirmations of liberation theologians regarding the Bible, the tradition, and the present activity of God as to render it absurd unless the liberation theologians are either exceedingly naive about their own method or exceedingly deceptive about their actual motives. A more convincing explanation is that McCann has overstated the role of conscienticization and ideology critique within the entire method of liberation theology.

Fourth, the logic of McCann regarding what liberation theologians must say if they are consistent to the method of conscienticization leads him to claim that liberation theology recognizes no "limit-situations," i.e., situations in which human beings are limited in their own ability to transcend them. This again is a deduction which McCann makes on the basis of his understanding of liberation theology's method. A more accurate presentation of its position might be to assert not that liberation theology rejects all limit-situations but rather that liberation theology does not agree that the present unjust social structures of Latin America constitute such a limit-situation. Instead liberation theologians affirm that a more just political and economic arrangement than the present one is a realizable human possibility.

---

[46]For example see the essays assembled in Wolfhart Pannenberg, ed., *Revelation as History*, trans. David Granskou (New York: Macmillan, 1968).

That does not mean they affirm that there exist no limits upon human capabilities. It does mean, however, they reject a cynical application of the theological anthropology of Christian realism which would negate all efforts to improve the situation of the Latin American poor by referring to the inescapable sinfulness of the human condition. While limit-situations may exist, the social injustice of Latin American society does not yet define such a limit-situation.

McCann is correct in noting that other limit-situations typical of traditional theology (e.g., human finitude and mortality) have not been given much attention by liberation theologians. This does not mean, however, they do not have their own legitimacy. It only means they are not central to the most urgent issues with which liberation theology has attempted to deal. Instead liberation theology may be seen to address other pseudo-limit-situations generally left undiscussed by traditional theology, e.g., fatalism, starvation, and political repression.

McCann's critique of liberation theology, in spite of its misunderstandings, nevertheless does raise three important questions in need of greater clarification by liberation theology. The first issue rightly concerns the method of liberation theology. While McCann exaggerates the importance of conscienticization for the method of liberation theology, his critique does indicate the need for greater clarity about the relationship of theological reflection to the entire praxis-oriented method of liberation theology. McCann is not alone in questioning whether theology plays a mere ideological role in justifying a course of social action already established on other grounds. Even Clodovis Boff has recognized this problem in liberation theology and has written his *Theology and Praxis* in an attempt, among other concerns, to lend theological reflection a legitimate, independent, and necessary place within a praxis-oriented theology. Liberation theologians already carry out theological reflection alongside of and within a commitment to praxis. The need remains for more clarity about how this takes place on the theoretical level.

The second issue raised not only by McCann but by Christian realism as a whole is the question of liberation theology's anthropology. By failing to articulate its own theological anthropology (McCann is most correct in this observation), liberation theology is vulnerable to criticism based upon more highly developed positions. In North America it is the theological anthropology of Niebuhr which has been especially influential and which in its "realism" raises critical questions about the capability of sinful human beings for improving their social condition. If liberation theology is to respond to its North American critics, it must elaborate its anthropological convictions.

The third and final issue called forth by McCann and the challenge of Christian realism is that of the concept of liberation. Again this question stems from the failure of liberation theology to articulate its anthropology. Is liberation an exclusively human task? If not, what is the legitimate human task within the scope of God's liberating activity? And what, if anything, in the liberation process must be attributed to God alone? Such questions about its concept of liberation are posed by Christian realism's critique of liberation theology.

4. Liberation Theology and the Kingdom of God

The critiques of Neuhaus and Braaten indicate some of the essential questions which contemporary Lutheran theologians have raised of liberation theology. Braaten, particularly in his book *The Flaming Center*, has demonstrated that his encounter with liberation theology has been a most serious one. In expressing their reservations about liberation theology both Neuhaus and Braaten have employed the New Testament idea of the kingdom of God as a primary criterion.

Perhaps the key question in beginning to discuss the criticisms of Neuhaus and Braaten is the following: Does liberation theology assert that through human activity it is possible to arrive at God's kingdom? Clearly liberation theology has left that impression with several of its critics. And it is undoubtedly true that liberation theologians have not always carefully enough differentiated between the divine initiative in ushering in the eschatological kingdom and the significant implications for human activity which they draw from the New Testament descriptions of that kingdom. In their concern for a liberating praxis, the distinction between the divine initiative and the human response has frequently become blurry and insofar as this has been the case, the criticism of Neuhaus and Braaten needs to be affirmed, particularly from a Lutheran perspective.

It is an inaccurate depiction of liberation theology, however, when it is universally claimed that liberation theologians equate the kingdom of God with human accomplishment. The positions of Gutierrez and Miguez Bonino demonstrate serious attempts to make a distinction of the kind which Neuhaus and Braaten claim to be totally absent from liberation theology—yet without disclaiming the

necessary relevance of the kingdom of God for human praxis. To
quote from Gutierrez, this time extensively:

> Not only is the growth of the Kingdom not reduced to temporal progress;
> because of the Word accepted in faith, we see that the fundamental obstacle
> to the Kingdom, which is sin, is also the root of all misery and injustice;
> we see that the very meaning of the growth of the Kingdom is also the
> ultimate precondition for a just society and a new man. One reaches this
> root and this ultimate precondition only through the acceptance of the
> liberating gift of Christ, which surpasses all expectations. But, inversely,
> all struggle against exploitation and alienation, in a history which is
> fundamentally one, is an attempt to vanquish selfishness, the negation of
> love. This is the reason why any effort to build a just society is liberating.
> And it has an indirect but effective impact on the fundamental alienation.
> It is a salvific work, although it is not all of salvation. As a human work it
> is not exempt from ambiguities, any more than what is considered to be
> strictly "religious" work. But this does not weaken its basic orientation
> nor its objective results.
>
> Temporal progress—or, to avoid this aseptic term, the liberation of
> man—and the growth of the Kingdom are both directed toward complete
> communion of men with God and of men among themselves. They have
> the same goal, but they do not follow parallel roads, not even convergent
> ones. The growth of the Kingdom is a process which occurs historically *in*
> liberation, insofar as liberation means a greater fulfillment of man.
> Liberation is a precondition for the new society, but this is not all it is.
> While liberation is implemented in liberating historical events, it also
> denounces their limitations and ambiguities, proclaims their fulfillment,
> and impels them effectively towards total communion. This is not an
> identification. Without liberating historical events, there would be no
> growth of the Kingdom. But the process of liberation will not have
> conquered the very roots of oppression and the exploitation of man by man
> without the coming of the Kingdom, which is above all a gift. Moreover, we
> can say that the historical, political liberating event *is* the growth of the
> Kingdom and *is* a salvific event; but it is not *the* coming of the Kingdom,
> not *all* of salvation. It is the historical realization of the Kingdom and,
> therefore, it also proclaims its fullness. This is where the difference lies.
> It is a distinction made from a dynamic viewpoint, which has nothing to
> do with the one which holds for the existence of two juxtaposed "orders,"
> closely connected or convergent, but deep down different from each
> other.[47]

Gutierrez states explicitly that "the growth of the Kingdom is not
reduced to temporal progress." The ultimate root of exploitation and
alienation in human selfishness is overcome only as "a gift." It may
well be that Neuhaus and Braaten object to Gutierrez's formulation of
the distinction between the kingdom as gift and as human work,
particularly his references to "the growth of the Kingdom." But there

---

[47]Gustavo Gutierrez, *A Theology of Liberation. History, Politics and
Salvation*, trans. Caridad Inda and John Eagleson (Maryknoll: Orbis, 1973),
pp. 176-177.

Critical Analysis 373

should be a recognition of the distinction he does make, regardless of their judgment of its adequacy.

Miguez Bonino has been even more circumspect when he writes:

> The positive relation between God's Kingdom and man's historical undertaking justifies us in understanding the former as a call to engage ourselves actively in the latter.[48]

Worthy of consideration in this context is also a formulation typical of the position of Leonardo Boff.

> The Kingdom is certainly the Christian utopia that lies at the culmination of history. But it must be repeated that this Kingdom is found in the process of history wherever justice and fraternity are fostered and wherever the poor are respected and recognized as shapers of their own destiny.[49]

The theologians of liberation insist that the kingdom of God has dynamic, even utopian, significance for human history already in the present. At the same time they seek to subordinate the human role to the priority of the divine. While critics of liberation theology may find such formulations overly ambiguous, there nevertheless needs to be greater attention given to the distinctions that have been made and the intention which lies behind them.[50]

An even more crucial issue, one which has long been debated but not yet resolved, becomes: What significance does the New Testament idea of the kingdom of God continue to have for Christian ethics, particularly since the arrival of the kingdom is now nearly 2000 years outstanding? Possible answers range along a continuum which has as its extreme poles the denial that the idea of the kingdom has any ethical significance at all at the one end, and the assertion that the kingdom is

---

[48]Jose Miguez Bonino, *Revolutionary Theology Comes of Age* (London: SPCK, 1975), p. 150.

[49]Leonardo Boff, *Church: Charisma and Power. Liberation Theology and the Institutional Church* (London: SCM, 1985), p. 10. Cf. also Leonardo Boff, "Integral Liberation and Partial Liberations," in Leonardo and Clodovis Boff, *Salvation and Liberation*, trans. Robert R. Barr (Maryknoll: Orbis, 1984), pp. 14-66.

[50]Consider, for example, the more careful formulation of Marc Kolden, "On Speaking of the Kingdom Today," *Word World* 2 (Spring 1982):155, who writes: "More significant criticisms engage liberation theologians in discussing the appropriateness of their interpretation of eschatology not for stressing its present dynamism but for the way in which they link God's Kingdom so closely with progress in history. To be sure, they usually make a distinction between historical liberation and salvation, but it may still be wondered whether liberation is not so closely linked to certain political positions that this theology does not see the penultimate character of all parties and movements in history. After all, the Kingdom also is to bring everything under judgment."

purely a matter of human construction on the other. It would appear that both the position of liberation theology and, for example, the "theology of vindication" referred to by Neuhaus and the "eschatopraxis" defended by Braaten fall at various points inbetween these extremes. Even as Neuhaus and Braaten criticize liberation theologians for drawing too near to the activist pole in identifying with one particular political program, they might well question Neuhaus and Braaten, as they have Moltmann, regarding the absence of sufficient mediation in their thought between the admitted significance of the kingdom of God and the often ambiguous business of leading one's life in the world. Modern theology has long struggled with the question of how to relate belief in a transcendent reality to the contingencies of human history. Whereas Neuhaus, Braaten, and many other Western theologians are cautious about premature identifications of the kingdom of God with this-worldly institutions and programs, and this for good reasons (e.g., National Socialism's pretensions to transcendent authority), liberation theologians in their context demand a much more contiguous relationship between the justice envisioned in the kingdom idea and the current misery experienced by the Latin American poor.

The entire discussion surrounding the ethical significance of the kingdom idea could be furthered by returning to and concentrating on the question regarding *what specific* significance the idea of the kingdom of God continues to have for Christian ethics. And to make the question even more precise: What significance does the idea of the kingdom of God have for Christian ethics *in a particular context*? Western theology has strongly emphasized that the kingdom of God proclaimed by Jesus was the kingdom *of God*. By so doing it has emphasized the apocalyptic nature of Jesus' proclamation and has insisted on the provisionality of all human action in relation to the coming of the kingdom. Liberation theology stresses, by contrast, that the kingdom of God is *a kingdom*. It is a kingdom which is not only to be fully realized in the eschaton but also a kingdom with a definite content, i.e., a model of human community in which all persons live under the loving rule of God. According to this content, a model is also disclosed which can serve as the ideal goal for the construction of human society until God's kingdom might one day arrive in its fullness. Even if "approximation" and "anticipation" define the preliminary nature of all human attempts to construct a community like unto the kingdom of God, the content of the kingdom disclosed in

the teaching and ministry of Jesus nevertheless remains a legitimate
ethical goal for society from a Christian perspective. The tension
within the New Testament itself between the kingdom "already"
present in the person and work of Jesus and "not yet" present in
fullness before the eschaton makes a definitive answer to the question
of the significance of the New Testament idea of the kingdom
unlikely. It is nevertheless along these lines that a constructive
dialogue might be initiated.

It is possible that behind the critique of liberation theology by
Neuhaus and Braaten, employing the criterion of the kingdom of God,
the root issue is finally their evangelical concern to preserve the
doctrine of justification by grace through faith alone. Braaten has been
most elaborate in pointing out the tendencies of liberation theology
toward "Pelagianism," "synergism," and "works righteousness."
Similarly both he and Neuhaus have criticized the Christology of
liberation theology for transforming the Christ who brings freedom
through the gospel, into a new law by reducing him to a model for
revolutionary activity. If it is true that this is the ultimate theological
concern of Neuhaus and Braaten, then it appears that once again their
critique is focusing upon the questions of liberation theology's
anthropology and its concept of liberation. What, if any, is the human
role in salvation? For Lutheran theologians this is the question which
takes priority over all others. In the case of liberation theology a
related question is also in order: What is the relationship between
salvation in Christ and the human project of liberation? For Neuhaus,
Braaten, and many others (e.g., Ogden) liberation theology has not yet
adequately answered these basic theological questions.

Braaten's critique of liberation theology for its use of Marxist
thought, particularly the Marxist idea of praxis, is not unrelated to
these questions. He understands liberation theology to have
uncritically appropriated the Marxist concept of praxis which makes of
salvation/liberation a purely human work. Braaten argues instead
that praxis must be seen as "a second step" which follows the
proclamation of the gospel in order to avoid "a legalization of the
Christian faith, whereby the kingdom of God generates no gospel, but
only the new law of transformative praxis."[51] Though it may be
questioned whether Braaten does not overestimate liberation theology's
reliance on Marx for its idea of praxis, the question which he raises

---

[51] Carl E. Braaten, "Praxis: The Trojan Horse of Liberation Theology,"
Dial 23 (Aug. 1984):279.

aims once more at liberation theology's anthropology and concept of liberation.

It is these two points which emerge again as the most significant issues raised by the critique of liberation theology by Neuhaus and Braaten. In calling upon the criterion of the New Testament idea of the kingdom of God, Neuhaus and Braaten would defend the gospel character of the gospel against what they are convinced is a false anthropology and an inadequate concept of liberation on the part of liberation theologians. While in presenting their critique one might have wished for a deeper recognition of the context of poverty and oppression in which the Latin American theology has arisen, a context which differs significantly from that of Luther in the sixteenth century and therefore leads to different theological emphases, their criticism, especially on these two points, needs to be taken seriously. By pointing to these difficulties in liberation theology the critique of Neuhaus and Braaten converges with that of several other North American theologians.

In questioning its anthropology, Neuhaus challenges the anthropological optimism of liberation theology expressed in such phrases as "the creation of a new man" or a "new society." Similarly Braaten points out the roots of human sinfulness which are deeper than its expressions in sinful social structures. Both then point to the person and work of Christ who is to be interpreted not as a mere model for revolutionary praxis but as the bringer of a gospel which speaks to and overcomes the innermost character of human alienation.

Their concern for an anthropology which accounts for the depths of human sinfulness and their interest in an understanding of the work of Christ commensurate with this human condition leads Neuhaus and Braaten to also criticize liberation theology's concept of liberation. Neuhaus indicates the need for an essential distinction between the attainment of individual freedom which finally can take place only through the work of Christ, and freedom's communal aspects which he understands to be the prevailing thrust of liberation theology. Likewise Braaten defends the indispensability of the theological distinction provided by a clear articulation of the *ordo salutis*. Such a distinction should make crystal clear that God's justification of the sinner is prior to the subsequent activation of faith in deeds of love. In this way the correct relationship is established between what Braaten also calls the "vertical" and "horizontal" dimensions of salvation. Only through a proper understanding of this relationship can Braaten advocate a "bifocal" approach to Christian mission which takes seriously both "evangelization and humanization," and "faith and political action." In outlining the *ordo salutis* in response to liberation theology, his theological concern approximates very closely that of Schubert Ogden who himself turns to Luther in distinguishing between "freedom in" and "freedom for," and between God as Redeemer and God the Emancipator, i.e., between God's work of redeeming the sinner and God's emancipative work in the world on behalf of all creatures held in bondage. As argued by Neuhaus and Braaten, who represent the perspective of a Lutheran theology, both the anthropology and concept of liberation thus far developed by liberation theology call for further reflection and clarification.

5. Question of Exegesis

The criticisms of the exegesis of liberation theology by North American theologians has unfortunately often been made in the form of generalizations which render closer examination and evaluation difficult. Needed are more specific studies of the exegesis of individual liberation theologians like those carried out by Phillips and Tambasco with regard to Segundo.[52] The conclusions of Phillips on the dangers that liberation theologies (1) sacrifice the Bible's critical function, (2) are selective in their choice of relevant texts, and (3) do not always pay sufficient attention to the original context, need to be taken seriously. Likewise Tambasco's pointing out the tendency toward eisegesis in certain interpretations of Segundo is an important insight. At the same time one should not overlook the generally appreciative judgments of Phillips and Tambasco as to the vitality and overall integrity of Segundo's exegesis.

Another approach which helps move beyond the level of generalization has been to examine the exegesis of a particular theme by liberation theology. Armerding and Yoder have employed this procedure in relationship to the Exodus theme and again arrive at mixed conclusions. While Armerding is very critical of Gutierrez's overall exegesis of the Exodus narrative, he confines his criticism of Miranda to specific technical points which are open for debate among scholars. Yoder, on the other hand, coming from the Mennonite

---

[52]The book by the British evangelical theologian J. Andrew Kirk, *Liberation Theology. An Evangelical View from the Third World* (Atlanta: John Knox, 1979), is another serious attempt to deal with the Scriptural interpretation by individual liberation theologians.

tradition renders an interpretation of the Exodus experience which raises as many questions as it answers. His emphases on non-violence and the role of a counter-community in his understanding of the Exodus event raise the question of whether his own theological presuppositions may not have shaped his interpretation even as he questions whether the presuppositions of liberation theologians have not colored their own exegesis. In light of these somewhat ambiguous conclusions, more elaborate studies which would critically examine the exegesis of a particular theme or paradigm by liberation theology could prove most helpful.

It should be noted in this context that not only commentators from outside Latin America have raised questions about the interpretation of the Bible by liberation theology. Similar questions have also been raised by those within the movement. Jose Miguez Bonino, for example, has called the task of biblical interpretation "a basic challenge for the theology of liberation."[53] He asks many of the same questions that have been raised by North American theologians about the legitimacy of liberation theology's exegesis. Miguez Bonino, however, also refers to the proposal that biblical texts contain "a reserve of meaning" which allows them to be legitimately interpreted in ever new historical contexts. Such a reference to "a reserve of meaning" shows that Miguez Bonino is familiar with the current discussion among those philosophers and theologians dealing with hermeneutics such as Paul Ricoeur. This reference furthermore indicates that the interpretation of biblical texts by many liberation theologians may not be as naive and uncritical as has sometimes appeared, but rather that their use of biblical texts moves beyond "mere" historical criticism to a more comprehensive hermeneutic which includes not only the meaning of a text in its original context but also the latent potential of a text to continue to speak in new situations.

This definitely appears to be the case with Raul Vidales as he writes of "a hermeneutic from the standpoint of liberation."[54] Vidales advocates a sophisticated hermeneutic which would incorporate both an understanding of the text in its historical particularity and in its

---

[53]Jose Miguez Bonino, "Theology and Theologians of the New World: II. Latin America. Five Theses Toward an Understanding of the 'Theology of Liberation'," *Expos T* 87 (Apr. 1976):199.

[54]Raul Vidales, "Methodological Issues in Liberation Theology," in Rosino Gibellini, ed., *Frontiers of Theology in Latin America*, trans. John Drury (Maryknoll: Orbis, 1979), p. 49.

vitality for the present.

The historical dimension of the message stems both from the fact that it arose in a specific historical milieu and from the fact that it is essentially related to human history. Only by salvaging this historical dimension can we maintain its prophetic character and function, its subversive undertones, and its provocative Christian originality: Only thus can we preserve the only field wherein God's message retains its validity for reflection and action.[55]

In a way which serves to counter the criticism voiced by several North American theologians, Vidales speaks of the need for the Bible to exercise a critical function as it moves "back and forth between the original Bible containing God's word and the other 'Bible' known as history."[56] Where this hermeneutic is particularly innovative is in its assertion that one move beyond historical-critical analysis of biblical texts to also thoroughly analyze contemporary reality. Thus the history, poverty, oppression, and injustice of the Latin American context also merit hermeneutical significance in this model for biblical interpretation.

This certainly does not mean that we are to go back and propose facile paradigmatic foundations, mechanical equations, fixist comparisons, inconsistent accommodations, and acritical parallels. It does mean we must try to work out a hermeneutic process that will enable us to establish the dialectical interrelationship between the historical reality of Jesus and his message on the one hand and present-day historical experience on the other. We cannot rest content with a theological effort that is merely concerned with interpreting God's salvific gesture or deed. We must proceed further to the actual work of relating it to an original and unassailable effort at historical collaboration. It is there that the much vaunted joint work of theology and exegesis take on flesh and bones.[57]

Whereas the theologians of liberation have been charged with undervaluing the original biblical context and in fact do need to be reminded of maintaining a critical point of view, perhaps their hermeneutic nevertheless also serves as a corrective to those interpretations which relegate the Bible exclusively to the past. The biblical interpretation of J. Severino Croatto is likewise indicative of a highly developed hermeneutical method.[58] Croatto in his approach to interpretation also seeks to emphasize both the original setting of biblical texts and their contemporary significance for the context of

---

[55]Ibid., p. 48.

[56]Ibid.

[57]Ibid., pp. 48-49.

[58]For the following cf. J. Severino Croatto, *Exodus. A Hermeneutics of Freedom*, trans. Salvator Attanasio (Maryknoll: Orbis, 1981).

liberation in Latin America. More than any other Latin American biblical scholar, Croatto has developed the insights of Ricoeur concerning the "surplus-of-meaning" of biblical texts in advocating the hermeneutical legitimacy of interpreting the Bible in light of contemporary Latin America. To this end Croatto has traced the liberating tradition of the Bible in a trajectory which originates in the Exodus and runs through the creation narratives, the prophetic witness, the liberating activity of Jesus, and the "paschal" theology of liberation of Paul. Throughout his exposition Croatto returns to the historical origins and development of the biblical tradition as the basis for his conclusions. At the same time, however, he insists on the ongoing significance of the biblical texts for the contemporary Latin American context as a legitimate function of the word itself. As is the case with Vidales, the biblical text grounded in one historical context must also continue to speak to present reality.

There are a great variety of ways in which theologians of liberation have interpreted the Bible in their theologies. Some of these, to be sure, are not so sophisticated as what Vidales and Croatto have advocated and at times their use does border on "proof-texting." When such is the case, the warning by Keck and others of the dangers of an ideological use of Scripture needs to be heeded. Similarly the insight of Tambasco regarding the importance of maintaining a dialectical tension between the original meaning of the biblical text and its contemporary relevance is an extremely important one. As David H. Kelsey has demonstrated, however, in examining the use of Scripture by other contemporary theologians, liberation theology is not alone in its need to be vigilant in examining its theological use of biblical interpretation.[59] Armerding's admission "that we all tend to come out of our exegetical house pretty much where we have gone in,"[60] thus serves as a word of caution not only to Latin American liberation theologians but to others as well. It needs to be emphasized, however, that there are a number of liberation theologians who operate with a highly developed exegetical and hermeneutical approach.

In concluding this discussion of the North American critique of liberation theology's exegesis, it might be added that in a number of

---

[59]Cf. David H. Kelsey, *The Uses of Scripture in Recent Theology* (Philadelphia: Fortress, 1975).

[60]Carl E. Armerding, "Exodus: The Old Testament Foundation of Liberation," in Carl E. Armerding, ed., *Evangelicals and Liberation* (Phillipsburg, NJ: Presbyterian and Reformed Publishing Co., 1979), p. 57.

cases liberation theology could be enriched by an encounter with the exegetical arguments and conclusions of North American scholars, for example, the extensive study of the history and sociology of Israel in the period 1250-1050 B.C. by Norman K. Gottwald or the discussions of the historical Jesus and his significance for human liberation by Peter C. Hodgson and Schubert M. Ogden.[61]

6. Evangelical Critiques

The evangelical theologians critical of liberation theology have independently raised many of the same arguments against liberation theology also developed by other North American theologians. For that reason their treatment here can be brief. What is unique about their argumentation is an appeal to biblical authority which often attempts to exclude a priori other appeals to the Bible as unbiblical. The division of evangelical theologians into those basically resonant to the concerns of liberation theology and those fundamentally opposed, indicates the need for evangelical theology to examine more closely the presuppositions which it brings to its own exclusive claim to biblical authority. Their dividedness on the question of liberation theology might point out to evangelical theologians that they too need to identify the presuppositions, theological and otherwise, which influence their own understanding of Scripture. Wagner, for example, brings the theology of "Church Growth" to his interpretation of the Bible. In this way his own understanding of ecclesiology and salvation may be as much in need of critical reflection as those of the liberation theology which he criticizes. Likewise Henry's presupposition, that the Bible consists of "propositional revelation," deserves examination in its own right before it can be accepted as the basis for criticizing liberation theology. To pursue an extensive critique of "Church Growth" or the notion of "propositional revelation," however, goes beyond the scope of the present work.

Setting to the side an examination of his understanding of the nature of Scripture and turning to his discussion of liberation theology, Henry employs several arguments against liberation theology already discussed in this chapter. He argues that liberation theology is an

---

[61] Cf. Norman K. Gottwald, *The Tribes of Yahweh. A Sociology of the Religion of Liberated Israel 1250-1050 B.C.E.* (Maryknoll: Orbis, 1979); Peter C. Hodgson, *New Birth of Freedom. A Theology of Bondage and Liberation* (Philadelphia: Fortress, 1976), pp. 208-264; and Schubert M. Ogden, *The Point of Christology* (San Francisco: Harper & Row, 1982), pp. 106-126.

attempt to erect the kingdom of God through human effort (revolution), that the exegesis of liberation theology is inadequate (Marxist), and that liberation theology is the attempt to reinterpret all of Christian doctrine in Marxist categories. In these arguments Henry shows little awareness of the attempt by liberation theologians to make a differentiated use of Marxist thought. He therefore interprets liberation theology through the lens of a preconceived understanding of Marxism and Communism which does not accurately represent the actual position of liberation theology.

By comparison, Bloesch's critique of liberation theology serves as a model for an evangelical approach which aims at fairly representing its views. Bloesch avoids exaggeration and caricature, and can even critically appreciate certain insights of liberation theology. For this reason the criticisms Bloesch makes of liberation theology deserve special attention. Once again they focus on two issues which have already emerged in the other North American critiques of liberation theology.

First, Bloesch refers to the doctrine of sin in criticizing the anthropology of liberation theology. Human misery, according to Bloesch, finds its ultimate ground in the sinfulness of the human heart and not in oppressive social conditions. On this point Bloesch is joined by Henry who in addition emphasizes the Marxist influence on liberation theology's anthropology. From the evangelical viewpoint of Bloesch and Henry, liberation theology has inaccurately appraised the influence of sin upon the human condition and thereby its capacity to establish a more just social order.

Second, and here Bloesch is joined in different ways both by Wagner and Henry, the evangelical critiques judge liberation theology to have a deficient soteriology. Liberation theology's inaccurate appraisal of the sinfulness of the human condition leads directly to a misunderstanding of the need for individual repentance and conversion. Bloesch insists that if liberation theology is to theologically ground its concern for liberation in the social realm, it must first pay adequate attention to salvation's individual dimension. With reference to Hans Küng he therefore proposes a clear differentiation in liberation theology between redemption and emancipation. For evangelical theology, the individual character of human sin and the individual dimension of conversion to Christ are paramount. It is especially on these two points that evangelical

theologians have credibly argued for the need for further clarification
on the part of liberation theology.

7. Proposals for a More Adequate Conceptuality

Migliore, Hodgson, Cobb, D. Brown, and Ogden have each
formulated a response to liberation theology which appreciates its basic
thrust while calling for greater conceptual clarity on certain specific
points. Moreover, they have gone beyond negative critique to offer
several constructive proposals for the development of what they believe
would be a more adequate conceptuality for liberation theology. By
formulating their critique in a constructive way, their approach
promises more for a future dialogue with liberation theologians than
those critiques which exhaust themselves in negative critique and an
unqualified rejection of liberation theology as a legitimate option for
Christian theology.

It should be noted, however, that the proposals of all five of these
North American theologians focus almost entirely on a more adequate
conceptuality for liberation theology. In this respect their proposals are
offered from the perspective of a primarily academic theology, a type of
theology which has been heftily criticized by liberation theology for its
disconnectedness from liberating praxis. It can be imagined that a
Latin American rejoinder to their conceptual proposals would not fail
to include renewed criticism of a theology which persists in refining
concepts while the demands of praxis are perceived to be so urgent. In
spite of their constructive approach, the gap between the procedure and
method of academic theology and the praxis method of liberation
theology is highlighted by their two vastly different understandings of
the present theological task. Nevertheless, it is to be hoped that
liberation theologians will take seriously the criticisms raised by their
North American critics even as North American academic theology
will be challenged to reexamine its relationship to praxis.

Before turning to the three most crucial criticisms of liberation
theology by this group of North American theologians, it is important to
mention a number of other salient points raised in the course of their
arguments. With regard to Migliore, it is interesting how once again
a theologian of the Reformed tradition, particularly those influenced
by the theology of Karl Barth, finds relevant liberation theology's
emphasis on the social implications of the Christian faith. In this
respect Migliore joins Shaull, Cone, Herzog, and R. Brown while
going beyond them in pointing out what he perceives to be the doctrinal

limitations of such a liberation orientation.

Moving next to Hodgson, reference has already been made to his implicit concurrence in the critique of liberation theology's anthropology insofar as it may have uncritically overtaken the Marxist idea. Likewise noted has been Hodgson's exposition of the historical Jesus which has immediate significance for the construction of a liberation Christology. An especially helpful insight in this regard is Hodgson's defense of the term "critical partisanship" as an appropriate description both of the posture of the historical Jesus and of those who seek to be faithful to his heritage. By preserving under the idea of critical partisanship not only the central concern of liberation theology for Jesus' partisan ministry to the poor and outcasts of his society but also the eschatological proviso which disallows any final identification of the kingdom of God with a particular political option, Hodgson's proposal merits serious consideration for mediating a basic conflict in understanding between liberation theology and several of its critics.

Delwin Brown's essay on freedom, *To Set at Liberty*, demonstrates in numerous ways the potential fecundity of process theology's idea of freedom for the liberation praxis advocated by liberation theologians. Although D. Brown himself never leaves the realm of academic discourse, his proposals for the reformulation of the doctrines of God, sin, and Christ, which articulate the specific realm in which human freedom can operate in the achievement of social liberation, are an important contribution to the current discussion that can only prove helpful to a future dialogue between Latin American and North American theologians. D. Brown's emphasis upon freedom's context is particularly important for recognizing that the meaning of freedom in the Latin American context of poverty and oppression may be different in other contexts where bondage takes on other forms. Also important is D. Brown's argument that Jesus' idea of the kingdom of God, stripped by Greek philosophy of its relevance for human history, needs to be restored. Its meaning for human action by means of process conceptuality, provides yet another position on the significance of the kingdom of God for Christian ethics, one with definite affinity to and relevance for liberation theology.

A major constructive contribution to liberation Christology has been offered by Ogden in his book *The Point of Christology*. Ogden's contention that a Christology of liberation is warranted by the apostolic witness provides within the North American academic context an argument which undergirds the legitimacy of formulating a liberation theology which is both appropriate to Christian origins and credible to the contemporary experience of social oppression. Ogden has in this way attempted to remain faithful to his dual criteria of an adequate theological statement while responding to the contemporary situation of those in bondage to unjust social structures. Like Hodgson and D. Brown, Ogden argues for an understanding of the kingdom of God which maintains its transcendent dimension while at the same time affirming its political implications. In arriving at this conclusion Ogden also argues for the importance of incorporating deideologizing into theological methodology, another concern which is responsive to the challenge of liberation theology to academic theology. Both Ogden's defense of the validity of a liberation Christology and his proposal for deideologizing within theological method demonstrate the influence of liberation theology upon one North American theologian. If these aspects of liberation theology have not been taken seriously by North American theologians on their own merit, then their meticulous exposition by a North American theologian of Ogden's stature lends them renewed vigor within the North American discussion of liberation theology.

In addition to these decidedly constructive proposals on behalf of a liberation theology, the North American theologians here under consideration also raise issues for liberation theology which they believe are in need of further reflection and clarification. These criticisms can be summarized under three points.

First, Hodgson, Cobb, D. Brown and Ogden each argue for the importance of a comprehensive philosophical framework for liberation theology. They are convinced that the truth claims of a liberation or any other theology cannot be demonstrated apart from the mode of argument characteristic of philosophical discourse. Only by means of such philosophical discourse and arguments can a liberation theology be taken seriously as a sound and reasonable theological option. For Hodgson that has meant the elaboration of what he describes as a foundational theology of freedom. A primary resource for Hodgson in elaborating such a foundational theology of freedom is Hegel's philosophy of history supplemented by insights from phenomenology, existentialism, and psychology. For Cobb, D. Brown and Ogden on the other hand, the primary resource is taken from process philosophy. It is particularly the idea of freedom expressed in process thought which they attempt to demonstrate could be of special value to the construction of a philosophically sound theology of liberation. Crucial to the process idea of freedom is its reformulation of the doctrine of God in establishing the legitimate place for human freedom in relationship to the divine. Lastly, Cobb and Ogden have both argued that a process conceptuality also incorporates a genuine concern for nature in its purview, a concern to which liberation theologians have not been sufficiently attentive.

A second issue for criticism, this one raised primarily by Ogden, is the need for liberation theology to more carefully articulate its method. Ogden has argued that liberation theology tends toward "the rationalization of positions already taken." This means that liberation theology has too often merely assumed the veracity of the Christian witness and its own claims for that witness. Ogden would, by contrast, distinguish much more rigorously between Christian *witness* and Christian *theology*. The task of theology is, according to Ogden, to critically apply the dual criteria of appropriateness and understandability/credibility to the claims of the Christian witness. This does not mean Christian witness is unimportant. But it does mean that the theological task is a different one. By confusing the two, Ogden believes liberation theology to have been negligent in carrying out its specifically theological duties. On this point he joins the somewhat different argumentation of McCann in challenging liberation theology to advance beyond rationalization.

The third and final point of major criticism is directed at liberation theology's concept of liberation. This point has been addressed in different ways by Hodgson and Ogden. Hodgson refers to a necessary distinction between Jesus' liberating work as it is addressed (1) to personal/psychic bondage and (2) to socio-economic/political bondage. Moreover, Hodgson recognizes a movement from liberation in the personal/psychic realm to participation in liberation movements in the socioeconomic/political sphere (cf. Braaten's emphasis on an *ordo salutis*).

Ogden calls explicitly upon Luther, especially his *The Freedom of a Christian*, in making a very similar point. Ogden would distinguish carefully, with regard to human freedom, between freedom *in* and freedom *for*. "Freedom in" refers to the incorporation of the individual into Christian existence which takes place through the love of God expressed in Jesus Christ. "Freedom for" refers to the outward directed character of Christian existence for the love and service of others. While Ogden insists that both "freedom in" and "freedom for"

belong inseparably to Christian existence, he also maintains that the
two need to be conceptually differentiated. Applying this distinction to
the doctrine of God, Ogden would correspondingly differentiate
between God the Redeemer and God the Emancipator. God's work of
redemption in unconditionally accepting sinful human beings needs
to be identified as God's work alone. God's work of emancipation,
however, in working to achieve interhuman justice allows for and
even invites the participation of human beings. Again Ogden insists
that both God's work as Redeemer and as Emancipator properly belong
to an adequate understanding of God's activity. Nevertheless, for the
sake of theological clarity the two need to be distinguished, yet without
separation. In asking for this clarification in liberation theology's
concept of liberation, Hodgson and Ogden join the ranks of other North
American theologians. They do so, however, by offering their own
constructive proposals for a more adequate conceptuality on the part of
liberation theology.

C. The Limitations of Latin American
Liberation Theology: Four Issues

The preceding analysis of the North American arguments in
criticism of liberation theology indicates four issues which before all
others require theological clarification. This is not to disregard the
other arguments so much as to propose that these four issues are, from
the side of North American academic theologians, the most crucial for
a future dialogue with Latin American liberation theology which takes
seriously the formulations it has thus far developed. These four issues
concern liberation theology's philosophical basis, theological method,
theological anthropology, and concept of liberation. In setting forth
these four issues it needs to be remembered that the liberation theology
movement is relatively young and itself still in the process of
development. Liberation theologians have never claimed to have
already arrived at a comprehensive theological statement. They have
never claimed for liberation theology the status of an all-
encompassing systematic theology.[62] Rather it has arisen in many
ways as an *ad hoc* theology, a theology seeking to respond to the urgent

---

[62]In an interview with Dow Kirkpatrick, "Liberation Theology and Third
World Demands," *Chr Cent* 93 (May 12, 1976):459-460, Gustavo Gutierrez makes
clear his objections to the misunderstanding that liberation theology is a
position which seeks to address all questions from its definite theological
perspective.

needs of the Latin American poor. For this reason these four issues can best be presented not as the refutation of liberation theology but instead as questions which need to be taken seriously in its future reflections.

The need for future clarification and reflection on these four points appears to be particularly important insofar as in each case the failure of liberation theology to elaborate its position has left it vulnerable to the charge that it is the Marxist understanding which underlies its position. For example, the failure to articulate its philosophical basis leaves open the question whether it is not Marx's deterministic philosophy of history with its dogmatic understanding of the necessity of revolution which actually undergirds liberation theology. Similarly the question arises whether it might not be a Marxist methodology, anthropology, and concept of liberation which finally are decisive for liberation theology. The assumption that this is the case has often been made by the North American critics of liberation theology and this too makes further clarification of these four issues significant.

1. Philosophical Basis

Although liberation theology has severely criticized what it understands to be the shortcomings of the Western philosophical tradition, it needs to be asked whether philosophical presuppositions of some sort are not an inevitable part of theological discourse (or any other kind of discourse for that matter). Philosophical assumptions, for example, about the existence of God, the relationship of God and the world, the origin and destiny of the world, the nature of freedom, etc., lie unavoidably behind theological statements. If such assumptions are not examined, that does not mean that they do not exist. Even granted that philosophical reflection is not, and moreover should not be, the highest priority for a theology in the context of Latin American poverty, nevertheless philosophical assumptions are made and therefore a blanket rejection of philosophical reflection seems inadequate.

It may well be that the subjectivistic and intellectualistic tendencies of philosophy in the Western tradition are in need of the critique which has been made by liberation theology and that this critique should be seriously pondered by those grounded in the Western tradition. Still, liberation theologians themselves continue to make philosophical assumptions and often they are assumptions which are a part of that Western tradition.[63] Two examples from the writings of liberation theologians can help illustrate this point.

Underlying Gustavo Gutierrez's *A Theology of Liberation* there appears a fundamental assumption about historical progress. While refusing to equate the kingdom of God with temporal progress, Gutierrez nevertheless makes a basic assumption about the reality of historical progress which is reflected in a phrase like "the liberation of man throughout history."[64] Throughout his book Gutierrez seems to share the very Western idea that history proceeds toward ever higher levels of realization.[65] While there is nothing intrinsically wrong with making such an assumption, it is nonetheless an assumption in need of recognition and critical reflection.

A second example is the reliance of several Latin American liberation theologians on the evolutionary philosophy of Teilhard de Chardin. Most elaborate in this regard has been Juan Luis Segundo.[66] Teilhard's vision of the evolutionary progression of human history lends Segundo a sense of hope and confidence about the future even in the midst of a historical reality which seems to contradict that hope. Likewise in the thought of other liberation theologians—Rubem Alves, Arturo Paoli, and Gutierrez among others—the evolutionary realization of history in Christ as described by Teilhard seems to provide a significant backdrop.[67] Again such philosophical assumptions need to be recognized and examined.

In the words of David Tracy (with reference to Aristotle), "the choice is not really between metaphysics or no metaphysics; the only real choice is between a self-conscious and explicit metaphysics or an

---

[63]Jürgen Moltmann, "An Open Letter to Jose Miguez Bonino. On Latin American Liberation Theology," *Chr Cris* 36 (Mar. 29, 1976):58-59, points out the ongoing dependence of Latin American liberation theology on the Western intellectual tradition.

[64]Gutierrez, *A Theology of Liberation*, p. 176.

[65]Robert Nisbet, *History of the Idea of Progress* (New York: Basic Books, 1980), has documented how thoroughly the idea of progress has interpenetrated Western thought, both in its liberal and the radical trajectories.

[66]Cf. esp. Juan Luis Segundo, *A Theology for Artisans of a New Humanity. Vol. 5: Evolution and Guilt,* trans. John Drury (Maryknoll: Orbis, 1974).

[67]Cf. Rubem Alves, "Towards a Theology of Liberation," Th.D. Dissertation (Princeton: Princeton Theological Seminary, 1968), pp. 107, 126-127, 249-250, and 261; Arturo Paoli, *Freedom to be Free* (Maryknoll: Orbis, 1973), pp. 184, 187, 213, 237, 244, and 263; and Gutierrez, *A Theology of Liberation*, pp. 32-33 and 173.

unconscious yet operative one."[68] Many North American theologians
like Tracy hold philosophical argumentation as a high priority not
only because philosophical assumptions are inevitable but also for two
other reasons. First, they hold philosophical reasoning to be the proper
mode of argumentation in their dialogue with the contemporary
secular world which does not share their convictions about the
existence and activity of God. Secondly, they believe philosophical
discourse can best serve in testing the truth claims of theology within
the scientific approach appropriate to the academy.[69] Since liberation
theology does not originate in an academic setting and does not see the
contemporary non-believer as its primary interlocutor, it is doubtful
that it can assent to the high priority given to philosophical
argumentation in many modern theologies. Similarly it remains to
be seen whether liberation theologians will find convincing the
constructive philosophical proposals such as those offered by Hodgson's
foundational theology of freedom or by the process theologians. If for
no other reason, however, liberation theologians would be well served
by a higher level of articulation of their philosophical assumptions and
basis in order to refute the claim that they uncritically operate within a
Marxist philosophical framework.

2. Theological Method

Liberation theology claims to have arrived at a theological method
grounded in Latin American history and experience, a method which
is essentially connected to a liberating praxis for the erection of more
just social structures. At the same time the articulation of a theoretical
understanding of that method has not yet been a high priority for the
majority of the liberation theologians. In attempting to understand the
method of liberation theology, several North American theologians,
especially Ogden, have noted that liberation theology approximates
more closely a form of Christian witness than what they would
normally describe as a theological method. Ogden insists that
theological method must incorporate reflection upon the truth claims of
Christianity and not only testify to the significance of the Christian
faith for contemporary experience. For this reason he has charged

---

[68]David Tracy, *Blessed Rage for Order. The New Pluralism in Theology*
(New York: Seabury, 1978), p. 68.

[69]Cf. David Tracy, *The Analogical Imagination. Christian Theology and
the Culture of Pluralism* (New York: Crossroad, 1981), pp. 62-64, on the task of
fundamental theology.

liberation theology with the tendency of being "the mere rationalization of positions already taken."[70]

Taking this criticism to its logical extreme by interpreting the method of liberation theology as being decisively shaped by Freire's understanding of conscienticization, Dennis P. McCann has attempted to unmask the method of liberation theology either as merely a new form of theological myth-making or as the radical abolition of theology according to the Marxist critique of religion. Although it has been argued that McCann overestimates the role of conscienticization for the method of liberation theology, it is significant that by failing to carefully elaborate its method, liberation theology is once again charged with having overtaken the Marxist position.

Another way to express this criticism might be to point out the facility with which liberation theology can be logically reduced to sheer activism. Given the five constitutive elements which comprise the method of liberation theology according to the second chapter of this work, should the fourth element, theological reflection and reformulation, be either deleted or insufficiently emphasized, then the method of liberation theology would collapse into a form of activism scarcely distinguishable from other forms of radical praxis. Such a reduction of liberation theology would appear to contradict the intentions of the liberation theologians themselves. Much effort has been given to the task of theological reflection and reformulation in their work. Yet the need remains for a clear theoretical articulation of the place of theological reflection and reformulation within the entirety of liberation theology's method.

An important contribution to this outstanding task has been made by Clodovis Boff in his work *Theology and Praxis.*[71] C. Boff argues that a clearly defined, epistemologically legitimate, and functionally independent place be assigned to theological reflection within the method of liberation theology. This proposal is one that has already been affirmed by other liberation theologians (e.g., Miguez Bonino) and could prove most helpful for clarifying the relationship of theological reflection to praxis within liberation theology.

One possible liability of C. Boff's formulation is his calling upon

---

[70]Schubert M. Ogden, "The Concept of a Theology of Liberation: Must a Christian Theology Today Be So Conceived?" in Mahan and Richesin, eds., *The Challenge of Liberation Theology,* p. 134.

[71]Clodovis Boff, *Theologie und Praxis. Die erkenntnistheoretischen Grundlagen der Theologie der Befreiung* (Munich: Kaiser-Grünewald, 1983).

the transcendental theological conceptuality of Thomas Aquinas (in dependence upon Aristotle) as a resource in exemplifying how liberation theology should maintain the integrity of theological reflection. Such a dependence upon the transcendental categories of scholastic theology, with its bifurcation of reality into imminent and transcendent, seems to contradict liberation theology's strong emphasis upon the oneness of human history. It would appear, however, that according to C. Boff's line of argumentation, a distinctive position can be given to the theological reflection within the method of liberation theology, without necessarily following him in returning to the scholastic understanding of history and theology originally worked out by Aquinas.

Liberation theologians have already given considerable effort to the task of constructive theological reformulation. Their contributions to rethinking the theology of history, Christology, ecclesiology, spirituality, and the idea of the kingdom of God are, for example, important contributions to the contemporary theological discussion. In examining their method, however, the issue needs to be addressed with greater intensity as to how their theological reformulations relate to the entire liberation project. Do their reformulations only function as the rationalization of positions already taken? A key question becomes: At what point does theological reflection not endorse but criticize a particular course of action? At this point the independence of theological reflection within a praxis-oriented theology would become evident. It is especially on this point that liberation theology needs to be challenged to clarify the place of theological reflection within its methodology.

3. Theological Anthropology

There would appear to be a certain irony in the fact that liberation theology has been accused of naivete about human nature when it is a theology which has been so insistent in pointing out the structural "sins" both of Western and of Latin American society—e.g., colonial exploitation, imperialism, militarism, political repression, economic dependency, and the disparity between rich and poor. If ever there were a theology which had reason to be skeptical about the human hubris and selfishness which expresses itself in unjust social structures, it would seem to be the theology of liberation.

Perhaps liberation theology's emphasis upon sinful structures rather than upon the sinfulness of the human heart can be explained at least in part by considering the context in which it has arisen. In many ways liberation theology has attempted to counter an often fatalistic attitude among the poor about the inevitability of their suffering by analyzing the social structures which oppress them— unjust social structures which have not in fact been established as such by God—and by emphasizing what the poor themselves can do to alter their condition. Before hastily accusing liberation theology of triumphalism, it is important to recognize that it may be the opposite extreme of a submissive fatalism and resignation (cf. D. Brown's description of sensuality as a form of sin[72]) which better characterizes the attitude of the poor than that of an overambitious pride which recognizes no limits. Certainly there are very few initiated into Western society who would be satisfied by an explanation which attributes an injustice committed against them to the will of God, without first exercising every means within their political power to correct that injustice.

If there is a theological understanding of sinfulness which affirms that fallen human beings ultimately twist circumstances for their own self-interest, there still remains the necessity of defining the legitimate sphere in which human freedom should be allowed to operate. If checks and balances need to be applied to prevent the abuses which result from human hubris, that is a different matter from denying that human freedom has a necessary role to play in structuring political affairs. Just as a particular system of social structures is the product of human construction, so too altering that system is a matter of human reconstruction. From the perspective of a traditionally Christian theological anthropology, it might well be argued that a system of social structures which establishes checks and balances to limit the abuses of human selfishness is preferable to a system which fails to establish such limits. Nevertheless, a specific system of social structures is a human construction and cannot be facilely attributed to the will of God. While government in general might still be seen as an "order of preservation" instituted by God, the historical evidence left by many specific twentieth-century governments argues against the identification of any particular system with the divine intention.

It might also be asked why several North American critics, particularly those influenced by Lutheran theology, have immediately

[72]See Delwin Brown, *To Set at Liberty. Christian Faith and Human Freedom* (Maryknoll: Orbis, 1981), pp. 70-73.

assumed that liberation theology has uncritically overtaken a Marxist anthropology. Those criticisms, for example, which accuse it of succumbing to a new form of works-righteousness would not only be applicable if liberation theology operates with a Marxist anthropology. Rather the suspicion of "semi-Pelagianism" would be just as applicable if liberation theology functions with the much more traditional Roman Catholic anthropology characterized by the phrase "grace perfects nature." It would appear far more cogent to assume, for example, that the Roman Catholic Gutierrez in his espousal of the creation of "a new man," is operating with the "super-added grace" anthropology of traditional Roman Catholic theology than that he has smuggled a Marxist anthropology into theological discourse.[73] A Lutheran criticism of liberation theology in this way returns to the age-old debate over an "optimistic" Roman Catholic anthropology versus a "pessimistic" Lutheran anthropology without exaggerating the influence of Marx upon the anthropology of liberation theology.

The preceding paragraphs attempt to discern the parameters within which a constructive discussion of liberation theology's anthropology can take place. As is the case for each of the four major issues remaining to be clarified by liberation theology, here too liberation theologians have not yet made theological anthropology a priority in their deliberations. The formulations they have made thus far have often been interpreted by their critics as presupposing an overly optimistic anthropology which fails to take the condition of human sin with sufficient seriousness. Frequently the "realistic" theological anthropology of Reinhold Niebuhr has been favorably contrasted with the overly optimistic anthropology of liberation theology. These criticisms can only be addressed by a more thorough elaboration and clarification by liberation theology of the theological anthropology with which it operates.

Would a more "pessimistic" or "realistic" apprehension of human sinfulness mean the abandonment of the fundamental thrust of liberation theology toward the construction of more just social structures in Latin America? It is only possible to speculate at this point what such a theological anthropology might mean for future formulations of liberation theology. It might mean, for example,

---

[73]For example, Braaten, "Praxis: The Trojan Horse of Liberation Theology," seems to unduly stress the Marxist influence upon liberation theology without considering explanations which are inherently Roman Catholic.

leaving behind some of the overly optimistic rhetoric which typified many of the earliest assertions of liberation theology about the construction of a "new man" in a "new society." Already the reality of ongoing hunger and social injustice coupled with increased political repression against the perspective of liberation theology has issued in a more sober appraisal of the difficulty of any liberation project in Latin America. The liberation theologians themselves have already begun to speak not only exclusively of a theology of liberation but also a theology of exile, martyrdom, and captivity.

A deeper recognition not only of the self-centered interests which oppose the erection of more just social structures in Latin America, but also of the potentially self-centered interests of those seeking to promote such social structures, might lead liberation theology into new vistas in its theological development. Without surrendering its option for the poor, the theologians of liberation, by virtue of a more skeptical estimation of the human possibilities for constructing a perfect society, might be forced to undertake, in further cooperation with economists, sociologists, and political scientists, a more extensive description and proposal of the kinds of social structures to which they aspire. What checks and balances are necessary for social structures in Latin America which adequately limit the excesses both of economic and political power? How can Latin American countries establish social structures which avoid not only what it perceives to be the economic exploitation of capitalism, but also the political totalitarianism of communism? Even granting in extreme cases the possible need for revolution in an individual country as the presupposition for establishing more just structures, much more critical work needs to be done in articulating a specific system of social structures which can better approximate the ideals which liberation theology envisions for the future of Latin America. While a utopian vision may be necessary, it is not in itself sufficient if new forms of oppression are not eventually to replace the old.

Thus far most liberation theologians have stopped short of the complex and difficult task of initiating and contributing to a discussion of specific structural proposals. One exception to this generalization is Juan Luis Segundo who in his book *Faith and Ideologies* begins to consider the possible contributions of religion, Marxism, and the Christian faith to the construction of a viable

cultural basis for the future of Latin American society.[74] While
Segundo's reflections are to be welcomed as a step in the right
direction, they too do not go far enough in describing the particular
nature of the new social structures which are needed to replace those
which already exist. Also Segundo's failure to examine democracy as
a possible resource for the future of Latin American society raises
questions about how not only economic power but also political power is
to be structurally held in check.

A strong argument might be made for the importance of the
establishment in Latin America not only of a more socialistic
economic system but also of a more democratic political system. Karl
Popper, for one, has made a substantial case for the significance of
democratic structures in setting limits upon both economic and
political power.

> I believe that the injustice and inhumanity of the unrestrained "capitalist
> system" described by Marx cannot be questioned; but it can be interpreted
> in terms of what we called, in a previous chapter, the *paradox of freedom.*
> Freedom, we have seen, defeats itself, if it is unlimited. Unlimited
> freedom means that a strong man is free to bully one who is weak and to
> rob him of his freedom. That is why we demand that the state should limit
> freedom to a certain extent, so that everyone's freedom is protected by law.
> Nobody should be at the *mercy* of others, but all should have a *right* to be
> protected by the state.[75]

Popper is operating here with what might be described as a "realistic"
anthropology. Translating his words into theological terms, one
might say, that he affirms an anthropology which takes seriously the
inclination of human beings toward selfishly manipulating
circumstances to their own advantage, i.e., that human beings are
inclined toward sin. For this reason there is a need to construct
systems of law which regulate human affairs, also in the economic
realm.

This does not mean for Popper, however, forgetting that human
hubris also is operative in the political realm. Just as "unrestrained
capitalism" must "give way to an economic interventionism,"[76] so
also unrestrained political power must be held in check by democratic
institutions.

. . . what Marxists describe disparagingly as "mere formal freedom"

---

[74]Juan Luis Segundo, *Jesus of Nazareth Yesterday and Today. Vol. 1:
Faith and Ideologies,* trans. John Drury (Maryknoll: Orbis, 1984), pp. 326-338.

[75]Karl R. Popper, *The Open Society and Its Enemies. Vol. 2: The High
Tide of Prophecy: Hegel, Marx, and the Aftermath,* p. 124.

[76]Ibid., p. 125 (emphases deleted).

becomes the basis of everything else. This "mere formal freedom," i.e., democracy, the right of the people to judge and to dismiss their government, is the only known device by which we can try to protect ourselves against the misuse of political power; it is the control of the rulers by the ruled. And since political power can control economic power, political democracy is also the only means for the control of economic power by the ruled. Without democratic control, there can be no earthly reason why any government should not use its political and economic power for purposes very different from the protection of the freedom of its citizens.[77]

Therefore, on the basis of a realistic view of human nature, both economic interventionism (i.e., a form of socialism) and democratic political structures seem imperative. A theological anthropology which takes seriously human sinfulness would do well to consider both elements in envisioning the types of structures needed to adequately order public affairs. It is in initiating and contributing to a discussion of the specific set of social structures appropriate to Latin America, structures governed by a rule of law against the abuses of both economic and political power, that liberation theology might make an important contribution in the future.

Taking Popper's insights one step further, there appears to be an equally urgent need for limiting structures which regulate the economic and political relations between nations. If human selfishness is also operative in international affairs—and there is no reason to believe it is not—then a form of economic interventionism and democratic control also appears to be warranted on the international level. The latter is one of the ideals of organizations like the United Nations and the World Court, organizations which in recent times have been severely hampered in their effectiveness by the noncooperation of member states. Based on a "realistic" view of human nature, a strong argument can be made, not for the weakening, but for the strengthening of the authority of such organizations. Likewise in the economic realm, elaborate proposals have been developed by the United Nations for the establishment of "A New International Economic Order," which proposes concrete measures for a more just regulation of international economic affairs.[78] Blocking

---

[77]Ibid., p. 127.

[78]Among the several pertinent United Nations documents cf. Resolution Adopted by the General Assembly, "Declaration on the Establishment of a New International Economic Order" (May 9, 1974), 5 pp.; Resolution Adopted by the General Assembly, "Programme of Action on the Establishment of a New International Economic Order" (May 16, 1974), 20 pp.; and United Nations, *International Development Strategy for the Third United Nations Development*

the implementation of such proposals, however, stands the self-interest of nations in seeking to promote their own advantages irrespective of the costs to others.

Other proposals of Popper, for example, the need for what he describes as a "piecemeal" approach to social change, might also be well considered by a liberation theology guided by a more skeptical theological anthropology.[79] Even in the extreme event of revolution, the subsequent structures which emerge do not suddenly appear from anew, but make use of the social fabric remaining from the previous social system. Holistic change is not only impossible but also brings about "unintended and largely unexpected repercussions, forcing upon the holistic engineer the expedient of piecemeal *improvization*"[80] regardless of other more radical intentions. For this reason, subscription to what Peter L. Berger has, in a parallel argument, described as "the postulate of ignorance in the formation of policy" might be appropriate for a liberation theology informed by a thoroughly "realistic" theological anthropology.[81]

The danger of suggesting to liberation theology these qualifications based on a theological anthropology skeptical of human self-interest is, that the urgency and necessity for change succumb to mere cynicism about human nature. This is a real danger and one which has often become reality when Christian realism has served as rationalization for an unjust status quo. Nevertheless the basis for successful social change, i.e., social change which delivers the more just society to which liberation theology aspires for Latin America, can only hope to be achieved on the basis of an anthropology which accurately depicts the vicissitudes of human nature. Such an anthropology must, from a theological perspective, entail a serious reckoning with the depths of human perversity.

4. The Concept of Liberation

The final issue to be considered, liberation theology's concept of liberation, is closely related to the preceding discussion of its theological anthropology. Insofar as liberation theology has stressed sin as a structural component of Latin American society, it has also

---

Decade (United Nations, NY: Department of Public Information, 1981), 27 pp.

[79]Cf. Karl R. Popper, *The Poverty of Historicism* (London: Routledge & Kegan, 1979), pp. 64-70.

[80]Ibid., p. 68.

[81]Peter L. Berger, *Pyramids of Sacrifice*, pp. 136-144.

primarily emphasized liberation as a socioeconomic and political reality. By so doing, liberation theology has accomplished much in raising theological awareness of the structural dimensions that sin does indeed assume. At the same time, especially in the attention it has given to spirituality, liberation theology has by no means ignored the personal dimensions of liberation. It has, however, done so in a less traditional way, referring, for example, to the "mystical and political dimensions of the Christian faith" to express its dual concern for both the personal and political ramifications of the gospel.

Several North American theologians, chief among them Braaten, Ogden, and the evangelical theologians, have found liberation theology's concept of liberation at least in need of further clarification if not fully unacceptable. Most constructive in his criticisms has been Ogden who has suggested a clear distinction between (1) liberation as redemption of the individual from sin and (2) liberation as emancipation for working to promote social justice—yet without separating the two aspects. Such a distinction might indeed help to sharpen and clarify an issue often misunderstood and criticized by those approaching the theological task with different presuppositions. This is especially the case for those North American theologians nurtured in Reformation theology. Ogden contends that such a distinction can only be an enrichment for liberation theology, not a reduction. A discussion of his constructive proposal among liberation theologians would be welcome from the side of North American theology.

There is a highly significant theological question underlying this entire issue, however, which also needs to be recognized and examined. In the debate between liberation theology and its North American critics over its concept of liberation, one question emerges to the forefront above all others: What is the gospel? When North American Protestant theologians make reference to "the gospel" it is almost certainly the case that they mean the Reformation understanding of "justification by grace through faith" as it has been primarily developed from Pauline theology. When Latin American liberation theologians, however, speak of "the gospel," it is almost certainly the case that they mean the "liberation trajectory" (Brueggemann) of "God's good news for the poor and marginals" drawn primarily from the Exodus narrative, the prophet corpus, and Jesus' proclamation of the kingdom of God. In view of its different understanding of the gospel, Shaull's allusion to the proponents of liberation theology as "heralds of a new reformation" may be very insightful. The problem arises, however, of reconciling the two understandings. Is one correct and the other false? Or, must not the meaning of the gospel be wide enough to incorporate both aspects?

There would appear to be biblical grounds for arguing for an understanding of the gospel large enough to incorporate both understandings. Both are deeply rooted in the biblical tradition and both continue to have immediate and ongoing relevance for contemporary Christian experience in a host of varying contexts. There is a pressing need for further reflection on the possible continuities between these two paradigmatic understandings of the gospel. As New Testament scholarship has long recognized, a key moment of transition is between the proclamation of the kingdom of God by the historical Jesus and the earliest Christian community's proclamation of Jesus as the crucified and risen Savior. In the light of the tension between a Pauline understanding of the gospel of justification and Jesus' proclamation of the kingdom of God, it is of theological importance to study possible links between the two. For example, the authority which Jesus claimed for himself in forgiving sins would appear to stand in continuity with the Pauline idea of the forgiveness of sins made available through Christ's death and resurrection. Or, Jesus' proclamation of a kingdom which is open to the sick and the demon-possessed, to tax collectors and sinners, and to women and children would seem to be a presupposition for the Pauline understanding of the Christian church which has broken down the barrier between Jew and Gentile. One of the ingenious aspects of Dietrich Bonhoeffer's theology, especially demonstrated in *The Cost of Discipleship*, is exactly his ability to bridge between the Pauline insistence upon justification by grace through faith and the synoptic call for discipleship.[82] For Bonhoeffer both theological emphases find their common focus in the centrality of Christ. Examining the New Testament for such continuities could do much to mediate between the Protestant and liberation theology understandings of the gospel.

There is a need for deeper theological reflection on the continuities between these two paradigmatically different understandings of the gospel. Thus far liberation theologians have tended to accuse a Protestant understanding of the gospel of serving ideological

---

[82]Cf. Geffrey B. Kelly, *Liberating Faith. Bonhoeffer's Message for Today* (Minneapolis: Augsburg, 1984), pp. 62-65.

purposes,[83] while theologians of the Reformation tradition have tended to accuse liberation theology of works-righteousness and/or a political reductionism of the gospel.[84] It is hoped that future dialogue between North American and Latin American theologians can address further this sensitive and vital theological question. For the purposes of future discussion, the constructive proposal for a distinction between liberation as redemption and liberation as emancipation would appear to be an excellent starting point.[85] In this understanding the traditionally Protestant theological affirmation of "faith becoming active in love" receives new contours as, in consideration of contemporary social inequities, "faith becomes active in justice."

In criticizing liberation theology's understanding of the concept of liberation for insufficiently apprehending and elaborating the need of the individual for redemption from sin, North American theologians, at the same time, might be challenged by liberation theology's insistence on the social dimensions of salvation. Salvation/liberation is too narrowly conceived when either the individual or the social dimensions remain undeveloped. Liberation theology serves as a constant reminder of the manifestations of sin in the economic and political structures of the modern world. The remaining task is one of theologically articulating an understanding of salvation/liberation which is attentive both to Christian origins and to contemporary experience—including the experience of poverty throughout the globe.

D. *The Validity of Latin American Liberation Theology*

To affirm at the conclusion of this work the validity of Latin American liberation theology is to render a judgment on the entirety of the preceding discussion. According to both its own formulations in the Latin American context and according to a critical evaluation of

---

[83]For example, see the criticism of Lutheran theology by Juan Luis Segundo, *The Liberation of Theology*, trans. John Drury (Maryknoll: Orbis, 1976), pp. 142-144.

[84]For example, see Carl E. Braaten, *Principles of Lutheran Theology* (Philadelphia: Fortress Press, 1983), pp. 107-108.

[85]Another constructive contribution to this discussion is Jürgen Moltmann (with M. Douglas Meeks), "The Liberation of Oppressors," *Chr Cris* 38 (Dec. 25, 1978):310-317, in which the distinction is made between the "root of all evil" expressed in the idea of "original sin" and the oppressive forms (e.g., racism, sexism, capitalism) which sin assumes in contemporary society. The liberation which God delivers in Christ from the presumptuousness and compulsions of sin becomes in turn the basis for a liberated and liberating "lifepraxis."

the North American responses, liberation theology can be affirmed as a valid and significant theological option. The criteria for such a judgment are twofold: (1) the rootedness of liberation theology in the Christian tradition and (2) the nature of the Latin American plausibility structure. This is not to dismiss the arguments which have been made in criticism of liberation theology. The four issues— philosophical basis, theological method, theological anthropology, and the concept of liberation—need to be further addressed and clarified by liberation theologians from the perspective of North American theology. They are issues which need to be taken most seriously. Nevertheless, in spite of these limitations, liberation theology emerges as a theological option with a vital role to play in awakening contemporary theology to aspects of global reality, and thereby aspects of the Christian tradition, long neglected in theology's preoccupation with the questions of modernity.

The position here taken approximates that of Schubert M. Ogden in his appraisal of the challenge of liberation theology.

> . . . the challenge presented by the various liberation theologies is that of working out a still more adequate theology of liberation than any of them has yet achieved.[86]

Ogden does not question that liberation theology is grounded in the Christian tradition. In fact, he understands it to be in continuity with the liberal theological tradition. Likewise he finds liberation theology's critique of academic theology, in its insistence upon commitment to practical action and justice, a challenge to which professional theologians need to respond. At the same time, Ogden seeks to constructively criticize what he perceives to be the "failures" of liberation theology so that it might develop a more adequate conceptuality. Through this kind of critical affirmation the North American exchange with liberation theology might move beyond the impasse of polarization to constructive dialogue.

1. Rootedness in the Christian Tradition

Liberation theology is, based on its own formulations and not on a caricature of its positions, a theology deeply rooted in the Christian tradition. The occasional accusation that liberation theology is mere Marxism in Christian guise cannot be sustained on the basis of its primary relatedness to the Christian tradition and its critical stance

---

[86]Schubert M. Ogden, *Faith and Freedom. Toward a Theology of Liberation* (Nashville: Abingdon, 1979), p. 32.

regarding several important aspects of Marxist thought. The theological reformulations of liberation theology in the area of Christology and ecclesiology, for example, illustrate the way in which liberation theologians make use of the Christian tradition in arriving at their interpretation of basic theological themes.

The primary resource for the theology of liberation is the Bible. Within the Bible it is what Brueggemann labels "the liberation trajectory" which has had primary significance for the formulations of liberation theology thus far in its development. The paradigm of the Exodus, the prophetic writings, and the proclamation and ministry of the historical Jesus have been found especially relevant for theology in the Latin American context. North American theologians such as Shaull, R. Brown, Ruether, Hodgson, D. Brown, Ogden and several evangelical theologians have each in their own way recognized the biblical rootedness of liberation theology and therefore affirmed its fundamental validity as a Christian theology. In its view of biblical history, liberation theology has returned to a position which emphasizes human history as the primary locus for divine revelation and therefore understands itself to be authorized to also pay strict attention to the historical context in which it is situated.

Liberation theology is also rooted in the Christian tradition by virtue of its constant references to past formulations of the Christian faith in articulating its own position. Often these references have been of a critical nature as liberation theology has questioned an other-worldly theological orientation, or the use of the church and/or theology to ideologically support oppressive governments. But liberation theology has been by no means exclusively critical of the Christian theological heritage. A few examples can help to briefly illustrate this point. Segundo, for instance, finds the Christological formulations of Chalcedon, especially in their preservation of Jesus' humanity, extremely relevant for the central concerns of a liberation Christology.[87] Likewise he finds the recovery of the trinitarian formulations which developed in the early centuries of the church an important component for the construction of a contemporary doctrine of God.[88] Jon Sobrino, in his Christology, devotes extended attention to

---

[87]Cf. Juan Luis Segundo, "Is Chalcedon Out of Date?" *American Academy of Religion. The Currents in Contemporary Christology Group. Newsletter* 3, No. 2, pp. 1-17.

[88]Cf. Juan Luis Segundo, *A Theology for Artisans of a New Humanity. Vol. 3: Our Idea of God*, trans. John Drury (Maryknoll: Orbis, 1974), pp. 63-66.

not only the Christological dogmas of the Christian tradition but also to the contemporary significance of the *Spiritual Exercises* of Ignatius Loyola.[89] Gutierrez draws extensively upon St. John of the Cross and other spiritual writers in describing the spirituality of the theology of liberation.[90]   Such examples from the writings of liberation theologians could be multiplied *ad infinitum* in pointing out the rootedness of liberation theology in the two thousand year history of Christian thought.

A final resource which needs to be noted with reference to liberation theology is its rootedness in the ecclesiastical documents of the Roman Catholic Church. Among the documents of Vatican II, it is to the "Pastoral Constitution on the Church in the Modern World" that liberation theology frequently turns in explaining the importance of a church which is a sign of love and service to the modern world, a church which is attentive to the "signs of the times."[91] The official documents of the Medellin and Puebla bishops conferences, moreover, are understood by liberation theologians to provide authorization for the basic insights from which their theology has been constructed. At Medellin, for example, in the document entitled "Peace," the Latin American bishops exercised a critique of Latin American economic injustice and institutionalized violence which undergirds the critique of Latin American social structures carried out by liberation theology.[92]   Also at Medellin, the Latin American bishops recognized the importance of the task of conscienticization in the pursuit of social justice[93] and the importance of evangelical poverty for the integrity of the church in Latin America.[94]   At Puebla, significant reaffirmations of the basic Christian communities and of "a preferential option for the

---

[89]Cf. Jon Sobrino, *Christology at the Crossroads. A Latin American Approach*, trans. John Drury (Maryknoll: Orbis, 1978), pp. 311-345 and 396-424.

[90]Cf. Gustavo Gutierrez, *We Drink From Our Own Wells. The Spiritual Journey of a People*, trans. Matthew J. O'Connell (Maryknoll: Orbis, 1984), esp. pp. 83-88.

[91]Cf. *"Gaudium et Spes*. Pastoral Constitution on the Church in the Modern World," in Joseph Gremillion, ed., *The Gospel of Peace and Justice. Catholic Social Teaching Since Pope John* (Maryknoll: Orbis, 1976), pp. 243-335.

[92]Cf. Medellin Documents, "Peace," in Gremillion, ed., *The Gospel of Peace and Justice*, pp. 455-464.

[93]Cf. Medellin Documents, "Justice," in Gremillion, ed., *The Gospel of Peace and Justice*, pp. 452-454.

[94]Cf. Medellin Documents, "Poverty of the Church," in Gremillion, ed., *The Gospel of Peace and Justice*, pp. 471-476.

poor" were made by the Latin American bishops in spite of attempts to achieve suppression of the viewpoint of liberation theology.[95] Even the Sacred Congregation for the Doctrine of the Faith's highly critical *Instruction on Certain Aspects of the "Theology of Liberation"* recognizes that liberation theology emerged as a theological and pastoral movement in accord with the legitimately Christian aspiration for liberation and identifies the biblical basis and voice of the Church's Magisterium which serve to warrant a theology of liberation.[96]

It is in light of the impugning of the Christian basis of liberation theology that this review of its resources appears necessary. The actual writings of the Latin American liberation theologians and, secondarily, those of their North American defenders should suffice to set aside misgivings about the rootedness of liberation theology in the Christian tradition.[97] One may certainly disagree about the accuracy of specific formulations made by liberation theologians. But to call into question the rootedness of liberation theology in the Christian tradition seriously misrepresents both their intention and the content of their formulations. Liberation theology has been motivated by nothing other than a concern for the poor and for justice which is deeply grounded within the Christian tradition. This affirmation provides the primary basis for asserting the validity of liberation theology as a significant contemporary theological option.

2. The Latin American Plausibility Structure

The second criterion which indicates the validity of liberation theology encompasses the nature of the Latin American plausibility structure. By "plausibility structure" is meant the sociological idea

---

[95]Cf. "Evangelization in Latin America's Present and Future. Final Document of the Third General Conference of the Latin American Episcopate," in John Eagleson and Philip Scharper, eds., *Puebla and Beyond. Documentation and Commentary*, trans. John Drury (Maryknoll: Orbis, 1979), pp. 210-214 (Nos. 617-657) and pp. 264-267 (Nos. 1134-1165).

[96]Cf. *Instruction on Certain Aspects of the "Theology of Liberation*," pp. 7-16.

[97]Among North American arguments for the rootedness of liberation theology in the Christian tradition see Robert McAfee Brown, *Theology in a New Key. Responding to Liberation Themes* (Philadelphia: Westminster, 1978), pp. 26-49 and 88-97; Rosemary Radford Ruether, *To Change the World. Christology and Cultural Criticism* (New York: Crossroad, 1983), pp. 19-30; and Richard Shaull, *Heralds of a New Reformation. The Poor of South and North America* (Maryknoll: Orbis, 1984), pp. 13-57.

that every convincing conception of the world and of reality "requires
a social 'base' for its continuing existence as a world that is real to
actual human beings."[98]

> ... it can be said that *all* religious traditions, irrespective of their several
> "ecclesiologies" or lack of the same, require specific communities for
> their continuing plausibility. . . .   The reality of the Christian world
> depends upon the presence of social structures within which this reality is
> taken for granted and within which successive generations of individuals
> are socialized in such a way that this world will be real *to them*. When this
> plausibility structure loses it intactness or continuity, the Christian world
> begins to totter and its reality ceases to impose itself as self-evident
> truth.[99]

The existence of a plausibility structure can be understood to be
functional not only in the case of comprehensive world-views like
those of the world religions, but also in the case of constructive
theological perspectives which offer themselves as interpretive
schemas for understanding reality.[100]

The theology of liberation intends to be a theology which has its
plausibility structure in the experience of the poor in Latin America.
Its theological interpretation of the world begins with reality as it is
experienced from a sociological base defined by those persons existing
at the margins of Latin American society. By attempting to articulate
a convincing theological world-view from the perspective of the poor,
liberation theology has begun to fill a void that has in the past been
adequately addressed neither by traditional Roman Catholic theology
nor by a contemporary theology which has its main interest in the
challenges of modernity. In the past it is what has been described as
"popular religion" that has most adequately filled the need for a
satisfactory world-view among the Latin American poor.[101] With the

---

[98]Peter L. Berger, *The Sacred Canopy*, p. 45.

[99]Ibid., p. 46.

[100]Peter L. Berger, *The Heretical Imperative. Contemporary Possibilities
of Religious Affirmation* (Garden City, NY: Doubleday Anchor, 1979), pp. 66-67,
77-80, 90-93, and 141-142, for example, applies the notion of plausibility structure
to the theologies of Barth, Bultmann, and his own inductive approach. It is
worth remarking that Berger's option for an inductive approach as appropriate
to a plausibility structure of what he considers to be a situation of "relative
normalcy" may be for the majority of persons living in Latin America not at
all their "normal" situation. Berger's distinctions between the "mellowness"
appropriate to "normalcy" and the "fanaticism" likely in a "marginal
situation" thus appear to be influenced by a definition of normalcy which may
not be normal for the majority of the world's population.

[101]For a concise definition and description of the phenomenon of "popular
religion" see Robert J. Schreiter, *Constructing Local Theologies* (Maryknoll:

advent of liberation theology, a new and highly convincing option in terms of Christian world-view appears to have emerged for the poor of Latin America.

The widespread reception of the perspective of liberation theology through the basic Christian community movement is one significant indication that for many of Latin America's poor, liberation theology provides a highly plausible description of reality including the participation of the biblical God in that reality. So too the general affirmation of the perspective of liberation theology by the majority of the Latin American bishops, first at Medellin in 1968 and again at Puebla in 1979, demonstrates a plausibility for the theology of liberation which must be recognized and taken seriously. It is, however, not only in Latin America where liberation theology has found a high level of plausibility among the poor. Throughout the Third World the basic insights of liberation theology have been accepted and then further adapted to local circumstances. In Africa and in Asia the basic perspective of liberation theology has been critically affirmed by many indigenous theologians.[102] Providing an important forum for theologians from throughout the Third World who represent a liberation theology viewpoint, has been the Ecumenical Association for Third World Theologians.[103] Also in the United States the plausibility of liberation theology among black and Hispanic minority populations is a significant development.[104]

The North American theologians who have offered the most resonant responses to liberation theology are highly cognizant of its plausibility for the poor of Latin America. Richard Shaull writes:

Orbis, 1985), pp. 124-131.

[102]Cf. the volumes Kofi Appiah-Kubi and Sergio Torres, eds., *African Theology en Route* (Maryknoll: Orbis, 1979); Virginia Fabella, ed., *Asia's Struggle for Full Humanity: Towards a Relevant Theology* (Maryknoll: Orbis, 1980); and The Commission on Theological Concerns of the Christian Conference of Asia, ed., *Minjung Theology. People as the Subjects of History* (Maryknoll: Orbis, 1983).

[103]The papers from the most recent meeting of the Ecumenical Association of Third World theologians held at Geneva in 1983 are published in book form as Virginia Fabella and Sergio Torres, eds., *Doing Theology in a Divided World* (Maryknoll: Orbis, 1985). Especially worthy of comparison for its affinity with the perspective of Latin American liberation theology is the "Final Statement of the Sixth EATWOT Conference," pp. 179-193.

[104]Cf. the work of James H. Cone and other black theologians in formulating a black theology of liberation and the contribution of Virgilio Elizondo, *Galilean Journey. The Mexican-American Promise* (Maryknoll: Orbis, 1983) to a theology of liberation among Hispanic Americans.

For those underneath the present is intolerable. It represents deprivation
and exploitation, suffering and death. When those underneath are not
only poor but also Christian, their unwillingness to accept the present order
of things can be greatly intensified. The Jesus whom they meet in the
Gospels exposes the injustices in the world and declares that his
identification with the poor goes so far that he shares their suffering. He
arouses their expectations by declaring that the messianic age is already
beginning.[105]

Perhaps the single most important factor which distinguishes the
resonant North American responses to liberation theology from those
highly critical of liberation theology is the ability of a particular
theologian to envision the world from the perspective of the poor and to
recognize the plausibility of liberation theology within that world-
view.

Liberation theology provides for many of the poor of Latin America
and for those attempting to see the world from the perspective of the poor,
a highly convincing and plausible understanding of the world. It is a
perspective which interprets Latin American history, analyzes the
causes of poverty, reformulates the basic themes of the Christian faith,
and proposes a course of action in a way which appears to be highly
credible for large numbers of marginal persons both in Latin America
and throughout the Third World. In addition to its rootedness in the
Christian tradition, it is the plausibility of liberation theology within
the context of the poor which speaks for the validity of the Latin
American theology of liberation.

3. Insufficiency of an Academic Theology

At the conclusion of this study there are many questions which
remain unanswered. For the ongoing dialogue between Latin
American liberation theology and North American theologians, none
of these questions may finally be so insolvable as their fundamental
disagreement over the very definition of the theological enterprise.
For most theologians trained either in Europe or North America, the
theological task is by definition an academic one. Theology is
understood as a critical science operating under the rigors of the
historical-critical method which has the university as its normative
context.[106] The goal of academic theology may be understood,
according to this definition, as the attainment of "sure knowledge."

---

[105]Shaull, *Heralds of a New Reformation*, pp. 81-82.

[106]For an elaboration of these characteristics of "academic theology" see
Jose Comblin, *The Church and the National Security State* (Maryknoll: Orbis,
1979), pp. 1-4.

Theology as sure knowledge, or *scientia*, is probably the most common form of theology in Roman Catholicism and mainline Protestantism in the West today. When people there think of theology, they think of this kind of theology. Theology as sure knowledge tries to give a critical, relational account of faith, using the tools of a discipline that can offer the most exact form of knowledge known to the culture. This has often meant the use of human reason, but also now includes disciplines in the social sciences and to some extent in the natural sciences. The knowledge gained in this kind of theological reflection is, first and foremost, *sure*.[107] Within the university context it is only to be expected that theology submit itself to the discipline of the academy in its pursuit of sure knowledge.

Liberation theology, however, does not primarily operate under the conditions established for academic theology. This should not be an excuse for indolence with regard to the question of truth. Liberation theology needs to be challenged by the commitment to truth which ideally underlies the methodological rigor of academic theology. Nevertheless, the context in which liberation theology has arisen is not that of the university. Liberation theology has rather arisen from a concern for the poor and thereby in criticism of the unjust social structures which oppress them. In this context the task of theology is understood in a radically different way. Instead of objectivity as the ideal for theological methodology, liberation theologians call for solidarity with the poor and partisan commitment to changing the unjust conditions under which they live. Instead of sure knowledge as the goal of the theological enterprise, liberation theologians insist on liberating praxis as the only legitimate measure of theological truth.

What are the tasks of a theology as praxis? Three can be mentioned specifically: (1) Theology as praxis is to help disentangle true consciousness from false consciousness. False consciousness arises out of accepting the oppressive relations within society as normative, either as an oppressor or as an oppressed person or group. Technically this task is known as ideology critique, "ideology" being a Marxist term for false consciousness. In theology the biblical-language style of prophecy is commonly used as a medium for carrying out this task. (2) Theology as praxis has to be concerned with the ongoing reflection upon action. What is the significance of the transformative praxis of a community? (3) Theology as praxis is concerned with the motivation to sustain the transformative praxis. In this it is especially distinguished from many other kinds of theological reflection that are devoted solely to clarification and amplification of experience. The adequacy of theology as praxis is measured in good part by the quality of action that emerges in its practical moment.[108]

---

[107]Schreiter, *Constructing Local Theologies*, pp. 87-88.
[108]Ibid., p. 92.

Due to its vastly different understanding of the theological task,
liberation theologians have sharply criticized what they perceive to be
the limitations of a theology undertaken primarily as an academic
discipline.[109]

This sharp divergence in the definition of theology itself goes far
in explaining the misunderstandings and mutual critiques
exchanged between North American and Latin American theologians.
Depending upon one's favored definition of what theology in fact is, the
contrasting position appears to be seriously inadequate. The Latin
American liberation theologians, attentive to the context in which they
live, have attempted to convey the urgency of the situation in which they
theologize, a situation which shatters the strictures of academic
"business as usual."

> The "Ouch!" or painful scream resulting from a blow, a wound or an
> accident indicates immediately not *something* but rather *somebody*. One
> who hears the cry of pain is astonished because the scream interrupts his
> commonplace and integrated world. The sound, the noise, produces a
> mental image of an absent-present somebody in pain. The hearer does not
> know as yet *what kind* of pain it is, nor the reason for the outcry. But the
> hearer will be disturbed until he knows who is crying out and why. What
> that cry says is secondary; the fundamental issue is the cry itself; one who
> is *somebody* is saying something. It is not what is said, but rather the
> saying itself, the person who cries out, who is important—that exteriority
> which calls out for help. . . .
>
> The cry of pain such as "I am hungry!" requires an urgent answer, an
> answer that issues from a sense of responsibility: to be responsible for the
> one who is crying out in his or her pain.[110]

For liberation theologians the suffering of the Latin American poor is a
"threshold" lying between their own training in the traditions of
academic theology and a liberation theology understood as "critical
reflection on praxis." In their context it is a threshold which they have
felt compelled to cross if they are to adequately respond to what they
perceive to be intolerable injustice.

In making reference to a "threshold" between academic theology
and theology as praxis, another theologian comes to mind who also felt
himself standing before a similar threshold in another context of
extreme injustice. Geffrey B. Kelly writes of the decision made by
Dietrich Bonhoeffer in the face of the evil of National Socialism.

---

[109]Cf. the critique of academic theology by Comblin, *The Church and the
National Security State*, pp. 4-9.

[110]Enrique Dussel, *A History of the Church in Latin America.
Colonialism to Liberation (1492-1979)*, trans. and rev. Alan Neely (Grand
Rapids: Eerdmans, 1981), p. 307.

The Christian church in Germany, in Bonhoeffer's opinion, had reached the situation of *ultima ratio*, or last resort, where "the exact observance of the formal law of a state . . . suddenly finds itself in violent conflict with the ineluctable necessities of the lives of men." Law and principle are of little help in such a conflict. Nor can guilt be avoided, because Christians must engage in action as forceful as the evil they are trying to destroy in order to restore the inner freedom needed to enable people to think clearly and to act responsibly. These are actions Bonhoeffer would hardly call Christian; but, given the historical situation, they are actions no responsible Christian would shirk.[111]

Though the situation of Bonhoeffer opting to participate in a conspiracy to overthrow Hitler is in detail different from the situation of Latin American liberation theologians, the threshold which they understand themselves to have crossed from an academic theology to a theology lived out in praxis, with all the inherent risks which that entails, appears to be very similar. The needs of others and the demand for effective action require, in their measured opinion, that the threshold be crossed.

In the context of Latin American poverty and its need for a praxis which addresses the root causes of social injustice, liberation theology deems an academic theology to be insufficient. That does not mean, however, that they deem all of the methodological contributions and substantive conclusions of academic theology to be irrelevant and unnecessary. It is to be hoped that liberation theology will take seriously the most important arguments raised by North American theologians in criticism of its own position. At the same time there needs to be a far deeper understanding on the part of academic theologians of the differentness of the context in which liberation theology has arisen and the validity of liberation theology within that context.

Liberation theology is a form of "advocacy scholarship" on behalf of the Latin American poor which is rooted in the Christian tradition.[112] In their identification with the poor, liberation theologians, motivated by the gospel, have attempted to construct a theological position which can lead to an increase in justice in Latin American social, economic, and political structures. If theologians in other contexts do not agree with either the theological method,

---

[111]Kelly, *Liberating Faith*, pp. 70-71. The secondary quote is from Dietrich Bonhoeffer, *Ethics*, trans. Neville Horton Smith (New York: Macmillan, 1965), p. 238.

[112]The term "advocacy scholarship" is employed, among others, by Ruether, *New Woman New Earth*, p. xii.

theological reformulations, or praxis advocated by liberation theology, they can at least be challenged to recognize the difference in context in which liberation theology has arisen and to reexamine the contextual nature of their own theology. They can, furthermore, be challenged to broaden their understanding of "reality" by discovering the reality of extensive poverty and social injustice which have not in the past been adequately addressed by theology.[113] On numerous occasions those North American theologians, missionaries, clergy, and lay persons who have immersed themselves in the Latin American context and who have experienced firsthand the situation of the Latin American poor have come to a new understanding of the validity of Latin American liberation theology. To those who have not yet been able to envision the context to which liberation theology seeks to respond, liberation theologians extend the invitation for them to come and see for themselves.

---

[113]Cf. Trutz Rendtorff, "Universalität oder Kontextualität der Theologie. Eine 'europäische' Stellungnahme," *Zeitschrift für Theologie und Kirche* 74 (1977):243-245.

Bibliography

BOOKS

Abbott, Walter M., ed. *The Documents of Vatican II*. New York: America Press, 1966.

Alves, Rubem A. *A Theology of Human Hope*. St. Meinrad, IN: Abbey Press, 1969.

Alves, Rubem A. *Tomorrow's Child. Imagination, Creativity, and the Rebirth of Culture*. New York: Harper & Row, 1972.

Alves, Rubem A. *What Is Religion?* Translated by Don Vinzant. Maryknoll: Orbis, 1984.

Anderson, Gerald H., and Stransky, Thomas F., eds. *Mission Trends No. 3. Third World Theologies*. New York: Paulist, 1976.

Anderson, Gerald H., and Stransky, Thomas F., eds. *Mission Trends No. 4. Liberation Theologies in North America and Europe*. New York: Paulist, 1979.

Armerding, Carl E., ed. *Evangelicals & Liberation*. Phillipsburg, NJ: Presbyterian and Reformed Publishing Co., 1979.

Assmann, Hugo. *Theology for a Nomad Church*. Translated by Paul Burns. Introduction by Frederick Herzog. Maryknoll: Orbis, 1976.

Avila, Rafael. *Worship and Politics*. Translated by Alan Neely. Maryknoll: Orbis, 1981.

Baran, Paul, and Sweezy, Paul. *Monopoly Capital: An Essay on the American Economic and Social Order*. New York: Monthly Review Press, 1966.

Baum, Gregory. *Religion and Alienation: A Sociological Reading of Theology*. New York: Paulist, 1975.

Barreiro, Alvaro. *Basic Ecclesial Communities. The Evangelization of the Poor*. Translated by Barbara Campbell. Maryknoll: Orbis, 1982.

Becker, Ernest. *The Denial of Death*. New York: Free Press, 1973.

Becker, Ernest. *Escape From Evil*. New York: Free Press, 1975.

Beeson, Trevor, and Pearce, Jenny. *A Vision of Hope. The Churches and Change in Latin America*. Philadelphia: Fortress, 1984.

Bellah, Robert N. *Beyond Belief. Essays on Religion in a Post-Traditional World*. New York: Harper & Row, 1970.

Bellah, Robert N. *The Broken Covenant. American Civil Religion in Time of Trial*. New York: Seabury, 1975.

Belo, Fernando. *A Materialist Reading of the Gospel of Mark.* Translated by Matthew J. O'Connell. Maryknoll: Orbis, 1981.

Bengu, Sibusiso. *Mirror or Model? The Church in an Unjust World.* New York: Lutheran World Ministries, 1984.

Benne, Robert. *The Ethic of Democratic Capitalism. A Moral Reassessment.* Philadelphia: Fortress, 1981.

Bennett, John C., ed. *Christian Social Ethics in a Changing World. An Ecumenical Theological Inquiry.* New York: Association Press, 1966.

Berger, Peter L. *Pyramids of Sacrifice. Political Ethics and Social Change.* Garden City, NY: Doubleday Anchor, 1974.

Berger, Peter L. *The Sacred Canopy. Elements of a Sociological Theory of Religion.* Garden City, NY: Doubleday Anchor, 1967.

Berger, Peter L., and Luckmann, Thomas. *The Social Construction of Reality. A Treatise in the Sociology of Knowledge.* Garden City, NY: Doubleday Anchor, 1967.

Berger, Peter L., and Neuhaus, Richard J. *Movement and Revolution.* Garden City, NY: Doubleday Anchor, 1970.

Berryman, Phillip E. *The Religious Roots of Rebellion: Christians in Central American Revolutions.* Maryknoll: Orbis, 1984.

Bigo, Pierre. *The Church and Third World Revolution.* Translated by Jeanne Marie Lyons. Maryknoll: Orbis, 1977.

Bloesch, Donald G. *Essentials of Evangelical Theology.* 2 vols. San Francisco: Harper & Row, 1978-1979.

Bloesch, Donald G. *Faith and Its Counterfeits.* Downers Grove, IL: Inter-Varsity Press, 1981.

Boff, Clodovis. *Theologie und Praxis. Die erkenntnistheoretischen Grundlagen der Theologie der Befreiung.* Translated by Egon Küter and Annelie Johannemann. Munich: Kaiser-Grünewald, 1983.

Boff, Clodovis, and Boff, Leonardo. *Salvation and Liberation.* Translated by Robert R. Barr. Maryknoll: Orbis, 1984.

Boff, Leonardo. *Church: Charism and Power. Liberation Theology and the Institutional Church.* Translated by John W. Diercksmeier. London: SCM, 1985.

Boff, Leonardo. *Jesus Christ Liberator. A Critical Christology for Our Time.* Translated by Patrick Hughes. Maryknoll: Orbis, 1978.

Boff, Leonardo. *Kleine Sakramentenlehre.* Translated by Horst Goldstein. Düsseldorf: Patmos, 1976.

Boff, Leonardo. *Liberating Grace.* Translated by John Drury. Maryknoll: Orbis, 1979.

Boff, Leonardo. *The Lord's Prayer. The Prayer of Integral Liberation*. Translated by Theodore Morrow. Maryknoll: Orbis, 1983.

Boff, Leonardo. *Saint Francis. A Model for Human Liberation*. Translated by John W. Diercksmeier. New York: Crossroad, 1982.

Bonhoeffer, Dietrich. *Nachfolge*. 14th ed. Munich: Chr. Kaiser, 1983.

Braaten, Carl E. *Eschatology and Ethics. Essays on the Theology and Ethics of the Kingdom of God*. Minneapolis: Augsburg, 1974.

Braaten, Carl E. *The Flaming Center. A Theology of the Christian Mission*. Philadelphia: Fortress, 1977.

Braaten, Carl E. *The Future of God. The Revolutionary Dynamics of Hope*. New York: Harper & Row, 1969.

Braaten, Carl E. *Principles of Lutheran Theology*. Philadelphia: Fortress, 1983.

Brockman, James R. *The Word Remains: A Life of Oscar Romero*. Maryknoll: Orbis, 1982.

Brown, Delwin. *To Set at Liberty. Christian Faith and Human Freedom*. Maryknoll: Orbis, 1981.

Brown, Robert McAfee. *The Bible Speaks to You*. Philadelphia: Westminster, 1955.

Brown, Robert McAfee. *Creative Dislocation: The Movement of Grace*. Nashville: Abingdon, 1980.

Brown, Robert McAfee. *Elie Wiesel: Messenger to All Humanity*. South Bend: University of Notre Dame Press, 1983.

Brown, Robert McAfee. *Frontiers for the Church Today*. New York: Oxford University Press, 1973.

Brown, Robert McAfee. *Gustavo Gutierrez*. Atlanta: John Knox, 1981.

Brown, Robert McAfee. *Is Faith Obsolete?* Philadelphia: Westminster Press, 1974.

Brown, Robert McAfee. *Making Peace in the Global Village*. Philadelphia: Westminster, 1981.

Brown, Robert McAfee. *The Pseudonyms of God*. Philadelphia: Westminster, 1972.

Brown, Robert McAfee. *P. T. Forsyth: Prophet for Today*. Philadelphia: Westminster, 1952.

Brown, Robert McAfee. *Religion and Violence. A Primer for White Americans*. Philadelphia: Westminster, 1973.

Brown, Robert McAfee. *The Significance of the Church*. Philadelphia: Westminster, 1956.

Brown, Robert McAfee. *The Spirit of Protestantism*. New York: Oxford University Press, 1965.

Brown, Robert McAfee. *Theology in a New Key. Responding to Liberation Themes.* Philadelphia: Westminster, 1978.

Brown, Robert McAfee. *Unexpected News. Reading the Bible with Third World Eyes.* Philadelphia: Westminster, 1984.

Brueggemann, Walter. *The Prophetic Imagination.* Philadelphia: Fortress, 1978.

Bultmann, Rudolf. *Existence and Faith.* Translated by Schubert M. Ogden. New York: Meridian, 1960.

Cabestrero, Teofilo, ed. *Faith: Conversations With Contemporary Theologians.* Translated by Donald D. Walsh. Maryknoll: Orbis, 1980.

Cabestrero, Teofilo. *Mystic of Liberation: Portrait of Bishop Pedro Casaldaliga of Brazil.* Translated by Donald D. Walsh. Maryknoll: Orbis, 1981.

Camara, Dom Helder. *Church and Colonialism.* London: Sheed and Ward, 1969.

Camara, Dom Helder. *The Desert Is Fertile.* New York: Jove Publications, 1976.

Camara, Dom Helder. *Hoping Against All Hope.* Translated by Matthew J. O'Connell. Maryknoll: Orbis, 1984.

Camara, Dom Helder. *A Thousand Reasons for Living.* Translated by Alan Neame. Philadelphia: Fortress, 1981.

Cardenal, Ernesto. *The Gospel in Solentiname.* 4 vols. Translated by Donald D. Walsh. Maryknoll: Orbis, 1976.

Casalis, Georges. *Correct Ideas Don't Fall From the Skies. Elements for an Inductive Theology.* Translated by Sister Jeanne Marie Lyons and Michael John. Maryknoll: Orbis, 1984.

Cobb, John B., Jr. *Process Theology as Political Theology.* Philadelphia: Westminster, 1982.

Cockcroft, James D.; Frank, Andre Gunder; and Johnson, Dale L. *Dependence and Underdevelopment: Latin America's Political Economy.* Garden City, NY: Anchor, 1972.

Colonnese, Louis Michael, ed. *The Church in the Present Day Transformation of Latin America in Light of the Council.* 2 vols. (Position Papers and Conclusions of CELAM II) Washington, DC: U.S. Catholic Conference, 1970.

Comblin, Jose. *The Church and the National Security State.* Maryknoll: Orbis, 1979.

Cone, James H. *Black Theology and Black Power.* New York: Seabury, 1969.

Cone, James H. *A Black Theology of Liberation.* Philadelphia/New York: J. B. Lippincott, 1970.

Cone, James H. *For My People. Black Theology and the Black Church*. Maryknoll: Orbis, 1984.

Cone, James H. *God of the Oppressed*. New York: Seabury, 1975.

Cone, James H. *My Soul Looks Back*. Nashville: Abingdon, 1982.

Cone, James H. *The Spirituals and the Blues: An Interpretation*. New York: Seabury, 1972.

Conway, James F. *Marx and Jesus: Liberation Theology in Latin America*. New York: Carlton Press, 1973.

Cordoso, Fernando Henrique, and Faletto, Enzo. *Abhängigkeit und Entwicklung in Lateinamerika*. Frankfurt am Main: Suhrkamp, 1976.

Costas, Orlando E. *Christ Outside the Gate. Mission Beyond Christendom*. Maryknoll: Orbis, 1982.

Cox, Harvey. *Just As I Am*. Nashville: Abingdon, 1983.

Cox, Harvey. *Religion in the Secular City. Toward A Postmodern Theology*. New York: Simon and Schuster, 1984.

Cox, Harvey. *The Secular City. Secularization and Urbanization in Theological Perspective*. London: SCM Press, 1965.

Croatto, J. Severino. *Exodus. A Hermeneutics of Freedom*. Translated by Salvator Attanasio. Maryknoll: Orbis, 1981.

Cussianovich, Alejandro. *Religious Life and the Poor. Liberation Theology Perspectives*. Translated by John Drury. Dublin: Grill and Macmillan, 1979.

De Santa Ana, Julio. *Good News to the Poor. The Challenge of the Poor in the History of the Church*. Translated by Helen Whittle. Geneva: World Council of Churches, 1977.

De Santa Ana, Julio, ed. *Separation Without Hope? The Church and the Poor During the Industrial Revolution and Colonial Expansion*. Maryknoll: Orbis, 1980.

De Santa Ana, Julio, ed. *Towards a Church of the Poor. The Work of an Ecumenical Group on the Church and the Poor*. Geneva: World Council of Churches, 1979.

Descartes, Rene. *Rene Descartes: The Essential Writings*. Translated and Introduction by John J. Blom. New York: Harper & Row, 1977.

Duchrow, Ulrich. *Christenheit und Weltverantwortung. Traditionsgeschichte und systematische Struktur der Zweireichelehre*. 2nd ed. Stuttgart: Klett-Cotta, 1983.

Dumas, Andre. *Political Theology and the Life of the Church*. Translated by John Bowden. Philadelphia: Westminster, 1978.

Dussel, Enrique. *Ethics and the Theology of Liberation*. Translated by Bernard F. McWilliams. Maryknoll: Orbis, 1978.

418   Orthopraxis or Heresy

Dussel, Enrique. *History and the Theology of Liberation.* Translated by John Drury. Maryknoll: Orbis, 1976.

Dussel, Enrique. *A History of the Church in Latin America. Colonialism to Liberation.* Translated by Alan Neely. Grand Rapids: Eerdmans, 1981.

Eagleson, John, ed. *Christians and Socialism.* Translated by John Drury. Maryknoll: Orbis, 1975.

Eagleson, John, and Scharper, Philip, eds. *Puebla and Beyond. Documentation and Commentary.* Translated by John Drury. Maryknoll: Orbis, 1979.

Elizondo, Virgilio. *Galilean Journey. The Mexican-American Promise.* Maryknoll: Orbis, 1983.

Elizondo, Virgilio and Greinacher, Norbert, eds. *Concilium 144: Tensions Between the Churches of the First World and the Third World.* New York: Seabury, 1981.

Ellacuria, Ignacio. *Freedom Made Flesh. The Mission of Christ and His Church.* Translated by John Drury. Maryknoll: Orbis, 1976.

Erdozain, Placido. *Archbishop Romero: Martyr of Salvador.* Translated by John McFadden and Ruth Warner. Foreword by Jorge Lara-Braud. Maryknoll: Orbis, 1981.

Fabella, Virginia, and Torres, Sergio, eds. *Doing Theology in a Divided World.* Maryknoll: Orbis, 1985.

Fabella, Virginia, and Torres, Sergio, eds. *The Emergent Gospel. Theology from the Developing World.* Maryknoll: Orbis, 1978.

Fabella, Virginia, and Torres, Sergio, eds. *Irruption of the Third World. Challenge to Theology.* Maryknoll: Orbis, 1983.

Fanon, Frantz. *The Wretched of the Earth.* Translated by Constance Farrington. New York: Grove Press, 1978.

Ferm, Deane William. *Contemporary American Theologies. A Critical Survey.* New York: Seabury, 1981.

Fiel, Ernst, and Weth, Rudolf, eds. *Diskussion zur "Theologie der Revolution".* Munich/Mainz: Chr. Kaiser, 1969.

Fierro, Alfredo. *The Militant Gospel. A Critical Introduction to Political Theologies.* Translated by John Drury. Maryknoll: Orbis, 1977.

Fischer, Gerd-Dieter. *Richard Shaulls "Theologie der Revolution". Ihre theologische und ethische Argumentation auf dem Hintergrund der Situation in Lateinamerika.* Frankfurt: Peter Lang, 1984.

Frank, Andre Gunder. *Dependent Accumulation and Underdevelopment.* New York/London: Monthly Review Press, 1979.

Frank, Andre Gunder. *Latin America: Underdevelopment or Revolution. Essays on the Development of Underdevelopment and the Immediate Enemy.* New York: Monthly Review Press, 1969.

Frank, Andre Gunder. *Lumpenbourgeoisie: Lumpendevelopment. Dependence, Class, and Politics in Latin America.* Translated by Marion Davis Berdecio. New York: Monthly Review Press, 1972.

Freire, Paulo. *Pedagogy of the Oppressed.* Translated by Myra Bergman Ramos. New York: Seabury, 1970.

Frieling, Reinhard. *Befreiungstheologien. Studien zur Theologie in Lateinamerika.* Göttingen: Vandenhoeck & Ruprecht, 1984.

Galilea, Segundo. *The Beatitudes. To Evangelize as Jesus Did.* Translated by Robert R. Barr. Maryknoll: Orbis, 1984.

Galilea, Segundo. *Following Jesus.* Translated by Helen Phillips. Maryknoll: Orbis, 1981.

Galtung, Johan. *Self-reliance: Beitrag zu einer alternativen Entwicklungsstrategie.* Munich: Minerva-Publikation, 1983.

Geffre, Claude, and Gutierrez, Gustavo, eds. *Concilium 96: The Mystical and Political Dimension of the Christian Faith.* New York: Herder and Herder, 1974.

Gerassi, John, ed. *Revolutionary Priest: The Complete Writings and Messages of Camilo Torres.* Translated by June de Cipriano Alcantara, et al. New York: Random House, 1971.

Gibellini, Rosino, ed. *Frontiers of Theology in Latin America.* Translated by John Drury. Maryknoll: Orbis, 1979.

Goldstein, Horst, ed. *Befreiungstheologie als Herausforderung. Anstöße—Anklagen der lateinamerikanischen Theologie der Befreiung an Kirche und Gesellschaft hierzulande.* Düsseldorf: Patmos, 1981.

Gottwald, Norman K., ed. *The Bible and Liberation. Political and Social Hermeneutics.* Maryknoll: Orbis, 1983.

Gottwald, Norman K. *The Tribes of Yahweh. The Sociology of the Religion of Liberated Israel 1250-1050 B.C.E.* Maryknoll: Orbis, 1979.

Goulet, Denis. *A New Moral Order. Studies in Development Ethics and Liberation Theology.* Maryknoll: Orbis, 1974.

Greinacher, Norbert. *Die Kirche der Armen. Zur Theologie der Befreiung.* Munich: Piper, 1980.

Grenholm, Carl-Henric. *Christian Social Ethics in a Revolutionary Age. An Analysis of the Social Ethics of John C. Bennett, Heinz-Dietrich Wendland and Richard Shaull.* Uppsala: Verbum, 1973.

Griffiths, Brian, ed. *Is Revolution Change?* Downers Grove, IL: Intervarsity Press, 1972.

Gutierrez, Gustavo. *The Power of the Poor in History*. Translated by Robert R. Barr. Maryknoll: Orbis, 1983.

Gutierrez, Gustavo. *A Theology of Liberation*. Translated and edited by Caridad Inda and John Eagleson. Maryknoll: Orbis Books, 1973.

Gutierrez, Gustavo. *We Drink From Our Own Wells. The Spiritual Journey of a People*. Translated by Matthew J. O'Connell. Maryknoll: Orbis, 1984.

Gutierrez, Gustavo, and Shaull, Richard. *Liberation and Change*. Edited and Introduction by Ronald H. Stone. Part One translated by Alvin Gutterriez. Atlanta: John Knox, 1977.

Hall, Douglas John. *Lighten Our Darkness: Toward an Indigenous Theology of the Cross*. Philadelphia: Westminster Press, 1976.

Harnack, Adolf. *History of Dogma*. 7 vols. Translated by Neil Buchanon. New York: Dover, 1961.

Heilbroner, Robert L. *An Inquiry into the Human Prospect. Updated and Reconsidered for the 1980s*. New York: W. W. Norton, 1980.

Hennelly, Alfred. *Theologies in Conflict. The Challenge of Juan Luis Segundo*. Maryknoll: Orbis, 1979.

Henry, Carl F. H. *God, Revelation and Authority*. 4 vols. Waco: Word Books, 1976-1983.

Herzog, Frederick, ed. *The Future of Hope*. New York: Herder and Herder, 1970.

Herzog, Frederick. *Justice Church. The New Function of the Church in North American Christianity*. Maryknoll: Orbis, 1980.

Herzog, Frederick. *Liberation Theology. Liberation in the Light of the Fourth Gospel*. New York: Seabury, 1972.

Herzog, Frederick, ed. *Theology of the Liberating Word*. Nashville: Abingdon, 1971.

Herzog, Frederick. *Understanding God. The Key Issue in Present-Day Thought*. New York: Charles Scribner's Sons, 1966.

Hodgson, Peter C. *Children of Freedom. Black Liberation in Christian Perspective*. Foreword by Gayraud S. Wilmore. Philadelphia: Fortress, 1974.

Hodgson, Peter C. *Jesus—Word and Presence. An Essay in Christology*. Philadelphia: Fortress, 1971.

Hodgson, Peter C. *New Birth of Freedom. A Theology of Bondage and Liberation*. Philadelphia: Fortress, 1976.

Hodgson, Peter C., and King, Robert H., eds. *Christian Theology. An Introduction to Its Traditions and Tasks*. Philadelphia: Fortress, 1982.

Hordern, William. *Experience and Faith. The Significance of Luther for Understanding Today's Experiential Religion.* Minneapolis: Augsburg, 1983.

Inch, Morris A. *Doing Theology Across Cultures.* Grand Rapids: Baker, 1982.

Is Liberation Theology for North America? The Response of First World Churches. New York: Theology in the Americas, n.d.

Kee, Alistair, ed. *A Reader in Political Theology.* Philadelphia: Westminster, 1975.

Kelsey, David H. *The Uses of Scripture in Recent Theology.* Philadelphia: Fortress, 1975.

Kirk, J. Andrew. *Liberation Theology. An Evangelical View from the Third World.* Atlanta: John Knox, 1979.

Kirk, J. Andrew. *Theology Encounters Revolution.* Leicester, England: Intervarsity, 1980.

Kirk, J. Andrew. *Theology and the Third World Church.* Downers Grove, IL/Exeter, England: Intervarsity/Paternoster Press, 1983.

Krass, Alfred C. *Evangelizing Neopagan North America. The Word That Frees.* Scottdale, PA: Herald Press, 1982.

Landsberger, Henry A., ed. *The Church and Social Change in Latin America.* South Bend/London: University of Notre Dame Press, 1970.

Lange, Martin, and Iblacker, Reinhold, eds. *Witnesses of Hope. The Persecution of Christians in Latin America.* Translated by William E. Jerman. Maryknoll: Orbis, 1981.

Lappe, Frances Moore; Collins, Joseph; and Kinley, David. *Aid As Obstacle. Twenty Questions About our Foreign Aid and the Hungry.* San Francisco: Institute for Food and Development Policy, 1980.

Lappe, Frances Moore, and Collins, Joseph. *Food First. Beyond the Myth of Scarcity.* 2nd ed. New York: Ballantine, 1978.

Lazareth, William H., ed. *The Left Hand of God.* Philadelphia: Fortress, 1976.

Lehmann, Paul L. *Ethics in a Christian Context.* New York: Harper & Row, 1963.

Lernoux, Penny. *Cry of the People.* New York: Penguin, 1980.

Lopez Trujillo, Alfonso. *Liberation or Revolution? An Examination of the Priest's Role in the Socioeconomic Class Struggle in Latin America.* Huntington, IN: Our Sunday Visitor, Inc., 1977.

McCann, Dennis P. *Christian Realism and Liberation Theology. Practical Theologies in Creative Conflict.* Maryknoll: Orbis, 1981.

McFadden, Thomas, ed. *Liberation, Revolution and Freedom: Theological Perspectives*. New York: Seabury, 1975.

McGovern, Arthur F. *Marxism: An American Christian Perspective*. Maryknoll: Orbis, 1980.

Mahan, Brian, and Richesin, L. Dale, eds. *The Challenge of Liberation Theology: A First World Response*. Maryknoll: Orbis, 1981.

Mannheim, Karl. *Ideologie und Utopia*. 6th ed. Frankfurt am Main: G. Schultz-Bulmke, 1978.

Marcuse, Herbert. *One Dimensional Man*. Boston: Beacon Press, 1964.

Marx, Karl. *Karl Marx: The Essential Writings*. Edited and introduction by Frederic L. Bender. New York: Harper & Row, 1972.

Metz, Johannes Baptist, ed. *Concilium 36: Faith and the World of Politics*. New York: Paulist Press, 1968.

Metz, Johannes Baptist. *The Emergent Church. The Future of Christianity in a Postbourgeois World*. Translated by Peter Mann. New York: Crossroad, 1981.

Metz, Johannes Baptist. *Faith in History & Society. Toward a Practical Fundamental Theology*. Translated by David Smith. New York: Seabury, 1980.

Metz, Johannes Baptist. *Poverty of Spirit*. Translated by John Drury. New York: Paulist Press, 1968.

Metz, Johannes Baptist. *Zur Theologie der Welt*. Mainz: Matthias-Grünewald, 1968.

Migliore, Daniel L. *Called to Freedom. Liberation Theology and the Future of Christian Doctrine*. Philadelphia: Westminster, 1980.

Miguez Bonino, Jose. *Christians and Marxists. The Mutual Challenge to Revolution*. Grand Rapids: Eerdmans, 1976.

Miguez Bonino, Jose, ed. *Faces of Jesus. Latin American Christ-ologies*. Translated by Robert R. Barr. Maryknoll: Orbis, 1984.

Miguez Bonino, Jose. *Revolutionary Theology Comes of Age*. London: SPCK, 1975.

Miguez Bonino, Jose. *Room to Be People: An Interpretation of the Message of the Bible for Today's World*. Translated by Vickie Leach. Philadelphia: Fortress, 1979.

Miguez Bonino, Jose. *Toward A Christian Political Ethics*. Philadelphia: Fortress, 1983.

Miranda, Jose Porfiro. *Being and the Messiah. The Message of St. John*. Translated by John Eagleson. Maryknoll: Orbis, 1977.

Miranda, Jose Porfiro. *Communism in the Bible*. Translated by Robert R. Barr. Maryknoll: Orbis, 1982.

Miranda, Jose Porfiro. *Marx Against the Marxists. The Christian Humanism of Karl Marx.* Translated by John Drury. Maryknoll: Orbis, 1980.

Miranda, Jose Porfiro. *Marx and the Bible: A Critique of the Philosophy of Oppression.* Translated by John Eagleson. Maryknoll: Orbis, 1974.

Moltmann, Jürgen. *The Church in the Power of the Spirit. A Contribution to Messianic Ecclesiology.* Translated by Margaret Kohl. New York: Harper & Row, 1977.

Moltmann, Jürgen. *The Crucified God. The Cross of Christ as the Foundation and Criticism of Christian Theology.* Translated by R. A. Wilson and John Bowden. New York: Harper & Row, 1974.

Moltmann, Jürgen. *The Experiment Hope.* Translated and edited with a Foreword by M. Douglas Meeks. Philadelphia: Fortress, 1975.

Moltmann, Jürgen. *Politische Theologie—Politische Ethik.* Munich: Chr. Kaiser, 1984.

Moltmann, Jürgen. *Religion, Revolution and the Future.* Translated by M. Douglas Meeks. New York: Scribner's, 1969.

Moltmann, Jürgen. *Theology of Hope. On the Ground and the Implications of a Christian Eschatology.* Translated by James W. Leitch. New York: Harper & Row, 1967.

Nash, Ronald H., ed. *Liberation Theology.* Milford, MI: Mott Media, 1984.

Neal, Marie Augusta. *A Socio-Theology of Letting Go. The Role of a First World Church Facing Third World Peoples.* New York: Paulist, 1977.

Nelson, Jack A. *Hunger For Justice: The Politics of Food and Faith.* Maryknoll: Orbis, 1980.

Neuhaus, Richard John. *The Naked Public Square.* Grand Rapids: Eerdmans, 1984.

Norman, Edward. *Christianity and the World Order.* Oxford: Oxford University Press, 1979.

Nouwen, Henri J. M. *Gracias. A Latin American Journal.* New York: Harper & Row, 1983.

Novak, Michael. *Freedom With Justice. Catholic Social Thought and Liberal Institutions.* San Francisco: Harper & Row, 1984.

Novak, Michael, ed. *Liberation South, Liberation North.* Washington/London: American Enterprise, 1981.

Novak, Michael. *The Spirit of Democratic Capitalism.* New York: Simon & Schuster, 1982.

Novak, Michael. *A Theology for Radical Politics.* New York: Herder and Herder, 1969.

Ogden, Schubert M. *Christ Without Myth: A Study Based on the Theology of Rudolf Bultmann.* New York: Harper & Row, 1961.

Ogden, Schubert M. *Faith and Freedom. Toward a Theology of Liberation.* Nashville: Abingdon, 1979.

Ogden, Schubert M. *The Point of Christology.* San Francisco: Harper & Row, 1982.

Ogden, Schubert M. *The Reality of God. And Other Essays.* New York: Harper & Row, 1966.

Pannenberg, Wolfhart. *Christian Spirituality.* Philadelphia: West-minster, 1983.

Pannenberg, Wolfhart. *Ethics.* Translated by Keith Crim. Philadelphia: Westminster, 1981.

Pannenberg, Wolfhart, ed. *Revelation As History.* Translated by David Granskou. New York: Macmillan, 1968.

Pannenberg, Wolfhart. *Theology and the Kingdom of God.* Philadelphia: Westminster, 1969.

Pannenberg, Wolfhart. *Theology and the Philosophy of Science.* Translated by Francis McDonagh. Philadelphia: Westminster, 1976.

Paoli, Arturo. *Freedom to Be Free.* Maryknoll: Orbis, 1973.

Pelikan, Jaroslav. *The Christian Tradition.* 5 vols. Chicago: University of Chicago, 1971-1989.

Perez Esquivel, Adolfo. *Christ in a Poncho. Testimonials of the Nonviolent Struggles in Latin America.* Edited by Charles Antoine. Translated by Robert R. Barr. Maryknoll: Orbis, 1983.

Peruvian Bishops' Commission for Social Action. *Between Honesty and Hope. Documents from and about the Church in Latin America.* Translated by John Drury. Maryknoll: Maryknoll Documentation Series, 1970.

Popper, Karl R. *The Open Society and Its Enemies.* 2 vols. Princeton: Princeton University Press, 1971.

Popper, Karl R. *The Poverty of Historicism.* London: Routledge & Kegan, 1957.

Prien, Hans-Jürgen. *Die Geschichte des Christentums in Lateinamerika.* Göttingen: Vandenhoeck & Ruprecht, 1978.

Prien, Hans-Jürgen, ed. *Lateinamerika: Gesellschaft, Kirche, Theologie.* 2 vols. Göttingen: Vandenhoeck & Ruprecht, 1981.

Rauschenbusch, Walter. *A Theology for the Social Gospel.* Nashville: Abingdon, 1945.

Rendtorff, Trutz. *Ethik. Grundelemente, Methodologie und Konkretionen einer ethischen Theologie.* 2 vols. Stuttgart: W. Kohlhammer, 1980-1981.

Rendtorff, Trutz, and Tödt, Heinz Eduard. *Theologie der Revolution. Analysen und Materialen*. Frankfurt am Main: Suhrkamp, 1969.

Richard, Pablo, et al. *The Idols of Death and the God of Life. A Theology*. Translated by Barbara E. Campbell and Bonnie Shepard. Maryknoll: Orbis, 1983.

Romero, Oscar. *Voice of the Voiceless. The Four Pastoral Letters and Other Statements*. Translated by Michael J. Walsh. Maryknoll: Orbis, 1985.

Ruether, Rosemary Radford. *Disputed Questions: On Being a Christian*. Nashville: Abingdon, 1982.

Ruether, Rosemary Radford. *Faith and Fratricide. The Theological Roots of Anti-Semitism*. New York: Seabury, 1974.

Ruether, Rosemary Radford. *Liberation Theology. Human Hope Confronts Christian History and American Power*. New York: Paulist Press, 1972.

Ruether, Rosemary Radford. *New Woman New Earth: Sexist Ideologies and Human Liberation*. New York: Seabury, 1975.

Ruether, Rosemary Radford. *The Radical Kingdom. The Western Experience of Messianic Hope*. New York: Paulist Press, 1970.

Ruether, Rosemary Radford, ed. *Religion and Sexism. Images of Woman in the Jewish and Christian Traditions*. New York: Simon and Schuster, 1974.

Ruether, Rosemary Radford. *Sexism and God-Talk. Toward a Feminist Theology*. Boston: Beacon Press, 1983.

Ruether, Rosemary Radford. *To Change the World: Christology and Cultural Criticism*. New York: Crossroad, 1981.

Ruether, Rosemary Radford, and McLaughlin, Eleanor, eds. *Women of Spirit. Female Leadership in the Jewish and Christian Traditions*. New York: Simon and Schuster, 1979.

Russell, Letty M. *The Future of Partnership*. Philadelphia: Westminster, 1979.

Russell, Letty M. *Growth in Partnership*. Philadelphia: Westminster, 1981.

Russell, Letty M. *Human Liberation in a Feminist Perspective—A Theology*. Philadelphia: Westminster, 1974.

Russell, Letty M., ed. *The Liberating Word. A Guide to Nonsexist Interpretation of the Bible*. Philadelphia: Westminster, 1976.

Sacred Congregation for the Doctrine of the Faith. *Instruction on Certain Aspects of the "Theology of Liberation"*. Vatican City: Vatican Polyglot Press, 1984.

Samuel, Vinay, and Sugden, Chris, eds. *Sharing Jesus in the Two Thirds World. Evangelical Christologies From the Contexts of Poverty, Powerlessness, and Religious Pluralism.* Grand Rapids: Eerdmans, 1983.

Schall, James V. *Liberation Theology in Latin America. With selected essays and documents.* San Francisco: Ignatius Press, 1982.

Schöpfer, Hans. *Lateinamerikanische Befreiungstheologie.* Stutt–gart: W. Kohlhammer, 1979.

Schöpfer, Hans. *Theologie der Gesellschaft. Interdisziplinäre Grundlagenbibliographie zur Einführung in die befreiungs- und polittheologische Problematik: 1960-1975.* Bern: Peter Lang, 1977.

Schreiter, Robert J. *Constructing Local Theologies.* Maryknoll: Orbis, 1985.

Schwarz, Hans. *The Christian Church. Biblical Origin, Historical Transformation, and Potential for the Future.* Minneapolis: Augsburg, 1982.

Schwarz, Hans. *On the Way to the Future. A Christian View of Eschatology in the Light of Current Trends in Religion, Philosophy, and Science.* 2nd ed. Minneapolis: Augsburg, 1979.

Scott, Waldron. *Bring Forth Justice.* Grand Rapids: Eerdmans, 1980.

Segundo, Juan Luis. *The Hidden Motives of Pastoral Action.* Translated by John Drury. Maryknoll: Orbis, 1978.

Segundo, Juan Luis. *Jesus of Nazareth Yesterday and Today. Vol. 1: Faith and Ideologies.* Translated by John Drury. Maryknoll: Orbis, 1984.

Segundo, Juan Luis. *The Liberation of Theology.* Translated by John Drury. Maryknoll: Orbis, 1976.

Segundo, Juan Luis. *Theology for Artisans of a New Humanity.* 5 vols. Translated by John Drury. Maryknoll: Orbis, 1973-1974.

Shaull, Richard. *Befreiung durch Veränderung. Herausforderungen an Kirche, Theologie und Gesellschaft.* Munich/Mainz: Kaiser/Grünewald, 1970.

Shaull, Richard. *Encounter With Revolution.* New York: Association Press, 1955.

Shaull, Richard. *Heralds of a New Reformation. The Poor of South and North America.* Maryknoll: Orbis, 1984.

Shaull, Richard, and Oglesby, Carl. *Containment and Change.* New York: Macmillan, 1967.

Sider, Ronald J. *Christ and Violence.* Scottdale, PA: Herald Press, 1979.

Sider, Ronald J., ed. *Evangelicals and Development. Toward a Theology of Social Change.* Philadelphia: Westminster, 1981.

Sider, Ronald J. *Rich Christians in an Age of Hunger.* Downers Grove, IL: Intervarsity Press, 1977.

Sider, Ronald J., and Taylor, Richard. *Nuclear Holocaust and Christian Hope: A Book for Christian Peacemakers.* Ramsey, NJ: Paulist, 1982.

Sobrino, Jon. *Christology at the Crossroads. A Latin American Approach.* Translated by John Drury. Maryknoll: Orbis, 1978.

Sobrino, Jon. *The True Church and the Poor.* Translated by Matthew J. O'Connell. Maryknoll: Orbis, 1984.

Sobrino, Jon, and Pico, Juan Hernandez. *Theology of Christian Solidarity.* Translated by Phillip Berryman. Maryknoll: Orbis, 1985.

Soelle, Dorothee. *Choosing Life.* Translated by Margaret Kohl. Philadelphia: Fortress Press, 1981.

Soelle, Dorothee. *Christ the Representative. An Essay in Theology after the "Death of God".* Translated by David Lewis. Philadelphia: Fortress, 1967.

Soelle, Dorothee. *Political Theology.* Translated by John Shelley. Philadelphia: Fortress, 1974.

Strharsky, Harry, ed. *Must We Choose Sides? Christian Commitment for the 80s.* U.S.A.: Inter-Religious Task Force for Social Analysis, 1979.

Strharsky, Harry, ed. *Which Side Are We On? Christian Commitment for the 80s.* U.S.A.: Inter-Religious Task Force for Social Analysis, 1980.

Stumme, Wayne, ed. *Christians & the Many Faces of Marxism.* Minneapolis: Augsburg, 1984.

Tambasco, Anthony J. *The Bible For Ethics: Juan Luis Segundo and First World Ethics.* London: University Press of America, 1981.

Tamez, Elsa. *Bible of the Oppressed.* Translated by Matthew J. O'Connell. Maryknoll: Orbis, 1982.

Tillich, Paul. *Systematic Theology.* 3 vols. Chicago: University of Chicago, 1951-1963.

Torres, Sergio, and Eagleson, John, eds. *The Challenge of Basic Christian Communities.* Translated by John Drury. Maryknoll: Orbis, 1981.

Torres, Sergio, and Eagleson, John, eds. *Theology in the Americas.* Maryknoll: Orbis, 1976.

Tracy, David. *The Analogical Imagination. Christian Theology and the Culture of Pluralism.* New York: Crossroad, 1981.

Tracy, David. *Blessed Rage for Order. The New Pluralism in Theology.* New York: Seabury, 1975.

Turner, Denys. *Marxism and Christianity*. Oxford: Basil Blackwell, 1983.

United Nations. *International Development Strategy for the Third United Nations Development Decade*. New York: United Nations Department of Public Information, 1981.

United Nations. *Towards a World Economy That Works. The World Economy; the Issues; the U.N. Role: Questions and Answers*. New York: United Nations, 1980.

Vaughan, Judith. *Sociality, Ethics, and Social Change. A Critical Appraisal of Reinhold Niebuhr's Ethics in the Light of Rosemary Radford Ruether's Works*. Lanham, MD: University Press of America, 1983.

Vekemans, Roger. *Caesar and God. The Priesthood and Politics*. Translated by Aloysius Owen and Charles Underhill Quinn. Maryknoll: Orbis, 1972.

Wagner, C. Peter. *Latin American Theology: Radical or Evangelical? The Struggle for the Faith in a Young Church*. Grand Rapids: Eerdmans, 1970.

Wallis, Jim. *Agenda for Biblical People*. New York: Harper & Row, 1976.

Wallis, Jim. *The Call to Conversion*. San Francisco: Harper & Row, 1981.

Wallis, Jim. *Revive Us Again. A Sojourner's Story*. Nashville: Abingdon, 1983.

West, Cornel; Guidote, Caridad; and Coakley, Margaret, eds. *Theology in the Americas. Detroit II. Conference Papers*. Maryknoll: Orbis, 1982.

Wilmore, Gayraud S. *Black Religion and Black Radicalism. An Interpretation of the Religious History of Afro-American People*. 2nd ed. Maryknoll: Orbis, 1983.

Wilmore, Gayraud S., and Cone, James H. *Black Theology: A Documentary History, 1966-1979*. Maryknoll: Orbis, 1979.

Wingren, Gustaf. *Creation and Gospel. The New Situation in European Theology*. New York: Edwin Mellen Press, 1979.

Wingren, Gustaf. *Creation and Law*. Translated by Ross Mackenzie. Philadelphia: Muhlenberg Press, 1961.

Wingren, Gustaf. *The Flight from Creation*. Minneapolis: Augsburg, 1971.

Wingren, Gustaf. *Gospel and Church*. Translated by Ross Mackenzie. Philadelphia: Fortress, 1964.

Yoder, John Howard. *The Original Revolution. Essays on Christian Pacifism*. Scottdale, PA: Herald Press, 1971.

Yoder, John Howard. *The Politics of Jesus. Vicit Agnus Noster.* Grand Rapids: Eerdmans, 1972.

Yoder, John Howard. *When War Is Unjust. Being Honest in Just-War Thinking.* Minneapolis: Augsburg, 1984.

Zambrano, Luis. *Entstehung und theologishes Verständnis der "Kirche des Volkes" (Iglesia Popular) in Lateinamerika.* Frankfurt: Peter Lang, 1982.

Zea, Leopoldo. *Latin America and the World.* Translated by Frances K. Hendricks and Beatrice Berler. Norman, OK: University of Oklahoma Press, 1969.

DISSERTATIONS

Alves, Rubem A. "Towards a Theology of Liberation." Th.D. Dissertation, Princeton Theological Seminary, 1968.

Garcia, Jose Rafael. "Liberation and Evil: A Critique of the Thought of Gustavo Gutierrez and Rubem Alves from the Standpoint of F. R. Tennant's Theodicy." Ph.D. Dissertation, Claremont Graduate School, 1975.

Gudorf, Christine Erhart. "Contested Issues in Twentieth Century Papal Teaching: The Position of the Vatican in Light of Challenges from Liberation Theology." Ph.D. Dissertation, Columbia University, 1979.

Hart, John William. "Topia and Utopia in Colombia and Peru. The Theory and Practice of Camilo Torres and Gustavo Gutierrez in their Historical Contexts." Ph.D. Dissertation, Union Theological Seminary, 1978.

Hermans, Karel. "Rückgewinnung des Glaubens in der Theologie des Volkes. Entwicklungen in der lateinamerikanischen Kirche als Frage nach Orten und Ort befreiender Theologie." Ph.D. Dissertation, University of Münster, 1981.

Herrera, Altagracia Marina, O.P. "Man and the Latin American Church in the Theology of Liberation." Ph.D. Dissertation, Fordham University, 1974.

Koh, Jae Sik. "A Comparison of Walter George Muelder's Christian Social Ethics of the Responsible Society and Jose Miguez Bonino's Liberation Ethics." Ph.D. Dissertation, Northwestern University, 1979.

Pantelis, Jorge. "Kingdom of God and Church in the Historical Process of Liberation: Latin American Perspectives." Ph.D. Dissertation, Union Theological Seminary, 1976.

Phillips, Steven. "The Use of Scripture in Liberation Theologies: An Examination of Juan Luis Segundo, James H. Cone, and Jürgen Moltmann." Ph.D. Dissertation, The Southern Baptist Theological Seminary, 1978.

Robb, Carol Sue. "Integration of Marxist Constructs into the Theology of Liberation from Latin America." Ph.D. Dissertation, Boston University Graduate School, 1978.

Schubeck, Thomas Louis. "Liberation and Imagination: A New Theological Language in Response to the Marxist Critique of Religion." Ph.D. Dissertation, University of Southern California, 1975.

Shejavali, Abisai. "The Idea of God in Liberation Theology." Ph.D. Dissertation, Aquinas Institute of Theology, 1978.

Snyder, Theodore Richard. "The Politics of Liberation and the Mission of the Church." Th.D. Dissertation, Princeton Theological Seminary, 1969.

ARTICLES

Abalos, David. "The Medellin Conference." Cross Currents 19 (Winter 1969): 113-132.

Adams, Daniel J. "Theological Method: Four Contemporary Models." Taiwan Journal of Theology 3 (Mar. 1981):193-205.

Aguilar-Monsalve, Luis Antonio. "The Separation of Church and State: The Ecuadorian Case." Thought 59 (June 1984):205-218.

Ainger, Geoffrey J. "The Gospel of Freedom." International Review of Mission 57 (Oct. 1968):417-423.

Albertine, Richard P. "Worship and the Theology of Liberation." St. Luke's Journal of Theology 20 (Mar. 1977):139-149.

Alves, Rubem A. "Christian Realism: Ideology of the Establishment." Christianity and Crisis 33 (Sept. 17, 1973):173-176.

Alves, Rubem A. "God's People and Man's Liberation." Communio Viatorum 14 (1971):107-116.

Alves, Rubem A. "Personal Wholeness and Political Creativity: The Theology of Liberation and Pastoral Care." Pastoral Psychology 26 (Winter 1977): 124-136.

Alves, Rubem A. "Theology and the Liberation of Man." In New Theology No. 9, pp. 230-250. Edited by Martin E. Marty and Dean G. Peerman. New York: Macmillan, 1972.

Anderson, Justice C. "The Church and Liberation Theology." Southwestern Journal of Theology 19 (Spring 1977):17-36.

Assmann, Hugo. "Basic Aspects of Theological Reflection in Latin America: a critical evaluation of 'Theology of Liberation'." Risk 9, No. 2 (1973):25-33.

Assmann, Hugo. "Theological Training and the Diversity of Ministries." International Review of Mission 66 (1977):22-28.

Bahmann, Manfred K. "Liberation Theology—Latin American Style." Lutheran Quarterly 27 (May 1975):139-148.

Banana, Canaan. "The Biblical Basis for Liberation Struggles." *International Review of Mission* 68 (Oct. 1979):417-423.

Banks, Robert. "A Christian Revolutionary Tradition?" *Journal of Ecumenical Studies* 9 (Spring 1972):285-300.

Banks, Robert. "How Revolutionary Is Revolutionary Theology?" *Theology Today* 27 (Jan. 1971):394-408.

Barndt, Joseph R. "Revolutionary Christians Confer in Santiago." *Christian Century* 89 (June 14-21, 1972):691-695.

Barr, William R. "The Shape of a White Liberation Theology." *Lexington Theological Quarterly* 9 (Oct. 1974):113-127.

Barr, William R. "The Struggle for Freedom in America: A Theological Critique." *Encounter* (Indianapolis) 37 (Summer 1976):229-244.

Barreiro, Alvara, S.J. "Grass-Roots Ecclesial Communities and the Evangelization of the Poor." *Foundations* 23 (Oct.-Dec. 1980): 294-331.

Bastian, Jean-Pierre. "Popular Religion. A Strategic Element for the Formation of a New Hegemonic Block in Latin America," *Foundations* 23 (Oct.-Dec. 1980):355-367.

Baum, Gregory. "Canadian Bishops Adapt Liberation Theology." *Cross Currents* 28, No. 1 (1978):97-103.

Baum, Gregory. "Liberation Theology and 'The Supernatural'." *The Ecumenist* 19 (Sept.-Oct. 1981):81-87.

Baum, Gregory. "Theology in the Americas: Detroit II." *The Ecumenist* 18 (Sept.-Oct. 1980):90-94.

Benjamin, Walter W. "Liberation Theology: European Hopelessness Exposes the Latin Hoax." *Christianity Today* 26 (Mar. 5, 1982):21-26.

Benne, Robert. "Capitalism in the World Economy." *Dialog* 20 (Fall 1981): 274-280.

Bennett, John C., and Bennett, Anne M. "The Church and the Struggles for Liberation." *Foundations* 18 (Jan.-Mar. 1975):53-60.

Bennett, John C. "Fitting the Liberation Theme Into Our Theological Agenda." *Christianity and Crisis* 37 (July 18, 1977):164-169.

Bennison, Charles E., Jr. "What Does it Mean to be a Church in an Age of Massive Hunger?" *Anglican Theological Review* 61 (July 1979):316-330.

Berryman, Phillip. "Illusions of Villainy. The U.S. Government's Propaganda Campaign Against Nicaragua." *Sojourners* 13, No. 7 (Aug. 1984):13-17.

Berryman, Phillip. "Latin American Liberation Theology." *Theological Studies* 34 (1973):357-395.

Bloesch, Donald G. "Soteriology in Contemporary Thought." *Interpretation* 35 (Apr. 1981):132-144.

Boff, Clodovis, and Boff, Leonardo. "Fünf grundsätzliche Bemerkungen zur Darstellung von Kardinal Ratzinger." *Orientierung* 48 (May 15, 1984): 99-102.

Boff, Leonardo. "Die Anliegen der Befreiungstheologie." *Theologische Berichte* 8 (1979):71-103.

Boff, Leonardo. "The Need for Political Saints." *Cross Currents* 30 (Winter 1980-1981):369-376, and 384.

Bonpane, Blase. "The Church in the Central American Revolution." *Thought* 59 (June 1984):183-194.

Borrat, Hector. "Liberation Theology in Latin America." *Dialog* 13 (Summer 1974):172-176.

Bowen, Starr. "Land Invasion and the Gospel." *Christian Century* 102 (Sept. 11-18, 1985):800-802.

Braaten, Carl E. "The Christian Doctrine of Salvation." *Interpretation* 35 (Apr. 1981):117-131.

Braaten, Carl E. "Editorial: Lutherans on Liberty and Liberation." *Dialog* 15 (Summer 1976):166-168.

Braaten, Carl E. "The Future As a Source of Freedom." *Theology Today* 27 (Jan. 1971):382-393.

Braaten, Carl E. "The Gospel of Justification Sola Fide." *Dialog* 15 (Summer 1976):207-213.

Braaten, Carl E. "Praxis: The Trojan Horse of Liberation Theology." *Dialog* 23 (Autumn 1984):276-280.

Bracken, Joseph A. "Faith and Justice: A New Synthesis? The Interface of Process and Liberation Theologies." *Process Studies* 14 (Summer 1985):73-75.

Brockman, James R. "Oscar Romero: Paradigm of the New Latin American Church." *Thought* 59 (June 1984):195-204.

Brockman, James R. "The Prophetic Role of the Church in Latin America. A Conversation with Gustavo Gutierrez." *Christian Century* 100 (Oct. 19, 1983):931-935.

Brown, Robert McAfee. "Appreciating the Bishops' Letter." *Christian Century* 102 (Feb. 6-13, 1985):129-130.

Brown, Robert McAfee. "The Debasement of Language." *Christian Century* 100 (Apr. 6, 1983):313-315.

Brown, Robert McAfee. "Drinking from Our Own Wells." *Christian Century* 101 (May 9, 1984):483-486.

Brown, Robert McAfee. "From Detroit to Nairobi and Beyond: The Fifth Assembly of the World Council of Churches." *Radical Religion* 2, No. 4 (1976):45-48.

Brown, Robert McAfee. "'Jesus Christ Frees and Unites' . . . And Divides." *The Ecumenical Review* 26 (1974):430-438.

Brown, Robert McAfee. "The Gospel According to Morley Safer." *Christian Century* 100 (Mar. 2, 1983):183-186.

Brown, Robert McAfee. "My Story and 'The Story'." *Theology Today* 32 (July 1975):166-173.

Brown, Robert McAfee. "Nicaragua: On Saving Us From Ourselves." *Christian Century* 102 (Jan. 2-9, 1985):6-7.

Brown, Robert McAfee. "Reflections on Detroit." *Christianity and Crisis* 35 (Oct. 27, 1975):255-256.

Brown, Robert McAfee. "Reflections on 'Liberation Theology'," *Religion in Life* 43 (Aug. 1974):269-282.

Brown, Robert McAfee. "The Rootedness of All Theology. Context Affects Content." *Christianity and Crisis* 37 (July 18, 1977):170-174.

Brown, Robert McAfee. "Theological Gamesmanship: Disposing of Liberation Theology in Eight Easy Lessons." *Christianity and Crisis* 38 (Aug. 21, 1978):200-202.

Brown, Robert McAfee. "Two Worlds: Beauty and Oppression." *Christian Century* 97 (Apr. 2, 1980):378-380.

Brown, Robert McAfee. "Who is this Jesus Christ who Frees and Unites?" *The Ecumenical Review* 28 (Jan. 1976):6-21.

Broz, Ludek. "Alves's Programme of Radical Utopianism." *Communio Viatorum* 15, No. 4 (1972):201-209.

Broz, Ludek. "Theological Reflection in Support of Liberation." *Communio Viatorum* 19, Nos. 1, 2 (1976):11-17.

Brueggemann, Walter. "Trajectories in Old Testament Literature and the Sociology of Ancient Israel." *Journal of Biblical Literature* 98 (June 1979):161-185.

Bucher, Glenn R. "Liberation in the Church: Black and White." *Union Seminary Quarterly Review* 29 (Winter 1974):91-105.

Bucher, Glenn R. "Liberation, Male and White: Initial Reflections." *Christian Century* 91 (Mar. 20, 1974):312-316.

Bucher, Glenn R. "Theological Method in Liberation Theologies: Cone, Russell, and Gutierrez." In *American Academy of Religion. Philosophy of Religion and Theology Proceedings 1976.* Pages 118-121.

Bucher, Glenn R. "Toward a Liberation Theology for the 'Oppressor'." *Journal of the American Academy of Religion* 44 (Summer 1976): 517-534.

"A Call to the Church in a Revolutionary World." *Study Encounter* 2, No. 3 (1966):110-112.

434   Orthopraxis or Heresy

Camara, Dom Helder. "CELAM: History Is Implacable." *Cross Currents* 28, No. 1 (1978):55-59.

Cardoso, Fernando Henrique. "0 Inimigo de Papel (The Paper Enemy)." *Latin American Perspectives* 1, No. 1 (Spring 1974):66-74.

Carmody, John T. "The Development of Robert McAfee Brown's Ecumenical Thought." *Religion in Life* 43 (Aug. 1974):283-293.

Castuera, Ignacio. "The Theology and Practice of Liberation in the Mexican American Context." *Perkins School of Theology Journal* 29 (Fall 1975): 2-11.

Cepeda, Rafael. "Christian Response to a Revolutionary Situation." *Reformed and Presbyterian World* 28 (Spring 1965):299-305.

Chapman, G. Clarke, Jr. "Black Theology and Theology of Hope: What Have They To Say To Each Other." *Union Seminary Quarterly Review* 29 (1973):107-129.

Chapman, G. Clarke, Jr. "Dear Theophilus—Now About 'Liberation Theology'..." *Dialog* 19 (1980):224-227.

Chatterji, Saral K. "Humanization As A Goal of Revolution." *Religion and Society* 20 (Mar. 1973):62-70.

Chilcote, Ronald H. "A Critical Synthesis of the Dependency Literature." *Latin American Perspectives* 1, No. 1 (Spring 1974):4-29.

Cobb, John B., Jr. "Points of Contact Between Process Theology and Liberation Theology in Matters of Faith and Justice." *Process Studies* 14 (Summer 1985):124-141.

Cogswell, Rob. "The Church in Cuernavaca." *Christian Century* 100 (Dec. 14, 1983):1161-1164.

Cogswell, Rob. "Poverty in Central America: Our Language Barrier." *Christian Century* 102 (May 8, 1985):470-472.

Collins, Sheila D. "Liberation Theology Conference in Detroit." *Journal of Ecumenical Studies* 13 (Winter 1976):183-184.

Collum, Danny. "Two Theologies In Contrast." *Sojourners* 12, No. 2 (Feb. 1983):35-36.

Cone, James H. "Asian Theology Today: Searching for Definitions." *Christian Century* 96 (May 23, 1979):589-591.

Cone, James H. "Biblical Revelation and Social Existence." *Interpretation* 28 (Oct. 1974):422-440.

Cone, James H. "A Black American Perspective on the Future of African Theology." *Theology in the Americas Documentation Series*, Document No. 4 (August 1978).

Cone, James H. "The Black Church and Marxism: What Do They Have to Say to Each Other?" *Theology in the Americas Documentation Series*, Document No. 14 (n.d.).

Cone, James H. "Black Theology and the Black Church: Where Do We Go From Here?" *Cross Currents* 27 (Summer 1977):147-156.

Cone, James H. "Black Theology and Ideology: A Response to my Respondents." *Union Seminary Quarterly Review* 31 (1975):71-86.

Cone, James H. "Black Theology on Revolution, Violence and Reconciliation." *Dialog* 12 (Spring 1973):127-133. Also in *Union Seminary Quarterly Review* 31 (1975):5-14.

Cone, James H. "Christian Theology and the Afro-American Revolution." *Christianity and Crisis* 30 (June 8, 1970):123-125.

Cone, James H. "A Critical Response to Schubert Ogden's *Faith and Freedom: Toward a Theology of Liberation.*" *Perkins School of Theology Journal* 33 (Fall 1979):51-55.

Cone, James H. "The Dialectic of Theology and Life or Speaking the Truth." *Union Seminary Quarterly Review* 29 (Winter 1974):75-89.

Cone, James H. "Freedom, History, and Hope." *Journal of the Interdenominational Theological Center* 1 (Fall 1973):55-64.

Cone, James H. "The Gospel and the Liberation of the Poor." *Christian Century* 98 (Feb. 18, 1981):162-166.

Cone, James H. "The Social Context of Theology: Freedom, History and Hope," *Risk* 9, No. 2 (1973):13-24.

Cone, James H. "The Story Context of Black Theology." *Theology Today* 32 (July 1975):144-150.

Cone, James H. "What Is Christian Theology?" *Caribbean Journal of Religious Studies* 3 (1980):1-12.

Cone, James H. "Who Is Jesus Christ For Us Today?" *Christianity and Crisis* 35 (Apr. 14, 1975):81-85.

Cooper, Burton. "How Does God Act in Our Time? An Invitation to a Dialogue between Process and Liberation Theologies." *Union Seminary Quarterly Review* 32 (Fall 1976):25-35.

Cormie, Lee; Stark, Robert; and Irarrazaval, Diego. "How Do We Do Liberation Theology?" *Radical Religion* 2, No. 4 (1976):25-31.

Cox, Harvey, and Sand, Faith Annette. "What Happened at Puebla?" *Christianity and Crisis* 39 (Mar. 19, 1979):57-60.

Davis, Charles. "Theology and Praxis." *Cross Currents* 23 (1973):154-168.

Decke, Gerd. "Perspectives for the Lutheran Churches in Chile and Argentina." *Dialog* 13 (Summer 1974):177-182.

DeHainaut, Raymond K. "New Alliance of Christians for Liberation in Colombia Comes into the Open." *Christian Century* 91 (July 17-24, 1974): 729-731.

De Santa Ana, Julio. "The Influence of Bonhoeffer on the Theology of Liberation." *The Ecumenical Review* 28 (Apr. 1976):188-197.

Dickinson, Richard D. N., Jr. "Notes Toward an Adequate Liberation Ethic." *Encounter* (Indianapolis) 34 (Autumn 1973):335-342.

Diocese of Vitoria, Brazil. "The Church We Want." *Cross Currents* 26 (Spring 1976):1-10.

Dombrowski, Daniel A. "Benne and Novak on Capitalism." *Theology Today* 41 (Apr. 1984):61-65.

Dorrien, Gary J. "A School of Humanity. Liberation Theology and Christian Political Ethics." *Sojourners* 12, No. 11 (Dec. 1983):36-38.

Duchrow, Ulrich. "The Church Facing Dependency Structures." *Dialog* 20 (Fall 1981):269-273.

Dussel, Enrique. "An International Division of Theological Labor." *Foundations* 23 (Oct.-Dec. 1980):332-354.

Dussel, Enrique. "The Kingdom of God and the Poor." *International Review of Mission* 68 (Apr. 1979):115-130.

Ebener, Dan R. "Is There a Future for Nonviolence in Central America." (and "A Latin American Response," by Mano Barreno). *Fellowship* 49, No. 10-11 (Oct.-Nov. 1983):6-7, and 28.

Escobar, Samuel. "Interview." *Sojourners* 5, No. 8 (Sept. 1976):15-18.

Feinberg, Richard E. "Dependency and the Defeat of Allende." *Latin American Perspectives* 1, No. 2 (Summer 1974):30-43.

Ferm, Deane William. "South American Liberation Theology." *Religion in Life* 48 (Winter 1979):474-491.

Fernandez, Raul A., and Ocampo, Jose F. "The Latin American Revolution: A Theory of Imperialism, Not Dependence." *Latin American Perspectives* 1, No. 1 (Spring 1974):30-61.

Fiorenza, Francis P. "Latin American Liberation Theology." *Interpretation* 28 (Oct. 1974):441-457.

"A First World Response to a Third World Challenge." *Theology in the Americas Documentation Series*, Document No. 2 (Apr. 1978).

Fitzpatrick, Joseph P. "The Latin American Church in the United States." *Thought* 59 (June 1984):244-254.

Frank, Andre Gunder. "Dependence is Dead, Long Live Dependence and the Class Struggle: A Reply to Critics." *Latin American Perspectives* 1, No. 1 (Spring 1974):87-106.

Freire, Paulo. "Education, Liberation and the Church," *Risk* 9, No. 2 (1973):34-48.

Frelick, J. P. "Peace and Progress (Reflections on the Ethics of Development)." *Communio Viatorum* 9 (1966):127-136.

Fry, John R., and Herzog, Frederick. "Liberation Theology: Continuing the Discussion." *Christianity and Crisis* 34 (Oct. 14, 1974):224-229.

Galilea, Segundo. "Between Medellin and Puebla." *Cross Currents* 28, No. 1 (1978):71-78.

Galtung, Johan. "A Structural Theory of Imperialism." *Journal of Peace Research* 8, No. 2 (1971):81-117.

Gaxiola, Manuel J. "The Pentecostal Ministry." *International Review of Mission* 66 (1977):57-63.

Gensichen, Hans-Werner. "From Minneapolis 1957 to Jakarta 1975. Variations on an Ecumenical Theme." *The Ecumenical Review* 26 (1974):469-482.

Gensichen, Hans-Werner. "Revolution and Mission in the Third World." *Lutheran World* 16 (1969):12-28.

"German Theologians Defend the Theology of Liberation." *IDOC Bulletin* No. 1 (Jan. 1978):7-9.

Gibbs, Eddie. "The Theology of Revolution." *Front* 16 (Autumn 1973): 141-145.

Gilbert, Guy J. "Socialism and Dependency." *Latin American Perspectives* 1, No. 1 (Spring 1974):107-123.

Girardet, Giorgio. "The Problem of Revolution and Christian Theology." *Communio Viatorum* 10 (1967):13-35.

Gold, Eva. "Central America: Time Bomb with a Lit Fuse." *Christian Century* 101 (Apr. 25, 1984):435-439.

Golden, Renny. "Sanctuary. Churches Take Part in a New Underground Railroad." *Sojourners* 11, No. 11 (Dec. 1982):24-26.

Gollwitzer, Helmut. "Liberation in History." *Interpretation* 28 (Oct. 1974): 404-421.

Goodwin, Bennie E. "Education as Liberation: An Analysis of Paulo Freire." *Journal of the Interdenominational Theological Center* 2 (Spring 1975): 89-99.

Gort, J. D. "Gospel for the Poor?" *Missiology* 7 (July 1979):325-354.

Griffin, David Ray. "North Atlantic and Latin American Liberation Theologians." *Encounter* (Indianapolis) 40 (Winter 1979):17-30.

Griffin, David Ray. "Values, Evil, and Liberation Theology." *Encounter* (Indianapolis) 40 (Winter 1979):1-15.

Griffiss, James E. "Some Current Literature on Political Theology " (Review Article). *Anglican Theological Review* 58 (Apr. 1976):217-228.

Grounds, Vernon C. "Bombs or Bibles? Get Ready for Revolution!" *Christianity Today* 15 (Jan. 15, 1971):4-6.

"Guatemala: Development or Liberation." *IDOC Bulletin* No. 13 (Nov. 1973): 5-10.

Gutierrez, Gustavo. "Faith as Freedom: Solidarity with the Alienated and Confidence in the Future." *Horizons* 2 (Spring 1975):25-60.

Gutierrez, Gustavo. "The Hope of Liberation." *Worldview* 17 (June 1974): 35-37.

Gutierrez, Gustavo. "The Meaning of Development. Working Paper IV." In *In Search of a Theology of Development*, pp. 116-179. Edited by Paul Loffler. Geneva: Committee on Society, Development and Peace, 1970.

Gutierrez, Gustavo. "Notes for a Theology of Liberation." *Theological Studies* 31 (1971):243-261.

Gutierrez, Gustavo. "A Retreat From Commitment. The 'Preparatory Document' for Puebla." *Christianity and Crisis* 38 (Sept. 18, 1978):211-218.

Gutierrez, Gustavo. "Talking About God." *Sojourners* 12, No. 2 (Feb. 1983): 26-29.

Hageman, Alice. "Liberating Theology Through Action." *Christian Century* 92 (Oct. 1, 1975):850-853.

Halvorsen, Loren. "The Power of the Powerless." *Dialog* 13 (Summer 1974): 195-200.

Ham, Adolfo. "Introduction to the Theology of Liberation." *Communio Viatorum* 16, No. 3 (1973):113-120.

Hammett, Jenny Y. "God 'As' . . . Image vs. Idol in Current Liberation Theology." *Religion in Life* 45 (Winter 1976):403-410.

Hanly, Elizabeth. "A Seventh Year of Unknowing. The Witness of Argentina's Mothers of the Plaza de Mayo." *Sojourners* 12, No. 4 (Apr. 1983):21-25.

Hanratty, Dennis M. "The Political Role of the Mexican Catholic Church: Contemporary Issues." *Thought* 59 (June 1984):164-182.

Harper, George Lea, Jr. "Roadblock to American Theology?" *Duke Divinity School Review* 38 (Fall 1973):135-138.

Harrison, Beverly Wildung. "The 'Theology in the Americas' Conference. Challenging the Western Paradigm." *Christianity and Crisis* 35 (Oct. 27, 1975):251-254.

"The Hartford Declaration. An Appeal For Theological Affirmation." *Theology Today* 32 (1975):94-97.

"The Hartford Declaration. Theological Table-Talk." *Theology Today* 32 (1975):183-191.

Hartman, Olov. "Development and Liberation." *Lutheran World* 20 (1973): 133-140.

Hearne, Brian. "Readings on Liberation Theology." *African Ecclesiastical Review* 21 (Apr. 1979):109-116.

Hebblethwaite, Peter. "How Liberating is Liberation Theology?" *Front* 18 (Winter 1975-1976):199-203.

Hefner, Philip. "Theology Engagee: Liberational, Political, Critical." *Dialog* 13 (Summer 1974):188-194.

Hellwig, Monika. "Liberation Theology: An Emerging School." *Scottish Journal of Theology* 30 (1977):137-151.

Hennelly, Alfred T. "Courage With Primitive Weapons." *Cross Currents* 28, No. 1 (1978):8-19.

Hennelly, Alfred T. "Theological Method: The Southern Exposure." *Theological Studies* 38 (Dec. 1977):709-735.

Henry, Carl. "The World Council and Socialism." *Christianity Today* 10 (July 8, 1966):3-7.

Herzog, Frederick. "Birth Pangs: Liberation Theology in North America." *Christian Century* 93 (Dec. 15, 1976):1120-1125.

Herzog, Frederick. "The Burden of Southern Theology: A Response." *Duke Divinity School Review* 38 (Fall 1973):151-170.

Herzog, Frederick. "Commentary on the Bishop's Call." *Perkins School of Theology: Journal* 27 (Summer 1974):5-12.

Herzog, Frederick. "From Good Friday to Labor Day." *Journal of Religious Thought* 34 (Fall-Winter 1977):15-22.

Herzog, Frederick. "God, Evil, and Revolution." *Journal of Religious Thought* 25, No. 2 (1968-1969):5-28.

Herzog, Frederick. "Interdependence on Spaceship Earth." *Christian Century* 92 (Mar. 26, 1975):304-307.

Herzog, Frederick. "Liberation and Imagination." *Interpretation* 32 (July 1978):227-241.

Herzog, Frederick. "Liberation Hermeneutic as Ideology Critique?" *Interpretation* 28 (Oct. 1974):387-403.

Herzog, Frederick. "Liberation Theology Begins at Home." *Christianity and Crisis* 34 (May 13, 1974):94-98.

Herzog, Frederick. "Liberation Theology or Culture Religion?" *Union Seminary Quarterly Review* 29 (Spring-Summer 1974):233-244.

Herzog, Frederick. "The Liberation of White Theology." *Christian Century* 91 (Mar. 20, 1974):316-319.

Herzog, Frederick. "Origins of Liberation Theology." *Duke Divinity School Review* 38 (Fall 1973):126-128.

Herzog, Frederick. "Political Theology." *Christian Century* 86 (July 23, 1969):975-978.

Herzog, Frederick. "Responsible Theology?" In *Philosophy of Religion & Theology: 1974 Proceedings*, pp. 159-173. Edited by William McClendon, Jr. Tallahassee, FL: American Academy of Religion, 1974.

Herzog, Frederick. "Theology at the Crossroads." *Union Seminary Quarterly Review* 31 (1975):59-68.

Herzog, Frederick. "Theology of Liberation." *Continuum* 7 (Winter 1970): 515-524.

Herzog, Frederick. "Which Liberation Theology?" *Religion in Life* 44 (1975):448-453.

Heyne, Paul. "A New International Economic Order?" *Dialog* 20 (Fall 1981): 281-286.

Heywood, Carter. "Ruether and Daly: Theologians. Speaking and Sparking, Building and Burning." *Christianity and Crisis* 39 (Apr. 2, 1979): 66-72.

Hinlicky, Paul R. "On the Need for Lutheran Political Thought." *Lutheran Forum* (Pentecost 1985):8-11.

Holland, Edward J. "The Significance of Liberation Theology for Christian Witness in the U.S.A." *Dialog* 13 (Summer 1974):183-187.

Hoops, M. H. "The Concept of Liberation." *Lutheran Quarterly* 28 (Aug. 1976): 240-256.

Hunt, Chester L. "Liberation Theology in the Philippines: A Test Case." *Christianity Today* 26 (Mar. 5, 1982):24-26.

Jenkins, David. "Who Is This Jesus Christ?" *The Ecumenical Review* 26 (1974):394-402.

Johnson, Paul. "The Almost-Chosen People: Why America Is Different." *The First Annual Erasmus Lecture.* Rockford, IL: The Rockford Institute, 1985.

Jones, Robert. "Four Churches in One: Latin American Catholicism." *Christian Century* 101 (Feb. 22, 1984):199-201.

Keck, Leander E. "The Church, the New Testament, and Violence." *Pastoral Psychology* 22 (Oct. 1971):5-14.

Kinsler, F. Ross, and Evans, Robert A. "Reflections on the Nicaraguan Election." *Christian Century* 102 (Feb. 20, 1985):186-188.

Kirk, Andrew. "Liberation Theology in Latin America Today." *The Modern Churchman* 23 (1980):161-171.

Kirk, Andrew. "A New Theology from Latin America." *The Modern Churchman* 18 (Apr.-June 1974):108-115.

Kirkpatrick, Dow. "Liberation Theologians and Third World Demands." *Christian Century* 93 (May 12, 1976):456-460.

Kirkpatrick, Dow. "What U.S. Protestants Need From CELAM III." *Cross Currents* 28, No. 1 (1978):90-96.

Knitter, Paul F. "Theocentric Christology." *Theology Today* (July 1983): 130-149.

Knoch, Michael. "'Jesus Christ Frees and Unites'—In a Socialist Society." *The Ecumenical Review* 26 (1974):439-452.

Kolden, Marc. "On Speaking of the Kingdom Today." *Word and World* 2 (Spring 1982):150-160.

Krass, Alfred. "Living in Resurrection Reality." *The Other Side* No. 110 (Nov. 1980):44-47.

Kress, Robert. "Theological Method: Praxis and Liberation." *Communio* (U.S.) 6 (Spring 1979):113-134.

Kuhn, Harold B. "Liberation Theology: A Semantic Problem." *Wesleyan Theological Journal* 15 (Spring 1980):34-45.

Lamb, Matthew L. "Liberation Theology and Social Justice." *Process Studies* 14 (Summer 1985):102-123.

Leech, Kenneth. "Letter to the Editor: Marxism and Liberation Theology." *Theology* 87 (May 1985):219.

Leech, Kenneth. "Liberating Theology: The Thought of Juan Luis Segundo." *Theology* 84 (July 1981):258-266.

Lehmann, Paul. "The Transfiguration of Jesus and Revolutionary Politics." *Christianity and Crisis* 35 (Mar. 3, 1975):44-47.

Lemert, Charles C. "Theorizing, Policy Making, and the Critique of Europeanism." *Review of Religious Research* 21 (Fall 1979):3-23.

LeMone, Archie. "Report on a Symposium: When Traditional Theology Meets Black and Liberation Theology." *Christianity and Crisis* 33 (Sept. 17, 1973):177-178.

Levine, Daniel H. "Religion and Politics: Dimensions of Renewal." *Thought* 59 (June 1984):117-135.

Livanio, J. B. "CELAM III: Fears and Hopes." *Cross Currents* 28, No. 1 (1978):20-33.

"Liberation Theology and Christian Realism" (Symposium). *Christianity and Crisis* 33 (Oct. 15, 1976):197-206.

Lincoln, C. Eric. "A Perspective on James H. Cone's Black Theology." *Union Seminary Quarterly Review* 31 (1975):15-22.

Lindley, Susan H. "A Crucially Necessary Risk?" *Duke Divinity School Review* 38 (Fall 1973):129-134.

Lochman, J. M. "Ecumenical Theology of Revolution." *Scottish Journal of Theology* 21 (June 1968):170-186.

Lochman, J. M. "Peace and Revolution." *Reformed and Presbyterian World* 30 (Spring 1968):108-114.

Lochman, J. M. "Social Theology in a Revolutionary Age." *Communio Viatorum* 10 (1967):53-60.

Lochman, J. M. "Violence. The Just Revolution." Responses by George Houser, James Cone, and Roger Shinn. *Christianity and Crisis* 32 (July 10, 1972):163-171.

McCann, Dennis P. "Liberation and the Multinationals." *Theology Today* 41 (Apr. 1984):51-60.

McCann, Dennis P. "Political Ideologies and Practical Theology: Is
    There a Difference?" *Union Seminary Quarterly Review* 36
    (1981):243-257.

McEoin, Gary. "The Church of the Poor?" *Cross Currents* 28, No. 1
    (1978):1-3.

McEoin, Gary, ed. "Puebla: Moment of Decision for the Latin
    American Church." *Cross Currents* 28, No. 1 (1978):1-112.

Mackie, Steven G. "Praxis as the Context for Interpretation. A Study
    of Latin American Liberation Theology." *Journal of Theology for
    South Africa* 24 (1978):31-43.

MacMichael, David. "Calling the Bluff. A Former C.I.A. Analyst
    Talks About Arms Shipments from Nicaragua to El Salvador."
    Sojourners 13, No. 7 (Aug. 1984):18-22.

"The Manipulation of CELAM." *Cross Currents* 28, No. 1 (1978):60-65.

Manley, Michael. "From the Shackles of Domination and
    Oppression." *The Ecumenical Review* 28 (Apr. 1976):49-65.

Marstin, Ronald. "A Look at 'Theology in the Americas'."
    Christianity and Crisis 38 (Aug. 21, 1978):198-200.

Martin, Earl, and Martin, Pat Hostetter. "Tell It to the Marines. First
    World Pacifism and Third World Violence." *Sojourners* 12, No. 4
    (Apr. 1983):18-20.

Mays, James Luther. "Justice. Perspectives from the Prophetic
    Tradition." *Interpretation* 37 (1983):5-17.

Meeks, M. Douglas. "God's Suffering Power and Liberation."
    Journal of Religious Thought 33 (Fall-Winter 1976):44-54.

Meeks, M. Douglas. "The Holy Spirit and Human Needs. Toward a
    Trinitarian View of Economics." *Christianity and Crisis* 40
    (Nov. 10, 1980):307-316.

"A Message from Concerned North Americans." *Cross Currents* 28,
    No. 1 (1978):4-7.

Metz, Johann Baptist. "Erlösung und Emanzipation." *Reformatorio*
    22 (Apr. 1973):208-224.

Miguez Bonino, Jose. "Doing Theology in the Context of the Struggles
    of the Poor." *Mid-Stream* 20 (1981):369-373.

Miguez Bonino, Jose. "Freedom Through Unity: Liberation Through
    Ecumenism in Latin America." *Thought* 59 (June 1984):255-264.

Miguez Bonino, Jose. "The Human and the System." *Theology Today*
    35 (Apr. 1978):14-24.

Miguez Bonino, Jose. "Liberation and Social Change." In *Today's
    Church and Today's World*, pp. 120-129. Edited by John Howe.
    London: CIO Publishers, 1977.

Miguez Bonino, Jose. "New Theological Perspectives." In *Theology
    in Action*, pp. 77-90. Edited by Jae Shik Oh. Bangkok: n.p., 1972.

Miguez Bonino, Jose. "New Trends in Theology." *Duke Divinity School Review* 42 (Fall 1977):131-142.

Miguez Bonino, Jose. "Poverty as Curse, Blessing and Challenge." *The Iliff Review* 34 (Fall 1977):3-13.

Miguez Bonino, Jose. "Protestantism's Contribution to Latin America." *Lutheran Quarterly* 22 (1970):92-98.

Miguez Bonino, Jose. "The Struggle of the Poor and the Church." *The Ecumenical Review* 27 (Jan. 1975):36-43.

Miguez Bonino, Jose. "Theology and Liberation." *International Review of Mission* 61 (Jan. 1972):67-72.

Miguez Bonino, Jose. "Theology and Theologians of the New World: II. Latin America. Five Theses Towards an Understanding of the 'Theology of Liberation'." *Expository Times* 87 (Apr. 1976):196-200.

Miguez Bonino, Jose. "Violence & Liberation." *Christianity and Crisis* 32 (July 10, 1972):169-172.

Minella, Mary. "Praxis and the Question of Revelation." *Iliff Review* 36 (Fall 1979):17-29.

Miranda, Osmundo Afonso. "Aspects of Latin American Revolutionary Theologies." *Journal of the Interdenominational Theological Center* 5 (Fall 1977): 1-22.

Moeller, Charles. "Jesus Christ, God's Dialogue with Mankind." *The Ecumenical Review* 26 (1974):380-393.

Moellering, Ralph. "North American Responses to Liberation Theology." *Currents in Theology and Mission* 7 (Aug. 1980):221-229.

Moltmann, Jürgen. "God in the Revolution." *Student World* 61 (1968): 241-252.

Moltmann, Jürgen. "God Reconciles and Makes Free." *Reformed and Presbyterian World* 31 (1970):105-118.

Moltmann, Jürgen. "Liberation in the Light of Hope." *The Ecumenical Review* 26 (1974):413-429.

Moltmann, Jürgen, with Meeks, M. Douglas. "The Liberation of Oppressors." *Christianity and Crisis* 38 (Dec. 25, 1978):310-317.

Moltmann, Jürgen. "The Liberation of Oppressors." *Journal of the Interdenominational Theological Center* 6 (Spring 1979):69-82.

Moltmann, Jürgen. "An Open Letter to Jose Miguez Bonino. On Latin American Liberation Theology." *Christianity and Crisis* 36 (Mar. 29, 1976):57-63.

Moltmann, Jürgen. "Die 'Religion der Freiheit' für das 'Reich der Freiheit'." *Communio Viatorum* 22, No. 1-2 (1968):21-28.

Morgan, Robert C. "Beyond Masochism: A White Male Primal Scream." *Christian Century* 94 (Dec. 7, 1977):1141-1143.

Moser, M. Theresa, RSCJ, and Schervish, Paul G. "Theology of Work—A Liberation Perspective." *Radical Religion* 3, No. 3-4 (1978):30-36.

Mottesi, Osvaldo Luis. "Doing Theology in the Latin American Context." *Journal of the Interdenominational Theological Center* 5 (Spring 1978): 76-90.

Nash, James A. "Politically Feeble Churches and the Strategic Imperative." *Christian Century* 99 (Oct. 6, 1982):983-987.

Nederhood, Joel H. "Christians and Revolution." *Christianity Today* 15 (Jan. 1, 1971):7-9.

Neely, Alan. "Liberation Theology in Latin America: Antecedents and Autochthony." *Missiology* 6 (July 1978):343-370.

Neuhaus, Richard John. "Liberation as Program and Promise: On Refusing to Settle for Less." *Currents in Theology and Mission* 2 (Apr. 1975): 90-99 (Part One); and 2 (June 1975):152-158 (Part Two).

Nicholls, William. "Liberation as a Religious Theme." *Canadian Journal of Theology* 16, No. 3-4 (1974):140-154.

Nouwen, Henri. "A Call to Peacemaking." *Pamphlet of World Peacemakers, Inc.* Washington, D.C.: Church of the Savior, 1983.

Novak, Michael. "Liberation Theology." *National Catholic Reporter* 12 (Apr. 9, 1976):9.

Novak, Michael. "Liberation Theology in Practice." *Thought* 59 (June 1984): 136-148.

Novak, Michael. "Liberation Theology: Latest Fad." *National Catholic Reporter* 12 (Feb. 27, 1976):7-8.

Novak, Michael. "Theology of Liberation." *National Catholic Reporter* 11 (Nov. 21, 1975):12.

Nunez, Emilio A. "The Theology of Liberation in Latin America." *Bibliotheca Sacra* 134 (1977):343-356.

Obayashi, Hiroshi. "Liberation Theology and the Problem of Religion's 'Sui Generis'," *Journal of Religious Thought* 31 (1974):33-49.

Ogden, Schubert M. "The Authority of Scripture for Theology." *Interpretation* 30 (1976):242-261.

Ogden, Schubert M. "Christology at the Crossroads: A Latin American Approach " (Review). *The Perkins School of Theology Journal* 31 (1978):47-49.

Ogden, Schubert M. "Faith and Freedom." *Christian Century* 97 (Dec. 17, 1980):1241-1244.

Ogden, Schubert M. "Faith and Truth." In *Frontline Theology*, pp. 126-133. Edited by Dean Peerman. Richmond: John Knox Press, 1967.

Ogden, Schubert M. "The Gospel We Hold in Common—Or Do We?" 1973 Faith and Order Conference of the Texas Conference of Churches, Oct. 19-21, 1973 (unpublished manuscript).

Ogden, Schubert M. "How Does God Function in Human Life?" *Christianity and Crisis* 27 (May 15, 1967):105-108.

Ogden, Schubert M. "The Metaphysics of Faith and Justice." *Process Studies* 14 (Summer 1985):87-101.

Ogden, Schubert M. "An Outline Still to Be Filled Out. In Retrospect: Books of the '60s." *Christian Century* 95 (May 17, 1978):538-539.

Ogden, Schubert M. "Prolegomena to Practical Theology." *The Perkins School of Theology Journal* 35 (Summer 1982):17-21.

Ogden, Schubert M. "The Task of Philosophical Theology." In *The Future of Philosophical Theology*, pp. 55-84. Edited by Robert A. Evans. Philadelphia: Westminster Press, 1971.

Ogden, Schubert M. "Theological Brief." In *Christian Theology: A Case Study Approach*, pp. 41-45. Edited by Robert A. Evans and Thomas D. Parker. New York: Harper & Row, 1976.

Ogden, Schubert M. "Theology and Religious Studies: Their Difference and the Difference It Makes." *Journal of the American Academy of Religion* 46 (Mar. 1978):3-17.

Ogden, Schubert M. "Theology in the University." In *Unfinished . . .: Essays in Honor of Ray L. Hart.* Edited by Mark C. Taylor. *Journal of the American Academy of Religion* 48, No. 1 (1981):3-13.

Ogden, Schubert M. "What is Theology?" *Journal of Religion* 52 (1972):22-40.

Ogden, Schubert M. "Women and the Canon: A Response to Elisabeth Schüssler Fiorenza " (unpublished paper).

Osborn, Robert T. "Jesus and Liberation Theology." *Christian Century* 33 (Mar. 10, 1976):225-227.

Osborn, Robert T. "Liberation Theology: Challenge to World, Church, and Academy. A Review Article." *Perspectives in Religious Studies* 6 (Summer 1979):152-161.

Osborn, Robert T. "A Poetic Act." *Duke Divinity School Review* 38 (Fall 1973):139-142.

Osborn, Robert T. "The Rise and Fall of the Bible in Recent American Theology." *Duke Divinity School Review* 41 (Spring 1977):57-72.

Osborn, Robert T. "Some Problems of Liberation Theology: A Polanyian Perspective." *Journal of the American Academy of Religion* 51, No. 1 (Mar. 1983):79-95.

Ostling, Richard N. "Deliberation at the Vatican. A Leftist Latin American Theologian Faces Interrogation." *Time* 124, No. 10 (Sept. 3, 1984): 49.

446 Orthopraxis or Heresy

Ostling, Richard N. "The New Missionary." *Time* 120, No. 26 (Dec. 27, 1982): 38-44.

"Our Martyrs Give Hope of Resurrection." *Cross Currents* 28, No. 1 (1978): 47-54.

Padilla, C. Rene. "The Theology of Liberation." *Christianity Today* 18 (Nov. 9, 1973):69-70.

Pantelis, Jorge. "Implications of the Theologies of Liberation for the Theological Training of the Pastoral Ministry in Latin America." *International Review of Mission* 66 (1977):14-21.

Peck, Jane Cary. "A Model for Ministry." *Christian Century* 100 (Feb. 2-9, 1983):94-97.

Peel, David R. "Juan Luis Segundo's, 'A Theology for Artisans of a New Humanity': A Latin American Contribution to Contemporary Theological Understanding." *The Perkins School of Theology Journal* 30 (Spring 1977):1-9.

Pereira Ramalho, Jether. "Basic Popular Communities in Brazil. Some Notes on Pastoral Activity in Two Types." *The Ecumenical Review* 29, No. 4 (Oct. 1977):394-401.

Perkins, Harvey L. "Issues of Contextual Theology: An Australian Perspective." *The Ecumenical Review* 28 (July 1976):286-295.

Phillip, T. M. "Liberation and Justice Motifs in Christianity." *Religion and Society* 27 (June 1980):13-23.

Pierard, Richard V. "A Reaganite in Nicaragua." *Christian Century* 100 (Mar. 9, 1983):204-205.

Pinnock, Clark H. "An Evangelical Theology of Human Liberation." *Sojourners* 5, No. 2 (Feb. 1976):30-33 (Part One); and 5, No. 3 (Mar. 1976): 26-29 (Part Two).

Pinnock, Clark H. "Liberation Theology: The Gains, The Gaps." *Christianity Today* 20 (Jan. 16, 1976):13-15.

Pixley, George V. "Pastoral Strategy for a 'People's Church.' Guest Editorial." *Foundations* 23 (Oct.-Dec. 1980):291-293.

Pixley, George V. "People of God. Popular Majorities in the Bible." *Foundations* 23 (Oct.-Dec. 1980):368-379.

Powelson, John P. "Holistic Economics." *Theology Today* 41 (Apr. 1984): 66-77.

Price, James L. "Unresolved Hermeneutical Questions?" *Duke Divinity School Review* 38 (Fall 1973):143-150.

Pronk, Jan. "A New International Order Is in the Interest of Developed Countries Too." *International Development Review* 18, No. 4 (1976): 8-14.

Quigley, Thomas E. "Latin America's Church: No Turning Back." *Cross Currents* 28, No. 1 (1978):79-89.

Ranly, Ernest W. "The Liberating Gospel According to Alfredo Fierro: A Review Article." *Encounter* (Indianapolis) 42 (Spring 1981): 189-196.

Reilly, Michael C. "Theologies of Liberation: Recent Translations." *Missiology* 6 (Jan. 1979):105-108.

Rendtorff, Trutz. "Universalität oder Kontextualität der Theologie. Eine 'europäische' Stellungnahme." *Zeitschrift für Theologie und Kirche* 74 (1977):238-254.

"Response to Revolution. A Symposium Based on 1966 WCC Conference Themes." *Social Action* 32 (1966):16-33.

Richard, Pablo. "The Latin American Church 1959-1978." *Cross Currents* 28, No. 1 (1978):34-46.

Riding, Alan. "Latin Church in Siege." *N.Y. Times Magazine* (May 6, 1979): 32-34ff.

Ritschl, Dietrich. "Westliche Theologie im Licht der Kritik aus der Dritten Welt. Kritisches zum Begriff 'Indigenous Theology'." *Evangelische Theologie* 39 (1979):451-465.

Roberts, J. Deotis. "A Black Theologian in Mexico." *Journal of Religious Thought* 37 (1980):15-22.

Roberts, J. Deotis. "Christian Liberation Ethics: The Black Experience." *Religion in Life* 48 (Summer 1979):227-235.

Roberts, J. Deotis. "Contextual Theology: Liberation and Indigenization." *Christian Century* 93 (Jan. 28, 1976):64-68.

Roberts, W. Dayton. "Where Has Liberation Theology Gone Wrong?" *Christianity Today* 23 (Oct. 19, 1979):26-28.

Romero, Oscar Arnulfo, and Damos, Arturo Rivera. "The Church, Political Organization and Violence." *Cross Currents* 29 (Winter 1979-1980): 385-408.

Rubio, A. Garcia. "Die lateinamerikanische Theologie der Befreiung (I)." *Internationale Katholische Zeitschrift* (Communio) 2 (Sept.-Oct. 1973): 400-423.

Ruether, Rosemary Radford. "Asking the Existential Questions." *Christian Century* 97 (Apr. 2, 1980):374-378.

Ruether, Rosemary Radford. "Consciousness-Raising at Puebla: Women Speak to the Latin Church." *Christianity and Crisis* 39 (Apr. 2, 1979): 77-80.

Ruether, Rosemary Radford. "Courage as a Christian Virtue." *Cross Currents* 33 (Spring 1983):8-16.

Ruether, Rosemary Radford. "Crisis in Sex and Race: Black Theology vs. Feminist Theology." *Christianity and Crisis* 34 (Apr. 15, 1974): 67-73.

Ruether, Rosemary Radford. "Feminism and Peace." *Christian Century* 100 (Aug. 31-Sept. 7, 1983):771-776.

Ruether, Rosemary Radford. "The Foundations of Liberation Languages: Christianity and Revolutionary Movements." *Journal of Religious Thought* 32 (1975):74-85.

Ruether, Rosemary Radford. "Individual Repentance Is Not Enough." *Explor* 2, No. 1 (1976):47-52.

Ruether, Rosemary Radford. "Monks and Marxists: A Look at the Catholic Left." *Christianity and Crisis* 33 (Apr. 30, 1973):75-79.

Ruether, Rosemary Radford. "Outlines for a Theology of Liberation." *Dialog* 11 (Autumn 1972):252-257.

Ruether, Rosemary Radford. "Paradoxes of Human Hope: The Messianic Horizon of Church and Society." *Theological Studies* 33 (June 1972): 235-252.

Ruether, Rosemary Radford. "Rich Nations/Poor Nations and the Exploitation of the Earth." *Dialog* 13 (Summer 1974):201-207.

Ruether, Rosemary Radford. "Sexism and the Theology of Libera‐ tion." *Christian Century* 90 (Dec. 12, 1973):1224-1229.

Ruether, Rosemary Radford. "What Is the Task of Theology?" *Christianity and Crisis* 36 (May 24, 1976):121-125.

Ruether, Rosemary Radford. "Why Socialism Needs Feminism, & Vice Versa." *Christianity and Crisis* 40 (Apr. 28, 1980):103-108.

Russell, George. "Taming the Liberation Theologians." *Time* 125, No. 5 (Feb. 4, 1985):44-45.

Sabant, Philippe. "Christ, Freedom and Salvation in the Thought of Nicholas Berdyaev." *The Ecumenical Review* 26 (1974):483-494.

Sanders, Thomas G. "Catholicism and Authoritarianism in Chile." *Thought* 59 (June 1984):229-243.

Sanders, Thomas G. "The Theology of Liberation: Christian Utopi‐ anism." *Christianity and Crisis* 33 (Sept. 17, 1973):167-173.

Sanders, Thomas G. "Thomas Sanders Replies." *Christianity and Crisis* 33 (Nov. 26, 1976):249-251.

Sanks, T. Howland, and Smith, Brian H. "Liberation Ecclesiology: Praxis, Theory, Praxis." *Theological Studies* 38 (Mar. 1977):3-38.

Sanks, T. Howland. "Liberation Theology and the Social Gospel: Variations on a Theme." *Theological Studies* 41 (Dec. 1980):668-682.

Sapezian, Aharon. "Ministry With the Poor. An Introduction." *International Review of Mission* 66 (1977):3-12.

Sapezian, Aharon. "Theology of Liberation—Liberation of Theology: Educational Perspectives." *Theological Education* 9 (Summer 1973): 254-267.

Saracco, J. Norberto. "The Type of Ministry Adopted by the Pentecostal Churches in Latin America." *International Review of Mission* 66 (1977):64-70.

Savolainen, James W. "A Communist's Reflection on the Intellectual History of Marx As a Critique of the 'Marxist Christian' Project." *Dialog* 23 (Autumn 1984):281-285.

Savolainen, James W. "Theology in the Shadow of Marx: The Theory-Practice Relationship in Liberation Theology and the Status of the Christian Specificum." *Dialog* 19 (1980):268-273.

Schrey, Heinz-Horst. "'Politische Theologie' und 'Theologie der Revolution'." *Theologische Rundschau* 36, No. 4 (1971):346-377; and 37, No. 1 (1972): 43-47.

Schwarz, Hans. "God's Cause for the Poor in the Light of the Christian Tradition." In *God and Global Justice: Religion and Poverty in an Unequal World*, pp. 169-184. Edited by Frederick Ferre and Rita H. Mataragnon. New York: Paragon House, 1985.

Segundo, Juan Luis. "Christianity and Violence in Latin America." *Christianity and Crisis* 28 (Mar. 4, 1968):31-34.

Segundo, Juan Luis. "Is Chalcedon Out of Date?" *American Academy of Religion*. The Currents in Contemporary Christology Group. Newsletter III, No. 2 (n.d.).

Shaull, Richard. "American Power and the Powerless Nations." In *What the Religious Revolutionaries Are Saying*, pp. 12-22. Edited by Elwyn A. Smith. Philadelphia: Fortress Press, 1971.

Shaull, Richard. "The Challenge to the Seminary." *Christianity and Crisis* 29 (Apr. 14, 1969):81-86.

Shaull, Richard. "Christian Faith and the Crisis of Empire." *The Witness* 67, No. 1 (Jan. 1984):4-6.

Shaull, Richard. "Christian Faith: The New Story." *The Witness* 58, No. 6 (Feb. 2, 1975):7-9.

Shaull, Richard. "Christian Faith as Scandal in a Technocratic World." In *New Theology No. 6*, pp. 123-134. Edited by Martin E. Marty and Dean G. Peerman. New York: Macmillan, 1969.

Shaull, Richard. "Christian Initiative in Latin American Revolution." *Christianity and Crisis* 25 (1966):295-298.

Shaull, Richard. "Christian Participation in the Latin American Revolution." In *Christianity Amid Rising Men and Nations*, pp. 91-118. Edited by Creighton Lacy. New York: Association Press, 1965.

Shaull, Richard, et al. "Christian Realism: A Symposium." *Christianity and Crisis* 28 (1968):175-190.

Shaull, Richard. "The Christian in the Vortex of Revolution." In *Projections: Shaping an American Theology for the Future*, pp. 50-69. Edited by Thomas F. O'Meara and Donald M. Weisser. New York: Doubleday, 1970.

Shaull, Richard. "The Christian World Mission in a Technological Era." *The Ecumenical Review* 17 (1965):205-218.

Shaull, Richard. "The Church and Revolutionary Change: Contrasting Perspectives." In *The Church and Social Change in Latin America*, pp. 135-153. Edited by Henry A. Landsberger. Munich: Chr. Kaiser, 1967.

Shaull, Richard. "The Church and the Struggle for Liberation in Latin America." *Slant* 4 (1968):15-17.

Shaull, Richard. "Crisis in the Young Churches." *World Encounter* 6 (1968): 10-11; and *National Christian Council Review* 89 (1969):22-26.

Shaull, Richard. "Discussion of Paul Lehmann: Ethics in a Christian Context." *Princeton Seminary Bulletin* 58 (1964):46-49.

Shaull, Richard. "Does Religion Demand Social Change?" *Theology Today* 26 (Apr. 1969):5-13.

Shaull, Richard. "The End of the Road and a New Beginning." In *Marxism and Radical Religion*, pp. 27-48. Edited by John C. Raines and Thomas Dean. Philadelphia: Temple University Press, 1970.

Shaull, Richard. "Evangelism and Proselytism in Latin America." *Student World* 46 (Second quarter, 1953):14-20.

Shaull, Richard. "Failure of a Mission." *Tempo* 1 (Dec. 15, 1968):11-12.

Shaull, Richard. "The Form of the Church in the Modern Diaspora." *Princeton Seminary Bulletin* 57 (1964):3-18.

Shaull, Richard. "Grace: Power for Transformation." In *Liberation, Revolution and Freedom: Theological Perspectives*, pp. 76-87. Edited by Thomas M. McFadden. New York: Seabury, 1975.

Shaull, Richard. "Human Rights and Economic Development." In *Sourcebook on Human Rights in World Perspective*, pp. 48-55. Edited by B. Levai. Kansas City: Methodist Church Board of Missions, 1968.

Shaull, Richard. "Letter to the Editor." *Student World* 46 (1953):49-51.

Shaull, Richard. "Liberal and Radical in an Age of Discontinuity." *Christianity and Crisis* 29 (Jan. 5, 1970):339-345.

Shaull, Richard. "The New Challenge Before the Younger Churches." In *Christianity and World Revolution*, pp. 190-206. Edited by Edwin H. Rian. New York: Harper & Row, 1963.

Shaull, Richard. "New Dimensions of International Education." *The Bowditch Review* 1 (1967):41-49.

Shaull, Richard. "New Forms of Church Life in a New Society." In *Raise a Signal. God's Action and the Church's Task in Latin America Today*, pp. 109-126. Edited by Hyla Stuntz Converse. New York: Friendship Press, 1961.

Shaull, Richard. "The New Latin Revolutionaries and the U.S." *Christian Century* 85 (Jan. 17, 1968):69-70.

Shaull, Richard. "A New Look at the Sectarian Option." *Student World* 61 (1968):294-299.

Shaull, Richard. "The New Revolutionary Mood in Latin America." *Christianity and Crisis* 23 (1963):44-48.

Shaull, Richard. "Next Stage in Latin America." *Christianity and Crisis* 27 (1967):264-266.

Shaull, Richard. "The Political Significance of Parabolic Action." *Motive* 28 (1968):27-29.

Shaull, Richard. "Reflections on My Years in Brazil." (unpublished manuscript, n.d.).

Shaull, Richard. "The Rehabilitation of Ideology." In *Religion and International Affairs*, pp. 99-107. Edited by J. Rose and M. Ignatieff. Toronto: n.p., 1968.

Shaull, Richard. "Repression Brazilian Style." *Christianity and Crisis* 29 (1969):198-199.

Shaull, Richard. "Response to President Bennett." *Theological Education* 3 (1967):291-293.

Shaull, Richard. "The Revolutionary Challenge to Church and Theology." *Theology Today* 23 (Jan. 1967):470-480.

Shaull, Richard. "Revolutionary Change in Theological Perspective." In *Christian Social Ethics in a Changing World*, pp. 23-43. Edited by John C. Bennett. New York: Association Press, 1966.

Shaull, Richard. "The Struggle for Economic and Social Justice." *Social Action* 32 (1966):27-30.

Shaull, Richard. "A Theological Perspective on Human Liberation." In *When All Else Fails: Christian Arguments on Violent Revolution*, pp. 52-63. Edited by Heinz-Dietrich Wendland. Philadelphia: Pilgrim Press, 1970.

Shaull, Richard. "Theology and the Transformation of Society." *Theology Today* 23 (Apr. 1968):23-36.

Shaull, Richard. "Toward a Reformation of Objectives." In *Protestant Crosscurrents in Mission. The Ecumenical-Conservative Encounter*, pp. 81-107. Edited by Norman A. Horner. Nashville: Abingdon, 1968.

Shinn, Roger L. "Liberation, Reconciliation, and 'Just Revolution'." *The Ecumenical Review* 30 (Oct. 1978):319-332.

Sider, Ronald J. "An Evangelical Theology of Liberation." *Christian Century* 97 (Mar. 19, 1980):314-318.

Snook, Lee E. "Review-Article: Ogden's '*The Point of Christology*'." *American Academy of Religion.* The Currents in Contemporary Christology Group. Newsletter III, No. 3 (n.d.).

Smolik, Josef. "Christian Co-Responsibility For the New Economic World Order." *Communio Viatorum* 20, No. 1 (1977):39-46.

Snyder, Howard A. "Missions From the Underside of History" (Review). *Sojourners* 13, No. 1 (Jan. 1984):36-38.

Sobrino, Jon. "The Historical Jesus and the Christ of Faith: The Tension Between Faith and Religion." *Cross Currents* 27 (Winter 1977-1978): 437-463.

Soelle, Dorothee. "Christians for Socialism." *Cross Currents* 25 (Winter 1976):419-434.

Soelle, Dorothee. "Faith, Theology and Liberation. Remembering Christ." *Christianity and Crisis* 36 (June 7, 1976):136-141.

Soelle, Dorothee. "Mysticism, Liberation and the Names of God." *Christianity and Crisis* 41 (June 22, 1981):179-185.

Soelle, Dorothee. "Resistance: Toward a First World Theology." *Christianity and Crisis* 39 (July 23, 1979):178-182.

Sontag, Frederick. "Coconut Theology: Is James Cone the 'Uncle Tom' of Black Theology?" *Journal of Religious Thought* 36, No. 2 (1979):5-12.

Stavenhagen, Rodolfo. "The Future of Latin America: Between Underdevelopment and Revolution." *Latin American Perspectives* 1, No. 1 (Spring 1974): 124-148.

Stover, Dale A. "Kerygma and Praxis." *Andover Newton Quarterly* 19 (Nov. 1978):111-120.

Strain, Charles R. "Ideology and Alienation: Theses on the Interpretation and Evaluation of Theologies of Liberation." *Journal of the American Academy of Religion* 45 (Dec. 1977):473-490.

Strain, Charles R. "Liberation Theology: North American Perspectives" (Review). *Religious Studies Review* 8 (July 1982):239-244.

Stumme, John R. "Luther's Doctrine of the Two Kingdoms in the Context of Liberation Theology." *Word and World* 3 (Fall 1983):423-434.

Sweeney, Ernest S. "The Nature and Power of Religion in Latin America: Some Aspects of Popular Beliefs and Practices." *Thought* 59 (June 1984): 149-163.

Talbot, Sylvia. "The Unity of Women and Men in the Struggle for Justice and Liberation." *Mid-Stream: An Ecumenical Journal* 19 (Apr. 1980): 190-201.

Taylor, Richard, and Sider, Ronald. "Fighting Fire with Water. A Call for Assertive Nonviolent Resistance." *Sojourners* 12, No. 4 (Apr. 1983): 14-17.

"Theological Education and Liberation Theology: A Symposium." *Theological Education* 16, No. 1 (Autumn 1979):5-68.

Thomas, Norman E. "Evangelism and Liberation Theology." *Theology* 9 (Oct. 1981):473-484.

Thompson, Tyler. "Theology as Liberation." *Explor* 2, No. 1 (1976): 56-59.

Thunberg, Anne-Marie. "The Egoism of the Rich." *The Ecumenical Review* 26 (1974):459-468.

Torres, Camilo. "A Message to Christians." *Slant* 4 (1968):17.

Toth, Karoly. "The Theology of Liberation and Its Relation to Antiracism." *Communio Viatorum* 18, No. 1-2 (1975):51-56.

"Towards a North American Theology of Liberation: Theology in the Americas Process." *Theology in the Americas Documentation Series*, Document No. 1 (Feb. 1978).

Trexler, Edgar R. "Editorial: The Fuss Over Liberation Theology." *The Lutheran* 22, No. 17 (Oct. 3, 1984):34.

Trojan, J. S. "The Theological Problem of Revolution." *Communio Viatorum* 10 (1967):45-52.

Tschuy, Theo. "Liberation of Latin American Christianity. A Review Article." *The Ecumenical Review* 30 (July 1978):260-265.

United Nations. "Charter of Economic Rights and Duties of States." (May 1975).

United Nations. "World Economic Perspective." *UN Chronicle* 19, No. 9 (Oct. 1982):33-48.

United Nations. "The World Economy in Crisis." *UN Chronicle* 20, No. 6 (June 1983):37-52.

United Nations Children's Fund. "The State of the World's Children 1984." Edited by James P. Grant, Executive Director. New York: UNICEF, 1984.

United Nations General Assembly. "Declaration on the Establish-ment of a New International Economic Order." (May 9, 1974).

United Nations General Assembly. "Programme of Action on the Establishment of a New International Economic Order." (May 16, 1974).

Vaillancourt, Pauline. "Nicaragua: Living a Revolution." *The Ecumenist* 19 (Sept.-Oct. 1981):88-90.

Vannucchi, Aldo. "Liturgy and Liberation." *International Review of Mission* 65 (Apr. 1976):186-195.

Vekemans, Roger. "Die lateinamerikanische Theologie der Befreiung (II)." *Internationale Katholische Zeitschrift* (Communio) 2 (Sept.-Oct. 1974): 434-448.

Vidales, Raul. "People's Church and Christian Ministry." *International Review of Mission* 66 (1977):36-48.

Volkmann, Martin. "Das Erbe Martin Luthers und die Theologie der Befreiung." Printed lecture from July 4, 1983 delivered at Strasbourg, France.

Wagner, Murray, Jr. "Toward a Theology of Revolution." *Brethren Life and Thought* 11 (Autumn 1966):49-60.

Wagner, Walter H. "Liberation Theology: Answers and Questions." *LCA Partners* 5, No. 6 (Dec. 1983):15-18.

Wall, James M. "Holding the Center Against 'Right' Rhetoric." *Christian Century* 102 (Feb. 27, 1985):203-204.

Wallis, Jim. "Liberation and Conformity." *Sojourners* 5, No. 8 (Sept. 1976):3-4.

Wallis, Jim. "The Rise of Christian Conscience." *Sojourners* 14, No. 1 (Jan. 1985):12-16.

"We Must Protest." *Cross Currents* 28, No. 1 (1978):66-70.

Weare, Kenneth M. "The Church in Castro's Cuba." *Thought* 59 (June 1984): 219-228.

Weir, J. Emmette. "Liberation Theology—Marxist or Christian?" *Expository Times* 90 (June 1979):60-61.

Wells, Harold. "Segundo's Hermeneutic Circle." *Journal of Theology for Southern Africa* 34 (Mar. 1981):25-31.

Wentz, Richard E. "Revolutionary Hope." *Encounter* (Indianapolis) 30 (Winter 1969):25-31.

Westhelle, Vitor. "Dependency Theory: Some Implications for Liberation Theology." *Dialog* 20 (Fall 1981):293-299.

"Whatever Happened to Theology?" (Symposium). *Christianity and Crisis* 35 (May 12, 1975):106-120.

Wilkens, Thomas G. "The Risk of Loving Boldly." *The Lutheran* 22, No. 17 (Oct. 3, 1984):13-14.

Williamson, Clark M. "Christ Against the Jews: A Review of Jon Sobrino's Christology." *Encounter* (Indianapolis) 40 (Fall 1979): 403-412.

Williamson, Rene de Visme. "The Theology of Liberation." *Christianity Today* 19 (Aug. 8, 1975):7-13.

Wright, Clifford. "Education for Community and Liberation." *Study Encounter* 11, No. 1 (1975):1-12.

Yoder, John Howard. "Probing the Meaning of Liberation." *Sojourners* 5, No. 8 (Sept. 1976):26-29.

Zahn, Gordon C. "The Bondage of Liberation: A Pacifist Reflection."
    Worldview 20 (Mar. 1977):20-24.